Footprint

Scotland Highlands & Islands Handbook

The travel guide

Alan Murphy

For there, among the flowers and grasses,
Only the mightier movement sounds and passes:
Only winds and rivers,
Life and death.

Robert Louis Stevenson, *In the Highlands*

Scotland Highlands & Islands Handbook
First edition
© Footprint Handbooks Ltd 2001

Published by Footprint Handbooks
6 Riverside Court
Lower Bristol Road
Bath BA2 3DZ. England
T +44 (0)1225 469141
F +44 (0)1225 469461
Email discover@footprintbooks.com
Web www.footprintbooks.com

ISBN 1 900949 94 6
CIP DATA: A catalogue record for this
book is available from the British Library

Distributed in the USA by
Publishers Group West

Credits

Series editors
Patrick Dawson and Rachel Fielding

Editorial
Editor: Stephanie Lambe
Maps: Sarah Sorensen

Production
Typesetting: Leona Bailey, Emma Bryers
and Richard Ponsford
Maps: Robert Lunn, Claire Benison and
Angus Dawson
Colour maps: Kevin Feeney

Cover: Camilla Ford

Design
Mytton Williams

Photography
Front cover: Scotland in Focus
Back cover: gettyone Stone
Inside colour section: Robert Harding
Picture Library, Impact Photo Library,
Scotland in Focus, James Davis Travel
Photography, Art Directors and Trip.

Print
Manufactured in Italy by LEGOPRINT

Every effort has been made to ensure
that the facts in this Handbook are
accurate. However, travellers should still
obtain advice from consulates, airlines
etc about current travel and visa
requirements before travelling. The
authors and publishers cannot accept
responsibility for any loss, injury or
inconvenience however caused.

Contents

Left: The appropriately-named Cape Wrath, in the far northwest of the Scottish mainland, looking uncharacteristically tranquil.

4

Right: The single-track road is a familiar sight throughout the Highlands and Islands. This one is heading off into the wilds of Mull.

A foot in the door

Right: One of Scotland's most recognizable peaks, Buachaille Etive Mór, stands guard over the entrance to Glen Coe.
Below: The harbourfront at Portree, the main town on the Isle of Skye.

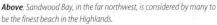

Above: Sandwood Bay, in the far northwest, is considered by many to be the finest beach in the Highlands.
Right: The Trotternish Peninsula, in the north of Skye, is a strange and prehistoric-looking land of bizarre rock formations.

Highlights

The Highlands and Islands of Scotland are Europe's last great wilderness: one of the few places in this increasingly cluttered continent where you can really get away from it all. Forget nightclubs or multi-screen cinemas. People come here for peace and quiet and an unequalled variety and quality of landscape: white beaches, turquoise seas, heather-clad mountains, magical glens, towering waterfalls and deep, mysterious lochs. When the rain stops falling and the mist clears there is no more beautiful place on Earth. Around every bend in the roads that wind their way through this vast region is a sight that leaves you (and me) testing the limits of your vocabulary in search of yet another appropriate adjective. The less eloquent amongst you may be reduced to a disbelieving grunt at the sheer wonder of it all. More emotional souls may even be reduced to tears. If there is a heaven, then it must look like the Scottish Highlands, but let's hope the petrol's cheaper.

About the only thing the Scottish Highlands doesn't have going for it is a dependable climate. If you want to lie on a beach all day soaking up rays, then you really ought to go somewhere else. Ironically, though, many of the greatest attractions are made even more appealing by the notoriously fickle weather conditions. And that's not just the whisky talking. Take all those medieval castles, for instance. Soaked in the blood of centuries and scarred from countless battles and feuds, these ruins are at their brooding best when shrouded in mist. The myriad prehistoric standing stones, burial chambers and brochs (ancient high-rise houses) are evocative enough places when the sun is shining, but under a bruised sky they take on a tangibly sinister feel, which only enhances their strange other-worldliness. And somewhere like Rannoch Moor, a huge expanse of petrified ancient forest, becomes a picture of utter desolation, totally in keeping with the tragic history of the place. **Under the weather**

The Scottish mainland is surrounded by hundreds of islands, each one with its own distinct history and culture. Crossing to these islands doesn't just feel like entering a different country but stepping into another time zone. Where else could you find a police station using gerbils as paper shredders or the swings in the playground padlocked to ensure strict observance of the Sabbath? Lying off the west coast are the Hebridean islands, home of the Gaelic culture, where the road signs include English spellings almost as an afterthought and the local people speak Gaelic as their native tongue. **The islands that time forgot**

Off the northern tip of the mainland is Orkney, an archipelago of 70 islands, which has spawned some of Scotland's greatest writers. Not surprising perhaps, given that Orkney has such a fascinating history and eventful history. The archipelago was ruled by the Vikings for 650 years until the 15th century and despite its remote location played a dramatic role at the end of the First World War when the German fleet was scuttled in Scapa Flow. But if you think Orkney seems remote, then you ain't seen nothing yet. The Shetland Isles are so far north they can only be included on maps as an inset. In fact, they still don't seem a part of Britain: the nearest mainland town is Bergen, in Norway, and Norwegian is taught in the schools. **Northern exposure**

Right: The remarkable Italian Chapel on the East Mainland of Orkney was built by Italian POWs and is fittingly known as 'The miracle of camp 60'.
Below: A lonely crofthouse stands under a bruised Hebridean sky on North Uist.
Previous pages: The sun filters through the autumn leaves in Glen More, Strathspey.

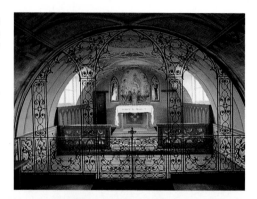

Above: The clearest expression of Highland culture comes through music, and a spontaneous outburst of furious playing can be expected at any time.
Right: The huge standing stones at Callanish on Lewis have been described as Scotland's answer to the pyramids of Egypt.
Next page: Springtime in Perthshire and the glens are carpeted in a blaze of colours.

Hit and myth

There's a lot more to the Scottish Highlands and Islands than bagpipes and whisky. Forget the clichéd image of *Brigadoon* and shortbread tins, the dreadfully twee tartan tat and Celtic kitsch that, sadly, still exists in the 21st century, and is too often passed off as a genuine Highland experience. The Scottish Tourist Board has been trying to change people's perceptions, and, thankfully has largely succeeded.

Of course, many Highland myths persist, and let's face it, the world would be a duller place without them. Loch Ness would just be another stretch of inland water were it not for Scotland's most sought-after resident. Nessie has even joined the information super-highway and now has her own website. At the other end of the scale, in Loch Morar, lives Morag, an altogether more discreet prehistoric monster, with not a single stuffed toy to her name.

Mor or Ness

One of the biggest myths is that the Scots are a tight-fisted bunch when it comes to money. This undeserved reputation is mainly due to the distinctly unfunny antics of some bloke in a kilt called Harry Lauder who laboured under the misconception that he was talented. Highland hospitality is legendary and you will become all too aware of this as you attempt to eat your own weight in bacon and eggs at breakfast.

Tight fit?

Another myth, that's more difficult to dispel, is that the Scots see life through a whisky-induced haze. This may be a bit of an exaggeration, but it cannot be denied that there's nothing the Scots love more than a good party, preferably involving lots of alcohol, singing and dancing. Music and dancing are an intrinsic part of Highland culture and you're never too far from a *ceilidh* (pronounced 'kay-lee'), a kind of Highland knees-up, which is somewhere between a barn dance and a rugby scrum. One of the most unforgettable experiences of a Highland holiday is to find yourself in a pub in the the middle of nowhere, consuming copious quantities of whisky with the locals and then being hurled by a bunch of total strangers around the room, to the accompaniment of a fiddle and accordian. By the time you reach the top of the nearest mountain the next day, you'll have forgotten all about the hangover.

Whisky galore

You'd have to be very unlucky not to experience at least one local festival. The calendar is bursting with them. Many have their roots in pagan ceremonies, others, such as *Up Helly-Aa* on Shetland, are of Viking origin, while some are downright crazy, like *The Ba'*, on Orkney. Amongst the most colourful events are the Highland Games, traditional gatherings involving dancing and various sporting competitions, the sound of massed pipe bands and acres of tartan (well, it had to feature somewhere). Much of the time is taken up by large, hairy men in kilts throwing around heavy objects of varying size and shape, but there are also track events and the prestigious individual piper's competition. There are over one hundred of these gatherings held in towns and villages up and down the country during the summer months. They range from the large and glitzy Braemar Gathering to more authentic events like the Lonach Highland Gathering, and attract both Royals and stars such as Billy Connolly, Robin Williams and Judy Dench.

Games with big names

A walk on the wild side

The Highlands greatest appeal is to those who love the outdoor life. There are mountains galore to climb or ski down, lochs to fish and wildlife to watch, or you can just sit back and take in all that stunning scenery. Okay, so you can't depend on the weather, but there's an old hikers' adage that states there's no such thing as bad weather, only inadequate clothing, which pretty much sums up the kind of attitude you'll need to enjoy the great outdoors in this part of the world.

Mountain high There are countless opportunities to leave civilization a long way behind. You could explore the long distance footpaths which snake through some of the country's finest scenery. These include the West Highland Way which starts in Glasgow and ends at Fort William and the less well-known Speyside Way, which passes through the heart of whisky country. The more adventurous can try their hand (or feet) at 'Munro Bagging', which is not some dubious public school practice but the name given to the popular pursuit of climbing Scotland's 284 mountains higher than 3,000 feet. This offers the chance to explore wild areas of unparalleled beauty such as Glen Coe, Torridon, Kintail or the Cairngorms, though not without the proper clothing, even in summer. In winter, the snow turns the Munros into major expeditions, but also brings the opportunity for downhill skiing. Resorts such as Glenshee, the Nevis Range, Glencoe, the Lecht and the Cairngorms are open from December to April and on a good day offer some superb skiing.

Eagle-eyed tourists Scotland's wide open spaces are rich in wildlife. In October the heather-clad mountains ring to the clashing antlers of rutting red deer and, depending on the time of year and where you are, you might see otters, pine marten, ptarmigan, buzzards, golden eagles and, if you're really lucky, sea eagles which have recently been re-introduced after having been wiped out by farmers angry at their predilection for domestic livestock. Wildlife-spotting tours, particularly marine cruises, are growing in popularity and the animals on view range from the ubiquitous seals to minke whales which are not an uncommon sight in the waters off the northwest coast. Less common are killer whales, which have been spotted in the wild Atlantic seas around the Outer Hebrides. Not to be outdone, on the east coast, in the Moray Firth, is Europe's largest colony of bottlenosed dolphins.

In-flight entertainment For keen birdwatchers, or twitchers, it's Orkney and Shetland which are the real attractions. The islands are an important crossroads for migrating birds and you can see just about every type of seabird, including rare and exotic species from Asia and America. Here, you can go on 'puffin patrols', or sail alongside porpoises while watching vast colonies of nesting seabirds rearing their young. The really adventurous can take the white-knuckle boat trip to the isolated and storm-battered Fair Isle, lying between Orkney and Shetland, a birdwatcher's paradise that really sorts out the men from the boys.

Left: Och aye, the coo! The clichéd image of Scotland is being swept away but these hairy beasts will always have a place in the hearts of visitors.
Below: Gone fishin'. An archetypal Highland image of peaceful contemplation.
Next page: Castlebay harbour on Barra. On an island in the middle is Kisimul Castle, ancient home of the Chief of the MacNeils.

Left: The majestic golden eagle is a fairly common sight throughout the Highlands and Islands.
Above: The winter snows make the Cairngorms a treacherous place for hikers and climbers but bring skiers and snowboarders in droves to the slopes of Scotland's largest ski area.

Essentials

2

18

Essentials

Planning your trip

Where to go

Which parts of Scottish Highlands and Islands you choose to visit will be determined by your own particular interests, as well as by the length of your stay and the size of your wallet. It goes without saying (but we'll say it anyway), that a longer trip will allow you to visit the wild, remote and beautiful parts of the country and get much more out of your holiday.

It is easy enough to visit the main towns and tourist sights by bus or train, but getting off the beaten track without your own transport requires careful planning and an intimate knowledge of rural bus timetables. Even if you're driving, getting around the remote Highlands and Islands can be a time-consuming business as much of this region is accessed only by a sparse network of tortuous, twisting, single-track roads. Be sure to allow plenty of time for getting around, especially for the countless impromptu stops you'll be making to admire the views, and be sure to book ferries in advance during the busy summer season.

If time is limited, it's only a short distance north from Edinburgh to **Perthshire**. Though not as dramatic as the northwest, the mountains, rivers, lochs and glens of the Perthshire Highlands are very beautiful and easily accessed. You could easily extend your route west to take in **Callander** and the **Trossachs**, another photogenic part of the Central Highlands with its own gentle beauty. The Trossachs is only a short distance from the historic town of **Stirling**. Continue north from Perth on the A9 and you'll reach **Inverness**, the largest town in the region. From here the Great Glen takes you southwest to Fort William, or you could make the short trip south to Aviemore, one of the main tourist centres of the Highlands and Islands and a mecca for outdoor sports enthusiasts.

To the north of Glasgow is **Loch Lomond**, gateway to the Western Highlands and a beautiful introduction to the spectacular sights which lie in wait farther north. From Loch Lomond you should head north through **Glencoe**, one of the main highlights of a visit to Scotland, to **Fort William**, the main tourist centre for the Western Highlands. From Fort William there are two routes to another of Scotland's most popular attractions, the **Isle of Skye**. The quickest route is by road and bridge, via **Kyle of Lochalsh**, but by far the most romantic and scenic route is by **train** from Fort William to **Mallaig**, and by **ferry** from there to **Armadale**. You should then leave at least three days to explore the island, or more if you plan to do any **walking**.

An alternative to Fort William and Skye, or in addition if you have more time, would be to head to **Oban**, the main ferry port of the west coast, and make the short trip to the beguiling **Isle of Mull**, which tends to be attract fewer visitors than Skye in the summer months. Or you could head south from Oban, through **Argyll**, with its many **prehistoric sites**, and take a ferry to the little-visited islands of **Islay**, famous for its **malt whiskies**, and **Jura**. Both are great places for **walking** holidays. Also within reach of Argyll, or Ayrshire, is the island of **Arran**, described as 'Scotland in miniature' and ideal for walking or **cycling**.

Those who have three or four weeks at their disposal, or who simply wish to skip the entrées and dive straight into the main course, should head north from Kyle of Lochalsh and make the stunningly beautiful trip along the coast to **Ullapool**. Most visitors don't make it north of Ullapool but those who do are rewarded with the most spectacular landscapes of the northwest. You can also sail from Ullapool across to the fascinating **Outer Hebrides**, a long, narrow archipelago stretching from **Lewis** and **Harris** in the north to **Barra** in the south. When planning your trip, note that most of the islands are fiercely religious and transport is non-existent on a Sunday.

British Tourist Authority offices abroad

The BTA represents the STB abroad. More information can be obtained from their **website** *(www.visitbritain.com), or from the offices listed below:*

Australia *Level 16, Gateway, 1 Macquarie Pl, Sydney NSW 2000, T02-93774400, F02-93774499.*

Belgium *Ave Louise 140, 1050 Brussels, T2-6262580, F2-6462726.*

Canada *5915 Airport Rd, Suite 120, Mississauga, Ontario LV4 1T1, T905-4051840, F905-4051835.*

Denmark *Montergade 3, 1116 Copenhagen K, T33-330142, F33-140136.*

France *Maison de la Gran-Bretagne, 19 rue des Mathurins, 75009 Paris, T1-44515622, F1-44515621.*

Germany, *Westendstr 16-22, 60325 Frankfurt, T69-971123, F69-97112444.*

Ireland *18/19 College Green, Dublin 2, T1-6708000, F1-6708100.*

Italy *Via Nazionale 230, 00184 Rome, T06-4620221, F06-72010086.*

Netherlands *Stadhouderskade 2 (5e), 1054 ES Amsterdam, T20-6077705, F20-6186868.*

New Zealand *17th Flr, 151 Queen St, Auckland 1, T09-3031446, F09-3776965.*

South Africa *Lancaster Gate, Hyde Park Lane, Hyde Park 2196, Johannesburg, T011-3250342, F011-3250344.*

Switzerland and Austria *Limmatquai 78, CH-8001 Zurich, T01-2662166, F01-2662161.*

USA *7th Flr, 551 Fifth Ave, New York, NY 10176-0799, T212-986-2200/ 1-800-GO-2-BRITAIN; 10880 Wilshire Blvd, Suite 570, Los Angeles, CA 90024, T310-4702782, F310-4708549; 625 North Michigan Ave, Suite 1510, Chicago, IL 60611, T1-800-4622748, F312-7870464.*

If you're fortunate enough to be spending even more time in the Scottish Highlands and Islands, or as an alternative to the above, you could include a trip to the wild and windy **Orkney Islands**, as much Scandinavian as they are part of the UK and home to myriad Stone Age ruins. And so far north of the mainland they can only be included on maps as an inset are the even windier and wilder **Shetland Isles**, famed for their incredible diversity of birdlife.

National Trust for Scotland Over 100 of the country's most prestigious sights, and 185,000 acres of beautiful countryside, are cared for by the *National Trust for Scotland* (NTS), 26-31 Charlotte Square, Edinburgh EH2 4ET, T243 9300, www.nts.org.uk National Trust properties are indicated in this guide as 'NTS' and entry charges and opening hours are given for each property. If you're going to be visiting several or more NTS sights in and around the city during your stay, then it's worth taking annual membership. This costs £28, £12 if you're aged under 25 and £47 for a family and gives free access to all NTS and NT properties. The *National Trust Touring Pass* costs £18 per adult and £28 for a family, and gives free admission to its properties for seven days. A 14-day pass costs £26 and £44 respectively. YHA and HI members and student-card holders get 50 % discount on NTS admission charges.

Historic Scotland *Historic Scotland* (HS), Longmore House, Salisbury Place, Edinburgh EH9 1SH, T0131-668 8800, www.historic-scotland.gov.uk, manages more than 330 of Scotland's most important castles, monuments and other historic sites. Historic Scotland properties are indicated as 'HS' and admission charges and opening hours are also given in this guide. Historic Scotland offer an *Explorer Ticket* which allows free entry to 70 of their properties including Edinburgh and Stirling castles. It costs £17 per adult and £35 for a family for seven days, and £22/£42 for 14 days. It can save a lot of money as entry to Edinburgh castle alone is £7.50 per adult.

Scottish tourist boards

Scottish Tourist Board Central Information Department *23 Ravelston Terr, Edinburgh EH4 3EU, T0131-3322433, www.visit.scotland.com*
In London *19 Cockspur St, London SW1 5BL, T020-79308661.*

Scottish area tourist boards

Aberdeen & Grampian Tourist Board *27 Albyn Pl, Aberdeen AB10 1YL, T01224-632727, www.agtb.org*
Angus & City of Dundee Tourist Board *7-21 Castle St, Dundee DD1 3AA, T01382-527527, www.angusanddundee.co.uk*
Argyll, the Isles, Loch Lomond, Stirling & Trossachs Tourist Board *7 Alexandra Pde, Dunoon, Argyll PA23 8AB, T01369-703785, www.visitscottish.heartlands.org*

Ayrshire & Arran Tourist Board *Burns House, Burns Statue Square, Ayr KA7 1UP, T01292-288688, www.ayrshire-arran.com*
The Highlands of Scotland Tourist Board *Peffery House, Strathpeffer IV14 9HA, T01997-421160, F421168, www.highlandfreedom.com*
Orkney Tourist Board *6 Broad St, Kirkwall, Orkney KW15 1NX, T01856-872856, www.visitorkney.com*
Perthshire Tourist Board *Lower City Mills, West Mill St, Perth PH1 5QP, T01738-450600, www.perthshire.co.uk*
Shetland Islands Tourism *Market Cross, Lerwick, Shetland ZE1 0LU, T01595-693434, www.shetland-tourism.co.uk*
Western Isles Tourist Board *26 Cromwell St, Stornoway, Isle of Lewis HS1 2DD, T01851-703088, www.witb.co.uk*

Essentials

When to go

The **high season** is from May to September and this is when Scotland receives the vast majority of visitors. Though the weather tends to be better during the summer months, prices for accommodation are higher in the high season and hotels and guesthouses in the most popular places need to be booked in advance. It's also a good idea to make reservations - at this time - on ferries to the islands, especially to Skye and Mull. A major advantage to visiting in the summer months is the long hours of daylight, especially farther north, where the sun doesn't set till around 2200 or later in June and July.

During the **low season**, from October to Easter, many tourist sights are closed and travelling around can be difficult as public transport services are limited. Many of the smaller tourist offices are also closed during the low season. Though some hotels and guesthouses close during the low season, the majority are now open all year round, as are most restaurants. Taking everything into consideration, May and September are probably the best months to visit.

Climate

The Scottish climate is notoriously unpredictable, especially on the west coast, where a bright, sunny morning can turn into a downpour in the time it takes to butter your toast. Predicting the weather is not an exact science and tables of statistics are most likely a waste of time. There's an old saying in Scotland that if you don't like the weather, then wait 20 minutes, and this just about sums up the climate.

The west coast receives far more rain than the rest of the country and the east coast gets more sunshine. The west coast is also milder in the winter due to the relatively warm waters of the Gulf Stream. Winters can be very harsh, especially in the mountains and glens, making hiking conditions treacherous. Winter storms also make it difficult to travel around the islands as ferry services are often cancelled.

Generally speaking, May to September are the warmest months, with an average summer high of around 18-19°C, and though they are often the driest months, you can expect rain at any time of the year, even in high summer. So, you'll need to come prepared, and remember the old hikers' adage that there's no such thing as bad weather, only inadequate clothing. For a seven-day weather forecast service, call *Weather Check*, T0891-3331111 plus 101 for the northwest and 102 for the northeast. Two excellent weather forecast websites are **www.met-office.gov.uk** and **www.bbc.co.uk/weather**

Tours and tour operators

There are many companies offering general interest or special interest tours of Scotland. Travel agents will have details, or you can check the small advertisements in the travel sections of newspapers or contact the *British Tourist Authority* or *Scottish Tourist Board* for a list of operators (see boxes for contact details).

   Two recommended **British** companies aimed at the more mature traveller are *Saga Holidays*, Saga Building, Middelburg Square, Folkestone, Kent CT20 1AZ, T0800-300500 and *Shearings Holidays*, Miry Lane, Wigan, Lancashire WN3 4AG, T01942-824824, www.shearingsholidays.co.uk *Saga* also operates in the USA, 222 Berkeley Street, Boston, MA 02116; and in Australia, Level 1, 10-14 Paul Street, Milsons Point, Sydney 2061. Other specialist tour operators in the **USA** are *Abercrombie & Kent*, T1-800-3237308, www.abercrombie keny.com, *Especially Britian*, T1-800-8690538 and *Prestige Tours*, T1-800-8907375. *Cross-Culture*, 52 High Point Dr, Amherst MA01002-1224, T800-4911148, www.cross cultureinc.com

Backpacker bus tours A great and cheap way to get around the Highlands is on one of these tours. As well as more general tours of Scotland, there are some excellent-value highland tours, leaving from Edinburgh. Prices start at £75 for three days, up to around £139 for six days. Prices

do not include accommodation or food. The main operators are *Haggis Backpackers*, 11 Blackfriars Street, Edinburgh EH1 1NB, T0131-5579393, www.haggis-backpackers.com; *Go Blue Banana*, T0131-5562000, www.gobluebanana.com and *Macbackpackers*, T0131-5589900, www.macbackpackers.com Several other companies run similar tours, including *Rabbie's Trail Burners*, 207 High Street, Edinburgh, T0131-2263133, www.rabbies.com

Bespoke Cycle Tours, the Bothy, Camusdarach, Arisaig, Inverness-shire, PH39 4NT , T01687-450272, www.scotland-info.co.uk/tours *Scottish Cycle Safaris*, 29 Blackfriars St, Edinburgh, EH1 1NH, T0131-5565560. *Scottish Cycling Holidays*, 87 Perth St, Blair-gowrie, Perthshire, PH10 6DT, T01250- 876100, www.sol.co.uk/s/scotcycl/ — Cycle tour companies

Golfing tours are organized from the USA by *Golf International Inc*, T1-800-8331389 and *Jerry Quinlan's Celtic Golf*, T1-800-5356148, www.jqcelticgolf. Com — Golfing tour companies

There are plenty of operators offering guided walks and walking holidays. A selection of companies is given below and the STB has a comprehensive list. — Walking tour companies

In Britain Assynt Guided Holidays, Birchbank, Knockan, Elphin, Sutherland, T/F01854-666215. Avalon Trekking Scotland, Bowerswell Lane, Kinnoull, Perth, PH2 TDL, T/F01738-624194. **C-N-Do Scotland**, Unit 32, STEP, Stirling, FK7 7RP, T/F01786-445703, www.btinternet.com/-cndo.scotland **Glen Coe Mountain Sport**, 37 Park Rd, Ballachulish, Glen Coe, Argyll, PA39 4JB, T01855-811472, www.glencoe-moun-tain-sport.co.uk Lomond Walking Holidays, 34c James St, Riverside, Stirling, FK8 1UG, T/F01786-447752, www.biggar-net.co.uk/lomond **North-West Frontiers**, 18A Braes, Ullapool, IV26 28Z, T/F01854-612628, www.nwfrontiers.com Ossian Guides, Sanna, Newtonmore, Inverness-shire, PH20 1DG, T/F01540-673402. *Rua Reidh Lighthouse*, Melvaig, Gairloch, Wester Ross, T/F01445-771263, ruareidh@netcomuk.co.uk

In North America Above the Clouds Trekking, T800-2334499, www.gorp.com/abvclds.htm **British Coastal Trails**, T800-4731210, www.bctwalk.com **Himalayan Travel**, T800-2252380, www.gorp.com/himtravel.htm

In Australia and New Zealand Adventure Specialists, 69 Liverpool St, Sydney, T02-92612927. **Adventure Travel Company**, 164 Parnell Rd, Parnell, East Auckland, T09-3799755. New Zealand agents for Peregrine Adventures. Peregrine Adventures, 258 Lonsdale St, Melbourne, T03-96638611, www.peregrine.net.au; also branches in Brisbane, Sydney, Adelaide and Perth.

Finding out more

The best way of finding out more information for your trip is to contact the **British Tourist Authority** (BTA) in your country or write (or email) direct to the head office of the **Scottish Tourist Board** (STB) (see boxes for contact details). The BTA and STB can provide a wealth of free literature and information such as maps, city guides, events calendars and accommodation brochures. Travellers with special needs should also contact their nearest BTA office. If you want more detailed information on a particular area, you should contact the area tourist boards.

At the time of writing, the foot-and-mouth crisis had not yet passed, though it has not affected tourist activities in the Highlands and Islands of Scotland. The STB website, **www.visitscotland.com**, gives an update on the latest situation as well as offering advice for those visiting the countryside.

Language

Some road signs are in Gallic, see page 45

Though the vast majority of Scots speak English, to the untutored ear, the Scottish dialect can be hard to understand, as many words and expressions are derived not from English but from **Lowland Scots**, or *lallans*, which is now recognized as a separate language as opposed to simply a regional dialect. Generally speaking, however, the Highland accent is very clear and east to understand. In fact, it is said that people from Inverness speak the clearest English in the UK.

In Orkney more people speak Cantonese than Gaelic

Scotland's oldest surviving language is **Scottish Gaelic** *(Gaidhlig*, pronounced 'Gallic'). Often referred to as the national language, it has been spoken the longest. Introduced to the country by Irish immigrants in the third and fourth centuries, its use soon spread and became well established. The language is spoken by about 85,000 people in Scotland (about 2% of the population). This is in the *Gaidhealtachd*, the Gaelic-speaking areas of the Outer Hebrides, parts of Skye and a few of the smaller Hebridean islands. Gaelic is one of the Celtic languages, which has included Irish Gaelic, Manx, Welsh, Cornish and Breton. Today, only Scottish and Irish Gaelic, Welsh and Breton survive.

Those wishing to **teach themselves Gaelic** could start with the BBC *CanSeo* cassette and book. A good phrasebook *is Everyday Gaelicby* Morag MacNeill (Gairm). Also, the Celtic Heritage Centre, based on Arran, has a great store of Gaelic and Celtic information and documents. They also publish a quarterly newsletter. Macbain's Etymological Dictionary of the Gaelic language contains a wealth of words and information.

Before you travel

Getting in

Visas

Visa regulations are subject to change, so it is essential to check with your local British Embassy, High Commission or Consulate before leaving home. Citizens of all European countries – except Albania, Bosnia, Bulgaria, Macedonia, Romania, Slovakia, Yugoslavia and all former Soviet republics (other than the Baltic states) – require only a passport to enter Britain and can generally stay for up to three months. Citizens of Australia, Canada, New Zealand, South Africa or the USA can stay for up to six months, providing they have a return ticket and sufficient funds to cover their stay. Citizens of most other countries require a visa from the commission or consular office in the country of application.

The **Foreign Office's website** (www.fco.gov.uk) provides details of British immigration and visa requirements. Also the **Immigration Advisory Service** (IAS) offers free and confidential advice to anyone applying for entry clearance into the UK: County House, 190 Great Dover Street, London SE1 4YB, T020-7357 6917, www.vois.org.uk

Longer stays & work permits

For **visa extensions** contact the Home Office, Immigration and Nationality Department, Lunar House, Wellesley Road, Croydon, London CR9, T020-8686 0688, before your existing visa expires.

Citizens of **Australia**, **Canada**, **New Zealand**, **South Africa** or the **USA** wishing to stay longer than six months will need an Entry Clearance Certificate from the British High Commission in their country.

British embassies abroad

Australia High Commission: Commonwealth Ave, Yarralumla, Canberra, ACT 2600, T02-62706666, www.uk.emb.gov.au

Belgium rue d'Arlon 85, 1040, Brussels, T2-2876211, www.british-embassy.be

Canada High Commission: 80 Elgin St, Ottowa, K1P 5K7, T613-2371530.

Denmark Kastelsvej 36/38/40, DK-2100 Copenhagen, T35-445200, www.britishembassy.dk

France rue de Faubourg St Honoré, 75383 Paris T01-4451 3100, www.amb-grandebretagne.fr

Germany Wilhelmstrasses 70, 10117, Berlin, T03-204570, www.britischebotschaft.de

Ireland 29 Merrion Rd, Ballsbridge, Dublin 4, T01-2053700, www.britishembassy.ie

Israel 192 Hayarkon St, Tel Aviv 63405, T3-7251222, www.britemb.org.il/

Italy Via XX Settembre 80a 1-00187 Roma RM, T06-4220 0001, www.ukinitalia.it

Netherlands Koningslaan 44, 1075AE Amsterdam, T020-6764343.

New Zealand High Commission: 44 Hill St, Wellington 1, T04-4726049, www.britain.org.nz

South Africa High Commission: 91 Parliament St, Cape Town 8001, T21-4617220.

Spain Calle de San Fernando el Santo 16, 28010 Madrid, T91-7008200, www.ukinspain.com

USA 3100 Massachusetts Ave NW, Washington DC 20008, T202-5886500, www.britaininusa.com

Essentials

Citizens of **European Union** (EU) countries can live and work in Britain freely without a visa, but **non-EU residents** need a permit to work legally. This can be difficult to obtain without the backing of an established company or employee in the UK. Visitors from **Commonwealth countries** who are aged between 17 and 27 may apply for a working holiday-maker's visa which permits them to stay in the UK for up to two years and work on a casual basis (ie non-career oriented). An option for citizens of some non-Commonwealth countries is to come to Scotland on an 'au pair' placement in order to learn English by living with a English-speaking family for a maximum of two years. Au pairs must be aged between 17 and 27, and come from one of the following countries: Andorra, Bosnia-Herzegovina, Croatia, Cyprus, Czech Republic, The Faroes, Greenland, Hungary, Macedonia, Malta, Monaco, San Marino, Slovak Republic, Slovenia, Switzerland or Turkey. This can be a good way to learn English, but check out the precise conditions of your placement before taking it up.

Visas should be obtained form a British mission overseas before entering the UK

If you want to **study** in Scotland you must forst prove you can support and accommodate yourself without working and without recourse to public. Your studies shgould take up at least 15 hours a week for aminimum of six months. Once you are studying, you are allowed to do 20 hours of casual work per week in the term time and you can work full-time during the holidays.

In **North America**, **full-time students** can obtain temporary work or study permits through the Council of International Education Exchange (CIEE), 205 E 42nd Street, New York, NY 10017, T212-8222600, www.ciee.org Also, **Commonwealth** citizens with a parent or grandparent born in the UK can apply for a **Certificate of Entitlement to the Right of Abode**, allowing them to work in Britain.

For more details, contact your nearest British embassy, consulate or high commission, or the Foreign and Commonwealth Office in London, T020-7270 1500.

Essentials

 ## Overseas consulates in Scotland

The following consulates are all in Edinburgh (phone code: 0131):
Australia *37 George St, T6243333.*
Canada *30 Lothian Rd, T2204333.*
Denmark *4 Royal Terr, T5564263.*
France *11 Randolph Cres, T2257954.*
Germany *16 Eglinton Cres, T3372323.*
Italy *32 Melville St, T2263631.*
Japan *2 Melville Cres, T2254777.*
Netherlands *53 George St, T2203226.*
Spain *63 North Castle St, T2203226.*

Sweden *22 Hanover St, T2206050.*
Switzerland *66 Hanover Pl, T2265660.*
USA *3 Regent Terr, T5568315.*

The following consulates are in Glasgow (phone code: 0141):
Germany *158 West Regent St, T2210304.*
Italy *24 St Enoch Square, T2263000.*
Norway *80 Oswald St, T2041353.*
Spain *389 Argyle St, T2216943.*
Sweden *16 Robertson St, T2217845.*

Customs regulations and tax

There is no longer any duty-free shopping

Visitors from EU countries do not have to make a declaration to customs on entry into the UK. The limits for **duty-paid goods** from within the EU are 800 cigarettes, or 1kg of tobacco, 10 litres of spirits, 20 litres of fortified wine, 90 litres of wine and 110 litres of beer. Visitors from non-EU countries are allowed to import 200 cigarettes, or 250g of tobacco, two litres of wine, and two litres of fortified wine or one litre of spirits.

There are various import restrictions, most of which should not affect the average tourist. There are tight **quarantine restrictions** which apply to animals brought from overseas (except for Ireland). For more information of British import regulations, contact HM Customs and Excise, Dorset House, Stamford Street, London, SE1 9PJ, T020-7928 3344, www.hmce.gov.uk

VAT Many goods in Britain are subject to a **Value Added Tax** of 17.5%. The major exceptions are books and food. Visitors from non-EU countries can save money through the Retail Export Scheme, which allows a refund of VAT on goods to be taken out of the country. Not all shops are participants in the scheme and that VAT cannot be reclaimed on hotel bills or other services.

Insurance

It's a good idea to take out some form of travel insurance, wherever you're travelling from. This should cover you for theft or loss of possessions and money, the cost of all medical and dental treatment, cancellation of flights, delays in travel arrangements, accidents, missed departures, lost baggage, lost passport and personal liability and legal expenses.

Insurance companies
There isn't one site for all travel insurance companies, but www.travelinsurance. co.uk is a good place to start your search

There are a variety of policies to choose from, so it's best to shop around to get the best price. Your travel agent can also advise you on the best deals available. *STA Travel* and other reputable student travel organizations often offer good value travel policies. Travellers from North America can try the *International Student Insurance Service* (ISIS), which is available through *STA Travel*, T1-800-7770112, www. sta-travel.com Some other recommended travel insurance companies in North America include *Travel Guard*, T1-800-8261300, www.noelgroup.com, *Access America*, T1-800- 2848300, *Travel Insurance Services* (1-800-9371387), *Travel Assistance International*, T1-800-8212828 and *Council Travel*, 1-888-COUNCIL, www.counciltravel. com Another company worth calling for a quote is *Columbus Direct*, T020-73750011, www.columbusdirect.co.uk/index.asp

Older travellers should note that some companies won't cover people over 65 years old, or may charge high premiums. The best policies for older travellers are offered by *Age Concern* (T01883-346964), though these may be expensive.

Points to note You should always read the small print carefully. Some policies exclude 'dangerous activities' such as scuba diving, skiing, horse riding or even trekking. Not all policies cover ambulance, helicopter rescue or emergency flights home. Find out if your policy pays medical expenses direct to the hospital or doctor, or if you have to pay and then claim the money back later. If the latter applies, make sure you keep all records. Whatever your policy, if you are unfortunate enough to have something stolen, make sure you get a copy of the police report, as you will need this to substantiate your claim.

What to take

You'll be able to find everything you could possibly need for your trip in Scottish cities, so you can pack light and buy stuff as you go along. Given the climate, however, you should bring warm and waterproof clothing, whatever the time of year. Also bring light clothes in the summer, preferably long-sleeved to protect you from the midges.

If you're planning on hill-walking you should come properly prepared as the weather can change rapidly in the mountains (for more details see page 53). It's worth treating your boots with a waterproofing agent as some of the trails cross boggy ground. A sleeping bag is useful in hostels. A sleeping sheet with a pillow cover is needed for staying in Scottish Youth Hostel Association (SYHA) hostels to save you the cost of having to hire one. A padlock can also be handy for locking your bag if it has to be stored in a hostel for any length of time. Other useful items include an alarm clock (for those early ferry departures), an adaptor plug for electrical appliances, an elastic clothes line and, if you're hillwalking or camping, a Swiss Army knife, torch (flashlight) and compass

Disabled travellers

For travellers with disabilities visiting the Highlands independently can be a difficult business. While most theatres, cinemas and modern tourist attractions are accessible to wheelchairs, **accommodation** is more problematic. Many large, new hotels do have disabled suites, but will charge more, and most B&Bs, guesthouses and smaller hotels are not designed to cater for people with disabilities. **Public transport** is just as bad, though newer buses have lower steps for easier access and some *ScotRail* inter-city services now accommodate wheelchair-users in comfort. Taxis, as opposed to minicabs, all carry wheelchair ramps, and if a driver says he or she can't take a wheel-chair, it's because they're too lazy to fetch the ramp.

Wheelchair users, and blind or partially-sighted people are automatically given 30-50% discount on train fares and those with other disabilities are eligible for the **Disabled Person's Railcard**, which costs £16 per year and gives a third off most tick-ets. There are no reductions on buses, however. For those travelling on *Calmac* ferries, there's 50% discount off the normal single car fare on presentation of an orange or blue card bearing the photograph of the disabled person, supported by a tax disc exemption certificate or proff of receipt of the Disabled Living Allowance at the higher level, and 10% discount on presentation of an orange or blue card with photograph.

Information and organizations If you are disabled you should contact the travel officer of your national support organization. They can provide literature or put you in touch with travel agents specializing in tours for the disabled. The *Scottish Tourist Board* produces a guide, *Accessible Scotland*, for disabled travellers and many local tourist offices can provide accessibility details for their area. For more information, contact **Disability Scotland**, Princes House, 5 Shandwick Place, Edinburgh EH2 4RG, T0131-229 8632. The **Royal Association for Disability and Rehabilitation (RADAR)**, Unit 12, City forum, 250 City Road, London, EC1V 8AF, T020-7250 3222, www.radar.org.uk, is a good source of advice and information and produces an annual guide on travelling in the UK (£7.50 including P&P). The **Holiday Care Service**, 2nd floor, Imperial Building, Victoria Road, Horley, Surrey RH6 7PZ, T-1293-774535, provides free lists of accessible accommodation and travel in the UK.

Gay and lesbian travellers

Don't assume that because men are wearing skirts in the Highlands that people take a relaxed attitude to homosexuality. The same prejudices apply as elsewhere in rural parts of the UK. There are no towns in the Highlands large enough to support an active gay scene, so overt displays of affection are not advised. *Gay Scotland* magazine, T0131-5572625, is a good source of information. For more information contact the **Gay Switchboard**, T0131-5564049 or the **Lesbian Line**, T0131-5570751.

For a good selection of gay events and venues, check out **www.whatsonwhen.com** or the UK gay-scene index at **www.queenscene.com** which as information on clubs, gay groups, accommodation, events, HIV/AIDS and cultural and ethical issues. Other good sites include: **www.gaybritain.co.uk**; **www.gaytravel.co.uk**; **www.rainbownetwork.com**; and **www.gaypride.co.uk**

Student travellers

There are various official youth/student ID cards available. The most useful is the **International Student ID Card** (ISIC). For a mere £6 the ISIC card gains you access to the exclusive world of student travel with a series of discounts, including most forms of local transport, up to 30% off international airfares, cheap or free admission to museums, theatres and other attractions, and cheap meals in some restaurants. There's also free or discounted internet access and a website where you can check the latest student travel deals (www.usitWORLD.com). You'll also receive the ISIC handbook, which ensures you get the most out of services available. ISIC cards are available at student travel centres (see page 32). US and Canadian citizens are also entitled to emergency medical coverage, and there's a 24-hour hotline to call in the event of medical, legal or financial emergencies.

If you're aged under 26 but not a student, you can apply for a **Federation of International Youth Travel Organisations** (FIYTO) card, or a **Euro 26 Card**, which give you much the same discounts. If you're 25 or younger you can qualify for a **Go-25 Card**, which gives you the same benefits as an ISIC card. These discount cards are issued by student travel agencies (see pages 33 and 34 for addresses) and hostelling organizations (see page 41).

Travel with children

Flying with kids
Visit:
www.babygoes2.com

Inform the airline in advance that you're travelling with a baby or toddler and check out the facilities when booking as these vary with each aircraft. British Airways now has a special seat for under 2s; check which aircraft have been fitted with them when booking. Pushchairs can be taken on as hand luggage or stored in the hold. Skycots are available on long-haul flights. Take snacks and toys for in-flight entertainment and remember that swallowing food or drinks during take-off and landing will help prevent ear problems.

Eating out
Sadly, eating out with children in Scotland can be a frustrating experience and too many establishments are downright unhelpful. Furthermore, the attitude to breastfeeding in public is still some way behind the rest of Europe.

Money

The British currency is the pound sterling (£), divided into 100 pence (p). Coins come in denominations of 1p, 2p, 5p, 10p, 20p, 50p, £1 and £2. (And a £5 coin is proposed for late 2000.) *Bank of England* banknotes are legal tender in Scotland, in addition to those issued by the *Bank of Scotland*, *Royal Bank of Scotland* and *Clydesdale Bank*. These Scottish banknotes (bills) come in denominations of £1, £5, £10, £20, £50 and £100 and are legal tender in the rest of Britain, though some shopkeepers south of the border may be reluctant to accept them.

Travellers' cheques

The safest way to carry money is in travellers' cheques. These are available for a small commission from all major banks. *American Express (Amex)*, *Visa* and *Thomas Cook* cheques are widely accepted and are the most commonly issued by banks. You'll normally have to pay commission again when you cash each cheque. This will usually be 1%, or a flat rate. No commission is payable on *Amex* cheques cashed at *Amex* offices. Keep a record of the cheque numbers and the cheques you've cashed separate from the cheques themselves, so that you can get a full refund of all uncashed cheques should you lose them. It's best to bring sterling cheques to avoid changing currencies twice.

Also note that in Britain travellers' cheques are rarely accepted outside banks, so you'll need to cash them in advance and keep a good supply of ready cash

Credit cards & ATMs

The easiest way to stay in funds whilst travelling is by using your credit card. Most hotels, shops and restaurants accept the major credit cards (*Access/MasterCard*, *Visa* and *Amex*), though some places may charge for using them. They may be less useful in more remote rural areas and smaller establishments such as B&Bs which will often only accept cash. You can withdraw cash from selected banks and ATMs (or cashpoints as they are called in Britain) with your cash card. Your bank or credit card company will give you a list of locations where you can use your card.

Visa card holders can use the *Bank of Scotland*, *Clydesdale Bank*, *Royal Bank of Scotland* and *TSB* ATMs; *Access/MasterCard* holders can use the *Royal Bank* and *Clydesdale*; *Amex* card holders can use the *Bank of Scotland*.

If you have an account with a High Street bank in England or Wales, you can use your cashpoint card in Scotland. *Bank of Scotland* and *Royal Bank* take *Lloyds* and *Barclays* cash cards; *Clydesdale* takes *HSBC/Midland* and *National Westminster* cards. *Bank of Scotland*, *Clydesdale* and most building society cashpoints are part of the Link network and accept all affiliated cards.

Banks & bureaux de change

Most towns and villages have a branch of at least one of the big four High Street banks – *Bank of Scotland*, *Royal Bank of Scotland*, *Clydesdale* and *TSB Scotland*. In small and remote places, and on some islands, there may only be a mobile bank which runs to a set timetable. This timetable will be available from the local post office.

Bank opening hours are Monday-Friday from 0930 to between 1600 and 1700. Some larger branches may also be open later on Thursdays and on Saturday mornings. Banks are usually the best places to change money and cheques. Outside banking hours you'll have to use a **bureau de change**, which can be found in most city centres and also at the main airports and train stations. Some *bureaux* charge high commissions for changing cheques. Those at international airports, however, often charge less than banks and will change pound sterling cheques for free. Avoid changing money or cheques in hotels, as the rates are usually very poor

Money transfers

If you need money urgently, the quickest way to have it sent to you is to have it **wired** to the nearest bank via *Western Union* (T0800-833833) or *Moneygram* (T0800-89718971). Charges are on a sliding scale: it will cost proportionately less to wire out more money. Money can also be wired by *Thomas Cook* or *American Express*, though this may take a day or two, or transferred via a bank draft, but this can take up to a week.

Costs The Highlands can be an expensive place to visit, especially in the more remote parts, though there is plenty of budget accommodation available and backpackers will be able to keep their costs down. Petrol in particular is very expensive: it can cost up to 10p per litre more than in other parts of the UK. Accommodation and restaurant prices also tend to be higher in more popular destinations and during the busy summer months.

The minimum daily budget required, if you're staying in hostels or cheap B&Bs, cycling or hitching, and cooking your own meals, will be around £20-25 per person per day. If you start using public transport and eating out occasionally that will rise to around £30-40. Those staying in slightly more upmarket B&Bs or guesthouses, eating out every evening at pubs or modest restaurants and visiting tourist attractions, such as castles or museums, can expect to pay around £40-50 per day. If you also want to hire a car and use ferries to visit the islands, and eat well, then costs will rise considerably and you'll be looking at least £75 per person per day. Single travellers will have to pay more than half the cost of a double room in most places and should budget on spending around 60% of what a couple would spend.

Getting there

Air

Inverness is the gateway airport to the Highlands, and just over 1 ½ hours from London. Daily services are operated by British Airways (through British Regional Airlines) from London Gatwick and by easyJet from London Luton. You can also fly to Inverness from Glasgow and Edinburgh. Services are avilable from Inverness and Glasgow to Shetland, Orkney and the Outer Hebrides.

There are direct flights from European cities to Edinburgh, Glasgow, Aberdeen and Prestwick, and from North America to Glasgow. There are no direct flights from North America to Edinburgh; these are usually routed via London or Dublin. There are also daily flights from Dublin and Belfast to Aberdeen, Edinburgh, Glasgow and Prestwick, and regular flights to most Scottish airports from other parts of the UK. There are limited flights to Africa, the Middle East and Asia. There are no direct flights to Scotland from Australia or New Zealand. You will have to get a connection from London.

Those wishing to also visit England should note that it is generally cheaper to fly to Scotland from the rest of Britain if you use an Airpass bought in your own country. This is offered by *British Airways* and *British Midland*. Airpasses are valid only with an international scheduled flight ticket.

Buying a ticket There is a mind-boggling number of outlets for buying your plane ticket and finding
Also worth trying are: the best deal can be a confusing business. **Fares** will depend on the season. Ticket
www.expedia.co.uk prices to Scotland are highest from around early June to mid-September, which is the
www.lastminute.com tourist high season. Fares drop in the months either side of the peak season –
www.e-bookers.com mid-September to early November and mid-April to early June. They are cheapest in
www.cheapflights. the low season, from November to April, when very few visitors are willing to brave the
co.uk Scottish winter. The exception is during Christmas and New Year when seats are at a
www.deckchair.com premium and prices rise sharply. It's also worth noting that flying at the weekend is
www.flynow.com normally more expensive. It is always worth spending a bit of time researching the var-
www.dialaflight.co.uk ious options available and starting early, as some of the cheapest tickets have to be
bought months in advance and the most popular flights sell out early. One of the best

ways of finding a good deal is to use the internet. There are a number of sites where you can check out prices and even book tickets. You can search in the travel sections of your web browser or try the sites of the discount travel companies and agents listed in this section.

Cheap flight tickets fall into two categories; official and unofficial. Official tickets are called budget fares, Apex, super-Apex, advance-purchase tickets, or whatever a particular airline chooses to call them. Unofficial tickets are discounted tickets which are released by airlines through selected travel agents. They are not sold directly by airlines. Discounted tickets are usually as low or lower than the official budget-price tickets.

Return tickets are usually a lot cheaper than buying two one-way tickets. **Round-the-World** (RTW) tickets can also be a real bargain and may even work out cheaper than a return fare. RTW prices start at around £900 (US$1,500), depending on the season. Note that it's easy to include London on a Round-the-World itinerary, but a stop in Scotland may be harder to arrange and may involve backtracking. It may be cheaper and easier to buy the London to Scotland leg separately or to travel overland to Scotland from London.

When trying to find the best deal, make sure you check the route, the duration of the journey, stopovers allowed, any travel restrictions such as minimum and maximum periods away, and cancellation penalties. Many of the cheapest flights are sold

Getting there

Airlines in Britain and Ireland

Aer Lingus, Ireland T01-8444777; UK T0645-737747, www.aerlingus.ie, flies from Dublin to Glasgow and Edinburgh . It also flies from Cork, Donegal and Shannon to Edinburgh and Glasgow.
British Airways, *T0845-7799977, www.britishairways.com, flies from London Heathrow, Gatwick and Stansted to Edinburgh, Glasgow and Aberdeen; also from Bristol, Belfast City and International, Birmingham, Cardiff and Manchester. They also fly from Gatwick to Inverness, Leeds/Bradford to Aberdeen, and from Jersey to Edinburgh and Glasgow.*
British Midland, *T08706-0705555, www.britishmidland.com, flies from London Heathrow to Edinburgh and Glasgow; from Manchester to Aberdeen, Edinburgh and Glasgow; from East Midlands to Edinburgh, Glasgow and Aberdeen; and from Amsterdam to Edinburgh.*

easyJet , T0870-600 0000, www.easyjet.com, flies from London Luton to Aberdeen, Edinburgh, Glasgow and Inverness.
Gill Airways, *T0191-214 666, www.gill-airways.com Flights from Newcastle to Wick.*
Go, *T0845-605 4321, www.go-fly.com, is BA's low-cost airline which flies from London Stansted to Edinburgh and Glasgow.*
KLM AirUK, *T08705-074074, www.klm.com, flies from London Stansted to Glasgow and Aberdeen, from London City to Edinburgh, and from Amsterdam to Edinburgh, Glasgow and Aberdeen.*
Ryanair , *T08701-569569; Ireland T01-609-7800, www.ryanair.com, flies from London Stansted to Glasgow (Prestwick) from £40 return.*
Scot Airways, *T08706-060707, www.scotairways.co.uk flies from London City airport to Dundee.*

Discount travel agents in Britain and Ireland

Council Travel, *28a Poland St, London, W1V 3DB, T020-7437 7767, www.destinations-group.com*
STA Travel, *86 Old Brompton Rd, London, SW7 3LH, T020-7361 6161, and 27 Forrest Rd, Edinburgh T0131-226 7747. www.statravel.co.uk Specialists in low-cost student/youth flights and tours,*

also good for student IDs and insurance.
Trailfinders, *194 Kensington High St, London W8 6FT, T020-7938 3939.*
Usit Campus, *52 Grosvenor Gardens, London SW1 0AG, T020-7730 3402, and 5 Nicolson Sq, Edinburgh, T0131-668 3303. www.campustravel.co.uk Student/youth travel specialists.*

by small agencies, most of whom are honest and reliable, but there may be some risks involved with buying tickets at rock-bottom prices. You should avoid paying too much money in advance and you could check with the airline directly to make sure you have a reservation. You may be safer choosing a better-known travel agent, such as **STA**, which has offices worldwide, or **Trailfinders** in the UK, or **Council Travel** in the USA. These and other reputable discount companies and agents are listed above.

Flights from Britain, Ireland & Europe
Details of the current best deals are given above, but note that prices may change by the time you read this

There are direct flights to Scotland's three main airports – Glasgow, Edinburgh and Aberdeen – almost hourly from London Heathrow, Gatwick, Stansted and Luton airports. There are also daily flights from provincial UK airports and from Dublin. To fly on to the smaller airports in the Highlands and Islands, you'll have to change planes (see page 43 for more details on domestic flights). The cheapest flights usually leave from Luton or Stansted. They are often subject to rigid restrictions but the savings can make the extra effort worthwhile. Cheaper tickets usually have to be bought at least a week in advance, apply to only a few mid-week flights and must include a Saturday night stayover. They are also non-refundable, or only partly refundable, and

Airlines flying from North America

Air Canada, T1-888-2472262,
www.aircanada.ca
American Airlines, T1-800-4337300,
www.americanair.com
British Airways, T1-800-2479297; in
Canada T1-800-6681059,
www.british-airways.com
Continental Airlines, T1-800-2310856,

www.flycontinental.com
Delta Airlines, T1-800-2414141,
www.delta-air.com
TWA, T1-800-8924141, www.twa.com
United Airlines, T1-800-5382929,
www.ual.com
Virgin Atlantic Airways, T1-800-8628621,
www.fly.virgin.com

Essentials

Discount travel agents in North America

Air Brokers International, 323 Geary St,
Suite 411, San Francisco, CA94102,
T1-800-8833273, www.airbrokers.com
Consolidator and specialist on RTW and
Circle Pacific tickets.
Council Travel, 205 E 42nd St, New York,
NY 10017, T1-888-COUNCIL,
www.counciltravel.com Student/budget
agency with branches in many US cities.
Discount Airfares Worldwide On-Line,
www.etn.nl/discount.htm A hub of
consolidator and discount agent links.
*International Travel Network/Airlines of
the Web*, www.itn.net/airlines Online air
travel information and reservations.

STA Travel, 5900 Wiltshire Blvd, suite 2110,
Los Angeles, CA 90036, T1-800-8364115,
www.sta-travel.com Discount
student/youth travel discount company
with branches in New York, San Francisco,
Boston, Miami, Chicago, Seattle and
Washington DC.
Travel CUTS, 187 College St, Toronto, ON
M5T 1P7, T1-800-6672887,
www.travelcuts.com Specialist in student
discount fares, IDs and other travel services.
Branches in other Canadian cities.
Travelocity, www.travelocity.com Online
consolidator.

---

non-transferable. A standard flexible and refundable fare from London to Glasgow or Edinburgh will cost at least £200 return.

Specialist agencies such as *Usit Campus* or *STA* (see above) offer Domestic Air Passes on *British Airways* flights to travellers under 26 years old. These give you substantial discounts on 'Hopper' flights to Inverness and the Hebrides.

There are flights from Edinburgh, Glasgow and Aberdeen to major cities in **Continental Europe** and some regional centres. Discount charter flights are often available to young travellers aged under 26 and holders of ISIC cards through the large student travel agencies listed above.

There are several daily non-stop flights to **Glasgow** from many US and Canadian cities, including Boston, Calgary, Chicago, Denver, Las Vegas, Los Angeles, Miami, Montreal, New York, Philadelphia, San Francisco, Seattle, Toronto, Vancouver and Washington. Transatlantic carriers are listed above. Flights to **Edinburgh** go via London or Dublin. Because of the much larger number of flights to London, it is generally cheaper to fly there first and get an onward flight (see 'Airlines in Britain and Ireland' box for the best deals).

Flights from North America

For low season Apex fares expect to pay around US$400-600 from New York and other East Coast cities and around US$500-700 from the West Coast. Prices rise to around US$700-900 from New York and up to US$1,000 from the West Coast in the summer months. Low season Apex fares from Toronto and Montreal cost around CAN$600-700, and from Vancouver around CAN$800-900, rising to CAN$750-950 and CAN$950-1150 respectively during the summer.

Essentials

 Airlines flying from Australia and New Zealand

Air France, T02-9321 1030 (Sydney), www.airfrance.com

Air New Zealand, T09-3573000, www.airnz.co.nz

British Airways, T02-9258 3200 (Sydney); T09-3568690 (Auckland), www.british-airways.com

Cathay Pacific, T02-9931 5500 (Sydney), www.cathaypacific.com

Gulf Air, Australia, T02-9244 2199 (Sydney).

Japanese Airlines (JAL), T02-9272 1111 (Sydney); New Zealand, T09-3799906.

Korean Air, T02-9262 6000; T09-3073687 (Auckland).

Qantas, T09-3578900, (Auckland), www.qantas.com.au

Singapore Airlines, T02-9350 0100 (Sydney); T131011 (reservations); T09-3793209 (Auckland).

South African Airways, T02-9223 4448 (Sydney), www.saa.co.za

Thai Airways, T02-9251 1922 (Sydney) T09-3773886 (Auckland), www.thaiair.com

United Airlines, T02-9292 4111 (Sydney); T131777 (reservations); T09-3793800 (Auckland), www.ual.com

Virgin Atlantic, T02-9352 6199, www.flyvirgin.com/atlantic/

Discount travel agents in Australia and New Zealand

Flight Centres, 82 Elizabeth St, Sydney, T13-1600; 205 Queen St, Auckland, T09-3096171. Also branches in other towns and cities.
STA Travel, T1300-360960, www.statravelaus.com.au, 702 Harris St, Ultimo, Sydney, and 256 Flinders St, Melbourne. In New Zealand: 10 High St, Auckland, T09-3090458. Also in major

towns and cities and University campuses.
Travel.com.au, 80 Clarence St, Sydney, T02-92901500, www.travel.com.au
UK Flight Shop, 7 Macquarie Place, Sydney, T02-92474833, www.ukflightshop.com.au They also have branches in Melbourne, T03-9600 3022 and Perth, T08-9266 1222.

Flights from Australia & New Zealand There are no direct flights to Scotland from Australia or New Zealand. You will have to get an onward flight from London. The cheapest scheduled flights to London are **via Asia** with *Gulf Air* or *Thai Airways*. They charge A$1300-1500 in low season and up to A$1800 in high season, and involve a transfer en route. Flights via **Africa** start at around A$2000 and are yet more expensive via **North America**. Flights to and from Perth via Africa or Asia are a few hundred dollars cheaper. The cheapest deal currently on offer is with *Britannia Airways/Airtours*, charter flights from Australia or New Zealand to London Gatwick or Manchester via Singapore and Bahrain. It's a 'no-frills' service which only runs between November and March. Fares start at around A$1100 in low season and up to A$1750 in high season. For more details contact the *UK Flight Shop* (see above).

The cheapest scheduled flights from **New Zealand** are with *Korean Air*, *Thai Airways* or *JAL*, all of whom fly via their home cities for around NZ$2000-2300. The most direct route is via North America with *United Airlines*, via Chicago or Los Angeles. Fares range from around NZ$2800 in low season to NZ$3200 in high season. *Britannia Airways*' charter flights from Auckland cost from around NZ$1600 in low season to NZ$2100 in high season.

A **Round-the-World** (RTW) ticket may work out just as cheap as a return ticket. Good deals are offered by *Qantas/British Airways*. As with North America, it may be cheaper to buy the London to Scotland leg of the trip separately.

Road

Road links to Scotland are excellent and several coach operators run daily services to the Highlands from Glasgow, Edinburgh and Aberdeen, with connections to all other parts of the UK. This is the cheapest form of travel to Scotland. The two main operators between England and Scotland are *National Express*, T0870-508080, www.gobycoach.com, and its sister company *Scottish Citylink*, T0870-5505050, www.city.link.co.uk

There are direct buses from most British cities to **Inverness**. Tickets can be bought at bus stations or from a huge number of agents throughout the country. Fares from London to Glasgow and Edinburgh with *National Express* are between £30-40 for an economy advance return. Fares to Inverness are a little higher. The London to Glasgow/Edinburgh journey takes around eight hours, while it takes around 11-12 hours for the trip to Inverness. Budget backpacker tours can be a cheap way of getting to and around the Highlands of Scotland (see page 22).

Bus travel passes Full-time students or those aged under 25 or over 50, can buy a **Coach Card** for £9 which is valid for one year and gets you a 30% discount on all fares. A **Family Card** costs £18 and allows two children to travel free with two adults, but children normally travel for half price. See page 43 for details of bus passes for travel within Scotland. The **Tourist Trail Pass** offers unlimited travel on all *Scottish Citylink* and *National Express* services throughout Britain. Passes cost from £49 for two days' travel out of three up to £190 for 14 days' travel out of 30. They can be bought from major travel agents, at Gatwick and Heathrow airports, as well as from bus stations in Scottish towns and cities. In **North America** these passes are available from *British Travel International*, T1-800-3276097, www.britishtravel.com, or from *US National Express,* T502-2981395.

The A82 (Glasgow-Fort William-Inverness, the A9 (Stirling-Perth-Inverness) and the A96 (Aberdeen-Nairn-Inverness) are the three main routes to and from the Highlands. There are two main routes to Scotland from the south: in the east the A1 runs to Edinburgh and in the west the M6 and A74(M) runs to Glasgow. The journey north from London to either city takes around eight to 10 hours. See 'Getting around' for more details of driving conditions in Scotland and for information on hiring vehicles.

Sea

The only direct route to Scotland from Europe is on the *Smyril Line* (Aberdeen T01224-572615; Faroe Islands T01-5900) service to **Lerwick** (Shetland) from Norway (Bergen), Iceland (Seydisfjordur) and the Faroe Islands (Torshavn). It sails from mid-May to early September only once a week and takes 12 hours. A sleeping berth one way from Norway and Faroe Islands costs £63 in high season. You then have to get from Lerwick to Aberdeen. *P&O Scottish Ferries* (T10224-572615) sail Monday-Friday from Lerwick to Aberdeen (14 hours; £55 per passenger in high season).

The *Argyll and Antrim Steam Packet Company*, T0990-523523, runs twice daily from Ballycastle in Northern Ireland to Campbeltown from mid-June to September. The crossing takes about three hours.

Train

Daily services to and from Inverness and Fort William connect the Highlands with Glasgow, Edinburgh, Aberdeen, Perth, Dundee and all the major UK cities. There are rail services from Inverness to Kyle of Lochalsh, Inverness to Wick and Thurso, Glasgow to

Oban and Fort William and Fort William to Mallaig (where steam trains run in the summer), many of which pass through spectacular scenery. There are fast and frequent rail services from London and other main towns and cities in England to Glasgow, Edinburgh and Inverness.

Two companies operate direct services from London to Scotland: *GNER* trains leave from Kings' Cross and run up the east coast to Edinburgh and Inverness; and *Virgin* trains leave from Euston and run up the west coast to Glasgow. Journey time from London is about four hours 30 minutes to Edinburgh, five hours to Glasgow and eight hours to Inverness. *Scotrail* operate the **Caledonian Sleeper** service if you wish to travel overnight from London Euston to Inverness and Fort William, with stops at Dalwhinnie, Newtonmore, Kingussie and Aviemore. This runs nightly from Sunday to Friday, and advance booking is essential.

Eurostar, T0990-186186, www.eurostar.com, operates high-speed trains through the channel tunnel to London Waterloo from Paris (three hours), Brussels (two hours, 40 minutes) and Lille (two hours). You then have to change trains, and stations, for the onward journey north to Scotland. If you're driving from continental Europe you could take **Le Shuttle**, which runs 24 hours a day, 365 days a year, and takes you and your car from Calais to Folkestone in 35-45 minutes. Fares range from £84 to £165 per carload, depending on how much in advance you book or when you travel. For bookings, T08705-353535.

Enquiries *National Rail Enquiries*, T0845-7484950, www.railtrack.co.uk, for information on rail services and fares. For online ticket purchases, www.thetrainline.com For advance credit/debit card bookings, T0845-7550033. *GNER*, T0845-7225225; *Virgin*, T0845-7222333; *ScotRail*, T0845-7550033, www.scotrail.co.uk

Fares The system of rail ticket pricing is very complicated. There are a series of discounted
For details of various fares, but restrictions are often prohibitive, which often explains the long queues and
discount rail passes delays at ticket counters in railway stations. The cheapest ticket is a **Super Apex**, which
and rail services within must be booked at least two weeks in advance. Next cheapest is an **Apex** ticket which
Scotland, see page 46 has to be booked at least seven days before travelling. Other discount tickets include a
Saver return, which can be used on all trains, and a **Super Saver**, which costs slightly less but cannot be used on a Friday or during peak times.

For example, a **GNER London-Edinburgh Saver** return costs £79, a **Super Saver** £69, an **Apex** £49 and a **Super Apex** £36. All discount tickets should be booked as quickly as possible as they are often sold out weeks, or even months, in advance, especially Apex and Super Apex tickets. The latter tickets guarantee seat reservations, but Saver and Super Saver tickets do not. These can be secured by paying an extra £1. A **Caledonian Sleeper** Apex return ticket to Edinburgh or Glasgow costs £79.

Touching down

Airport information

Airport tax All air tickets are subject to a passenger service charge and airport tax. For economy fare flights within the UK and from EU countries the tax is £5. For all other flights it is £20. Taxes on first or club-class flights are £10 for UK and EU and £40 for other destinations. The service charge varies from one airport to another.

Touching down

Electricity *The current in Britain is 240V AC. Plugs have three square pins and adapters are widely available.*

Emergencies *For* **police**, **fire brigade**, **ambulance** *and, in certain areas,* **mountain rescue** *or* **coastguard**, *dial 999.*

Laundry *Most towns have coin-operated launderettes. The average cost for a wash and tumble dry is about £3. A service wash where someone will do your washing for you, costs around £4-5. In more remote areas, you'll have to rely on hostel and campsite facilities.*

Time *Greenwich Mean Time (GMT) is used from late October to late March, after which time the clocks go forward an hour to British Summer Time (BST). GMT is five hours ahead of US Eastern Standard Time and 10 hours behind Australian Eastern Standard Time.*

Toilets *Public toilets are found at all train and bus stations and motorway service stations. They may charge 20p but are generally clean with disabled and baby-changing facilities. Those in town centres are often pretty grim.*

Weights and measures *Imperial and metric systems are both currently in use. Distances on roads are measured in miles and yards, drinks are poured in pints and gills, but generally nowadays, the metric system is used elsewhere.*

Essentials

Glasgow T0141-8871111. The main departure point in Scotland for flights to North America and the Caribbean. There are also regular flights to many European destinations, and domestic flights to and from London, Manchester, Bristol and Belfast. Terminal facilities include car hire, bank ATMs, currency exchange, left luggage, tourist information, T8484440, and shops, restaurants and bars. There's also an *SPT Travel Centre*, T8484330, in the UK Arrivals concourse, (open daily 0800-2200 in summer and till 1800 in winter) and a Thomas Cook Hotel & Travel Reservations desk in the International Arrivals concourse, T8877220.

Scottish airports *For more information visit www.highlands-and-islands.airports.uk.com*

    Edinburgh T0131-3331000. There are flights to Edinburgh from all over Europe, Ireland and the UK. Edinburgh airport has all facilities, including a tourist information desk, Bureau de Change, ATMs, restaurants and bars (first floor) and shops (ground floor and first floor). For car hire, **Avis**, **Budget**, **Europcar**, **Hertz** and **National** car hire desks are located in the terminal in the main UK arrivals area.

    Aberdeen T01224-722331. There are regular daily flights to Aberdeen from other parts of the UK as well as flights from Amsterdam, Copenhagen, Esbjerg and Stavanger.

    Inverness T01667-464000. The region's main airport, with daily direct flights from Glasgow, Edinburgh, London Gatwick and London Luton. There are also flights to **Dundee**, T01382-643242, from London City Airport, to **Prestwick**, T01292-722331, from London Stansted, and to **Wick**, T01955-602215, from Aberdeen and Newcastle.

Rules, customs and etiquette

Visitors will find their Highland hosts to be friendly and obliging. The level of hospitality should be a significant part of the enjoyment of your trip and visitors from south of the border should encounter little of the anti-English sentiment which is prevalent throughout the Central Lowlands. However, those visiting the Outer Hebrides need to be aware of the strict observance of the Sabbath on those islands.

Sustainable or Eco-Tourism has been described as:" … ethical, considerate or informed tourism where visitors can enjoy the natural, historical and social heritage of

Responsible tourism

Essentials

The Countryside Code

- Drive carefully and behave courteously to other motorists and cyclists on narrow, winding island roads. Park vehicles where it will not be a hazard or disruption to other motorists, residents or businesses
- Respect local people and their observance of the Sabbath
- Keep to public paths through farmland to minimise crop damage and avoid 'short-cuts' on steep terrain to prevent soil erosion and damage to natural vegetation
- Litter is an eye-sore, harmful to farm animals, wildlife and the water supply – leave no waste and take all your rubbish home
- Protect wildlife, plants and trees
- Respect ancient monuments, buildings and sites of religious importance – do not vandalise or cause graffiti
- Many of the abandoned crofts are derelict and dangerous – keep out for your own safety
- Avoid damaging crops, walls, fences and farm equipment and fasten all gates
- Do not collect wildflowers, seabird eggs or historical artefacts for souvenirs
- Avoid pollution of water supplies - there are few toilets outside of villages so when walking in the countryside bury

- human waste and toilet paper in the ground and at least 30 metres from water courses
- Guard against all risk of fire from matches, cigarettes, cooking stoves and campfires
- Keep dogs under careful control, especially when near to sheep at lambing-time, seabird nesting sites at cliff edges and avoid dog-fouling in public places
- Respect the peace, solitude and tranquillity of the islands for others to enjoy – keep noise to a minimum
- The landscape can be spectacular but dangerous – take particular care along precipitous cliff edges, hilltops and slippery coastal rocks
- Stay away from working areas on the moors and hills during grouse-shooting, lambing season, deer culling, heather burning and respect other locally or nationally imposed access restrictions
- Report any damage or environmental concerns to the landowner or the Scottish Environment Protection Agency (SEPA) in Stornoway (T: 01851 706477)
- Be adequately prepared when you walk in the hills – check the weather forecast, carry warm, waterproof clothing, adequate food and water supplies and know how to use map and compass

an area without causing adverse environmental, socio-economic or cultural impacts that compromise the long-term ability of that area and its people to provide a recreational resource for future generations and an income for themselves ..."

The Highlands and Islands of Scotland is beautiful, dramatic and wild but also a living, working landscape and a fragile and vulnerable place. By observing the simple guidelines outlined on the following page and behaving responsibly you can help to minimise your impact and protect the natural and cultural heritage of this unique island environment so that it can continue to be appreciated by other visitors.

For further information on what action is being taken either in Scotland, throughout UK or across the world to control against the negative aspects of tourism on the natural environment and traditional cultures contact **Tourism Concern** in London (or T020-7753 3330) or the **Tourism and Environment Forum** (www.greentourism.org.uk).

Tipping Tipping in Scotland is at the customer's discretion. In a restaurant you should leave a tip of 10-15% if you are satisfied with the service. If the bill already includes a service charge, you needn't add a further tip. Tipping is not normal in pubs or bars. Taxi drivers will expect a tip for longer journeys; usually of around 10%. As in most other countries, porters, bellboys and waiters in more upmarket hotels rely on tips to supplement their meagre wages.

Safety

The major safety issue when visiting the Highlands and Islands relates to the notoriously unpredictable weather conditions. Everyone should be aware of the need for caution and safety preparations when walking or climbing in the mountains (see page 53.

Tourist information

Tourist offices, known as Tourist Information Centres (TICs), can be found in most towns. Their addresses, phone numbers and opening hours are listed in the relevant sections of this book. Opening hours vary depending on the time of year, and many of the smaller offices are closed during the winter months. All tourist offices provide information on accommodation, public transport, local attractions and restaurants, as well as selling books, local guides, maps and souvenirs. Many also have free street plans and leaflets describing local walks. They can also book accommodation for you for a small fee. Addresses of the main office of the **Scottish Tourist Board** and the *Area Tourist Boards* are given on page 21

Where to stay

Accommodation will be your greatest expense. It ranges from hostels and cheaper Bed and Breakfasts (B&Bs) to upmarket hotels, many of which are converted castles and country mansions.

Hotels and other places to sleep are identified by a ∎ symbol on maps.

Tourist Information Centres will help find accommodation for you. They can recommend a place within your particular budget and give you the number to phone up and book yourself, or will book a room for you. Some TICs charge a small fee (usually £1) for booking a room, while others ask you to pay a deposit of 10% which is deducted from your first night's bill. Most TICs also offer a **Book-a-Bed-Ahead** service, which reserves accommodation for you at your next destination. This costs £3 per booking and is particularly useful in July and August, or if you'll be arriving in a town late.

Single rooms are in short supply and many places are reluctant to let a double room to one person, even when they're not busy. They are usually more than the cost per person for a double room and in some cases cost the same as two people sharing a double room.

Hotels, guesthouses and B&Bs

Regional tourist boards publish accommodation lists which include campsites, hostels, self-catering accommodation and STB approved hotels, guesthouses and B&Bs. Places participating in the STB system will have a plaque displayed outside which shows their grading, determined by a number of stars ranging from one to five. These reflect the level of facilities, as well as the quality of hospitality and service. However, do not assume that a B&B, guesthouse or hotel is no good because it is not listed by the tourist board. They simply don't want to pay to be included in the system and some of them may offer better value.

Accommodation price codes

Accommodation prices in this book are graded with the letters below and are based on the cost per person for two people sharing a double room with en suite bathroom during the high season. Cheaper rooms with shared bathrooms are available in many hotels, guesthouses and B&Bs. Many places, particularly larger hotels, offer substantial discounts during *the low season and at weekends. All places listed are recommended as providing good quality and value within their respective price category.*

L *£80 plus*	**A** *£66-80*
B *£46-65*	**C** *£36-45*
D *£26-35*	**E** *£16-25*
F *£15 and under*	

Hotels

A company specialising in arranging accommodation in castles is Scotts Castle Holidays, T0131-2297111, www.scottscastles.com

At the top end of the scale, there are some fabulously luxurious hotels, often in spectacular locations. Many of them are converted baronial mansions or castles and offer a chance to enjoy a taste of aristocratic grandeur and style. At the lower end of the scale, there is often little to choose between cheaper hotels and guesthouses or B&Bs. The latter often offer higher standards of comfort and a more personal service, but many smaller hotels are really just guesthouses, and are often family-run and every bit as friendly. Some hotels, especially in town centres or in fishing ports, may also be rather noisy, as the bar can often be the social hub. Rooms in most mid-range to expensive hotels almost always have bathrooms en suite. Many upmarket hotels offer excellent room-only deals in the low season.

Guesthouses Guesthouses are often large, converted family homes with up to five or six rooms. They tend to be slightly more expensive than B&Bs and though they are often less personal, usually provide better facilities, such as en suite bathroom, colour TV in each room and private parking. In many instances, they are more like small budget hotels. Many guesthouses offer evening meals, though this may have to be requested in advance.

Bed & Breakfasts B&Bs provide the cheapest private accommodation. At the bottom end of the scale, you can get a bedroom in a private house, a shared bathroom and a huge cooked breakfast for around £14-18 per person per night. Small B&Bs may only have one or two rooms to let, so it's important to **book in advance** during the summer season and on the islands where accommodation options are more limited. More upmarket B&Bs have en suite bathrooms and TVs in each room and usually charge from £20-24 per person per night. In general, B&Bs are more hospitable, informal, friendlier and offer better value than hotels. Many B&B owners, particularly in the Highlands and Islands, are a great source of local knowledge and can even provide OS maps for local walks. B&Bs in the Outer Hebrides also offer dinner, bed and breakfast, which is useful as eating options are limited, especially on a Sunday.

Some places, especially in ferry ports, charge room-only rates, which are slightly cheaper and allow you to get up in time to catch an early morning ferry. However, this means that you miss out on a huge **cooked breakfast**. If you're travelling on a tight budget, you can eat as much as you can at breakfast time and save on lunch as you won't need to eat again until evening. This is particularly useful if you're heading into the hills, as you won't have to carry so much food. Many B&B owners will even make up a packed lunch for you at a small extra cost.

Youth Hostel Associations

Australia *Australian Youth Hostels Association, 422 Kent St, Sydney, T02-92611111.*

Canada *Hostelling International Canada, Room 400, 205 Catherine St, Ottawa, ON K2P 1C3, T800-6635777.*

England & Wales *Youth Hostel Association (YHA), Trevelyan House, 8 St Stephen's Hill, St Albans, Herts AL1 2DY, T0870-8708808, www.yha/ england/wales/org.uk*

France *FUAJ, 7 Rue Pajol, 75018 Paris, T1-4498727.*

Germany *Deutsches Jugendherbergswerk, Hauptverband, Postfach 1455, 32704 Detmold, T5231-74010.*

Ireland *An Oige, 61 Muntjoy St, Dublin 7, T01-8304555, www.irelandyha.org*

New Zealand *Youth Hostels Association of New Zealand, PO Box 436, Christchurch 1, T03-379970.*

Northern Ireland *Youth Hostel Association of Northern Ireland, 22 Donegal Rd, Belfast, BT12 5JN, T01232-324733.*

Scotland *Scottish Youth Hostel Association (SYHA), 7 Glebe Cres, Stirling FK8 2JA, T01786-451181, www.syha.org.uk*

USA *Hostelling International-American Youth Hostels (HI-AYH), 733 15th St NW, Suite 840, PO Box 37613, Washington DC 20005, T202-7836161, www.hostel.com*

Essentials

Hostels

For those travelling on a tight budget, there is a large network of hostels offering cheap accommodation. These are also popular centres for backpackers and provide a great opportunity for meeting fellow travellers. Hostels have kitchen facilities for self-catering and some include a continental breakfast in the price or provide cheap breakfasts and evening meals. **Advance booking** is recommended at all times, and particularly from May to September and on public holidays.

The *SYHA* is separate from the *YHA* in England and Wales. It has a network of over 80 hostels which are often better and cheaper than those in other countries. They offer bunk-bed accommodation in single-sex dormitories or smaller rooms, kitchen and laundry facilities. Prices range from £4 for juniors (under 18) and £5 for seniors (over 18) for the cheapest up to £11.25 for juniors and £12.75 for seniors for the most expensive. Those in large towns and cities and main tourist centres are more expensive. The average cost is £7-9 per person per night. Though some rural hostels are still strict on discipline and impose a 2300 curfew, those in larger towns and cities tend to be more relaxed and doors are closed as late as 0200. Some larger hostels provide breakfasts for around £2.50 and three-course evening meals for around £4.

The *SYHA* produces a handbook (free with membership) giving details of all their youth hostels, including transport links. This can be useful as some hostels are difficult to get to without your own transport. You should always phone ahead, as many hostels are closed during the day. Phone numbers are listed in this guide. Many hostels are closed during the winter. Details are given in the *SYHA Handbook*.

For Scottish residents, adult membership costs £6, and can be obtained at the SYHA National Office (see box for address), or at the first SYHA hostel you stay at. SYHA membership gives automatic membership of *Hostelling International* (HI). The *SYHA* also offers an **Explore Scotland** and **Scottish Wayfarer** ticket, which can save a lot of money on transport and accommodation, especially if you're not a student (see page 43).

Scottish Youth Hostel Association (SYHA) *Youth hostel members are entitled to half-price entry to all National Trust for Scotland properties*

The *Gatliff Hebridean Hostels Trust* (GHHT) is a non-profit making charitable organization which cheap basic traditional croft-style accommodation in the Outer Hebrides.They currently have four hostels, at Garenin (Isle of Lewis), Rhenigidale (Isle of Harris), Berneray (Isle of North Uist) and Howmore (South Uist). Further information including contact details, hostel locations and photographs and places of interest to visit in the surrounding area can be found at www.gatliff.org.uk

Independent backpackers hostels The *Independent Backpackers Hostels of Scotland* is an association of over 90 independent hostels/bunkhouses throughout Scotland. They charge between £6 and £15 per person per night, though the average is around £7.50-9.50. They tend to be more laid-back, with fewer rules and no curfew. They all have dormitories, hot showers and self-catering kitchens. Some include continental breakfast, or provide cheap breakfasts. All these hostels are listed in the *Independent Hostel Guide*, which is available from tourist offices or send an A5 SAE to: Pete Thomas, Croft Bunkhouse & Bothies, Portnalong, Isle of Skye, IV47 8SL. They also have a **website**: www.hostel-scotland.co.uk

Camping and self-catering

Camping There are hundreds of campsites around Scotland. They are mostly geared to caravans and vary greatly in quality and level of facilities. The most expensive sites, which charge up to £10 to pitch a tent, are usually well-equipped. Sites are usually only open from April to October. If you plan to do a lot of camping, you should buy *Scotland: Camping & Caravan Parks* (£3.95), available from most tourist offices. It lists around 150 camping and caravan parks graded by the STB.

North Americans planning on camping should invest in an **international camping carnet**, which is available from home motoring organizations, or from *Family Campers and RVers* (FCRV), 4804 Transit Road, Building 2, Depew, NY 14043 (T1-800-2459755). It gives you discounts at member sites.

Self-catering There is plenty of STB-approved self-catering accommodation available, ranging from remote farmhouse cottages to city centre apartments. The minimum stay is usually one week in the summer peak season, or three days or less at other times of the year. Expect to pay at least £150 per week for a two-bedroom cottage in the winter, rising to £250 in the high season. Places in the city range from around £200 to over £700 per week. A good source of self-catering accommodation is the STB's guide (£5.95), which lists over 1,200 properties and is available from any tourist office.

The *National Trust for Scotland* owns many historic properties which are available for self-catering holidays. Prices start at around £250 per week in high season. Contact them at 5 Charlotte Square, Edinburgh EH2 4DU, T0131-2265922. For something a bit different, *Highland Hideways* has a range of more individual self-catering properties. For a free brochure write to them at 5-7 Stafford Street, Oban, Argyll PA34 5NJ, T01631-526056.

Getting around

Public transport is generally good and efficient, but it can be a slow and difficult process getting to more remote parts of the Highlands and Islands. Public transport can also be expensive, but there's a whole range of discount passes and tickets which can save you a lot of money. To get off the beaten track, you may have to consider hiring a car, but with a combination of buses, trains, ferries, walking, hiring a bike, plenty of time and careful planning, you can get almost anywhere.

Air

As well as the main airport at Inverness, there are many small airports, many of them on the islands (one of them, on Barra, uses the beach as an airstrip). However, internal flights are expensive: a return flight from Edinburgh or Glasgow to Shetland costs over £250. There are discounted tickets available, such as Apex fares, which must be booked at least 14 days in advance, and special offers on some services. *British Airways'*, **Highland Rover** costs under £200 and allows you to take any five flights within seven days (except inter-island flights within Orkney or Shetland).

The majority of flights are operated by *British Airways/Loganair*, T0845-7799977 www.british-airways.com For inter-island flights in Shetland, you should book direct through *Loganair*, T01595-840246. Other carriers are *Gill Air*, T0191-2146666, www.gil-airways.com and *British Midland*, T08706-070555, www.britishmidland.com For information on flight schedules, call the airports listed on page 37 , or *British Airways*. The *British Airports Authority* (BAA) publishes a free *Scheduled Flight Guide*.

Essentials

Road

Travelling around by bus takes longer than the train but is much cheaper. There are numerous local bus companies but the main operator is *Scottish Citylink*, T0990-505050, www.citylink.co.uk, part of the *National Express* group. Bus services between towns and cities are good but far less frequent in more remote rural areas. Note that long-distance express buses are called coaches.

Bus & coach

Passes and discounts There are a number of discount and flexible tickets for bus/coach travel in Scotland. Full-time students or those aged under 25 or over 50, can buy a **Coach Card** for £9 which is valid for one year and gets you a 30% discount on all National Express fares within the UK. A **Family card** costs £18 and allows two children to travel free with two adults, but children normally travel for half price.

The **National Express Explorer Pass** offers unlimited travel within a specified period on *Scottish Citylink* buses. It is available to overseas visitors but must be bought outside Britain. It costs £59 for three days travel within a five-day period, £110 for seven days in a 21-day period and £170 for 14 days in a 30-day period. Smart Card and Discount Coach Card holders can get a 30% discount on these prices.

The **Tourist Trail Pass** offers unlimited travel on all *Scottish Citylink* and *National Express* services throughout the UK. Passes cost from £49 for two days' travel out of three, up to £190 for 14 days' travel out of 30. They can be bought from major travel agents, as well as from bus stations in Scottish towns and cities. In **North America** these passes are available from *British Travel International*, T1-800-327 6097, www.britishtravel.com, or from *US National Express,* T502-298 1395.

The SYHA sells its own **Explore Scotland** bus pass, which allows free travel on *Citylink* services. It costs £155 for five days and £250 for eight days and includes seven nights hostel accommodation, free SYHA membership and free entry to many *Historic Scotland* properties. They also sell a **Scottish Wayfarer** ticket which is similar but also includes rail travel, *CalMac* ferries and discounts on many *P&O Ferries*. It costs £160 for four days, £270 for eight days and £299 for 12 days.

Postbus services Many rural areas, particularly in the Highlands and Islands, can only be reached by Royal Mail postbuses. These are minibuses that follow postal delivery routes and carry between four and 14 fare-paying passengers. They set off early in the morning from the main post office and follow a circuitous route as they deliver and collect mail in the most far-flung places. They are often very slow on the outward morning routes but quicker on the return routes in the afternoons, but although it can be a very

Essentials

 ## Car hire companies

Britain Arnold Clark, T0800-838245; Avis, T0990-900500; **Budget**, T0800-181181; **EuroDollar**, T01895-233300; **Europcar**, T0345-222525; **Hertz**, T0990-996699; **Holiday Autos**, T0990-300400; **National Car Rental**, T0990-365365; **Thrifty**, T0990-168238. **North America** Alamo, T800-5229696, www.goalamo.com; **Avis**, T800-3311084, www.avis.com; **Budget**, T800-5270700, www.budgetrentacar.com; **Dollar**,

T800-4216868, www.dollar.com; **Hertz**, T800-6543001, www.hertz.com; **Holiday Autos** , T800-4227737, www.holiday/colauto.com; **National**, T800-CAR-RENT, www.nationalcar.com; **Thrifty**, T800-3672277, www.thrifty.com **Australia** Avis, T1800-225533; **Budget**, T1300-362848; **Hertz**, T1800-550067. **New Zealand** Avis, T09-5262847; Budget, T09-3752222; Hertz, T09-3676350.

slow method of getting around but you get to see some of the country's most spectacular scenery and it is useful for walkers and those trying to reach remote hostels or B&Bs. There's a restricted service on Saturdays and none on Sundays. A free booklet of routes and timetables is usually available at local Tourist Information Centres. For more information on Postbuses call the Royal Mail in Edinburgh, T0131-228 7407.

Car
Note that petrol here is a lot more expensive than in other parts of the UK and that petrol stations and garages are few and far between

Travelling with your own private transport allows you to cover a lot of the country in a short space of time and to reach remote places. Roads are generally a lot less busy than those in England and driving is relatively stress-free, especially on the B-roads and minor roads. Many roads in the Highlands and Islands are **single track** with passing places indicated by a diamond-shaped signpost. These should also be used to allow traffic behind you to overtake. Remember that you may want to take your time to enjoy the stupendous views all around you, but the driver behind may be a local doctor in a hurry. Don't park in passing places. A major driving hazard on single track roads are the huge numbers of sheep wandering around, blissfully unaware of your presence. When confronted by a flock of sheep, slow down and gently edge your way past. Be particularly careful at night, as many of them sleep by the side of the road (counting cars perhaps). **Rules and regulations** To drive in Scotland you must have a current driving licence. Foreign nationals also need an **international driving permit**, available from state and national motoring organizations for a small fee. Those importing their own vehicle should also have their vehicle registration or ownership document. Make sure you're adequately insured. In all of the UK you **drive on the left**. **Speed limits** are 30 miles per hour (mph) in built-up areas, 70 mph on motorways and dual carriageways and 60 mph on most other roads.

Motoring organizations It's advisable to join one of the main UK motoring organizations during your visit for their **24-hour breakdown** assistance. The two main ones in Britain are the *Automobile Association* (*AA*), T0800-448866, www.theaa.co.uk, and the *Royal Automobile Club* (*RAC*), T0800-550550, rac.co.uk. One year's membership of the *AA* starts at £46 and £39 for the *RAC*. They also provide many other services, including a reciprocal agreement for free assistance with many overseas motoring organizations. Check to see if your organization is included. Both companies can also extend their cover to include Europe. Their **emergency numbers** are: *AA* T0800-887766; *RAC* T0800-828282. You can call these numbers even if you're not a member, but you'll have to a pay a large fee. In remote areas you may have to wait a long time for assistance. Also note that you may be stranded for ages waiting for spare parts to arrive.

Getting around the islands in Gaelic

Aside from the fact that nothing moves on a Sunday, the biggest problem facing visitors to the Outer Hebrides is that road signs and place names are almost exclusively in Gaelic; except for English-speaking Stornoway and Benbecula, where signs are also in English. This means that it's essential, particularly if you're driving, to buy the tourist board's bilingual 'Official Map of the Western Isles', which is available at most tourist offices and many tourist sight gift shops. Also note that the brown tourist sight signs are in both languages, but the Gaelic spelling is much more prominent, so you'll need to be attentive!

In order to reflect the Gaelic-only policy, place names in the text are in Gaelic first, with the English spelling in brackets, and thereafter the names appear in Gaelic only. The exceptions to this are the names of the islands and ferry terminals, which are in English after they are first mentioned in both English and Gaelic.

Car hire This is expensive and you may be better off making arrangements in your home country for a fly/drive deal through one of the main multi-national companies. The minimum you can expect to pay is around £150 per week for a small car. Small, local hire companies often offer better deals than the larger multi-nationals. Most companies prefer payment with a credit card, otherwise you'll have to leave a large deposit (£100 or more). You'll need your driver's licence and to be aged between 21 and 70. **Motorcycle hire** is very expensive, ranging from around £200 up to £350 per week.

As in the rest of the UK, hitching is never entirely safe, and is certainly not advised for anyone travelling alone, particularly women travellers. Those prepared to take the risk should not find it too difficult to get a lift as people in the Highlands and Islands are often very willing to stop for you. Bear in mind, though, that you will probably have to wait a while to actually see a vehicle in more remote parts.

Hitching

Sea

There are around 60 or so inhabited islands off the coast of Scotland, and nearly 50 of them can be reached by a scheduled ferry service. Most ferries carry vehicles and can be booked in advance. If you're travelling to the islands by car, it's a good idea to book ferries in advance whatever the time of year, particularly to the more popular islands.

The majority of ferry services on the west coast are operated by *Caledonian MacBrayne*, or *CalMac* as they're more commonly known. They sail from **Oban**, **Mallaig** and **Ullapool** to over 20 islands in the **Inner** and **Outer Hebrides**. They also run services on the **Firth of Clyde**. Fares are expensive, especially with a car, but if you're planning on using ferries a lot, you can save a lot of money with an **Island Hopscotch** ticket, which offers reduced fares on 17 set routes. The ticket is valid for one month and you need to follow your set itinerary, though this can be changed en route without too much fuss. For more details and some sample fares, see under the relevant destination. A more flexible option is the **Island Rover**, which offers unlimited travel on *CalMac* ferries for a set period, though you still need to make reservations. An eight-day pass costs £43 per passenger and £210 for a car, and a 15-day pass costs £63 per passenger and £315 for a car. *CalMac* schedules are complicated, but fares and frequency of sailings are given under each relevant destination in this guide. *Western Ferries* runs services between **Gourock** and **Dunoon** and **Islay** and **Jura**.

P&O Scottish Ferries run car ferries to **Orkney** and **Shetland**. Ferries to Orkney depart from **Aberdeen** once or twice weekly and take eight to 10 hours, or from **Scrabster**, near Thurso, a few times daily and take two hours. Fares from Aberdeen are

Essentials

Ferry companies

Caledonian MacBrayne
The Ferry Terminal, Gourock, PA19 1QP,
T01475-650100, reservations T08705-
650000, www.calmac.co.uk
John O' Groats Ferries T01955-
611353.
Orkney Ferries Shore St, Kirkwall, KW15

1LG, T01856-872044,
www.orkneyislands.com
P&O Scottish Ferries PO Box 5,
Jamieson's Quay, Aberdeen AB11 5NP,
T01224-572615, www.poscottish
ferries.co.uk
Western Ferries T0141-3329766.

about £80-85 return for passengers and £140 for a car; from Scrabster it costs around £30-35 per passenger and £80-85 for a car. There's also a passenger ferry from **John O' Groats** to Orkney which sails daily during the summer only (May-September) and is run by **John O' Groats Ferries** (see above).

   P&O Ferries run an overnight ferry from **Aberdeen** to **Shetland** daily except Saturday during the summer months. The journey takes 14-20 hours. Fares are around £115-120 per passenger and £180 for a car. You should also book in advance on these routes if you're travelling by car.

   The **Orkney** islands are linked by services run by **Orkney Ferries**, T01856-872044, while **Shetland's** inter-island ferries are run by **Shetland Islands Council**, T01806-244234. There are also numerous small operators offering day-trips to various islands. Details are given in the relevant chapters.

Train

*For information on
fares and timetables,
see page36*
The rail network in the Scottish Highlands is limited and train travel is comparatively expensive, but trains are a fast and effective way to get around and also provide some beautifully scenic journeys. The West Highland line to Fort William and Mallaig and the journey from Inverness to Kyle of Lochalsh are amongst the most beautiful rail journeys in the world and well worth doing. There are frequent trains between Inverness and Perth and Aberdeen and also from Inverness up the northeast coast to Wick and Thurso.

   ScotRail operates most train services. Details of the different rail passes and railcards available are given below. Details of the different types of tickets are on page 35.

   Cyclists should note that though train comapnies have a more relaxed attitiude to taking bikes on trains, reservations for bikes (£3.50) are still required on some services.

Entertainment and nightlife

People don't come to the Highlands and Islands for nightclubs and multi-screen cinemas, but that isn't to say that everyone is safely tucked up in bed by 2200. There's nothing Highlanders love more than a good party, preferably involving lots of alcohol, singing and dancing.

Pubs & bars As in the rest of Britain, pubs are the main focus of social life and entertainment for most Scots. These vary greatly, from traditional old inns (or *howffs*) full of character (and often full of characters) to the depressingly ubiquitous chain pubs which are appearing on the high streets of every town. In remote parts of the Highlands and Islands the local hotel bar is often the only watering hole for miles around. Pubs generally are open from 1100 till 2300 Monday-Saturday and Sunday from 1100-1200 till 2230. Note that many pubs in more remote parts close for a couple of hours between 1400 and 1600, which can be very annoying on a wet afternoon.

Discount rail passes

ScotRail offers a couple of worthwhile travel passes. The most flexible is the **Freedom of Scotland Travelpass**, *which gives unlimited rail travel within Scotland. It is also valid on all CalMac ferries on the west coast and many Citylink bus services in the Highlands. It also gives 33% discount on P&O Ferries from Scrabster to Orkney and 20% discount on P&O Ferries from Aberdeen to Orkney and Shetland. It costs £69 for four days' travel out of eight consecutive days, £99 for any eight out of*

15 consecutive days and £119 for any 12 out of 15 consecutive days. The **Highland Rover** *is more limited. It allows unlimited rail travel in the Highlands region, plus the West Highland line from Glasgow and travel between Aberdeen and Aviemore. It also allows free travel on Citylink buses between Oban, Fort William and Inverness. It costs £49 for any four out of eight consecutive days. Holders of Senior Citizen's or Young Person's Railcard get a 30% discount on these passes*

Celtic culture is alive and well and you'll be able to hear traditional folk music in many pubs. At weekends you may also happen across a **ceilidh** (pronounced "kay-lee") in the local village hall or hotel. These traditional dances, somewhere between a barn dance and a rugby scrum, can be raucous affairs but great fun, even if you don't have a clue what you're doing. Ask for details at the local tourist office. One of the most unforgettable experiences of a Scottish trip is to find yourself in a pub in the back of beyond, consuming copious quantities of whisky with the locals and then hurling a bunch of total strangers around the room, to the accompaniment of a fiddle and accordion. By the time you reach the top of the nearest mountain the following day, you'll have forgotten all about the hangover.

Live music

Food and drink

While Scotland's national drink is loved the world over, Scottish cooking hasn't exactly had a good press over the years. This is perhaps not too surprising, as the national dish consists of a stomach stuffed with diced innards and served alongside root vegetables, in other words **haggis** served with mashed tatties (potatoes) and neeps (turnips). Not a great start. And things got even worse when the Scots discovered the notorious deep-fried Mars bar.

Places to eat are marked on maps in this book with the symbol ●

But Scottish cuisine has undergone a dramatic transformation in recent years and Scotland now boasts some of the most talented chefs, creating some of the best food in Britain. The heart of Scottish cooking is local produce, which includes the finest fish, shellfish, game, lamb, beef, vegetables and a vast selection of traditionally-made cheeses. What makes Scottish cooking special is ready access to these foods.

Anyone staying at a hotel, guesthouse or B&B will experience the hearty **Scottish breakfast**, which includes bacon, egg, sausage and black pudding (a type of sausage made with blood), all washed down with copious quantities of tea, Scotland's staple drink. Although coffee is readily available everywhere, do not expect *cappuccinos* and *café lattes*: filter coffee is the staple 'tea-substitue' in most hotels and B&Bs. You may also be served kippers (smoked herring) or **porridge**, an erstwhile Scottish staple, which is now eaten by few people. Porridge is made with oatmeal and has the consistency of Italian polenta. It is traditionally eaten with salt, though heretics are offered sugar instead. **Oatcakes** (oatmeal biscuits) may also be on offer, as well as potato scones, baps (bread rolls), bannocks (a sort of large oatcake) or butteries (butter-laden

Essentials

 The price of a feed

*In this book places to eat are divided into three categories: **expensive** (over £20 a head); **mid-range** (£10-20 a head); and **cheap** (under £10 a head). These prices are based on a two-course meal (main course plus starter or dessert) without drinks. We have tried to include an equal number of choices in each category, though this is not always possible. All places listed are recommended as offering relatively good value, quality and standards of service within their respective price category.*

bread similar to a croissant). These local baked goodies can be spread with marmalade, brought to the world's breakfast tables by the city of Dundee.

After such a huge cooked breakfast you probably won't feel like eating again until **high tea**, taken between 1700 and 1800. This national institution consists of a cooked main course (usually fish and chips) and a *smorgesbord* of scones and cakes, washed down with pots of tea.

Scottish dishes Fish, meat and game form the base of many of the country's finest dishes. Scottish **beef**, particularly Aberdeen Angus, is the most famous in the world and largely escaped the worst of the BSE scares of recent years. This will, or should, usually be hung for at least four weeks and sliced thick. **Game** is also a regular feature of Scottish menus, though it can be expensive, especially **venison** (deer), but delicious and low in cholesterol. **Pheasant** and **hare** are also tasty, but **grouse** is, quite frankly, overrated.

Fish and **seafood** are fresh and plentiful and if you're travelling around the northwest coast you must not miss the chance to savour local mussels, prawns, oysters, scallops, langoustines, lobster or crab. **Salmon** is, of course, the most famous of Scottish fish, but you're more likely to be served the fish-farmed variety than 'wild' salmon, which has a more delicate flavour. Trout is also farmed extensively, but the standard of both remains high. **Kippers** are also a favourite delicacy, the best of which come from Loch Fyne or the Achilitibuie smokery. **Arbroath smokies** (smoked haddock) are a tasty alternative.

Haggis, has made something of a comeback and small portions are often served as starters in fashionable restaurants. Haggis is traditionally eaten on *Burns Night* (25 January) in celebration of the great poet's birthday, when it is piped to the table and then slashed open with a sword at the end of a recital of Robert Burns' *Address to the Haggis*. Other national favourites feature names to relish: **cock-a-leekie** is a soup made from chicken, leeks and prunes; **cullen skink** is a delicious concoction of smoked haddock and potatoes; while at the other end of the scale of appeal is **hugga-muggie**, a Shetland dish using fish's stomach. There's also the delightfully-named **crappit heids** (haddock heads stuffed with lobster), **partan bree** (a soup made form giant crab's claws, cooked with rice) and **stovies**, which is a mash of potato, onion and minced beef. Rather more mundane is the ubiquitous **Scotch broth**, made with mutton stock, vegetables, barley, lentils and split peas.

Waist-expanding **puddings** or desserts are a very important part of Scottish cooking and often smothered in butterscotch sauce or syrup in order to satisfy a sweet-toothed nation. There is a huge variety, including **cranachan**, a mouth-watering mix of toasted oatmeal steeped in whisky, cream and fresh raspberries, and **Atholl Brose**, a similar confection of oatmeal, whisky and cream.

Eaten before pudding, in the French style, or afterwards, are Scotland's many home-produced **cheeses**, which have made a successful comeback in the face of mass-produced varieties. Amongst the tastiest examples are **Lanark Blue**, made from unpasteurized ewe's milk and similar to Roquefort, and **Teviotdale** and **Bonchester**, which both come from the Borders. Many of the finest cheeses are

How malt whisky is made

Malt whisky is made by first soaking dry barley in tanks of local water for two to three days. Then the barley is spread out on a concrete floor or placed in cylindrical drums and allowed to germinate for between eight and 12 days, after which it is dried in a kiln, heated by a peat fire. Next, the dried malt is ground and mixed with hot water in a huge circular vat called a 'mash tun'. A sugary liquid called 'wort' is then drawn from the porridge-like result and piped into huge

containers where living yeast is stirred into the mix in order to convert the sugar in the wort into alcohol. After about 48 hours the 'wash' is transferred to copper pot stills and heated till the alcohol vaporizes and is then condensed by a cooling plant into distilled alcohol which is passed through a second still. Once distilled, the liquid is poured into oak casks and left to age for a minimum of three years, though a good malt will stay casked for at least eight years.

Essentials

produced on the islands, especially Arran, Mull, Islay and Orkney. **Caboc** is a creamy soft cheese rolled in oatmeal and is made in the Highlands.

For a **cheap** meal, you're best bet is a **pub**, **hotel bar** or **café**, where you can have a one-course meal for around £5 or less, though don't expect gourmet food. The best value is often at lunch time, when many restaurants offer three-course **set lunches** or business lunches for less than £10. You'll need a pretty huge appetite to feel like eating a three-course lunch after your gigantic cooked breakfast, however. Also good value are the **pre-theatre dinners** offered by restaurants in the main towns (you don't need to have a theatre ticket to take advantage). **Vegetarians** are increasingly well catered for, especially in the larger towns, where exclusively vegetarian/vegan restaurants and cafés are often the cheapest places to eat. Outside the main tourist centres, vegetarian restaurants are thin on the ground, though better quality eating places will normally offer a reasonable vegetarian selection.

Eating out

The biggest problem with eating out in Scotland, as in the rest of the UK, is the ludicrously limited serving hours in most pubs and hotels. These places only serve food between 1230 and 1400 and 1700 and 1900, seemingly ignorant of the eating habits of foreign visitors, or those who would prefer a bit more flexibility during their holiday. In small places especially, it can be difficult finding food outside these strictly-enforced times. Places which serve food all day till 2100 or later are restaurants, fast-food outlets and the many chic bistros and café-bars, which can be found not only in the main cities but increasingly in smaller towns. The latter may not be to everyone's taste, but they often offer very good value and above-average quality.

Those who prefer to eat to live, rather than the other way round, need never spend more than £5-6 for lunch and £7-10 for dinner, excluding drinks. It is generally not difficult to find a **cheap** meal, though on many of the islands and in more remote parts of the northwest Highlands, there is less choice and prices tend to be higher. Also, if you're on a tight budget avoid those restaurants at visitor centres or other such tourist traps, as they tend to charge exorbitant prices for very average food.

At the other end of the scale, there are many excellent **restaurants**. These are often found in hotels, where you can enjoy the finest of Scottish cuisine, often with a continental influence. You can expect to pay from around £25 a head up to £40 or £50 in the very top establishments. Many of the best restaurants in the country are included in the *Taste of Scotland* guide (£7.99), which is better than most eating guides (though restaurants have to pay to be included) but certainly not comprehensive.

Which whisky?

*Opinions vary as to what are the best single malts and as to when you should drink them, but generally speaking a Speyside malt such as Glenmorangie or Glenlivet is best supped **before dinner** and one of the Islay malts – Ardbeg, Bowmore, Bunnahabhain (pronounced 'bun-a-haven'), Lagavulin, or the very wonderful Laphroaig (pronounced 'la-froig') – **after dinner**.*

If the Islays are not to your taste, then you could try instead Highland Park from Orkney or perhaps Tamdhu or Aberlour from Speyside. Those eternal favourites, Glenfiddich and The Macallan, can be enjoyed at any time.

Drinks

Beer Beer is the staple alcoholic drink in Scotland. The most popular type of beer is lager, but connoisseurs should sample one of the many excellent types of **heavy**, which is a thick, dark ale served at room temperature with a full, creamy head. Types of heavy are graded by the shilling, which indicates its strength; the higher the number the stronger the beer. The usual range is 60 to 80 shillings (written 80/-). The best ales are hand-pumped from the cask under pressure. Beer is served in pints, or half pints, and you'll pay between £1.50 and £2.20 for a pint, depending on the brew and location of the pub.

The market is dominated by the large brewers – *Youngers*, *McEwan's*, *Scottish & Newcastle* and *Tennet's*. They produce smooth, strong beers, but the country's best seller is, strangely enough, *Tartan Special*, which is weak and tasteless by comparison. For the best of Scottish beers, however, you should try one of the small **local breweries**. Edinburgh's *Caledonian* produces a wide range of excellent cask ales. Others worth trying are *Belhaven*, brewed in Dunbar near Edinburgh, *Maclays*, brewed in Alloa, and the very wonderful *Greenmantle*, brewed in the Borders.

Whisky
More than 700 mn bottles a year are exported, mainly to the United States, France, Japan and Spain

No visit to Scotland would be complete without availing oneself of a 'wee dram'. There is no greater pleasure on an inclement Highland evening than enjoying a malt whisky in front of a roaring log fire whilst watching the rain outside pelt down relentlessly. The roots of Scotland's national drink (*uisge beatha*, or 'water of life' in Gaelic) go back to the late 15th century, but it wasn't until the invention of a patent still in the early 19th century that distilling began to develop from small family-run operations to the large manufacturing business it has become today.

There are two types of whisky: **single malt**, made only from malted barley; and **grain**, which is made from malted barley together with unmalted barley, maize or other cereals, and is faster and cheaper to produce. Most of the popular brands are blends of both types of whisky – usually 60-70% grain to 30-40% malt. These **blended** whiskies account for over 90% of all sales worldwide and most of the production of single malts is used to add flavour to a blended whisky. Amongst the best known brands of blended whisky are *Johnnie Walker*, *Bells*, *Teachers* and *Famous Grouse*. There's not much between them in terms of flavour and they are usually drunk with a mixer, such as water or soda.

Single malts are a different matter altogether. Each is distinctive and should be drunk neat to fully appreciate its subtle flavours. Single malts vary enormously. Their distinctive favours and aromas are derived from the peat used for drying, the water used for mashing, the type of oak cask used and the location of the distillery.

Single malts fall into four groups: Highland, Lowland, Campbeltown and Islay. There are over 40 distilleries to choose from, most offering guided tours. The majority are located around Speyside, in the northeast. The region's many distilleries include that perennial favourite, *Glenfiddich*, which is sold in 185 countries. A recommended alternative is the produce of the beautiful and peaceful Isle of Islay, whose malts are lovingly described in terms of their peaty quality. Scots tend to favour the 10 year-old *Glenmorangie*, while the most popular in the USA is *The Macallan*.

Shopping

The shelves of gift shops in every tourist attraction from Lerwick to Loch Lomond are stuffed full of dreadful tartan tat such as 'See-you-Jimmy' wigs and bonnets, Loch Ness monster replicas and those scary-looking tartan dolls with flickering eyelashes. All very harmless (except for the dolls which give you nightmares) but don't do much for Scotland's image. But amongst all this tourist kitsch are many excellent high-quality goods on offer.

See also individual towns for tips on local bargains

Scottish **textiles**, especially the tartan variety, are popular and worth buying. Everything from a travelling rug to your own kilt outfit. Shops throughout the Highlands and Islands, especially in Inverness, can tell which clan your family belongs to and make you a kilt in that particular tartan. For the full outfit, including kilt, sporran, jacket, shoes and *skeann dhu* dagger expect to pay in the region of £600, or more if you want more elaborate accessories. There are mill shops making tweeds and cloths in many parts of Scotland. **Harris Tweed** is also a good buy and you can watch your cloth being woven on the Hebridean islands of Harris and Lewis.

Knitwear is also good value and sold throughout Scotland. Shetland is a good place to find high-quality wool products. Note that Aran jumpers are not from the island of Arran, but from Aran (with one 'r') in Ireland.

Jewellery is another popular souvenir and there are many excellent craft shops throughout the Highlands and Islands making beautiful jewellery with Celtic designs.

Food is another good souvenir and not just the ubiquitous shortbread is sold in tartan tins. If you haven't far to travel home, **smoked salmon**, or any other smoked product, is good value. One of the best places for food products is the island of **Arran**, where you can buy their delicious local mustards and preserves, smoked fish and game, and cheeses. And, of course, there's **whisky**. Most distilleries will refund the cost of their guided tour in the form of a discount voucher on a bottle of their brand whisky.

Shop hours in Scotland are generally Monday to Saturday from 0900-1730 or 1800. However, in more remote parts opening hours are slightly reduced. Few shops are open on Sunday, most notably in the Outer Hebrides, when nothing is open on a Sunday and in many rural areas there is an early-closing day when shops close at 1300. This varies from region to region but the most common day is Wednesday.

Shopping hours

Sport and special interest travel

Scotland is a great country for outdoor activities and many visitors come specifically to enjoy the magnificent scenery as they walk in the hills, cycle through forests, ski down mountains or head off in search of rare wildlife. The coastline, lochs and rivers are ideal for fishing and offer plenty of opportunities for a whole range of watersports, including windsurfing, sailing and scuba diving, and there are lots of beautiful beaches.

Hillwalking

The Scottish Highlands and Islands is a walker's paradise. There are numerous marked trails, ranging from short walks to long-distance treks from one side of the country to the other. Whatever your taste or level of fitness and experience, you'll find plenty opportunities to get off the beaten track and explore the countryside.

The best time is usually from May to September for hiking in the mountains, though in the more low-lying parts, April and October should also be safe. Winter walking in the Highlands requires technical equipment such as ice axes and crampons and a lot of experience. July and August are the busiest times, though only the most popular routes, such as Ben Nevis, get really crowded. Another problem during these months are midges (see page 62). May to mid-June is probably the most pleasant time overall, as the weather can often be fine and the midges have yet to appear. September is also a good time, though it can be a lot colder.

Access
The Highlands and islands is free of foot-and-mouth and open for outdoor pursuits

Scotland has a long tradition of generally free responsible access to mountain and moorland. This free access, of course, relies on walkers behaving responsibly and recognizing that the countryside is a place of work as well as recreation (see page38). Most land in Scotland is privately owned and at certain times of the year, such as the main shooting seasons, walkers may be asked to respect certain restrictions on access. The main **deer stalking** season runs from mid-August to 20 October and the **grouse shooting** season is between 12 August (referred to as the 'Glorious Twelfth') and 10 December. For more information on this, see *Heading for the Scottish Hills*, which is published by the Mountaineering Council of Scotland (see below) and the Scottish Landowners Federation and gives estate maps and telephone numbers to call for local advice. There may also be restricted access during the lambing season (March-May).

It is not an offence to walk over someone's land but, especially during the stalking and shooting seasons, you may be asked to take a different route, though this rarely happens. There are no national parks but there is free access at all times of the year to areas owned by the **National Trust for Scotland** (address on page 20). These areas include Torridon and Glencoe. There is also free access to most land owned by the *Forestry Commission*, and there is good public access to land owned by the *John Muir Trust*, *Scottish Natural Heritage*, the *Royal Society for the Protection of Birds* (address on page 57) and the *Woodland Trust*, though these areas are not marked on *Ordnance Survey* (OS) maps. Also not shown on OS maps are **Rights of Way**, which are signposted by the Scottish Rights of Way Society's green metal signs. The society publishes maps of rights of way, many of which follow ancient 'drove roads' through the hills.

Information & advice

The *Scottish Tourist Board* is a useful source of information for walkers (address on page 21). Local tourist offices have details of interesting local walks. The organizations listed opposite are also useful sources of information.

Many walk descriptions and maps are given in this guidebook, but these should ideally be used in conjunction with a good map, such as the *Ordnance Survey* (OS) *Landranger* series. The relevant map numbers have been listed, where possible, with the route description. OS maps can be found at tourist offices and also at **outdoor shops**, which are usually staffed by experienced climbers and walkers who can give good advice about the right equipment. The best equipped shops are *Tiso*, www.tiso.co.uk, who have branches in the main towns and cities, and *Nevisport* in Fort William. For a list of recommended walking guidebooks and maps, see page 62.

Long distance walks

There is a network of long walking trails carefully prepared to provide ideal walking conditions together with sufficient places for accommodation and supplies en route. These walks can be attempted in full or sampled in part by less experienced walkers. Area tourist boards and local tourist offices can provide information and advice for their own particular sections. One of the three main trails, the **Speyside Way** (see page 180), is covered in this handbook. The best known, and busiest, long distance trail is the **West Highland Way**, which runs for 95 miles from Milngavie (pronounced 'mull-guy'), just north of Glasgow, to Fort William. The route progresses steadily from the lowlands, along the eastern shore of **Loch Lomond** and the traverse of the western edge of **Rannoch Moor**, to enter **Glencoe** at White Corries. It continues along the Devil's Staircase, past Kinlochleven, and through **Glen Nevis** to Fort William. Many walkers finish off with an ascent of **Ben Nevis** (4,406 ft), the highest mountain in Britain (see page226). **Further information**, including a trail leaflet with accommodation and facilities guide, is available from *West Highland Way Ranger Service*, Balloch Castle, Balloch, G53 8LX, T01389-758216.

Many of the most popular short walks, including the ascent of Ben Nevis, are described in this guidebook. They range from gentle strolls through forest glades to strenuous hikes, steep hills and mountains, and also include some beautiful coastal trails. One of the most popular pastimes is Munro-bagging (see page 55), which involves climbing as many peaks over 3,000 ft as possible. The Highlands is the best area for this providing many challenging peaks and it's possible to climb several in a day. Many of these hills are straightforward climbs, but many also require a high level of fitness and experience, and all require proper **clothing** (see 'safety' below).

Short walks

Other good areas for walking include the **Isles of Arran**, **Mull**, **Islay** and **Skye**, **Perthshire**, **Stirling** and the **Trossachs**. The mighty **Cairngorms** are better known as a winter ski area, but provide excellent year-round hillwalking and climbing. This is extremely wild terrain, however, and suitable only for experienced walkers. There are many opportunities for less experienced walkers in Rothiemurchus Estate and Glenmore Forest Park around **Aviemore**. Other areas which are best left to serious climbers are **Torridon**, **Kintail** and **Glencoe**, though the latter also offers a few more straightforward walks through spectacular scenery.

Climbing

The Cairngorms, Cuillins on Skye, Glencoe and Torridon offer the most challenging climbing in Scotland. For a list of climbing **guidebooks**, see page 62. For more detailed information, contact the *Mountaineering Council of Scotland*, 4a St Catherine's Road, Perth, T01738-638227. A recommended rock climbing and mountaineering instructor is Gary Latter, Kinalty Cottage, By Kirriemuir, Angus, DD8 5LY, T01575-530308.

Visitors should be aware of the need for caution and safety preparations when walking or climbing in the mountains. The nature of Scottish weather is such that a fine sunny day can turn into driving rain or snow in a matter of minutes. Remember that a blizzard can be raging on the summit when the car park at the foot of the mountain is bathed in sunshine. It is essential to get an up-to-date weather forecast before setting off on any walk or climb.

Mountain safety
A weather phone-line service is available from the following numbers:
East Highlands T0891-333197;
West Highlands T0891-333198

Whatever the time of year, or conditions when you set off, you should always carry or wear essential items of clothing. A basic list for summer conditions would be: **boots** with a good tread and ankle support and a thick pair of socks; **waterproof jacket and trousers**, even on a sunny day; **hat and gloves** are important if the weather turns bad; **warm trousers** should be worn or carried, tracksuit bottoms are okay if you also have waterproof trousers; **spare woolly jumper or fleece jacket** will provide an extra layer; **map and compass** are essential to carry and to know how to use. Other essentials are **food and drink**, a simple **first aid kit**, a **whistle** and a **torch**. A small 25-30 litre rucksack should be adequate for carrying the above items. Also remember to leave details of your route and expected time of return with someone, and remember to inform them on your return.

Essentials

Cycling organizations

Cyclists' Touring Club (CTC), *Cotterell House, 69 Meadrow, Godalming, Surrey, GU7 3HS, T01483-417217, www.ctc.org.uk The largest cycling organization in the UK, providing a wide range of services and information on transport, cycle hire and routes, from day rides to longer tours.*
Forestry Enterprise, 21 Church St, Inverness, IV1 1EL, T01463-232811. Provides information on Scotland's extensive network of forest trails.

The Scottish Cyclists' Union (SCU), The Velodrome, Meadowbank Stadium, London Rd, Edinburgh, EH7 6AY, T0131-6520187, www.btinternet.com/~scottish.cycling Produces an annual handbook and calendar of events for road racing, time trialling and mountain biking.
SUSTRANS, 53 Cochrane St, Glasgow, G1 1HL, T0141-5720234, www.sustrans.co.uk Provides information on new cycle trails.

In the winter extra warm clothing is needed, as well as an **ice axe** and **crampons** (and the ability to use them). The skills required for moving over ice or snow should be practised with an experienced and qualified mountain guide/instructor.

Cycling and mountain biking

The bicycle was invented in Scotland so it seems appropriate that travelling by bike is one of the best ways to explore the country. Most towns are not particularly cycle-friendly. Very few have proper cycle routes and there's the added problem of security. It's best to stick to rural backroads, especially unclassified roads and country lanes, which are not numbered but are signposted and marked on OS maps. There are also forest trails and dedicated routes along canal towpaths and disused railway tracks. The main problem in rural areas, though, is the availability of spare parts.

The remote and wild Highlands are understandably popular with cyclists but as it is also walking country cyclists should stick to tracks where a right to cycle exists and be considerate towards walkers. The *Forestry Commission* has 1150 miles of excellent off-road routes up and down the country. These are detailed in a series of *Cycling in the Forest* leaflets, which are available from Forestry Enterprise offices (see above) and from most tourist offices. These are best used by **mountain bikes** with multi gears, though easier routes can be attempted on hybrid or standard bikes.

You can cut down on the amount of pedalling you have to do by **transporting your bike** by train. Bikes can be taken free on most local rail services on a first come-first served basis (call *ScotRail* bookings, T0845-550033). On long-distance routes you'll have to make a reservation (£3.50 charge) and pay a small charge. Space is limited on trains so it's a good idea to book as far in advance as possible. **Bus and coach** companies will not carry bikes, unless they are dismantled and boxed. **Ferries** transport bikes for a small fee and **airlines** will often accept them as part of your baggage allowance. Check with the ferry company or airline about any restrictions.

Bike rental is available at cycle shops in most large towns and cities and tourist centres. Expect to pay from around £6-15 per day, or from £50 a week, plus a refundable deposit. There's also the option of a **cycling holiday package**, which includes transport of your luggage, prebooked accommodation, route instructions, food and backup support. A list of specialists is given above.

The STB publishes a free booklet, *Cycling in Scotland*, which is useful and suggests routes in various parts of the country, as well as accommodation and repair shops. Many area tourist boards also provide cycling guides for their own areas. A list of useful **cycle guides and books** is given on page 62.

Munros, Corbetts and Grahams

There are 284 mountains over 3,000 ft (914 m) in Scotland, known as 'Munros', after Sir Hugh Munro, first president of the Scottish Mountaineering Club (SMC), who published the first comprehensive list of these mountains, in 1891. In the 1920s a further list was published, of the 221 summits between 2,500 and 3,000 ft, by

J Rooke Corbett, and these became known as 'Corbetts'. A third list, of summits between 2,000 and 2,500 ft was compiled by Fiona Graham and published in 1992. This list was subsequently revised and corrected and now all peaks of between 2,000 and 2,500 ft are called Grahams.

Essentials

Golf

Scotland has over 400 golf courses, with more being built all the time, and, therefore has more courses per head of population than any other country in the world. Any decent sized town will have a golf course nearby and most, if not all, are available for play. There are many public courses, which tend to be both cheap and extremely busy often have excellent layouts. The majority of private clubs allow visitors, although many have restrictions as to what days these visitors can play. Weekends are usually reserved for club competitions for the members and it is best to try to play on a week-day. All private clubs have a dress code and it is inadvisable to turn up for a round in a collarless shirt and jeans. These minor caveats aside, you are more than likely to receive a warm and courteous welcome.

Green fees for one of the top courses will cost from around £40 upwards. Many clubs offer a daily or weekly ticket. A **Golf Pass Scotland** costs between £50 and £70 for five days (Monday-Friday), depending on the area. *Golf in Scotland* is a free brochure listing 400 courses and clubs with accommodation details. For a copy contact the *Scottish Tourist Board*. The *British Tourist Authority* (BTA) has a very useful *Golfing Holidays* booklet which provides details of golfing holidays and major golf tournaments in Britain. (BTA and STB address on page 21). For a list of recommended golf books, see page 62.

Skiing

Conditions in Scotland are not as good or reliable as anywhere in the Alps, but on a clear, sunny day, and with good snow, you can enjoy some decent skiing. However, at weekends, in conditions like these, expect the slopes to be very busy. Scotland offers both **alpine** (downhill) and **nordic** (cross-country) skiing, as well as the increasingly-popular **snowboarding**. The high season is from January to April, but it is possible to ski from as early as November to as late as May. Ski packages are available but it's easy to arrange everything yourself and there's plentiful accommodation and facilities in and around the ski centres.

There are **five ski centres** in Scotland. The largest are **Glenshee**, which has the largest network of lifts and selection of runs, as well as snow machines, and **Cairngorm**, which has almost 30 runs spread over an extensive area. **Glencoe** is the oldest of the ski resorts, and the **Nevis Range**, at Aonach Mor near Fort William, has the highest ski runs and only gondola in Scotland, as well as a dry slope. **The Lecht** is the most remote centre and is good for beginners and families and for nordic skiing. Access to all five centres is easiest by car. Each resort has a ski patrol and facilities for snowboarding.

Ski equipment and clothing can be hired at all resorts but lessons should be booked in advance. Prices vary from centre to centre, but on average expect to pay around £15

Costs

per day for hire of skis, sticks and boots, and around £12 per day for ski clothes. Snowboard hire is around £18 per day for board and boots. Lift passes cost around £20 per day, or £70-80 for five days. Ski lessons are around £18-20 for four hours. Packages including ski hire, tuition and lift pass cost from around £125 to £155 for five days. These prices are for adults; prices for juniors are less.

Information Details for each of the five resorts, including phone numbers, are given in the appropriate place in the main text. For further general information contact the **Scottish Tourist Board** for its *Ski Scotland* brochure and accommodation list, or visit their website, www.ski.scotland.net, which is updated daily. Or you can contact the **Scottish National Ski Council**, T0131-3177280, www.snsc.demon.co.uk They produce a useful *Snowsport Scotland Handbook*.

The **ski hotline** weather-report service gives the latest snow and weather conditions plus a five-day forecast. Phone 0891-654 followed by: 655 for Cairngorm; 656 for Glenshee; 657 for The Lecht; 658 for Glencoe; 660 for Nevis Range; and 659 for cross-country skiing.

Fishing

Scotland's rivers, streams, lochs and estuaries are among the cleanest waters in Europe and are filled with salmon, trout (sea, brown and rainbow) and pike. Not surprisingly, then, fishing (coarse, game and sea) is hugely popular.

There is no close season for **coarse fishing** or **sea angling**. For **wild brown trout** the close season is early October to mid-March. The close season for **salmon** and **sea trout** varies from area to area and between net and rod fishing. It is generally from late August to early February for net fishing, and from early November to early February for rod fishing.

No licence is required to fish but most of the land and rivers are privately owned so you must obtain a **permit** from the owners or their agents. These are often readily available at the local fishing tackle shop and usually cost from around £15, though some rivers can be far more expensive.

The STB's booklet *Fish Scotland* is a good introduction and a source of all kinds of information. It is available free from tourist offices, or by post (see page 21). Also contact the **Scottish Federation of Sea Anglers**, Brian Burn, Flat 2, 16 Bellevue Road, Ayr, KA7 2SA, T01292-264735, or **Scottish National Anglers Association**, David Wilkie, Administration Office, Caledonia House, South Gyle, Edinburgh, EH12 9DQ, T0131- 3398808.

Pony trekking and horse riding

Pony trekking is a long-established activity and miles of beautiful coastline, lochsides, and moorland are accessible on horseback. There are numerous equestrian centres catering to all levels of riders. The Scottish Tourist Board produces a *Trekking & Riding* brochure listing riding centres, all approved by the **Trekking and Riding Society of Scotland** (TRSS) or the **British Horse Society** (BHS). Centres offer **pony trekking** (leisurely strolls at walking pace for novices), **hacks** (short rides at a fast pace for experienced riders) and **trail riding** (long distance rides at no more than a canter). For general information contact the TRSS, Horse Trials Office, Blair Atholl, Perthshire, T01796-481543.

Birdwatching

Over 450 species have been recorded throughout Scotland, including vast colonies of seabirds, birds of prey and many rare species. Among the best places in Scotland to see birds are **Handa Island**, off the coast of Sutherland, and the **Treshnish Islands**, off Mull, where you'll see colonies of shags, razorbills, guillemots, pulmars, kittiwakes and puffins. Other good places for birdwatching are **Loch Garten** and **Abernethy Forest**, by Boat of Garten, famous for its ospreys and the only place in the world to see the Scottish crossbill, **Culbin Sands**, not far from the Moray Firth, the mudflats of **Udale Bay**, and **Forsinard**. Many of the Hebridean islands, such as **Islay** and **Mull**, are home to a rich variety of seabirds and you can also see golden eagles. **Orkney** and **Shetland** are famous for their rich variety of birdlife and are home to large colonies of seabirds and migratory birds. There are puffins, kittiwakes, fulmars, shags, razorbills, guillmeots and even auks.

Further information can be obtained from the *Royal Society for the Protection of Birds*, 17 Regent Terrace, Edinburgh EH7 5BT, T0131-5573136, the *Scottish Ornithologists Club*, 21 Regent Terrace, Edinburgh EH7 5BT, T0131-5566042, *Scottish Natural Heritage*, 12 Hope Terrace, Edinburgh EH9 2AS, T0131-4474784 and the *Scottish Wildlife Trust*, Cramond House, Cramond Glebe Road, Edinburgh EH4 6NS, T0131-3127765, which owns and runs over 100 nature reserves.

Dolphin, seal, whale and otter spotting

Almost anywhere around the coast of the Highlands and Islands there is a chance to see dolphins and occasionally porpoises, seals and whales. The most popular place to see **dolphins** is in the Moray Firth area which has a resident population of about 150, most frequently seen in the summer months. Other good places to catch glimpses of the creatures are at the entrance to the Caledonian Canal at Inverness, Nairn beach, Arderseir, Fort George, Fortrose and Cromarty. **Seals** can be seen in abundance. They can often be observed lolling about on sandbanks when the tide is out and there are plenty of seal spotting boat trips on offer from spring to autumn. **Otters** are more elusive. They tend to live on undisturbed remote stretches of the seashore or quiet areas of a river. If you are determined to spot the creatures, for further information contact *Skye Environmental Centre* (home to the *International Otter Survival Fund*) T01471-822487. **Whales**, Minke and Orcas, inhabit the Atlantic, Pentland Firth and the Moray Firth. Contact the *Highlands of Scotland Tourist Board*, T0870-5143070, www.highlandfreedom.com, for details of boat trips.

Diving

There are thousands of dive sites around Scotland' shores with a rich variety of marine life and plenty of wrecks to explore. The **West Coast** offers the best diving, as the water is warmed by the effects of the Gulf Stream and is not cold, even without a dry suit. Among the best sites are the **west coast of Harris**, the **Summer Isles** and the remote island of **St Kilda**. There lots of wrecks in the **Sound of Mull** and the chance to find a Spanish Galleon off **Tobermory**. **Scapa Flow** in Orkney is world renowned as the burial site of the German First World War fleet.

Contact *Scottish Sub Aqua Club*, 40 Bogmoor Place, Glasgow, G51 47Q, T0141-4251021 or *British Sub Aqua Club (Scottish Federation)*, 67 Moredun Park, Gilmerton, Edinburgh EH17, T0131-6644381. A recommended dive operator is *Dive Scotland*, T0131-4412001, in Edinburgh.

Surfing

Scotland has some of the best surfing beaches in Europe. This is no Hawaii, with its sunbleached hair and bronzed bodies. Surfing in Scotland is strictly for the hardy, with water temperatures rarely above 15°C and often as low as 7°C. A good wet suit is

The main season is Sep-Dec

therefore essential. The waves though make up for the freezing waters comparing with those in Hawaii and Australia.

The best beaches on the **West Coast** are to be found at the northern tip of the **Isle of Lewis** and at **Machrihanish**, down near the Mull of Kintyre. On the **North Coast** the top spot is **Thurso**, especially at Dunnet Head to the east of town. Another recommended place is **Strathy Bay**, near Bettyhill, halfway between Thurso and Tongue. **Nigg Bay**, just south of Aberdeen, between Montrose and Arbroath, is also good.

There is a bi-monthly surf magazine, *Surf*, which is a good source of information. Also try the surf shops, which sell equipment and provide information on the best breaks. If you visit either Glasgow, Edinburgh or Aberdeen there is *Clan*, 45 Hyndland Street, Partick, T0141-3396523 and *Boardwise*, 1146 Argyle Street, T0141-3345559 in Glasgow and *Momentum*, 22 Bruntsfield Place, T0131-2296665 in Edinburgh and *Granite Reef*, 45 Justice Street, T01224-621193 in Aberdeen.

Windsurfing

As you'd expect of a country which experiences more than it'as fair share of strong winds, Scotland is a popular destination for windsurfers. The more sheltered lochs such as Loch Earn and Loch Tay offer good facilities and opportunities for novices to get to grips with the sport, but the wild west coast gives experienced windsurfers the chance to really test their abilities, particularly the Isle of Tiree, the 'windsurfing capital of Scotland'.

Canoeing

Scotland's rivers, lochs and deeply indented coastline offer great opportunities for canoeing or kayaking. For information, contact the *Scottish Canoe Association*, Caledonia House, South Gyle, Edinburgh EH12 9DQ, T0131-3177314, www.scotcanoe.org They organize tours, including introductory ones for beginners. Also try *Splash Rafting* of Aberfeldy, splashraft@compuserve.com

Paragliding

If you fancy getting high during your visit, you can try your hand at the exciting sport of paragliding. *Flying Fever*, No 2 Coastguard House, Kildonan, Isle of Arran, T01770-820292, www.arran.uk.com/kildonan/flyingfever are a company offering such trips.

Curling

Curling is nothing to with hairdressing, but is in fact a winter game which involves sliding smooth circular granite stones across the ice as close to the centre of a target as possible, while your team-mates use brooms to sweep away the loose white flakes (a bit like hairdressing, in fact). It is still played on frozen ponds occasionally but more commonly played in indoor ice rinks.

Spectator sports

Football   Football (soccer) is Scotland's most popular spectator sport. The **Scottish Football League**, established in 1874, is the main competition, but is dominated, and always has been, by the two main Glasgow teams, *Rangers* and *Celtic*, known collectively as the 'Old Firm', who regularly attract crowds of over 50,000. The top 12 teams make up the Premier League. Teams in the lower divisions mostly exist on a shoestring budget, though the other major competition, the Scottish FA Cup, still throws up occasional upsets, such as Celtic's defeat a few years back at the hands of lowly *Inverness Caledonian Thistle*, who also managed to reach the last eight of the competition in 2001. The domestic football **season** runs from early August to mid-May. Most matches are played on Saturdays at 1500, and there are often games through the week, on Tuesday and Wednesday evenings at 1930. There is usually a match on a Sunday afternoon, which is broadcast live on satellite TV. **Tickets** range from £10 up to £20 for big games.

The **national** team play at the recently-renovated Hampden Park in Glasgow. Their passionate supporters, known as the 'Tartan Army', have gained something of an international reputation for their fun-loving attitude and self-deprecating humour in the face of defeat. This has stood them in good stead over the years, for despite qualifying for every World Cup final save one since 1974, Scotland have never managed to reach the second round, failing against such footballing giants as Iran and Costa Rica along the way.

Rugby is one of the major sports of the country but lags a long, long way behind football in terms of popularity. The national team plays at Murrayfield in Edinburgh and during match weekends there's always a great atmosphere in the city. Every year, in February and March, Scotland takes part in the **Six Nations Championship**, along with the other home teams, plus France and Italy. The most important game, though, is the clash with the 'Auld enemy', England. Tickets for games are hard to come by, but you can contact the *Scottish Rugby Union* (*SRU*), T0131-3465000, for details of upcoming home fixtures and where to find tickets. **Rugby Union**

Shinty (or *camanachd* in Gaelic) is an amateur sport similar to Ireland's hurling. It's a physical game played at a fast and furious pace, and is a bit like hockey, but with more blood. The game is played mostly in the Highlands and the highlight of the season is the **Camanachd Cup Final**, which attracts a large crowd and is televised. **Shinty**

Keeping in touch

Communications

Many hotels have internet access and some hostels also offer internet access to their guests. Websites and email addresses are listed where appropriate in this guide. The Scottish Tourist Board and area tourist boards have their own websites and these are given on page 21. **Cybercafés** are also listed under each relevant section. In the absence of any cybercafés listed under a particular town try the public library for internet access or ask at the tourist office. **Internet**

Most **post offices** are open Monday-Friday 0900 to 1730 and Saturday 0900 to 1230 or 1300. Smaller sub-post offices are closed for an hour at lunch (1300-1400) and many of them operate out of a shop. Post offices keep the same half-day closing times as shops. **Post**

Stamps can be bought at post offices, but also from vending machines outside and also at many newsagents. A first-class letter to anywhere in the UK costs 26p and should arrive the following day, while second-class letters cost 20p and take between two to four days. Airmail letters of less than 20g cost 30p to Europe. To the USA and Australia costs 43p for 10g and 63g for 20g. For more information about *Royal Mail* postal services, call T0845-7740740.

Essentials

Telephone
Operator: T100
International
operator: T155
Directory enquiries:
T192
Overseas directory
enquiries: T153

Most public **payphones** are operated by *British Telecom* (*BT*) and are fairly widespread in towns and cities, though less so in rural areas. *BT* payphones take either coins (20p, 50p and £1) or **phonecards**, which are available at newsagents and post offices displaying the *BT* logo. These cards come in denominations of £2, £3, £5 and £10. Some payphones also accept credit cards.

For most countries (including Europe, USA and Canada) calls are cheapest between 1800 and 0800 Monday-Friday and all day Saturday and Sunday. For Australia and New Zealand it's cheapest to call from 1430 to 1930 and from midnight to 0700 every day.

Phone codes for towns and cities are given in the margin by the town's heading throughout this book. You don't need to use the area code if calling from the same area. Any number prefixed by 0800 or 0500 is free to the caller; 0845 numbers are charged at local rates and 0990 numbers at the national rate.

To call Scotland from overseas, dial 011 from USA and Canada, 0011 from Australia and 00 from New Zealand, followed by 44, then the area code, minus the first zero, then the number. To call overseas from Scotland dial 00 followed by the country code. **Country codes include**: Australia 61; Ireland 353; New Zealand 64; South Africa 27; USA and Canada 1.

Media

Newspapers

The main British daily and Sunday newspapers are widely available in Scotland and some of them publish special Scottish editions, among them the *Scottish Daily Mail*, *Scottish Daily Express* and Rupert Murdoch's notorious scandal sheet, *The Sun*.

The **Scottish press** produces two main 'quality' newspapers, the liberal-leaning *The Scotsman*, published in Edinburgh, and *The Herald*, published in Glasgow (the oldest daily newspaper in the English-speaking world dating from 1783). The biggest-selling daily is the *Daily Record*, a tabloid paper. The Sunday equivalents of the dailies are *Scotland on Sunday* from the *Scotsman* stable, the *Sunday Herald* and the *Sunday Mail*, published by the *Daily Record*. DC Thomson, who also produce *The Beano* and *Dandy* kids' comics, publish Scotland's most successful Sunday newspaper, the *Sunday Post*, which is fascinating to read but seems incongruous in the 21st century as it has changed little in the last 50 years. Provincial newspapers are widely read in Scotland. In the highlands, the main papers are the weekly *Oban Times* and the radical, crusading *West Highland Free Press* published on Skye. *Time* and *Newsweek* are also available in larger newsagents and bookstores.

Television

There are five main television channels in Scotland; the publicly-funded BBC 1 and 2, and the independent commercial stations, Channel 4, Channel 5 and ITV. The ITV network in Scotland is formed by *STV*, which serves central Scotland and parts of the West Highlands, the Aberdeen-based Grampian TV which produces a lot of Gaelic programmes.

Radio
There is a large
number of local
commercial radio
stations

The BBC network also broadcasts several radio channels, most of which are based in London. These include: **Radio 1** aimed at a young audience; **Radio 2** targeting a more mature audience; **Radio 3** which plays mostly classical music; **Radio 4** which is talk based and features arts, drama and current affairs; and **Radio 5 Live** which is a mix of sport and news. **Radio Scotland** (92-95 FM, 810 MW) provides a Scottish-based diet of news, sport, current affairs, travel and music. It also provides a Gaelic network in the northwest and local programmes in Orkney and Shetland. Some of the local Highland radio stations include **Moray Firth Radio** (97.4 FM) based in Inverness, **Nevis Radio** (96.6 FM), **Lochbroom FM** (102.2 FM), **Speysound and Ski FM** (96.6 FM) and **CaithnessFM** (102.5 FM).

Calendar of events

New Year's Day *A variety of ancient local celebrations take place, including the Kirkwall Ba' Game, a mixture of football and mud wrestling.*
Up-Helly-Aa *Re-enactment of the ancient Viking fire festival held on Shetland on the **last Tuesday in January** (see page 389).*
Burns Night *Burns suppers held on **25th January** all over the country to celebrate the poet's birthday. Lots of haggis, whisky and poetry recitals.*
Braemar Highland Gathering
*Attended by the Royal Family in **September***.
National Mod *Competitive Gaelic music festival held at various locations in*

October (check with the Tourist Board).
Tour of Mull Rally *The highlight of the Scottish rally season, run over the island's public roads (no wonder they're in such appalling condition) in **October**.*
Hogmanay *Old year's night and the most important national celebration. Possible derivations of the word include Holag Monath, Anglo Saxon for 'holy month' and Hoog min dag, which is Dutch for 'great love day'.*
The Highland Festival *Held over 2 weeks from late May till early June at venues throughout the Highland region. For details, T01463-719000, www.highlandfestival.org.uk*

Holidays and festivals

New Year's Day and **2 January, Good Friday** and **Easter Monday, May Day** (the first Monday in May), **Victoria Day** (the last Monday in May), 25 and 26 December (**Christmas Day** and **Boxing Day**). There are also local public holidays in spring and autumn. Dates vary from place to place. Banks are closed during these holidays and sights and shops may be affected to varying degrees. Contact the relevant area Tourist Board for more details.

Bank holidays

There is a huge range of organized events held throughout the Highlands and Islands every year, ranging from Highland Games to humble sheepdog trials. Many of the more obscure traditional events featuring ancient customs dating back many centuries. The Scottish Tourist Board (STB) publishes a comprehensive list, *Events in Scotland*, twice a year. It's free and available from the main tourist offices. Also check out **whatsonwhen.com** and the Highland Tourist Board website, **www.highlandfreedom.com**

Events
Details of local festivals are given in the individual towns

The most popular tourist events are the *Highland Games* (or Gatherings), a series of competitions involving lots of kilts, bagpipes and caber-tossing which are held across the Highlands and Islands from **June to September**. The best known is the *Braemar Gathering* (see page 174), which is attended by various members of the Royal Family. Those at Oban and Dunoon are also large events, but smaller gatherings are often more enjoyable and 'authentic'. *Folk festivals* are also great expressions of Celtic culture and a list of the best and most popular is given on page 425.

Health

No vaccinations are required for entry into Britain. Citizens of **EU** countries are entitled to free medical treatment at National Health Service hospitals on production of an E111 form. Also, Australia, New Zealand and several other non-EU European countries have reciprocal health-care arrangements with Britain.

Medical emergency: dial 999 or 112 (both free) for an ambulance

Essentials

The midge

The major problem facing visitors to the Highlands and Islands of Scotland during the summer months is Culicoides Impunctatus – or the midge, as it's more commonly known. These tiny flying creatures are savage and merciless in the extreme and hunt in huge packs. No sooner have you left your B&B for a pleasant evening stroll, than a cloud of these bloodthirsty little devils will attack from nowhere, getting into your eyes, ears, nose and mouth – and a few places you forgot you even had. The only way to avoid them is to take refuge indoors, or to hide in the nearest loch.

Midges are at their worst in the evening and in damp, shaded or overcast conditions and between late May and September, but they don't like direct sunlight, heavy rain, smoke and wind. Make sure you're well covered up and wear light-coloured clothing (they're attracted to dark colours). Most effective is a midge net, if you don't mind everyone pointing and laughing at you. Insect repellents have some effect, particularly those with DEET, but herbal remedies such as bog myrtle, lavender, citronalla or eucalyptus are considered equally effective. Once you've been attacked the best treatment is antihistamine creams or dock leaves –

Citizens of other countries will have to pay for all medical services, except accident and emergency care given at Accident and Emergency (A&E) Units at most (but not all) National Health hospitals. Health insurance is therefore strongly advised for citizens of non-EU countries.

Pharmacists can dispense only a limited range of drugs without a doctor's prescription. Most are open for normal shop hours, though some are open late, especially in larger towns. Local newspapers will carry lists of which are open late.

Doctors' surgeries are usually open from around 0830-0900 till 1730-1800, though times vary. Outside surgery hours you can go to the casualty department of the local hospital for any complaint requiring urgent attention. For the address of the nearest hospital or doctors' surgery, T0800-665544.

You should encounter no major problems or irritations during your visit. The only exceptions to this are the risk of **hypothermia** if you're walking in the mountains in difficult conditions (see page 53), and the dreaded **midge** (see page62).

Further reading

The books listed below are non-fiction and reference guides. For a list of the best in Scottish fiction and poetry, see **Scottish Writers**, on page 421.

History, politics & culture

The best general overview of Scottish social history is given by **Professor Chris Smout** in his excellent *A History of the Scottish People (1560-1830)* and *A Century of the Scottish People (1830-1950)*. A worthy new contender is *Scotland A New History*, by **Michael Lynch** (Pimlico, 1999). Also *Scotland the Story of a Nation*, by **Magnus Manusson** (Harper Collins, 2000) is a mighty tome, and after reading it you're unlikely to pass on any questions on Scottish history.

For a more emotive and subjective view of highland history, read any of **John** Prebble's books, including *1,000 years of Scotland's History*, *The Lion in the North*, *Glen Coe*, *Culloden* and *The Highland Clearances* (Penguin), or **Nigel Tranter**'s *The Story of Scotland*. Two excellent biographies of the most romantic figures in Scottish history are **Antonia Fraser**'s *Mary, Queen of Scots* (UK Mandarin) and **Fitzroy Maclean**'s *Bonnie Prince Charlie* (Canongate). An entertaining account of Scotland's often turbulent relationship with England is given by **Sir Ludovic Kennedy**'s *In Bed with an Elephant*. **Tom Nairn**'s *The Break-up of Britain* gives a radical perspective of Scottish independence and *Scotland's Story* (Fontana) is also insightful. A comprehensive guide to Scottish culture is **David Daiches'** *The New Companion to Scottish Culture* (Arnold). For a light-hearted and refreshing take on Scottish myths and little-known facts, read *Emperor's New Kilt* by **Jan-Andrew Henderson** (Mainstream, 2000).

If you only read one, then make it **James Boswell** & **Samuel Johnson**'s *A Journey to the Western Islands of Scotland* (UK Penguin). Other notables include *In Search of Scotland* by **HV Morton** (Methuen), *A High and Lonely Place* and *Gulfs of Blue Air – A Highland Journey* (Mainstream) by **Jim Crumley** and **Elizabeth Grant** of Rothiemurchus, *Memoirs of a Highland Lady* (Canongate). One of the best known Highland memoirs is *A Ring of Bright Water* by **Gavin Maxwell**; a tale of otters and other wildlife set in Glenelg. *A Last Wild Place* by naturalist **Mike Tomkies** is a fascinating account of life in a remote West Highland croft. Also interesting is *Queen Victoria's Highland Journal*, edited by **David Duff** (UK Hamlyn). For a selection of the best, including Daniel Defoe, Edwin Muir and Jan Morris, there's *The Road North - 300 years of Classic Scottish Travel Writing*, Ed June Skinner Sawyers (The Inn Pinn, 2000).

Travelogues & memoirs

There are numerous **walking guides** available and this is only the briefest of selections. Two of the best are *Great Walks Scotland* by **Hamish Brown** and *100 Best Routes on Scottish Mountains* by **Ralph Storer**. Two helpful hill-walking guides published by the Scottish Mountaineering Trust are *The Munros* by **Donald Bennett** and *The Corbetts* by **Scott Johnstone** et al. The SMT also publishes a range of district guides listing mainly high level walks. Also useful are *The Munro Almanac* and *The Corbett Almanac* by **Cameron McNeish**. A healthy antidote to all those climbing anoraks is **Muriel Gray**'s entertaining and clean-shaven *The First Fifty: Munro Bagging without a Beard* (UK Corgi). Those wishing to attempt one of the long distance walks should read *The West Highland Way* or *The Southern Upland Way*, both highly informative guides by **Roger Smith** (HM Stationery Office).

Outdoor activities

An excellent guide for both walkers and **mountain bikers** is Ralph Storer's *Exploring Scottish Hill Tracks*. Other recommended cycling guides include: *The Scottish Cycling Guide*, by **Brendan Walsh**; *101 Bike Routes in Scotland*, by **Henry Henniker** (Mainstream); and *Cycling in Scotland* by **John Hancox** (Collins Pocket Reference, Harper Collins).

For a comprehensive guide to Scotland's **golf courses** try *Scotland – Home of Golf*, a Pastime publication produced by the Scottish Tourist Board and *The Scottish Golf Guide* by **David Hamilton** (Canongate Press). An outsider's view of golf in Scotland can be found in American **Michael Bamberger**'s highly entertaining book *To the Linksland* (Mainstream Publishing), ideal if the Scottish weather keeps you from playing!

A good **birdwatching** guide is *Where to Watch Birds in Scotland*, by **Michael Madders** and **Julia Welstead** (UK Christopher Helm).

The Collins pocket guides to *Clans and Tartans*, *Scottish Surnames* and their *Scots Dictionary* are handy and informative. For more detailed genealogical study, look at *Tracing your Ancestors* by **Cecil Sinclair** (HM Stationery Office). *Exploring Scotland's Heritage* is a beautifully-illustrated series of books on historic buildings and archaeological sites in different regions of Scotland (HM Stationery Office). Those wishing to bone up on their malt whiskies should refer to the *Malt Whisky Companion* by **Michael Jackson** (UK Dorling Kindersley). An excellent Scottish recipe book is the *Claire MacDonald Cookbook* by **Lady Claire MacDonald** (UK Bantam) who runs a hotel on Skye.

Miscellaneous

Maps

You'll find a good selection of maps of Scotland in many bookshops and at the main tourist offices. **Road atlases** can be bought at most service stations. The best of these are the large-format ones produced by the *AA*, *Collins* and *Ordnance Survey* which cover all of Britain at a scale of around three miles to one inch and include plans of the major towns and cities. The *Michelin* and *Bartholomew* fold-out maps are also excellent, as are the official regional tourist maps published by *Estate Publications*, which are ideal for driving and which are available from most tourist offices.

The best detailed maps for walking are the *Ordnance Survey* maps, which are unsurpassed for accuracy and clarity. These are available at different scales. The *Landranger* series at 1:50,000 (1¼ inches to a mile) covers the whole of Britain and is good for most walkers. The new *Explorer* and *Outdoor Leisure* series are 1:25,000 and offer better value for walkers and cyclists. An excellent source of maps is *Stanfords* at 12-14 Longacre, London WC2E 9LP.

Useful websites

The official Scottish Tourist Board site and the various area tourist board sites listed on page 21 contain information on accommodation, transport and tourist sights as well as outdoor activities such as walking, skiing, fishing etc. Other recommended sites include:

www.scotland.net Scotland Online: with good information on golf, walking and climbing and also features **www.travelscotland.co.uk** Run in conjunction with STB, with magazine-style features and reviews.

www.scotland-info.co.uk Good for local information on hotels, shops and restaurants.

www.aboutscotland.co.uk Useful for accommodation.

www.travelscotland.co.uk Run in conjunction with STB, with magazine-style features and reviews.

www.historic-scotland.gov.uk Home pages for Historic Scotland, the body in charge of many important historic monuments up and down the country.

www.walkscotland.com Suggested walks, contacts and practical information for hikers and climbers.

www.golfscotland.co.uk Everything you need to know on golf in Scotland.

www.geo.ed.ac.uk/home/scotland/scotland/html Background information on history, politics and geography.

www.scottish.parliament.uk Easy to use guide to the Scottish Parliament.

www.ski.scotland.net Information on ski conditions at all centres, updated daily. Also **www.ifyouski.com**

www.golfscotland.co.uk Everything you need to know on golf in Scotland.

www.hebrides.com Comprehensive site for the islands.

www.geo.ed.ac.uk/home/scotland/scotland/html Background information on history, politics and geography.

www.ceolas.org Celtic music site with lots of information and sounds.

Argyll

3

Argyll

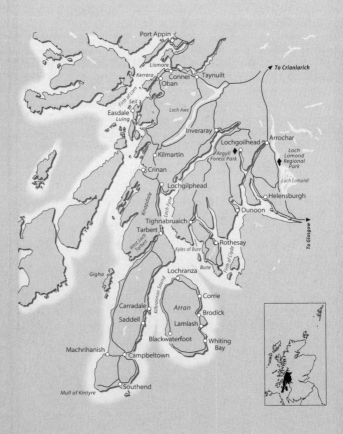

Stretching north from the Mull of Kintyre almost to Glencoe and east to the shores of Loch Lomond, the region of Argyll marks the transition from Lowland to Highland. It's a region of great variety, containing all the ingredients of the classic Scottish holiday: peaceful wooded glens, heather-clad mountains full of deer, lovely wee fishing ports, romantic castles and beautiful lochs.

Argyll also has its own particular attractions in the shape of its numerous prehistoric sites. Much of the region was once part of the ancient **Kingdom of Dalriada**, *established by the Irish Celts (known as the Scotti, hence Scotland) who settled here in the fifth century. Their capital was at* **Dunadd**, *near Lochgilphead, from where they gained ascendancy over the native Picts. Argyll has since been ruled by Norse invaders, then by Somerled, whose successors, the powerful MacDonalds, Lords of the Isles, were in turn dislodged by the Campbells, allies of Robert the Bruce. They became the* **Dukes of Argyll**, *and even today are still one the largest landowners in the region.*

Despite its proximity to the massive Glasgow conurbation, Argyll is sparsely populated. Its largest town, **Oban**, *has only 8,000 inhabitants. Oban is also the main ferry port for Argyll's Hebridean islands.*

This chapter covers mostly mainland Argyll, plus the smaller coastal islands. Also included are the Firth of Clyde islands of **Bute** *and* **Arran**, *the most accessible of Scotland's more southerly islands, and the most popular. Bute is actually part of Argyll and Bute, created in the recent regional government reorganization, while Arran was tacked onto Ayrshire to form Ayrshire and Arran.*

Ins and outs

Getting there Most visitors' approach to Argyll is west from Glasgow. At Dumbarton there's a choice of route: the more popular one is north on the busy A82 along the west bank of **Loch Lomond** (see page 150); the other route is along the north shore of the Firth of Clyde, through **Helensburgh** and along the shores of **Gare Loch** and **Loch Long**. Both routes converge at **Arrochar**, the gateway to the real Argyll. The latter road is much quieter but is not exactly a scenic alternative, as it passes through an industrial wasteland that includes the submarine base at Faslane and the oil tanks at Finnart.

Getting around
During the peak summer months it's essential to book ferry tickets in advance
Public transport is limited in much of Argyll, though the main towns are served by **buses**. The main bus operators are *Scottish Citylink*, T0990-505050, and *Oban & District Buses*, T01631-562856. The Oban to Glasgow rail line passes through the northern part of the region. For rail enquiries, T0345-484950. For general public transport enquiries contact Argyll & Bute Council, T01546-604695. Times of local buses and trains can also be checked at local tourist offices.

Most **ferries** to the islands and remote peninsulas are run by *CalMac*, T01475-650100, www.calmac.co.uk If you're planning on taking more than 1 or 2 ferries, especially with a car, it may be more economical to buy an **Island Hopscotch** ticket. They can be used on a variety of route combinations and are valid for 1 month. They require advance planning but are better value than buying single tickets. For example, the Bute-Cowal-Kintyre Hopscotch ticket allows you to travel by ferry from Wemyss Bay to Rothesay, from Rhubodach to Colintraive and from Portavadie to Tarbert for £6.30 per passenger plus £29.50 for the car.

Tourist information Most of this chapter is covered by the *Argyll, the Isles, Loch Lomond, Stirling & Trossachs Tourist Board*, F01369-706085, www.scottish.heartlands.org The main offices, which are open all year round, are in **Oban**, **Inveraray**, **Dunoon**, **Rothesay** and **Campbeltown**. There are smaller seasonal offices in **Lochgilphead**, **Tarbert**, **Ardgarten** and **Helensburgh**. The island of **Arran** is covered by the *Ayrshire & Arran Tourist Board*, T01292-262555, F269555, www.ayrshire-arran.com

Climate As with the rest of the west of Scotland, the weather is highly unpredictable. It rains a lot on the west coast of Argyll and the summer months are no guarantee of good weather. It's best to avoid the busiest months of Jul and Aug, when the single-track roads can become frustrating and accommodation is harder to find. You'll also have more chance of avoiding the dreaded midge (see page 62).

Firth of Clyde

Helensburgh

Phone code: 01436
Colour map 2, grid A1
Population: 14,000

On the west coast, the lowlands and highlands are separated by the Firth of Clyde, which leads eventually into the heart of the city of Glasgow. Twenty-three miles northwest of Glasgow on the A814, overlooking the Clyde, is the town of Helensburgh, its wide, grid-plan streets lined with elegant Georgian houses. The town boasts a few very notable connections; both **Henry Bell**, originator of the steamship, and **John Logie Baird**, who invented the television, were born here.

★

Things to do in Argyll

- Take a cruise on **Loch Etive**, inaccessible except by boat, and one of Scotland's great hidden treasures .
- Explore the archaeological treasures of **Kilmartin Glen**.
- Drive down to **Tighnabruaich** in

Southwest Cowal and enjoy the wonderful views across the Kyles of Bute.
- Take a look round the magnificent Gothic fantasy of **Mount Stuart** .
- Enjoy the finest of piscine cuisine at the **Inverawe Fisheries and Smokery**.

Getting there   There is a daily ferry service to and from Gourock. There are also 2 train stations: one for Glasgow trains, and the other for trains to Oban and Fort William. See transport below.

Ins & outs

Argyll

The **tourist information centre** is in the clock tower on the waterfront, T672642. Open Apr to mid-May daily 1000-1700; mid-May to Jun daily 0930-1800; Jul-Sep daily 0930-1900; early Oct Mon-Fri 1000-1630, Sat-Sun 1000-1700.

Helensburgh is more famously known for its connection with the great Glasgow architect, **Charles Rennie Mackintosh**. In the upper part of the town, on Upper Colquhoun Street, is **Hill House**, one of the best examples of Mackintosh's work. The house was designed for Glasgow publisher, Walter Blackie in 1902-04, and is now owned by the National Trust for Scotland. The house is a masterpiece of balanced perfection and artistry and there's much to admire. The attention to detail, the use of natural light and the symbolism of the floral patterns and use of light and dark, hallmarks of his personal Art Nouveau style, are all very much in evidence. After exploring the house, you can visit the kitchen, which has been tastefully converted into a tearoom (open 1330-1630). ■ *T673900. Daily 1330-1730 Apr-Oct. Adult £6, concession/children £4.50. To get there from the central train station, walk about a mile and a half up Sinclair St, then turn left at Kennedy St and follow the signs. From Helensburgh Upper station (see below) it's a 5-min walk.*

The most upmarket place to stay is **C-D** *The Commodore Hotel*, 112-117 West Clyde St, T676924, F677112. 45 rooms. West Clyde Street overlooks the loch and is where you'll find most of the hotels and guest houses, including **E** *Ardmore Guest House*, T673461, www.scoot.co.uk/ardmore_guest_house There are lots of B&Bs, including **E** *Ava Lodge*, 44 Glasgow St, T677751, norma@cantello.prestel.co.uk

Sleeping

There's a daily passenger-only *Calmac* **ferry** service from Helensburgh to **Kilcreggan** (30 mins) and **Gourock** (42 mins), from where there are regular trains to Glasgow Central and other ferries to Dunoon (see page 71). Helensburgh has 2 **train** stations. The Central station has a regular service (every 30 mins) to and from **Glasgow** (45 mins), while the Upper station serves **Oban** (3 times daily; 2 hrs 15 mins) and **Fort William** (4 daily Mon-Sat, 3 on Sun; 3 hrs). For times, contact *Scotrail*, T08457-484950.

Transport

Cowal Peninsula

The Cowal Peninsula reaches out into the Firth of Clyde, framed by Loch Fyne and Loch Long. This is the most visited part of Argyll, due to its proximity to Glasgow, but despite the summer hordes, much of it is undisturbed. Most people head straight for **Dunoon***, the main ferry port and one of the major Clyde seaside resorts, leaving* *more adventurous souls to enjoy the forests and mountains of **Argyll Forest Park** in the north or the peace and tranquillity of the southwest coastline.*

North Cowal

Colour map 3, grid C6   The northern part of the peninsula is largely covered by the sprawling **Argyll Forest Park** which extends from Loch Lomond south to Holy Loch. This area contains the most stunning scenery in Cowal, and includes the **Arrochar Alps**, a range of rugged peaks north of Glen Croe which offer some of the best climbing in Argyll. The most famous of these is Ben Arthur (2,891 ft), better known as "**The Cobbler**", but this, and the other "Alps" are only for the more serious hill walker. Rather less imposing are the hills south of Glen Croe, between Loch Goil and Loch Long, in an area known as **Argyll's Bowling Green** (not because it's flat, but an English corruption of the Gaelic *Baile na Greine*, meaning "Sunny Hamlet"). There are also numerous footpaths and cycle tracks threading their way through the park, and details of these can be found in the Forestry Commission leaflets available at the **tourist office** in Ardgarten (see below).

Arrochar   The gateway to Cowal sits at the head of Loch Long on the main A83, only a few
Phone code: 01301   miles west of Tarbet and the shores of Loch Lomond. It's a small, unremarkable
Colour map 3, grid C6   place but the setting is dramatic, with The Cobbler towering overhead.

Sleeping and eating   There are plenty of hotels and B&Bs, including **D** *The Village Inn*, T702279, F702458, www.maclay.com, which also serves decent grub, and the very friendly **E** *Lochside Guest House*, T/F702467, lochsidegh@aol.com, which also serves food and which is very close to the village's main pub.

Transport   *Scottish Citlink* **buses** between Glasgow and Oban stop off at Arrochar (1 hr 10 mins to Glasgow; 1 hr 40 mins to Oban), 3 daily in each direction (twice on Sunday). Arrochar shares a **train** station with Tarbet, on the main west coast line. Trains heading north to Oban (1 hr 45 mins) or Fort William (2 hrs 30 mins) or south to Glasgow (1 hr 15 mins) stop 3-4 times daily.

Ardgarten,   A few miles beyond Arrochar, on the shores of Loch Long, is **Ardgarten**, where
Glen Croe &   there's a **tourist office and visitor centre**, T702342, which is open daily
Lochgoilhead   April-October 1000-1700, till 1800 in July and August, and provides useful advice and information on hillwalking and wildlife, as well as organizing various activities.

From Ardgarten the A83 climbs steeply up **Glen Croe** to reach one of Scotland's classic viewpoints at the top of the pass, the **Rest and be Thankful**. The hordes of like-minded tourists, eager for that memorable photograph, cannot detract from the majestic views of the surrounding craggy peaks.

Here the road forks. The A83 continues towards **Inveraray** (see page 77) and the single-track B828 heads southwest to meet the B839, which runs down to the village of **Lochgoilhead**, in a beautiful setting on Loch Goil. There are several **hotels** and **B&Bs** as well as an unsightly village of self-catering holiday chalets next door. At the end of the road, several miles down the west side of Loch Goil, are the ruins of 15th-century **Castle Carrick**.

Sleeping   In Ardgarten there's a an **SYHA youth hostel**, T702363, open Feb-Dec, and Forestry Commission **campsite**, T702293; open Easter-Oct.

The A83 meanwhile runs down through **Glen Kinglas** to reach the village of **Cairndow**, at the head of Loch Fyne. Nearby is the Ardkinglas Woodland Garden, which contains an impressive collection of exotic rhododendrons, as well as the largest conifers in Europe, over 120-ft high and 30-ft in girth. ■ *Daily dawn till dusk. Free. T01499-600263.*

Ardkinglas Woodland Garden

A mile or so further on towards Inveraray, at **Clachan**, at the head of Loch Fyne, is the highly-acclaimed *Loch Fyne Oyster Bar* (see page 79).

Just before Cairndow, the A815 branches left and runs south down the eastern shore of Loch Fyne. At **Strachur** it turns inland and heads down to **Loch Eck**, a very beautiful and narrow freshwater loch, popular with trout fishermen. At the southern end of Loch Eck, at **Benmore**, is Younger Botanic Garden, a lovely woodland garden and offshoot of the Royal Botanic Garden in Edinburgh. Its 140 acres are laid out with over 250 species of rhododendrons and feature an avenue of Giant Redwoods. ■ *1 Mar-31 Oct daily 0930-1800. Adult £3, concession £2.50, children £1. T01369-706261.*

Younger Botanic Garden

Dunoon

The largest town in Cowal, and indeed the largest in Argyll, with 13,000 inhabitants, is Dunoon, one-time favourite holiday destination for Glaswegians, who came in their hordes on board the many paddle steamers that sailed "doon the watter" from Glasgow. Dunoon still attracts visitors, albeit in much smaller numbers, but the town has fallen on desperately hard times with the recent closure of the US nuclear submarine base on nearby Holy Loch, which was the town's life blood.

Phone code: 01369
Colour map 2, grid A1

Nevertheless, the town still comes to life during the **Cowal Highland Gathering**, held on the last weekend of August. This is the world's largest Highland Games and culminates in a spectacular march of massed pipes and drums through the streets.

Getting there There are 2 **ferry** crossings to Dunoon from Gourock, with **train** connections to and from Gourock to Glasgow. There are also buses to Colintraive, Inveraray and Lochgoilhead.

Ins & outs

Cowal's main **tourist information centre** is on Alexandra Parade, T703785. Open Apr Mon-Fri 0900-1700, Sat 1100-1730, Sun 1100-1500; May Mon-Fri 0900-1730, Sat-Sun 1000-1700; Jun and Sep Mon-Fri 0900-1800; Jul-Aug Mon-Sat 0900-1900; Oct Mon-Fri 0900-1730.

There's not much to keep you in Dunoon, but if the weather's bad and you need to kill time, you could head for the **Castle House Museum**, on Castle Hill, which dominates the town centre, where you can bone up on Cowal's often grisly past. ■ *Easter-Oct 1030-1630 Mon-Sat, 1400-1630 Sun. Adult £1.50, concession/children free.* A mile northwest, along the A855 to Sandbank, is the **Cowal Bird Garden**, an aviary with exotic birds such as parrots and macaws and a small rare-breeds farm. ■ *Easter-Oct daily 1030-1800, Nov-Easter Sun only 1100-1600. Adult £3, children £2.*

Sights

There are more than enough hotels and guesthouses to choose from. One of the best is the **A** *Enmore Hotel*, Marine Parade (near Hunter's Quay), T702230, F702148, www.enmorehotel.com A small, family hotel in its own grounds overlooking the sea and with a reputation for good food (restaurant open to non-residents; mid-range-expensive). Also good is **B** *Ardfillayne House*, a mile south of town on the Innellan Rd,

Sleeping & eating

Argyll

T702267, F702501, www.argyll-business.directory.com   A Victorian country house offering fine Scottish/French cooking (booking required). 3 miles north of Dunoon, on the A815, is **C** *The Anchorage Hotel & Restaurant*, T/F705108, www.anchorage.com Also has a reputation for fine food (lunch mid-range; dinner expensive).

There's lots of **B&B** accommodation, which can be booked at the tourist office (see below), and there are 2 **campsites** nearby: *Cot House Caravanan & Campsite* is at Kilmun, a few miles north of town, on the shores of Holy Loch, T840351; open Apr-Oct; and a few miles further north, at the southern end of Loch Eck, is *Stratheck Caravan Park*, T/F840472; open Mar-Dec.

Aside from the hotels listed above, the best food can be found at *Chatters*, at 58 John St, T706402, an informal and outstanding little restaurant offering French-style Scottish cuisine (lunch mid-range; dinner mid-range-expensive). Open Mon-Sat.

Sport **Cycle hire** *Highland Stores*, 156 Argyll St. **Pony trekking** *Velvet Path Riding & Trekking Centre*, Rowan House, Innellan, by Dunoon, T830580.

Transport The most popular ferry crossing is the *CalMac* car and passenger ferry which makes the 20-min trip daily all year round every 30 mins. The first leaves Gourock at 0620 and the last returns from Dunoon at 2105. There's also a *Western Ferries* service every 30 mins which arrives at Hunter's Quay, a mile north of the town centre, T01369-704452. For times and details of **train** connections from **Gourock** to **Glasgow**, T01475-650100. There are **buses** to **Colintraive** 2-3 times daily Mon-Sat (40 mins), to **Inveraray** (on Tue, Fri-Sat; 1 hr 15 mins) and to **Lochgoilhead** (Mon and Fri; 1 hr 15 mins). For times, contact *Western Buses*, T01700-502076.

Southwest Cowal

One of the most beautiful parts of Argyll is the southwest of Cowal, particularly the route down to the little village of **Tighnabruaich**. The A8003 runs down the west side of Loch Riddon and there are few lovelier sights than the view from this road across the **Kyles of Bute**, the narrow straits that separate Cowal from the island of Bute.

Tighnabruaich
Phone code: 01700
Colour map 5, grid A3

Tighnabruaich gets busy in the summer with visitors who come here to enjoy some of the best sailing on the west coast. Much of the accommodation is booked up by those enrolled at the **Tighnabruaich Sailing School**, T811717, which offers dinghy sailing and windsurfing courses at all levels. There is a bank in the village and buses leave from here to **Portavadie** (1-3 times daily; 25 minutes), **Colintraive** (see below) and **Rothesay** (1-2 times daily Monday-Thursday; one hour).

Sleeping The **SYHA youth hostel**, T811622, open Apr-Sep, sits high above the village with great views across the Kyles and is often full. There's also **D** *The Royal Hotel*, T811239, F811300, royalhotel@btinternet.com, on the waterfront, with a multi-gym and sauna and excellent restaurant serving cheap lunches and mid-range-expensive dinners. There are a couple of cheap **B&Bs** in the village, including **E-F** *Ferguslie*, T811414, open Apr-Sep. In neighbouring **Kames**, there's the **C** *Kames Hotel*, T811489, F811283, tcandrew@aol.com, with great views and live music in the bar.

It's also possible to reach **Bute** from southwest Cowal. The A8003 turns off the main A883, which runs right down the west of the peninsula and the east side of Loch Riddon to **Colintraive**, at the narrowest point in the Kyles, only a few hundred yards wide. A small car and passenger *CalMac* ferry crosses to

Rhubodach on Bute (for details, see next page). There are buses from **Colintraive** to **Tighnabruaich** (1-2 times daily Monday-Thursday; 35 minutes), and to **Dunoon** (see previous page).

South of Tighnabruaich

A few miles southwest of Kames, is **Portavadie**, on the west coast of Cowal. A *CalMac* car and passenger **ferry** sails from here to **Tarbert**, on the Kintyre Peninsula, saving a lot of time if you're heading for the islands of **Islay, Jura** or **Colonsay**. The ferry to Tarbert makes the 25-minute crossing, every hour, daily, from 0800 till 1915. The one way trip costs £3.15 per passenger and £13.35 per car.

About 10 miles further up the deserted west coast of Cowal is **Otter ferry**. There used to be a ferry link from here to Lochgilphead, but not for the small, amphibious mammals. It gets its name from the gravel bank that juts out into Loch Fyne (*An Oitir* means gravel bank in Gaelic). It's still worth stopping here, if only for the excellent oyster bar and pub, *The Oystercatcher*, T01700-821229, which overlooks the lovely sandy beach.

Argyll

Isle of Bute

Barely a stone's throw off the south coast of Cowal is the island of Bute, another favourite holiday destination for people from Glasgow and Ayrshire, who come here in droves during the busy summer months. But though the island is small (15 miles long by five miles wide), it's deceptively easy to escape the hordes, who tend to congregate around the east coast resort of Rothesay, leaving the delights of the sparsely populated west coast free for those who enjoy a bit of peace and quiet.

Phone code: 01700
Colour map 5, grid A3
Population 7,500

Bute has been a popular place since late Victorian times, when a gaggle of Glasgow grannies could be seen being pushed along the promenade in their bath-chairs under tartan blankets, taking the invigorating sea air. Now, the island is successfully reinventing itself as a haven for walkers and cyclists. Some of the island's walks are described below.

Bute

Ins and outs

Bute is easily accessible from Glasgow. Take a **train** from Glasgow Central to the **ferry** terminal at Wemyss Bay (1 hr 10 mins), and from there it's a 35-min crossing to Rothesay. There are also **buses** to Rothesay from Tighnabruaich in Southwest Cowal (see above) once or twice a day Mon-Thu (1 hr). For times, contact *Western Buses*, T502076. See also Transport on page 77.

Getting there

The *Western Buses* service around Bute is fairly good, though limited on Sun. The best way to see Bute is by **bicycle**. The island is fairly flat and the roads are quiet and in good condition. See also Transport on page 77.

Getting around

Argyll

Tourist Information Centre The Tourist Information Centre has recently moved into The Winter Gardens on the Promenade, in Rothesay, T502151. Open Apr and Oct Mon-Fri 0900-1730, Sat 1000-1730, Sun 1100-1500; May Mon-Fri 0900-1730, Sat-Sun 1000-1700; Jun and Sep Mon-Fri till 1800; Jul-Aug Mon-Sat till 1900; Nov-Mar Mon-Thu 0900-1730, Fri 0900-1700.

Rothesay

Rothesay was the hometown of child singing sensation, Lena Zavaroni, who died tragically in 1999 from Anorexia The sole town on Bute is Rothesay, which, like Dunoon, is a hugely popular holiday destination. There the similarity ends, however, for Rothesay is a genteel and tasteful Victorian seaside resort, with its handsome period mansions lining the broad sweep of bay, its elegant promenade lined with palm trees and the distinctive 1920s **Winter Gardens**, now refurbished and housing a cinema and restaurant.

Sights One thing you must do before leaving Rothesay is spend a penny in the palatial **Victorian public toilets**. Rather more than that (£300,000 to be exact) has already been spent on restoring this architectural gem to its former glory. Gents get the best deal but the ladies can also take a peek. ■ *Daily Easter-Oct 0800-2100, Nov-Easter 0900-1700. 10p.*

Rothesay Castle is also worth visiting. Built around the 12th century, the castle was attacked by Vikings, before becoming a favourite with the Stewart kings. It fell into English hands during the Wars of Independence and was retaken by Robert the Bruce in 1311. It was also occupied by Cromwell's New Model Army after the Civil War and partly dismantled, but restoration work has helped preserve much of this impressive circular, moated ruin. ■ *Apr-Sep Mon-Sat 0930-1830, Sun 1400-1830; Oct-Mar Mon-Sat 0930-1630, Sun 1400-1630 (closed Thu-Fri afternoon). Adult £1.80, concession £1.30, children £0.75. To get there, follow the signs from the pier.*

Behind the castle is **Bute Museum**, which features interesting displays covering the island's history, wildlife and archaeology. ■ *Oct-Mar Tue-Sat 1430-1630; Apr-Sep Mon-Sat 1030-1630, Sun 1430-1630. Adult £1.20, children £0.40.*

Around Bute

Mount Stuart One of Bute's main attractions is Mount Stuart, a unique Victorian Gothic house set in 300 acres of lush woodland gardens, three miles south of Rothesay. This magnificent architectural fantasy reflects the Third Marquess of Bute's passion for astrology, astronomy, mysticism and religion and the sheer scale and grandeur of

Rothesay Castle

Kilchattan Bay to Glencallum Bay walk

The route is waymarked, but if you want to take a map, it's OS Landranger sheet 63
A longer walk is the circular route from **Kilchattan Bay** *south to* **Glencallum Bay** *and back, via* **St Blane's chapel**. *The walk is five miles in total. Allow about three hours. For buses to and from Rothesay, see 'Getting around' above.*

Follow the signpost for 'Kelspoke Path' beside Kiln Villas and take the track which climbs steadily before turning sharply back on itself. Go through a gate and shortly before the next gate turn right. Follow the rough track, which swings right, then left over open ground to the ruins of **Kelspoke Castle**.

Continue along the grassy path, past a reservoir on your right, then cross the stile and go down and across a small burn. Turn left and follow the burn, before heading right to join the shore path and follow this past the lighthouse on your left and around the headland to Glencallum Bay. Continue round the shoreline and at the far end of the bay follow the waymarks as the path climbs to cross the headland. The path then levels out and from here

there are great views across to the mountains of **Arran**.
The path then reaches the col above **Loch na Leighe**. *Drop down to the loch and follow the waymarks south over open ground. Before reaching a farm called 'The Plan', go right over two footbridges, then left below a low ridge. Keep to the right of the buildings, following the waymarks across open ground to the stile that crosses to the ruins of St Blane's Chapel (see above). Leave the chapel by the gap in the boundary wall and go through a gate, turning left on a clear track which climbs steadily to a stile. Cross the stile and turn right, following the edge of the field down to a gate. Walk uphill on the left side of the field to Suidhe Hill. At the top of the field, cross the fence and keep going, turning right at the corner of the fence. Go through a gate at the next corner and look for a waymark about 100 m downhill. Follow the path steeply downhill, passing through a kissing gate and staying close to the wall. You then reach a drying green at the foot of the hill; turn left and follow a path around the buildings and back onto the road at Kilchattan.*

---

the place almost beggars belief. This is truly one of the great country houses of Scotland and displays breathtaking craftsmanship in marble and stained glass, as well as a fine collection of family portraits and Italian antiques. Much of the existing house dates from 1877, and was built following a terrible fire which destroyed the original, built in 1719 by the Second Earl of Bute.

Equally impressive are the **landscaped gardens** and woodlands, established by the Third Earl of Bute (1713-92), who advised on the foundation of Kew Gardens in London. It's worth spending a whole day here in order to take in the amazing splendour of the house and to explore the beautiful gardens. And if the weather's fine, why not bring a picnic and enjoy the wonderful sea views.

■ *Easter weekend and 1 May-17 Oct, daily except Tue and Thu. Gardens open 1000-1700; House open 1100-1630. Admission to House/gardens: adult £6.50, concession £5, children £2.50. Gardens only: adult £3.50, concession £3, children £2. T503877, www. Mountstuart.com A regular bus runs from Rothesay to the gates of the House (see 'Getting around' above).*

Just before Mount Stuart is the tidy little village of **Kerracroy**, designed by the wife of the Second Marquess of Bute and featuring an interesting mix of building styles. South of Mount Stuart and the village of Kingarth is **Kilchattan Bay**, an attractive bay of pink sands and the start of a fine walk down to Glencallum Bay, in the southeastern corner of the island (see below). There's accommodation at Kilchattan Bay, at **E** *St Blane's Hotel*, T/F831224.

Southwest of Kilchattan Bay is **St Blane's Chapel**, a 12th century ruin in a beautifully peaceful spot near the southern tip of the island. The medieval church stands on the site of an earlier monastery, established in the sixth century by St Blane, nephew of St Catan, after whom Kilchattan is named. The ruin can be reached by road from Rothesay, or as part of the walk from Kilchattan Bay (see below).

Four miles north of St Blane's, on the west coast, is **Scalpsie Bay,** the nicest beach on the island and a good place for seal-spotting. A little further north is **St Ninian's Point**, looking across to the island of Inchmarnock. At the end of the beach are the ruins of a sixth-century chapel, dedicated to St Ninian.

Walks on Bute The Highland-Lowland dividing line passes through the middle of Bute at **Loch Fad**, which separates the hilly and uninhabited northern half of the island and the rolling farmland of the south. The highest point on the island is **Windy Hill** (281 m) in the north, from where there are great views across the island.

A less strenuous walk is up **Canada Hill**, a few miles southwest of Rothesay, above Loch Fad. Walk along Craigmore promenade and turn off at the old pier to Ardencraig Gardens. Then continue uphill along the golf course to the top of the hill for great views of the Firth of Clyde.

Essentials

Sleeping Most of the island's accommodation is in and around Rothesay, and the tourist office will book your hotel or B&B. Convenient for the ferry is **B** *Cannon House Hotel*, Battery Pl, T502819, F505725. A comfortable Georgian townhouse. Also central is **E** *The Commodore*, 12 Battery Pl, T/F502178, spearcommodore@aol.com One of the nicest guest houses. There are lots of other guest houses and B&Bs on Battery Place. North of town, in **Ardbeg**, is the **D** *Ardmory House Hotel & Restaurant*, T502346, F505596, ardmory.house.hotel@dial.pipex.com, with a restaurant open to non-residents. 3 miles south of town, at **Ascog**, is the excellent value **E-F** *Ascog Farm*, T503372.

Eating The best place to eat on the island is the *New Farm Restaurant*, T831646, which is 6 miles south of Rothesay, near Mount Stuart House and Gardens (see below). This whitewashed cottage farmhouse is set on a working sheep farm and dairy and uses local produce to great effect. The atmosphere is friendly and informal. Booking is essential for lunch (mid-range) and dinner (expensive). They also offer B&B (**E**, or **D** including dinner). In town, there's *Fowler's*, housed in the Winter Gardens, T500505, offering good value lunches and dinners. It is an absolute culinary must while you are on Bute to sample the superb fish and chips at the award-winning *West End Café*, 1-3 Gallowgate, T503596. It's open for takeaways all year round, and for sit-down meals Easter-Sep 1200-1400 and 1600-2400 (closed Mon).

Festivals The island holds its own *Highland Games* on the last weekend in **Aug**. There's also the *Isle of Bute International Folk Festival* and *World Ceilidh Band Championships*, a massive festival of music and dance held over the third weekend in **Jul**, and the *Isle of Bute Jazz Festival*, during the **May** Bank Holiday weekend.

Sport **Golf** *Rothesay Golf Course*, T503554, scenic 18-holes with great views at Canada Hill. **Pony trekking** *Rothesay Riding Centre*, at Ardbrannan Farm, Canada Hill, T504791. **Sailing** *Bute Sailing School*, Cannon House, Battery Pl, T502819. Open Mar-Nov. Runs all RYA courses, as well as cruises on their own luxury yacht.

Buses connect with the arriving ferries at Rothesay and run to: Mount Stuart (hourly; **Transport** 15 mins), Kilchattan Bay (4 daily Mon-Sat, 3 on Sun; 30 mins) and Rhubodach (1-2 daily Mon-Sat; 20 mins). For **cycle hire** try *Mountain Bike Centre*, 24 East Princes St, Rothesay, T503554, open daily 0800-2000 Apr-Sep, or at *Mount Stuart House*, T502333.

Ferries sail daily every 45 mins from 0715 till 1945 (later on Fri, Sat-Sun). For times, T01700-502707. The one-way trip costs £3.25 per passenger and £13.15 per car. There's also a ferry to Rothesay from Brodick on Arran (2 hrs), once a day on Mon, Wed and Fri in the summer only. Bute can also be reached from the Cowal Peninsula. A small car/passenger ferry makes the 5-min crossing from Colintraive to Rhubodach, at the northern end of Bute, daily every half hour or hour; from 0530-1955 Mon-Sat and 0900-1955 Sun in the summer (21 Apr-27 Aug). The one-way trip costs £1 per passenger and £6.60 per car.

Argyll

Inveraray

Inveraray is the classic 18th-century planned village, with its straight wide streets and dignified Georgian houses, and enjoys the most stunning of settings, on the shores of Loch Fyne. It was rebuilt by the third Duke of Argyll, head of the Campbell clan, at the same time as he restored the nearby family home, which now attracts hordes of summer visitors. As well as its natural beauty and elegance, and fine castle, Inveraray has several other notable attractions in and around the town and you could quite happily spend a few days here, whatever the weather.

Phone code: 01499
Colour map 3, grid C6
Population: 700

Ins and outs

Inveraray is on the main Glasgow-Oban and Glasgow-Campbeltown bus routes and *Scottish Citylink* **buses** from Glasgow (1 hr 45 mins) stop in Front St, 6 times daily Mon-Sat (4 on Sun). Three of these buses (2 on Sun) continue to Oban (1 hr 5 mins), and 3 continue (2 on Sun) to Lochgilphead and Campbeltown (2 hrs 30 mins). For times, T0990-505050.

Getting there

Inveraray is a small village and most of the sights below are within easy walking distance. **Getting around**

The tourist office is on Front St, T302063. Open Apr Mon-Sat 0900-1700, Sun **Tourist office** 1200-1700; May-Jun Mon-Sat 0900-1700, Sun 1100-1700; Jul-Aug Mon-Sun 0900-1800; Sep-Oct Mon-Sat 0900-1700, Sun 1200-1700; Nov Mon-Fri 1100-1600, Sat-Sun 1200-1600; Dec-Jan Mon-Fri 1000-1500, Sat-Sun 1100-1500; Feb-Mar Mon-Fri 1100-1600, Sat-Sun 1200-1600.

Sights

One of Argyll's most famous castles, Inveraray has been the clan seat of the **Inveraray** Campbells for centuries and is still the family home of the Duke of Argyll. The **Castle** present neo-Gothic structure dates from 1745, and its main feature is the magnificent armoury hall, whose displays of weaponry were supplied to the Campbells by the British government to quell the Jacobite rebellion. The elaborately furnished rooms are also on display, as is the fascinating and troubled family history in the Clan room. There are extensive grounds with fine walks, particularly up to the hill-top folly. ■ *Apr-Jun, Sep-Oct Mon-Thu and Sat 1000-1300 and 1400-1745, Sun 1300-1745; Jul-Aug Mon-Sat 1000-1745, Sun 1300-1745. Adult £5.50, concession £4.50, children £.50. T302203.*

Inveraray Jail The Georgian prison and courthouse in the centre of the village has been brilliantly restored as a thoroughly fascinating museum that gives a vivid insight into life behind bars from medieval times up till the 19th century. You can sit in on an 1820 courtroom trial, then visit the cells below and learn all about some of the delightful prison pursuits, such as branding with a hot iron, ear nailing and public whipping. The whole experience is further enhanced by the guides, who are dressed as warders and prisoners. Makes you want to stay on the right side of the law, though, thankfully, conditions have improved – as you will see for yourself. ■ *Daily Apr-Oct, 0930-1800, Nov-Mar 1000-1700. Adult £4.90, concession £3.10, children £2.40. T302381.*

Inveraray Maritime Museum Another worthwhile diversion, especially if you've got kids in tow, is the *Arctic Penguin*, one of the world's last iron sailing ships, which is moored at the loch-side pier. Below decks are lots of interesting displays on Clyde shipbuilding and the Highland Clearances, as well as various 'hands-on' activities. ■ *Daily Apr-Sep 1000-1800, Oct-Mar 1000-1700. Adult £3, concession £2, children £1.50. T302213.*

All Saints Church One sight which has great appeal is the **Bell Tower** of All Saints Church, which attracts campanologists from near and far to ring the second heaviest set of church bells in the world. It's worth a visit, not just to dangle from the end of a rope, but to climb the tower and admire the panoramic view of the town below. ■ *Daily mid-May to end-Sep 1000-1300 and 1400-1700. Tower: adult £2, children £0.75.*

Argyll Wildlife Park A few miles southwest of town, on the A83 to Lochgilphead, Argyll Wildlife Park is another great place for kids. Amongst the native wildlife wandering around the forest-clad hills are pine martens, badgers, foxes, deer, wildcats, wild goats, a variety of wildfowl and birds of prey, racoons and wallabies, though the more informed of you will have noted that the last two are not native to Scotland. There's also the obligatory tearoom and gift shop. ■ *Daily 1000-1700. Adult £3.75, concession £2.50, children £1.95. T302264.*

Auchindrain Township Three miles beyond Argyll Wildlife Park is Auchindrain, a complete reconstruction of an original West Highland village. The thatched cottages, barn and blacksmith have all been perfectly restored and are all furnished and equipped to give a real insight into what rural life must have been like in the Highlands before the Clearances. There's also an informative visitor centre, with a bookshop and tearoom. ■ *Daily 1 Apr-30 Sep 1000-1700. Adult £3.80, concession £3, children £1.80. T500235.*

Crarae Gardens
Note that the gardens may close in 2001 prior to being taken over by the NTS
Four miles further down the A83 is one of Scotland's very best public gardens, dramatically set in a deep wooded glen on the shores of Loch Fyne. There are marked woodland walks winding their way through a spectacular array of rhododendrons, azaleas and numerous other exotic plants towards the tumbling waterfalls of the "Himalayan Gorge". May is a good time to see the gardens in full bloom, as is Autumn for the vast variety of deciduous trees, but any time of year is worth it. ■ *Mar-Oct 0900-1800, from dawn till dusk in winter. Adult £2.50, children £1.50. T01546-886614.*

Essentials

There are several good **hotels** to choose from, such as the historic **A-B** *Argyll Hotel*, Front St, T302466, F302389, formerly the *Great Inn*, or the **B** *Loch Fyne Hotel*, just of town on the A83, T302148, F302348. Also good is the **C** *Fernpoint Hotel*, T302170, F302366, fernpoint.hotel@virgin.net, a lovely Georgian house overlooking the loch, and the **D** *George Hotel*, T302111.

There's also lots of **B&Bs** in town, including **E** *Newton Hall*, Main St, T302484, a converted church, open Mar-Dec, as well as a **F** *SYHA Youth Hostel*, Dalmally Rd, T302454, open mid-Mar to end-Oct, and a **campsite**, at *Argyll Caravan Park*, T302285, 2½ miles south of town on Loch Fyne, with excellent facilities.

The best place to eat for miles around is the *Loch Fyne Oyster Bar*, T600264, about 9 miles east of town on the A83 near Clachan. This restaurant, shop and smokehouse attracts customers from miles around to enjoy their famous oysters and other "Fyne" foods such as the renowned smoked kippers. Open daily all year 0900-1800 Nov-Mar, 0900-2100 from mid-Mar onwards (booking essential at weekends). The *George Hotel* in town offers good, cheap bar food and good ale in a lively atmosphere. The *Loch Fyne Hotel* also does good food, but is a bit more expensive.

Pony trekking *Argyll Riding & Activities*, Dalchenna Farm, T302611.

Loch Awe and Loch Etive

North of Loch Fyne is Loch Awe, the longest freshwater loch in Scotland and, further north, the beautiful Loch Etive. There's enough here to justify a couple of days exploration, particularly the little-visited west shore of Loch Awe, but if you're pressed for time, there are a few conveniently placed sights along the A85 from Glasgow to Oban.

Colour map 3, grid B/C 6

The A819 north from Inveraray joins the A85 at the northeastern tip of Loch Awe, between the villages of of **Dalmally** and **Lochawe**. Just west of the junction is the romantic ruin of **Kilchurn Castle**, on a promontory jutting out into the loch. The castle ruin can be visited by boat from the pier in Lochawe village.

Kilchurn Castle

Argyll

 Piscine cuisine

The whole philosophy of smoking fish varies from one producer to another. At **Inverawe Fisheries and smokery** (see below) they buy smaller farmed salmon because they believe the lower fat content makes them tastier than larger ones. Traditional methods prevail here. The fish are dry salted, washed, smoked over oak logs for anything from 16 to 24 hours depending on conditions and then hand-sliced. The result is a rich and freshly oaky taste in a huge range of formats from a 112 g sliced pack (£5.95) to a whole side (£20.65), as well as gravadlax, smoked trout, eel and halibut, plus a whole range of pre-packed hampers.

Knipoch Smokehouse, in South Lorn near Oban (T01852-316251, www.knipochsmokehouse.co.uk) on the other hand, believes that large salmon, weighing 6-7 kg, produce the best quality. Its more approach involves a dry salt cure strengthened with sugar, whisky, juniper and rowan berries, plus a lengthy 2-3 day smoke. The fish comes out so black it has to be washed and trimmed to look presentable and the taste is a rather unusual one: strong, sweet, sharp and almondy. A whole side costs £45, but it can be cut to any size: sliced at £17.60 per 500 grams, unsliced at £15.95.

Sleeping There's a good selection of places to stay in Dalmally and Lochawe. A place with an especially nice view is the **D** *Loch Awe Hotel*, T01838-200379, open Feb-Dec.

Transport Both Dalmally and Lochawe are on the Glasgow-Oban rail and bus routes. **Trains** in either direction stop 3 times daily and there are several *Scottish Citylink* **buses** daily. These buses also stop at **Inveraray** (see above) and **Taynuilt** (see below) en route from Glasgow to Oban and vice versa.

Ben Cruachan & Pass of Brander
Colour map 3, grid B6

A few miles west of Lochawe, and almost a mile inside Ben Cruachan (3,695 ft) is the underground **Cruachan Power Station**, or "Hollow Mountain". From the visitor centre on the shores of Loch Awe, a guided bus trip takes you deep into the heart of the mountain through massive tunnels until you reach the generating room. ■ *Apr-Nov 0930-1700; Jul-Aug 0930-1800. Adult £3, children £1.50.*

Between Loch Awe and Loch Etive runs the River Awe, which squeezes through the dark and ominous **Pass of Brander**, so steep and narrow that legend has it that it was once held against an entire army by an old woman brandishing a scythe.

Taynuilt
Phone code: 01866
Colour map 3, grid B5

Further west, and 12 miles east of Oban, is the tiny village of Taynuilt, near the shore of Loch Etive. Just before the village, at **Bridge of Awe**, is a sign for **Inverawe Fisheries, Smokery & Country Park**, T822446, www.smokedsalmon.co.uk, where you can take fishing lessons, learn about traditional smoking techniques, or wander along a series of nature trails. If the weather's fine, you can buy some of their delicious smoked products and have a picnic (see box above).

The main attraction though, is **Bonawe Iron Furnace**, north of the village on the shores of Loch Etive. Founded in 1753 by a group of Cumbrian ironmasters, Bonawe used the abundant woodlands of Argyll to make charcoal to fire its massive furnace. At its height, it produced 600-700 tons of pig-iron a year. This was then shipped out to the forges of England and Wales. Iron production ceased at Bonawe in 1876 and it has now been restored as an industrial heritage site, with displays explaining the whole production process. ■ *Daily Apr-Sep, daily 0930-1830. Adult £2.50, concession £2, children £1. T822432.*

Beyond the Bonawe Heritage Site is the pier from which **Loch Etive Cruises** depart. The loch is inaccessible except by boat, and the three-hour cruise of one of Scotland's great hidden treasures is definitely worth it. You'll see the mountains of Glencoe, seals on the rocks, deer on the hillsides and maybe even a golden eagle flying above, and you won't stop talking about it for weeks, or months. ■ *Cruises depart at 1000, 1200 and 1400 (except Easter-30 Apr, Sat-Sun, 1-14 Oct, at 1400 only). ADULT £8, children £4, no booking necessary but arrive in plenty of time. T822430.*

Running south from the village is the very lovely and very quiet **Glen Lonan**. About four miles along the Glen Lonan road is **Barguillean's Angus Garden**, one of Argyll's youngest and smallest gardens, but also one of the most peaceful and evocative, set around the shores of little Loch Angus. It was created in 1957, in memory of Angus MacDonald, a journalist and writer killed in Cyprus in 1956. ■ *Daily 0900-1800. No admission charge but there's an honesty box. T822333.*

Sleeping and eating There's a good selection of accommodation in and around Taynuilt. On the main road is the welcoming **D-E** *Taynuilt Hotel*, T822437, F822721, and there are also several B&Bs. The most luxurious places to stay, and the best places to eat, are in **Kilchrenan**, south of Taynuilt on the shores of Loch Awe. **L** *Ardanaiseig Hotel*, T833333, F833222, www.ardanaiseig-hotel.com 3 miles east of Kilchrenan village on an unclassified road. Open Feb-Dec. Offers opulence and style, beautiful surroundings and views and exquisite food (lunch mid-range; dinner expensive). **B** *Taychreggan Hotel*, T833211/833366, F833244. Not as grand as the *Ardanaiseig Hotel*, but with equally wonderful views and superb cuisine (lunch mid-range; dinner expensive.)

A single-track road runs southwest of Kilchrenan, along the shores of Loch Awe, to the tiny villages of **Dalavich** and **Ford**, through the very beautiful **Inverinan Forest**, a Forestry Commission property which has a series of undemanding marked trails running through the hills overlooking the loch.

Walking around Loch Awe
These routes are all outlined, with accompanying maps, in the Forestry Commission leaflet, 'A Guide to Forest Walks and Trails in North Argyll', available at tourist offices

The first walk starts out from the little hamlet of **Inverinan**. Red waymarkers lead you from the car park into the woods surrounding the gorge of the River Inan. Part of the route follows the old drove road along which cattle were driven from the Highlands down to the markets in south and central Scotland. The walk is three miles long and should take around an hour and a half.

Further along the road, half a mile north of Dalavich, is a car park at **Barnaline Lodge**, the starting point for a nine-mile bike route, a waymarked walk through the **Caledonian Forest Reserve** and a couple of other woodland walks. The longest of the walks is the five-mile route that leads along the river Avich, then along the shores of Loch Avich before returning to the lodge.

Two and a half miles south of Dalavich is a car park, which marks the starting point for a blue waymarked walk along the shores of Loch Awe. The route passes through **Mackenzie's Grove**, a sheltered gorge containing some of the largest conifers on the west coast. The route then runs along the shores of the loch, from where you can see the remains of a *crannog*, one of over 40 of these Iron-Age settlements on Loch Awe. The route then heads back to the car park; about three miles in total.

Argyll

Oban

Phone code: 01631
Colour map 3, grid B5
Population: 8,500

Oban lies at the centre of the northerly part of Argyll, known as Lorn, which stretches north as far as Appin, south to Ardfern and east to the shores of Loch Awe. It also comprises several relatively peaceful islands, including Lismore, Kerrera, Seil and Luing. It's a busy little place: not only is it the largest port in northwest Scotland and the main departure point for ferries to the Hebrides, it is also the main tourist centre in Argyll. Not surprisingly, it gets very crowded in summer, with passing traffic and people using it as a base for exploring the region. It has a wide range of hotels, guest houses, B&Bs, restaurants and shops and a number of tourist attractions, which is useful to know if you're stuck here in bad weather. The town lies in the beautiful setting of a wide, crescent-shaped bay, backed by steep hills, with the island of Kerrera, just offshore, providing a natural shelter. It has been a favourite with tourists since Victorian times, when Queen Victoria pronounced it as 'one of the finest spots we have ever seen'. More recent royal comments, made by Prince Philip (who else?), in relation to the drinking habits of the local populace, have been less than flattering.

Ins and outs

Getting there
See page 86 for transport details

Oban is reasonably well served by **buses** and **trains** from Glasgow, Fort William and Inverness, and there are a number of west coast local bus services to and from Lochgilphead, Dalmally and Kilmartin.

Getting around

There are regular local buses around town and around Lorn, including to Clachan **Seil**, North Cuan, Isle of Luing, North Connel, Dalavich, Bonawe, and Ganavan Sands. These are mostly operated by *Oban & District Buses* or *Royal Mail Postbuses*, T01463-256200.

Tourist office

The **Tourist Information Centre** is on Argyll Sq, T563122. Open 1-29 Apr Mon-Fri 0900-1700, Sat-Sun 1200-1700; 30 Apr-17 Jun Mon-Sat 0900-1730, Sun 1000-1700; 18 Jun-1 Jul Mon-Sat 0900-1830, Sun 1000-1700; Jul-Aug Mon-Sat 0900-2000, Sun 0900-1900; 1 Sep-23 Sep Mon-Sat 0900-1830, Sun 1000-1700; 24 Sep-28 Oct Mon-Sat 0900-1730, Sun 1000-1600; 29 Oct-31 Mar Mon-Fri 0930-1700, Sat-Sun 1200-1600.

Sights

The town's great landmark is **McCaig's Folly**, an incongruous structure that resembles Rome's Coliseum and which dominates the skyline. The tower was built by local banker John Stuart McCaig in the late 19th century, as a means of providing work for unemployed stonemasons. Unfortunately, McCaig died before the project was complete, and to this day no one is quite sure of his intentions. There's not much to see, apart from the exterior walls, but the views of the town and bay are quite magnificent and well worth the climb up. There are various routes on foot, but the most direct is to go up Argyll Street and on the left beside the church climb the set of steps, known as Jacob's Ladder, which lead to Ardonnel Terrace. Turn left here and the tower soon comes into view and is well signposted.

Another good walk is to the ruins of **Dunollie Castle**, north of town on the Corran Esplanade towards Ganavan, from where there are also wonderful views. The castle was built on the site of an ancient stronghold of the King of Scots, and was then taken over in the 13th century by the MacDougalls, Lords of Lorn.

The principal seat of the MacDougalls was **Dunstaffnage Castle**, three miles north of Oban, off the A85. The 13th-century fort is built on an impressive site and much of the huge curtain wall remains intact. The ruins

Oban

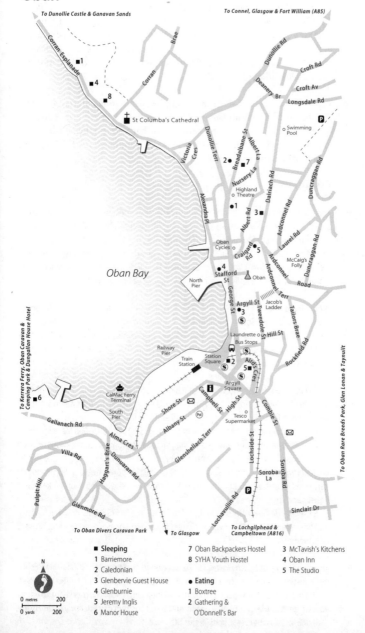

Argyll

of the little chapel nearby are worth a look. The castle served as a temporary prison for Flora MacDonald. ■ *Apr-Sep daily 0930-1830, Oct-Mar 0930-1630. Adult £1.80, concession £1.30, children £0.75. T562465.*

Two miles east of Oban along the Glencruitten Road is the **Rare Breeds Farm Park**. It's a fun place, especially for kids, with lots of strange-looking, yet familiar animals native to these shores. The animals are in pens, or roam free, and are very friendly and approachable. ■ *Daily late Mar to late Oct 1000-1730 (till 1930 mid-Jun to end of Aug). Adult £5, concession/children £3. There are 3 buses daily Mon-Fri to and from Oban train station. T770608.*

If the weather's bad you can take a tour round the **Oban Distillery**, at the end of Stafford Street, which is opposite the North Pier. ■ *Mon-Fri 0930-1700, and Sat 0930-1700 from Easter to Oct (Jul-Sep Mon-Fri 0930-2030). Adult £3.50. T572004.*

Boat trips   Boat trips can be made from Oban, to **Mull, Iona, Staffa,** and **The Treshnish Islands** with *Gordon Grant Tours*, on Railway Pier, T562842. There are other boat operators around the harbour, on the North, South and Railway Piers. You can also rent boats from *Borro Boats*, Dungallan Parks, Gallanach Road, T563292.

Essentials

Sleeping   There's no shortage of hotels, guest houses and B&Bs, most of which are very reason-
■ *on map*   ably priced, and many of which are on or near the seafront. There are also lots of B&Bs
Price codes: in the streets below McCaig's Folly. Though it shouldn't be a problem finding a room
see inside front cover   for the night, Oban is the main ferry port for the islands and gets very busy in the summer with through traffic. It's often a good idea, therefore, to get the tourist office to find
a place, which costs a little more, but can save a lot of time and effort.

There are dozens of   **A** *Caledonian Hotel*, Station Sq, T563133, F562998, www.miltonhotels.com 70 rooms.
B&Bs on Ardconnel Rd   Huge old Victorian Gothic building which is hard to miss. Full of 'character', which
hides a multitude of sins, but it's very handily placed for the ferry and train station.
A *Manor House Hotel*, Gallanach Rd, T562087, F563053. 11 rooms, open Feb-Dec.
Overlooking the bay on the road south out of town towards the Kerrera ferry. Offers
comfort, style and superb cuisine.

   C *Dungallan House Hotel*, Gallanach Rd, T563799, F566711, dungallanhotel-
oban.co.uk   13 rooms, open Jan, Mar-Oct and Dec. A Victorian house set in 5 acres of
woodland, offering great views, hospitality and fine food.

   D *Barriemore Hotel*, Corran Esplanade, T/F566356. 13 rooms, open Mar-Nov, more
of a guesthouse, and a superior one at that, Victorian style and elegance coupled with
great views and a friendly atmosphere mean that this is much more than all right.
D *Glenburnie Hotel*, Corran Esplanade, T/F562089. 15 rooms, open Apr-Oct, another
very good guesthouse along the seafront, which is lined with more upmarket guest
houses and small hotels.

   E *Glenbervie Guest House*, Dalriach Rd, T564770, F566723. 8 rooms, lovely Victorian house high above the town on a street full of good quality accommodation, very
good value.

   The official **F** *SYHA Youth Hostel*, T562025, open all year from Mar, is on Corran Esplanade, just beyond St Columba's Cathedral. Cheaper and more central is the independent hostel, **F** *Oban Backpackers*, T562107, on Breadalbane St. Open all year and where
you can get breakfast for £1.40. Cheaper still is the much smaller **F** *Jeremy Inglis Hostel*,
T565065, at 21 Airds Cres, opposite the TIC.

There are 2 **campsites** nearby: the *Oban Divers Caravan Park*, T/F562755, open Mar-Nov, on the Glenshellach Rd, about 1½ miles south of the ferry terminal; and the *Oban Caravan & Camping Park*, T562425, F566624, open Apr to mid-Oct, on Gallanach Rd, 2 miles south of town near the Kerrera ferry.

Expensive The best food in Oban can be found at the excellent *Manor House Hotel* (see above). Mid-range *The Boxtree*, 108 George St, T563542. Very good bistro-style lunches and dinners and a wide vegetarian selection, open daily 1130-2200 in summer. *The Studio*, Craigard Rd, T562030. Good value 3-course set dinner and good à la carte menu, popular with locals, so you'll need to book, open daily 1700-2200 (cheap 'early bird special' served 1700-1830). A few miles south at Lerags, is *The Barn Bar*, T564618. Good pub food and children-friendly, open daily 1100-2100 Apr-Oct. *The Gathering*, Breadalbane St, T564849/565421/566159. Good, honest home cooking in one of Oban's oldest restaurants. Downstairs is *O'Donnell's* (see below).

Eating
There are numerous cheap options around town, none of which are particularly memorable

Argyll

Cheap Bar meals are available at pubs and hotels, and there are the ubiquitous fish and chip shops, the best of which is *Onorio's* on George St. Perhaps the best place in this category is the much-publicised *McTavish's Kitchens*, at 34 George Street, T563064. There's a self-service cafeteria downstairs (open from 0900) and the restaurant upstairs (open 1200-1400 and 1800-2230) has a 'Scottish Show' (see below).

The town is not exactly the party capital of Scotland, so don't expect much in the way of late night diversion. Your best bet is *O'Donnell's*, an Irish pub which has live music most nights, including ceilidhs, serves bar meals till 2300 and stays open till 0100. There's also Scottish music and dancing every night at *McTavish's Kitchens* 0830-2230 May-Sep (£3 admission, £1.50 if dining). Otherwise, there's the *Oban Inn*, by the north pier, which is the nicest pub in town and serves bar food.

Bars & entertainment

The local cinema, confusingly called *The Highland Theatre*, is at the north end of George St, T562444, and shows most of the popular current releases.

The *Highlands & Islands Music & Dance Festival* is held att the end of **Apr/beginning of May**. At the beginning of **Jun** is the *Oban Mod*, and at the beginning of **Aug** it's the *Lorn Agricatural Show*. The *Argyllshire Gathering* (Oban Games) is held at the end of **Aug** in Mossfield Park.

Festivals
Precise dates change annually: check the latest details at the TIC

Cycling You can rent bikes from *Oban Cycles*, 9 Craigard Rd, T566966. For details of cycle routes through the forests of Argyll, see the Forest Enterprise leaflet, *Cycling in the Forest*, available free at the tourist office.

Sport

Diving *Puffin Dive Centre*, Gallanach Port, Gallanach Rd, T566088. Diver training centre and facilities (open 0800-2000).

Fishing Excellent trout and coarse fishing on Loch Awe and Avich. Permits and boat hire from *The Angler's Corner*, 2 John St, T566374 (open daily 0930-1700).

Golf *Glencruitten Golf Club*, T562868/564115, is an 18-hole course on the edge of town; £16 per round per day.

Pony trekking *Melfort Riding Centre*, Melfort Village, Kilmelford by Oban, T01852-200322. Also at *Achnalarig Farm*, Glencruitten, T562745.

Swimming *Atlantis Leisure*, Dalriach Rd, T566800.

Walking The *Oban Walkers* organize walks throughout Argyll and beyond every fortnight. For more details contact the tourist office, where you can also pick up the Forestry Commission guides to *Forest Walks and Trails in North Argyll and Knapdale, Kintyre & Kilmichael*.

Windsurfing *Oban Windsurfing* at Ganavan, T564380, also at *Linnhe Marine Watersports Centre* at Lettershuna (see under North of Oban below).

Argyll

Transport **Bus** There are regular daily buses to and from **Fort William**, via Benderloch and Appin (1 hr 45 mins) with *West Coast Motors*, T01586-552319, *Highland Country Buses*, T01463-233371 and *Oban & District Buses*, T562856. There's a regular daily service to and from **Glasgow** (3 hrs) with *Scottish Citylink Coaches*, T0990-505050, and to **Inverness** (1 hr 15 mins). There are regular daily buses to and from **Dalmally**, via Cruachan Power Station, Lochawe and Taynuilt Hotel, operated by *Oban & District*, *Scottish Citylink*, *Awe Service Station*, T01866-822612 and *LF Stewart*, T01866-833342. There's a service to **Lochgilphead**, via Kilmartin, a couple of times a day (Mon-Sat), operated by *Oban & District*, *Scottish Citylink* and *West Coast Motors*.

Car hire *Flit Van & Car Hire*, Glencruitten Rd, T/F566553. From £20 per day. *Practical Car & Van Rental*, Robertson's Motor Repairs, Lochavullin Industrial Estate, T570900. From £30 per day. *Hazelbank Motors*, Lynn Rd, T566476, F566783. From £30 per day.

Ferry Oban is the main ferry port for many of the Hebridean islands. The *CalMac* ferry terminal, T566688 is on Railway Pier, to the south of the town centre. Only 100 yds away is the train station, T563083, which is next to the bus terminal. Details of ferries out of Oban are on page 114. For ferries to Lismore, see page 88.

Train There are 3 trains daily to **Glasgow**, via Crianlarich, where the Oban train connects with the Mallaig/Fort William-Glasgow train. For times, contact *Scotrail* (T08457-484950).

Directory **Banks** All the major banks have branches in the town centre and you can also change foreign currency at the tourist office.

Isle of Kerrera A good place to get away from the crowds and enjoy some peace and quiet and some fine walking is the island of Kerrera, which protects Oban Bay. It's only five miles by two, so can be explored easily on foot or by bike.

Phone code: 01631
Colour map 3, grid C5

The highest point on the island is 600 ft, from where there are great views across to Mull, the Slate Islands, Lismore and Jura. Otherwise, there's a good trail down to the ruins of **Gylen Castle**, built by the MacDougall's in 1582, which is perched on a cliff-top on the south coast. Near the castle is the F *Kerrera Bothy*, T570223, which has six beds, is open April-September, and can also arrange a lift to and from the ferry. There's also a tearoom here, which serves tea, coffee, juices, cakes and snacks.

The ferry lands at the spot where King Alexander II was mortally wounded while defeating the Vikings in battle, in 1249. A mile northwest of here is **Slatrach Bay**, a nice sandy beach and a great place for a picnic.

Getting there The departure point for ferries to Kerrera is 1½ miles along the Gallanach Rd. They leave several times daily between 0845 and 1800 (between 1030 and 1700 on Sun). The trip takes 5-10 mins and costs £2.50 return (£1.50 for children and 50p for bikes), T563665.

North of Oban

Phone code: 01631
Colour map 3, grid B5

Five miles north of Oban an impressive steel cantilever bridge carries the A828 across the mouth of Loch Etive at **Connel**. It's worth stopping here to see the **Falls of Lora**, a wild tide-race created by the narrow mouth of the sea loch and the reef that spans most of it, thus restricting the flow of water. The result is the impressive rapids, which are best seen from the shore in the village or from halfway across the bridge. There are several cheap **B&Bs** in Connel village, should you wish to stay, but the nicest place is the **D** *Ards House*, T710255, which offers good food.

Five miles east of Connel Bridge, on the north shore of Loch Etive, **Archattan Priory Garden** is worth a detour if the weather's fine. You can wander amongst the 13th century priory ruins and the gardens, which are at their best between July and September, though Spring is also a good time. There's also a tearoom. ■ *1 Apr-31 Oct 0900-1800. T750274.*

A few miles north of Connel Bridge at **Benderloch**, a road turns west (signed South Shian) to the *Tralee Dive Centre*, T/F720262, where you can charter boats for fishing. Nearby is *Tralee Rally Karting*, T720297, which is open daily July-September 1000-1800.

Continue on this road to reach Barcaldine Castle, built by the Campbells in the late 16th century. The tower house is still occupied by Campbells, having been sold in the mid-19th century and the bought back as a ruin 50 years later. It's now open to the public and though there are no real treasures, there are interesting stories to be told, secret passages to explore, a dungeon (with ghost) and a tearoom where you can try Mrs Campbell's home baking. You can also spend the night: there are two **D-E** rooms for B&B from June-September. ■ *Castle open Jul-Aug Tue-Sun 1200-1700. Adult £3.25. T720598.*

Barcaldine Castle

Argyll

Sleeping If the thought of a night in a haunted castle doesn't appeal, there are several B&Bs in the village of Benderloch. If money's no object, then treat yourself to the luxurious **L** *Isle of Eriska Hotel*, T720371, F720531. 17 rooms. Argyll's only five-star hotel, situated on its own private 300-acre island off the northern point of Benderloch.

Near Barcaldine Castle, on the main A828, is the Oban Sealife Centre, on the shore of Loch Creran. It's enormous fun and also environmentally-friendly as they rescue seals and other aquatic life and then release them back into the wild at the end of the season. You can see lots of strange underwater creatures at close quarters and even touch some of them. It's the ideal place to come with kids, or if it's raining. There's also a self-service restaurant. ■ *Daily 0900-1800 (1000-1700 in the winter months). Adult £6.50, concession £5.50, children £4.50. Various discount vouchers are in operation. Ask at the TIC or phone directly; T720386. Buses to Fort William pass by the Sealife Centre (see under 'Oban Transport' above).*

Oban Sealife Centre

The road runs around Loch Creran and enters the district of Appin, made famous in Robert Louis Stevenson's *Kidnapped*, which was based on the 'Appin Murder' of 1752. A road turns southwest off the main Fort William road to Port Appin, on the western tip of the peninsula, the departure point for the passenger ferry to **Lismore.**

Port Appin
Phone code: 01631
Colour map 3, grid B5

Sleeping and eating There are a couple of hotels in this attractive little fishing village, the best of which is the superb **L** *Airds Hotel*, T730236, F730535. 12 rooms, this classy little roadside hotel boasts one of the very best restaurants in the whole country and is recommended in all the best guide books. There's also the **C** *Pierhouse Hotel*, T730302, F730400. Sitting right by the tiny pier, this cosy little hotel has a deserved reputation for excellent, moderately-priced local seafood. If your budget doesn't stretch that far, then there's the **E** *Fasgadh Guest House*, T730374.

To the north of Port Appin is the irresistibly photogenic Castle Stalker. Standing on its own tiny island with a background of islands and hills, it's probably

Castle Stalker

second only to the famous Eilean Donan, in its portrayal of Scotland's romantic image. It was built in the 16th century by the Stewarts of Appin before falling into Campbell hands after the ill-fated 1745 rebellion. The current owners open it to the public for a limited period in July and August. Check opening times at the tourist office in Oban.

At **Lettershuna**, just beyond Port Appin, is the **Linnhe Marine Watersports Centre**, where you can hire motor boats, sailing dinghies or windsurfing boards, take sailing or windsurfing lessons, or try water-skiing, pony trekking or even clay pigeon shooting. ■ *May-Sep 0900-1800. T730227, Cell 0421-503981.*

Isle of Lismore

Phone code: 01631
Colour map 3, grid B5

The island of Lismore lies only a few miles off the mainland, in Loch Linnhe, yet feels a world away. It makes an ideal day trip and offers great opportunities for walking and cycling, as well as wonderful views across to the mountains of Morvern and Mull, the Paps of Jura to the south and Ben Nevis to the north. It's a fertile little island (the name *leis mór* is Gaelic for "the big garden") and once supported a population of 1,400, though the present population is about a tenth of that.

Lismore has a long and interesting history. It was the ecclesiastical capital of Argyll for several centuries and the **Cathedral of St Moluag** was founded here in the 12th century, just north of Clachan. All that remains is the choir, which is now used as the parish church. The occupies the site of a church founded by the Irish saint, who established a religious community on the island about the same time as St Columba was busy at work in Iona. Legend has it that the two saints were racing to the island, in an attempt to be the first to land and found a monastery. Such was Moluag's religious zeal that he cut off his finger and threw it on to the shore, thus claiming possession.

Not far from the church, is the 2,000-year-old **Broch of Tirefour**, one of the best-preserved prehistoric monuments in Argyll with surviving circular walls up to 16-ft high. Other interesting sights include **Castle Coeffin**, a 13th-century fortress built by the MacDougalls of Lorn, on the

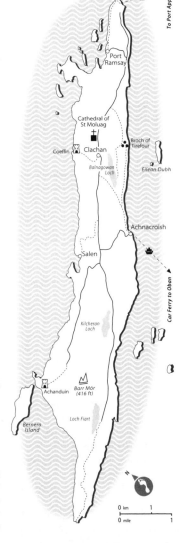

Lismore

To Port Appin

Port Ramsay

Cathedral of St Moluag

Coeffin · Clachan · Broch of Tirefour

Balnagowan Loch · Eilean Dubh

Achnacroish

Salen

Car Ferry to Oban

Kilcheran Loch

Achanduin · Barr Mór (416 ft)

Bernera Island · Loch Fiart

N

0 km   1
0 mile   1

west coast, and in the southwest of the island, the 13th-century **Achadun Castle**, built for the Bishops of Argyll. It's a short walk from here to **Bernera Island**, which can be reached at low tide (but don't get stranded).

Sleeping and eating There are a couple of B&Bs on the island, including **F** *The Schoolhouse*, T760262, juest beyond Clachan, 1½ miles north of the ferry pier. There's also a shop and post office at Clachan.

Transport There's a limited postbus service which runs Mon-Sat (see the *Lorn Area Transport Guide* for times), or you can hire bikes from *Mary MacDougall*, T760213). The *CalMac* car ferry from Oban lands at **Achnacroish**, about halfway up the east coast (2-4 daily Mon-Sat; 50 mins). A passenger ferry leaves from Port Appin pier to the island's north point (daily every 1-2 hrs; 10 mins).

South Lorn and the Slate Islands

Eight miles south of Oban the B884 turns west off the A816 to the tiny Slate Islands, so called because in the mid-19th century, the island's slate quarries exported millions of roofing slates every year. The quarrying industry has long since gone, leaving behind dilapidated old buildings as well as pretty little villages of whitewashed cottages built for the slate workers.

Phone code: 01852
Colour map 3,
grid C4/5

Getting there A passenger **ferry** sails from Ellanbeich on Seil to Easdale, making the 5-min trip at regular intervals between 0745 and 1900 Mon-Sat (between 0930 and 1500 on Sun), partly to schedule, partly on request. Check times at Oban tourist office. A car ferry to Luing (South Cuan) sails from South Cuan on Seil (5 mins), Mon-Sat every 15-30 mins from 0745 to 1815 (later in summer) and on Sun every 30 mins from 1100-1800. Check times at Oban tourist office.

Ins & outs
It can be a rough crossing & times are subject to sailing conditions

Getting around A *Postbus* service runs from Oban train station to Clachan Seil, Balvicar, Ellenbeich and North Cuan on Seil. There's also a circular postbus service on Luing, from South Cuan to Cullipool and Toberonochy. Check times at Oban tourist office. Fares for both routes are £1 adults, 50 p children.

The most northerly of the Slate Islands is Seil, which is reached from the mainland across the impressive Clachan Bridge, better known as the 'Bridge over the Atlantic', built in 1792, with its elegant, high arch to allow ships to pass beneath. Beside the bridge is an old inn, *Tigh an Truish*, or 'House of the Trousers', where islanders would have to swap kilt for trousers in order to conform to the post-1745 ban on the wearing of Highland dress.

Isle of Seil
Phone code: 01852

Two miles south, at **Balvicar**, the road turns right and climbs up and over to the main village of **Ellanbeich**, an attractive wee place with rows of white cottages around the harbour. This was once a tiny island itself until the intensive slate quarrying succeeded in silting up the narrow sea channel. The village is also, rather confusingly, known by the same name as the nearby island of **Easdale**, so renowned was the latter for its slate deposits. Another road runs south from Balvicar to **North Cuan**, from where the car ferry sails across the treacherous Cuan Sound to **Luing** (see below).

Sleeping There's B&B accommodation on Seil, at **E** *Mutiara* , T300241, open May-Nov.

Argyll

Isle of Easdale
Phone code: 01852

Easdale is separated from Seil by a 500-yard-wide channel which has to be dredged to keep it open. The island, only 800 yards by 700 yards, was the centre of the slate industry and the old dilapidated workers' cottages can still be seen, lending an air of melancholy to the place. There was once a population of over 450 here, but the quarries were flooded during a great storm in 1881 and the industry collapsed. The present population numbers around 50. The old quarries can still be seen, filled with water, with the derelict work buildings standing forlorn as the surrounding vegetation takes over. The fascinating history of the island is explained at the **folk museum** near the main square in the village. ■ *Apr-Oct daily 1030-1730. Adult £2. T300370.*

There are no roads on the island, which only takes about half an hour to walk around. There's a tearoom by the pier and some of the old cottages have been modernized and turned into self-catering accommodation (details from the tourist office in Oban).

Isle of Luing
Phone code: 01852

The long, thin island of Luing (pronounced 'Ling') once had a population of around 600 which was drastically reduced during the Clearances to make way for cattle. The island is still well known for its beef and is the home of a successful new breed named after it.

The island is small, six miles by two, and mostly flat, making it ideal for exploring by bike. Bikes can be hired in the pretty little village of **Cullipool**, a mile or so southwest of the ferry (contact *Isle of Luing Bike Hire*, T314256). There's also a tearoom, post office and general store. On the road to Cullipool is the island's only B&B, **E-F** *Bardrishaig Farm*, T314364.

The only other village is **Toberonochy**, three miles from Cullipool on the east coast. It's another village of attractive white cottages built for slate workers and nested below a ruined church.

South Lorn

Phone code: 01852

South of the turn-off to the Slate Islands is **Arduaine Garden**, a beautiful place and an absolute must for all gardening enthusiasts. The 20-acre garden, now owned by the National Trust for Scotland, is best visited in May and June when you can enjoy the spectacular rhododendrons, but there are also beautiful herbaceous borders, ponds filled with water lilies, woodland and sweeping lawns to admire, as well as great views across to Jura and the

Atlantic Bridge,
Clachan,
Isle of Seil

Slate Islands. ■ *Daily all year 0930 till sunset. Adult £3, concession £2, children £1. T200366.*

Sleeping If you want to stay around here, there's the superb **B-A** *Loch Melfort Hotel*, T01852-200233, F200214, www.loch-melfort.co.uk 26 rooms. Open all year. It enjoys great views and a reputation for the finest seafood. If you can't afford such luxury, there's a **campsite** nearby, or **B&B** at **E-F** *Willow Cottage*, T200202.

This is boating country, and just south of Arduaine, on the northern coast of the **Craignish Peninsula**, is surreal **Croabh Haven**, a yachting marina, built in the style of a reproduction 18th-century fishing village. You can go for comfort and stay at the **D-E** *Buidhe Lodge*, T01852-500291, www.buidlodge.com or opt for the faded charm of **E-F** *Lunga*, T01852-500237, F500369, coline@lunga.demon.co.uk

South of Croabh Haven is another yachting marina at **Ardfern**, where there's a hotel and B&B accommodation, a popular pub, restaurant and delicatessen. You can arrange boat trips from Ardfern around Loch Craignish and to the offshore islands with *Ruby Cruises*, T/F500616.

Mid-Argyll

The area south of Oban and north of Kintyre is commonly known as Mid-Argyll, a very attractive region of sea lochs, rolling hills and the huge forest of Knapdale, which offers some fine walking. The greatest attraction in Mid-Argyll, though, is Kilmartin Glen, which is littered with Neolithic, Bronze Age and Iron Age monuments, and is one of the most interesting and least known prehistoric sites in Europe.

Ins and outs

Getting there *Scottish Citylink*, T0990-505050, runs a daily service from Glasgow to Campbeltown which stops in Lochgilphead.

Getting around Public transport is thin on the ground, but with a little time and patience it is possible to explore the area by bus. You can find out times of buses at the tourist office in Lochgilphead (see below), or pick up a free copy of Argyll & Bute Council's Mid-Argyll timetable. For details of shared taxis, or to book a taxi, contact *Mid Argyll Taxis*, 4 Slockavullin, Kilmartin, T01546-510318.

For bus details, see Transport below

Lochgilphead

Phone code: 01546
Colour map 3, grid C5

The main town in the area, and administrative centre for the entire Argyll and Bute region, is Lochgilphead, a sleepy little place at the head of Loch Gilp, an arm of Loch Fyne. Lochgilphead started life as a planned town, but the industries came and went, leaving it with the customary grid plan of wide streets but little else. Today, it serves as a useful base for exploring the area, with a decent range of accommodation, a bank, supermarket and **tourist office** on Lochnell Street, T602344; open April-October.

South of Lochgilphead and almost a continuation of the town, is the village of **Ardrishaig**, where you'll find the *Castle Riding Centre*, at Brenfield Estate & Farm, T603274. Here you can enjoy cross country horse riding, beach gallops, pub rides or hire mountain bikes, sail boards, boats, or even try clay pigeon shooting and archery. There's a nice easy walk from the car park at **Kilmory Castle Gardens**, about a mile east of town, up to **Kilmory Loch**. It takes about an hour there and back and is well marked. The gardens also make a pleasant stroll and there are other marked walks, including up to Dun Mór (360 ft).

Sleeping & eating

There are several hotels, guesthouses and B&Bs in and around Lochgilphead. Best of the bunch is **B** *Cairnbaan Hotel*, T603668, F606045, a lovely 18th-century coaching inn overlooking the Crinan Canal in the village of Cairnbaan, just north of Lochgilphead. In the town itself is **E** *The Argyll Hotel* on Lochnell St, T602221, F603576, argyll.hotel@btclick.com which has a moderately-priced restaurant and lively bar. Just outside of town, at Bank Park, is a **caravan park**, where you can pitch a tent. It has the full range of facilities and also hires out mountain bikes, T602003.

Mid-Argyll, Knapdale & Kintyre

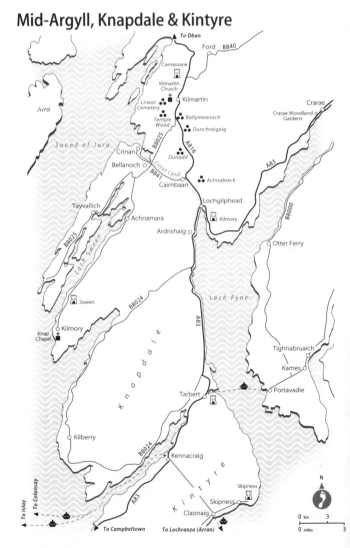

In **Ardishaig** is the recently refurbished **F-E** *Grey Gull Inn*, T606017, F606167, www.greygull.co.uk which is very good value and serves snacks and meals all day. A cheaper alternative for eating out is *The Stables*, or the bar of the *Stag Hotel*, both on Argyll St. If you fancy a picnic, then try the *Alba Smokehouse*, an excellent deli in Kilmory, just east of town.

Cycle hire *Crinan Cycles*, The Pier, Ardrishaig, T603511. Also *Lochgilphead Caravan Park* (see above).

Sport

There are **buses** from Lochgilphead to Cairnbaan, Crinan, Achnamara and Tayvallich several times daily Mon-Sat. There are buses and shared taxis to Oban via Kilmartin (Mon-Sat) and a postbus to Inveraray (Mon-Sat). There's also a local service to and from Ardrishaig.

Transport

Banks *Bank of Scotland*, Poltalloch St.

Directory

Kilmartin Glen

North of Lochgilphead, on the A816 to Oban, is Kilmartin Glen, an area of Neolithic and Bronze Age chambered and round cairns, stone circles, rock carvings, Iron Age forts and duns, Early Christian sculptured stones and medieval castles. Most notable of all is the **linear cemetery**, a line of burial cairns that stretch southward from Kilmartin village for over two miles. The largest and oldest of the group is the Neolithic cairn, **Nether Largie South**, which is over 5,000 years old and big enough to enter. The other cairns, **Nether Largie North**, **Mid Nether Largie** and **Ri Cruin**, are Bronze Age and the huge stone coffins show carvings on the grave slabs. Nearby are the **Temple Wood Stone Circles**, where burials took place from Neolithic times to the Bronze Age.

Phone code: 01546
Colour map 3, grid C5

On the other side of the A816, and visible from the road, is a group of monuments which can all be reached from **Dunchraigaig Cairn**. This is a huge Bronze Age cairn with some of the covering stones removed to reveal three stone coffins. From here a path is signed to **Ballymeanoch Standing Stones**, the tallest of which is 12-ft high. Two of the stones are decorated with cup marks, prehistoric rock carvings that can be found at numerous locations throughout the Kilmartin area. There's also a henge monument in the same field. These were generally round or oval platforms with an internal ditch and it's thought they were used for ceremonial purposes.

The best example of rock carvings is at **Achnabreck**, near Cairnbaan village, the largest collection anywhere in Britain. The purpose and significance of these cup- and ring-marked rocks is still a matter of debate.

Before exploring this fascinating area, it's a good idea to stop off at **Kilmartin House**, the multi award-winning interpretive centre, housed in the old manse next to the parish church in the village of Kilmartin. The imaginative and interesting museum helps to explain the bewildering array of prehistoric sites lying all around and includes artefacts from the various sites and prehistoric music. Upstairs is an audio-visual display which tells the story of this unique corner of Scotland. The café/restaurant does not disappoint either and serves cheap snacks and meals, using local produce, and excellent coffee from 1230 till 1700. ■ *Daily all year 1000-1730. Adult £3.90, concession £3.10, children £1.20. T510278.*

Kilmartin

Next door in the church graveyard are the **Kilmartin crosses**, dating from as far back as the ninth and 10th centuries. Also within the graveyard is one of the largest collections of medieval grave slabs in the West Highlands.

Two miles north of Kilmartin, sitting high above the A816, is **Carnasserie Castle**, an imposing 16th-century tower house built by John Carswell, Bishop of the Isles, who translated *The Book of the Common Order* in 1567, the first book to be printed in Gaelic. Entry to the castle is free, but it's a little way from the car park.

Dunadd   A few miles south of Kilmartin village is the Iron Age hill fort of Dunadd, which stands atop a rocky outcrop and dominates the surrounding flat expanse of Moine Mhór (Great Moss), one of the few remaining peat bogs in the country and now a Nature Reserve. Dunadd Fort became the capital of the ancient kingdom of Dalriada around 500 AD and is one the most important Celtic sites in Scotland. The views from the top are wonderful and worth the visit alone, but you can also see carved out of the exposed rock, a basin and footprint, thought to have been used in the inauguration ceremonies of the ancient kings of Dalriada. There's also an inscription in *ogham* (a form of early writing from Ireland) and the faint outline of a boar, possibly of Pictish origin.

Sleeping & eating   If you want to spend more time exploring Kilmartin Glen, there are a few accommodation options. Opposite the church is **D** *Kilmartin Hotel*, T510250, F606370, which is comfortable and serves meals all day. There are also a couple of cheaper B&Bs to choose from, including **E** *Burndale*, T510235 and **F-E** *Tibertich*, T/F810281, www.tibertich.com, a working sheep farm just north of the village. A good place for lunch is the café at Kilmartin House (see above), otherwise, there's *The Cairn* restaurant, T510254, which serves very good, moderately-priced Scottish and European dishes using local produce (open Mar-Oct from 1700).

Crinan Canal

Phone code: 01546
Colour map 3, grid C5

Kilmartin Glen is bordered to the south by the Crinan Canal, a nine-mile stretch of waterway linking Loch Fyne at Ardishaig with the Sound of Jura. It was designed and built by Sir John Rennie in 1801, with the assistance of the ubiquitous Thomas Telford, to allow shipping to avoid the long and often hazardous journey round the Mull of Kintyre and to help stimulate trade in the islands. These days, you're more likely to see pleasure yachts and cruisers sailing on the canal than the cargo vessels which once transported coal and other goods to the islands and returned with livestock. You don't need to come in a boat to appreciate the canal. You can walk or cycle along the towpath that runs the entire length of the canal, from Ardrishaig to Crinan, and watch boats of all shapes and sizes negotiating a total of 15 locks. The best place to view the canal traffic is at **Crinan**, a pretty little fishing port on Loch Crinan at the western end of the canal. Here you can take a boat trip with *Gemini Cruises*, based at Crinan harbour, T/F01546-830238. They offer two-hour wildlife spotting cruises round Loch Craignish (£9 per person), or longer trips out to the Gulf of Corrievreckan.

Sleeping & eating   Crinan boasts one of Scotland's finest hotels, the **A** *Crinan Hotel*, T830261, F830292, www.crinanhotel.com Not only is this one of the most beautifully-located hotels in the country, but its celebrated restaurants are amongst the best on the west coast. The bar next to the *Lock 16* restaurant on the top floor offers cheaper lunches, for those who can't afford such indulgence. A cheaper **B&B** alternative is **E-D** *Tigh-Na-Glaic*, T830245, F830243.

Knapdale

Phone code: 01880
Colour map 5, grid A2

Running south from the Crinan Canal down to Kintyre is Knapdale, a forested, hilly area that gets its name from its Gaelic description, *cnap* (hill) and *dall* (field). It's an area worth exploring, for there are many walking trails and superb views from the west coast across to the Paps of Jura.

Immediately south of the canal is **Knapdale Forest**, which stretches from coast to coast over hills dotted with tiny lochs. The Forestry Commission has marked out several lovely trails. Three fairly easy circular trails start from the B8025 which runs south from **Bellanoch**, just east of Crinan. One sets out from the car park at the Barnluasgan Interpretation Centre and runs up to a point beyond Loch Barnluasgan, with great views over the forest and the many lochs. It's a mile in total. A second trail, also a mile long, starts from a car park a little further along the B8025 and heads through the forest to the deserted township of Arichonan. The third trail starts out from the car park between the starting points for the first and second trails. It runs right around Loch Coille-Bharr and is three miles long. A more strenuous walk starts from a car park about 100 yds into the forest, off the B841, about half a mile west of Cairnbaan, and climbs up to the peak of **Dunardy** (702 ft).

At the Barnluasgan Interpretation Centre a little side road turns south down the eastern shore of beautiful **Loch Sween**, past the village of **Achnamara**, to the 12th century **Castle Sween**. First impressions of the castle, situated on the shores of the lovely loch with the forested hills all around, are completely ruined by the criminally distasteful caravan park nearby. Unfortunately, the caravans were not there when Robert the Bruce attacked the castle, otherwise he might have done us all a favour by razing them.

Three miles south is the ruined 13th-century **Kilmory Knap Chapel**. A new glass roof protects the carved stones inside. The most notable of these is the 8-ft high, 15th-century MacMillan's Cross, which shows the Crucifixion on one side and a hunting scene on the other.

The best place to stay in Knapdale is the highly recommended **C** *Kilberry Inn*, **Sleeping**
T01880-770223, www.kilberryinn.com, west of Tarbert on the B8024. 3 rooms, open Easter-Oct, it offers superb food and perfect peace.

Kintyre

Colour map 5, grid A/B2

The long peninsula of Kintyre is probably best known as the inspiration for Paul McCartney's phenominally successful 1970s dirge, Mull of Kintyre, but don't let that put you off. Kintyre has all the usual Highland ingredients, such as great scenery, wildlife, bags of history, golf and whisky, but also has the added attraction of being one of Scotland's least explored spots.

The peninsula would be an island, were it not for the mile-long isthmus between West and East Loch Tarbert, a fact not lost on King Magnus Barefoot of Norway. In the 11th century, he signed a treaty with the Scottish king, Malcolm Canmore, giving him all the land he could sail round, so he promptly had his men drag his longboat across the narrow isthmus, thus adding Kintyre to his kingdom.

Ins and outs

Getting there It's about a 3-hr drive from Glasgow to Campbeltown. The most direct route is by the A82 to Tarbert on Loch Lomond, then the A83 via Inveraray and Lochgilphead. There are several daily **buses** from Glasgow to Campbeltown (4 hrs 20 mins), via Inveraray, Lochgilphead, Kennacraig and Tarbert. For details: T01586-552319 or T0141-3329191, or *Scottish Citylink* (T0990-505050). Kintyre can also be reached by car and passenger **ferry** from Portavadie on the Cowal peninsula (20 mins). They leave daily every hour all year round. There are buses between Portavadie and Dunoon, Tarbert and Kennacraig (details from Argyll & Bute Council, T01546-604695, or the tourist office). A summer ferry (April to mid-October) leaves from Lochranza in the north of Arran, to Claonaig (30 mins), on the west coast of Kintyre, south of Kennacraig. For details, see page 102. Ferries leave from Kennacraig, 5 miles south of Tarbert, to Islay (see page 135 and to Colonsay (see page 133). There's also a summer service from Ballycastle in Northern Ireland to Campbeltown; for details T0990-523523. There are 2 **flights** daily, all year round from Glasgow to Machrihanish airport near Campbeltown (35 mins). For times and reservations, contact *British Airways Express*, T08457-222111.

Getting around Getting around Kintyre without your own transport requires time and patience. There's a **bus** service running up and down the west coast (see above), and also a limited service from Campbeltown to places around the peninsula (see page 99).

Tarbert

Phone code: 01880
Colour map 5, grid A3

The fishing village of Tarbert sits at the head of East Loch Tarbert, in a sheltered bay backed by forested hills, and is one the most attractive ports on the west coast. Tarbert (the name derives from the Gaelic *An Tairbeart* meaning "isthmus") has a long tradition of fishing and in the 18th and 19th centuries was a major herring port. Today, prawns and other shellfish are the main catch and though there is still a sizeable fleet, fishing has declined in importance to the local economy. Tourism, meanwhile, is a growing source of income, and Tarbert attracts its fair share of yachties, particularly in May, when the village hosts the second largest racing series in the UK, after Cowes, attracting hundreds of boats and thousands of visitors. The town also hosts an excellent **folk music festival**, over a weekend at the end of September (for details, T820343).

Ins & outs There are **buses** from Kennacraig and Tarbert to Claonaig and Skipness (2-3 daily Mon-Sat), and from **Tarbert** to **Kennacraig** (several times daily Mon-Sat).

The **Tourist Information Centre** is on Harbour St, T820429. Open 6-29 Apr Mon-Fri 1000-1700, Sat-Sun 1200-1700; 30 Apr-1 Jul Mon-Sat 1000-1700, Sun 1100-1700; 2 Jul-2 Sep Mon-Sat 0930-1800, Sun 1000-1700;3 Sep-28 Oct Mon-Sat 1000-1700, Sun 1200-1700.

Sights Overlooking the harbour is the dramatically-sited ruin of **Robert the Bruce's** 14th-century castle. There's not much left to see, other than the five-storey 15th-century keep. It's unsafe to investigate the ruins too closely, but the view alone is worth the walk. There are steps leading up to the castle, next to the *Ann Thomas Gallery*, on Harbour Street. Behind the castle, there are several marked trails leading up into the hills, with great views over Loch Fyne and the islands. Less strenuous is the short walk at the end of Garvel Road, on the north side of the harbour, which leads to the beach. At the end of East Pier road, beyond the Cowal Ferry, is another interesting walk, to the Shell Beaches. You can also explore the lovely gardens at *Stonefield Castle Hotel* (see below).

Just south of town, on the main A83, is the **An Tairbeart Heritage Centre**, which tells you all you need to know about the area's fascinating history, as well as providing a whole host of activities such as woodturning and sheep shearing. There's also a good, moderately-priced restaurant offering local specialities such as venison and oysters. ■ *Easter till early Jan daily 1000-1900. Free. T820190, www.an-t.co.uk*

Sleeping

Three miles north on the A82 to Lochgilphead is the sumptious **A** *Stonefield Castle Hotel*, T820836, F820929, a magnificent Baronial Victorian mansion set in 60 acres of beautiful woodland garden, with great views across the loch and an acclaimed restaurant to boot.

There's a good selection of places to stay in Tarbert itself, including the **B** *Columba Hotel*, T/F820808, www.columbahotel.com, on East Pier Rd. 10 rooms. This refurbished and comfortable Victorian hotel is on the waterfront and features fine cooking. The restaurant is moderately priced and the popular bar offers cheap, imaginative meals.

Just outside the village is the **D** *West Loch Hotel*, T820283, F820930, a traditional 18th-century coaching inn on the main A83 overlooking West Loch Tarbert. There's also plenty B&B accommodation, mostly **E**, and a **campsite**, at Escart Bay in a secluded spot overlooking West Loch Tarbert, T820873.

Eating

Pick of the bunch is *The Anchorage*, on Harbour St, T820881. Wonderful food, particularly the local seafood and fish, and mid-range prices. Small and cosy so book in advance. Otherwise the best food is available at the hotels. There's the above-mentioned *Columba and Stonefield Castle Hotels* but also recommended is the *Victoria Hotel*, T820236, aliatvic@aol.com, which is on the right as you enter the village from Lochgilphead.

As you'd expect with a place popular with yachties, Tarbert boasts some very fine restaurants

Shopping

Earra Gael Craft Shop, T820428, in the old Weighbridge on Harbour St. Open daily Apr-Oct 1000-1730. *Ann Thomas Gallery*, Harbour St, T820390. Good selection of books, local prints and stationery; open daily (Mon-Sat 0900-1830, Sun 1100-1830 in summer).

Directory

Banks *Bank of Scotland* and *Clydesdale Bank are both on Harbour St, and both have ATMs.*

Isle of Gigha

The small island of Gigha (pronounced "Gee-a" with a hard "g") translates from Norse as "God's Island". A grand claim, perhaps, but there's no question that this most accessible of islands is also one of the loveliest and most romantic. It's only a 20-minute ferry ride away, and only six miles by one mile, so it can be visited easily in a day, which is just about enough time to appreciate why the Vikings loved it so much. Like so many of the Hebridean islands, Gigha has had a long list of owners, including various branches of the MacNeils and, more recently, in 1944, Sir James Horlick, he of bedtime drink fame.

It was Horlick who created the island's single greatest attraction, the wonderful **Achamore Garden**, one mile south of the ferry terminal. Thanks to Gigha's mild climate, the 50-acre woodland garden has an amazing variety of tropical plants, including rhododendrons, azaleas, camellias as well as other, more exotic, species. There are two marked walks through the gardens, which start out from the walled garden. The gardens are best seen in early summer, when the rhodies are in full bloom. ■ *Daily all year 0900 till dusk. Adult £2, children. Also rooms to let, T505254, F505244.*

Population: 120
Phone code: 01583

Argyll

Walks on the island The island's other delights include some good **walks**, white sandy **beaches** and fantastic views across to Jura on one side and Kintyre on the other. One of the best walks is to take the path left after the **nine-hole golf course**, signed Ardaily, past Mill Loch to the Mill on the west shore. The views from here are just magnificent. Another good idea is to walk, or cycle (see below for bike hire) to the peninsula of **Eilean Garbh** at the north of the island. About half a mile beyond Kinererach Farm a path leads left to the peninsula where two crescent-shaped beaches are separated by a thin spit of land. And if the weather's good enough for a picnic, make sure you try some of the island's famously distinctive cheese.

Sleeping & eating The ferry port and only village is **Ardminish**. Here you'll find the **C** *Gigha Hotel*, T505254, F505244, open Mar-Oct, which offers comfort, great views and good bar food. Another option is the **E** *Post Office House*, T505251, a short walk from the ferry. The McSporrans also run the post office and general store, provide good home cooking and even rent out bikes.

A good alternative to staying on the island, at the ferry port of **Tayinloan**, is the **C** *Tayinloan Inn*, T441233, a small and cosy 18th-century coaching inn offering the best food south of Tarbert.

Transport The small *CalMac* car and passenger ferry leaves from Tayinloan to the ferry pier at Ardminish, daily all year round (hourly 0800-1800 Mon-Sat, 1100-1700 Sun). The return trip costs £4.75 per passenger and £17.90 per car (though a car is totally unnecessary).

Campbeltown

Phone code: 01586
Colour map 5, grid B2
Population: 6,500

At the southern end of the Kintyre Peninsula is the "metropolis" of Campbeltown, originally called Kinlochkilkerran (*Ceann Loch Cille Ciaran*) but renamed in the 17th century by the Earl of Argyll, who was, of course, a Campbell. This may be the largest town by far in this part of Argyll, but it has a real end-of-the-line feel, due in part to its geographical isolation, but also because the town has long since lost its *raison d'être* – whisky.

Ins & outs There are several daily **buses** to and from Glasgow. Also to Machrihanish, Carradale, Saddell, Southend and the airport (see page 99).

The **Tourist Information Centre** is on the Old Quay, T552056. Apr Mon-Fri 0900-1730; May-Sep Mon-Fri 0900-1730, Sat-Sun 1100-1700; Oct Mon-Fri 0930-1730, Sat-Sun 1000-1600; Nov-Mar Mon-Fri 1000-1600.

There was once a lot of whisky distilled in Campbeltown. So much so, in fact, that local fishermen were able to smell their way home. That may be apocryphal but there's no doubting that the place did inspire tartan crooner Andy Stewart (a man responsible for such dubious classics as *Donald, Whar's yer Troosers*) to

Campbeltown

sing *Campbeltown Loch I wish you were whisky*. But even Andy Stewart might have had problems trying to consume the total production of the town's whisky at its 1886 peak; no fewer than two million gallons.

It's not only whisky that's in decline; shipbuilding and fishing have also suffered. But it's hoped that the new car ferry link to Ballycastle in Northern Ireland will help to stimulate the local economy.

Sights

Campbeltown's whisky production was such that the town even has its own particular regional subgroup of single malt named after it, but of the 34 distilleries once in production, only one remains, the **Springbank distillery**. This family-run distillery is in Well Close, off Longrow, and guided tours are by appointment only, T552085. Whisky aficionados should also pay a visit to **Eaglesome** on Longrow South, where you can choose from over 400 single malts.

To find out more on the town's history, you can visit the **Campbeltown Heritage Centre**, on the Southend road, housed in the former Lorne Street church, or "Tartan Kirk" as it is known locally, due to its distinctive facade of alternating stone and red brick. ■ *Apr-Oct Mon-Sat 1100-1700, Sun 1400-1700. Adult £2.*

The most interesting sight in town is the wonderfully evocative **"Wee Picture House"**, on Hall Street, first opened in May 1913. This rare art deco treasure was closed in 1983, but such was the storm of local protest that it was lovingly refurbished and reopened in 1989. No visit to Campbeltown would be complete without witnessing the glories of a bygone era in the oldest surviving cinema in Scotland. Films are shown six nights a week (Friday night is bingo night).

Sleeping & eating

There's plenty of accommodation in town. There's the comfortable **C** *Ardshiel Hotel*, T552133, F551422, on Kilkerran Rd, or the **D** *White Hart Hotel*, T552440, F554972, on Main St. There are also several cheap **B&Bs**. Aside from the aforementioned hotels, the culinary scene is not worth mentioning.

Festivals

If you're around at the end of **Aug**, don't miss the *Mull of Kintyre Music Festival*, 3 days of the best in traditional Celtic music, held in various venues throughout the town, with numerous impromptu pub sessions.

Sport

Horse riding   *Mull of Kintyre Equestrian Centre*, Homeston Farm (2 miles south on the B842 to Southend), T552437. Dinner and B&B also available.

Transport

There are buses from Campbeltown to **Machrihanish** (hourly Mon-Sat, 3 on Sun; 15 mins), to **Carradale** (45 mins) and **Saddell** (4 daily Mon-Sat, 2 on Sun; 25 mins), to **Southend** (several daily; 25 mins), and also to the **airport** (2 daily Mon-Fri; 10 mins). If you want to hire a car, there's *Campbeltown Motor Company*, T01586-552030 or *Fona taxis & minibuses*, T01586-554001.

Around Campbeltown

If the weather's good, it's worth taking a walk up to **Beinn Ghulean**, which overlooks the town and loch. Follow the signs for the A83 to Machrihanish until you reach Witchburn Road. After passing the creamery on your left, turn left into Tomaig Road and continue till you come to a wooden gate. Cross over the stile and follow the track through the fields, crossing two more stiles, before you reach the Forest Enterprise sign which marks the start of the walk. It's about four miles there and back from the end of Tomaig road.

One of the most popular day trips is to the uninhabited **Davaar Island**, connected to the peninsula by a tidal breakwater. Here you can see the cave painting of the Crucifixion, completed in secret by a local artist in 1877. The island can be visited at low tide from Kildalloig Point, a couple of miles east of town. Check tide times at the tourist office before setting out.

Machrihanish
Phone code: 01586
Colour map 5, grid B2

Six miles from Campbeltown, on the west coast of Kintyre, is Machrihanish, site of Campbeltown's airport and a magnificent beach. Five miles of glorious unspoiled sand backed by dunes and washed by gigantic Atlantic breakers. Not surprisingly, this is a cracking place for **windsurfing** and **surfing**; one of the very best in the country, in fact. It also boasts a dramatic 18-hole championship golf course, whose first hole was described by Jack Nicklaus as the world's greatest opening hole. The beach can be approached either by walking north from the village, or south from the car park on the main A83 to Tayinloan and Tarbert, where it leaves the coast.

Sleeping There are a couple of options if you wish to stay here, the best of which is **D** *Ardell House Hotel*, overlooking the golf course, T/F810235. Open Mar-Oct, 10 rooms. Cheaper and simpler is **E** *Kilgour House*, T/F810233, which has a lively bar/restaurant next door. There's also a **campsite** at East Trodigal, T810366; open Mar-Sep, with full facilities. It's on the right just before the village heading west from Campbeltown.

Southend and the Mull of Kintyre

It's only a short drive south from Campbeltown to the tip of the peninsula, the Mull of Kintyre, eulogised by one-time resident Paul McCartney in the irritating eponymous hit single. There's nothing much to see in this bleak, storm-battered place, apart from the coast of Ireland, a mere 12 miles away and clearly visible on a good day. The road out to the lighthouse, built in 1788 and remodelled by Robert Stevenson, grandfather of Robert Louis, is pretty hairy, to put it mildly. It's possible to walk from here up to Machrihanish (about 10 miles), past the ruined township of Balmavicar and the Largiebaan Bird Reserve. The views are great and there's a chance of seeing Golden Eagles.

The southernmost village on Kintyre is **Southend**, a bleak, windswept place with a wide sandy beach. At the east end of the beach, jutting out on a rocky promontory, are the scant remains of **Dunaverty Castle**, once a MacDonald stronghold, where 300 Royalists were brutally massacred in 1647 by the Covenanting army of the Earl of Argyll, despite having already surrendered. To the west of Southend, below the cliffs, is the ruined 13th-century **Keil Chapel**, which is said to mark the spot where **St Columba** first set foot on Scottish soil, before heading north to Iona. Close by is a pair of footprints carved into the rock, known as **Columba's footprints**.

Sleeping Should you wish to spend time here, there are a couple of good **B&Bs** in Southend, including **E** *Ormsary Farm*, T830665, open Apr-Sep.

The east coast

The slow and winding single track B842 meanders up the east coast from Campbeltown to Skipness and Claonaig, departure point for the ferry to Arran (see below). The scenery en route is gentle and pleasant with nice views of Arran, and there are some worthwhile places to stop, but public transport is somewhat limited (see Campbeltown 'Transport' above).

Ten miles up the coast are the idyllic ruins of **Saddell Abbey**, a Cistercian establishment, founded by Somerled in 1160. The abbey fell into ruin in the early 16th century and much of the stone was used in the building of Saddell Castle for the Bishop of Argyll. Though little remains, there are some impressive medieval grave slabs, depicting knights, monks, ships, animals and other images.

A few miles further north is the village of Carradale, the only place of any size on the east coast, nestling in the sandy sweep of beautiful Carradale Bay. There are several pleasant marked walks through the woods between the B842 and the shore. The shortest of these walks (with green waymarkers) starts from the Network Centre (see below) and is a mile long. There's a three-mile walk with red waymarkers which starts at the Port Na Storm car park and follows the forest road to the left. After 150 yards the route turns left again at the road junction. A mile further on, you turn right off the road and follow the track up to the summit of Cnoc-nan Gabhor, from where there are great views of Kintyre and across to Arran. A third walk (six miles; blue waymarkers) also starts from the Port Na Storm car park. This time the route heads right at the junction 150 yds beyond the car park and then runs north along the shore, with a chance of seeing dolphins and basking shark. The path then swings west towards the road, then turns south with views of Carradale Glen.

Carradale
Phone code: 01583
Colour map 5, grid B2

If the weather's bad, there's the **Network Carradale Heritage Centre**, which features displays of fishing, farming and forestry. ■ *Easter to mid-Oct Mon-Sat 1030-1700, Sun 1230-1600.* A little further north is the **Grogport Tannery**, which produces organically tanned, naturally coloured sheepskins. ■ *Daily 0900-1800.*

Twelve miles north of Carradale the B842 ends at **Claonaig**, which is actually nothing more than a slipway for the ferry to Arran (see below). From here, the B8001 heads west to meet the A83 near the Kennacraig ferry pier. A dead-end road runs north for a few miles to the tiny village of **Skipness**, where you can visit the substantial ruins of the 13th-century **Skipness Castle** and nearby chapel. You might want to stop here and enjoy some fresh seafood or good home baking at the *Seafood Cabin*, T01880-760207, open daily 1100-1800 from end May-end September.

Sleeping and eating There are a couple of hotels in Carradale, including the **D** *Carradale Hotel*, T/F431223, carradaleh@aol.com, which offers excellent food and a lively bar with a good selection of local malts and cask ales. There are also several **B&Bs** and a **campsite** at Carradale Bay with full facilities T431665; open Easter-Sep.

Isle of Arran

In the wedge of sea between Ayrshire and Kintyre lies the oval-shaped and very beautiful island of Arran. It manages to combine the classic features of the North-west Highlands with the more sedate pleasures of the Southern Lowlands, thus earning the sobriquet, "Scotland in Miniature". This obvious appeal, coupled with its easy accessibility, makes Arran a very popular destination, but it remains unspoiled and at 25 miles long, is big enough to never feel crowded.

Phone code: 01770
Colour map 5, grid B3

The island attracts all sorts of visitors: hillwalkers and climbers come to tackle the 10 summits over 2,000 ft and dozens of ridge routes; golfers are driven by their desire to play on no fewer than seven courses; the beaches of the southeast are popular with the bucket and spade brigade; and the island is a big hit with geology students, who come here in droves to marvel at the unique rock formations.

Although tourism has become Arran's main income earner, the island is large enough to sustain a relatively stable population of around 4,500, only slightly more than the number of red deer which roam wild in the beautiful mountain glens. Arran was tacked onto North Ayrshire in the recent local government reorganisation, but its geological, historical and cultural links are with the Highlands and Islands, hence its inclusion here.

Ins and outs

Getting there

The main **ferry** route to Arran is from the distinctly unappealing Ayrshire town of Ardrossan to the island's main town, Brodick. The *CalMac* car/passenger ferry makes the 55 min journey 6 times daily Mon-Sat, 4 times on Sun. A 1-way fare costs £4.40 per passenger and £25.50 per car. A 'Day Saver' return (available Apr-Oct) costs £60 for a car and up to 4 passengers. There's a train connection between Ardrossan and Glasgow Central (5 times daily Mon-Sat, 4 times on Sun). There's also a bus connection to/from Edinburgh twice daily Mon-Sat. By **car**, from the south the main route to Arran is from the M74 motorway, on to the A71 via Kilmarnock, to Irvine and Ardrossan. For more ferry information, contact Ardrossan ferry office, T01294-463470, or Brodick, T01770-302166. There's also a car/passenger ferry to Brodick from

Arran

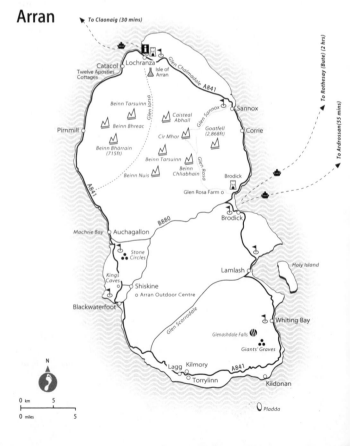

Rothesay, on the island of Bute, a 2-hour journey. It sails once a day on Mon, Wed and Fri, in the summer only.

The other **ferry** route to Arran is from Claonaig, near Tarbert on Loch Fyne (see page 96), to Lochranza in the north of the island. The non-bookable car/passenger ferry makes the 30-min trip 8-11 times daily during the summer (Apr-Oct). A 1-way journey costs £4 per passenger and £18.05 per car. A 'Day Saver' return costs £36 for a car and up to 4 passengers. For ferry times, T08705-650000. For details of **bus** services to Claonaig, see page 96, or T01546-604695.

Getting around

Fifty-seven miles of main road run right around the coastline and pass through every village, making it easy to see much of the island by **car** in a short space of time. There are also 2 roads, "The String" and "The Ross", which bisect the island. Arran is best appreciated on a **bike**, however, and for details of bike hire, see below under Brodick.

It's possible to explore the island using public transport, as there are regular **bus** and postbus services. There are regular daily buses from Brodick to Blackwaterfoot (30 mins) via "The String"; to Lamlash (10 mins) and Whiting Bay (25 mins) and on to Blackwaterfoot (1 hr 10 mins); to Corrie (20 mins), Sannox (25 mins), Lochranza (45 mins), Catacol (50 mins), Pirnmill (1 hr), Machrie (1 hr 10 mins) and Blackwaterfoot (1 hr 20 mins). There's also a postbus service from Brodick to Corrie, Sannox, Lochranza, Catacol, Pirnmill, Machrie, Blackwaterfoot and back to Brodick; and from Brodick to Lamlash, "The Ross", Kildonan, Whiting Bay and back to Brodick.

A rural daycard gives you unlimited travel on Arran for £3. For bus times and more information contact the tourist office in Brodick, where you can pick up a free copy of the *Arran Transport Guide*, or contact *Western Buses*, T302000, or, for postbuses, *Royal Mail*, T0131-228 7407.

Brodick

The largest and busiest settlement on Arran, and main ferry port, is Brodick, lying in a wide bay (hence its Norse name *breidr vik*, meaning "broad bay") backed by a range of steep crags. It's not the most attractive village on the island, and consists of little more than one long street that sweeps round the bay, but you'll find a wide range of tourist facilities and services here. Brodick also makes a convenient base from which to explore the island, particularly if you intend climbing Goatfell, Arran's highest mountain, or walking in Glen Rosa (see page 108).

Ins & outs

For ferry details, see above. The **Tourist Information Centre** is beside the ferry pier and bus terminal, T302140, F302395. Open May-Sep Mon-Sat 0900-1930, Sun 1000-1700; Oct-Apr Mon-Sat 0900-1700.

Sights

A few miles north of town is the impressive **Brodick Castle**, one of the island's top sights and a flagship National Trust for Scotland property. Until recently, this was the family seat of the Dukes of Hamilton, erstwhile owners of the island. The oldest part of the castle dates from the 13th century, with extensions added in the 16th, 17th and 19th centuries. The hour-long tour of the sumptuously-furnished rooms and huge kitchens is very interesting and can perfectly rounded off with a visit to the Castle restaurant, where you can enjoy cheap and tasty home-cooked meals or light snacks and excellent home baking. On a good day you even sit outside on the castle terrace and have lunch whilst admiring the views over Brodick Bay. The walled garden is also worth a look and the surrounding country park includes 11 miles of way-marked trails. ■ *Castle open 1 Apr-30 Jun and 1 Sep-31 Oct, daily 1100-1630; 1 Jul-31*

Argyll

Aug, daily 1100-1700. Walled garden open all year, daily 0930-1700. Country Park open all year daily 0930-sunset. Restaurant open 1000-1700. Castle and garden: adult £6, concession £4.50, child £1. Garden and country park only: adult £2.50, concession £1.70, child £1. *T302202*.

Halfway between the village and the castle is the **Arran Heritage Museum**, which consists of a pile of old tools and furniture in a converted 18th- century farm. Strictly for the enthusiast or the terminally bored. ■ *3 Apr-end of Oct, Mon-Sat 1000-1700. Adult £2.25, concession £1.50, children £1.*

Sleeping Brodick boasts some pretty high-class accommodation, the best of which is the **A** *Kilmichael Country House Hotel*, T302219, F302068, www.kilmichael.com 9 rooms. Take the road north to the castle, turn left at the golf course and follow the signs for about a mile. Refined elegance and gracious living in the heart of the countryside in the island's oldest house. Their award-winning restaurant is quite simply the best on the island, and that's really saying something, and booking is essential for non-residents.

Just beyond the turning to Kilmichael is the road leading to **B-C** *Auchrannie Country House Hotel*, T302234, F302812, www.auchrannie.co.uk 28 rooms (also self-catering and time-share lodges). May lack the charm of *Kilmichael* but makes up for it with superb facilities and state-of-the-art leisure complex. Their *Garden Restaurant* is also highly-rated and the popular *Brambles Bistro* offers less expensive bar meals.

There are several hotels closer to the ferry along the seafront, and best of these is the **D** *Dunvegan House Hotel*, T/F302811, which offers good quality cooking for residents only. There is also plentiful **B&B** accommodation, including the secluded **E** *Glen Cloy Farmhouse*, Glen Cloy Rd, T302351, www.arran.net/brodick/tighnamara, open Mar-Oct, which is a cut above the rest, or the consistently-good **E** *Tigh-na-Mara*, on the seafront, T302538, open Apr-Oct. The nearest **campsite** is *Glen Rosa*, T302380, open Apr-Oct, 2 miles from town on the road to Blackwaterfoot.

Eating Aside from the hotels, and the castle restaurant, mentioned above there's the excellent *Creelers Seafood Restaurant*, at Home Farm, a mile or so north of town on the road to the castle, T302810. Some of the best seafood in the whole country served in an informal atmosphere. Taste their Scandinavian smoked salmon which is the ultimate in piscine pleasure. Cheap lunch specials and moderate 3-course dinners on Tue only. For a cheaper alternative try the *Brodick Bar*, behind *Wooley's bakery* and opposite the post office. Superior pub grub served in the bar or restaurant next door at cheap-mid-range prices.

Shopping Arran has an enviable reputation for producing fine foods and at *Home Farm*, just north of the village, are a couple of places you won't want to miss if you're looking for a tasty souvenir. The *Island Cheese Company*, T302788, produces a range of cheeses for sale, including soft cheeses, flavoured cheddars and the famous Arran Blue Cheese. You can also watch the whole process of cheese making. On the opposite side of the courtyard is *Creelers Smokehouse*, T302797, where you can find a vast range of delicious smoked fish, shellfish, poultry and game, and an excellent restaurant (see above). Next door is *Arran Aromatics*, T302595, open daily 0930-1730, which produces a wide range of unique and beautifully-packaged natural soaps and body care products. A rare treat for the olfactory organ.

On the main street is the excellent *Wooley's of Arran*, a highly-acclaimed bakers producing great rolls and their own oatcakes. For more basic provisions, there's the *Co-op supermarket* near the ferry terminal.

Cycle hire *Mini Golf Cycle Hire*, T302272, F302903, *Brodick Cycles*, T/F302460, and   **Transport**
Brodick Boat & Cycle Hire, T302868, are all on the seafront and all charge around £9 per
day for mountain bikes.

Banks The *Bank of Scotland* and *Royal Bank* are both on the seafront, both with   **Directory**
ATMs. **Communications** Post office: Just off the seafront, opposite the petrol station
and pharmacy.

The South

The south of Arran is a fertile landscape of rolling hills and pretty little seaside
villages. Here you'll find the bulk of the island's population and tourists.

A few miles south of Brodick is Lamlash, a quiet and attractive place set in a   **Lamlash**
wide, sheltered bay but with an unappealing mud beach. Lying just offshore
is the humpbacked **Holy Island**, which is owned by a group of Scottish Bud-
dhists, who have retired here for peace and meditation. A ferry runs to and
from the island several times daily from 1 May to 4 September (limited service 5 September to 30 October), and costs £6 return. The first ferry departs
Lamlash at 1000 and the last one returns at 1700, leaving you just enough
time to climb up to the highest point, **Mullach Mór** (1,030 ft). Boats can be
hired for **fishing trips** from the pier, T600998 or 600349. For fishing supplies or information on **scuba diving**, contact *Johnson's Marine Stores* at the
Old Pier, T600333.

   The main reason for visiting Lamlash is the excellent *Arran Fine Foods*,
at the Old Mill, at the southern entrance to the village, T600606. Here you'll
find a mouth-watering selection of locally-produced mustards, preserves and
chutneys. Don't leave Arran without them!

Sleeping and eating The **C** *Lilybank Guest House*, T600230, www.smoothHound.co.uk,
also serves good food, and the **D** *Glen Isle Hotel*, T600559, does a good, moderately-priced
3-course dinner. There are several cheaper **B&B** options and also a **campsite** T600251,
open mid-Apr to mid-Oct, a short way south of town.

   The best place to eat by far is the superb *Carraig Mhor Restaurant*, T600453,
whose Austrian chef specializes in local seafood. Open for dinner only (1900-2130),
closed Sun. Booking is essential. Moderate-expensive.

Down in the southeast of Arran, Whiting Bay enjoys a beautiful setting and   **Whiting Bay**
makes a pleasant alternative to Brodick as an island base with some good
accommodation and restaurants. Whiting Bay is also the starting point for the
lovely walk up to **Glenashdale Falls** (see page 109).

Sleeping and eating C-D *Argentine House Hotel*,   T700662,   F700693,
www.argentinearran.co.uk 5 rooms, on the seafront and easily recognisable by the flags
flying outside, Swiss owners are friendly, hospitable and professional, excellent cooking
with a continental touch. Dinner is also available to non-residents but booking is essential. **C-D** *Burlington Hotel*, T700255, F700232, www.milfrod.co.uk/go/burlington.html 9
rooms, open Easter-Oct, comfortable rooms and a reputation for superb seafood, moderately-priced set 3-course dinner in dining room or a la carte in bistro.

   There are also **B&Bs** and **guesthouses**, such as the lovely **D** *Grange House*,
T/F700263; open mid-Mar to end-Oct, and a *SYHA Youth Hostel* on the seafront by
the bridge, T700339; open end-Feb to end-Oct.

Argyll

Argyll

A cheaper alternative to the hotels mentioned above is the *Coffee Pot* on Golf Course Rd, T700382, where you can enjoy tasty but cheap snacks and home baking. Open daily Easter-Oct, 1000-1700 (Jul/Aug 1000-1900).

Transport Car hire/taxis/island tours *Whiting Bay Garage*, T/F700345. **Cycle hire** *Whiting Bay Hires*, on the jetty, T700382.

South of Whiting Bay The main road runs south from Whiting Bay, then swings west along the south coast of Arran, with great views south across to the distinctive mound of Ailsa Craig, lying off the coast of South Ayrshire.

There are some good sandy beaches along this stretch, particularly at **Kildonan**, a village set back off the main road and with a ruined castle looking out to the island of **Pladda**. Anyone with a sudden urge to throw themselves off the nearest cliff can try their hand at **paragliding**, at *Flying Fever*, No 2 Coastguard House in Kildonan, T820292. A half day course costs £30 and full day is £50.

About four miles west of Kildonan are the tiny villages of **Torrylinn**, **Lagg** and **Kilmory**, where you can stop off at the **Torrylinn Creamery** to buy some excellent local cheese and watch it being made, T/F870240, open daily 1000-1600. You can stay here at the **C** *Lagg Hotel*, T870255, an 18th-century coaching inn set in acres of woodland by the river, or at the local **campsites**, at *Breadalbane Lodge*, T820210, and *Kildonan Hotel*, T820207, where there's also a **bunkhouse**.

Just beyond these villages "The Ross" branches off northeast up Glen Scorrodale to Lamlash. The A841 meanwhile continues north to Blackwaterfoot, on the southwest coast.

Blackwaterfoot The little fishing village of Blackwaterfoot is set round an attractive bay with a tiny harbour – smaller than some people's jacuzzis. The village maintains its quiet charm, even at the height of the summer, and is the ideal place to escape the crowds and enjoy some peace and quiet.

There's plenty to do around these parts. Two miles north along the coast are the **King's Caves**, where, according to legend, Robert the Bruce watched a spider try, try and try again and was thus inspired to secure his own and Scotland's destiny. It's a 20-minute walk from where you leave the car to the cathedral-like main cave which has an iron gate to keep out wandering sheep.

There's also **pony trekking** at *Cairnhouse Riding Centre*, T860466, which caters for beginners and experienced riders, and **fly fishing**, at *Port-Na-Lochan Fishery* (contact the *Kinloch Hotel*, see below).

A couple of miles northeast of Blackwaterfoot, at **Shiskine**, on the "String Road" which cuts across the middle of the island to Brodick, is the **Balmichael Visitor Centre**, it's a good place to bring the kids, with a motor museum, adventure playground and a quad bike track. ■ *Mon-Sat 1000-1700, Sun 1200-1700. T860430.*

Four miles north of Blackwaterfoot, off the main coast road, is **Machrie Moor**, site of the most impressive of Arran's Bronze Age **stone circles**. Park by the Historic Scotland sign and then walk for 1½ miles along the farm track to reach an area boasting no fewer than six stone circles. Many of them are barely visible above the ground, but the tallest is over 18 ft high.

A few miles further on, just south of the turn-off to Machrie village, is another Historic Scotland sign, this time for **Moss Farm Road Stone Circle**, which lies about a half mile walk along the farm track. There's another Bronze Age site nearby, at **Auchagallon**.

Sleeping There are a couple of options should you wish to stay here. **B** *Kinloch Hotel*, T860444, F860447, www.kinloch_arran.com The largest hotel on the island with 51 rooms and full leisure facilities including swimming pool, sauna, gym and squash court. The are also plenty of **B&Bs**, which are cheaper and of rather more modest proportions, including **E** *Morvern House*, T860254.

The North

The north half of Arran contrasts sharply with the southern part. It looks and feels more like the Scottish Highlands – desolate, unspoiled and much of it accessible only to the serious hillwalker. But though the north is scenically more spectacular, it attracts relatively few visitors.

Corrie Six miles north of Brodick is Arran's loveliest village, Corrie; a row of perfect, whitewashed fishermen's cottages lining the seafront. Corrie has a couple of hotels and B&Bs, a good pub, and makes an attractive alternative to Brodick as a starting point for the ascent of Goatfell (see page 108).

The main coastal road continues north from Corrie to **Sannox,** with its sandy beach, then it cuts inland and climbs steeply northwest towards Lochranza. It's worth taking your time on this part of the road to admire the wonderful views of the mountains and on the other side of the pass, in **Glen Chalmadale,** you can see red deer heading down to the shore at dusk.

Sleeping D *Tigh-na-Achaidh*, T810208. 3 rooms, superior B&B with sea views. **E** *Corrie Hotel*, T810273. Friendly, unassuming and good value with a lively bar. **E** *Blackrock Guest House*, T810282. Open Mar-Oct.

Lochranza The most spectacular introduction to Arran is to arrive at Lochranza, the most northerly village and second ferry port. This charming village is guarded by its ruined 13th-century castle and backed by looming mountains. **Lochranza Castle** can be visited free of charge (the key is available from the *Lochranza Stores*).

Lochranza is also the site of Scotland's newest distillery, **Isle of Arran Distillers**, which opened in 1995 and is the first legal whisky distillery on the island for over 150 years. There are guided tours of the distillery, followed by the obligatory dram, and an excellent restaurant (see below). ■ *Daily 1000-1700 Apr-Oct. Adult £3.50, £2.50 concession, children under 12 free. T830264, www.arranwhisky.com*

A couple of miles southwest of Lochranza is the tiny village of **Catacol**, whose whitewashed cottages are know as 'The Twelve Apostles'. Here, the bar of the *Catacol Bay Hotel* serves good, cheap pub food and also puts on live music, as well as hosting a week-long **folk festival** in early June.

Sleeping and eating Lochranza has a decent selection of places to stay, best of which is **C** *Apple Lodge*, T/F830229, applelodge@easicom.com A lovely country house with 4 double rooms, offering high quality home cooking (for residents only). Around the same price but lacking the charm, is **D** *Lochranza Hotel*, T830223, www.lochranza.co.uk, whose bar is the social hub of the village. A cheaper option is **E** *Castlekirk*, T830202, a converted church opposite the castle, or the slightly austere **E** *Benvaren*, T830647. Cheaper still is the *SYHA Youth Hostel*, T830631, open Feb-Dec, overlooking the castle. There's a beautifully-situated **campsite** next to the golf course, with full facilities, T820273, office@lochgolf.demon.co.uk, open Apr-Oct.

Argyll

The best place to eat is **Harold's Restaurant**, T830264, arranvc@aol.com, on the upper floor of the distillery visitor centre. Here you can enjoy innovative Scottish/Caribbean cuisine in bright, modern surroundings. Open till 2100. Mid-range prices (cheap lunch menu). The only alternative is the **Lochranza Hotel** which does cheap bar meals.

Walks on Arran

OS map No 69 covers these walks. Ask local advice during the deer stalking season (late Aug-late Oct)

Arran is a hillwalker's paradise. The north part of the island boasts 10 peaks of over 2,000 ft and dozens of ridge walks while the gentler south features a variety of less strenuous forest walks.

You should only attempt these routes in good weather and avoid climbing any rockfaces. Some ridge walks (A'Chir, Witches Step, Suidhe Fherghas and Cioch Na Oighe) involve quite a lot of scrambling and should only be attempted by fit and experienced climbers.

Goatfell

Arran's most popular peak, Goatfell, is also its highest, at 2,866 ft. There's a path leading up from Corrie, but most people begin the walk from the car park at **Cladach sawmill**, near Brodick Castle. The path is well marked, easy to follow and, apart from the final section, relatively easy. It runs initially through the **Brodick Country Park**, then follows the **Cnocan burn** as it rises steadily through woodland before crossing the **Mill burn**. Beyond the burn is a deer fence which runs across the entire island to keep the deer from the north away from the farming in the south. Above the deer fence the landscape changes to heather moorland and the path begins to climb the flanks of the mountain. The final 650 ft up to the top is steep and rocky and the path is not always clear. The last section requires some scrambling on loose scree but the views that greet you at the top on a clear day are magnificent, stretching right across from Ireland to Mull.

The walk to the summit and back should take about five hours. Though it's considered a fairly straightforward ascent, it should be treated with the same caution as any Scottish mountain. You should be dressed and equipped appropriately and be prepared for any sudden change in the weather. There are also numerous ridge walks around Goatfell as well as other high peaks to climb.

Glen Rosa

Many of the walks start from **Glen Rosa Farm**. One of these takes in the three Bheinns; **Beinn Nuis**, **Beinn Tarsuinn** (2,681 ft) and **Beinn A'Chliabhain**. Start at Glen Rosa Farm and go up the Wood Road to the High Deer Gate, then to Torr Breac and the 'Y' junction at the top of the Garbhalt and on to the path which runs round the Three Beinns. This is a full day's walk.

Another excellent walk is from Glen Rosa to the head of the Glen; then take the path up into the **Coire Buidhe** and onto the ridge between **Cir Mhor** (2,617 ft) and **A'Chir** (known as the **Ceems Ridge**). Then follow the path around the west side of A'Chir. This is not easy to find, but takes you around the back of A'Chir to **Bowman's Pass** and the north end of **Beinn Tarsuinn**. From here take the path to **Beinn A'Chliabhan** and down to the foot of **Garbhalt Ridge** and back down to Glen Rosa.

Cir Mhor can also be climbed from Glen Rosa. Before going over into Glen Sannox take the steep path straight up. On the way back down, head into Coire Buidhe and back down the glen. You can also continue from the top of Cir Mhor and take the path around the west side of A'Chir to the north end of the Bowman's Pass up onto Beinn Tarsuinn and along the ridge to Beinn Nuis, then down the path to the Garbhalt Bridge.

Walk to Glenashdale Falls and Giant's'Graves

This is one of the most popular walks on the island. It's a steady, easy climb through woodland with the considerable incentive of a beautiful waterfall at the end of it. Both walks can be done together and should take around two to three hours in total, though you should allow some time to enjoy the falls. If you want to take a picnic, then pop into the Village Shop which has a wide range of deli-type foods and local cheeses.

The trail starts by the bridge over **Glenashdale Burn**, *next to the Youth Hostel. There's a map board here showing the route. Walk up the track alongside the burn till you see the sign for the path leading to the left up to the* **Giants' Graves**. *It's about 40-45 minutes up to the graves and back to this point, but it's a stiff climb up a steep staircase of 265 steps. At the top continue left along a path through the trees, which then curves right till you*

reach a clearing and the graves, which are chambered tombs, believed to be around 5,000 years old. Depending on the light, this can be a very eerie, but almost magical place.

Return back down the steps, and head left along the main path as it climbs steadily above the burn, past smaller falls, till you reach the main falls. The setting is stunning and the falls are spectacular as they plummet 140 ft into the pools below. You can rest and have a picnic at the top of the falls, or follow the paths down to the pools below which you can swim.

The path back down to **Whiting Bay** *passes the scant remains of an* **Iron Age fort**, *then turns back uphill to reach a broad track. Turn right, cross a small burn by stepping stones, then follow the track downhill all the way to the main road, a short way along from the car park.*

Argyll

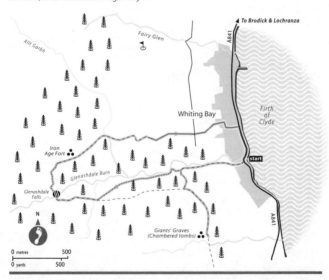

Finally, you can also climb **Caisteal Abhail** (2,818 ft) from Glen Rosa. Go straight up into Coire Buidge on to the Ceems Ridge. Then take the path round the west side of the A'Chir through the Bowman's Pass and on to Beinn A'Chliabhain down the side of the Garbhalt to Glen Rosa.

There are also several walks in and around lovely Glen Sannox. It's a pleasant walk just to head up the head of the Glen and return the same way. You can walk up the Glen to beyond the old mine then make your way up towards the

Glen Sannox

Devil's Punchbowl until you reach the main path and follow that down into the Coire. Take the main path back down into Glen Sannox instead of trying to climb out of the Devil's Punchbowl. You can also walk from **Glen Sannox** to **Glen Rosa**, which takes around four hours.

Inner Hebrides

4

Inner Hebrides

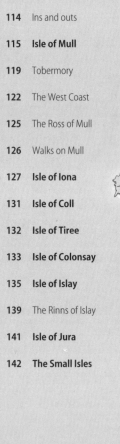

The Inner Hebrides comprise the great swathe of islands lying off the western coast of Scotland – east of the Outer Hebrides, south of Skye and west of the Kintyre peninsula. Each is very different in appearance and atmosphere and each has its own distinct appeal.

The most accessible of the islands is **Mull**, a short ferry ride from Oban. It's also the most popular by far, and with some justification. The variety of scenery on offer is astounding and its capital, Tobermory, is the most attractive port in western Scotland. A stone's throw from Mull is tiny **Iona**, one of the most important religious sites in Europe, whose abbey attracts hordes of pilgrims all year round. Boat trips can be made from Mull or Iona to the dramatic island of **Staffa**, looming out the sea like a great cathedral and the inspiration for Mendelssohn's 'Hebrides Overture'. Further west, windswept **Coll** and **Tiree** offer miles of unspoilt beaches and some great windsurfing and, to the south, **Colonsay** is a stress-free zone that makes Mull seem hectic.

Those who enjoy a good malt whisky should head for **Islay**. There are over half a dozen distilleries on this attractive island, as well as a rich variety of wildlife, while neighbouring **Jura**, famous for its three shapely mountains, the Paps of Jura, is a wild and beautiful place, perfect for some off-the-beaten-track hiking. If you're after some peace and quiet on Jura then you're in good company, for this where George Orwell came to write '1984'. Furthest north are the "small islands" of **Eigg**, **Muck**, **Rùm** and **Canna**, reached from Mallaig, but ignored by most tourists. People come here for the fine bird watching and superb walking.

Things to do in the Inner Hebrides

- *Take a boat trip to the spectacular island of **Staffa** and the cathedral-like **Fingal's cave**, which inspired Mendelssohn.*
- *Hire a bike and explore the island of **Iona**, especially the very wonderful **Bay at the Back of the Ocean**.*

- *Take a walk on the wild side on the remote and windswept island of **Jura**.*
- *If you're a golfer tee off at **Machrie**, a memorable golfing experience.*
- *If you're into windsurfing head for the island of **Tiree** for the ultimate challenge.*

Inner Hebrides

Ins and outs

Getting there

Car space on ferries is limited during the summer months, so it's advisable to book ahead

There are **flights** from Glasgow to Port Ellen (**Islay**): 2 daily Mon-Fri and 1 on Sat (40 mins), all year round. From Glasgow to **Tiree**: 1 flight daily Mon-Sat (45 mins) all year round. For flight times, call *British Airways Express*, T0345-222111, the local **tourist offices**, or Port Ellen airport, T01496-302022, and Tiree airport, T01879-220309.

CalMac car and passenger **ferries** sail to and from Mull, Islay, Coll, Tiree, Colonsay and Gigha, and passenger-only ferries sail to Iona and the Small Isles (Eigg, Muck, Rùm and Canna). The departure point for ferries to Mull, Coll, Tiree and Colonsay is **Oban**. Ferry times change according to the day of the week and time of the year, so they aren't listed in full below. Services listed below under each separate island are for the summer period (2 Apr-16 Oct). For full details see the *CalMac* Ferry Guide or call *CalMac*; T08705-650000, reservations@calmac.co.uk (reservations) T01475-650100, www.calmac.co.uk (general enquiries).

For details of **bus** connections from Oban to Glasgow, contact *Scottish Citylink*, T0990-505050. For **train** services from Mallaig to Fort William and Glasgow, contact *Scotrail*, T0345-484950. See also 'Essentials', page 45. There are regular daily train and bus services from Glasgow. For full details, see under Oban (page 82), or contact the tourist office in Oban, T01631-563122. The departure point for ferries to Islay (and on to Jura), and some ferries to Colonsay, is **Kennacraig**. There are daily bus services from Glasgow, via Tarbert (see page 96). **Mallaig** is the ferry port for the Small Isles of Eigg, Muck, Rùm and Canna. There are regular bus and train services from Glasgow, via Fort William (see page 226). For bus, train and ferry times, pick up Argyll & Bute Council's free *Area Transport Guides to Lorn, Mull and Islay & Jura*, available at most tourist offices. For times of buses and trains to Mallaig, for the Small Isles, see the *South Highland Public Transport Travel Guide* (£1) and is available at main tourist offices. For details on how to get around the Inner Hebrides by public transport, see under the relevant island destination.

Getting around Island Hopscotch Tickets are a cheaper way to get around the islands with a **car**. There are various route options and tickets give you 30 days unlimited travel on each route. For example, a ticket for the Oban-Craignure-Tobermory-Kilchoan-Mallaig-Armadale route, allowing you to visit Mull and Skye, costs £8.85 per passenger and £53 per car. See the *CalMac* guide or call the numbers above for full details of the Island Hopscotch Tickets, and the **Island Rover Ticket**, which gives unlimited travel on most *CalMac* routes for 8 or 15 days.

Orientation & information There are **Tourist Information Centres** in Oban (see page 82), Craignure and Tobermory (Mull), Bowmore (Islay), and Mallaig (see page 242). Oban tourist office has information on all the islands covered in this chapter, with the exception of the Small Isles, information on which can be got from Mallaig tourist office.

Isle of Mull

The island of Mull is the third largest of the Hebridean islands and, after Skye, the most popular. Everyone has their own particular favourite island, but Mull has enough going for it to appeal to most tastes: spectacular mountain scenery; 300 miles of wild coastline; castles; wildlife; a narrow-gauge railway; some of the best fishing in Scotland; and some of the prettiest little villages; all in an area roughly 24 miles from north to south and 26 miles from east to west. It's worth spending time on Mull to really appreciate its pleasures, and take advantage of the great hospitality of an island where people don't even have to lock their doors at night.

Colour map 3, grid B3/4

Ins and outs

Mull is well served by **ferry** services. From Oban to Craignure (40 mins) 6-8 times daily Mon-Sat and 5 times daily on Sun. One way tickets cost £3.55 per passenger and £24.55 per car. *CalMac* offices: Oban, T01631-566688, and Craignure, T01680-812343. From Kilchoan to Tobermory 7 times daily Mon-Sat and 5 times daily on Sun (Jun-Aug). A one-way tickets cost £3.40 per passenger and £18.05 per car. From Lochaline to Fishnish (15 mins) hourly 0700-1910 Mon-Sat and 0900-1800 Sun. A one- way tickets cost £2.15 per passenger and £9.65 per car. Some ferries from Oban to Coll and Tiree call in at Tobermory.

Getting there
Mull is one of the most accessible of the Hebridean islands

You can get to most parts of the island by **bus**. Services given below are for Apr-Oct. Winter services are less frequent. There's a bus from Tobermory post office to Dervaig and Calgary, 5 times a day Mon-Fri and twice on Sat (operated by *RN Carmichael*, T01688-302220). The Craignure to Tobermory via Salen service runs 5 times a day Mon-Fri, 8 times on Sat and 3 times on Sun (operated by *Bowman's Coaches*, T01680-812313, and *Highlands & Islands Coaches*, T01680-812510). There's a bus from Craignure to Fionnphort (for Iona) 6 times a day Mon-Fri, 4 times on Sat and 1 on Sun (*Bowman's* and *Highlands & Islands*). There's also a postbus service from Salen to Burg (Kilninian) via the Ulva Ferry twice a day Mon-Sat (*Royal Mail*, T01463-256200). For bus times, contact the operators or pick up a free copy of the *Mull Area Transport Guide* at the tourist office in Oban, Tobermory or Craignure. This also includes ferry times.

Getting around

The island's 140 miles of **roads** are almost all single-track and mostly in poor condition, so allow plenty of time to get from place to place. The best sections are from Craignure to Salen and the few miles south from Tobermory towards Salen. Petrol stations are few and far between, so it's best to fill up before leaving Oban, on arrival in Craignure, or in Tobermory. Another point worth noting is that the sheep on Mull are even more fearless and stubborn than in other parts of the Highlands and Islands and regard the roads very much as their own, which can slow you down even more.

Cycling is a good way to get around and there are a number of places to rent bikes. In Tobermory there's *Tom-a' Mhuillin* on the Salen Rd, T01688-302164, or try the youth hostel (see page 119). In **Salen** there's *On Yer Bike*, T01680-300501, which also has a shop by the ferry terminal in **Craignure**, T01680-812487. Expect to pay around £8-10 per day.

The best time to visit is generally May and Jun and late Aug to Sep. At these times midges and clegs (horse flies) are not so much of a problem. But Mull is the wettest of the Hebridean islands and rain can fall at any time, even in the summer months, so you'll need to come prepared.

Climate

Like many of the Hebridean islands, the people of Mull, or *Muileachs*, suffered greatly during the Clearances, when they were forced off their land to make way for sheep. The subsequent decline in population was exacerbated by the terrible potato famine of 1846 and the population fell dramatically from a peak of 10,600 in 1820. Numbers have stabilized to around 2,500 in recent years, mainly through the replacement of native islanders by English and Scottish incomers, known as 'White Settlers'. This is something of a sore point and the locals sarcastically refer to their island as 'The Officer's Mess', when the resident population rises to around 8,000 during the summer.

With around 600,000 visitors a year, tourism is an important contributor to the island's economy, supplementing the traditional fishing, crofting and whisky distilling. Despite the numbers, Mull remains unspoiled, though the main roads become congested at the height of the season and accommodation can be hard to find, as there are few large hotels or campsites on the island.

Festivals & events A great time to be on Mull is during the annual **Mull Music Festival**, held on the last weekend of April, when you can enjoy a feast of Gaelic folk music. The focus of the festival is the bar of the *Mishnish Hotel* in Tobermory (for details T01688-302383). Another great musical event is the **Mendelssohn on Mull Festival**, held over 10 days in early July to commemorate the famous composer's visit here in 1829. On 22 July are the **Tobermory Highland Games**. Rally enthusiasts should not miss the **Tour of Mull Rally** held in early October, which is part of the Scottish Championship. Anyone who's complained about the state of Mull's roads (and who hasn't?) should watch the professionals hurtle around the island at over 60 miles per hour!

Mull

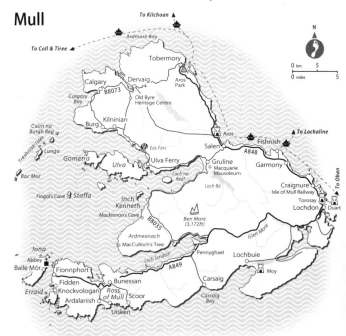

Things to do on Mull when it's wet

*It rains a lot on Mull, but luckily there's a fairly large number of indoor options to keep you nice and dry until the weather changes. If you've just arrived off the ferry from Oban and it's chucking down, then head straight for **Torosay Castle**, just to the south of Craignure. And if the weather changes whilst exploring the interior, don't miss the gardens. Nearby is Mull's greatest fortification, **Duart Castle**, which is also worth a peek. If all that history gets too much then you could do worse than hole up in the bar of the **Craignure Inn** and relax in front*

of their roaring log fire.

*In the north of the island, the most appealing option by far is the **Old Byre Heritage Centre**, not far from the picturesque village of Dervaig. When in Tobermory do as the locals do, and get yourself down to the bar of the Mish, though you shouldn't really need the excuse of inclement weather. Meanwhile, over in Fionnphort, the departure point for the pilgrimage to Iona, you can seek spiritual assistance with a wee dram in the cosy **Keel Row Bar**.*

Craignure and around

Phone code: 01680

The arrival point for most visitors is the tiny village of Craignure, which is little more than a row of houses scattered along the seafront. There are are a few places to eat, a tourist office and some basic services, but precious little else in the way of diversions, though Torosay Castle is just down the road.

Directly opposite the pier is the **Tourist Information Centre**, in the same building as the *CalMac* office, T812337. Open Easter to end of October, Monday-Thursday and Saturday 0900-1900 (Saturday till 2015 in July and August), Friday 0900-1700, Sunday 1030-1700 (till 1900 June-August). Next to the tourist office is a craft shop where you can rent cars or bikes, and there's also a garage on the road to Torosay Castle.

Sleeping & eating

Not far from the pier, on the main road heading south, is **D** *Craignure Inn*, T812305, www.craignure-inn.co.uk 3 rooms, open all year, it's cosy bar serves decent cheap-moderately priced food and is a good place to seek refuge on a wet day. There are also several guesthouses and B&Bs around Craignure, all in the **E** category (details from the tourist office). A little further south of the *Craignure Inn*, on the opposite side, is the turning to *Shielings Holiday Campsite*, T812496, which is beside the terminal for the little steam railway to Torosay Castle (see below). As well as a campsite with full facilities, there's accommodation in self-catering "shielings", which are carpeted cottage tents (**F**). On the north side of the ferry pier is the *Ceilidh Place* restaurant, T812471, a general store and post office.

Three miles south of Craignure, at Lochdon, is **D** *Old Mill Guest House & Restaurant*, T/F812442. 3 rooms, their cosy little restaurant has a deserved reputation for fine cuisine, so you'll need to book in advance.

Torosay Castle

One and a half miles south of Craignure is **Torosay Castle**, more of a baronial family home than a full-blown castle. Inside everything is informal and, refreshingly, there are invitations to sit down, or touch things, or even look through old family scrapbooks. There is some fine Edwardian furniture and paintings by Landseer and Sargent. The real attraction is though, the fabulous garden, designed by Lorimer, especially the Italianate statue walk. In the castle grounds you can watch traditional weaving methods at the **Isle of Mull Weavers**, or visit the gallery and workshops of **Kells gold and Silversmiths**, T812526, open daily

Inner Hebrides

0900-1800. You can walk to the castle along a forest path starting just to the south of Craignure, but the best way to arrive at the castle is by the **Mull and West Highland Railway**. The little steam and diesel engine pulls the miniature carriages along the narrow-gauge track on the 20 minute journey from Craignure. ■ *The castle is open Easter-mid Oct daily 1030-1730. Gardens open all year daily 0900-1900. Admission to house and gardens £4.50, £1.50 child; gardens only £3.50, child £1. Free parking, tearoom and shop. T812421. Isle of Mull Weavers open daily all year 0900-1700. Free. Mull and West Highland Railway open Easter-mid Oct (T812494 for times). Fares: £2.30 adult single, £3.30 return.*

Duart Castle A couple of miles east of Torosay is **Duart Castle**. The 13th-century ancestral seat of the Clan Maclean stands imperiously at the end of a promontory, commanding impressive views over Loch Linnhe and the Sound of Mull. The castle's main feature is the tower house, built in the late 14th century when it became the main residence of the Macleans of Duart. Mull belonged to the clan until it was forfeited when the Macleans supported young Prince Charles Edward Stuart, who was defeated at Culloden in 1746. The castle was deserted for the next century and a half, then in 1911, Colonel Sir Fitzroy Donald Maclean, chief of the clan, bought the castle from Murray Guthrie of Torosay and restored it as the clan chief's residence. Today, it's a fascinating place to visit, with many relics and artifacts on display. There's also an excellent tearoom serving delicious home-baked scones. ■ *May-mid Oct daily 1030-1800. Adult £3.80, concession £3, children £1.90. T812309.*

Salen

Phone code: 01680 Midway between Craignure and Tobermory on the main A849 is the pretty village of Salen. It stands on the east coast at the narrowest point on the island, and is only three miles from the west coast, making it a good base from which to explore the island. **Bicycles** can be hired from *On Yer Bike* (T300501) for around £10 per day.

Sights There are a couple of interesting sights around Salen. Just to the north, overlooking the bay, is the ruin of **Aros Castle**, built in the 14th century and one of the strongholds of the Lords of the Isles. Tradition holds that the treasure of the Spanish galleon sunk in Tobermory Bay in 1588 (see page 119) was recovered by the Macleans and still lies buried beneath the ruins of Aros Castle.

Four miles southwest of Salen, near **Gruline** and **Loch Ba**, is the **MacQuarrie Mausoleum**, which houses the remains of Major-General Lachlan MacQuarrie (1761-1824). He took over as Governer-General of New South Wales from the unpopular William Bligh, formerly of the *Bounty*, and became known as the "Father of Australia". The mausoleum is maintained by the National Trust for Scotland, on behalf of the National Trust of Australia.

Wildlife tours Tours can be made from Aros, just to the north of Salen, with Richard Atkinson at *Island Encounter Wildlife Safaris*, Arla-Beag, Aros, T300441. Full-day wildlife safaris with a local guide cost £22 including lunch. You'll see golden eagles, white-tailed sea eagles, hen harriers, divers, merlins, peregrine falcons, seals and porpoises to name but a few.

Sleeping In the village is **B-C** *Salen Hotel*, T300324, F300599. 18 rooms, open all year. Near the
& eating MacQuarrie Mausoleum, at Gruline, is **D** *Gruline Home Farm*, T300581, F300573. There are also several **B&Bs** in and around Salen, mostly in the **E** category. About 5 miles

Inner Hebrides

south, just before the turn-off to the Fishnish to Lochaline Ferry, is *Balmeanach Park Caravan & Campsite*, with full facilities, and *Cynthia's Tearoom*, T300342, which serves snacks, lunches and a cheap to mid-range 3-course dinner. In the village itself is *The Puffer Aground*, T300389; closed Sun and Mon, which does very good cheap meals and snacks.

Tobermory

There is no prettier port in the west of Scotland than Tobermory, Mull's main village, which is set on the side of a steep hill in a wooded, sheltered bay. The brightly-painted houses that line the harbour front date from the late 18th century when the British Fisheries Society built Tobermory as a planned herring port. It never really took off as a fishing port, however, and nowadays you're more likely to see pleasure yachts anchored in the protected waters of the natural harbour. Lying at the bottom of the harbour is a galleon of the Spanish Armada, which sank in mysterious circumstances, along with its treasure of gold doubloons, which has eluded salvage crews ever since (see box on page 123).

Phone code: 01688
Population: 800
Tobermory is the only
Highland town to
have a Womble
named after it

Ins & outs

Getting there Tobermory is a 30-40 min drive north from the ferry pier at Craignure. There are regualr daily buses from Craignure which coincide with ferry arrivals. For more details see page 115.

The **Tourist Information Centre** is in the same building as the *CalMac* ticket office, at the far end of Main St, T302182. It's open Apr Mon-Fri 1000-1700, Sat-Sun 1200-1700; May-Jun Mon-Sat 1000-1700, Sun 1100-1700; Jul-2 Sep Mon-Sat 0930-1800; Sep-Oct Mon-Sat 1000-1700, Sun 1200-1700.

Sights

The harbour front – known as **Main Street** – is where you'll find most of what you want: hotels, guesthouses, restaurants, pubs and shops and the tourist office. Mercifully, though, it's free from the tartan tat that blights so many other tourist hot-spots. Here you'll find the **Mull Museum**, housed in an old bakery. It's worth visiting on a rainy day and you'll learn all about the island's history. ■ *Mon-Fri 1030-1630, Sat 1030-1330. Adult £1, children £0.20.*

At the foot of the main road down to the harbour is the tiny **Tobermory Distillery** which offers a guided tour rounded off with a sampling of the island's single malt. ■ *Easter to end-Oct, Mon-Fri 1000-1700. Adult £2.50, concession £1, under 18 free. T302645.* At the top of Back Brae, on Argyll Terrace, is **An Tobar**, the new arts centre housed in an old schoolhouse and featuring a varied programme of exhibitions, music and workshops. Or you can just have a coffee and admire the view. ■ *Mon-Sat all year 1000-1800. T302211.*

Essentials

The accommodation on Main St tends to be a bit more expensive than that in the higher part of the village, but it saves you the steep walk uphill after the obligatory night in the *Mish* (see below).

Sleeping
*The tourist office can
book you into a B&B
for a small fee*

L *Western Isles Hotel*, T302012, F302297. 23 rooms. Open all year, the biggest and grandest hotel on the island, set high above the harbour with great views from the

Inner Hebrides

comfortable rooms, has 3 excellent restaurants, including the lovely conservatory bar. **B-C** *Tobermory Hotel*, 53 Main St, T302091, F302254. Good value and great location. Also on the harbour front, close to the ferry port is the famous **D** *Mishnish Hotel*, Main St, T302009, www.mishnish.co.uk Open all year, 10 rooms. Its bar is the live music focus of the town and social hub (see below).

Best of the guesthouses on the harbour front is the excellent **E** *Failte Guest House*, T/F302495. Open Mar-Oct, 7 rooms. Also on Main St is the **F** *SYHA Youth Hostel*, T302481. Open end-Feb to end-Oct and rents out bikes.

There are many guesthouses and B&Bs uphill from the harbour, which are often better value. These include: **E** *Copeland House*, Jubilee Terr, T302049/302422. 3 *en*

Inner Hebrides

Tobermory

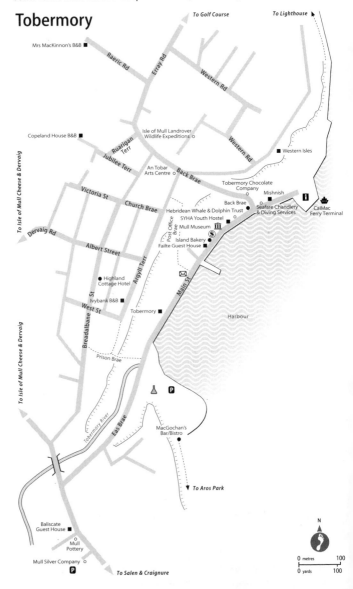

To Golf Course

To Lighthouse

Mrs MacKinnon's B&B

Raeric Rd

Erray Rd

Western Rd

Copeland House B&B

Isle of Mull Landrover
Wildlife Expeditions

Western Rd

Western Isles

Ruaroan Terr

Jubilee Terr

An Tobar
Arts Centre

Back Brae

Tobermory Chocolate
Company

Mishnish

Victoria St

Church Brae

Back Brae

Hebridean Whale & Dolphin Trust

Seafare Chandlery
& Diving Services

CalMac
Ferry Terminal

SYHA Youth Hostel

Dervaig Rd

Mull Museum

Post Office

Island Bakery

Albert Street

Failte Guest House

Argyll Terr

Main St

Highland
Cottage Hotel

Ivybank B&B

West St

Tobermory

Harbour

Breadalbane St

Prison Brae

To Isle of Mull Cheese & Dervaig

To Isle of Mull Cheese & Dervaig

To Isle of Mull Cheese & Dervaig

Tobermory River

Eas Brae

MacGochan's
Bar/Bistro

To Aros Park

N

Baliscate
Guest House

Mull
Pottery

Mull Silver Company

To Salen & Craignure

0 metres 100
0 yards 100

suite rooms with seaviews. **E** *Mrs Mackinnon*, 'Ardsorn' Raeric Rd, T302214, F302148. Open Apr-Oct, 2 *en suite* rooms with great seaviews, parking. **F-E** *Ivybank*, Argyll Terrace, T302250. Friendly and comfortable. A short walk from town is **E** *Baliscate Guest House*, T302048, F302666. 4 en suite rooms. They also organize fishing and wildlife trips (see 'Trips from Tobermory' below).

The best eating in town is to be had in the ***Western Isles Hotel*** (see above), where you **Eating** can choose between 3 restaurants. A 3-course à la carte in the dining room or the oriental *Spices Bistro* is expensive to mid-range, while cheap bar meals are served in the excellent *Conservatory Bar*. Not so stylish or tasty, but cheaper is the *Highland Cottage Hotel* on Breadalbane St, which does a moderately-priced 4-course dinner.

The harbour front is filled with places where you can fill yourself, including the moderately-priced *Back Brae Restaurant*, T302422, open daily from 1800. Cheaper still is the bar of the *Mishnish Hotel*, where you can attempt to munch your way through their monumental portions and, if you're not sleeping on the same street, also attempt the walk uphill on an over-filled stomach. Also on the harbour front is the excellent *Island Bakery*. A worthwhile detour is to walk to the edge of town to the excellent *Green Barn* which is run by *Isle of Mull Cheese* (see below). Here you can enjoy good old home baking in the unusual surroundings of a plant-filled glass barn.

An absolute must when in Tobermory is a night in the *Mish*. After one of their pub **Entertainment** meals and several pints of ale, bending over the pool table is an effort, not to mention getting down to some good live folk music. For the sake of choice, other pubs and live music venues are available, namely *MacGochan's*, at the other end of the harbour, near the distillery. There are also music events at *An Tobar* (see 'Sights' above).

Despite its popularity, Tobermory hasn't succumbed to the dreaded tartan disease that **Shopping** afflicts so many other tourist hot-spots. You're more likely to find shops selling fishing tackle or diving gear than tacky souvenirs and the ones that do cater for the tourist market, such as *Mull Pottery* , T302057, and the *Mull Silver Company*, T302345, open 0900-1730, are tastefully done and enjoyable places to browse in on a wet afternoon. At the foot of Back Brae, which leads steeply up from the harbour to the upper part of the village, is the *Tobermory Chocolate Company*, T302526, open Mar-Jan Mon-Sat 0930-1700, where you can try out their speciality of chocolate made with the local whisky . On the edge of town, 500 yds off the Dervaig Rd, at Sgriob-Ruadh Farm, is *Isle of Mull Cheese*, T302235, where you can savour their award-winning traditionally-made cheese and their wonderful glass barn (see 'Eating' above). Open Apr to end-Sep Mon-Fri 1000-1600.

Banks Mull's only permanent bank is the *Clydesdale Bank* on Main St. There's also a **Directory** mobile bank which tours the island; for details T0345-826818.

Trips from Tobermory

Trips can be made from Tobermory with *Sea Life Surveys*, T302787. A full-day tour costs **Whale &** £42 (£45 in Jul/Aug), and there's a maximum of 12 people per trip. Proceeds from the **dolphin** trips go to the *Hebridean Whale and Dolphin Trust*, a charity which aims to protect the **watching** marine environment through education. You can visit the trust at 28 Main St, Tobermory, T302620, F302728, www.gn.apc.org/whales Mon-Fri 1000-1700, Sat/Sun 1100-1600.

Trips can be made on the *Silver Swift*, leaving from the ferry pier 1200-1500 and **Fishing** 1800-2100. Trips cost £12.50 per person (tackle supplied). Book at the tourist office or after hours T302182, www.silverswift.co.uk The *Silver Swift* can also be chartered for

£300 per day, T302390. Fishing trips are also available with *Amidas Sea Fishing & Wildlife Trips*, based at Baliscate House (see 'Sleeping' above), or book at *Tackle & Books*, T302336. **Fishing permits** for trout fishing are available from *A Brown & Son*, 21 Main St, Tobermory, T302020, F302454. For more details pick up the *Tobermory Angling Association* leaflet from the tourist office.

Diving   Trips and courses are available with *Seamore Diving*. Book through *Seafare Chandlery & Diving Service*, Main St, Tobermory, T/F302277.

Wildlife   Expeditions with *Isle of Mull Landrover Wildlife Expeditions*, at *Ulva House Hotel*, T302044 (David Woodhouse). Full day tour costs £24.50/£18.50 per person.

The West Coast

Mull's west coast is where you'll find some of the island's most stunning scenery. The B8073 winds its way anti-clockwise from Tobermory in a series of tortuous twists and turns as it follows the contours of the deeply-indented coastline. It starts off in terrible condition and soon deteriorates into something resembling a poorly-maintained farm track.

Dervaig

Phone code: 01688   The road climbs west from Tobermory then makes a dramatic descent, with innumerable hairpin bends, to Dervaig. This section of road is closed to the public for the annual car rally in October. Dervaig is a lovely village of white-washed cottages, beautifully situated at the head of Loch Cuin, where the old folk still converse in Gaelic.

It has two very notable features (quite a lot for such a tiny place). One is **Kilmore Church**, which has a very unusual pencil-shaped spire (the only other one in Scotland is at Dunfermline in Fife). Dervaig's real claim to fame, though, is the **Mull Little Theatre**, the smallest professional theatre in Britain, with only 43 seats. It puts on an impressive programme of plays throughout the summer (May-September), and common sense dictates that advance booking is essential (T400245).

One mile beyond Dervaig take the turn-off to Torloisk to reach the **Old Byre Heritage Centre**, which stands out as one of the few genuinely interesting examples of these places. It also features a video of Mull's history and an excellent tea-room (see below). ■ *Easter to end-Oct daily 1030-1830. Adult £3, concession £2, children £1.50. T400229.*

Sleeping   Dervaig has a wide choice of places to stay. The nicest is **A** *Druimard Country House*
& eating   *Hotel*, T400291, F400345, www.druimard.co.uk 6 rooms, open end Mar-Oct, this Victorian country house offers peace and comfort in beautiful surroundings and is right beside the *Mull Little Theatre*, the room rate includes dinner in the excellent restaurant. They offer a pre-theatre 4-course dinner for non-residents (expensive). **E-D** *Ardbeg House Hotel*, T/F400254, iona@abnett.freeserve.co.uk 4 rooms, open all year, not as stylish as the *Druimard* but with plenty of charm. There are several B&Bs and guesthouses in and around the village, including the excellent **D** *Cuin Lodge*, overlooking Loch Cuin, T400346, cuin-lodge@mull.com, open Mar-Oct.

Aside from the *Druimard Country House*, probably the best food around is at the *Old Byre Heritage Centre* (see above), whose tearoom serves delicious but cheap snacks and home baking. There's also the 16th-century *Bellachroy Hotel*, where you

Shiver me timbers!

The history of 16th-century Europe is littered with the remains of carefully forged and hastily broken political alliances between the various superpowers. One such deal between England and Spain was broken in 1588, prompting Philip II of Spain to send the Spanish Armada, a massive force of 130 ships, to take on the English navy. Originating in Cadiz, the Spanish force moved north and left Lisbon on 20 May. They met Queen Elizabeth's ships in the English Channel, where they were duly routed.

A number of Spanish ships fled up the east coast, chased by the British fleet as far as the Firth of Forth. Denied entry into the estuary by further British naval forces, the tattered remnants of these great Spanish galleons were considered to no longer pose a threat and were left to their own fate.

Many continued up the east coast of Scotland, only to be wrecked in the perilous North Sea. Not all the crews drowned, however, and several integrated into local communites, where their descendants still live to this day. Their offspring were most distinctively black haired, there is strong facial resemblance even today between some on the north east coast of Scotland and the residents of Cadiz, from where the Armada originally sailed.

Some Spanish ships headed for the west coast, but were lost in a violent storm in the Hebrides. One galleon, the Florida, was lost in Tobermory, harbour, reputedly carrying £300,000 worth of gold bullion. However, during recent dives, all that was found on the seabed were rotted timbers, a sailor's bangle and a silver spoon.

can get decent bar meals. Opposite is *Coffee and Books*, for good coffee and, funnily enough, books.

Five miles west of Dervaig is Calgary Bay, ringed by steep wooded slopes with views across to Coll and Tiree. Any Canadians reading this, may be interested to note that the large city in Alberta was named after the former township. Many emigrants were forcibly shipped to Canada from here during the Clearances.

Calgary Bay
Mull's most beautiful beach

Sleeping and eating Near Calgary Bay is the wonderfully peaceful and relaxing **D** *Calgary Farmhouse Hotel*, T01688-400256. 9 rooms, open Apr-Oct. This restored farmhouse is one of Mull's gems and the adjoining *Dovecote Restaurant* serves excellent, moderately-priced food using the best of local seasonal produce. There's also a tea-room, *The Carthouse*, which offers cheap and delicious light lunches and home baking. There can be no better end to a day than dinner at the *Dovecote* followed by a stroll along the beach at sunset.

The road down the west coast passes through a series of tiny settlements before reaching the turn-off to Ulva Ferry. A couple of miles before the turning, it's worth stopping at **Eas Fors**, a spectacular waterfall that tumbles straight into the sea from under the road bridge. There's a path down to the bottom and you can swim in the sea, below the falls.

If you have the time and need to escape the hectic bustle of Mull, then take a day out on idyllic Ulva (meaning 'wolf island' in Norse), just off the west coast. You won't see any wolves around, but you're almost guaranteed to spot deer, golden eagles, buzzards and seals offshore. There are several well-marked walks that criss-cross the island, including one to the southwest where there are basalt columns similar to those on Staffa. Or you can cross to its smaller neighbour **Gometra** by a causeway.

Isle of Ulva
Colour map 3, grid B3
No accommodation but ask the ferry operators about camping

It's hard to believe, but the island once sustained a population of over 850, until they were completely cleared between 1846 and 1851. The derelict crofts can still be seen around the island, along with the lovely little church, which still holds services for the remaining population of around 20. For more information on the island walks and on its history, visit the *Boathouse Heritage Centre* close to the ferry slip on Ulva. There's also a licensed tea-room where you can try the local oysters with Guinness. ■ *Easter-Oct Mon-Fri 0900-1700 and Sun Jun-Aug only. The entry price is included in the ferry fare (see below). T01688-500241, ulva@zetnet.co.uk*

Transport A small bicycle/passenger-only ferry makes the 2 min crossing on demand from Ulva Ferry, Apr-Oct Mon-Fri 0900-1700, and on Sun from June-Aug; £4 adult return, £2 children (£0.50 for bikes). At other times, phone to make arrangements, T500226.

Staffa and the Treshnish Isles

Colour map 3, grid B3

The tiny uninhabited island of Staffa, five miles off the west coast of Mull, is one of the most spectacular sights not just in Scotland but anywhere in the world. It consists of immense, hexagonal, basalt pillars which loom up out of the sea, like a giant pipe organ.

Staffa was formed 60 million years ago by the slow cooling of Tertiary basalt lavas. These have been carved by the pounding sea into huge cathedral-like caverns such as the mightily impressive **Fingal's Cave**. The sound of the sea crashing against the black crystalline columns made such an impression on Felix Mendelssohnn in 1829 that he immortalized the island in his *Hebrides Overture*. The composer was obviously aware of its original name in Gaelic, which means 'The Melodious Cave'.

You can land on the island – if the weather is good enough – and walk into the cave via the causeway; an experience not be missed. But even if the seas are too rough, it's worth making the 90-minute boat trip just to witness the huge columns and gaping black hole of the cave.

Treshnish Isles Most boat trips to Staffa include a memorable tour of the uninhabited Treshnish Isles to the northwest. The two most northerly islands, **Cairn na Burgh** and **Cairn na Burgh Beg** have ruined castles, while another, **Bac Mór**, is better known as **Dutchman's cap** because of its curious shape. The largest island, **Lunga**, is the main bird sanctuary and a haven for thousands of seabirds, including razorbills, guillemots, kittiwakes, shags, fulmars, skuas and puffins so tame you'll need to tread carefully to avoid them. In the surrounding seas there are seals, dolphins, minke whales, porpoises, and maybe even basking sharks and killer whales! Most boat trips include time ashore on Lunga and all are dependent on sea conditions.

Boat trips Boat trips to Staffa and the Treshnish Isles leave from Oban, Dervaig, Ulva Ferry, Iona or Fionnphort, weather permitting. A full day cruise including Staffa and the Treshnish Isles costs £25-30 per person (half fare for children); a cruise to Staffa only costs around £15. *Turus Mara*, T08000-858786 (freephone), www.turusmara.com/timetabel.html leave from Ulva Ferry, daily May-Sep and Sep-Oct subject to weather and demand . They also run this trip from Oban; £33.50 including ferry and courtesy bus form Craignure to Ulva Ferry. *Inter-island Cruises* leave from Croig near Dervaig, T/F01688-400264. They're a little bit more expensive than the others, but also have trips to Coll and Muck. *Gordon Grant Marine* leave from Fionnphort and Iona, T01681-700338. *Staffa Trips* sail to Staffa on the *MB Iolaire* from Iona and Fionnphort, T01681-700358.

Ben More and the Ardmeanach Peninsula

From Ulva Ferry the B8073 heads east along the north shore of **Loch na Keal** then enters a wide flat valley, where the road forks east to Salen (see page 118) and west along the south shore of Loch na Keal. This part of Mull is dominated by **Ben More** (3,170 ft), the island's highest mountain. All around is a spectacular region of high jutting mountains and deep glens, extending west to the **Ardmeanach Peninsula**. The road passes Dishig, the best point from which to begin the steep walk to the summit (see page 126), then cuts through the towering Gribun cliffs, with the tiny island of **Inch Kenneth** lying offshore. There are also great views of Ulva, Staffa and the Treshnish Isles. The road then turns south across the peninsula as it climbs over the pass and down to Loch Scridain, where it joins the A849 which runs through the beautiful and dramatic **Glen More** to Craignure.

The peninsula may look impenetrable but with the proper walking gear can be explored on foot. On the north coast, about a mile from the road, is the massive entrance to **MacKinnon's Cave**, which runs for about 100 yards back under the cliffs. Make sure to visit only at low tide and also watch out for the evil spirits who live inside and who are said to have caused the deaths of an entire party of adventurous – or foolish – men. The area around the headland, now owned by the National Trust for Scotland, is known as '**The Wilderness**'. Near the headland is **MacCulloch's Tree**, a remarkable fossilized tree 40 ft high and thought to be 50 million years old, which was discovered in 1819. The tree is only accessible by a seven mile footpath which begins at Burg Farm. You should call in at the farm to let them know of your intentions and also to get directions. You should have a good map of the area and also time your arrival with low tide.

Inner Hebrides

The Ross of Mull

Mull's southernmost peninsular stretches west for 20 miles from the head of Loch Scridain as far as Iona. Most visitors use it merely as a route to Iona, but if you've got the time and the weather's good, there are a couple of interesting little detours along the way. The Ross of Mull also makes a sensible alternative to trying to find a bed for the night on Iona.

Phone code: 01681

The first village is **Pennyghael**, which has two hotels overlooking the loch, **D** *Pennyghael Hotel*, T704288, F704205, which is open from Easter to October and has an excellent restaurant, and **D** *Kinloch Hotel*, T704204, which serves cheap bar meals. A tortuous, twisting side road leads south from Pennyghael over the hills and down to **Carsaig Bay**, from where you can head east or west along the shore for some dramatic coastal scenery. For a description of these walks, see 'Walks on Mull' (page 126).

Pennyghael to Carsaig Bay

The next village is **Bunessan**, fairly unappealing, but the largest place around with a wide range of inexpensive B&B accommodation and very convenient for an early ferry to Iona. There are also a couple of superb hotels around Bunessan. In the village itself is the excellent **A-B** *Assapol House Hotel*, T700258, F700445. Five rooms, open from Easter to October. A few miles west of Bunessan is the turning to **B** *Ardfenaig House*, T/F700210. Five rooms, open April-October, the former shooting lodge offers style and elegance and expensive but superb food.

Bunessan

You can find out everything about local history and culture at the **Ross of Mull Historical Centre**, on Pier Road. ■ *Daily 1000-1630. £1.*

A mile east of Bunessan is the **Isle of Mull Angora Rabbit Farm**, where you can cuddle the cute fluffy bunnies, watch them being shorn and then listen to someone rabbiting on about the history of angora. ■ *Easter to end-Oct daily 1100-1770 (except Sat). Adult £2.*

Two roads lead south from Bunessan. One leads to **Scoor**, near where is a great beach at Kilveockan. The other road splits near the coast: the left branch leads to **Uisken Bay**, where there's a nice beach; the righthand branch leads to **Ardlanish Bay**, which also has a good beach. You can spend the night at Uisken Bay at the idyllic **E** *Uisken Croft*, T700307, open from April to October.

Fionnphort The road ends at Fionnphort, the departure point for the small passenger-only ferry to Iona, just a mile across the Sound of Iona. The village is little more than a car park, a row of houses, a pub and a shop, but there are several inexpensive B&Bs for those arriving too late to make the crossing. Even if you're not staying, it's worth stopping off in the village to visit the **Columba Centre**, a museum which relates the saint's life story. ■ *Mid-May to end-Sep, Mon-Sat 1000-1800, Sun 1100-1800. Adult £2, children £1.*

Just before the village is **E** *Achaban House*, T700205, F700649, www.achabanhouse.co.uk 7 rooms, this former manse is comfortable and well-furnished and also offers dinner. **E-F** *Burnside*, T700208. 1 room, 2 mins from ferry pier, friendly with great views of Iona. Eating options are limited to the *Keel Row Bar & Restaurant*, where you can get moderately-priced meals and enjoy a drink by the fire in the cosy bar.

A road runs south from Fionnphort a mile to a **campsite** at *Fidden Farm*, T700427. Further south is **Knockvologan**, opposite **Erraid island**, which is accessible at low tide. The island has literary connections, for it was here that Robert Louis Stevenson is believed to have written *Kidnapped*. **Balfour Bay** on the south of the island is named after the novel's hero who was shipwrecked here.

Walks on Mull

OS Landranger Nos 47, 48 & 49 Mull presents numerous walking opportunities, ranging from gentle forest trails to wild and dramatic coastal routes, or even a spot of Munro-bagging for the more intrepid.

Ben More With the exception of the Cuillins on Skye, Mull's highest peak (3,169 ft) is the only Munro not on the mainland. The trail starts at a lay-by on the B8035, at Dishig, and is fairly clear, though it can be tricky near the top. Return the same way or more experienced climbers could continue down the narrow ridge to the eastern summit, **A'Chioch**, then descend the eastern face to the road that skirts **Loch Ba**. The views from the top are magnificent, across the other Hebridean islands and even as far as Ireland. If it's a cloudy day, it's worth postponing the ascent until there's clear weather. Allow around six hours for the round trip.

Coastal walks There are a couple of excellent coastal walks which start out from Carsaig Bay. A good path heads west along the shore to **Carsaig Arches** at Malcom's Point. The path runs below the cliffs out to the headland and then around it, and after about a mile reaches **Nun's Cave**, a wide and shallow cave where the nuns of Iona took refuge after being expelled during the Reformation. The path continues for another mile or so, but becomes a bit exposed in places and traverses a steep slope above a sheer drop into the sea. The famous arches are columnar basalts worn into fantastic shapes. One is a free-standing rock stack and another is a huge cave with two entrances. You'll need to allow about four hours in total plus some time at the arches.

Heading east from Carsaig Bay is a spectacular 4½ mile walk to **Lochbuie**, past Adnunan stack. It starts out through woodland, then follows the shore below the steep cliffs, with waterfalls plunging straight into the sea. It's easy at first but then gets very muddy in places and there's quite a bit of wading through boggy marsh, so make sure you've got good walking boots. Allow about five to six hours in total.

There are a few marked trails through Forestry Commission land on Mull. The first walk is to **Aros Park**, on the south side of Tobermory Bay. Start out from the car park near the distillery in Tobermory and follow the shoreline for about a mile to Lochan a'Ghurrabain, which is good for trout fishing (see page 121). From here there is also a marked path around the loch (1 mile).

A longer walk is to **Ardmore Bay**, three miles north of Tobermory. The trail/cycle path starts at the car park by the road that runs northwest from Tobermory. From here, it runs out almost to Ardmore point and back again, passing a couple of ruined villages on the way. There's a good chance of seeing seals and lots of sea birds in Ardmore Bay. The trail is four miles in total.

Four miles north of Craignure is the car park and picnic site at **Garmony Point**, where a two-mile trail leads to the Ferry terminal at **Fishnish**, hugging the shore all the way. Another trail (four miles) runs out to Fishnish Point and back through the forest to the car park by the old harbour.

Forest walks
For detailed maps and more information pick up the free Guide to Forest Walks and Trails in North Argyll leaflet at any tourist office

Inner Hebrides

Isle of Iona

Iona is a small island – barely three miles long and a little over a mile wide – but its importance to Christianity is out of all proportion to its size. Iona's place in religious history was guaranteed when **St Columba** *arrived with his 12 disciples and founded a monastery there in 563 AD. The Irish monk then set about converting practically all of pagan Scotland and much of northern England. Iona went on to become the most sacred religious site in Europe and has been a place of pilgrimage for several centuries. Today that pilgrimage has turned into more of an invasion, with hordes of daytrippers making the five-minute ferry trip from Mull to visit the abbey. Few, however, venture beyond the main village,* **Baile Mór***, and it's easy to find a quiet spot, particularly on the west coast with its sparkling silver beaches washed by turquoise sea. It's worth spending a day or two here to soak up the island's unique spiritual peace, so well conveyed in the words of Dr Johnson: "that man is little to be envied whose…piety would not grow warmer among the ruins of Iona".*

Phone code: 01681
Colour map 3, grid C3
Population: 130

Ins and outs

Passenger-only **ferry** only from **Fionnphort**, Mull, (5 mins) frequently T0845-1815 Mon-Sat and hourly 0900-1800 Sun; return trip £3.10.

Getting there

The Story of St Columba

St Columba (Colum Cille in Gaelic), a prince of Ireland and grandson of the Irish King, Niall of the Nine Hostages, came to Scotland, not as a missionary, but as an act of self-imposed penance for his actions. He stubbornly refused to hand over his copy of the Gospels, illegally copied from St Finian's original, which led to a bitter dispute with the king. This ended in a pitched battle, in which Columba's supporters prevailed, but he was so overcome with remorse at the bloodshed he had caused that he fled Ireland, finally settling on Iona, as it was the first place he found from where he couldn't see his homeland.Columba, however, was not retiring into obscurity.

His missionary zeal drove him to begin work on building the abbey. He also banished women and cows from the island, declaring that "where there is a cow there is a woman, and where there is a woman there is mischief". Workers at the abbey had to leave their womenfolk on nearby Eilean nam Ban (Women's Island). Not content with that, he also banished frogs and snakes from Iona, though there are plenty on Mull. He is even said to have pacified the Loch Ness Monster during a visit to Inverness.He went on to found the Celtic Church, or the Church of the Culdees, with centres throughout Scotland, which differed in many ways from the Church of Rome.

Getting around Iona is small enough to get around easily on foot, or you can **hire mountain bikes** at *Finlay Ross (Iona) Ltd*, in Baile Mór village (see also Sleeping and eating below), T700357, F700562, for around £10 per day.

History

Iona is known as 'Cradle of Christianity in Scotland' and was a centre of the arts. The monks produced elaborate carvings, manuscripts, ornate gravestones and Celtic crosses. Their greatest work was the beautiful *Book of Kells*, which dates from 800 AD and which is now on display in Dublin's Trinity College. This proved to be the high point of the church's history. Shortly after, came the first of the Viking raids, in 806, when many monks were slaughtered at Martyrs' Bay, followed by another in 986 which destroyed the work of many years. The relentless pressure from the established church ended with the suppression of the Celtic Church by King David in 1144.

In 1203 Iona became part of the mainstream church with the establishment of a nunnery for the Order of the Black Nuns as well as a Benedictine Abbey by Reginald of the MacDonalds of the Isles. Iona became overshadowed by the royal city of Dunfermline and its final demise came with the Reformation, when buildings were demolished and all but three of the 360 carved crosses destroyed.

The abbey lay in ruins until in 1899 the island's owner, the eighth Duke of Argyll, donated the buildings to the Church of Scotland on condition that the abbey church was restored for worship. Then in 1938 the Reverand George Macleod founded the Iona Community as an evangelical Church of Scotland brotherhood, with the abbey buildings as its headquarters, and by 1965 had succeeded in rebuilding the remainder of the monastic buildings. Now the abbey complex has been completely restored and the island of Iona, apart from the abbey buildings, is owned by the National Trust for Scotland.

Inner Hebrides

The Abbey

The present abbey dates from around 1200, though it has been rebuilt over the centuries and completely restored in the 20th century. The oldest part is the restored **St Oran's Chapel**, to the south of the abbey on the right, which is plain and unadorned save for its splendid 11th-century Norman doorway. It is said that Columba was prevented from completing the building of the original chapel until a living person had been buried in the foundations. His friend Oran volunteered and was duly buried. Columba later asked for the face to be uncovered so that he could bid a final farewell to his friend, but Oran was found to be alive and claimed he had seen Heaven and Hell, describing them in such blasphemous terms that Columba ordered he be covered up immediately!

Surrounding the chapel is the **Reilig Odhrain**, the sacred burial ground, which is said to contain the graves of 48 Scottish kings, including Macbeth's victim, Duncan, as well as four Irish and eight Norwegian kings. The stones you see today are not the graves of kings but of various important people from around the West Highlands and Islands. The most recent is that of **John Smith**, leader of the British Labour Party from 1992 until his untimely death in 1994.

Beside the **Road of the Dead**, which leads from the abbey church to St Oran's Chapel, stands the eighth-century **St Martin's Cross**. This is the

Inner Hebrides

Iona

■ **Sleeping**
1 Finlay Ross B&B

● **Eating**
1 Martyrs' Bay

finest of Iona's Celtic high crosses and is remarkably complete, with the Pictish serpent-and-boss decoration on one side and holy figures on the other. Standing in front of the abbey entrance is a replica of **St John's Cross**, the other great eighth century monument. The restored original is in the **Infirmary Museum**, at the rear of the abbey, along with a fine collection of medieval gravestones.

No part of St Columba's original buildings survives, but to the left of the main entrance is **St Columba's Shrine**, the small, steep-roofed chamber, which almost certainly marks the site of the saint's tomb. You get a good view of the whole complex from the top of the small grassy knoll opposite the abbey entrance. This is **Torr an Aba**, where Columba's cell is said to have been. The **Abbey** itself has been carefully restored to its original beautiful simplicity and inside, in a side chapel, are marble effigies of the eighth Duke of Argyll and his third wife, Duchess Ina. ■ *The abbey is open all year and at all times. Admission is free but you're asked to give a £2 donation at the entrance where you can pick up a plan of the abbey.*

Baile Mór

The passenger ferry from Fionnphort on Mull lands at Baile Mór, Iona's main village, which is little more than a row of cottages facing the sea. There are several places to stay, but as demand far exceeds supply during the busy summer, it's best to book in advance at one of the tourist offices on Mull, or in Oban. There's also a post office, a very good craft shop and general store in the village.

Just outside the village, on the way to the abbey, are the ruins of the **Augustinian nunnery**. Just to the north, housed in the parish church manse, built by Thomas Telford, is the **Iona Heritage Centre**, which features displays on the island's social history. ■ *Apr-Oct Mon-Sat 1030-1630. Adult £1.50.* Nearby stands the intricately-carved 15th-century **Maclean's Cross**.

Sleeping & eating
B-C *Argyll Hotel*, T700334, F700510, www.argyllhoteliona.co.uk 17 rooms, open Apr-Oct, this is the better of the island's 2 upmarket hotels and its very good restaurant serves cheap lunches and mid-range-expensive 4-course dinners. There are a couple of B&Bs in and around the village, including **D** *Bishop's House*, T/F700306, open Mar-Oct, overlooking the Sound of Iona. There's also **E** *Finlay Ross (Iona) Ltd*, T700357/365, F700562. 15 rooms, open all year. **Camping** is possible but ask permission first.

Apart from the *Argyll Hotel*, there's the *Martyrs' Bay Restaurant*, which serves soup and snacks. Opposite the abbey is a coffee house run by the Iona Community (open Mon-Thu 1100-1630, Fri 1200-1630, Sat 1130-1630, Sun 1200-1600), serving soup, filled rolls and cakes.

Around the island

Do yourself a real favour by taking the time to explore the island and enjoy its natural beauty as well as its spiritual peace. On the west coast, are some lovely beaches of white sand and colourful pebbles.

The best of the lot is the **Bay at the Back of the Ocean**, beside the golf course, and only a mile and a half walk from the ferry. This was one of John Smith's favourite places and it's easy to see why. At the southern tip of the island is another sandy beach at **St Columba's Bay**, believed to be the spot where the saint first landed. The small cairns here are said to have been built by the monks as penance for their sins. They obviously had a lot on their conscience. Around the corner, at Rubha na Carraig-géire on the southeastern tip, is the **marble quarry**, disused since 1915. The rusting remains of the cutting equipment are still lying around.

Another good walk is to the top of **Dun I**, the only real hill, which rises to a height of 300 ft. To get there, continue on the road north from the abbey, past MacDougal's Cross, then go through a gate to the right of Bishop's Walk Farm and follow the fence up to where you join a footpath up to the top. It's only about half an hour up and down and there are great views from the top of the entire island and the coastline of Mull.

Isle of Coll

The low-lying, treeless and windswept island of Coll offers the simple pleasures in life and is so peaceful and quiet that it makes some of the more popular islands appear crowded by comparison. There's little to do here other than stroll along the magnificent, deserted beaches and enjoy the relatively long hours of sunshine. Tourism, though, remains low on the list of priorities and those who do come prefer it that way. Even by Hebridean standards there are few facilities and accommodation is scarce.

Phone code: 01879
Colour map 3,
grid B3
Population: 170

Inner Hebrides

Ins and outs

There's a **ferry** from Oban to Coll (2 hrs 40 mins) and Tiree (55 mins) once daily on Mon, Tue, Wed, Fri and Sat. One way ticket to Coll or Tiree costs £11.40 per passenger and £65 per car. From Coll to Tiree costs £2.90 and £16.65.

Getting there

The CalMac ferry from Oban calls in at Coll's only village, Arinagour, where half of the island's population live and where you'll find the post office and a few shops. There's no petrol station but that's probably a hint to leave the car behind. The island is only 13 miles long by 4 miles wide and the best way to get around is on foot or by bike.

Getting around

Around the island

The best of Coll's beaches are on the west coast, at **Killunaig**, **Hogh Bay** and **Feall Bay**. The latter is separated from the nearby **Crossapool Bay** by giant sand dunes up to 100 ft high. These are now owned by the RSPB to protect the resident corncrake population. Nearby, at the head of Loch Breachacha, is the restored medieval **Breachacha Castle**, built by the Macleans of Coll and once owned by them but now used as an adventure-training school for young overseas aid volunteers. The castle is sometimes open to the public; check with the tourist office in Oban for details. The dilapidated 18th-century mansion nearby is where Boswell and Dr Johnson stayed when they were stranded here for 10 days during their grand Highland tour in 1773.

It's worth taking a walk up **Ben Hogh** (341 ft), the island's highest point, overlooking Hogh Bay on the west coast, to get a good overview. The east coast, north from Arinagour to **Sorisdale**, is an uninhabited wilderness which is ideal for some gentle hillwalking.

Essentials

Sleeping
& eating
In Arinagour is the **D** *Coll Hotel*, T230334, F230317. A family hotel with a good restaurant and which is the social hub of the island. Also in the village is **E** *Taigh Solas*, T/F230333. A few miles to the west is **E-F** *Achamore*, T230430. A lovely old farmhouse. Down in the southwest, at Breachacha Bay, is **E** *Garden House*, T/F230374. Nearby, in the walled garden of the castle, is the island's **campsite** (open Apr-Oct; phone as for *Garden House*). The only alternative to hotel or guesthouse food is the trendy bistro in Arinagour.

Isle of Tiree

Phone code: 01879
Colour map 3,
grid B2
Population: 800

Inner Hebrides

Tiree claims to be the sunniest place in Scotland, and has a comparatively low average rainfall, but it's also one of the windiest places in the country. So windy, in fact, that Tiree has become the windsurfing capital of Scotland and is known as the 'Hawaii of the North'. International windsurfers are attracted by the huge Atlantic rollers that break on the island's countless, long, clean and silver beaches.

Ins and outs

Getting there
Tiree has an **airport** and there are regular daily flights (except Sun) all year round from Glasgow. The airport is at The Reef, Crossapol (T220309). For full details, see page 114.
      There are *CalMac* car and passenger **ferries** to the island from Oban, via Coll and, occasionally, Tobermory. The ferry port is at Scarinish (T220337). From Oban to Tiree (55 mins) once daily on Mon, Tue, Wed, Fri and Sat. One-way ticket to Tiree costs £11.40 per passenger and £65 per car. From Coll to Tiree costs £2.90 and £19.90.

Getting around
There's a **shared taxi** service which operates on request Mon-Fri 0930-1500 (limited service on Sat), also Mon-Wed and Fri 1600-1730. There's also a Tue evening service for arriving ferries, but only in the summer. For private taxi hire call *Island Cabs*, T220344 (evenings and weekends only). There's a **postbus** service around the island, including to and from the airport. The timetable is available at Scarinish Post Office. **Bicycle hire** is available at the *Tiree Lodge Hotel* (see below), or contact Mr N Maclean, T220428.

Compared to Coll, Tiree is heavily populated, with over 800 inhabitants. It's also much greener and more fertile than its neighbour. Tiree was once known as the breadbasket of the Hebrides and its Gaelic name, *tir-iodh*, means 'Land of Corn'. The island supported a population of 4,450 in 1831, but was ruthlessly cleared by its owner, the Duke of Argyll, so that by 1881 the population had been halved. Not content to stop there, he even drafted in the marines, in 1885, to evict those crofters who dared to protest. Today, Tiree enjoys relative prosperity and crofting is the mainstay of the economy, with cattle and sheep grazing the miles of rich machair. Tourism is also a major contributor and during the height of the season, the island's population approaches the levels of the early 19th century.

Around the island

Tiree is a low, flat island, only about 11 miles long and six miles across at its widest, and is also known by the nickname *Tir fo Thuinn*, or "Land below the waves". When seen from a distance most of it disappears below the horizon save its two highest hills, **Ben Hynish** (462 ft) and **Beinn Hough** (390 ft), on the west coast. Being flat and small, it obviously makes good sense to explore it by bicycle, but remember that the constant wind varies from strong to gale force.

The ferry port is at **Gott Bay**, half a mile from **Scarinish**, the island's main village and home to a *Co-op* supermarket, post office and bank (there's a garage at the pier head). About four miles from Scarinish, is Vaul Bay, where the well-preserved remains of **Dun Mor**, a Pictish Broch built around the first century AD, stand on rocky outcrop to the west of the bay. A few miles west of here is the **Clach a'Choire**, or 'ringing stone', a huge glacial granite boulder covered in Bronze Age cup marks which makes a metallic sound when struck. Legend has it that should it ever shatter, or fall off its pedestal, then Tiree will sink beneath the waves.

The island's main road runs northwest from Scarinish, past the beautiful beach at **Balephetrish Bay** to **Balevullin**, where you can see some good examples of restored traditional thatched houses. Just to the south, at **Sandaig**, is the **Thatched House Museum** which tells of the island's social history. ■ *Jun-Sep, Mon-Fri 1400-1600.*

In the southwestern corner of the island is the most spectacular scenery of all, at the headland of **Ceann a'Mara**, or Kenavara. The massive sea cliffs are the home of thousands of sea birds and you can see seals on the rocky shore. East from here, across the golden sands of Balephuil Bay, is the island's highest hill, **Ben Hynish**, topped by a radar-tracking station resembling a giant golf ball. Despite this, it's worth the climb to the top for the magnificent views over the island and, on clear days, across to the Outer Hebrides. Below Ben Hynish, to the east, is the village of **Hynish**, where you'll find the **Signal Tower Museum**, which tells the fascinating story of the building of the **Skerryvore Lighthouse** (1840-44) by Alan Stevenson, an uncle of Robert Louis Stevenson. This incredible feat of engineering was carried out from Hynish, where a dry dock/reservoir was built for shipping materials by boat to the Skerryvore reef, 10 miles to the southwest.

Essentials

There are several guesthouses and B&Bs, the best of which is the wonderful **C** *Kirkapol House*, T/F220729, in a converted Victorian church overlooking Gott Bay. Best of the 2 hotels is **D** *Tiree Lodge*, T220368, F220994, at Gott Bay. The other is the **E** *Scarinish Hotel*, T220308, F220410, in the village itself. **It's possible to camp** free on the island, but ask for permission first. | **Sleeping & eating**

The best food on offer is at the moderately-priced ***The Glassary***, T/F220684, at Sandaig. It also offers accommodation (**D-E**). There's also the option of bar lunches and suppers at the *Tiree Lodge* and *Scarinish Hotels*. For afternoon tea or coffee you're limited to the ***Alan Stevenson Centre*** in Hynish, open 1430-1630, or *Glebecraft* in Scarinish.

Windsurfing tuition is available at Loch Bhasapol, T220559 (summer only). The major windsurfing event is the *Wave Classic*, held annually in **Oct**. | **Sports**

Isle of Colonsay

Colonsay is the epitome of the island haven: remote, tranquil and undemanding. It has abundant wildlife (150 species of resident or migrant birds), beautiful plants and flowers (over 500 species) and glorious beaches. All this has become accessible to daytrippers, with a ferry round trip (see below), leaving you six hours ashore. This does scant justice to the island's peculiar charms, however, and judging by the ever-growing number of holiday homes and self-catering accommodation on Colonsay, it's a view shared by many.

Phone code: 01951
Colour map 3, grid C3
Population: 100

Ins and outs

Getting there   There are **ferry** sailings from Oban (2 hrs) once daily Wed, Fri and Sun, arriving at Scalasaig on the east coast. From Kennacraig there is 1 sailing (3 hrs 35 mins) on Wed. From Port Askaig there is 1 sailing (1 hr 10 mins) also on Wed. One-way Oban/Kennacraig-Colonsay costs £10.10 per passenger and £48.50 per car; Port Askaig-Colonsay £3.55 and £18.75. Ferries need to be booked well in advance during the summer months.

Getting around   There's a limited **bus** and postbus service around the island Mon-Sat, for those without their own transport. On Wed in the summer, a tour bus meets the ferry and takes visitors round the island. As the island is only 8 miles long by 3 miles wide, you might want to consider hiring a bicycle. **Bike hire** from *A McConnel*, T200355.

Around the island

The island is rich in archaeological & historical remains   Colonsay's population lives in the three small villages, the largest of which is **Scalasiag**, the ferry port. The island's only hotel is here and there's also a restaurant, a post office/shop, a petrol pump and a heritage centre by the pier. A few miles north of the ferry, in the middle of the island, is **Colonsay House**, dating from 1772. The house was sold, along with the rest of the island, in 1904 to Lord Strathcona, who had made his fortune in Canada with the Hudson Bay Company and went on to found the Canadian Pacific Railway. The house is not open to the public but the lovely gardens and woods, full of rhododendrons, giant palms and exotic shrubs, are worth a stroll. The estate cottages are now self-catering holiday homes.

There are several standing stones, the best of which are **Fingal's Limpet Hammers**, at Kilchattan, southwest of Colonsay House. There are also Iron Age forts, such as **Dun Eibhinn**, next to the hotel in Scalasaig (see below). Colonsay is also home to a wide variety of **wildlife**. You can see choughs, one of Britain's rarest birds, as well as corncrakes, buzzards, falcons, merlins and perhaps even the odd golden eagle or sea eagle. There are also otters, seals and wild goats (said to be descended from the survivors of the Spanish Armada ships wrecked in 1588).

The jewel in the island's crown, though, lies six miles north of Scalasaig, past Colonsay House, at **Kiloran Bay**. The beach here is described as the finest in the Hebrides, and who could argue? The magnificent half mile of golden sands, backed by tiers of grassy dunes, with massive breakers rolling in off the Atlantic is worth the two-hour ferry crossing alone.

Essentials

Sleeping & eating   Accommodation on Colonsay is limited and must be booked up well in advance. **B** *Isle of Colonsay Hotel*, T200316, F200353, www.colonsay.org.uk A few hundreds yards from the ferry, 11 rooms, a cosy 18th-century inn with a friendly bar and excellent food, they also arrange various trips around the island. Attached to the hotel is *Viragos*, a coffee house and well-stocked bookshop. A cheaper option is the excellent **E** *Seaview*, T200315, at Kilchattan, near the standing stones. Open Apr-Oct. There's also a B&B near the hotel, at **E** *Smiddy Cottage*. Aside from the hotel bar, you can eat at *The Pantry*, T200325, near the ferry pier. It is open Mon-Sat and offers simple home cooking as well as teas and cakes.

Apart from 1 hotel and a couple of B&Bs, all accommodation is self-catering. Caravans and camping are not allowed on the island

Isle of Oronsay

Just off the southern tip of Colonsay is the island of Oronsay, two miles square with a population of six and one of the highlights of a visit to Colonsay. The name derives from the Norse for 'ebb-tide island', which is a fitting description as Oronsay can be reached on foot at low tide, across the mud flats known as 'The Strand'. It takes about an hour to walk from the south end of Colonsay to the ruins of 14th-century **Augustinian Priory**. This was the home of some of the most highly-skilled medieval craftsmen in the Western Highlands. A surviving example of their work is the impressive Oronsay Cross and the beautifully-carved tombstones, on display in the **Prior's House**.

Legend has it that St Columba first landed here after leaving his native Ireland, but he could still see his homeland from the top of Ben Oronsay and so decided to continue north to Iona, where he founded the community that was to become the centre of Christianity in northern Britain (see page 127).

Make sure you take wellies for the walk across The Strand and check on the **tides**. Tide tables are available at the hotel or shop. Spring tides (new and full moon) allow about three to four hours to walk across and back, which is just enough time to see the priory but little else. Fest walkers may have time to also pop into *The Barn*, T200344, for home cooking and crafts.

Inner Hebrides

Isle of Islay

Islay (pronounced eye-la), the most southerly of the Hebridean islands and one of the most populous, with around 4,000 inhabitants, has one very important claim to fame – single malt whisky. Islay produces a very distinctive, peaty malt and connoisseurs are in for a treat, as the island has no fewer than seven working distilleries. Aside from whisky, people also come here to watch birds. The island is something of an ornithologist's paradise and from October to April plays host to migrating barnacle and white-fronted geese flying down from Greenland in their thousands for the winter.

Phone code: 01496
Colour map 5, grid A1

If that leaves you cold, then there's always the spectacular coastal scenery, from the wild Mull of Oa to the glorious beach at Laggan Bay. Compared to other islands like Skye, Mull or Arran, Islay receives few visitors, mainly due to its distance from the mainland, giving it a really isolated feel. And because the island is partially Gaelic-speaking the road signs are bilingual, which only enhances the feeling of being far from home.

Ins and outs

Islay can be reached by **air** from Glasgow (for flight details, see page 114). The airport is at Glenegedale, a few miles north of Port Ellen on the road to Bowmore.

Getting there

It takes about 2½ hrs to **drive** to Kennacraig from Glasgow, and there's a daily **bus** from Glasgow to Kennacraig (with *West Coast Motors*) which connects with the ferry to Islay (for bus times, contact Buchanan Street bus station, T0141-3327133).

The **ferry** to Islay (and Jura) from Kennacraig to Port Ellen (2 hrs 10 mins) sails once daily on Mon and Sun and twice daily on Tue, Thu, Fri and Sat. Also to Port Askaig (2 hrs) once daily on Tue, Wed, Thu, Fri and Sat and twice daily Mon. One-way to Port Ellen/Port Askaig costs £7.05 per passenger and £37.50 per car. The ferry from Oban to Port Askaig sails on Wed (4 hrs 15 mins); one-way £10.10 per passenger and £48.50 per car. From Colonsay to Port Askaig (1 hr 10 mins) there is a sailing on Wed; one-way

£3.55 and £18.75. *CalMac* offices: Kennacraig, T01880-730253; Port Ellen, T01496-302209.

Getting around For those without their own transport, there's a regular bus service around the island, with *Islay Coaches*, T840273, and *Royal Mail Postbuses*, T01463-256200. There are buses from Portnahaven to Port Ellen, via Port Charlotte, Bridgend, Bowmore and the airport; from Port Askaig to Port Ellen via Ballygrant, Bridgend, Bowmore and the airport; from Port Ellen to Ardbeg, Bowmore, Port Askaig and Portnahaven, and also a **postbus** to Bunnahabhain. Buses run hourly at least from Mon-Sat, but only once on Sun. For bus times, pick up a copy of the *Islay & Jura Area Transport Guide* from the tourist office in Bowmore, Tarbert, Lochgilphead or Oban.

For **car hire** there's *D&N Mackenzie* at Glenegedale, T302300, and *Bowmore Engineering*, T810206. **Taxi hire** at *Carol's Cabs*, Frederick Cres, Port Ellen, T302155. **Bicycle hire** at *Macauley & Torrie*, Frederick Cres, Port Ellen, T302053, and Mick Stuart, Lennox St, Port Ellen, T302391, who is also a wildlife guide.

Tourist Islay's only official Tourist Information Centre is in Bowmore, T810254. Open Apr-Jun
Information Mon-Fri 0930-1730 (and Sun 1400-1700 in Jun); Jul-Sep Mon-Sat 0900-1745, Sun
Centre 1100-1700; Oct-Mar Mon-Fri 1000-1600. They'll find accommodation for you.

Islay

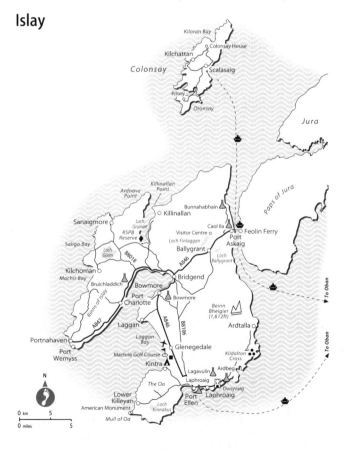

Port Ellen

Port Ellen is the largest place on Islay and the main ferry port, yet it still has the feel of a sleepy village. It was founded in 1821 by the laird, Walter Frederick Campbell, and named after his first wife. There are shops, hotels, B&Bs, restaurants, bank, a couple of filling stations, a post office and an information centre of sorts, based in a caravan beside the *White Hart Hotel*, making Port Ellen a good base from which to explore the delights of the southern half of Islay.

Four miles to the north, overlooking Laggan Bay, is **A** *Machrie Hotel*, T302310, F302404. 18 rooms, this golfing hotel is right by a great beach and a great golf course,. The bar and restaurant make the perfect end to 18 perfect holes. Also by the golf course is the excellent **B-C** *Glenmachrie*, T/F302560, www.isle-of-islay.com/group/ guest/glenmachrie A genuine farmhouse offering genuine hospitality and superb food. 5 rooms. The price includes dinner, but you'd be crazy to book B&B only and deny yourself the pleasure. Nearby is **D** *Glenegedale House Hotel & Restaurant*, T302147, F302210, which is very handy for the airport. At Kintra beach (take the Oa road and follow the signs for Kintra) is **E-F** *Kintra Farmhouse*, T302051. Open Apr-Sep, 3 rooms. There's also an independent hostel, the **F** *Kintra Bunk Barns Hostel* and a very good restaurant (see below). This is a great place for camping and there's a **campsite** with full facilities (open Apr-Sep).

    There are several places to stay in the village itself. **E** *The Trout-Fly Guest House*, T/F302204, is right beside the ferry terminal and has a decent restaurant (for residents only). **E** *The Bothy*, 91 Lennox St, T302391. Run by the versatile Mick Stuart who also hires out bikes and acts as a wildlife guide. Keen divers might want to try the *Islay Dive Centre*, 10 Charlotte St, T302441, which has apartments to rent (**E**).

    Apart from the places mentioned above, there's very good, cheap food available at the *Old Granary* at Kintra Farm (open 1730-2300, Jul/Aug 1200-2300).

Sleeping & eating
The places listed are in and around Port Ellen

Inner Hebrides

Around Port Ellen

There are a number of excellent day trips from Port Ellen. A road runs east out to **Ardtalla**, where it ends. Along the way, it passes three distilleries, first **Lapgroaig**, then **Lagavulin** and lastly, **Ardbeg**, all of which offer guided tours (see 'The Whisky Trail'). Between the Lagavulin and Ardbeg distilleries is the dramatically-sited 16th-century ruin of **Dunyvaig Castle**, once the main naval base and fortress of the Lords of the Isles (see also page 140). A mile further on is the impressive **Kildalton Cross**, standing in the graveyard of the ruined 13th-century chapel. The eighth-century cross is remarkably well preserved and one of Scotland's most important Early Christian monuments, and the carvings depict biblical scenes. At the end of the road is Ardtalla, from where you can begin the ascent of **Beinn Bheigeir** (1,609 ft), the island's highest hill, with spectacular views from the summit.

    Southwest of Port Ellen a road runs out to a little, rounded peninsula known as **The Oa**, an area of varied beauty, both wild and pastoral, and with a wonderful coastline. The road runs as far as **Upper Killeyan**, from where it's about a mile uphill to the spectacular headland at the **Mull of Oa**. Here you'll see the strange-looking **American monument**. The obelisk commemorates the shipwrecks offshore of two US ships, the *Tuscania* and the *Ontranto*, both of which sank in 1918 at the end of the war. There's a great walk north from the Mull of Oa up to Kintra, but it's best to start out from Kintra (see below).

    A turn-off from the road to The Oa leads north to **Kintra**, at the south end of **The Big Strand** at Laggan Bay, with five miles of glorious sands and

The Whisky Trail

Though the whisky distilling process is basically the same everywhere, some distilleries have more beautiful locations and more interesting tours. Islay's seven distilleries enjoy the most scenically stunning settings and are full of character and history. Islay also offers the unique opportunity to visit several of Scotland's most impressive distilleries in one day, and their distinctive peaty malts are considered to be among the finest.

__Laphroaig__ (pronounced 'la-froyg') is the closest to Port Ellen and its wonderful setting is summed up by its name, meaning "The beautiful hollow by the broad bay" in Gaelic. According to many (including the author) this is the ultimate in malt whisky and is at its best after dinner. The distillery's tours are by appointment only, T302418. Free.

__Lagavulin__ (pronounced 'laga-voolin') is a mile along the shore by the romantic ruin of Dunyveg Castle. Their 16-year-old single malt is one of the classics and also makes the ideal after-dinner tipple. They also offer a very interesting tour, Monday-Friday by appointment only, T302400. £3.

__Ardbeg__ distillery is a mile further east and produces a robust and powerful single malt. Established in 1815, it was closed for a while,

but was recently acquired by Glenmorangie and runs tours Monday-Friday from 1030 till 1530, and also on Saturday and Sunday June-August, T302244. £2.

__Bowmore__ is the oldest distillery on Islay and still uses all the old traditional methods to produce its fine single malt, also at its best after dinner. Their hour-long tours are the most professionally done and even include a video. Tours all year round from Monday-Friday at 1030 and 1400, in the summer months at 1030, 1130, 1400 and 1500, T810441. £2.

__Caol Ila__ (pronounced 'coal-eela') was founded in 1846 and lies close to Port Askaig with great views across the Sound of Islay to Jura. Unlike most of its island peers, this single malt is best before dinner. Tours of the distillery all year round by appointment only, T840207. £3.

__Bunnahabhain__ (pronounced 'bun a havan') is the most northerly of the distilleries, set in a secluded bay with great views across to Jura. Tours are also by appointment only, T840646. Free.

__Bruichladdich__ (pronounced 'broo-laddie') is in the village of the same name on the road south to Port Charlotte. They offer tours all year round Mon-Sat at 1030, 1130 and 1430. £3.

dunes. There's a restaurant and accommodation here, and it's a great place for camping (see 'Sleeping & eating' below). The restaurant is at the end of the road, with the beach on one side and on the other a wild and spectacular coastal walk to the **Mull of Oa**. There's a detailed map of the route in the restaurant. Just to the north of Kintra is the **Machrie golf course**, a memorable golfing experience. The *Machrie Hotel* does golfing packages (see Sleeping & eating above).

Bowmore

The A846 runs north from Port Ellen, straight as a pool cue, to Bowmore, the island's administrative capital and second largest village. Founded in 1768 by the Campbells, it's an appealing place, laid out in a grid plan with the main street running straight up the hill from the pier to the unusual **round church**, designed to ward off evil spirits, who can hide only in corners. Thankfully, there's also a nice spirit here, which can be found at the **Bowmore Distillery**, just to the west of Main Street. This is the oldest of the island's distilleries, founded in 1779, and the most tourist-friendly.

D *Harbour Inn*, Main St, T810330, F810990, hrbour@harbour-inn.co.uk 4 rooms, completely refurbished to a high standard, great views across the bay and superb food in their acclaimed restaurant (mid-range-expensive). **D** *Lochside Hotel*, Shore St, T810244, F810390. 8 rooms, friendly and good value hotel with a mind-boggling selection of single malts. On the road between Bowmore and Port Charlotte, at Bridgend, is **C** *Bridgend Hotel*, T810212, F810960. 10 rooms, nice and peaceful and good bar meals, there are also several B&Bs in Bowmore. **Sleeping & eating**

The Rinns of Islay

North of Bowmore, at **Bridgend**, the A846 joins the A847 which runs west to the hammerhead peninsula known as the Rinns of Islay ("rinns" is derived from the Gaelic for promontory). A few miles west of Bridgend the B8017 turns north to the **RSPB Reserve** at **Loch Gruinart**. The mudflats and fields at the head of the loch provide winter grazing for huge flocks of barnacle and white-fronted geese from Greenland, arriving in late October. There's an RSPB visitor centre at **Aoradh** (pronounced "oorig") which houses an observation point with telescopes and CCTV, and there's a hide across the road. In total there are about 110 species of bird breeding on Islay, including the rare chough and corncrake. Keen bird watchers can stay close by at **E** *Loch Gruinart House*, T/F850212 (**D** including dinner).

The coastal scenery around the Rinns is very impressive, particularly at **Killinallan Point**, a beautiful and lonely headland at the far northeast of Loch Gruinart. Also impressive is **Ardnave Point**, west of Loch Gruinart, and further west along the north coast, **Sanaigmore**. The best beaches are at **Saligo** and **Machir Bay** on the west coast, past Loch Gorm. Both are lovely, wide, golden beaches backed by high dunes, but swimming is forbidden due to dangerous undercurrents.

You can stay at **Kilchoman**, near Machir Bay, at the excellent **E** *Kilchoman House*, T850382, F850277, a former Georgian Manse with a reputation for fine cooking. Open April-October, book in advance.

Port Charlotte

Port Charlotte is without doubt the most charming of Islay's villages, with rows of well-kept, whitewashed cottages stretched along the wide bay. It, too, was founded by the prolific Walter Frederick Campbell, in 1828, and named after the other important woman in his life, his mother.

But Port Charlotte is not just a pretty face. The **Islay Wildlife Information and Field Centre** is a must for anyone interested in flora and fauna. It's very hands-on, with good displays on geology and natural history, a video room and reference library. It's also a great place for kids and has activity days when staff take tours of the surrounding area. ■ *Easter-Oct Tue and Thu 1000-1700, Fri and Sun 1400-1700. Adult £2, concession £1.20, children £1.*

Also worth visiting is the compact **Museum of Islay Life**, to the east of the village, where you can find out all about illegal whisky distilling on the island. ■ *Easter-Oct Mon-Sat 1000-1630, Sun 1400-1630. Adult £2, concession £1.20, children £1.* Across the road is the **creamery**, where you can see the local cheeses being made. There are also a few good beaches around.

Accommodation is somewhat limited in Port Charlotte. The best place to stay is the **C** *Port Charlotte Hotel*, T850360, F850361, carl@portcharlottehot.demon.co.uk 10 **Sleeping & eating**

Inner Hebrides

rooms, restored Victorian inn with gardens and conservatory on seafront, their restaurant features local seafood and is the best around. There's also a **B&B** run by *Mrs Wood* (T850225), **E**, open April-October, and a *SYHA youth hostel* (T850385; open Mar to end-Oct), next to the Wildlife Information Centre.

Aside from the hotel, the best place to eat is the *Croft Kitchen* (T850230). It's a coffee and gift shop by day and moderately-priced restaurant by night, open Mar-Oct daily 1000-2030, best to book in season.

Portnahaven At the southern end of the Rinns is the picturesque little fishing and crofting village of Portnahaven, its Hebridean cottages rising steeply above the deeply-indented harbour. A mile south is Portnahaven's twin settlement, **Port Wemyss**, also named after the laird's wife, would you believe (she was a daughter of the Eighth Earl of Wemyss). Amenities are few and far between in this remote corner. If you want to stay, you can find a bed at **E** *The Old School House*, in Portnahaven, T860242.

Port Askaig and around

Port Askaig Port Askaig is Islay's other ferry port, with connections to the mainland and to the islands of Jura and Colonsay. It's little more than a dock, a car park and a few buildings huddled at the foot of a steep, wooded hillside. If you're arriving by the late ferry, there's accommodation at **C-D** *Port Askaig Hotel*, T840245.

A short walk north along the coast is the **Caol Ila Distillery** and a couple of miles further north, at the end of the road which branches left before you enter Port Askaig, is the beautifully-situated **Bunnahabhain Distillery**.

Ballygrant The A846 runs east from Bridgend out to Port Askaig passing a couple of interesting sights on the way. A mile and a half beyond Bridgend is the **Islay Woollen Mill**, which was established in 1883 on the site of a 17th- century mill. The road then passes through **Ballygrant**, just to the south of **Loch Finlaggan**. Here, on two crannogs (artificial islands) were the headquarters of the Lords of the Isles, the ancestors of Clan Donald. The MacDonalds ruled from Islay for nearly 350 years, over a vast area covering all of the island off the west coast and almost the whole of the western seaboard from Cape Wrath to the Mull of Kintyre. There's a new **visitor centre** to the northeast of the loch, where you can learn more about the history of the site and see some of the archaeological remains. ■ *Easter-Oct, Tue, Thu and Sun 1430-1700. T840644.* You can walk across the fen to **Eilean Mor**, where there's a collection of carved gravestones near the ruins of a medieval chapel. A smaller island, **Eilean na Comhairle** ('The Council of the Isle'), is where the Lords of the Isles met to decide policy.

Sleeping There's accommodation at the superb **B** *Kilmeny Farmhouse*, T/F840668, www.kilmeny.co.uk Comfort, style, excellent food and a warm, friendly atmosphere. The only drawback is that there are only 3 rooms, so book well in advance. Otherwise, there's the **D** *Ballygrant Inn*, T/F840277, which is comfortable and serves great pub grub.

Isle of Jura

The words 'wild' and 'remote' tend to get overused in describing the many Hebridean islands, but in the case of Jura they are, if anything, an understatement. The short ferry crossing from neighbouring Islay takes you into another world, pervaded by an almost haunting silence. Jura has one road, one hotel, six sporting estates and 5,000 red deer, which outnumber the 200 people by 25:1, the human population having been cleared to turn the island into a huge deer forest. Rather appropriately, the name Jura derives from the Norse 'dyr-ey', meaning deer island.

Phone code: 01496
Colour map 5,
grid A1/2

Ins and outs

A small car and passenger **ferry** makes the regular 5-min crossing daily from Port Askaig on Islay to Feolin Ferry. For times, contact *Western Ferries*, T01496-840681. A one-way ticket costs £6.40 per car and £0.90 per passenger.

Getting there

Amazingly enough, there is a **bus** service on Jura, which runs from Feolin Ferry to Craighouse several times a day, Mon-Sat. A few buses continue to Lagg and Inverlussa and return to Craighouse. Note that some journeys are by request only and must be booked the day before, T820314. For bus times, see the *Islay & Jura Area Transport Guide*, available free at tourist offices.

Getting around

Inner Hebrides

Jura

Around the island

The Paps Jura is one of the last, great wildernesses in the British Isles and perfect for some real off-the-beaten-track walking. Its main attractions are the beautiful **Paps of Jura**, three breast-shaped peaks that dominate not only the island itself but also the view for miles around. From Kintyre, Mull, Coll and Tiree, and from the mountains of mainland Scotland from Skye to Arran, they can be seen on the horizon. The Paps provide some tough hillwalking and require good navigational skills, or a guide. It takes a good eight hours to cover all three peaks, though during the Paps of Jura fell race they are covered in just three hours. A good place to start is by the three-arch bridge over the Corran river, north of **Leargybreack**. The first pap you reach is **Beinn a'Chaolais** (2,408 ft), next is the highest, **Beinn an Oír** (2,571 ft) and the third is **Beinn Shiantaidh** (2,476 ft). To find out about guides, ask at the hotel in Craighouse (see below). The island's west coast is completely uninhabited and inaccessible to all but the hardiest and most dedicated of walkers.

Corryvreckan One of the island's main draws is the Corryvreckan whirlpool at the very
whirlpool & northern tip, between Jura and the uninhabited island of **Scarba**. The noto-
the north rious whirlpool, the most dangerous tide race in Scotland, is best appreciated one hour after low tide and its awesome roar can be heard long before you reach it. It is named after a Viking, Bhreacan, who anchored his boat here for three days and nights by a rope woven from the hair of virgins. Unsurprisingly, the rope parted under the strain, casting doubt on the status of one of the contributors, and Bhreacan drowned. To get there, follow the rough track from **Ardlussa** to **Kinuachdrach**, or get someone to drive you, then it's a two-mile walk. Before setting out, ask at the hotel for information and directions.

Also in the north of the island is **Barnhill**, the completely isolated and forlorn-looking cottage where **George Orwell** wrote *1984* between 1946 and 1948 (hence the book's title). Though the house attracts literary pilgrims, it remains closed.

Craighouse The only village on Jura is Craighouse, eight miles from Feolin Ferry on the southeast coast. Here you'll find the **Jura distillery** which welcomes visitors. Tours are by appointment, T820240. Beside the distillery is the island's one and only hotel, the **C** *Jura Hotel*, T820243, F820249, overlooking the lovely small isles bay. They'll provide information on island walks and the pub is the social hub. There's cheaper accommodation with **E** *Mrs Boardman*, T820379, open April-September.

Three miles south of the village, at **Ardfin**, is **Jura House**, with its beautiful walled garden, filled with wild flowers and Australasian plants and trees. ■ *Daily during daylight hours. £2. T820315.*

The Small Isles

Phone code: 01687 *The Small Isles is the collective name given to the four islands of Eigg, Muck, Rùm*
Colour map 3 *and Canna, lying south of Skye. Seen from the mainland, they look a very tempting prospect, especially the jagged outline of Rùm and the curiously-shaped Eigg. But visiting the islands is not easy, as ferry transport is purely designed for the inhabitants and not geared towards the convenience of island-hopping tourists.*

Furthermore, the island populations are small and accommodation and facilities are limited. But the determined traveller with time on their hands will be well rewarded, particularly on mountainous Rùm, with its superb walking and abundant wildlife.

Ins and outs

A *CalMac* passenger-only **ferry** sails from Mallaig to all 4 islands. From Mallaig to **Eigg** (1½ hrs) on Mon, Tue, Thu and Sat; Mallaig to **Muck** (2 ½ hrs) on Tue, Thu and Sat; Mallaig to **Rùm** (1¾ -3½ hrs) on Mon, Wed and Sat; Mallaig to **Canna** (3 hrs) on Mon, Wed, Fri and Sat. One way Mallaig to: Eigg £4.75; Muck £7.25; Rùm £7.10; Canna £8.10. From May-Sep the *CalMac* ferries from Mallaig are supplemented by cruises from Arisaig with *Arisaig Marine*, T01687-450224. For details, see page 240. **Getting there**

There are ferries between Eigg, Muck, Rùm and Canna; for details contact the *CalMac* office in Mallaig, T01687-462403. On Sat in the summer a ferry leaves at 0500 and sails Mallaig-Canna-Rùm-Muck-Eigg, allowing those with limited time to **Getting around**

Inner Hebrides

Eigg

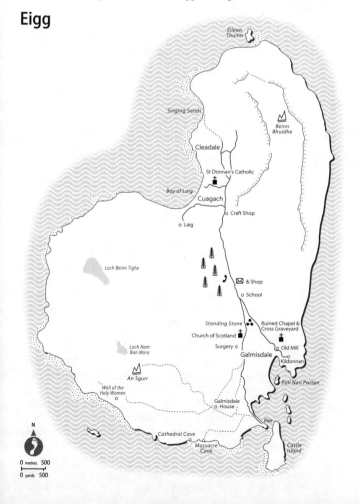

at least see the islands from close up. A second ferry leaves on summer Sat, making it possible to spend either 9½ hrs on Canna, or 7½ hrs on Rùm, or 5 hrs on Muck, or 3½ hrs on Eigg. At Eigg, Muck and Rùm passengers are transferred to small boats as there are no suitable piers.

Eigg

Colour map 3, grid A/B 4

Little Eigg has had something of a chequered past. In 1577 it was the scene of one of the bloodiest episodes in the history of Clan warfare, when 395 MacDonalds, almost the entire population, were trapped in a cave and suffocated by a raiding party of Macleods from Skye, who lit a fire at the entrance. More recently it has been at the heart of a bitter land ownership debate. Having endured a succession of absentee landlords, ranging from the merely eccentric to the criminally negligent, the 65 remaining islanders seized the moment and bought the island themselves, in conjunction with the Scottish Wildlife Trust. Now everyone can enjoy the island's wildlife, which includes otters, seals, eagles and many other birds, such as the Manx shearwater, guillemots and black-throated divers.

Around the island

The island is dominated by **An Sgurr**, a 1,289 ft flat-topped basalt peak with three vertical sides. It can be climbed easily by its western ridge and there's a superb view from the summit. Sitting in the shadow of the Sgurr, at the southeastern corner, is the main settlement, **Galmisdale**. This is where the ferries drop anchor (passengers are transferred to a smaller boat), and there's a post office, shop and tearoom, all by the pier. At the northern end is the small township of **Cleadale**, on the Bay of Laig. Just to the north are the "**Singing Sands**", a beach that makes a strange sound as you walk across it.

Sleeping

Two croft houses at Cleadale offer B&B: **D** *Lageorna*, T482405, www.isleofeigg.org also offers full board with pack lunch and caters for vegetarians; and **D** *Laig Farm*, T482437. There's also an independent **hostel** with 24 beds, *The Glebe Barn*, T482417.

Muck

Colour map 3, grid B3

Tiny Muck is the smallest of the four islands and is flat and fertile, with a beautiful shell beach. It has been owned by the MacEwan family since 1879. The island gets its unfortunate name (*muc* is Gaelic for pig) from the porpoises, or "sea pigs", that swim round its shores. The ferry drops anchor near **Port Mór**, and you can stay at **D** *Port Mór House*, T462365. The price includes dinner which is also available to non-residents. Alternatively, you can ask permission to camp at the tearoom, which does snacks and sells fresh bread.

Rùm

Colour map 3, grid A3

Rùm, or Rhum (the extra 'h' was added to avoid alcoholic associations) is the largest of the islands and the most wild, beautiful and mountainous. The island is owned and run by *Scottish Natural Heritage* as an enormous outdoor laboratory and research station, and most of the 30 or so inhabitants are employed by them. Studies of the red deer population is one the most important areas of their work and access to parts of the island is restricted. This is not prohibitive, though, and there are many marked nature trails, walks and bird-watching spots. The island is a haven for wildlife and perhaps its most notable resident is the magnificent white-tailed sea eagle, successfully re-introduced onto Rùm in the 1980s and now spreading beyond the island. Rùm is also home to golden eagles, Manx shearwaters and, less appealingly, millions of midges. The island is the wettest of the Small Isles and a haven for the little pests.

Rùm's other great attraction is its mountain range, which rivals that of the Cuillins of Skye. The highest point is **Askival** (2,664 ft), which can be reached by the main ridge from **Hallival**, though the route involves some rock scrambling and is only advised for fit and experienced walkers. Before setting out, you'll need to ask permission from the manager of the reserve office at the *White House* (T462026).

Though it looks like a wilderness, Rùm once supported a population of 300. Most of them were shipped off to Canada in the mid-19th century, leaving behind an uninhabited deer forest for sporting millionaires. One of these, John Bullough, bought it in 1888 and passed it on to his son, Sir George Bullough, who built the extravagant and extraordinary **Kinloch Castle**. No expense was spared on this massive late-Victorian mansion, constructed of red sandstone from Arran in a bizarre combination of styles, and to describe it as over-the-top would be a gross understatement. It is currently undergoing a £14 million refurbishment.

The castle stands at the head of narrow Loch Scresort by the little hamlet of **Kinloch**, where you'll find a well-stocked shop, a post office and a coffee shop in the community hall. Ferries are anchored in the loch and passengers are transferred to a smaller craft and dropped a few minutes' walk along the shore from Kinloch.

Rùm

The Bullough family mausoleum, built in the style of a Greek Doric temple, stands incongruously on the west coast at **Harris Bay**. It's an interesting 7½ mile walk across to the mausoleum from Kinloch.

Sleeping

Accommodation on the island is limited: most people visit on a day trip

If you plan to stay longer than the day book well in advance. Rooms in *Kinloch Castle* are no longer available but there is cheap hostel accommodation in the old servants' quarters, including double rooms; open Mar-Oct. For bookings and more information, T462037, castlemanager@rumcastle.free_/online.co.uk There are also a couple of cheap and basic **bothies** (F), and **camping** is allowed at Kinloch. Contact the reserve manager, T462026.

Canna

Colour map 3, grid A3

There are no shops on Canna, so you'll need to bring your own supplies

Canna is the most westerly of the Small Isles and is owned by the *National Trust for Scotland*. It's a small island, five miles long by one mile wide, bounded by cliffs and with a rugged interior, fringed by fertile patches. It's attached to its smaller neighbour, **Sanday**, by a narrow isthmus which is covered, except at low tide. The main attraction for visitors is some fine walking. It's about a mile from the ferry jetty up to the top of **Compass Hill** (458 ft), so called because its high metallic content distorts compasses. The highest point on the island is **Carn a' Ghaill** (690 ft).

During the summer, a day trip from Mallaig allows you over nine hours in which to explore Canna and enjoy the fantastic views across to Rùm and Skye.

The population of 20 mostly work on the island's farm. Canna was gifted to the National Trust by its benevolent owner, Dr John Lorne, a notable Gaelic scholar who still lives there. The island continues to be run as a single working farm and, since it was sold in 1938, has been an unofficial bird sanctuary with 157 recorded bird species, including Manx shearwater and puffins.

Sleeping Those wishing to stay put, can **camp** rough, with permission from the National Trust for Scotland, or rent out their self-catering cottage, T0131-226 5922.

Canna & Sanday

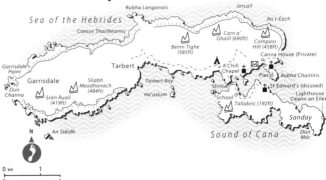

Central Highlands

5

Central Highlands

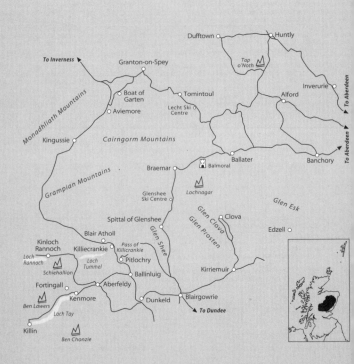

The vast swathe of Central Highlands is not a distinct region but rather the sum of disparate parts of other regions, including Perthshire, the Trossachs, Angus Glens, Deeside, Don Valley, the Grampians, Speyside and Strathspey and Loch Lomond. The historically important regions of Perthshire and Stirling straddle the Highland Boundary Fault, the dividing line between the heavily-populated Central Lowlands and the wild, remote Highlands. Just across this 'border' is the **Trossachs**, *a beautiful area of mountains, forests, lochs and steep-sided glens that stretches west from* **Callander**, *and the glens of* **Perthshire**, *marinated in the rich sauce of Scottish history and seasoned with lochs and mountains.*

The spectacular and varied landscape ranges from the gentle pleasures of **Loch Tay** *to the rugged peaks of the* **Grampian Mountains**, *where there are Munros aplenty for the bagging and decent winter skiing. In the far west, on the eastern shores of* **Loch Lomond**, *is the* **West Highland Way**, *Scotland's most popular long-distance hike. In the northeast, in the* **Spey valley**, *are those tasty staples of a Highland tourist diet – whisky and salmon – while to the east, not far from Aberdeen, are some of Scotland's most notable castles, one of which plays host every year to the most famous family in the UK.*

Ins and outs

Getting there **By air** This region is served by airports at Aberdeen, Dundee and Inverness, which receive flights from London, as well as the major airports at Glasgow and Edinburgh.

By road The the main route north from the Central Lowlands to the Highlands is the A9 which runs from Perth to Inverness. It continues south from Perth almost as far as Stirling, where it becomes the M9 and runs all the way to Glasgow. The M90 north from Edinburgh meets the A9 at Perth. These routes are well served by regular buses from Edinburgh and Glasgow.

By rail There is also a regular train service from Edinburgh and Glasgow north to Inverness, via Perth and Aviemore.

Getting around Though the more remote northerly parts of the region are difficult to reach by public transport, much of the region is easily accessible. The towns of Perth and Stirling are transport hubs and one of the country's main train lines, from Perth passes through the region. A good network of intercity and local buses connects all the main towns and villages. The main road north to Inverness, the A9, runs through the eastern part of the region, and the main route north from Glasgow, the A82, forms its western boundary.

Tourist information The area north of Perth to Loch Tay, and from Glenshee in the east to Rannoch Moor in the west, is covered by the *Perthshire Tourist Board*, www.perthshire.co.uk, with Tourist Information Centres in Aberfeldy, Blairgowrie, Crieff, Dunkeld, Perth and Pitlochry. The Trossachs and Loch Lomond are all covered by the *Argyll, the Isles, Loch Lomond, Stirling & the Trossachs Tourist Board*, www.scottish.heartlands.org, with Tourist Information Centres in Aberfoyle, Callander and Killin. The Angus Glens are covered by the *Angus & Dundee Tourist Board*, with offices in Dundee, Kirriemuir, Forfar and Brechin, www.angusanddundee.co.uk Strathspey and the Cairngorms are covered by the *Highlands of Scotland Tourist Board*, with an office in Aviemore, www.host.co.uk Deeside, the Don Valley and Speyside are covered by the *Aberdeen & Grampian Tourist Board*, with offices in Banchory, Ballater, Inverurie, Tomintoul and Dufftown. The various tourist boards can provide information and literature on accommodation and various outdoor activities such as walking, cycling, golf and fishing.

Loch Lomond

Colour map 4, grid C1 *Britain's largest inland waterway, measuring 22 miles long and up to five miles wide, is Scotland's most famous (uninhabited!) loch, thanks to the Jacobite ballad about its "bonnie banks". These same banks are now one of the busiest parts of the Highlands, due to their proximity to Glasgow, (only 20 miles south on the congested A82). During the summer the loch becomes a playground for day-trippers who tear up and down the loch in speedboats and on jet skis, obliterating any notion visitors may have of a little peace and quiet.*

The **west bank** of the loch, from Balloch north to Tarbet, is one long, almost uninterrupted development of marinas, holiday homes, caravan parks and exclusive golf clubs. The most picturesque village on the west bank, **Luss**, is the setting for the Scottish TV soap *Take the High Road*, and is full of visitors buying souvenir tea towels and hoping to catch a glimpse of one of the 'stars'. The **Loch Lomond Authority Visitor Centre**, T01436-860601, next to the

★

Things to do in the Central Highlands

- *Visit the beautiful Perthshire village of* **Fortingall**, *said to be the birthplace of Pontius Pilate.*
- *Take the High Road to* **Loch Lomond**, *but stick to the quiet east bank.*
- *Travel the road from Aberfoyle to Callander, through the spectacular* **Duke's Pass**, *one of the most*
- *beautiful routes in the country.*
- *Climb to the summit of mysterious* **Lochnagar**, *subject of a book by Prince Charles.*
- *Visit the* **Strathisla whisky distillery**, *the oldest working distillery in the Highlands.*

large car park in the village, has information on the loch's natural history, flora and fauna. ■ *Easter-Oct daily 1000-1800.*

Balloch to Tarbet

At the southern end of the loch is the resort town of **Balloch**, packed full of hotels, B&Bs, caravan parks and any number of operators offering **boat trips** around the loch's overcrowded waters. Try *Sweeney's Cruises*, T01389-752376 or *Mullen's Cruises*, T01389-751481, which both offer a wide range of trips, starting at around £5 for an hour. A daily 2½-hour cruise from Balloch to Luss, leaves at 1430. There's also a **tourist information centre**. ■ *Apr-Jun, Sep and Oct daily 1000-1700; Jul and Aug 0930-1930.* T01389-753533.

North of **Tarbet**, at the narrow northern end of the loch, things quieten down a great deal and the road to **Ardlui**, at its northern tip, is very beautiful and peaceful. The A82 continues north of Ardlui, past **Inverarnan**, to meet the A85 at **Crianlarich** (see page 157). There's a **tourist information centre** in Tarbet. ■ *Apr-Oct. T01301-702260.*

East bank and Ben Lomond

The tranquil **east bank** of Loch Lomond is a great place for walking. The **West Highland Way** (see page 52) follows the east bank all the way from **Drymen**, through **Balmaha**, **Rowardennan** and **Inversnaid**. Beyond Rowardennan this is the only access to the loch's east bank, except for the road to Inversnaid from the Trossachs. From Rowardennan you can climb **Ben Lomond** (3,192 ft), the most southerly of the Munros. It's not too difficult and the views from the top (in good weather) are astounding. There are two routes: the easier one starts from the car park at the end of the road just beyond the *Rowardennan Hotel*; the other route, known as the 'Ptarmigan Route', starts from beyond the youth hostel. You can also go up by one route and return by the other. Allow about five to six hours there and back.

OS Landranger map 58

An easier climb is **Conic Hill**, on the Highland fault line and very close to Glasgow. The route starts from the Balmaha car park. It takes about 1½ hours to reach the top, from where the views of the loch are stunning.

Essentials

There are numerous hotels and B&Bs in Balloch, Luss, Inverbeg and Tarbet. In **Balloch**, the best of the B&Bs is the **E** *Gowanlea Guest House*, on Drymen Rd, T752456, gowanlea@aol.com There's a good **campsite** at *Tullichewan Holiday Park*, T759475,

Sleeping & eating

Central Highlands

on the Old Luss Rd, where you can hire **mountain bikes**. A few miles further on up the west bank, in **Arden**, is **F** *Loch Lomond SYHA Youth Hostel* , T850226, a grand 19th-century turreted mansion complete with the obligatory ghost. A few miles north of Luss, at **Inverbeg**, is the **C-B** *Inverbeg Inn*, T01436-860678, which does good food.

On the **eastern shore** there's a **F** *SYHA Youth Hostel* at **Rowardennan**, T01360-870259, open Jan-Oct. There's also the **C** *Rowardennan Hotel*, T01360-870273, which offers a bit more comfort and serves bar meals. There are a couple of **campsites** on the east bank, at *Milarrochy Bay*, T01360-870236, open end Mar to Oct, near Balmaha, and the Forestry Commission campsite at *Cashel*, T01360-870234, a few miles further north. On the northeast shore, and only accessible by road via the B829 from Aberfoyle, is the splendidly isolated **D** *Inversnaid Hotel*, T01877-386223.

In **Ardlui**, at the northern tip of the loch, is the comfortable **C** *Ardlui Hotel*, T01301-704243. A few miles north, at **Inverarnan**, is the *Drover's Inn*, T01301-704234, the famous Highland watering hole, with smoke-blackened walls, low ceilings, bare floors, open fires, a hall filled with stuffed animals, barman in kilt and a great selection of single malts. The perfect place for a wild night of drinking in the wilderness. It simply doesn't get any better than this.

Transport *Scottish Citylink*, T0990-505050, **buses** run regularly from Glasgow to **Balloch** (45 mins) and on to **Luss** and **Tarbet** (1 hr 10 mins). Some buses go to **Ardlui** (1 hr 20 mins) and on to **Crianlarich**.

There's a passenger **ferry service** across the loch between **Inverbeg** and **Rowardennan**, T01360-870273, 3 times daily. There are also ferries between **Inveruglas** and **Inversnaid**, T01877-386223.

There are 2 **rail** lines from Glasgow to Loch Lomond. One runs to **Balloch** every 30 mins (35 mins). the other is the West Highland line to Fort William and Mallaig, with a branch line to Oban. It reaches Loch Lomond at **Tarbet** and there's another station further north at **Ardlui**.

The Trossachs

Strictly speaking, the Trossachs is the narrow wooded glen between **Loch Katrine** *and* **Loch Achray**, *but the name is now used to describe a much larger area between Argyll and Perthshire, stretching north from the* **Campsies** *and west from* **Callander** *to the eastern shore of Loch Lomond. It's a very beautiful and diverse area of sparkling lochs, craggy mountains and deep, forested glens and for this reason is often called the 'Highlands in miniature'. Visit in the autumn when the hills are purple and the trees are a thousand luminous hues, from lustrous gold to flaming scarlet and blazing orange.*

The Trossachs was one of the country's first holiday regions, and remains a major tourist destination. Its enduring appeal is due in no small measure to Sir Walter Scott, who eulogized its great natural beauty in his epic poem, Lady of the Lake, *and whose historical novel,* Rob Roy *brought to public attention the region's other great attraction, Rob Roy MacGregor, one of the great romantic Highland figures.*

Ins and outs

Getting there Stirling is the nearest large town to the Trossachs and there are regular **buses** to and from Callander and Aberfoyle. There's also a daily bus service to Aberfoyle from Glasgow. There are frequent **trains** to Stirling from Glasgow and Edinburgh.

The *Trossachs Trundler* is an old vintage **bus** which makes a circuit of the Trossachs, linking Stirling, Callander, Loch Katrine, Aberfoyle and Port of Menteith and stopping off at various scenic places *en route*. It also connects with departures of the *SS Sir Walter Scott* on Loch Katrine. It runs from Jun-Sep, Mon-Fri and Sun and costs £8.10 for a day ticket. Contact the local tourist office for details

Walking in the Trossachs

The Trossachs is superb walking country. The two most challenging peaks are *OS Landranger maps* **Ben Venue** and **Ben A'an** around Loch Katrine and Loch Achray, about 10 *56 and 57* miles west of Callander. **Ben Venue** (2,385 ft) is the more difficult climb. It starts from behind the *Loch Achray Hotel* and is waymarked, but it's a strenuous climb which requires hill walking experience, proper clothing and all the usual safety precautions (see page 53). Allow about five hours for the return trip. **Ben A'an** (1,520 ft) isn't a giant of a hill but it's a steep climb from the car park on the north bank of Loch Achray, west of the former *Trossachs Hotel* (now a timeshare development), and there's a bit of scrambling involved near the summit. It takes about 1½ hours to the top. The views from both hills are stupendous on clear days, but remember that the weather is as unpredictable in the Trossachs mountains as anywhere else in the Highlands. A useful guide is Bartholomew's *Walk Loch Lomond and the Trossachs*.

Both these mountains lie within the **Queen Elizabeth Forest Park**. This vast and spectacular wilderness of 75,000 acres borders Loch Lomond to the west and incorporates Loch Ard, Loch Achray and Loch Lubnaig, as well as Ben Venue, Ben A'An and **Ben Ledi** which overlooks Callander. The park is run by the Forestry Commission and is criss-crossed by a network of less difficult waymarked trails and paths which start from the Queen Elizabeth Park **Visitor Centre**, about half a mile north of Aberfoyle on the A821. Available at the centre are audio-visual displays on the park's flora and fauna and information on the numerous walks and cycle routes around the park. ■ *Apr-Oct daily 1000-1800; Nov-Mar Sat and Sun only 1000-1600 (parking £1). T01877-382258. Full details of the park are available from the* **Forest Enterprise** *in Aberfoyle, (same tel no).*

Aberfoyle

The sleepy little village of Aberfoyle suddenly bursts into life in the summer *Phone code: 01877* with the arrival of hordes of tourists. It lies on the edge of Queen Elizabeth *Colour map 4, grid C1* Forest Park and, along with Callander to the east, is one of the main tourist centres for the Trossachs. It makes an ideal base for walking and cycling in the surrounding hills. There's plentiful accommodation, though you'll have to book during the busy summer season. The **tourist office** is on the main street. ■ *Mar-Jun, Sep and Oct daily 1000-1700; Jul and Aug 0930-1900. T382352.*

Three miles east of Aberfoyle is the **Lake of Menteith**, the only lake in Scotland (as opposed to loch). On Inchmahome island in the middle of the lake are the beautiful and substantial ruins of **Inchmahome Priory**, the 13th-century Augustinian priory where the four-year-old Mary, Queen of Scots was sent in 1547, safe from the clutches of Henry VIII. A **ferry** takes visitors over to the island from **Port of Menteith**. ■ *Apr-Sep daily 0930 till last sailing at 1715. Adult £3.30, concession £2.50, children £1.20. Ferry included in admission price. T385294 (HS).* The lake is also a popular spot for **fly-fishing** and you can rent boats from *Lake of Menteith Fisheries*, T385664, April-October.

To the south of Aberfoyle is Doon Hill, better known as the **Fairy Knowe**. The tree at the top is said to be the home of the 'People of Quietness' and in

1692 a local minister was less than discreet in telling the world of their secrets. As punishment, he was taken away to fairyland and his spirit has languished there ever since. If you go round the tree seven times, your wish will be granted, but go round it backwards and... well, we won't be held responsible. It's about an hour up and back. Cross the bridge over the Forth River and head past the cemetery, then follow the signs.

Sleeping The best place to stay in the area is the **A-B** *Lake Hotel*, in Port of Menteith, situated on the lakeshore overlooking Inchmahome, T385258, www.lake-of-menteith-hotel.com It's stylish, comfortable, very romantic and boasts a fine restaurant (lunch mid-range; dinner expensive). Across the river is the **D** *Covenanters Hotel*, T382347, F382785. **C** with excellent dinner, friendly and comfortable, serves a good breakfast, good value. There are dozens of **B&Bs** in and around Aberfoyle, including **E** *Tigh-na-Cruinn*, T382760, open Apr-Sep, and the lovely **C** *Creag-Ard House* in Milton, 2 miles west of Aberfoyle overlooking Loch Ard, T382297, with fishing and boat hire available. **Camping** is available at *Cobeland Campsite*, T382392, open Apr-Oct, 2 miles south of Aberfoyle on the edge of Queen Elizabeth Forest Park, and the excellent *Trossachs Holiday Park*, T382614, open Mar-Oct, set in 40 acres with **mountain bike hire**.

Eating There are several decent **eating** places in the village. The *Forth Inn*, on Main St, T382488, is a cosy wee pub with a good restaurant and rooms to let (**E**). Also on Main St is *The Coach House*, T382822, which serves good pub food. Best place to eat is the excellent and very popular *Braeval Old Mill*, T382711, a few miles east on the A873 to Port of Menteith.

Transport There are regular **buses** to and from **Stirling** with *First Edinburgh*, T01324-613777. There are also daily services from **Glasgow**, via Balfron. There's a **postbus service**, T01463-256200, from Aberfoyle to **Callander** via Port of Menteith (Mon-Fri in the afternoon) and another (Mon-Sat) from Aberfoyle to **Inversnaid** on Loch Lomond (see page 151).

Aberfoyle to Callander The A821 route north from Aberfoyle, through the spectacular **Duke's Pass**, and then east past Loch Achray and Loch Vennachar, is one of the most beautiful routes in the country and not to be missed. There are a couple of worthwhile diversions along the way. About five miles north of Aberfoyle, a track branches to the right and runs through Achray Forest and along the shores of Loch Drunkie, before rejoining the A821 further north. A few miles further on, a road turns left to **Trossachs Pier** on the eastern shore of **Loch Katrine**. This is the departure point for **cruises** on the *SS Sir Walter Scott*, T376316. In the mornings (Sunday to Friday) it sails to the remote settlement of **Stronachlachar** on the far western shores of the loch and back. In the afternoons it only sails around the loch for an hour. ■ *Cruises depart end of Mar to end of Oct: to Stronachlachar and back Sun-Fri at 1100, arriving at 1145 and returning at 1200; around the loch at 1345 and 1515. Morning cruises cost £6 return, £4.40 one way (£4.20 and £2.90 for OAPs and under 16s); afternoon cruises £5.20, concessions £3.60.*

There's a road and cycle path around the loch as far as Stronachlachar and you could take the morning cruise there and then cycle back to the pier. **Cycle hire** from *Trossachs Cycle Hire*, T382614, for around £8 per half day and £16 per full day.

The road then swings east along the northern shores of luscious Loch Achray and Loch Venachar, past the village of **Brig o' Turk**, which was the backdrop for the classic film of John Buchan's 39 Steps. There's a nice *Tearoom & Restaurant* in the village, T376267.

Callander

Callander sits at the eastern end of the Trossachs, 14 miles northwest of Stirling, its wide streets totally and unashamedly devoted to tourism and lined with tearooms, restaurants and craft shops. The town's overworked **Tourist Information Centre** is on the main street, in Ancaster Square. ■ *T330342. Same opening times as visitor centre below.* It shares the same building as the **Rob Roy and Trossachs Visitor Centre** which gives an entertaining account of the life of Rob Roy MacGregor. ■ *Mar-May and Oct-Dec daily 1000-1700; Jun and Sep 0930-1800; Jul and Aug 0900-1900; Jan and Feb weekends only 1000-1700. Adult £3.25, students £2.50, children & OAPs £2.25.*

Phone code: 01877
Colour map 4, grid C2
Population: 2,500

Sleeping

If you want something a wee bit special, then head for the **A** *Roman Camp Country House Hotel*, T330003, www.roman-camp-hotel.co.uk An exquisite 16th-century hunting lodge set in extensive grounds by the river, away from the hoi polloi. Queen Victoria was quite taken with the place. Also superb Scottish cuisine (expensive). For something a bit more down-to-earth, there's a huge selection of B&B accommodation, including the highly recommended **C-D** *Arran Lodge*, open Mar-Oct, on Leny Rd. Also recommended are: **D-E** *Brook Linn Country House*, T330103, open Mar-Nov, a fine Victorian house overlooking the town; **D-E** *Arden House*, T/F330235, open Mar-Nov, on Bracklinn Rd; **D-E** *The Priory*, T/F330001, open Easter-Oct, also on Bracklinn Rd; and **D-E** *Dunmor Guest House*, T330756, open Apr-Oct, on Leny Rd.

A couple of miles out of town, along the Invertrossachs Rd, which turns off the A81, is the **F** *Trossachs Backpackers*, T331200, trosstel@aol.com, an independent hostel which also **rents bikes**. There's also **camping** at *Gart Caravan Park*, Stirling Rd, T330002, open Apr to mid-Oct.

Eating

The best place to eat is the *Roman Camp Hotel* (see above). Otherwise the hotels and pubs offer bar meals. Most of the places along the main street are overpriced, but the *Ben Ledi Café* offers good-value basic grub. A few miles north of town, at Kilmahog, is the highly-rated *Lade Inn*, T330152.

Transport

There are regular **buses** to and from **Stirling** (45 mins). There's a *Scottish Citylink* service once daily between Edinburgh and Fort William which stops in Callander. A **postbus** leaves daily, except Sun, at 0915 to **Trossachs Pier** and connects with **cruises** on Loch Katrine (see 'Aberfoyle to Callander' above). There's also a postbus between Callander and **Aberfoyle**, via **Port of Menteith** (Mon-Fri in the afternoon).

Central Highlands

Callander

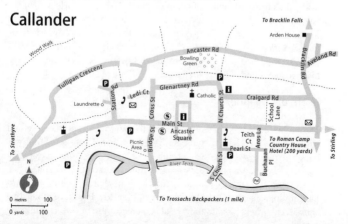

Rob Roy

As the tourist board never tires of reminding us, the Trossachs is Rob Roy country. Rob Roy ('Red Robert' in Gaelic) was one of Scotland's most notorious outlaws or one the bravest Highland heroes, depending on your point of view. It is true that he was a freebooter, but he was also defending Highland clan culture and more specifically fighting for the very survival of his own clan against proscription and persecution by government and its supporters.

Rob Roy MacGregor (1671-1734) was born in Glengyle, to the northwest of Loch Katrine. The MacGregors' lands included those previously owned by the rival Campbells but bestowed on the MacGregors for services rendered to Alexander II in his conquest of Argyll. For a long time the clan kept possession of their lands by right of the sword, but the constant attempts by neighbouring clans to displace them led to retaliation by the MacGregors and earned them a reputation for being aggressive. Rob Roy did little to change this image and his bitter feud with the powerful Duke of Montrose led to his being outlawed and eventually captured and sentenced to transportation. He was pardoned and returned to Balquhidder, where he stayed for the rest of his life. He now lies buried in the churchyard.

The Rob Roy story was first popularized by Sir Walter Scott's eponymous 19th-century novel and his life continues to be romanticized, most recently in the 1995 film starring Liam Neeson and Tim Roth. Like Robin Hood before him, his courage in refusing to bow to the forces of authority seems to strike a chord with people.

Walks & cycle routes around Callander
OS Landranger No 57

Callander is also a good base for exploring the Trossachs. A recommended local walk is to **Bracklinn Falls**, reached by a woodland trail which leads from Bracklinn Road. It's about 30 minutes each way. Another trail from Bracklinn Road leads up to **Callander Crags**, from where there are great views of the surrounding area. Allow 1½ hours there and back. The most challenging walk in the area is to the summit of **Ben Ledi** (2,857 ft), but it's a tough climb and you'll need to be fit, experienced and prepared (see page 53).

Two miles north of Callander, on the A84 route to the Highlands, are the **Falls of Leny**, in the narrow and dramatic Pass of Leny. The falls are accessible from the car park by the roadside or via the **Callander to Strathyre Cycleway**, which follows the old train line to Oban, from Callandar north along the west bank of **Loch Lubnaig**. This forms part of the **Glasgow to Killin Cycleway**, which runs from the centre of Glasgow, via Balloch, Aberfoyle, Callander, Balquhidder and Lochearnhead, to Killin. This is the best way to see the Trossachs. For more details on cycle routes in the area, get a copy of *25 Cycle Routes: Stirling & Trossachs* by Erl B. Wilkie (HMSO), available at the tourist office or good bookshops. You can **hire bikes** in Callander from *Wheels*, Invertrossachs Road (T331100) for around £10-12 per day.

North of Callander

Colour map 4, grid C2

The A84 heads north from Callander, along the east bank of Loch Lubnaig, and beyond towards **Loch Earn**. At the northern end of Loch Lubnaig, in **Strathyre**, is **C-D** *Creagan House*, T384638, a family-run 17th-century farmhouse offering excellent food (mid-range-expensive) and comfortable accommodation.

A few miles further north, a side road branches left to the tiny village of **Balquhidder**, famous as the burial place of Rob Roy. His grave in the little churchyard, where his wife and two of his sons are also buried, is thankfully understated. The road continues west along the north shire of Loch Voil to **Inverlochlarig**, from where there are numerous excellent opportunities for experienced hillwalkers. The best place by far to stay in these parts is the small, family-run **C** *Monachyle Mhor Hotel*, T384622, on the road to Inverlochlarig. It offers great views of the loch, peace and quiet and fabulous Scottish/French cuisine (lunch mid-range; dinner expensive).

A few miles north of the Balquhidder turn-off, where the A84 meets the A85 from Crieff to Crianlarich, is Lochearnhead, at the western tip of Loch Earn. The loch is a highly popular **watersports centre** and at *Lochearnhead Watersports*, T830330, you can try water-skiing, windsurfing, canoeing and kayaking. Lochearnhead is also a good base for walking in the surrounding hills.

Lochearnhead
Phone code: 01567

Sleeping and eating D *Clachan Cottage Hotel*, T830427, www.clachancottagehotel.com Most other options are **self-catering** cabins and caravans and include *Earnknowe*, T/F830238, cottages for rent, from £120-355 per week for up to 6 people. The best place to eat is the *Four Seasons Hotel*, T685333, at St Fillans, at the east end of the loch.

In the far northwestern corner of Stirling region, just to the west of Loch Tay, is little village of Killin, which makes a good base for walkers wishing to explore the wild mountains and glens of the ancient district of **Breadalbane** (pronounced Bread-*al*binn). Killin's picture-postcard setting, with the beautiful **Falls of Dochart** tumbling through the centre of the village, make it a popular destination for tourists.

Killin
Phone code: 01567

The **Tourist Information Centre** overlooks the falls. In the same building is the **Breadalbane Folklore Centre**, which has displays on local clan history and contains the sacred healing stones of the seventh-century missionary, St Fillan. ■ *TIC and Folklore Centre both open Mar-May and Oct daily 1000-1700; Jun and Sep till 1800; Jul and Aug 0930-1830; Feb weekends only 1000-1600. Adult £2, students £1.50, children & OAPs £1.25. T820254.*

Sleeping and eating The best place to stay is the **C** *Dall Lodge Country House Hotel*, T820217, wislon@dalllodgehotel.co.uk, open Mar-Oct, which offers idiosyncratic style and very good food. Next best choice is the **D** *Killin Hotel*, T820296. Amongst the dozens of **B&Bs** is **E** *Invertay House*, T820492, invertay@btinternet.com There's also a **F** *Youth Hostel*, T820546, open end Feb to end Oct, at the northern end of the village. The **outdoor centre**, T820652, on the main road hires out mountain bikes, as well as climbing equipment.

Transport There are **buses** to Killin (on schooldays only) from **Stirling** via **Callander** (1 ¾ hrs). There's a **postbus** from **Callander** once daily except Sun (1 hr), which continues to **Crianlarich** and **Tyndrum**. There's also a postbus service from **Aberfeldy** (see page 166).

Twelve miles west of Killin is Crianlarich, at the crossroads of the A82 Glasgow-Fort William road and the A85 to Perth, and at the junction of the Glasgow to Fort William and Oban **rail lines**. It is a staging post on the **West Highland Way**. There are many places to stay, including an *SYHA Youth Hostel*, T300260, open all year.

Crianlarich & Tyndrum
Phone code: 01838
Colour map 4, grid C1

Six miles further north is tiny **Tyndrum**, which shot to prominence recently after the discovery of gold in the surrounding hills. There's a **tourist office**, T400246, in the car park of the *Invervey Hotel*. Next to the filling station is a craft/food shop which sells a vast range of single malts, many at discounted prices.

Central Highlands

Transport *Scottish Citylink* **buses**, T0990-505050, between **Glasgow** and **Oban** and Fort William stop in both villages. There's also a **postbus** service between Crianlarich and Tyndrum and **Killin** (Mon-Sat). There are 2 **train stations** at Tyndrum. One serves the Glasgow to Oban line and the other the Glasgow to Fort William line. There are **trains** from both villages to **Fort William**, **Oban** and **Glasgow** (T0345-484950).

Perthshire and Angus

Perth is the main gateway to the eastern side of the Central Highlands and the road north, the A9, is a gentle introduction to the wild northern reaches of Scotland. The Perthshire Highlands may lack the sheer magisterial grandeur of the northwest but they have their own serene beauty.

Dunkeld

Phone code: 01350
Colour map 4,
grid B3

Twelve miles north of Perth is the attractive village of Dunkeld, standing right on the Highland line. Dunkeld is surrounded by beautiful scenery offering excellent walking opportunities, details of which are available from the **Tourist Information Centre**, at The Cross, T727688, in the heart of the village. It's open all year round: April-June, September and October Monday-Saturday 0930-1730, Sunday 1100-1600; July and August Monday-Saturday 0900-1930, Sunday 1100-1900; November and December Monday-Saturday 0930-1330.

It's definitely worth making a stop here, if only to admire the **cathedral**, in the most idyllic situation on the banks of the fast-flowing, silvery Tay. Half of it is still in use as a church and the other half is in ruins. The oldest part of the cathedral is the 14th-century choir which now forms the parish church, while the 15th-century nave and tower are also still standing. Much of the original was damaged during the orgy of ecclesiastical destruction that sadly accompanied the Reformation, then it was damaged again in the Battle of Dunkeld, in 1689, fought between supporters of the protestant William of Orange and the Stuart monarch James VII. ■ *Apr-Sep 0930-1830 (HS), free.* On your way to the cathedral you'll pass a collection of lovely little whitewashed cottages, beautifully restored by the National Trust for Scotland. More details are available at the *Ell Shop* nearby.

Across the bridge from Dunkeld is **Birnam**, made famous by Shakespeare's *Macbeth*, though the play's protagonist was in reality a very different character from the evil villain portrayed by the Bard. Birnam was the inspiration for another famous literary figure, **Beatrix Potter**, who spent her childhood summers here. Visitors can explore the origins of the *Peter Rabbit* stories in the **Beatrix Potter Garden**.

A short distance north of Dunkeld on the A9, is the turning to **The Hermitage**. A marked woodland walk starts from the car park and follows the river Braan to the Black Linn Falls, overlooked by Ossian's Hall, an 18th-century folly built by the Duke of Atholl. It's a lovely spot, which has inspired the likes of Wordsworth and Mendelssohn. Further on is Ossian's Cave. Buses to Pitlochry (see below) stop at the turning for The Hermitage.

A few miles northeast of Dunkeld, off the A923 to Blairgowrie, is the **Loch of the Lowes Visitor Centre**, managed by the Scottish Wildlife Trust. There's a hide with binoculars for viewing a pair of ospreys which breed here and which can be seen on the loch from early April to early September. ■ *Apr-Sep daily 1000-1700. Free (donation advised), T727337.*

The top hotel in the area is **L** *Kinnaird House*, at Dalguise, about 8 miles north via the A9, T01796-482440. The setting, the style and the service are all unbeatable. In the village is the luxurious **L** *Hilton Dunkeld*, T727771, former home of the Duke of Atholl, now with full leisure and outdoor activity facilities. More modest options include **D** *Atholl Arms Hotel* , T727219, by the bridge, or **B&B** at **D** *The Pend*, 5 Brae St, T727586, www.thepend.com, and **E** *Birnam Guest House*, 4 Murthly Terr, Birnam, T727201. There's also a **hostel**, the **F** *Western Caputh Independent Hostel*, at Caputh, 5 miles east of Dunkeld, on the A984 to Coupar Angus, T01738-710617. It has 18 beds and is open all year. **Eating** options are mostly limited to the hotels. The best bar meals are offered by the *Atholl Arms* (see above) and the *Birnam House Hotel*, T727462, on the main road through Birnam.

Citylink **buses** between Perth and Inverness stop at the train station by Birnam several times daily in either direction. *Stagecoach* buses from Perth to Pitlochry and Aberfeldy stop in Dunkeld, and *Strathtay Scottish* buses between Blairgowrie and Aberfeldy also stop in the village (twice daily Mon-Sat). There are several **trains** daily, T08457-484950, to and from Perth and Inverness.

Pitlochry and around

Despite being one of the busiest Highland tourist towns in the summer, Pitlochry's lovely setting on the shores of the river Tummel, overlooked by Ben y Vrackie makes it a pleasant base for exploring this beautiful area. The town also has a few worthwhile attractions of its own.

Getting there The **bus** and **train stations** are on Station Rd, south of the main street. There are regular buses to Perth, Inverness, Edinburgh and Glasgow. Pitlochry is on the main Perth-Inverness rail line, with regular services in either direction.

The **Tourist Information Centre** is at 22 Atholl Rd, T472215.Open 9 Apr-20 May Mon-Sat 0900-1800, Sun 1100-1700; 21 May-9 Sep Mon-Sat 0900-1900; 10 Sep-28 Oct Mon-Sat 0900-1800, Sun 1100-1700; 29 Oct-24 Mar Mon-Fri 0900-1700, Sat 1000-1400. They sell a useful leaflet *Pitlochry Walks* (£0.50), which describes four long local walks, but there are many other fine walks in the surrounding area.

Sights

There are two whisky distilleries to visit. The larger of the two is Bell's **Blair Atholl Distillery**, at the southern end of town, heading towards the A9 to Perth. ■ *Easter-Sep Mon-Sat 0900-1700, Sun 1200-1700; Oct-Easter Mon-Fri only, tours every 10 mins. £3. T482003.* A couple of miles east of town, on the A924, is the **Edradour Distillery**, the smallest in Scotland. ■ *Mar-Oct Mon-Sat 0930-1700, Sun 1200-1700; Nov and Dec Mon-Sat 1000-1600. Free. T472095.*

Pitlochry's main attraction is the **fish ladder**, part of the **power station and dam** which formed man-made **Loch Faskally** when it was constructed on the River Tummel. The ladder allows salmon to swim up to their spawning grounds and you can watch them leap spectacularly in the spring and summer. The best months are May and June. The fish ladder is across the river, a short distance from the *Pitlochry Festival Theatre* (see below).

Essentials

Sleeping
There's plenty of accommodation to choose from

The best hotel in town is the superb **A** *Pine Trees Hotel*, Strathview Terr, T472121. This Victorian country house is set in 10 acres of gardens away from the tourist bustle. Its *Garden Restaurant* has a fine reputation. A few miles north of Pitlochry, in the village of Killiecrankie, is the **B** *Killiecrankie Hotel*, T473220, www.btinternet.com/~killie-crankie.hotel/index.html Open Mar-Dec, 11 rooms, it's a quiet, cosy country house hotel which offers quite possibly the very finest food in the area. Another top-class hotel is the **C-D** *Dunfallandy Country House Hotel & Restaurant*, T472648, dunfalhse@aol.com, a mile out of town on the Logierait road. 9 rooms, this Georgian mansion offers great views, peace and quiet and superb cuisine, no smoking, excellent value. There are numerous guesthouses and B&Bs, far too many to list here. The tourist office will provide a full list. Among the most recommended are **D** *Craigroyston House*, 2 Lower Oakfield, T472053, **E** *Arrandale House*, Knockfarrie Rd, T472987, and **E** *Tordarroch*, T472136, which also has the bonus of a lovely garden. There's a **F** *SYHA Youth Hostel*, T472308, open all year, on Knockard Rd overlooking the town centre.

Eating

The *Killiecrankie Hotel* (see above) is expensive but the best place to eat. The best restaurant in town is *Port-na-Craig Inn & Restaurant*, T472777, which is just below the Festival Theatre on the banks of the river Tummel. It offers great Scottish cooking at mid-range prices in a bistro ambience. Another good choice is the *Old Smiddy*, at 154 Atholl Rd, T472356, which is mid-range open daily till 2100. A couple of miles south of Pitlochry on the old A9 road is the *East Haugh Country House Hotel & Restaurant* , T473121, www.world-traveller.com/scotland.east.html, a 17th-century country house with excellent and elegant dining and great bar lunches (lunch mid-range; dinner expensive). A few miles north of Pitlochry, at Moulin on the A924 is the wonderful *Moulin Inn*, T472196, which serves good, hearty and cheap pub food, fine real ales (try their 'Braveheart') and a great atmosphere. Food daily till 2130.

Entertainment

The *Pitlochry Festival Theatre*, T472680, is across the river from the town centre. It stages a different play every night for 6 nights a week during its season from May to Oct.

Shopping

MacNaughton's, Station Rd. A vast range of everything tartan and lots more besides. Come here first.

Transport

Scottish Citylink **buses** run almost every hour between **Glasgow** (2 hrs 15 mins), **Edinburgh** (2 hrs 45 mins) and **Inverness** (2 hrs) via Pitlochry. *Stagecoach* buses run daily except Sun to **Aberfeldy**, **Dunkeld** and **Perth**. Pitlochry is on the Perth-Inverness rail line and there are several daily **trains** (Mon-Sat; fewer on Sun) to and from Perth (30 mins). **Cycle hire** *Escape Route*, 8 West Moulin Rd, T/F473859. Touring and off-road bikes for around £15 per day. **Taxi** *Elizabeth Yule Transport*, T472290.

Around Pitlochry

Killiecrankie

Four miles north of Pitlochry the A9 cuts through the **Pass of Killiecrankie**, a spectacular wooded gorge which was the dramatic setting for the Battle of Killiecrankie in 1689, when a Jacobite army led by Graham of Claverhouse, Viscount 'Bonnie Dundee', defeated the government forces under General Hugh Mackay. One government soldier evaded capture by making a jump of Olympic gold medal-winning proportions across the river Garry at **Soldier's Leap**. An National Trust for Scotland **visitor centre** has displays on the battle and the local natural history. ■ *Apr-Oct daily 1000-1730. Free (honesty box; £1 donation advised). T473233.*

The greatest walking attraction is **Ben y Vrackie** (2,758 ft), a steep six-mile walk (there and back) from the tiny hamlet of Moulin, a mile north of Pitlochry on the A924 (turn left at the *Moulin Inn*). The path is well trodden and the going is relatively easy, across bleak moorland, until the steep final ascent on scree. On a clear day the views from the summit of the Trossachs are wonderful, so it's best not to attempt this on a cloudy day. In spite of its proximity to Pitlochry, you need to be properly equipped and take the usual safety precautions (see page 53).

Another excellent walk from Pitlochry, described in the tourist office leaflet, leaves town on the north road and turns left past the boat station. It then crosses the Cluanie footbridge and follows the road to Loch Faskally and up the river Garry to Garry Bridge over the **Pass of Killiecrankie** (see page 160). The path returns to Pitlochry along the west banks of the river Garry, before turning west up the river Tummel, passing close by the **Linn of Tummel**, then crossing the Tummel and following the west shore of Loch Faskally to the dam and fish ladder.

Walks around Pitlochry
OS Landranger maps Nos 43 and 52 cover all the walks & the OS Explorer map No 21 (Pitlochry & Loch Tummel) covers them in greater detail

Seven miles from Pitlochry, and a mile from the village of Blair Atholl, is Blair Castle, traditional seat of the Earls and Dukes of Atholl. This whitewashed, turreted castle dates from 1269 and presents an impressive picture on first sight. This is the headquarters of Britain's only private army, the Atholl Highlanders, and one of them usually pipes in new arrivals. Thirty-two rooms in the castle are open for public viewing and are packed full of paintings, furniture, armour, porcelain and much else besides, presenting a startling picture of aristocratic Highland life in previous centuries. The most outrageously sumptuous of the rooms are the Tapestry Room and the ballroom. The surrounding landscaped grounds are home to peacocks and Highland cattle, and there are woodland walks and a walled Japanese water garden to enjoy. ■ *Apr-Oct 1000-1800 (last admission 1700). Adult £6.25, concession £5.25, children £4; plus £2 parking charge. T481207.*

There's a **caravan park** within the castle grounds, T481263, open April-October, with good facilities. A very good **walk** starts from the caravan park and heads up into **Glen Tilt**. It's about 10½ miles there and back along estate roads, though this can be shortened by four miles or lengthened by six miles. A leaflet describing the routes is available from the castle or caravan park.

Blair Atholl & Blair Castle
Phone code: 01796
Colour map 4, grid B3

Sleeping There's a selection of accommodation in Blair Atholl village. The **B** *Atholl Arms Hotel*, T481205, near the train station does B&B and serves bar meals.

Transport Not all **trains** stop at Blair Atholl. *Elizabeth Yule Transport* (see Pitlochry Transport above) runs a service between Pitlochry and Blair Atholl, via Killiecrankie, a few times daily, except Sun. You can **hire bikes** from *Atholl Mountain Bikes*, T473553, for around £12 per day. They have a leaflet listing various cycle routes, including the Glen Tilt route above.

Eight miles from Blair Atholl, just off the A9, are the Falls of Bruar. There's a short walk from the car park to the lower falls, but it's worth continuing to the more dramatic upper falls, which are less visited (see above). By the car park is the excellent **House of Bruar**, a huge shopping emporium designed like a Victorian hunting lodge where you can buy just about any kind of souvenir and enjoy some very fine Scottish cooking.

Falls of Bruar

Central Highlands

Blair Atholl to Glen Fincastle walk

A lovely three-mile linear walk leads from Blair Atholl village to Glen Fincastle, passing through woodland and across moorland and pasture. Starting in the village, head down past the watermill and stay on the road until it ends at the river. Then follow a path left till it takes you to a footbridge over the River Garry. Cross the footbridge and then over two stiles till you reach the main A9. Cross the road, taking care as it's usually busy, to another stile, then continue through trees to a gate with a footprint sign. On the otherside of the gate, the path zigzags up through a wood which thins out as you reach the top of the hill. Here, the path fords a stream then continues across open moorland to the other side of the hilltop, where there's a gate. Go through the gate and follow the grassy track down to Tomanraid cottage. From here you can see down into Glen Fincastle. Before the cottage go left over a stile and then down to a gate. Through the gate, head straight along the track till you reach a junction. Go through the gate ahead and donw a grassy lane to another gate. Then the path curves diagonally to the left down to a metal gate at the end of a public road. To return to BlairAtholl simply retrace your steps.

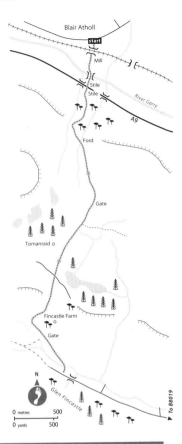

Central Highlands

Loch Tummel & Loch Rannoch
Phone code: 01796
Colour map 4, grid B2

The B8019 turns off the B8079 road from Pitlochry to Blair Atholl and runs west along the shores of beautiful lochs Tummel and Rannoch, best seen in the autumn when the trees change their colours. At the eastern end of Loch Tummel is **Queen's View**, a spectacular viewpoint which looks down the loch and across to Schiehallion. There's a **visitor centre** here, with displays and audio-visual programmes about the area. ■ *Apr-Oct daily 1000-1730. Free, but £1 parking charge. T473123.*

Kinloch Rannoch
Colour map 4, grid B2

Beyond Loch Tummel is the little village of Kinloch Rannoch, where backpackers can stock up on supplies before heading into the hills. There are a few **places to stay** in the village, including the characterful **C** *Dunalastair Hotel*, T01882-632323, and **E** *Bunrannoch House*, T01882-632407, a former Victorian shooting lodge which offers good cooking.

Sixteen miles west of the village the road ends at Rannoch station, where you can catch trains north to Fort William or south to Glasgow. Beyond the west end of Loch Rannoch is bleak Rannoch Moor which extends all the way to Glen Coe. By the station is the **E-D** *Moor of Rannoch Hotel*, T01882-633238, which does good, moderately priced meals. There's a daily

Pass of Killiecrankie walk

A three-mile waymarked trail around the RSPB Killcrankie Nature Reserve starts from the Balrobbie Farm car park. Follow the signs for the reserve from Killiecrankie village, take the minor road over the River Garry, then take the left fork up a steep hill. Turn right at the sharp bend into the farm car park. Access to the reserve is free, but there's a cairn for donations and a parking charge.

Head down the driveway, then turn right along the road which climbs uphill below wooded crags. Turn right through as gate, opposite a cottage and follow a grassy track to a gate in a stone wall. Through the gate, the path climbs diagonally under the crags to an iron gate beside a bench. Go through the gate and the path zigzags steeply up to an area of open marsh. The path curves right and continues to climb across a heather moor and past a ruin. At the crest of the hill, from where there are wonderful views down to Blair Atholl, go downhill, over a stile and enter woodland. Beyond the trees is another bench, then the trail turns to the right. After another two stiles the path heads left downhill, then zigzags down a rocky slope, before heading diagonally downhill to the right to an iron gate. Pick up the path again by a stone wall and follow it back to the car park.

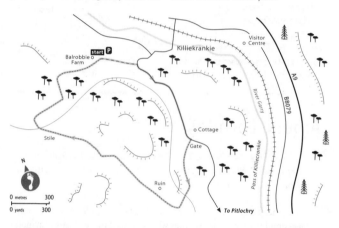

Central Highlands

(except Sunday) **postbus** service, T472386, from Pitlochry to Rannoch station, via Kinloch Rannoch, or check with *Elizabeth Yule Transport* (see Pitlochry **Transport**).

The car park on the B846 Kinloch Rannoch to Aberfeldy road, near Braes of Foss, is the starting point for the route to the summit **of Schiehallion** (3,552 ft), one of Scotland's best-loved mountains whose distinctive conical peak made it ideal for use in early experiments in 1774 to judge the weight of the earth. These were not an unqualified success, but led to the invention of contour lines as an aid to surveying the mountain. The walk to the summit is fairly straightforward, except for the very rocky final stretch. You'll need to be properly clothed and equipped (see page 53) and take a map and compass.

OS sheet No 51

Falls of Bruar walk

A well-maintained path leads from the lower falls along the gorge of the Bruar River to the upper falls and back down the other side. It's a 1½ mile round trip.

From the House of Bruar, turn right by the adventure playground, then left up the river bank. The path passes under a railway arch and through a kissing gate. It then heads through open forest to a rocky outcrop, from where you can see the lower falls.

A series of wooden steps leads down from the outcrop, then a ricky path climbs up till it forks. Go right, then cross the bridge, from where there's a good view of the lower falls. From here a clear path leads up the far side till it reaches a deer fence. Climb up to the gate, go through it and continue uphill through trees till the path levels out high above the gorge. Further on there's a picnic area, then the path curves left down to the upper bridge, which is a great vantage point from which to admire the stunning view.

The path heads left through more trees. It then crosses a stream before descending to the lower bridge and then back to the car park.

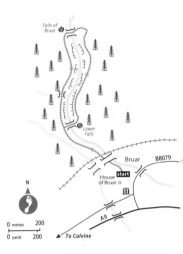

Around Loch Tay

The 14 mile-long Loch Tay is surrounded by some of the loveliest scenery in Perthshire and is well worth exploring, though public transport around its shores is limited to one postbus service a day.

Kenmore
Phone code: 01887

At the northeast end of Loch Tay is **Kenmore**, a neat little village of whitewashed cottages dominated by a huge archway which stands at the gateway to Taymouth Castle, built by the Campbells of Glenorchy in the early 19th century and now a very fine **golf course**, T830228. Near the village, on the southern bank of the loch, is **The Scottish Crannog Centre**, an authentic reconstruction of a *crannog*, an artificial Bronze Age island-house built for defensive purposes. ■ *Apr-Oct daily 1000-1730 (last tour at 1630). Adult £3.85, children £2.85. T830583.*

Sleeping and eating   The best place to stay in Kenmore is the **C** *Kenmore Hotel*, T830205, www.kenmorehotel.com, which claims to be Scotland's oldest coaching inn, dating from 1572. Whether or not that's true, there's no denying it's full of character and very comfortable. There's also a **campsite** at the *Kenmore Caravan and Camping Park*, T830226, complete with its very own golf course.

Sports   Loch Tay is a major **watersports** centre and close by the Crannog Centre is *Croft-Na-Caber*, T830588, Scotland's best watersports and activities centre, where you can try water-skiing, windsurfing, sailing, rafting, jet biking, river sledging (!), fishing, parascending, clay-pigeon shooting, hill walking and Nordic skiing. You can hire speed-boats, fishing boats and canoes at the *Loch Tay Boating Centre*, T830291, open Apr-Oct, and **hire bikes** from *Perthshire Mountain Bikes*, T830291. See also 'sleeping' above.

Climbing Ben Lawers

*The north side of Loch Tay is dominated by
Ben Lawers (3,987 ft), the highest mountain
in Perthshire. Its massif of seven summits
includes six Munros which are linked by an
eight-mile ridge which can be walked in one
day by fit and experienced hill walkers. The
best access to the ridge is from Glen Lyon.
You'll need OS sheet No 51. The trek to the
main summit starts from the **National
Trust for Scotland Visitor Centre** (£1
admission), two miles along a track which
turns off the main A827 about halfway
between Kenmore and Killin (see page 157).
This track continues over a wild pass to
Bridge of Balgie in Glen Lyon. Leaflets
describing the climb are available from the*

*visitor centre. It's a seven-mile walk there
and back and though the route is
straightforward and easy to follow, it's a
very steep, tough climb of 2,700 ft from the
centre to the summit. Allow five to six hours.
You should be fit, properly clothed (see page
53) and have some previous hill-walking
experience, but the views from the top on a
clear day are amazing, across to the North
Sea in the east and the Atlantic Ocean in the
west. There's also a much easier one-mile
nature trail and an accompanying booklet
describing the rare Alpine flora is available
at the centre. Near the turn-off to the
National Trust for Scotland Visitor Centre is
the E Ben Lawers Hotel, T01567-820436.*

For those with their own transport, one of the most scenic routes in this part of
the country is the spectacular road which winds its way south from Kenmore
high up into the mountains, across a bleak and barren plateau and down the
other side to the tiny hamlet of **Amulree**. This road is often closed in the winter and there are gates at either end. From Amulree you can continue south to
Crieff, through the gentler, but equally stunning, scenery of the **Sma' Glen**.
Alternatively, you could head north to Aberfeldy and then complete the circuit back to Kenmore.

**Kenmore to
Amulree**
*Colour map 4,
grid B2*

A few miles west of Kenmore an unclassified road turns off the A827, which
runs along the north bank of the loch, and heads to Fortingall, a tiny village of
classic beauty which features on many a calendar. It's little more than a row of
thatched cottages which wouldn't even get a mention were it not for two
amazing claims. The 3,000-year-old yew tree in the churchyard is claimed to
be the oldest living thing in Europe. More astonishing is the claim that this is
the birthplace of **Pontius Pilate**, said to be the son of a Roman officer who was
stationed here. Furthermore, it is believed that Pilate returned here to be buried, and a gravestone in the churchyard bears the initials 'PP'. There's **accommodation** in the village at the wonderful, and very popular, D *Fortingall
Hotel*, T01887-830367, next to the churchyard.

**Fortingall &
Glen Lyon**
*Colour map 4,
grid B2*

If you have your own transport, make a detour up Glen Lyon, one of the most
beautiful of all Scottish glens. On a summer's day, there can be few lovelier
places on earth as the river Lyon tumbles through corries and gorges, and
through flowering meadows, with high mountain peaks on either side and
eagles soaring overhead. It's no surprise that Wordsworth and Tennyson
waxed lyrical over its qualities. The road from Fortingall runs all the way to the
head of the glen, at Loch Lyon. This is walking and fishing paradise. There are
several Munros to 'bag' and fishing permits are available at the *Fortingall Hotel*
(see above).

Central Highlands

Aberfeldy

Phone code: 01887
Colour map 4, grid B2
Population: 2,000

The little town of Aberfeldy stands on the banks of the river Tay, on the A827 which runs between the A9 and Loch Tay. It's well placed geographically for exploring the northern part of Perthshire, though Pitlochry has better tourist facilities. The **Tourist Information Centre** is housed in an old church on The Square, in the centre of town. ■ *Apr-Jun Mon-Sat 0930-1730, Sun 1100-1600; Jul-2 Sep Mon-Sat 0930-1830, Sun 1100-1700; 3 Sep-28 Oct Mon-Sat 0930-1730, Sun 1100-1600; winter Mon-Sat 0930-1730. T820276.*

Sights   The river Tay is spanned by **Wade's Bridge**, built by General Wade in 1773 during his campaign to pacify the Highlands. Overlooking the bridge is the **Black Watch Monument** which commemorates the famous regiment becoming part of the British Army's peacekeeping force here, in 1739. In Mill Street is the **Aberfeldy Water Mill**, built in 1825 and restored in 1983 to produce stone-ground oatmeal in the traditional Scottish way. ■ *Easter-Oct Mon-Sat 1000-1700, Sun 1100-1700. Adult £2.50, children £1. T820803.*

A mile west of Aberfeldy, across the Tay at Weem, is **Castle Menzies**, an impressive, restored 16th-century, 'Z-plan' fortified tower house and former seat of the chief of Clan Menzies. ■ *Apr-Oct Mon-Sat 1030-1700, Sun 1400-1700. Adult £3.50, concession £3, children £2. T820982.*

A popular local walk is to the **Falls of Moness**, through the famous **Birks of Aberfeldy**, forever associated with the poet Robert Burns who was inspired by the birks (birch trees) to write his eponymous song. It's a fairly easy walk along a marked trail (see map) up to the impressive falls and the views of Strathtay and the surrounding hills on the descent also make it worthwhile. It's about four miles there and back.

Sleeping   There are several hotels in and around town, best of which is the magnificent 15th-century
& eating   **L-A** *Farleyer House Hotel* in Weem, T820332, 100127.222@compuserve.com Also recommended is **B** *Guinach House*, T820251, a family-run country house hotel in a lovely setting by the Birks and with a superb restaurant (expensive); and the very friendly **C** *Weem Hotel* T820381, in Weem, about a mile west of Aberfeldy on the B846 to Strathtummel. There are many **guesthouses** and **B&Bs**, including **D-E** *Fernbank House*, Kenmore St, T820345, **E** *South Lodge*, T820115, by Castle Menzies and **E** *Tigh'N'Eilean Guest House*, T820109, on Taybridge Drive, all of which are recommended and offer good value.

There's not a great deal of choice for **eating**, other than the hotels in town or a bar lunch in one of the pubs. The *Breadalbane Bakery*, at 37 Dunkeld St on the way out of town, is recommended for home baking and their Aberfeldy Whisky Cake.

Transport   *Stagecoach* **buses** run regularly (Mon-Sat) to **Pitlochry** (45 mins), **Dunkeld** (1 ¼ hrs) and **Perth** (1 ¾ hrs). *Strathtay Scottish* has twice daily (except Sun) buses to **Blairgowrie**, via Dunkeld. There's also a **postbus** service to **Killin** and another to **Glen Lyon** once a day, except Sun, T01463-256200.

Glenshee Ski Centre

Glenshee ski centre is at the crest of the Cairnwell Pass (2,199 ft), the highest main road pass in Britain, on the border of Perthshire and Aberdeenshire. It is the most extensive skiing area in Scotland, with 38 pistes, as well as Nordic skiing. **Ski rental** is around £13 per day (£12 for snowboards) and lessons are £18 for four hours. A day **lift pass** costs £18, or £72 for five days,

including tuition and hire. For more information, call Ski Glenshee (T01339-741320, www.ski.scotland.net) For the latest snow and weather conditions, call the Ski Hotline (T0900-1-654656).

The only public transport is a daily **postbus** service (Monday-Saturday only) from Blairgowrie to Spittal of Glenshee, or to the ski resort from Braemar and Ballatar.

Blairgowrie and Glenshee

The other major road running north from Perth is the A93, which passes Blairgowrie, centre for the Glenshee ski resort, on its way to Braemar and then heads east through Deeside to Aberdeen.

Blairgowrie

The respectable town of Blairgowrie, or Blairgowrie and Rattray to give it its full title, lies amidst the raspberry fields of Strathmore and is conveniently placed to serve as an accommodation centre for Glenshee Ski Centre (see below). There's little of real interest to detain passing tourists but **Keathbank Mill**, off the A93 to Braemar, is worth a look. This huge 19th-century jute mill has an 1862 steam turbine driven by the largest water wheel in Scotland. There's also a heraldry museum, model railway and woodcarving workshops. ■ *Apr to early Oct daily 1030-1700. Adult £2.95. T872025.*

The **Tourist Information Centre** is at 26 Wellmeadow in the centre of town, T872960. It's open all year: Easter-June, September and October Monday-Saturday 0930-1730, Sunday 1100-1600; July and August Monday-Saturday 0900-1900, Sunday 1000-1800; November-Easter Monday-Friday 0930-1730, Saturday 1000-1400

Three miles south of Blairgowrie, just off the A93 by **Meikleour**, is a 100-ft high **beech hedge**, the highest in the world, which must take some trimming.

Phone code: 01250
Colour map 4, grid B4
Near Blairgowrie is the highest hedge in the world

Central Highlands

Sleeping There's a good selection of accommodation. Top of the range is the **L** *Kinloch House Hotel*, T884237, www.kinlochhouse.com, a luxurious country house 3 miles west of town on the A923 to Dunkeld. It offers excellent cuisine (expensive) and sporting facilities. More affordable is the **B** *Altamount House Hotel*, T873512, on the Coupar Angus Rd, which also offers top-class cooking (mid-range-expensive). There are plenty of cheaper options, including **E** *Rosebank House*, T872912, on Balmoral Rd. **Camping** is available at the *Blairgowrie Holiday Park*, T872941, in Rattray, across the River Ericht.

Some 20 miles north of Blairowrie, at **Spittal of Glenshee** is *Gulabin Lodge*, T885256, a **hostel/bunkhouse** run by Cairnwell Mountain sports which rents out skis, boards and mountain bikes and also gives skiing tuition. Nearby is one of the area's top hotels, **B-C** *Dalmunzie House Hotel*, T885224, a grand old Highland sporting lodge set in a 6,000-acre estate and boasting the highest 9-hole golf course in Britain.

Eating   There are several decent eating places, best of which is *Cargills*, T876735, a nice-looking bistro housed in a converted mill store by the river. Moderate prices. Closed Mon. The *Angus Hotel* and *Brig o'Blair* pub, both on Wellmeadow, serve decent bar meals, as does the lovely **D-E** *Bridge of Cally Hotel*, T886231, 6 miles north of town on the A93.

Transport   *Strathtay Scottish*, T01382-228054, **buses** run hourly (Mon-Sat; less frequently on Sun) to and from **Perth** (45 mins) and **Dundee** (1 hr).

The Angus Glens

Colour map 4, grid B4   *East of Perthshire, south of the Grampians and north of Dundee are the Angus Glens, a series of five glens running parallel to each other and all of them beautiful, peaceful and offering plenty of relatively painless hillwalking opportunities.*

Ins & outs   **Getting there and around**   Kirriemuir is the gateway to **Glens Isla, Prosen** and **Clova**, while the other two, **Glens Lethnot** and **Esk**, are reached via Brechin. There are regular **buses** to Brechin and Kirriemuir from Dundee, but getting around the glens is not easy without your own transport as there is only a limited postbus service.

Glen Isla   Running parallel to Glen Shee (see page 167), lovely Glen Isla is the furthest *Phone code:01575*   west of the Angus Glens and can also be reached from the little town of Alyth, east of Blairgowrie. At the southern end of the glen, five miles north of Alyth by Bridge of Glenisla, is **Reekie Linn**, a series of waterfalls that plunge through a deep, wooded gorge. A path leads for 200 yards from the car park and picnic site on the road between Bridge of Glenisla and Bridge of Lintrathen. Nearby is the excellent *Lochside Lodge* restaurant and *Peel Farm Coffee and Craft Shop*.

Six miles north, at **Kirkton of Glenisla**, on the B951, is the **C-D** *Glenisla Hotel*, T582223, glenislahotel@sol.co.uk, an impossibly cosy 17th-century inn with log fires, real ales, good grub and plenty of local characters. It's worth the trip just to spend a night here. Further north a side road turns off the B951 and runs to **Auchavan**, at the head of the glen. There are paths from here into the wild and mountainous **Caenlochan Forest**.

At the mouth of the glen, in the tiny village of **Meigle**, home to Scotland's most important collection of early Christian and Pictish carved stones. They are housed in the superb **Meigle Museum**. ■ *Apr-Sep daily 0930-1830. Adult £1.80.*

Transport   A **postbus** runs Mon-Sat from Blairgowrie to Auchavan.

Glen Prosen   Five miles north of Kirriemuir is the tiny village of **Dykehead**, at the foot of *Phone code: 01575*   Glen Clova, where a side road branches northwest and runs into Glen Prosen. Both glens penetrate deep into the Grampian Mountains and are blessed with a rugged beauty, but Glen Prosen carries little of the cachet of its neighbour and is consequently a much more peaceful option for hillwalkers. The little road runs deep into the glen but it's best explored on foot.

A good walk is the relatively straightforward four-mile **Minister's Path**, which connects the two glens. It starts from behind the kirk in Glenprosen village and heads over the hilly moorland and down to the B955 just before Clova village.

Transport   You can catch the **postbus** back to Kirriemuir from the *Clova Hotel* (see below). The Kirriemuir to Glen Prosen postbus runs once daily except Sun.

Central Highlands

Glen Clova is only 30 miles north of Dundee yet you could be in the heart of the Highlands, with craggy mountains towering overhead and heather-clad slopes populated by deer and grouse. Glen Clova leads north into Glen Doll, from where you can follow the old **drove roads** which lead to Ballater and Braemar in Deeside. These ancient routes were used by whisky smugglers, government troops and rebels, as well as cattle drovers, and though they may look straightforward on the map, they can be as treacherous as any of the Scottish mountains. Only fit and experienced walkers should attempt these walks.

Glen Clova & Glen Doll
Phone code: 01575
OS Landranger
Nos 43 & 44

One of the best walks in the famous **Jock's Road** to Braemar. The 14-mile route starts from the Glen Doll youth hostel and it's a tough seven-hour hike up to the summit at Crow Craigies (3,108 ft) and down to the head of Loch Callater. The descent is very steep and may require crampons in winter. From the loch, the path follows the Callater Burn till it reaches the main A93, two miles from Braemar (see page 174). Another excellent walk is the **Loops of Brandy**, which starts from behind the *Clova Hotel* and climbs up into the mountains, around Loch Brandy and back again. It's a four-hour walk there and back.

Drivers should note that the B955 from Dykehead divides just before the bridge of the river South Esk. The west branch is traditionally used by vehicles heading up the glen, while the east branch should be for traffic returning down the glen. The two roads meet up again six miles further on, at the tiny hamlet of **Clova**, which consists of little more than the **D-E** *Clova Hotel*, T550222, which is a very friendly and popular climbers' retreat. As well as bar meals, the hotel lays on regular barbecues, ceilidhs and a multitude of various activities. There's also an eight-bed bunkhouse outside (**F**) which is open all year. It has a kitchen, but no shower.

Four miles further north, near the end of the road, in Glen Doll, is a campsite, T550233, by the bridge. It's open during the summer and has only basic facilities. A few hundered yards north is **F** *Glendoll Youth Hostel*, T550236, open 10 March-31 October. It has 45 beds and boasts a squash court as well as the standard facilities. Note that access is limited to between 1030 and 1700.

Transport There's a **postbus** service to Glen Clova from Kirriemuir twice a day Mon-Fri and once on Sat. The 0830 departure runs as far as the hostel and the 1500 departure (Mon-Fri only) stops at the *Clova Hotel*. The afternoon service leaves from the hotel at 1530.

North from Edzell, the road runs 13 miles to the head of beautiful **Glen Esk**, the most easterly of the Angus Glens and, like the others, quiet and empty. Nine miles north of Edzell along the Glen road is the **Glenesk Folk Museum**, housed in an old shooting lodge known as 'The Retreat'. The museum's extensive local folk history collection gives a fascinating insight into the lives of the Glen's inhabitants. It also has a good tearoom (try their rhubarb jam and home baking). ∎ *Easter-May Sat-Mon 1200-1800, Jun to mid-Oct 1200-1800. Adult £2. T670254.*

Glen Esk
Phone code: 01356

Four miles further on, beyond Tarfside village, the public road ends at **Invermark Castle**. This is the start of one of the Mounth Roads, ancient rights of way leading from the Angus Glens across the mountains to Deeside. This route leads eventually to Ballater or **Glen Tanar**, near Aboyne. For a description of the latter route in reverse, see under **Deeside** (page175). You can also hike from here to the summit of **Mount Keen** (3,081ft), Scotland's most easterly Munro, but like the Mounth Road, this is a tough walk and you'll need full

OS Landranger No 44

Central Highlands

hill-walking equipment and a map. An easier walk is to the **Queen's Well**, three miles from the car park across the river from Invermark Castle. It's about three hours there and back. Altenatively, you can head west from the castle, past the lovely old church and along the north shore of **Loch Lee.**

Deeside

Colour map 4, *The river Dee rises in the Cairngorms and flows down through the surrounding*
grid A4-6 *hills, eastwards to the sea at Aberdeen. The valley of the Dee is known as Deeside, or rather Royal Deeside, for its connections with the royal family, who have holidayed here, at Balmoral, since Queen Victoria first arrived in 1848. Originally, Queen Victoria and Prince Albert were looking for an estate further west, but were advised that the Deeside climate would be better for Albert's delicate constitution. The queen fell in love with this area and its people, and following Albert's death she sought out the company of straight-talking northerners, preferring their down-to-earth honesty to the two-faced toadies she endured at court.*

Today, Deeside's royal associations have made it the tourist honeypot of the northeast, but the royal presence has also saved it from mass development. There's an air of understated affluence and refinement in the villages strung out along the A93 that runs along the north bank of the Dee and, as well as the obvious attraction of Balmoral, there are many other fine examples of baronial castles. Deeside is also a great area for various outdoor activities, such as hiking in the surrounding mountains, mountain biking, canoeing and skiing.

Ins and outs

Getting there & All the main tourist attractions on Deeside can be reached by **bus** from Aberdeen.
getting around *Bluebird Northern* service No 201, T01224-212266, runs every 30 mins (Mon-Sat) to Banchory, via Cults and Crathes, and every hour to Braemar, via Aboyne, Dinnet, Ballater and Crathie (for Balmoral). On Sun, the bus runs every hour and 2 hrs respectively. If you wish to explore Deeside along a less popular route (though even in the summer, crowds are never great) take the B976 along the south bank of the river Dee.

Information For details of the **Castle Trail**, **Victorian Heritage Trail** and **Deeside Tourist Route**, contact the tourist office in Aberdeen, or in any of the towns along the way.

Aberdeen to Banchory

Colour map 4, The first sight of interest heading west from Aberdeen is **Drum Castle**, three miles
grid A5/6 west of **Peterculter** (pronounced 'Petercooter'). It's a combination of a 13th-century square tower, Jacobean mansion house and later Victorian additions. It was given to one William de Irvine by Robert the Bruce for service rendered at Bannockburn and was in the family's hands for over 650 years, until taken over by the National Trust for Scotland in 1976. There's a beautiful walled garden and a trail through the 100-acre ancient Wood of Drum which forms part of the castle grounds. ■ *Mid-Apr-31 May and 1-30 Sep daily 1330-1730; Jun-31 Aug daily 1100-1730; weekends in Oct 1330-1730. Gardens same dates daily 1000-1800. Grounds all year daily 0930 till dusk. Castle, gardens and grounds, adult £6, concession £4.50; garden and grounds only £1 (honesty box). T01330-811204.*

A few miles southeast of Peterculter is its sister village, **Maryculter** (pronounced 'Marycooter') where you'll find **Storybook Glen**, the northeast's

Braemar Gathering

There has been a gathering (or games) of some sort at Braemar for 900 years, ever since Malcolm Canmore set contests for the local clans so that he could pick the strongest and bravest of men for his army. These events take place up and down the country throughout the summer but none are as famous, or well attended, as Braemar's. Queen Victoria attended in 1848 and the Gathering is still patronized by the royal family. Crowds come from all over the world to proclaim the monarch as Chieftain of the Braemar Gathering.

At the gathering the visitor will see contests in traditional Scottish events, such as tossing the caber, Highland dancing and bagpipe competitions and displays. There is an inter-services tug o' war championship, a medley relay race and a hill race up Morrone. The sounds of the massed pipes echoing around the encircling heather-clad hills and a plethora of tartan also help to make this a real tourist highlight. The royal connection (and the crowds) apart, many other local communities hold similar games.

answer to Disneyland. This very attractive and tasteful 'theme park' is a great place to take the kids and features giant tableaux and lifesize characters from many childhood fairy tales and nursery rhymes. ■ *Daily Mar-Oct 1000-1800, Nov-Feb weekends only 1100-1600. Adult £3.50, children £1.75. T01224-732491.*

Fifteen miles west of Aberdeen, where the A93 meets the A957 from Stonehaven, is Crathes Castle, a perfect 'fairytale' castle built over 40 years in the mid-16th century. The turreted tower-house is still furnished with many period pieces and wall hangings, and is notable for its superb painted ceilings. **Crathes Castle & gardens**

There are narrow spiral staircases leading to tiny rooms, one of which is said to be inhabited by the obligatory ghost. The castle is well worth exploring but is almost overshadowed by the exceptional gardens which shouldn't be missed. There are no fewer than eight of them, so take your time. There's also a visitor centre, restaurant and shop. ■ *Castle, visitor centre and shop open 1 Apr-30 Sep daily 1030-1730; 1-31 Oct daily 1030-1630 (last admission to castle 45 mins before closing). Licensed restaurant open 10 Jan-31 Mar and 1 Nov-23 Dec Wed-Sun 1030-1600; 1 Apr-31 Oct daily 1030-1730. Grounds and garden open all year daily 0900-dusk. Castle only dault £3.50, concession £3; castle and grounds combined adult £7, concession £5. T01330-844525.*

Opposite the castle gates is *The Milton Restaurant*, T01330-844566, serving excellent, moderately priced food daily till 2200 (lunch only on Sunday).

Banchory

Banchory makes a very pleasant base for exploring the area, with the river Dee burbling through, but there's not a great deal to do here, apart from salmon fishing, which is popular in these parts. You can watch salmon leaping spectacularly at the **Bridge of Feugh**, to the south of town. There is a sad tale, though, of a lady-in-waiting who was staying at Balmoral when the royal family were in residence some years ago. She was standing fishing in the river, in quite deep water, and wearing chest-height waders, when the sovereign rode by. Seeing the king, she curtsied, whereupon the water flowed quickly into her waders and she sank beneath the water and drowned. *Phone code: 01330 Colour map 4, grid A5*

The **Tourist Information Centre** is in the local museum, on Bridge Street, behind the High Street. It can provide information on walking and fishing in the area. It's open April-June Monday-Saturday 1000-1300, 1400-1700;

Central Highlands

July-19 August Monday-Saturday 0930-1800, Sunday 1300-1800; 20 August-27 October Monday-Saturday 1000-1300, 1400-1700.

Sleeping & eating

There are some very fine places to stay in and around Banchory. Three miles north of town on the A980 is the very wonderful **B** *Raemoir House Hotel*, T824884. A country mansion set in 3,500 acres of woods and parkland, 20 rooms. Another excellent choice is the **B** *Banchory Lodge Hotel*, T822625, a sporting lodge-type hotel superbly situated on the banks of the river near the town centre. It's also a great place to stop and have a bite to eat for lunch. The river runs past the lawn and you can watch the salmon leap as you perhaps enjoy the fruits of their labour. Also recommended is the **B** *Tor-na-Coille Hotel*, T822242, tornacoille@ btinternet.com, outside town on the Inchmarlo Rd. This tastefully furnished Victorian country house hotel is set in lovely grounds and boasts a considerable reputation for its modern Scottish cooking (lunch mid-range; dinner expensive).

There are also plenty of good guesthouses and B&Bs, including **E** *Towerbank House*, at 93 High St, T824798, diane@dawps.fsnet.co.uk, and **D** *The Old West Manse*, 71 Station Rd, T822202. There's also a **campsite**, *Silver Ladies Caravan Park*, T822800, at Strachan, just outside Banchory.

Aside from the hotels listed above, the best place to **eat** is probably the *Burnett Arms Hotel* on the High St, T824944. There's also *Le Bistroquet*, which has a varied menu.

Tour operators

Adventure Scotland, T850332, dlatham@netcomuk.co.uk, is a Banchory-based company offering a wide range of adventure activities, including white-water rafting, mountain biking, skiing and hiking.

Lumphanan
Colour map 4, grid A5

From Banchory you can head northwest on the A980 to Alford, in the Don Valley (see page 178). Roughly halfway is the village of Lumphanan, which was thought to be the burial place of Macbeth, the Scottish king so misrepresented by Shakespeare (he is actually buried on Iona). **Macbeth's Cairn** is instead a prehistoric cairn. Just to the south of the village is the **Peel Ring**, a 12th-century Motte, or castle mound, and one of Scotland's earliest medieval sites.

Aboyne
Phone code: 01339
Colour map 4, grid A5

The attractive little village of Aboyne is 30 miles west of Banchory on the A93. There are a couple of very good places to eat in and around Aboyne. In the village itself is *The Black-faced Sheep*, T887311, a coffee shop with excellent home baking. A few miles back down the road to Banchory is *The White Cottage*, T886265, an award-winning restaurant which uses the very best local produce in its creative Scottish cooking (expensive; closed Monday). South of Aboyne, in **Glen Tanar** (see 'Walks in Deeside' below), is *Glen Tanar Equestrian Centre*, T886448, which offers riding in the forests and hills.

Dinnet
Colour map 4, grid A4

A few miles further on is Dinnet. In the **Muir of Dinnet National Nature Reserve** you can explore the Burn o' Vat, a sheltered valley which attracts many butterflies and dragonflies. During the walk, you'll come to a huge circular stone chamber and, in nearby Loch Kinord, there are crannogs, which are ancient man-made islands.

Ballater

Phone code: 01339
Colour map 4, grid A4

The neat little town of Ballater is proud of its royal connections. You can buy meat from the butcher with his 'By Royal Appointment' sign, or clothes from royal outfitters. This is where Lizzie and Phil pop down to the shops for a pint of milk or perhaps to choose a video. Ever since Queen Victoria first arrived by train from Aberdeen in 1848, the royal family have been spending their holidays here in their summer residence, Balmoral. She was not amused at the prospect of having an unsightly rail station on her doorstep, so the line ended eight miles east, at Ballater. The line has been closed for some time, but you can still visit the old train station, which now houses an elegant tearoom.

The **Tourist Information Centre** in Ballater is in Station Square, opposite the old station, T755306. It's open Easter-May and October Monday-Saturday 1000-1300, 1400-1700, Sunday 1300-1700; June and September Monday-Saturday 1000-1300,1400-1800, Sunday 1300-1800; July-August Monday-Saturday 1000-1300, 1400-1900, Sunday 1300-1900.

The royals are not the only famous summer visitors. The poet Byron (who attended Aberdeen Grammar School) spent many childhood summer holidays at Ballaterach, a few miles east of Ballater. He had a narrow escape when he slipped and nearly fell into the fast flowing stream at the Linn of Dee, beyond Braemar. He was rescued just in time and went on to reminisce in *The Island*,

> He who first met the Highlands' swelling blue
> Will love each peak which shows a kindred hue.

Those beautiful hills of which Byron waxed poetic are Ballater's other great attraction. The town makes the ideal base for **hiking** (see below) as well as a number of other outdoor activities. Many of the walks set off from **Loch Muick** (pronounced 'Mick'), nine miles southwest of Ballater, at the head of Glen Muick. (For details, see 'Walks in Deeside' below). There's a visitor centre and car park at Spittal of Glenmuick. From here a track leads along the west shore of the loch to the lodge where Queen Victoria met John Brown. For guides and equipment for canoeing, climbing, mountain biking and skiing, contact *Adventure Scotland* in Banchory (see above).

Sleeping There's plenty of accommodation in Ballater, from expensive hotels to reasonably priced B&Bs. Pick of the bunch is the **A-B** *Darroch Learg Hotel*, T755443, darroch.learg @exoams.wk.com, half a mile from town, off the A93 heading west to Braemar. 18 rooms, open Feb-Dec, friendly country house hotel with fine views and a reputation for superb food (expensive), good value. **A-B** *Hilton Craigendarroch*, on the Braemar Rd, T755858, www.hilton.com 44 rooms, Victorian country house converted into a modern resort hotel with full leisure and sports facilities, 2 good restaurants. **B** *Balgonie Country House Hotel*, T/F755482, on the western outskirts of town, off the A93. 9 rooms, open Feb-Dec, friendly and comfortable country house hotel, excellent food (expensive). **C** *Glen Lui Hotel*, Invercauld Rd, T755402, www.glen-lui-hotel.co.uk 19 rooms, another comfortable hotel offering fine food (lunch cheap; dinner mid-range). **E** *Deeside Hotel*, set back from the A93 heading out of town towards Braemar. T755420, www.royal-deeside.org.uk Friendly, good value and good food (mid-range). Among the many B&Bs is the recommended **E** *Inverdeen House*, 11 Bridge Sq, T755759, www.inverdeen.com French, German and Polish spoken, great breakfasts, no smoking. Also good is **E** *Moorside House*, T/F755492, on the Braemar Rd. There's a **campsite** at *Anderson Road Caravan Park*, T755727, open Apr-Oct.

Eating Apart from the hotels listed above, there are lots of places to eat. Best of all is *The Green Inn*, T/F755701, on the green in the town centre. It boasts a well-deserved reputation as one of the very best restaurants in the region, classic Scottish cooking with an imaginative and health-conscious twist, expensive, open daily (closed Sun Oct-Mar), also has 3 rooms upstairs (**B-C** full board). Also good is the *Hayloft Restaurant*, T/F755999, on Bridge Square (lunch cheap-mid-range; dinner mid-range to expensive).

Balmoral Castle

Colour map 4, grid A4 Eight miles west of Ballater is the area's main attraction, Balmoral Castle. The 16th-century tower house, formerly owned by the local Gordon family, was bought for Queen Victoria by Prince Albert in 1852 and converted into today's baronial mansion. It has been the royal family's summer retreat ever since. Only the ballroom and the grounds are open to the likes of you and me, and only for three months of the year. **Pony trekking** and **pony cart rides** are available around the estate grounds and are favourite ways of enjoying the wonderful scenery. Opposite the castle gates is **Crathie Church**, which is used by the family when they're in residence. There's a small souvenir shop next to the main gates and a visitor centre which gives a lot of information on the castle and its owners. ■ *Mid-Apr to end Jul, daily 1000-1700 (closed on Sun in Apr-May). Adult £4.50, concession £3.50, children £1. T742334. Buses to Braemar from Aberdeen stop by the gates.*

Braemar

Phone code: 01339 Nine miles west of Balmoral, is Braemar, the final town on Deeside, lying at
Colour map 4, the foot of the awesome, brooding **Cairngorm** massif, which dominates the
grid A3 Eastern Highlands. Even at the height of summer you can see a dab of snow still lying in a hollow in the surrounding mountains, and Braemar is an excellent base for **hiking** (see below), and winter **skiing** at Glenshee (see page 167). It's an attractive little place, much loved by Queen Victoria and much visited during its annual **Braemar Gathering** (or games), which attracts tens of thousands of visitors each year, amongst them members of the royal family. ■ *The games are held on the first Sat in Sep. Booking is essential and tickets can be bought in advance from the Booking Secretary, BRHS, Coilacreich, Ballater, AB35 5UH, T755377. Or contact the Tourist Information Centre for details.*

Just north of the village, and well signposted, is **Braemar Castle**, dating from 1628. This impressive fortress was used by Hanoverian troops after the Jacobite Rising of 1745. It is L-shaped with a star-shaped defensive wall and a central round tower with a spiral stair. There are barrel-vaulted ceilings and an underground prison. The world's largest cairngorm (a semi-precious stone, a variety of quartz, which is yellow, grey or brown in colour) weighing 52 lbs is on display in the morning room. There's also a piece of tartan worn by Prince Charles Edward, Bonnie Prince Charlie. ■ *Mid-Apr to end Oct Sat-Thu 1000-1800. Adult £3, concession £2.50, children £1. T741219.*

The **Braemar Highland Heritage Centre** in Balmoral Mews by the tourist office, includes informative talks (in several languages) on the area, an exhibition and shops. ■ *Daily Apr-Sep 0900-1800 (Jul-Aug till 2000), Oct-Mar 1000-1700. Free. T741944.*

A very scenic side trip from Braemar is to the **Linn of Dee**, six miles west of the village, at the end of the road. Here, the river thunders through a narrow gorge to spectacular effect. There are numerous walks from here along the river, or for the more adventurous, the famous **Lairig Ghru**, which runs through the Cairngroms to Aviemore (see below). Between the Linn of Dee and the tiny settlement of **Inverey**, a mile to the east, there's a very basic **youth hostel** (open mid-May to early October), which has no phone, so book through Braemar hostel (see below). A postbus runs in the afternoon (Monday-Saturday) from Braemar to the Linn of Dee, via the hostel.

The **Tourist Information Centre** in Braemar is in Balmoral Mews, on Mar Road. It's open daily January-May and September-December 1000-1700,

June 0930-1800, July-August 0930-1900. T741600. For rental of **ski** equipment, try the The *Braemar Ski School Hire*, in Victoria Hall on Glenshee Road.

Central Highlands

Best of all is the **C** *Braemar Lodge Hotel*, T741627, on the outskirts of the village on the road south to Glenshee and Blairgowrie. There's also the **B** *Invercauld Arms Hotel*, T741605, and the **D-E** *Callater Lodge Hotel*, Glenshee Rd, T741275, www.hotel-braemar.co.uk Small and comfortable. There are plenty of guesthouses and B&Bs, including **E** *Schiehallion House*, T741679, open Jan-Oct on Glenshee Rd, and **E** *Clunie Lodge*, T741330, on Cluniebank Rd. There's a **F** *SYHA Youth Hostel*, T741659, open all year, at Corrie Feragie on Glenshee Rd, and also **F** *Rucksacks*, 15 Mar Rd, T741517, a cheap and friendly bunkhouse that's popular with hikers and also rents out **mountain bikes**. There's **camping** at *Invercauld Caravan Site*, T741373, open Dec-Oct, on Glenshee Rd.

   The only real places to eat are the bars of the larger hotels, which are a bit on the expensive side. Otherwise, try the *Braemar Takeaway*, 14 Invercauld Rd, for some cheap stodge.

Sleeping & eating
Accommodation is hard to find before and during the Braemar Gathering, but at other times of the year there's plenty to choose from

Walks in Deeside

Ballater and Braemar are ideal bases for walking in the surrounding Grampian Mountains, and if you feel like 'bagging a Munro' (ie climbing a mountain over 3,000 ft), there are some close at hand.

The best walk in the area is to the summit of Lochnagar (3,786 ft), made famous by Prince Charles in the book he wrote for his brothers when young, *The Old Man of Lochnagar*. The noble and mysterious mountain dominates the Royal Forest of Balmoral and takes its name from a small loch at its foot (it's also known as the White Mounth). This fine granite mass is approached from the car park by the Rangers' **visitor centre** at Spittal of Glen Muick. For information on their free guided walks, T755377. The path to the top is well trodden and well marked, though steep as you near the summit. It's 10 miles there and back, so allow a full day for the climb. You'll need to be properly equipped and take a map.

Lochnagar
OS Landranger No 44

An easier walk is to Cambus o' May, on the river, about four miles east of Ballater. It's a great spot for a picnic, or to swim in the river, or to enjoy a stroll along the riverbank. A good walk from Braemar is to the summit of Morrone (2,818 ft), the mountain to the southwest. The walk takes about four hours in total.

Cambus o' May & Morrone
OS Landranger No 43

Another good climb is the route up **Mount Keen** (3,077 ft), the most easterly Munro, which lies between Deeside and Glen Esk, the loveliest of the Angus glens (see page 169). Again, you should allow a whole day for this expedition.

   It can be approached from the Visitor Centre in **Glen Tanar**, at the end of the little road that runs southwest off the B976, across the river from Aboyne. You can climb to the summit and return by the same route, but if your party has two cars, it is well worth walking over to Glen Esk, 14 miles away. Drive around to the Invermark car park at the head of Glen Esk and park one car there. From Glen Tanar follow the old drove road which at times runs with the Mounth road. Skirting the Home Farm with its Arboretum and its dammed lake, the fairly flat track winds along Glen Tanar through the forest for about four miles. Then comes the Halfway Hut, used for rest and repast by former shooting parties. You will pass shooting butts *en route*. The next stretch is through open country with the **Clachan Yell** (626 ft) on the left.

Glen Tanar to Glen Esk
OS Landranger No 44

The walk proper then begins to take shape. Cross the stone bridge of Etnach, and then the path begins to lead up to the Shiel of Glentanar. The second bridge forks left and the track heads for the summit. The rough path continues along a ridge, the shoulder of Mount Keen. From the summit with its stone marker, Dinnet and its two lakes is visible to the north, and the river Esk glints its way down the valley to the south. Watch out for adders around here. On the descent, you'll pass the **Queen's Well**, used by Queen Victoria when she and her party went down to Fettercairn posing as a wedding party. The well is decorated with a graceful granite crown which was erected in 1861. The royal party covered much of the climb on hill ponies. The stone arch at Fettercairn commemorates this visit. Perhaps the queen saw the stone, dated 1799, in the ancient graveyard by the ruined church at Loch Lee, which reads:

The grave, great teacher, to one level brings
Heroes and beggars, galley slaves and kings.

The Don Valley

Colour map 4, grid A4/5 *North of Royal Deeside is the lesser-known valley of the Don, Aberdeen's second river. This relatively little-visited corner of the northeast is an historian's and archaeologist's dream, as it's littered with medieval castles, Pictish stone circles and Iron Age hillforts. A quarter of all Britain's stone circles can be found here (if you look hard enough). Local tourist offices have free leaflets on the region's archaeological sites, with background information and details of how to find them. The main sites are included in the tourist board's 'Stone Circle Trail'. There's also a well-signposted 'Castle Trail', which includes the area's main castles. One of these castles, Corgarff, stands at the southern end of the notorious Lecht Road, which runs from Cock Bridge to Tomintoul. This area, known as The Lecht, is one of Scotland's main ski centres.*

Ins and outs

Getting there   There are regular **trains** and **buses** to Inverurie, from Aberdeen and Inverness. *Bluebird Northern*, T01224-212266, No 220 runs regularly every day from Aberdeen to Alford (1 hr 15 mins).

Getting around   Travelling around the Don Valley without your own transport is not easy. Bus No 219 runs from Alford to Strathdon (Mon-Sat), but services beyond Strathdon are virtually non-existant.

Inverurie and around

Phone code: 01467
Colour map 4, grid A5 The solid farming town of Inverurie is 17 miles northwest of Aberdeen, on the A96 to Inverness. It makes a useful base for visiting the numerous castles and ancient relics dotted around the area. There's little of specific interest in the town itself, though the **Victoria cinema** is a wonderful throwback to the golden days of the movies. Films are only shown occasionally, T621436. The **Thainstone Mart**, south of town just off the A96, is one of the largest livestock markets in the country and interesting, if you like that sort of thing. It's held Monday, Wednesday and Friday around 1000.

The **Tourist Information Centre** is in the Town Hall on Market Place. T625800. Open April-June and September Monday-Saturday 0930-1700; July-August 0930-1800.

Central Highlands

About six miles southwest of Inverurie, off the B993 (turn first left after the village of Kemnay) is the magnificent **Castle Fraser**, built in 1575 by the 6th Earl of Mar and similar in style to Crathes and Craigievar. The interior was remodelled in 1838 and many of the furnishings date from that period. There's a walled garden, tearoom and trails through the estate. ■ *Castle open Mid-Apr-31 May and 1-30 Sep daily 1330-1730; 1 Jun-31 Aug daily 1100-1730; weekends in Oct 1330-1730. Garden oen all year daily 0930-1800. Grounds all year daily 0930 till dusk. Castle, garden and grounds adult £6, concession £4.50. Garden and grounds only adult £2, concession £1.30. T01330-833463 (NTS).*

Close by, and signed off the B993, is the 4,000 year-old **Easter Aquhorthies Stone Circle**. This archaeological site is overshadowed by **Bennachie** (1,732 ft), by far the best hill in the area and thought to be the site of Mons Graupius, in 83 AD, when the Romans defeated the Picts. It's a straightforward two-hour walk to the summit and the views from the top are great. There are various trails, though the most commonly used route starts from the **Bennachie Centre**, at Esson's car park, a mile beyond **Chapel of Garioch** (pronounced 'Geery'), signposted off the A96 at Pitcaple, and about five miles northwest of Inverurie. ■ *Apr-Oct, Tue-Sun 1000-1700; Nov-Mar Wed-Sun 1000-1700. For more details of the various Bennachie Hill walks and the 'West Gordon Way', T794161. Bennachie Centre, T681470.* Near here is the **Maiden Stone**, a 10-ft high Pictish gravestone with relief carvings showing what looks like an elephant, along with other creatures not normally found around these parts.

A few miles west of the turn-off to Chapel of Garioch, the B9002 heads west off the A96 to the village of **Oyne**, site of the **Archaeolink Prehistory Park**. This state-of-the-art interpretive centre takes you on a journey back in time. It's a great introduction to the numerous ancient sites in the area and explains why the stone circles were built and what the various carved symbols mean. The 40-acre park includes various interesting features such as a reconstructed Iron Age farm, Stone Age settlement and Roman camp, as well as a hilltop Iron Age fort. The Archeodrome features audio-visual presentations which bring to life the ancient history of the area. ■ *Daily Apr-Oct 1000-1700. Adult £3.90, children £2.35. T01464-851544, www.archaeolink.co.uk*

Near the village of **Daviot**, north of the A96 off the B9001 from Inverurie, or reached via the A920 west of **Oldmeldrum**, is the **Loanhead of Daviot Stone Circle**. This impressive 6,000 year-old site is 500 yards from the village

Castle Fraser

and consists of two stone circles, the smaller of which encloses a cremation cemetery dating from 1500 BC.

Thirteen miles north of Inverurie is **Fyvie Castle**, off the A947 between Oldmeldrum and Turriff. This grandest of Scottish baronial piles is a major feature on the 'Castle Trail' and shouldn't be missed if you're in the vicinity. The castle's five towers are each named after one of the five families who have had the pleasure of living here over the centuries. The last lot only moved out in 1980 so it has a rare lived-in feel to it. The oldest part of the castle dates from the 13th century and, apart from the great wheel-stair and the 17th-century morning room, the extravagantly opulent interior largely dates from the Edwardian era. There's a superb collection of portraits including works by the likes of Raeburn, Batoni, Gainsborough and Hoppner, as well as 17th-century tapestries and collections of arms and armour. The landscaped grounds and Fyvie Loch are also worth exploring and even the tearoom is great. ■ *Easter to 31 May and 1-30 Sep daily 1330-1730; 1 Jun-31 Aug 1100-1730; weekends only in Oct 1330-1730. Grounds open all year daily 0930-dusk. Adult £6, concession £4.50, children £1. T01651-891266 (NTS).*

Sleeping & eating The best place to stay around Inverurie is the magnificent **B** *Pittodrie House Hotel*, near Chapel of Garioch, T681444, www.macdonald.hotels.co.uk 27 rooms, this fine baronial mansion originally belonged to the Earls of Mar and the 2,000-acre estate was granted to them by Robert the Bruce for their loyalty at the Battle of Bannockburn. The opulent surroundings are matched by the superb cuisine. **B** *Thainstone House Hotel*, to the south of Inverurie off the A96, T621643, is a luxurious country mansion offering excellent cuisine and leisure facilities. There's also a decent selection of cheaper guesthouses and B&Bs, including **E** *Breaslann Guest House*, Old Chapel Rd, T621608.

Alford and around

Phone code: 01975
Colour map 4, grid A5 The main tourist centre on Donside is the little country town of Alford (pronounced 'Ah-ford'), 25 miles west of Aberdeen. The principal point of interest in town is the **Grampian Transport Museum**, which features a comprehensive and fascinating display of transport history, with collections of cars, buses, trams, steam engines and some more unusual exhibits. ■ *Daily end Mar to end Oct, 1000-1700. Adult £3.80, concession £3.10, children £1.60. T562292.* Almost next door is the terminus for the **Alford Valley Railway**, a narrow-gauge passenger steam railway that runs for about a mile to Murray Park and back again (total journey time one hour). ■ *Apr-May and Sep, Sat-Sun 1300-1700, Jun-Aug daily 1300-1700. Adult £2, children £1. T562811.*

The railway station is also where you'll find the **Tourist Information Centre**.T562052. Open April-May and September Monday-Saturday 1000-1300, Sunday 1300-1700; June-August Monday-Saturday 1000-1200, 1230-1700, Sunday 1300-1700. Also in town is the **Alford Heritage Centre**, on Mart Road, which has a large display of agricultural and domestic items. ■ *Apr-Oct Mon-Sat 1000-1700, Sun 1300-1700. T562906.*

Alford is close to The Lecht winter ski centre (see below) but you can ski here all year round on the local dry ski slope at the **Alford Ski Centre**, on Greystone Road, T563024. There's also snowboarding, instruction and equipment hire.

Craigievar Castle Six miles south of Alford is one of the northeast's most gorgeous castles, the classic tower house of Craigievar, with its impressive turrets, balustrades and cupolas. The castle remains much as it was when it was built in 1626 by

The Lecht

The Lecht is a ski resort for all seasons. It offers dry-slope skiing throughout the year and its snowmaking facilities mean that the winter season can be extended beyond January and February. The Lecht's gentler slopes make it ideal for beginners and intermediates and the emphasis is on family skiing. There's a snowboard fun park with half pipe, log slide, gap jump and table top. However, there are also more difficult runs for the more experienced skier, and extensive off piste skiing.

*A **day ticket** costs £15 for adults, and £8 for children; a half-day ticket costs £12. There's a ski school and equipment hire at the base station, T01975-651440, thelecht@sol.co.uk For latest snow and weather conditions call the base station, or the Ski Hotline, T09001-654657.*

---

wealthy local merchant, William Forbes. Unfortunately, though, its popularity led to its deterioration and the NTS now restricts entry to only a small number of visitors at a time to prevent further damage. The castle stands in well-tended grounds. ■ *Castle open Mid-Apr-30 Sep daily 1330-1730 (last admission 1645). Grounds open daily all year 0930-dusk. Adult £7, concession £5. Grounds only £1 (honesty box). T01339-883280.*

About a mile west, at Bridge of Alford, is the **D** *Forbes Arms Hotel*, T562108, where you can get decent bar food (prices cheap to mid-range). There's also **B&B** accommodation in Alford at **E** *Dunvegan*, 26 Gordon Rd, T563077, and **E** *Bydand*, 18 Balfour Rd, T563613.

Sleeping & eating

West of Alford

Six miles west of Alford, the A944 meets the A97 which heads north towards the town of Huntly, on Speyside (see page 184). A few miles south of the junction stand the extensive and impressive ruins of Kildrummy Castle, Scotland's most complete 13th-century castle. Amongst the most infamous events in the castle's long and bloody history was the treacherous betrayal of Robert the Bruce's family to the English during the Wars of Independence. It was the seat of the Earls of Mar and used as an HQ for the Jacobite rebellion of 1715, after which the sixth Earl of Mar ('Bobbing John') fled to exile in France and the castle fell into ruin. ■ *Daily Apr-Nov 0930-1830. Adult £2, concession £1.50, children £0.75. T571331.*

Kildrummy Castle
Phone code: 01975

Across the other side of the river from the castle ruins is one of the very best hotels in the northeast, the spectacularly sited **L-A** *Kildrummy Castle Hotel*, T571288, www.kildrummycastelhotel.co.uk, a baronial country mansion set in beautiful grounds (see above). It also has an excellent restaurant.

The tiny village of Strathdon, 10 miles southwest of Kildrummy, is famous for its **Highland Games**, known as the *Lonach Highland Gathering*, held on the third Saturday in August, and a healthy blast of authenticity in comparison to the rather more glitzy affair at Braemar on Deeside (see page 171).

Strathdon
Phone code: 01975
Colour map 4, grid A4

As you head west through Strathdon, you'll see a sign which appears to tell you that you're lost, but in fact is pointing the way to the wonderfully named village of **Lost**, four miles north of Strathdon, in the middle of nowhere. Take the turning off the A944 at Bellabeg. This road also leads to the excellent **Lost Gallery**, which shows work by contemporary artists and is well worth visiting. ■ *Wed-Sun 1100-1700. T651287.*

Central Highlands

The Speyside Way

The Speyside Way follows the River Spey from its mouth at Spey Bay inland as far as Ballindalloch, then crosses high moorland to Tomintoul. The 45-mile route takes three to five days to complete. Much of it is on an old railway line and passes close to several small villages, meaning that it can easily be broken down into shorter walks. It also passes several distilleries along the way. There are plans to extend the route in the next few years, from Buckie, on the Moray coast, to Aviemore.

There is no guidebook to the Speyside Way, but OS Landranger maps Nos 28 & 36 cover the entire route. Further information and route leaflets are available from the **Moray Council Ranger Service**, at Boat of Fiddich, Craigellachie. The office is open Easter-Oct, daily 0900-1700 (T01340-881266, www.moray.org/area.speyway/webpages/swhome.htm)

Corgarff Castle Five miles west of Strathdon, the A944 meets the A939 Ballater-Tomintoul road. A few miles beyond the junction is the austere Corgarff Castle, a 16th-century tower house, later turned into a garrison post, with an eventful and gruesome history. Here Margaret Forbes and her family were burned alive by the Gordons in 1571 during the bitter feud between the two families. In the wake of the ill-fated 1745 rebellion, the government remodelled the castle, building a star-shaped defensive wall, and garrisoned 60 men to maintain order and communications in this part of the Highlands. Corgarff continued in use into the 19th century when English Redcoats were stationed here in order to prevent whisky smuggling. Today, it's managed by Historic Scotland. ■ *Daily Apr-Sep 0930-1830; Oct-Mar weekends only. Adult £2.80, concession £2, child £1. T651460.*

Just before the castle, an old military road leads for about a mile to **F** *Jenny's Bothy*, T651449. Open all year, a basic but wonderfully remote bunkhouse.

Tomintoul
Phone code: 01807
Colour map 4, grid A4

Beside Corgarff is the hamlet of **Cock Bridge**, standing at one end of one the most beautiful and notorious stretches of road in the country. In winter, the Tomintoul to Cock Bridge road is almost always the first road in Scotland to be blocked by snow (you have been warned!). From Cock Bridge, the A939 rises steeply to the Lecht Pass (2,089 ft) before dropping dramatically to **Tomintoul**, one of the highest villages in Scotland, at 1,600 ft.

Tomintoul is a bit of a one-horse town, and like so many others in this area, is an 18th-century planned village, built by the local laird to keep an eye on his tenants. It lies roughly midway between the Don Valley and Speyside, and is therefore well-placed for both the Whisky and Castle Trails. It is also the nearest settlement of any size to **The Lecht**, one of Scotland's top five ski resorts (see above), and it marks the end of the long-distance **Speyside Way** (see page 180), so is popular with walkers and skiers.

The **Tourist Information Centre** is in the village square, T580285, tomintoul@agtb.ossian.net It's open 2 April-2 June Monday-Saturday 0945-1300, 1400-1700; 4 June-8 July Monday-Saturday 0930-1300, 1400-1700; 9 July-19 August Monday-Saturday 0930-1800, Sunday 1300-1800; 20 August-1 September Monday-Saturday 0930-1300, 1400-1700; 3 September-27 October Monday-Saturday 0945-1300, 1400-1700.

On the village square is the **Museum & Visitor Centre**, which has a display of local history, wildlife, landscape and outdoor activities. ■ *Jun-Sep Mon-Sat 1000-1600, Oct-May Mon-Fri 1000-1600. Free. T673701.*

Ten miles north of Tomintoul on the B9008 is the **Glenlivet Crown Estate** (see also page 181), with an extensive network of hiking paths and cycle trails, as

The Malt Whisky Trail

*Speyside is Scotland's most prolific whisky-producing region and the **Malt Whisky Trail** is a well-signposted 70-mile tour around seven of the most famous distilleries, plus the Speyside Cooperage. Most of the distilleries offer guided tours, and most (with the exception of Glenfiddich) charge an entry fee, which can then be discounted, in full or in part, from the cost of a bottle of whisky in the distillery shop. Tours also include a free dram. Those listed below are the most interesting.*

***Strathisla**, in Keith, is the oldest working distillery in the Highlands (1786) and perhaps the most atmospheric, in a beautiful setting on the River Isla. This is a relatively rare malt, which is also used in the better-known Chivas Regal blend. T01542-783044. Open Feb to end Nov, Mon-Sat 0930-1600, Sun 1230-1600. £4 (includes £2 discount voucher).*

***Speyside Cooperage** is near Craigiellachie, four miles north of Dufftown. Here you can watch the oak casks for whisky being made. T01340-871108. Open Jun-Sep Mon-Sat 0930-1630; Oct-May Mon-Fri 0930-1630. £2.25.*

***Dallas Dhu** is a bit off the beaten track, a mile south of Forres, off the A940. It no longer produces whisky but it's a beautifully preserved Victorian distillery which you can explore on your own. T01309-676548. Open daily Apr-Sep 0930-1830; Oct-Mar Mon-Wed and Sat 0930-1630, Thu 0930-1200, Fri and Sun 1400-1630. Adult £3, concession £1.90, children £1.*

***Cardhu** is seven miles west of Craigiellachie,*

at Knockando on the B9102. This lovely little distillery is now owned by United Distillers and their fine malt is one of many used in the famous Johnny Walker blend. T01340-872555. Open Mar-Nov Mon-Fri 0930-1630, Sun 1100-1600; Jul-Sep also Sat 0930-1630 and Sun 1100-1600; Dec-Feb Mon-Fri 1000-1600. £3 (includes £2 discount voucher).

***Glen Grant** is in Rothes, on the A941 to Elgin. The distillery is not in production but tours are still offered, with the added attraction of a Victorian garden and orchard, woodland walks by the burn and the rebuilt 'Dram Pavilion'. T01542-783318. Open mid-Mar to end Oct Mon-Sat 1000-1600, Sun 1130-1600; Jun-Sep Mon-Sat 1000-1700, Sun 1130-1700. £3 (includes £2 discount voucher).*

***Glenfiddich** is just north of Dufftown, on the A941. Probably the best known of all the malts and the most professionally run operation. It's the only distillery where you can see the whisky being bottled on the premises, and the only major distillery that's free (including the obligatory dram). T01340-820373. Open all Apr to mid-Oct Mon-Sat 0930-1630 and Sun 1200-1630; mid-Oct to Mar Mon-Fri only. Free.*

*The **Glenlivet** is 10 miles north of Tomintoul, on the B9008. This was an illicit whisky until it was licensed in 1824. The distillery was later founded in 1858 and this malt has gone on to become one of the world's favourites. It was then taken over in 1978 by Seagram's. T01542-783220. Open mid-Mar to end Oct Mon-Sat 1000-1600, Sun 1230-1600; Jul-Aug till 1800. £3 (includes £2 discount voucher).*

well as lots of wildlife, including reindeer. Information and free maps are available from the **ranger's office** in Tomintoul, T580283.

Sleeping and eating There are a few hotels around the main square, the nicest of which is the **D-E** *Glenavon Hotel*, T580218. It is also the best place for a drink and popular with après-skiers, tired walkers and locals. There's also a **F** *SYHA Youth Hostel*, on Main St, T580282, open mid-May to end Oct. Other than the hotels, the best place to eat is the *Clockhouse* on the Square.

The Tap o' Noth walk

OS Landranger No 37 covers the route. The total distance is three miles. Allow at least two hours there and back.

*Eight miles south of Huntly on the A97 is the village of **Rhynie**, where you turn off for one of the best walks in the northeast. The Tap o' Noth (1,851 ft) dominates this part of rural Aberdeenshire and the panoramic views from the top make it a worthwhile climb. It's also a fairly easy walk to the conical summit, where there's a vitrified fort.*

It's believed that the name derives from the Gaelic taip a'nochd, *which translates as look-out top. But there's also a local legend that the hill's giant, Jack o'Noth, stole the sweetheart of his neighbour, Jack o'Bennachie. In retaliation, the cuckolded neighbour hurled a huge boulder and flattened Jack on his own hilltop.*

*Start the walk from the car park at **Scurdargue**, a few miles west of Rhynie, off the A941. Leave the car park and head straight up the track to a gate. Go through the gate and cross some rough pasture into woodland. At the northwest corner of the wood, go through another gate and turn*

left onto a track. Follow this grassy track uphill beside a fence until you see another area of forestry ahead, with rough pastureland on the right. Follow the faint track across the pasture to the broad track which then climbs up the Tap's western slopes. Follow this all the way to the top, up the tight zig-zag on the southern flank and through the eastern entry to the hillfort, into a large enclosure. On the way back down look out for a subsidiary path under the fort's western ramparts. This path descends steeply to the left, south of the main track. It then joins the main track and you can retrace your steps back to the car park.

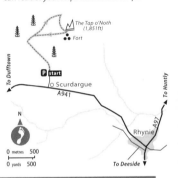

Transport There are **buses** to Tomintoul from **Keith** via **Dufftown**, (Tue and Sat only), from **Elgin** (Thu only) and from **Aberlour** (on schooldays, with connection to Elgin). For details call **Roberts of Rothiemay**, T01466-711213.

Speyside

Colour maps 2, grid C3/4

The river Spey is Scotland's second longest river, rising in the hills above Loch Laggan and making its way northeast to where it debouches at Spey Bay, on the Moray coast. Speyside is one of Scotland's loveliest valleys and is synonymous with two of Scotland's greatest products, salmon and whisky. The upper part, Strathspey, is equally famous for its hiking, skiing and watersports. It is covered in the Highlands chapter (see page 184). This section covers the lower part of the valley and comprises the famous Malt Whisky Trail. There are more malt whisky distilleries in this small area than in any other part of the country, and some of the famous brands include Glenlivet and Glenfiddich. It's not all whisky in these parts. There's also some fine walking along the 45-mile Speyside Way, which runs from Spey Bay south to Tomintoul.

Dufftown

A good place to start your whisky tour is Dufftown, founded in 1817 by James Duff, the fourth Earl of Fife, and the self-proclaimed 'Malt Whisky Capital of the World'. There's more than a grain of truth in that assertion, for there are no fewer than seven working distilleries here. This is indeed the town that was built on seven stills.

Phone code: 01340
Colour map 2, grid C4

Dufftown's **Tourist Information Centre** is inside the Clock Tower in the centre of the main square, T820501. They have maps and information on the whisky trail. Open Apr-8 July Monday-Saturday 1000-1300, 1400-1700; 9 July-19 August Monday-Saturday 1000-1800, Sunday 1300-1800; 20 August-27 October Monday-Saturday 1000-1300, 1400-1700.

Just outside of town, on the A941 to Craigellachie, is the **Glenfiddich Distillery**, the town's most famous distillery and one of the best known of all malt whiskies (see box, page 181). Behind the distillery are the 13th-century ruins of **Balvenie Castle**, built by Alexander 'Black' Comyn, then added to in the 15th and 16th centuries, and visited by Mary, Queen of Scots in 1562. ■ *Daily Apr-Sep 0930-1830. Adult £1.50, concession £1.10, children £0.50. T820121 (HS).*

Sights

Four miles north of Dufftown, at the junction of the A941 and A95, is the little village of **Craigellachie**, site of the **Speyside Cooperage** (see below) and where you can see Thomas Telford's beautiful bridge over the river Spey. At nearby Aberlour is the home of *Walkers Shortbread*, T01340-871555.

About eight miles southwest of Craigiellachie, on the A95 to Grantown-on- Spey, is beautiful **Ballindalloch Castle**, a mile west of the village of Marypark. The castle is one of the loveliest in the northeast and has been lived in continuously by its original family, the Macpherson-Grants, since 1546. It houses a fine collection of Spanish paintings and the extensive grounds are home to the famous Aberdeen-Angus herd of cattle, bred here since 1860. ■ *Easter-Sep daily 1000-1700. £4 entry plus £1 parking. T01807-500206.*

Also in Ballindalloch is the **Glenfarclas Distillery**. ■ *Tours Apr-Sep Mon-Fri 0930-1700; Jun-Sep also Sat 0930-1630; Oct-Mar Mon-Fri 1000-1600. Adult £3.50, under 18s free. T01807-500245, www.glenfarclas.co.uk*

The best place to stay is the superb **A** *Craig iellachie Hotel*, T881204, in the village of Craig iellachie. Also recommended is the **B** *Minmore House Hotel*, T01807-590378, minimorehouse@ukonline.co.uk, open May-Oct, 10 miles southwest of Dufftown, in the village of Glenlivet, it stands right beside the distillery and is the former home of the owner. Also in Craig iellachie is the **E** *Highlander Inn*, on Victoria St, T/F881446. Popular and serves decent bar meals. There's a fairly wide selection of accommodation in Dufftown itself. Two good **B&Bs** are **E** *Davaar*, T820464, on Church St, and **E** *Tullich House*, T821008. Both also provide dinner.

Sleeping & eating

The best place to eat is the moderately priced **A** *Taste of Speyside*, on Balvenie St, T820860. *The Fife Arms Hotel*, T820220, on the square does cheap bar meals. As far as entertainment goes, the *Commercial Hotel*, T820313, on Church St has ceilidhs on Thu nights during the summer.

Bluebird Buses, T01224-212266, runs a daily service from **Elgin** (No 336). There's also a bus (Nos 360 & 361) which connects Dufftown with **Keith** and **Aberlour** (Mon-Fri). For details call *W W Smith*, T01542-882113.

Transport

Central Highlands

Huntly

Phone code: 01466
Colour map 2, grid C5

Ten miles east of Dufftown is the pleasant and prosperous-looking little town of Huntly. Close to the Whisky Trail and on the main Aberdeen to Inverness train route, it makes a convenient base from which to explore this area. The **Tourist Information Centre** is on the main square, T792255. It's open daily April-October 1000-1700; July-August till 1900.

The town also boasts a lovely little castle all of its own. The 16th-century **Huntly Castle** stands in a beautiful setting on the banks of the river Deveron, on the northern edge of town. It was built by the powerful Gordon family and is notable for its fine heraldic sculpture and inscribed stone friezes, particularly over the main door. ■ *Apr-Sep daily 0930-1830; Oct-Mar Mon-Wed and Sat 0930-1630, Thu 0930-1200, Fri and Sun 1400-1630. Adult £2.80, concession £2, children £1. T793191 (HS).*

Near the castle is the **Nordic Ski Centre**, T794428, the only year-round cross-country ski centre in the UK. The centre also hires out ski equipment and mountain bikes.

Seven miles south of town, near the village of Kennethmont, is **Leith Hall**, an unprepossessing mid-17th-century mansion house. The house contains the personal possessions of successive Leith lairds, most of whom saw military service overseas, but more interesting are the extensive grounds which include a six-acre garden, 18th-century stables and ice house, two ponds, a bird observation hide and countryside walks. ■ *Easter and 1 May-30 Sep daily 1330-1730; weekends in Oct 1330-1730. Garden and grounds open all year, daily 0930-dusk. Adult £6, concession £4.50, children £1. T01464-831594 (NTS).*

Sleeping & eating

There's a decent selection of accommodation in and around Huntly. The most impressive place to stay is **C** *The Castle Hotel*, T792696, castlehot@enterprise.net The former home of the Duke of Gordon, it's approached through the castle entrance and then over the river. There are several good **B&Bs** in town, including **E** *Greenmount Guesthouse*, 43 Gordon St, T792482 and **E-F** *Strathlene*, on MacDonald St, T792664. The hotels in town serve bar food, as does the *Auld Pit*, which is a good pub. Another good pub, especially for real ale, is the *Borve Brew House*, in Ruthven, a few miles off the A96 to Keith.

Strathspey and the Cairngorms

One of Scotland's busiest tourist areas is Strathspey, the broad valley of the river Spey, Scotland's second longest river, which rises high in the hills above Loch Laggan and flows northeast to its mouth on the Moray Firth. The lower reaches are famous for salmon fishing and whisky and are covered in the Speyside section of this (see page 182), while the upper reaches attract outdoor sports enthusiasts in droves. Hemmed in between the mighty Monadhliath Mountains to the north and the magnificent Cairngorms, Britain's second highest range, to the south, this is an area which offers excellent hiking, watersports, mountain biking and above all, winter skiing.

The main focus of the area is the tourist resort of Aviemore, a name synonymous with winter sports. It's a fairly tawdry place, but people don't come here for the architecture. Aviemore is surrounded by towering peaks, lochs, rivers and forests of native Caledonian pine which are home to rare wildlife such as pine martens, wildcats, red squirrels, ospreys and capercaillie, and Britian's only herd of wild reindeer. Most of upper Strathspey is privately owned by the Glen More Forest Park and Rothiemurchus Estate which has been in the possession of the Grant family since the 16th century, but both owners allow free access to their lands and provide generous outdoor facilities.

Outdoor sports

Cairngorm is Scotland's longest-established ski resort and though it cannot compare to anything in the Alps or North America, it remains Scotland's largest ski area, with 28 runs and over 20 miles of pistes. When the sun shines, the snowfall is good and the crowds are thin, it can be a very satisfying experience. The season normally runs from January until the snow disappears, which can be as late as April.

Skiing
Phone code: 01479
For latest snow conditions call the Ski Hotline T0900-1654655

The **Cairngorm Ski Area** is about nine miles southeast of Aviemore, above Loch Morlich in Glen More Forest Park and reached by a frequent bus service. You can rent skis and other equipment from the Day Lodge at the foot of the ski area (T861261), where you can also buy a lift pass (£20 per day). Ski hire (skis, poles and boots) costs £13 per day, and snowboard hire is £16. There are plans to replace the chair-lift with a funicular railway, much to the anger of environmentalists, but this may be a few years away.

If there's enough snow, the area around **Loch Morlich** and **Rothiemurchus Estate** provides good **cross-country** skiing, though in recent years snowfall has been below average. For more information, see page 55. The tourist office provides a free *Cairngorm Piste Map & Ride Guide* leaflet and a *Ski Scotland* brochure which lists ski schools and rental facilities.

The Cairngorms provide some of Scotland's most challenging walking, with no fewer than 49 Munros and half of Britain's eight mountains over 4,000 ft (**Ben MacDrui**, **Braeriach**, **Cairn Toul** and **Cairn Gorm**). These mountains come into their own in winter, providing experienced climbers with a wide range of classic ice climbs. They should not be taken lightly. They require a high degree of fitness, experience and preparation (see page 53 for safety precautions).

Walking
The walks around Strathspey are covered by OS Landranger map No 36 (1:50,000 scale) or OS Outdoor Leisure Map No 3 (1:25,000 scale)

The summit of Cairn Gorm (4,084 ft) is readily accessible as you take the chair-lift up to the Day Lodge (see above) and from there it's a relatively short climb to the top, though you should be prepared for a sudden change in weather conditions.

There are 50 miles of footpaths through this area, including some lovely walks through the forests. There are also ranger-led guided walks. You can find out more at the **Rothiemurchus Estate Visitor Centre**, T810858, which is a mile from Aviemore along the Ski Road. It's open daily 0900-1700 and can provide a free *Visitor Guide and Footpath Map*. Another good area for walking is around **Glen More Forest Park**. The **visitor centre**, T861220, near Loch Morlich has a *Glen More Forest Guide Map* which details local walks.

The best known of the long-distance trails is the **Lairig Ghru**, a 25-mile hike from Aviemore over the Lairig Ghru Pass to Braemar. The trail is well marked but can take at least eight hours and is very tough in parts, so you'll need to be properly equipped and prepared.

In summer, the main activities are watersports and there are two centres which offer sailing, canoeing and windsurfing tuition and equipment hire. The **Loch Morlich Watersports Centre** (T861221, lochmorlichw-s@sol.co.uk; open

Watersports

Central Highlands

Loch an Eilein walk

As well as the many tough hill walks, there are some excellent low-level walks. An easy circular walk of about four hours around Loch an Eilean in Rothiemurchus Estate starts from the end of the side road which turns east off the B970 two miles south of Aviemore.

From the car park at the end of the road head for the lochside. The route around the loch is clearly marked and it's difficult to lose your way as it follows the loch shore. It's a very pleasant walk through woodland with views of a 14th century castle ruin on an island in the middle of the loch. You can extend the walk by around a mile by including the circuit around Loch Gamhna. The paths around Loch an Eilein are also connected with the massive network of trails around Rothiemurchus. OS Sheet 36.

Apr-Oct) is five miles east of Aviemore. The **Loch Insh Watersports Centre**, T651272, user@lochinsh.dial.netmedia.co.uk, open Apr-Oct, offers the same facilities, plus fishing, mountain bike hire and ski instruction on a dry ski slope.

Fishing Fishing is a major pursuit in the area. You can fish for trout and salmon on the **River Spey** and the Rothiemurchus Estate has trout fishing on its stocked loch at **Inverdruie**, where you can hire rods. Fishing permits cost around £10-15 per day for the stocked lochs and £20-30 per day for the River Spey. They are sold at local shops such as *Speyside Sports* in Aviemore, and at *Loch Morlich Watersports Centre* which also hires out rods and tackle. **Alvie Estate**, T01540-651255, near Kingussie also hires rods.

Mountain biking Rothiemurchus and Glen More estates are great areas for mountain biking with lots of excellent forest trails. The **Rothiemurchus Visitor Centre** (see above) at Inverdruie has route maps and you can also hire bikes. Bike hire and good advice on routes is also available at *Bothy Bikes*, Unit 7, Grampian Rd, Aviemore, T810111, open daily 0900-1800. *Aviemore Mountain Bikes*, T811007, at 45a Grampian Rd, organises guided bike tours.

Horse riding Horse riding and pony trekking are on offer at various places throughout Strathspey. There's *Alvie Stables*, at Alvie near Kincraig, T01540-651409, mobile T0831-495397, *Carrbridge Trekking Centre*, Station Rd, Carrbridge, T841602, and *Strathspey Highland Pony Centre*, Rowanlea, Faebuie, Grantown-on-Spey, T873073.

Loch Morlich to Lairig Ghru walk

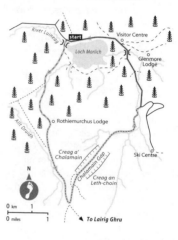

The famous Lairig Ghru is an ancient route through the Cairngorms which passes between Ben Macdui and Braeriach. It is a very strenuous walk and only for fit and experienced hikers. An easier propostion is a 12-mile loop which leads to the start of the Lairig Ghru pass, starting from Loch Morlich. To reach Loch Morlich take the B970 east from the southern end of Aviemore, beyond Coylumbridge. The route starts at the western end of Loch Morlich where a forestry track runs south from the road. It leads to a bridge over the River Luineag. Cross the bridge and continue along the track, keeping straight on where another track heads off left. About a mile further on, another track heads off to the right, but keep to the left fork, signposted for Rothiemurchus Lodge.

The track climbs up towards the lodge. Just before it, turn right onto a clear track which leads up to a reservoir. Soon another track heads off to the right signposted for the Lairig Ghru. Follow this path through heather moorland. The path then heads left, climbing up through open moorland to the lip of the glen. The entrance to the Lairig Ghru is straight ahead.

After about a mile, as the hills begin to encroach on either side, a rough path almost doubles back to the left. Follow this

path up the slope to the gap between Creag a' Chalamain and Creag an Leith-choin. The deep gully, the Chalamain Gap, is filled with huge boulders and requires great care when clambering through it. Beyond the gully a path leads through heather and pine saplings, dropping down to the side of a burn, then climbing up on the other side of the burn. Continue on this path, which then drops steeply down to the side of the burn. Cross the footbridge and climb the slope beyond to reach the main road. Turn left along the road to return to the start of the route.

Aviemore and around

In the 1960s Aviemore was transformed from a sleepy Highland village into the jumble of concrete buildings, tacky gift shops and sprawling coach parks that it is today. The extent of the tourist tat here is so awful it makes Fort William seem charmingly understated by comparison, and there can be few more depressing and hideous sights than Santa Claus Land children's theme park on a drizzly afternoon in November. In saying that, however, the town is the most important tourist centre in the area and has a wide range of facilities.

Phone code: 01479
Colour map 4, grid A3
Population: 2,500

The town lies just off
the A9, 33 miles
south of Inverness

The train station, banks, restaurants and pretty much everything else are all found along Grampian Road. Buses stop here too (see 'Transport' below).

Ins and outs

There are **buses** to and from Inverness Perth and Edinburgh and direct **trains** to and from Glasgow, Edinburgh and Inverness.

Getting there

Tourist Information Centre The TIC is on Grampian Rd, about 400 yds south of the train station, T810363. They will book accommodation as well as provide free maps and leaflets on local attractions and change foreign currency. Apr-Oct Mon-Fri 0900-1800, Sat 1000-1700, Sun 1000-1600; Nov-Mar Mon-Fri 0900-1700, Sat 1000-1700.

Essentials

Sleeping
There's no shortage of accommodation around Aviemore

The best choice in the area is the **A** *Corrour House Hotel*, at Inverdruie, 2 miles southeast of Aviemore, T810220, www.corrourhouse.co.uk, open Dec-Oct. This Victorian country house oozes charm, enjoys wonderful views and offers superb cuisine. Also recommended is the **D** *Rowan Tree Restaurant & Guest House*, at Loch Alvie, 1½ miles south of Aviemore on the B9152, T810207, enquiries@rowantreehotel.com, open Dec-Oct. This is one of the oldest hotels in the area and offers excellent food (lunch cheap; dinner moderate). One mile south of Aviemore, at Lynwilg, is the beautiful **D** *Lynwilg House*, T811685, marge@lynwilg.co.uk, a charming, friendly guesthouse with a reputation for good food. There are lots of **B&Bs** in Aviemore itself, including and **C** *Vermont Guest House*, T810470, and **E** *Ravenscraig Guest House*, T810278, ravenscrg@aol.com, both on Grampian Rd.

There are a couple of good hostels in Aviemore. The large **F** *SYHA hostel*, T810345, is on Grampian Rd near the tourist office and open all year. There's also the **F** *Aviemore Independent Bunkhouse and Backpackers Hostel*, T811137, on Dalfaber Rd. There are several good **campsites**, including the *Rothiemurchus Camping & Caravan Park*, T812800, at Coylumbridge, and a *Forest Enterprise* site at Glenmore, T861271.

Eating Apart from the hotels and guesthouses listed above, the best place to eat in Aviemore is the *Old Bridge Inn*, T811137, on Dalfaber Rd. This lovely old pub serves excellent value food and hosts ceilidhs and Highland dinner dances in the summer months. There's a good lochside restaurant at the *Loch Insh Watersports Centre* at Kincraig, between Aviemore and Kingussie, which doubles as a café during the day.

Transport There are *Scottish Citylink* **buses**, T0990-505050, between Aviemore and **Inverness** (45 mins), **Kingussie** (20 mins), **Pitlochry** (1¼ hrs), **Perth** (2 hrs), **Glasgow** (3½ hrs) and **Edinburgh** (3½ hrs). For **Aberdeen**, change at Inverness. **Car hire** from *MacDonald's Self Drive*, 13 Muirton, T811444.

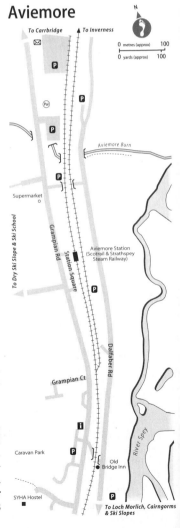

Aviemore

There are direct **trains** to and from **Glasgow** and **Edinburgh** (3 hrs) and **Inverness** (40 mins). For details T0345-484950. The *Strathspey Steam Railway*, T810725, runs between Aviemore, Boat of Garten and Nethy Bridge. The station is just to the east of the main train station. The *Cairngorm Chairlift Company*, T861261, runs daily buses between Aviemore and Cairngorm Ski Centre from late Oct to Apr.

Around Aviemore

There's nothing of real interest in Aviemore. The real enjoyment lies in the surrounding mountains and forests, though there are a few interesting places close at hand. A great place for kids is the **Cairngorm Reindeer Centre**, in Glen More Forest Park, on the road from Coylumbridge, seven miles from Aviemore. ■ *Guided walks to see the herd and feed them leave daily at 1100 and also at 1430 during the summer. Adult £5, children £3. T861228.*

Eight miles northeast of Aviemore is the tiny village of Boat of Garten which suddenly shot to fame when a pair of **ospreys**, which had disappeared from these shores, reappeared on nearby **Loch Garten**, two miles east of the village. Now these beautiful birds of prey have established themselves here and elsewhere and there are thought to be well over 100 pairs throughout the Highlands. The **Abernethy Forest RSPB Reserve** on the shore of Loch Garten is best visited during the nesting season, between late April and August when the RSPB opens an **observation centre**. This is the only place in the world to see Scottish crossbills. ■ *Daily in season 1000-1800. £2.50 for non-members.* You can also see ospreys at the Rothiemurchus trout loch at Inverdruie, and maybe even on Loch Morlich and Loch Insh. The reserve is also home to several other rare species such as capercaillie, whooper swans and red squirrels. Guided walks leave from the observation centre at 0930 on Wednesdays.

Boat of Garten
*Phone code: 01479
Colour map 4,
grid A3*

Sleeping and eating There's a good selection of accommodation in the village. **C-D** *Heathbank – The Victorian House*, T831234, is a must for Art Nouveau lovers and offers good French cuisine, while the **C-D** *Boat Hotel*, T831258, offers cheap and tasty meals. **D-E** *Glenavon House*, T831213, open Apr-Oct, is a lovely guesthouse on Kinchurdy Rd, and **D-E** *Moorfield House*, on Deshar Rd, T831646, moorfieldhouse@msn.com, is also a good choice. You can also **camp** at *Campgrounds of Scotland*, T831652.

Transport The best way to get to Boat of Garten is on the *Strathspey Steam Railway* which runs at least 5 times daily from Aviemore, T810725. Loch Garten is not easy to reach without your own transport, but check with one of the local TICs about tours.

At Carrbridge, a pleasant little village seven miles north of Aviemore, is the **Landmark Forest Heritage Park**, a woodland theme park which combines entertainment, education and shopping. There's a raised Treetop Trail for viewing wildlife, a fire tower, maze and various nature trails and fun rides. It manages to avoid being tacky and is good fun for kids. ■ *Daily Apr to mid-Jul 0930-1800; mid-Jul to Aug 0930-2000; Sep and Oct 0930-1730; Nov-Mar 1000-1700. Adult £6.85, Adult with children £6.50, children £4.55. T841614.* In the village itself is the decidedly fragile-looking 18th-century **Bridge of Carr**, which is not for vertigo sufferers.

Carrbridge

Sleeping and eating There are several places to stay in Carrbridge. Top of the range is the stylish **B** *Dalrachney Lodge Hotel*, T841252, www.dalrachney.co.uk, a former

Victorian hunting lodge with a good restaurant. More down to earth, but nonetheless comfortable is the **E** *Cairn Hotel*, T841212, cairn.carrbridge@talk21.com, which serves good-value bar meals. There's also the much cheaper option of the *Carrbridge Bunkhouse Hostel*, T841250, at Dalrachney House, half a mile north of the village on the road to Inverness.

Transport There are several **buses** daily (except Sun) to Carrbridge from **Inverness** and **Grantown-on-Spey** with *Highland Country Buses*, T01463-233371.

Kingussie

Phone code: 01540
Colour map 4, grid A2
Population: 1,500

The quiet village of Kingussie (pronounced King-yoosie) lies 12 miles southwest of Aviemore and makes a pleasant alternative as a place to stay. The **Tourist Information Centre** (T661297) is housed in the Folk Museum (see below) and has the same opening hours.

Sights The main attraction here is the excellent **Highland Folk Museum** which contains a fascinating collection of traditional highland artefacts, as well as a farming museum, an old smokehouse, a water mill and traditional Hebridean 'blackhouse'. During the summer there are also demonstrations of spinning, woodcarving and peat-fire baking. ■ *T661307. May-Aug Mon-Fri 0930-1730, Sat and Sun 1300-1700; Apr, Sep and Oct guided tours only Mon-Fri 1030-1630. Adult £4, concession and children £2.40.*

Another worthwhile attraction is **Ruthven Barracks**, standing on a hillock across the river. This former barracks was built by the English Redcoats as part of their campaign to tame the Highlands after the first Jacobite rising in 1715. It was destroyed by the Jacobites in the wake of defeat at Culloden to prevent it from falling into enemy hands and it was from here that Bonnie Prince Charlie sent his final order which signalled the end of his doomed cause. Access is free and the ruins are particularly attractive at night when floodlit.

At nearby **Kincraig** village, between Kingussie and Aviemore, is the **Highland Wildlife Park**, which has a captive collection of rare native animals. ■ *Daily Apr, May, Sep and Oct 1000-1800; Jun-Aug till 1900; Nov-Mar 1000-1600. Park tours: adult £6.50, concession £5.40, children £4.35. T651270.* Those who mourn the loss of the hit TV show, *One Man and His Dog*, will be excited at the prospect of visiting the **Working Sheepdogs Show** at the nearby Leault Farm, where you can see demonstrations of dogs rounding up a flock of sheep. ■ *Daily. Adult £3.50. T651310.*

Sleeping **B** *The Osprey Hotel*, Ruthven Rd, T661510, www.ospreyhotel.co.uk, is a comfortable little hotel with a very good restaurant (expensive). The **D** *Scot House Hotel*, Newtonmore Rd, T661351, www.scothouse.com, is another good choice and also offers great food (lunch cheap; dinner midrange to expensive). There are several good guesthouses, all on Newtonmore Rd, including: **E** *Arden House*, T661369, **E** *Avondale House*, T661731, walsh.lorraine@talk21.com, and **E** *Homewood Lodge*, T661507, homewood@kingussie.ndirect.co.uk There's also **B&B** at **E** *Glengarry*, T661386, www.scots98.freeserve.co.uk, on East Terrace, and **E** *Greystones*, on Acres Rd, T661052, greystones@ lineone.net

There are several decent **hostels** in the area (all **F**): *The Laird's Bothy*, T661334, is on the High St next to the *Tipsy Laird* pub; *Bothan Airigh Bunkhouse*, T661051, is at Insh, a few miles east of Ruthven Barracks on the B970; *Kirkbeag Hostel*, T651298, is in Kincraig, between Kingussie and Aviemore; and at Balachroick House in Glen Feshie, near Kincraig, is *Glen Feshie Hostel*, T651323. In Newtonmore, a few miles west of

Kingussie on the A86, is the *Newtonmore Independent Hostel*, T673360, hostel.newtonmore@dial.pipex.com, and at Laggan Bridge, 8 miles further west on the A86, is the *Pottery Bunkhouse*, T01528-544231, attached to the *Caoldair Pottery*.

The *Osprey Hotel* and *Scot House Hotel* both have very good restaurants, but the outstanding place to eat in this area is the award-winning *The Cross*, T661166, on Tweed Mill Brae, a private drive leading off Ardbroilach Rd. This restaurant with rooms (**L** for dinner, B&B) is expensive but well worth it. Open Mar-Nov & Christmas; closed Tue. The *Tipsy Laird* pub serves good meals and real ales and *La Cafetière* is a nice café. **Eating**

Kingussie is on the main Inverness to Perth/Glasgow/Edinburgh routes. All **Perth-Inverness trains** stop here and most *Citylink* **buses**. For rail enquiries, T0345-484950. There's also an infrequent school bus service run by *Highland Country Buses* between Kingussie, **Aviemore**, **Newtonmore** and **Dalwhinnie**. **Transport**

Grantown-on-Spey

This genteel Georgian holiday town is 15 miles northeast of Aviemore and attracts the more mature tourist by the coach-load. Everything here is geared towards fishing and anyone wishing to get kitted out in proper style should get themselves down to either *Mortimers* or *Ritchies* on the High Street. The **Tourist Information Centre**, T872773, is also here, open daily from April to October 0900-1800.

Phone code: 01479
Colour map 4,
grid A3
Population: 3,250

Central Highlands

As you'd expect in such a respectable place, there's a wide range of upmarket accommodation and a number of very good places to eat. The best places in town are all on Woodlands Terr: **L** *Culdearn House*, T872106, www.culdearn.com, and **D** *Ardconnell House*, T872104, enquiry@ardconnel.com, both of which offer excellent food. **Sleeping & eating**

At **Dulnain Bridge**, a few miles southwest of town, is the elegant **C** *Auchendean Lodge Hotel*, T851347, www.auchendean.com, and the handsome **B-C** *Muckrach Lodge Hotel & Restaurant*, T851257, muckrachlodge@sol.co.uk, both of which have superb restaurants. There are lots of other very good guesthouses and B&Bs to choose from, as well as the *Speyside Backpackers*, T873514, an independent hostel, also known as *The Stop-Over*, at 16 The Square.

There are several **buses** daily (Mon-Sat) between Grantown and **Aviemore** (35 mins) and 2 or 3 buses daily, except Sun, to and from **Inverness** (1 ¼ hrs). **Transport**

North and Northwest Highlands

North and Northwest Highlands

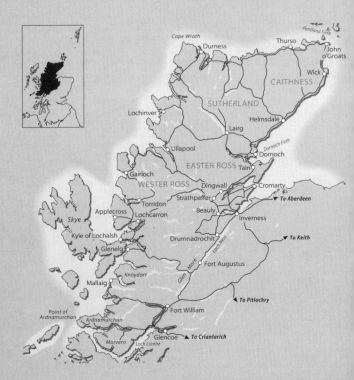

The northwest coast is the part which reflects most perfectly people's romantic image of Scotland. The main town is Fort William, which lies in the shadow of **Ben Nevis**, Britain's highest mountain. North from here stretches a dramatic shoreline of deep sea lochs and sheltered coves of pure white sand backed by towering mountains and looking across to numerous Hebridean islands. West of Fort William, via the lyrical 'Road to the Isles', is Mallaig, now the main departure point for ferries to **Skye**. Further north is Ullapool, one of the main ferry ports for the **Outer Hebrides** and the ideal base from which to explore the wild and near-deserted far northwest.

    Inverness is the largest town in the region and 'capital of the Highlands'. It lies at the northeastern end of the Great Glen, which cuts diagonally across the southern Highlands to Fort William, linking deep and mysterious **Loch Ness** with the west coast and giving access to **Glencoe**, one of the most beautifully evocative Highland glens and a major climbing and skiing centre. Inverness is also ideally situated for exploring the northeast coast, with its charming old fishing ports, and the storm-lashed north coast, running west from John O'Groats to **Cape Wrath**, as wild and remote a place as you could ever wish for.

Ins and outs

Getting there
For more transport details, see pages 36 & 197

Inverness is linked to the south by the fast A9 from Edinburgh and Perth, to Aberdeen by the A96 and to Fort William by the A82, and is well served by buses. Wick, Thurso, Ullapool and Kyle of Lochalsh can all be reached by bus from Inverness. The rail line from Edinburgh closely follows the A9 to Inverness, and there are connections north to Wick and Thurso, west to Kyle of Lochalsh and east to Aberdeen. **Fort William** is easily reached from Glasgow by buses and trains, which continue to Mallaig for the ferry to Skye.

Getting around
By far the most scenic route to the Highlands is the spectacular West Highland Railway, one of the world's great rail journeys, particularly the section from Fort William to Mallaig

Getting around in the Highlands is a lot easier with your own transport, especially in the more remote parts, but it's not difficult to reach the main tourist centres by bus or train. Getting off the beaten track can be a little more complicated, but with forward planning is easily achievable. Much of the time you'll need to rely on the local postbus service, which runs between the various remote post offices throughout the region. Timetables are available at most post offices or Tourist Information Centres (see also page 43). A good idea is to purchase the Public Transport Travel Guides, for South Highland and/or North Highland and Orkney. These are available at main tourist offices for £1. Note that details of ferries from the mainland ports to Skye, the Outer Hebrides and Orkney are given in the respective island chapters.

Information

Roughly speaking, this chapter covers the northern half of mainland Scotland. It includes the Highland administrative region, minus the Isle of Skye, which has its own chapter, and is covered by the **Highlands of Scotland Tourist Board**, T01997-421160, www.highlandfreedom.com, which publishes free accommodation guides for the region. They will also book accommodation for a nominal fee. Note that many of the smaller offices are closed during the low season. There's also a local website which has lots of information, including maps, at www.cali.co.uk/highexp/

Climate

The beauty of the northwest Highlands is only enhanced by the notoriously unpredictable weather and that ever-present travelling companion, the midge. That's a lie. The midge is the scourge of many a Highland holiday. A ferocious, persistent and unbelievably irritating little beast who will drive you to the edge of insanity. For details on how best to combat this little terror, see page 62.

The only predictable thing about the weather is its unpredictability. You can have blazing sunshine in Apr, pouring rain in Jul and a blizzard in May. So, you'll need to be prepared for everything. Climbers and walkers especially must take heed of all weather warnings. It can be hot enough for bikinis in the car park at the foot of a 2,000-ft mountain, and 2 hrs later near the summit you're faced with driving, horizontal hail, rain or snow and unable to see further than the end of your nose. People die every year on the Scottish mountains, simply because they are ill-prepared, and it is essential to take proper precautions (see page 53). Even those who are not intent on bagging the odd Munro should remember the old adage, that there's no such thing as bad weather, only inadequate clothing.

★

Things to do in the north and northwest Highlands

- Go for a drive up glorious Glen Affric, one of the very loveliest of Highland glens.
- Choose the West Highland choo-choo, one of the world's great train journeys.
- Take a trip from Shiel Bridge to the splendidly isolated village of Glenelg.
- Travel the stunning route to Applecross and enjoy some wonderful seafood in the cosy Applecross Inn.
- Go for a walk along the beach at Sandwood Bay and watch the sun set with a loved one.

Inverness

Inverness is the largest town in the Highlands and the busy and prosperous hub of the region. All main routes through the Highlands pass through here at some point, so it's a hard place to avoid. The town's position at the head of the Great Glen and on the shores of the Moray Firth have made it a firm favourite with tourists, who flock here in their legions during the summer months to look for the evasive Loch Ness Monster. Though Inverness has little in the way of major sights, it's a pleasant place to base yourself as you explore the other, more visible attractions on offer in the surrounding area, including the resident population of dolphins in the Moray Firth. The town, though, is not without its own appeal, particularly the leafy banks of the River Ness, which runs through its heart, linking Loch Ness with the Moray Firth.

Phone code: 01463
Colour map 2, grid C2
Population: 42,000

Ins and outs

There are daily **flights** to and from London Gatwick, Glasgow and Edinburgh with *British Airways* (continuing to Kirkwall and Sumburgh), and daily flights to and from London Luton with *easyJet*. There are also flights to and from Stornoway Mon-Sat with *British Airways Express*. The airport is 7 miles east of the town, at Dalcross (T232471). A twice-daily airport bus to and from the town centre connects with London and Stornoway flights. It takes 20 mins and costs £2.50. A taxi to/from the airport costs £10.

Getting there
For further details see page 204. Inverness is 109 miles from Aberdeen, 161 miles from Edinburgh & 117 miles from Perth

The **bus station** is nearby, just off Academy St (T233371). Left luggage costs £1 per item, open Mon-Sat 0830-1800, Sun 1000-1800.

The **train station** is at the east end of Academy St (T238924). There are regular services to Aviemore, Perth, Glasgow, Edinburgh and Kyle of Lochalsh (for Skye). Left luggage lockers at the train station cost £2-4 per 24 hrs.

Inverness town centre is compact and easy to explore on foot and most of the hotels and guesthouses are within a 15-min walk of the TIC. Loch Ness is not within walkable distance, so you'll need your own transport, or alternatively book a tour (see page 198).

Getting around

The TIC, T234353, is on Castle Wynd, near Ness Bridge, 5-mins walk from the train station. It stocks a wide range of literature on the area, can book accommodation and transport and gives out free maps of the town and environs. Tickets for all the tours listed on the next few pages are available from the TIC. Open 2 Apr-27 May Mon-Sat 0900-1700, Sun (Easter and from 6 May) 1000-1600; 28 May-24 Jun Mon-Sat 0900-1800, Sun 0930-1700; 25 Jun-22 Jul Mon-Sat 0900-1900, Sun 0930-1700; 23 Jul-19 Aug Mon-Sat 0900-2030, Sun 0930-1800; 20 Aug-2 Sep Mon-Sat 0900-1900, Sun 0930-1700; 3 Sep-30 Sep Mon-Sat 0900-1800, Sun 1000-1600; 1 Oct-21 Oct Mon-Sat 0900-1700, Sun 1000-1600; 22 Oct-Apr Mon-Fri 0900-1700, Sat 1000-1600.

Tourist Information Centre

☞ **Monster tours**

There are various monster-spotting tours of **Loch Ness** *which leave from the tourist office. Guide Friday are based at the train station, T224000. They run half-day coach trips right round the loch, at 1030 and 1430, lasting 3 hours. Tickets: adult £14.50, concession £11.50, children £6.50, available from booking office at the train station or the tourist office.*

Coach tours, boat cruises and combined coach and cruise trips round the loch are offered by Jacobite Cruises (T233999, *jacobite@cali.co.uk) Half day cruises cost £10, half day coach and cruise trips cost £14.50 (including entry to the Loch Ness Monster Exhibition and Urquhart Castle). Trips run from April-October and leave from Tomnahurich Bridge on Glenurquhart Road, 1½ miles south of the town centre. Free buses leave from the TIC 20 minutes before sailing, if tickets are bought here. Otherwise, to get there take Inverness Traction buses Nos 3, 3A, 4 and 4A every 15 minutes from Church Street.*

History

One of the town's first visitors was that much-travelled cleric, St Columba, who came in AD 565 to confront the Pictish King Brude, whose fortress was reputedly at **Craig Phadraig**, a few miles west of Inverness. Around the mid-12th century King David I built the original castle and made Inverness a royal burgh on the strength of its growing importance as a trading port. Furs, hides, wool and timber were all exported as far afield as the Mediterranean. The town's economic prosperity and status as the most important northern outpost, however, made it a prime target for marauding Highland clansmen, and during the Wars of Independence in the 13th century, Inverness was also a regular target for both English and Scots armies.

The town's renaissance came with the completion of the Caledonian Canal and rail links with the south in the 19th century. These improved communications heralded something of a tourist boom amongst the wealthy and fashionable who came north to the Highlands to shoot anything that moved in the name of sport. In the mid-19th century Queen Victoria decided to embrace all things Scottish, which only boosted the town's popularity. Over recent decades, Inverness has grown rapidly, not only as a prime base for visiting tourists, but also as the main administrative and commercial centre for the Highlands.

Sights

The castle The town is dominated by its red sandstone castle. Built in 1834, this Victorian edifice is very much the new kid on the block in terms of Scottish castles. The original castle dates from the 12th century and was built on a ridge to the east of the present structure. Nothing remains of the old castle, which is unsurprising given its bloody and eventful history. It was here that King Duncan of Scotland was slain by Macbeth, an event dramatically (and erroneously) portrayed in Shakespeare's eponymous work. The castle was occupied three times during the Wars of Independence in the 13th century and when Robert the Bruce recaptured it in 1307, he destroyed it. In the mid-17th century Cromwell ordered his men to build a stone version on the same site. In 1715 James Francis Edward was proclaimed king there, but not

Tours of Inverness

*An open-top double-decker **Bus Tour** around Inverness and Culloden is run by Guide Friday. Tours leave from Bridge Street near the tourist office at 1000 and then every 45 minutes till 1645, from May to October. Tickets can be bought at their booth in the train station, T224000; open Mon-Fri 0900-1730, Sat 0830-1745, or on board the bus. A full day ticket: adult £7.50, concession £6 , children £2.50. The city only tour costs £5.50/£4/£2.50.*

The Inverness Terror Tour leaves from outside the tourist office at 1900 nightly and tells the tale of the town's horrific past, complete with witches, ghosts, torture and murders.

long after, it was destroyed by the Jacobites to prevent it from falling into enemy hands following the defeat of Bonnie Prince Charlie at Culloden (see page 219).

The present castle houses the Sheriff Court and also stages the **Castle Garrison Encounter**, where you can sign up as a mid-18th century soldier. New recruits (that's you) pass through the Quartermaster's Store and are introduced to the Sergeant of the Guard, before being accosted by a female camp follower and finally led out through the garrison shop. ■ *Mar-Nov Mon-Sat (Sun only in Jul/Aug) 1030-1730. Adult £3, concession £2.70, children £2. T243363.*

On the castle terrace is a statue of **Flora MacDonald**, to honour her part in helping the prince to escape (see page 299). Below the castle is **Inverness Museum and Art Gallery**, on Castle Wynd beside the Tourist Information Centre . The museum gives a decent overview of the history of the town and the region, while the gallery is eminently missable. ■ *Mon-Sat 0900-1700. Free.*

Around the castle

Just around the corner, on High Street, is the Gothic-style **Town House**, where Prime Minister Lloyd George held an emergency cabinet meeting in 1921, the first ever to be held outside London.

Opposite, on the corner of Bridge Street and Church Street, is the **Tolbooth Steeple** which dates from 1791 and which had to be repaired after an earth tremor in 1816. Church Street also boasts the town's oldest building, **Abertarff House** (built around 1592), which is now owned by the National Trust but not open to the public. Almost opposite is the much-restored **Dunbar's Hospital**, built in 1688 as an almshouse for the town's poor. At the end of Church Street, where it meets Friar's Lane, is the **Old High Church**, founded in the 12th century and rebuilt in 1772, though the 14th-century vaulted tower remains intact. In the adjoining graveyard, prisoners taken at Culloden were executed and you can still see the bullet marks left by the firing squads on some of the gravestones. ■ *The church is open on Fri 1200-1400 and during services; guided tour at 1230.*

Church Street

At the corner of Huntly Street and Ness Bridge, is the **Kiltmaker Centre**, where you can learn everything you ever wanted to know about tartan (including what Scotsmen wear under their kilts). You can also see kilts being made in the factory and, in the shop downstairs, be measured up for one of your own. ■ *Mid-May to end of Sep Mon-Sat 0900-2100, Sun 1000-1700; Oct to mid-May Mon-Sat 0900-1700. Adult £2. T222781, www.hector-russell.com*

West Bank

Nearby, directly opposite the castle, is the neo-Gothic **St Andrews Cathedral** which dates from 1869, and is worth a peek if you're passing by.

North & Northwest Highlands

Continuing south along Ness Bank, past the **Eden Court Theatre** (see 'Entertainment' below), you reach **Bught Park** (see 'Sleeping'), which overlooks the **Ness Islands**, joined by footbridge to both banks. The islands are attractively laid out as a park and are a favourite with local anglers. This also happens to be a lovely place for a peaceful evening stroll.

Inverness

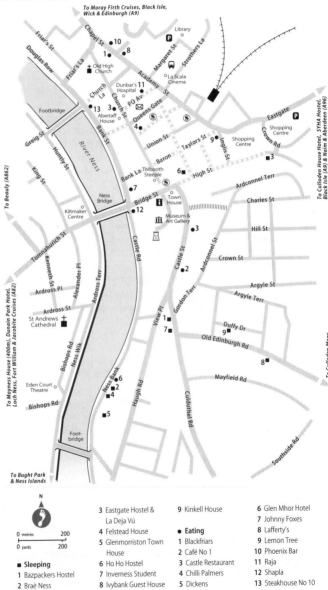

North & Northwest Highlands

■ **Sleeping**		
1 Bazpackers Hostel	3 Eastgate Hostel & La Deja Vú	9 Kinkell House
2 Braè Ness	4 Felstead House	● **Eating**
	5 Glenmorriston Town House	1 Blackfriars
	6 Ho Ho Hostel	2 Café No 1
	7 Inverness Student	3 Castle Restaurant
	8 Ivybank Guest House	4 Chilli Palmers
		5 Dickens
		6 Glen Mhor Hotel
		7 Johnny Foxes
		8 Lafferty's
		9 Lemon Tree
		10 Phoenix Bar
		11 Raja
		12 Shapla
		13 Steakhouse No 10

Essentials

Sleeping

You shouldn't have much trouble finding somewhere to stay in Inverness, though in Jul and Aug it's advisable to book ahead. This can be done through the tourist information centre, or in the train station at the Thomas Cook booth, but you'll be charged a booking fee (see page 39). There are several good quality hotels in and around town and plenty of B&Bs. The best places to look are along both banks of the river south of the Ness Bridge, Old Edinburgh Rd, Southside Rd, Culduthel Rd and Ardconnel St, all to the east of the castle, and on the west bank, behind Balnain House, around Kenneth St and Fairfield Rd. There are also several budget hostels in and around the centre, and a couple of large campsites.

■ *on map*
Price codes:
see inside front cover

L *Culloden House Hotel*, Milton of Culloden, about 3 miles east of town near the A9. T790461, F792181. 28 rooms, superb Georgian mansion with 1st-class facilities, service and restaurant. **L** *Dunain Park Hotel*, about 3 miles southwest of the town centre, just off the A82 Fort William Rd. T230512, F224532, dunainparkhotel@btinternet.com 12 rooms, in an elegant Georgian mansion house with its own grounds, lovely and peaceful with an excellent restaurant (see below) and its own indoor pool. **L** *Glenmoriston Town House Hotel*, 20 Ness Bank. T223777, F712378. 15 rooms. Recently refurbished and now one of the classiest places in town with a superb Italian restaurant (see below). **L** *Inverness Marriot*, Culcabock Rd, 1 mile south of the town centre near A9, T237166, F225208. 81 rooms, large, modern hotel with excellent rooms, service and facilities.

B *Glenruidh House Hotel*, Old Edinburgh Rd South, 2 miles from the town centre (phone for directions). T226499, F710745, glenruidhhousehotel@btinternet.com 6 rooms, no smoking. Comfortable and peaceful hotel in secluded setting, with friendly service and excellent food.

D *Moyness House Hotel*, 6 Bruce Gardens. T/F233836, kayjonesmoyness@msn.com Fine Victorian villa in a quiet area near the theatre, with comfortable rooms and very good food. **D** *Brae Ness Hotel*, 17 Ness Bank. T712266, F231732. 10 rooms, no smoking. Family-run Georgian hotel overlooking the river and Eden Court with a licensed restaurant for residents. **D** *Felstead House*, 18 Ness Bank. T/F231634, felstead@jafsoft.com 8 rooms, 5 with bathroom en suite. Family-run Georgian guesthouse, large and comfortable rooms, good breakfast and overall good value. **D** *Ivybank Guesthouse*, 28 Old Edinburgh Rd. T/F232796. 5 rooms, 3 with en suite bathroom. Georgian house with lots of character, nice garden and friendly welcome. **D** *Kinkell House*, 11 Old Edinburgh Rd. T235243, F225255, clare@kinkell. freeserve.co.uk 7 rooms, 3 with en suite bathroom. Comfortable Victorian family home with spacious rooms, decent value, £2 charge for credit card payment.

F *Bazpackers Hostel*, 4 Culduthel Rd (at the top of Castle St), T717663. 48 beds in dorms of 4-8, twin and double rooms available, cooking facilities and garden for barbecues, also has laundrette, good atmosphere. **F** *Eastgate Hostel*, 38 Eastgate (above *La Déjà Vu* restaurant). T/F718756. 38 beds in 8 dorms, free tea and coffee and continental breakfast for £1.50. **F** *Inverness Student Hotel*, 8 Culduthel Rd, next door to *Bazpackers*. T236556. 9 dorms with 57 beds, some dorms have good views. Friendly and laid-back atmosphere with all the usual facilities. **F** *SYHA Youth Hostel*, Victoria Drive, off Millburn Rd. T231771, F710349. 166 beds, huge hostel in former school hall of residence. Another cheap option is the **F** *Ho Ho Hostel*, T221225, at 23a High St. *Bught*

North & Northwest Highlands

The big blue

There are various **dolphin-spotting cruises** around the Moray Firth, but there is a code of conduct for boat operators. Before you choose a cruise, make sure the company is part of the Accreditation Scheme. One such company, based in Inverness, is **Moray Firth Dolphin Cruises**, T717900, morayfirth.cruises@virgin.net Trips are £10 (£8 concession), last 1½ hours and leave from Shore Street Quay (beyond the roundabout at the far end of Chapel St). Buses run from the tourist information centre 15 minutes before sailings. Also in Inverness are **McAuley Charters**, Harbour offices, Longman Drive, T717337. Dolphin-spotting cruises also leave from Cromarty (see page 276) and Buckie. Buckie is also the home of the **Moray Firth Wildlife Centre**, which houses a **dolphin exhibition**, where you can find out evrything you ever wanted to know about them.

Caravan and Camping Site, Bught Park, on the west bank of the river near the sports centre, T236920. The largest and most centrally located campsite, with good facilities, charges £4.30-11.40 per pitch.

Eating

No shortage of places to eat in Inverness — As you'd expect in a major tourist centre, there's the usual plethora of pubs, cafés and restaurants serving cheap and basic food for the non-discerning palate, but those looking for a higher standard of cuisine won't be disappointed either. There are also loads of takeaways, particularly on Academy St and the Eastgate around the train station, and on Young St, just across the Ness Bridge. A good bakery is *Asher's* in Church St.

Expensive *Dunain Park Hotel* (address as above). Award-winning Scots-French cuisine in elegant surroundings and a superb list of malts, take a stroll in the lovely gardens afterwards. *Glen Mhor Hotel*, 9-12 Ness Bank, T234308. *Riverview* restaurant at the front is good, especially for seafood. *La Riviera*, at the *Glenmoriston Town House Hotel* (see above). Excellent Italian food.

Mid-range *Café No 1*, 75 Castle St, T226200. Stands head and shoulders above everything else in the town centre in terms of quality and imagination, has nice contemporary décor, good selection of vegetarian options, open for lunch and 1800-2200. *Dickens*, 77 Church St. T713111. Offers a mix of oriental and international dishes with an emphasis on fish, business lunch for £6.50, open 1200-1400 and 1730-2300. *La Déjà vu*, 38 Eastgate. T231075. Very good French provincial cooking in an informal atmosphere, their 3-course business lunch is great value at £7, open daily 1200-1400 and 1700 till late. *Nico's Bistro* at the back is also good for traditional Scottish dishes. *Raja*, behind the post office on Post Office Av. T237190. Highly rated Indian restaurant. *Shapla*, 2 Castle Rd, T241919. Good Indian restaurant with Tandoori and Balti menu, good views of the river in the upstairs lounge, open till 2330. *Steakhouse No 10*, 10 Bank St. T714884. Specializes in crêpes and steaks, offers reasonably priced snacks 1100-1500, and à la carte lunch and dinner.

Cheap *Castle Restaurant*, 41 Castle St. Glorified greasy spoon serving huge portions of stodgy, filling grub, convenient for backpacker's hostels, open till 2100. *The Lemon Tree*, 18 Inglis St. Located in the pedestrianized town centre, family-run café offering good home baking and basic but filling meals. The best bet for a cheap lunch or evening meal is one of the city's many pubs and bars, where you can get a main course for £5-6. The most favoured options are *Johnny Foxes*, *Chilli Palmers* and *No 27* (see below).

Entertainment

At 108 Academy St is the *Phoenix*, one of the best pubs in town and always lively. Next **Bars**
door is an Irish theme pub, *Lafferty's*, which features Scottish/Celtic live music on Fri
and Sat. Across the street is *Blackfriars*, which is another good pub. *Gellions*, on Bridge
St, has varied live music throughout the week and *Johnny Foxes*, at 26 Bank St, features
Irish folk music every night in summer as well as boasting one of the most unusual pub
menus around. *Chilli Palmers*, on the corner of Queensgate and Church St, is a trendy
new bar offering decent food and a DJ at weekends, and you can enjoy a Jazz Lunch on
Sun at *No 27*, on Castle St.

Eden Court Theatre is on Bishops Rd, overlooking the river Ness. It offers a varied **Theatre &**
programme of theatre, dance and all kinds of music. There's also a bar and self-service **cinema**
restaurant with good food and views over the river. The attached cinema shows a
programme of art-house and newly released movies, for information: T234234. Prices
vary depending on the performance. *La Scala* on Strother's Lane, just off Academy St,
has 2 screens, and the 7-screen *Warner Village* is on the A96 Nairn Rd, about 2 miles
from the town centre. Cinema tickets cost from £4.

There are numerous events held in and around Inverness throughout the year. These **Festivals**
range from a humble pub ceilidh to a full-blown Highland Games. For details contact the
Tourist Information Centre or visit their website. The best of the local folk festivals are
held over the Easter weekend (T01738-623274) and the excellent *Highland Festival*
takes place over 3 days at the end of **Jun** (T711112, www.highlandfestival.demon.co.uk).
There's also a festival of *folk music* in **Jul** and **Aug** at Balnain House (see 'Sights' above).

Shopping

Inverness is a good place to buy a **kilt**, or practically anything else in tartan. To find out
your own clan tartan, head for the *Scottish Kiltmaker Visitor Centre* (see 'Sights'
above). Other places which sell highland dress and traditional gifts are *Chisholm's
Highland Dress*, 47-51 Castle St, T234599, open 0900-1730 and 1900-2130 in Jul and
Aug; and *Hector Russell*, 4-9 Huntly St, T222781. At *James Pringle Weavers* (Holm
Mills, Dores Rd, T223311) you can see tartan rugs being made in the weaving mill, then
spend your cash in their extensive mill shop and eat in the restaurant. The Eastgate
Shopping Centre houses all the usual high street branches and the Victorian Market on
Church St has a wide range of shops. The largest **bookshop** in town is *James Thin*, 29
Union St, T233500, which has an excellent range of Scottish books and maps. There's
also a branch of *Waterstone's*, at 50-52 High St, T717474.

Sports

10-pin bowling at *Roller Bowl*, 167 Culduthel Rd, T235100. Open Mon-Fri 1200 till late, **Bowling**
Sat-Sun 1100 till late.

Barney's Bicycle Hire & Shop, 35 Castle St, T232249. Open 0900-2100. Mountain bike **Cycle hire**
hire from £7 per day. Also bikes for hire from *Bazpacker's Hostel* (see 'Sleeping').

The best golf course in the area is at Nairn (see page 208). There's an 18-hole municipal **Golf**
course at Torvean, 2 miles from town on the A82 to Fort William. T711434.

The *Highland Riding Centre* is at Borlum Farm, Drumnadrochit, T/F01456-450358. **Horse riding**

North & Northwest Highlands

Tours from Inverness

Orkney Islands Day Tours leave from Inverness every day throughout the summer. The tour departs daily 1 Jun-2 Sep from Inverness bus station at 0730; returns 2100. Booking essential; £44 per person, under 16

*half price. Details from the tourist office, or contact **John O'Groats Ferries**, Ferry Office, John O'Groats, Caithness. T01955-611353, F611301, www.jogferry.co.uk (for tours from John O'Groats, see page 274).*

Leisure centres The *Aquadome Leisure Centre* is at Bught Park (T667500). Open Mon-Fri 0730-2200, Sat-Sun 0730-2100. Competition sized pool, flumes, wave machine and kiddies' pool, also health suites, gym and other indoor sports facilities.

Tennis The *Inverness Tennis and Squash Club* is at Bishop's Rd (T230751).

Transport

Bus There are regular daily buses to **Glasgow** and **Edinburgh** via **Aviemore, Pitlochry** and **Perth** with *Scottish Citylink* (T0990-505050). Change at Perth for **Dundee**. There are regular daily *Citylink* buses to **Ullapool**, connecting with the ferry to **Stornoway**; also to **Fort William** and **Oban**. There are daily *Citylink* buses to **Kyle of Lochalsh, Portree** and **Uig** (connecting with ferries to **Tarbert** and **Lochmaddy**). There are regular *Citylink* buses to **Fort Augustus** via **Drumnadrochit** and **Urquhart Castle** (also with *Highland Bus & Coach*, T233371), and to **Scrabster**, for the ferry to **Stromness**, via **Wick** and **Thurso**; also with *Morrison's Coaches*, T01847-821241.

To **Ullapool** via **Gairloch** and **Aultbea**, there are daily buses with *Spa Coaches* (T01997-421311), *Bluebird Northern* (T239292) and *Westerbus* (01445-712255). To **Tain** and **Lairg** there are daily services with *Bluebird* and *Rapson's* (T710555). To **Tain** and **Helmsdale**, via **Dornoch** there are regular daily buses with *Citylink, Morrison's* and *Bluebird*. To **Lochinver** via **Ullapool** there's a daily service with *Spa* coaches and *Rapson's of Brora* (01408-621245). To **Durness** via **Lairg** and **Tongue**, or via **Ullapool** (not in winter) there's a daily service with *Royal Mail Postbuses* (T0131-228 7407). To **Grantown-on-Spey**, daily service with *Highland Country Buses* (T233371) and *Highland Bus & Coach. Inverness Traction* and *Highland Country Buses* have services to places around Inverness, including **Nairn, Forres, Culloden, Beauly** and **Dingwall**. *Bluebird* have regular buses to **Aberdeen**, via **Nairn**.

Car hire *Avis* is at the airport (T01667-462787); *Budget* is on Railway Terr behind the train station (T713333); *Europcar* has an office at the Highlander service station on Millburn Rd (T235337) and at the airport; *Thrifty* is at 33 Harbour Rd (T224466). Expect to pay from around £30 per day.

Ferry For details of connections to Stornoway (Lewis) see page 318, or contact the *CalMac* office in Inverness, T717681. For Scrabster to Stromness, see page 356.

Taxi *Rank Radio Taxis*, T221111/220222; *Tartan Taxis*, T233033.

Train There are direct trains to/from **Aberdeen, Edinburgh** via Aviemore and **Glasgow** . There are several daily services to/from **London King's Cross**, via Perth and Edinburgh, including a sleeping car service (see page 35). There is also a regular service to **Wick** and **Thurso**, via Tain, Lairg and Helmsdale. The journey from Inverness to **Kyle of Lochalsh** (for Skye) is one of the most scenic in Britain. There are 3 trains daily (none on Sun). Phone T0845-7484950 for all rail enquiries.

North & Northwest Highlands

Battle of Culloden

The second Jacobite rebellion of 1745 was ill-fated from the start. Bonnie Prince Charlie's expedition south lacked sufficient support and was turned back at Derby. After their long and dispiriting retreat north, the half-starved, under-strength army, exhausted after an abortive night attack on Hanoverian forces at Nairn, faced overwhelmingly superior forces under the command of the ambitious Duke of Cumberland at Culloden.

The open, flat ground of Culloden Moor was hopelessly unsuitable for the Highlanders' style of fighting, which relied on steep hills and plenty of cover to provide the element of surprise for their brave but undisciplined attacks. In only 40 minutes the Prince's army was blown away by the English artillery and the Jacobite charge, when it finally came, was ragged and ineffective. Cumberland's troops then went on to commit the worst series of atrocities ever carried out by a British Army. 1,200 men were slain, many as they lay wounded on the battlefield. Prince Charlie, meanwhile, fled west where loyal Highlanders protected him until he made his final escape to France.

But the real savagery was to come. Cumberland resolved to make an example of the Highlands. Not only were the clans disarmed and the wearing of Highland dress forbidden, but the Government troops began an orgy of brutal reprisals across the region. Within a century the clan system had ended and the Highland way of life changed forever.

Directory

Banks All the major banks can be found in the town centre. The *Royal Bank* is opposite the post office on Queensgate; the *Bank of Scotland* is opposite the Town House on the High St; the *Clydesdale* is opposite the train station; and *Lloyds TSB* is on Church St. Foreign currency can also be exchanged at the tourist office's bureau de change at 2.5% commission (see below for address and opening hours). Also *Thomas Cook*, 9-13 Inglis St, T711921, Mon-Fri 0900-1700; and *Alba Travel* (American Express agents), 43 Church St, T239188, Mon-Sat 0900-1700.

Communications Internet: *MTC Internet*, 2 Grant St, T715450. *Invernet* is in the process of moving premises, agrainger@yahoo.com *The Gate* café bar, opposite the post office, has internet facilities and serves drinks and snacks from 1000-2100. **Post office:** the main branch is at 14-16 Queensgate, T234111. Open Mon-Thu 0900-1730, Fri 0930-1730, Sat 0900-1320.

Cultural centres Inverness library is just around the corner from the bus station. It has an excellent genealogical research unit. Consultations with the resident genealogist cost £12 per hr; T236463 for an appointment. The library also houses the highland archives, where you can research the history and culture of the region. Open Mon-Fri 1100-1300 and 1400-1700; 1400-1700 only during Oct-May.

Medical facilities *Raigmore Hospital* is on the southeastern outskirts of town near the A9 (T704000) for accidents and emergencies. **Pharmacies:** *Boots* is in the Eastgate Shopping Centre; open daily 0900-1730, Thu till 1900.

North & Northwest Highlands

The Moray Firth

Colour map 2, grid C2   *East of Inverness along the Moray Firth stretches a long coastline of cliff-top walks, fine beaches, attractive old towns and many historic sites and castles. The Moray Firth is perhaps best known for its large resident population of **bottlenose dolphins**, the largest dolphins in the world. Over 100 of these beautiful and intelligent mammals live in the estuary, the most northerly breeding ground in Europe, and there's a very good chance of seeing them, particularly between June and August. The Moray Firth dolphins have become a major tourist attraction and several companies run dolphin-spotting boat trips. You can also see them from the shore. Two of the best places are **Chanonry Point**, on the southern shore of the Black Isle (see page 275), and **Fort George**, on the opposite shore (see below). The **Kessock Bridge**, which crosses the Moray Firth to the Black Isle, is another good dolphin-spotting location and also has a **visitor centre**, where you listen in to their underwater conversations.*

The busy A96 parallels the coast and the region is well served by public transport. The attractions listed below can be visited as day-trips from Inverness.

Culloden

Colour map 2, grid C2   The eerie and windswept Culloden Moor, five miles to the east of Inverness on the B9006, was the site of the last major battle fought on the British mainland. The Jacobite cause was finally lost here, on 16 April 1746, when the army of Prince Charles Edward Stuart was crushed by the superior Government forces, led by the Duke of Cumberland, whose savagery earned him the nickname 'Butcher'. Now owned by the National Trust for Scotland, Culloden is a melancholy place and by far the most painfully evocative of Scotland's battlefields, particularly on a bleak and windy winter's day.

The battlefield has been restored to its original state (minus the dead bodies). The Visitor Centre is the obvious starting point and gives a graphic audio-visual description of the gruesome episode. From the Visitor Centre paths lead across the field to the clan graves, marked by simple headstones which bear the names of the clans who fought. Next to the Visitor Centre, the restored cottage of Old Leanach – which was used by the Jacobites as a headquarters, and where 30 Highlanders were burnt alive – is now a museum. A memorial cairn, erected in 1881, is the scene each April of a commemorative service organized by the Gaelic Society of Inverness.

To get there by public transport, Highland Country Bus No 12 leaves from Inverness Post Office Monday-Saturday (last bus back at 1830). The *Guide Friday* tour bus leaves from Bridge Street, May to September from 1030, last bus returns at 1745.

■ *Site open daily all year. Visitor Centre and shop open 15 Jan-31 Mar and 1 Nov to 31 Dec, daily 1000-1600; 1 Apr-31 Oct daily 0900-1800. Visitor centre, including audio-visual presentation, and Old Leanach cottage: adult £4, concession £3, children £1. Wheelchair access, bookshop, restaurant.*

Clava Cairns

This impressive and important Bronze Age site lies only a mile southeast of Culloden and is well worth a short detour. The 5,000 year-old site consists of three large burial cairns encircled by standing stones, set in a grove of trees.

The less imaginative visitor may see it as merely a pile of stones but no one can fail to be affected by the spooky atmosphere of the place. This is even more perceptible when no one else is around!

To get there, continue on the B9006 past Culloden Moor, then turn right at the Culloden Moor Inn and follow the signs for Clava Lodge. Look for the sign on the right of the road.

Fort George

Standing proudly on a sandy spit that juts out into the Moray Firth is Fort George, Europe's finest surviving example of 18th-century military architecture. Begun in 1748, it was the last in a chain of three such fortifications built in the Highlands – the other two being Fort Augustus and Fort William – as a base for George II's army to prevent any potential threats to Hanoverian rule. It was completed in 1769, by which time the Highlands were more or less peaceful, but was kept in use as a military barracks. Today, it remains virtually unchanged and there are even armed sentries at the main gate.

*Colour map 2, grid C2
Fort George is 11 miles NE of Inverness and 6 miles W of Nairn*

You can walk along the ramparts to get an idea of the sheer scale of the place and also enjoy the sweeping views across the Moray Firth. You may even be lucky enough to see a school of dolphins. Within the fort are the barracks, a chapel, workshops and the Regimental Museum of the Queen's Own Highlanders, which features the fascinating Seafield Collection of arms and military equipment, most of which dates from the Napoleonic Wars.

Highland Bus and Coach No 11 from the Post Office in Inverness, several daily except Sun, also buses from Nairn.

■ *Apr-Oct daily 0930-1830; Oct-Mar Mon-Sat 0930-1630, Sun 1400-1630. Adult £4.50, concession £3.50, children £1.50. Wheelchair access, café.*

Cawdor

Though best known for its legendary association with Shakespeare's *Macbeth*, Cawdor Castle post-dates the grisly historical events on which the great Bard based his famous tragedy. The oldest part of the castle, the central tower, dates from 1372, and the rest of it is mostly 16th or 17th century. But despite the literary disappointment, the castle is still one of the most appealing in Scotland. The castle has been in the hands of the Cawdor family for over six centuries and each summer they clear off, leaving their romantic home and its glorious gardens open for the enjoyment of ordinary folks like us. There's also a nine-hole golf course.

Cawdor Castle
Highlights include the impressive paintings and tapestries, fascinating kitchen and the genuinely witty captions that have visitors laughing all over the castle

According to family legend, an early Thane of Cawdor, wanting a new castle, had a dream in which he was told to load a donkey with gold, let it wander around for a day and watch where it lay down, for this would be the best spot for his new castle. He duly followed these instructions and the donkey lay down under a thorn tree, the remains of which can still be seen in the middle of a vaulted chamber in the 14th-century tower. ■ *May to mid-Oct daily 1000-1730. Adult £5.40.* To get to Cawdor by public transport, take the **Highland Country Buses** No 12 from Inverness Post Office. It runs several times daily (except Sunday), the last bus returns around 1800. There are also regular buses from Nairn.

In the village of Cawdor, close by the castle, is the *Cawdor Tavern*, T/F01667-404777, a traditional country pub serving excellent food in a friendly atmosphere. Perfect for lunch or dinner after visiting the castle. Prices are cheap to mid-range.

North & Northwest Highlands

Just to the west of Cawdor is **Kilravock Castle**, a lovely 15th-century stately home which is closed to the public, but can be visited by prior appointment. The castle (pronounced 'Kilrawk') is still the seat of the Rose family, who now run it as a guesthouse on strictly Christian principles. ■ *T01667-493258. The castle gardens are open to the public Mon-Sat 1000-1600, and worth visiting. Free.*

Nairn

Phone code: 01667
Colour map 2, grid C2
Population: 11,190

The genteel seaside resort of Nairn claims the driest and sunniest climate in the whole of Scotland. This alone should be reason enough to pay a visit, but there are other attractions besides the sunshine. There are miles of sandy beach stretching east to the Culbin Forest, a **championship golf course** (which hosted the 1999 Walker Cup), and two of the best castles in the country are within easy reach – **Cawdor Castle** (see above) and **Brodie Castle** (see below).

Nairn began life as an important commercial centre in the 12th century and by the early 17th century had grown to such an extent that King James VI was able to boast of a town in his northern kingdom so large that people at one end of the High Street didn't understand the language spoken by those at the other end (the different languages being English and Gaelic). The town was a major fishing port in the 19th century and the tiny houses of the **Old Fishertown**, huddled together around the harbour, are very different from the town centre, which is known as **New Fishertown**. Both lie apart from the substantial villas and hotels of the seaside resort that developed with the arrival of the Highland Railway in the mid-19th century.

Today, Nairn is still a tourist favourite with its seafront full of people munching chips and ice cream. There are banks with ATMs in the High Street, a post office in Cawdor Street, a swimming pool on Marine Road and cinema on King Street. The **Tourist Information Centre** is at 62 King St, T452753. Open Easter-May and September-October Monday-Saturday 1000-1700; June-August daily 0900-1800.The town hosts its annual **Highland Games** in August.

Sights   The **Fishertown Museum** in old Fishertown is interesting and tells of the building of the harbour by Thomas Telford in 1820 and the subsequent decline of the herring industry. The harbour is now mainly used by pleasure craft. ■ *The museum is open from Jun to Aug, Mon-Sat 1000-1700. Free.*

About two miles east of Nairn, in the little village of **Auldearn**, is a 17th-century doocot (dovecote) from where the royal standard was flown, in 1645, by the victorious troops of Charles I led by the Marquis of Montrose against the Covenanters. Displays in the doocot tell of the battle (entry £1.50).

Sleeping   The most luxurious here is **L** *The Golf View Hotel*, on Seabank Rd next to the golf
There's lots of   course, T452301, scotland@morton-hotels.demon.co.uk 47 rooms, pool, sauna, spa,
accommodation to   gym, tennis courts and fine restaurant. **B** *Clifton House*, Viewfield St, T453119. This
choose from right   genuinely unique hotel offers superb hospitality and a touch of class, every room is dif-
across the range   ferent and the place is full of antiques, they also host musical and theatrical evenings and dinner is also quite an event.

There are lots of guesthouses and B&Bs, including the very fine **E** *Bracadale House*, Albert St, T452547, neil.macleod@ lineone.net There's a good **campsite** 1½ miles from town; *Spindrift Caravan & Camping Park*, at Little Kildrummie, T453992, open Apr-Oct.

Eating   Aside from the hotels in town, one of the best places to eat is the *Boat House*, T455469, 2 miles east of Nairn in the little village of Auldearn (prices mid-range). If you fancy a fish supper, try *Friar Tuck's*, at 30 Harbour St. For a hot snack there's *Asher's Bakery*, 2 Bridge St, which is recommended and run by the same folk as the one in Inverness.

Cycling Bike hire from *The Bike Shop*, 178 Harbour St. **Pony trekking** *Heatherfield* **Sport** *Riding Centre*, Lochloy Rd, T456682.

There are regular daily **buses** from Inverness (30 mins) with *Highland Country Buses* **Transport** and *Bluebird* (see Inverness Transport above). Nairn is on the **Inverness-Aberdeen** rail line and there are several **trains** daily from Inverness (20 mins).

Around Nairn

Ten miles south of Nairn on the A939 to Grantown is Dulsie Bridge, a very **Dulsie Bridge** popular local beauty spot which is a great place for a summer picnic or to swim in the river Findhorn.

On the southern shores of the Moray Firth, just east of Nairn, is this stretch of **Culbin Sands** sand home to a host of birdlife. The best time to visit is from autumn to spring when bar tailed godwits, oystercatchers, knots, dunlins, ringed plovers, redshanks, curlews, shellducks, red breasted mergansers, greylag geese and snow buntings, to name but a few, come here in their droves.

Here is one of Scotland's finest castles still lived in by the Brodie family. The old- **Brodie** est part of the castle, the Z-plan tower house, is 16th-century, with additions **Castle** dating from the 17th and 19th centuries, giving it the look of a Victorian coun- *the castle is 8 miles* try house. The interior of the house is the epitome of good taste, with some fab- *E of Nairn, just off* ulous ceilings, and you can look round several rooms, including the huge *the main A96* Victorian kitchen. The collections of furniture and porcelain are wonderful but *to Forres* most notable are the outstanding paintings, which include Edwin Landseer and Scottish Colourists. The grounds, too, are a delight, especially in spring when the daffodils are in bloom. There's also a tearoom. *Bluebird* buses run to Brodie from Inverness, via Culloden and Nairn; 45 mins. ■ *Castle open 1 Apr-30 Sep Mon-Sat 1100-1730, Sun 1330-1730; Oct weekends only, Sat 1100-1730, Sun 1330-1730. Grounds open all year daily 0930-sunset. Castle: adult £6, concession £4.50, children £1; grounds only £1 (honesty box). T01309-641371.*

West of Inverness

*West of Inverness, the Moray Firth becomes the **Beauly Firth**, a relatively quiet little corner despite its proximity to Inverness, as most traffic heading north crosses the Kessock Bridge on the main A9. The A862 west to Beauly offers a more scenic alternative, and the chance to visit a **13th-century priory**, and a **distill-ery**. South of Beauly, the A831 leads to two of Scotland's most beautiful glens, **Glen Strathfarrar**, and **Glen Affric**.*

Beauly

The sleepy little market town of Beauly is 10 miles west of Inverness, where the *Phone code: 01463* Beauly River flows into the Firth. It's a lovely wee place – hence its name. *Colour map 2, grid C1* According to local legend, when Mary, Queen of Scots stayed here, at the pri- ory, in 1564, she was so taken with the place that she cried (in French, of course) "Ah, quel beau lieu!" (What a beautiful place!).

North & Northwest Highlands

At the north end of the marketplace is the ruin of **Beauly Priory**, founded in 1230 for the Valliscaulian order, but like so much else of Scotland's ecclesiastical heritage, destroyed during the Reformation. ■ *11 June-30 Sep daily 0930-1830. Adult £1.20, concession £0.90, children £0.50.*

Sleeping & eating The most expensive place to stay is **L** *The Priory Hotel*, on the main street, T782309. At the opposite end of on the main street is the **C** *Lovat Arms Hotel*, T782313, lovat.arms@cali.co.uk, which is the best place to stay. A relaxed and comfortable place with an excellent restaurant and great bar food, lots of tartan and the occasional ceilidh. A cheaper **B&B** option is **F** *Ellengowan*, Croyard Rd, T782273 (open Apr-Oct).

The best food is at the *Lovat Arms Hotel*, which offers cheap meals in the bar or an expensive 4-course dinner in the restaurant. Otherwise, you could try the *Beauly Tandoori* on The Square, T782221, for a cheap curry, or the *Friary* for an even cheaper fish supper.

Transport There are *Inverness Traction* **buses**, T239292, every hour to Beauly, and on to Muir of Ord, from Inverness and from Dingwall. There's also a *Ross's Minibus* service from Beauly 3 days a week, T761250.

Around Beauly

Four miles east of Beauly, at Balchraggan just off the main Inverness road, is **Moniack Castle Winery**, where you can try a whole range of wines, including elderflower and birch. ■ *Mon-Sat 1000-1700.* Four miles to the north is the **Glen Ord Distillery**, on the outskirts of **Muir of Ord**, just off the A832. ■ *Mar-Oct Mon-Fri 0930-1700; Jul-Sep also Sat 0930-1700 and Sun 1230-1700. T01463-872004. Take a bus from Inverness or the train.*

The river Beauly is one of Scotland's best salmon-fishing rivers, and five miles south of Beauly, at **Aigas**, is a fish lift, where you can watch salmon bypass the dam with the aid of technology. ■ *Mon-Fri 1000-1500.*

Glen Strathfarrar and Glen Affric

Colour map 1, grid C6
Most of the walks and cycle routes around glens Strathfarrar and Affric are covered by OS Landranger Nos 25 and 26

Southwest of Beauly are glens Affric and Strathfarrar. **Glen Strathfarrar**, the lesser known of the two, is unspoiled and considered by some to be the more beautiful. To get there, take the A831 nine miles south from Beauly to **Struy** and follow the signs. Access to the glen is restricted by the owners, Scottish Natural Heritage, to 12 cars at a time and you have to leave by 1900. The glen is also closed from mid-August to October. But once you're in, there is a tremendous feeling of peace and there's good climbing, fishing and walking. The little ungraded road runs for 14 miles all the way to the impressive Monar Dam at the head of the glen. Glen Strathfarrar can also be reached from Drumnadrochit, via Cannich (see below).

Colour map 3, grid A6

The A831 continues south from Struy, through **Strathglass**, to the village of **Cannich**, gateway to glorious **Glen Affric**, a dramatic and beautiful gorge, with the river Affric rushing through it, and surrounded by Caledonian pine and birch forest (this is one of the few places where you can still see the native Scots pine). There are few, if any, more stunning sights in the Scottish Highlands and it's perfect for walking, or even just to drive through and stop for a picnic on a nice, sunny day.

Glen Affric reaches west into the very heart of the Highlands and is great for a spot of Munro-bagging. Beyond Loch Affric the serious walking starts.

From Affric Lodge, nine miles west of Cannich, begins a 20-mile trail west to Morvich, near **Shiel Bridge**, on the west coast near Kyle of Lochalsh (see page 243). This strenuous walk is for experienced hikers only, and takes around 10 hours. You can stop off halfway at one of the most remote **youth hostels** in Scotland, *Glen Affric Youth Hostel*, at Allt Beithe (no phone; open mid-March till end October).

There are also many shorter, easier walks around Glen Affric. There are some short, circular marked trails at the end of the road which runs west from Cannich almost to Loch Affric, and also from the car park at the impressive **Dog Falls**, 4½ miles from Cannich and a great place to stop for a picnic and swim. Cycling in the forests around Cannich is good too – you can hire bikes at *Cannich Caravan and Camping Park*.

Glen Affric can also be reached from **Drumnadrochit** (see page 212) by heading west on the A831 through **Glen Urquhart** to Cannich. Just before Cannich, on the road from Drumnadrochit, a single track road leads left (south), past the Caravan and Camping Park, to the tiny village of **Tomich**. From here, it's a three-mile hike up a woodland trail to a car park. A few hundred yards down through the trees takes you to the lovely **Plodda Falls**. An old iron bridge affords a spectacular view of the waterfall as it plunges 150 yards into the foaming waters below.

There are several options in and around **Cannich**. One of the best hotels in the area is the **B** *Mullardoch House Hotel*, in Glencannich, on the road to Beauly, T/F01456-415460. An excellent B&B is **C-D** *Kerrow House*, in Cannich village, T415243, F415425, stephen@kerrow-house.demon.co.uk There are also a couple of **hostels**: the **F** *SYHA Cannich Youth Hostel*, T415244, open mid-Mar to end Oct; and the slightly cheaper independent **F** *Glen Affric Backpackers*, T/F415263, which is open all year.

In the village of **Tomich** is **B** *The Tomich Hotel*, T01456-415399, F415469. The price includes dinner, it's a comfortable place with good food and free use of the nearby indoor heated pool, also great for fishing holidays. Near Tomich is the independent hostel **F** *Cougie Lodge*, T01456-415459, which is open Apr-Sep and will pick you up from Tomich or Cannich if you phone ahead.

Highland Bus & Coach, T01463-233371, runs buses 3 days a week Mon-Fri from Inverness to Cannich and Tomich, via Drumnadrochit. There are also buses from Inverness to Cannich and Tomich, via Beauly (2 on Tue and Fri, and 1 on Sat).

Sleeping

Transport

North & Northwest Highlands

Loch Ness to Fort Augustus

*One of Scotland's biggest attractions is the narrow gash of Loch Ness, Britain's deepest body of fresh water, stretching 23 miles from Fort Augustus in the south, almost to Inverness in the north. The loch is scenic in its own right, with rugged hills rising steeply from its wooded shores, but visitors don't come here for the views. They come every year, in their hundreds of thousands, to stare across the dark, cold waters in search of its legendary inhabitant, the **Loch Ness Monster**. A huge tourist trade has grown up around 'Nessie', as the monster is affectionately known, and every summer, the main A82 which runs along its western shore is jam packed with bus loads of eager monster-hunters, binoculars trained on the loch surface, desperate for one glimpse of the elusive beast.*

Colour map 4, grid A1/2

The Great Glen

The Great Glen, which splits the Scottish mainland from Fort William in the south to Inverness in the north, is one of the world's major geological fault lines. The Glen was formed millions of years ago when the northern part of the Caledonian mountains 'slid' more than 60 miles south, leaving behind a massive glen, with four freshwater lochs – **Loch Linnhe, Loch Lochy, Loch Oich** *and* **Loch Ness**.

The most famous of these is Loch Ness, which attracts hordes of visitors eager to catch a glimpse of its elusive monster. The renowned engineer, Thomas Telford, succeeded in connecting all these lochs when he built the impressive **Caledonian Canal**. *The canal took 22 years to complete, and when it was opened in 1822 was the first in Britain to take ships from one coast to the other. It remains the only canal in the country capable of carrying ships of up to 500 tons. The best way to appreciate the glen is by boat, through the 38 miles of natural lochs and rivers and the 22 miles of canal, and every summer, pleasure craft of all shapes and sizes ply its length. The main A82 runs from Inverness south to Fort William. The southern section, from Fort Augustus, follows the original line of the road constructed in 1727 by General Wade to link the military garrisons at Fort William and Fort Augustus (hence their names). There are regular daily* **bus services** *between Inverness and Fort William, with additional buses between Invergarry and Fort Augustus. Another way to travel through the Great Glen is along the excellent* **cycle route**, *which follows the canal towpaths, forest trails and quiet minor roads to avoid the busy main road. The route is outlined in the Forestry Commission leaflet, available from most Tourist Information Centres.*

The best way to see the loch is on a cruise from Inverness (see the Monster Tours box on page 198). There are also boat trips from Drumnadrochit and Fort Augustus (see below). Most of the tourist traffic uses the congested A82, which offers few decent views of the loch. By far the best views of the loch are from the quiet and picturesque B862/852 which runs along its eastern shore, from Fort Augustus up to Inverness. It's possible to make a complete circuit of the loch, which is best done in an anti-clockwise direction heading south from Inverness on the A82, but you'll need your own transport (or take a tour), as there are no buses between Fort Augustus and Foyers.

Drumnadrochit

Phone code: 01456
Colour map 2, grid C1

The Nessie tourist trade is centred on the village of Drumnadrochit, 15 miles south of Inverness, where the canny locals have cashed in on the enduring popularity of the monster myth. The monster hype is almost overpowering, with two rival Monster Exhibitions and the inevitable souvenir shops selling all manner of awful tartan tack, including those scary-looking tartan dolls with flickering eyelids, the "See-You-Jimmy" tartan bonnet, complete with ginger 'hair' and not forgetting the Loch Ness Monster novelty hat.

Of the two aforementioned Monster Exhibitions, the **Original Loch Ness Visitor Centre** is the least worthwhile. It's a glorified gift shop with a rather amateurish audiovisual show attached. ■ *T450342. daily Apr to end of Oct 1000-1800 (Jul-Aug till 2100). Adult £3.50, students £3, children and OAPs £2.75.*

Those genuinely interested in the fascinating history of the search for 'Nessie' should visit the recently refurbished **Official Loch Ness Monster Exhibition**. Though it's considerably more expensive, it gives a detailed

The Great Monster Hunt

In a country full of myths and legends, the Loch Ness Monster is the greatest of them all. As elusive as a straight answer from a politician, Nessie has single-handedly sold more tins of tartan-wrapped shortbread to foreign visitors than Edinburgh castle.

Tales of Nessie go way back to the sixth century, when St Columba is said to have calmed the beast after she had attacked one of his monks. But the monster craze only really took off with the completion of the A82 road along the loch's western shore in 1933. Since then, there have been numerous sightings, some backed up with photographic evidence, though the most impressive of these – the famous black-and-white movie footage of Nessie's humps *moving through the water, and the classic photograph of her head and neck – have been exposed as fakes.*

In recent decades, determined monster hunters have enlisted the help of new technology, such as sonar surveys, but have failed to come up with conclusive evidence. Enter Cyber Nessie, the latest attempt to end the years of rumours, hoaxes and speculation. Nessie's very own website – www.lochness.scotland.net/ camera.htm – is a 24-hour real-time video watch of Loch Ness, and has already produced a couple of claimed sightings. But nothing could compare with the excitement of seeing the monster in the flesh.

---

description of the many eye-witness accounts over the years and also explains the recent research projects carried out in the loch. ■ *T450573. Easter-end May 0930-1730; Jun and Sep 0930-1830; Jul-Aug 0930-2030; Oct 0930-1800; Nov-Mar 1000-1600. Adult £5.95, students £4.50 , children £3.50.*

Loch Ness Cruises operate from the Original Loch Ness Visitor Centre, from April to October and run daily from 0930-1800. They last one hour and cost £8 per adults and £5 per children.

There's a wide range of accommodation on offer in and around the village of Drumnadrochit. If you can afford it, your best bet is to head for **B** *Polmaily House Hotel*, 3 miles from Drumnadrochit on the A831 to Cannich, in Glen Urquhart, T450343, F450813, polmailyhousehotel@btinternet.com 10 rooms, a comfortable, child-friendly country house far enough away from the madding crowd to offer peace and quiet, many walks nearby, also tennis courts, horse riding and covered pool, good restaurant. In the village itself is **D** *The Benleva Hotel*, T450288, F450781. Small, family-run hotel with bar and dining room. There are numerous **B&Bs**, including the excellent **E** *Drumbuie Farm*, T450634, F450595, a modern farmhouse on the right as you enter the village from Inverness, with its own erd of Highland cattle. **D** *Gillyflowers*, T/F450641, gillyflowers@cali.co.uk, is good value. Cheaper still is the **F** *Loch Ness Backpackers Lodge*, at Coiltie Farmhouse in East Lewiston, T450807, immediately south of Drumnadrochit, on the left. It's open all year, has excellent facilities and arranges boat trips and local walks.

Other than the hotels, which all serve decent bar food, there's the *Glen Restaurant*, T450282, which offers simple fare and, next door, the more upmarket *Fiddler's Bistro*, T450678, where you can also hire **mountain bikes**.

Citylink **buses** between Inverness and Fort William stop at Drumnadrochit several times daily in either direction. Additional services run between Inverness and Urquhart Castle during the summer months. There are also buses from Inverness to Cannich and Tomich, via Drumnadrochit (see page 211).

Sleeping & eating

Transport

North & Northwest Highlands

Around Drumnadrochit

If it all gets too much, then fear not, for Drumnadrochit gives easy access to one of the most beautiful corners of Scotland. The A831 heads west from the village, through **Glen Urquhart**, to **Cannich** about 12 miles away, at the head of **Glen Affric**, a great place for walking or enjoying a picnic (see page 210). If the weather's good, hiring bikes in Drumnadrochit (see below) and cycling into Glen Affric makes for a great day out. There's also **pony trekking** at the *Highland Riding Centre*, T450358, at Borlum Farm.

Castle Urquhart   A few miles south of Drumnadrochit are the ruins of Castle Urquhart. The castle bears the scars of centuries of fighting but its setting, perched on a rocky cliff on the loch's edge, is magnificent, and not surprisingly, one of the most photographed scenes in Scotland. Dating from the 14th century, the castle was a strategic base, guarding the Great Glen during the long Wars of Independence. It was taken by Edward I, held by Robert the Bruce against Edward II, and was then almost constantly under siege before being destroyed in 1692 to prevent it from falling into Jacobite hands. Most of the existing buildings date from the 16th century, including the five-storey tower, the best-preserved part of the complex, from where you get great views of the loch and surrounding hills. At the time of writing, there are plans to build a new visitor centre. ■ *Apr-Sep daily 0930-1830; Oct-Mar daily 0930-1630. Adult £3.80, concession £2.80, children £1.20. T450551.*

Invermoriston

Phone code: 01320
Colour map 4, grid A1

Between Drumnadrochit and Fort Augustus is the tiny village of Invermoriston, probably the nicest spot on the entire Inverness to Fort Augustus stretch of the A82. It's a beautiful little piece of Highland scenery, with a photogenic old stone bridge over foaming river rapids. There are marked woodland trails leading off into the hills past some lovely waterfalls.

At Invermoriston the A887 heads west through **Glen Moriston** to meet the A87 which runs from **Invergarry** (see below) all the way through the rugged and dramatic **Glen Shiel** to the awesome mountains of **Kintail** on the west coast near **Kyle of Lochalsh**. *Citylink* buses between Inverness and Kyle of Lochalsh stop at Invermoriston.

Sleeping   There are several B&Bs in the village and, a few miles to the north on the main A82 overlooking Loch Ness, is the **F** *SYHA Loch Ness Youth Hostel*, T351274, open mid-Mar to end Oct. 1½ miles south of Invermoriston, and 6 miles north of Fort Augustus, is the *Loch Ness Caravan & Camping Park*, T351207, right on the shores of the loch with great views and excellent facilities (open Easter-Oct).

Fort Augustus

Phone code: 01320
Colour map 4, grid A1

At the more scenic southern end of Loch Ness stands the village of Fort Augustus, originally set up as a garrison after the Jacobite rebellion of 1715 and headquarters of General Wade's campaign to pacify the Highlands. Today, Fort Augustus is a busy little place, full of monster-hunting tourists and boats using the flight of five locks to enter or leave Loch Ness on their journey along the **Caledonian Canal**.

The village hosts **Highland Gatherings** in late June and July, mid-August and early September, featuring traditional dancing and piping competitions, tossing the caber and sheep dog trials.

The **Tourist Information Centre**, T366367, is in the car park next to the petrol station and *Bank of Scotland*. It's open April-June Monday-Saturday 1000-1700; July-August 0900-2000; September-October 0900-1800.

On the shores of Loch Ness is **Fort Augustus Abbey**, a Benedictine Monas- **Sights** tery founded in 1876 on the site of the original fort. The abbey closed in 1998 but there are tours of the grounds and cloisters. ■ *Daily Easter-Oct 0900-1700; Nov-Mar 1000- 1600. Adult £3, concession £2. T366233.*

By the canal locks is **The Clansman Centre**, where young guides in tradi- tional dress provide a lively and entertaining presentation of 17th-century Highland family life in an old turf house. There follows a display of weaponry and a mock sword fight in the garden. You can even have your picture taken wearing traditional highland costume. There's also a craftshop selling the more tasteful kind of souvenirs. ■ *Daily Apr, May, Jun and Sep 1100-1700; Jul-Aug 1000-1800. Adult £3, concession £2.50. T366444.*

Loch Ness Cruises with *Loch Ness Ferry Co Ltd*, on board the *Royal Scot* set off from the jetty in the abbey grounds. ■ *Hourly from 1000 between Apr and Oct. The trip lasts 50 mins and costs £6 per adult. Also boat and bike hire. T01223-208939.*

There's a good selection of places to stay in Fort Augustus, but perhaps the best, and **Sleeping &** certainly the most unique, is the **D** *Lovat Arms Hotel*, T366206, F366677. 23 rooms, a **eating** beautiful old mansion house standing above the village. There are lots of **B&Bs** to choose from, including the wonderfully named **D-E** *Mrs Service*, at *Sonas* on the Inver- ness Rd, T366291, and the friendly **E** *Kettle House* on Golf Course Rd, T366408; open Feb-Nov. The newly-converted **F** *Morag's Lodge*, T366289, offers baclpacker accom- modation between Mar and Oct.

Other than the hotels in the village, there's the cosy *Bothy Bite* (T366710) by the canal bridge, which serves cheap meals from 1200-2100. The *Loch Inn*, by the canal, is the best place for a drink, and also serves decent pub grub.

Cycle hire at *Loch Ness Ferry Co Ltd* (see above). **Pony trekking** *Fort Augustus* **Sport** *Riding Centre*, Pier House, T366418.

Fort Augustus is a convenient stopover between Fort William and Inverness and there **Transport** are several **buses** daily in either direction. It takes 1 hr to both towns. There is an addi- tional service between Fort Augustus and Invergarry (see below) once a day Mon-Sat.

Fort Augustus to Dores

A worthwhile detour from Fort Augustus is to take the B862/852 up the **east** *Colour map 4, grid A1/2* **shore of Loch Ness** on a mostly single-track road that skirts the loch for much of its length to the village of Dores. It's a much quieter and more scenic route than the busy A82 and follows General Wade's original (and very straight) military road which linked Fort Augustus with Fort George. Though it makes a more interesting alternative to the more popular A82 route from Inverness to Fort Augustus, it's best done from south to north, if you have the time.

The road winds its way up into rugged hills before returning to the lochside at **Foyers**, where there's accommodation at **E-F** *Intake-House*, T01456- 482258, open April-October, and the small independent youth hostel **F** *Foyers House*, T01456-486623. It's worth stopping here to see the impres- sive **waterfall** where the river Foyers plunges into Loch Ness. To get there, fol- low the steep (and slippery) track down from opposite the shops.

Three miles further north, at **Inverfarigaig**, is the spooky and sinister **Boleskine House**, once home of Alastair Crowley, who is said to have practised Devil worship here. In the 1970s the house was bought by Jimmy Page of Led Zeppelin, but sold some years later after the tragic death of his daughter. Those of a nervous disposition may wish to pass on quickly and continue to the little village of **Dores**, at the northeastern end of the loch, where you can enjoy a good pint of ale and some decent grub at the *Dores Inn*. You can then continue to Inverness, or return via the beautiful hill road that leads up to **Loch Mhor** and back to Fort Augustus via the **Stratherrick** valley. From **Errogie**, at the northern end of Loch Mhor, there's a dramatic section of road that winds down to the loch through a series of tight, twisting bends, reminiscent of an Alpine pass, and great for cyclists. There are also some interesting marked woodland trails around Errogie.

Transport This route is only possible if you have your own transport. There are buses south from Inverness, but they only run as far as Foyers (3 times Mon-Fri, twice on Sat). Alternatively, it can be done by **bike**, as a full-day circular trip from Fort Augustus or from Inverness.

Fort Augustus to Fort William

*South of Fort Augustus, the A82 leaves behind Loch Ness and runs along the west shore of **Loch Oich** and then the east shore of **Loch Lochy**, till it reaches **Spean Bridge**. Here, the A82 continues south to **Fort William**, while the A86 branches east, through **Glen Spean** to finally join the A9 Perth to Inverness road at **Kingussie**. All along this route are many opportunities to get off the beaten track and explore huge chunks of real wilderness, deserted since the Clearances and soaked in the blood of history.*

Invergarry and around

Phone code: 01809
Colour map 4, grid A1

The old village of Invergarry stands where the A82 turns west to meet the A87. There's not much to see or do in the village, but the surrounding area merits some exploring, particularly the route west through Glen Garry (see next page), and there are several places to stay.

Sights Inside the entrance to the *Glengarry Castle Hotel* (see 'Sleeping' below) stand the ruins of **Invergarry Castle**, once the stronghold of the MacDonnells of Glengarry and later destroyed by the Duke of Cumberland as he wreaked revenge on the Highlands in the aftermath of Culloden (see page 39). The hotel was later built as the main house of the Ellice family, who made their fortune from the *Hudson Bay Company* in Canada and who were the main driving force behind the creation of the Victorian planned village.

A mile or so south of the village, at **North Laggan**, is a monument by the side of the road standing over **The Well of the Seven Heads**. This tells the grisly story of the Keppoch Murders, one of the most infamous clan murders which took place at **Roy Bridge** (see below) in the 17th century. It all began when the chief of the clan MacDonnell died, leaving two young sons, who were sent away to complete their education before returning to Roy Bridge to celebrate the elder brother's accession to the chiefship. Another branch of the

Getting shirty

One the bloodiest battles in Scottish clan history was the Battle of the Shirts, fought in 1544. It was so named because it was fought on a hot day and the combatants took off their shirts before proceeding to butcher each other. One side – the Frasers – were almost wiped out and their opponents – a combined force of MacDonalds, MacDonnells and Camerons – suffered less heavy losses and claimed victory. In total, over 1,000 were killed and a plaque beside the canal locks describes the terrible events.

clan present at the celebrations started a fight in which both brothers were killed. Believing they had been murdered, one of their cousins persuaded a fellow clan member to raise 50 men and march on the murderers' house at nearby Inverlair. The accused murderers – a father and his six sons – were duly slaughtered and their heads cut off, to be displayed before the local laird at Glengarry. On the way to his lodge, the heads were washed here in this well.

A few miles further south, at **Laggan**, where the A82 crosses to the east bank of Loch Lochy, is the site Battle of the Shirts. On the east shore of Loch Oich, near North Laggan, is the **Great Glen Water Park**, T501381, an outdoor activities centre offering numerous adventure sports, including white-water rafting, canoeing, mountain biking, rock climbing, sailing, windsurfing, hill walking and water skiing. There are also self-catering lodges for rent.

Sleeping There are various options for sleeping in and around Invergarry, but none can match the splendour of **A** *Glengarry Castle Hotel*, T501254, F501207, castle@glengarry.net, set in 60 acres of woodland running down to Loch Oich. 26 rooms, open Mar-Nov. The hotel has been in the MacCallum family for over 40 years and continues to be one of the best in the Highlands. Rather less luxurious but still comfortable and good value is **D** *Invergarry Hotel*, T501206, F501400, hotel@invergarry.net

South of Invergarry, at South Laggan, is the **F** *SYHA Loch Lochy Youth Hostel*, T501239, open mid-Mar to end-Oct. There are a couple of **campsites** near the village: *Faichem Park*, T501226, open Easter-Oct; and *Faichemard Farm Camping Site*, T501314, open Apr-Oct, which is off the A87.

Tour companies *Glengarry Mini Tours*, T501297 run various minibus day tours around in the Great Glen, Glen Coe and Glen Nevis.

Transport Invergarry is on the Fort William to **Inverness** bus route (see Fort Augustus above). It is also on the main **Fort William** to **Kyle of Lochalsh** (and **Skye**) *Citylink* route and a couple of buses pass through daily in both directions. For times: T0990-505050.

West of Invergarry The A87 leads west from Invergarry, through Glen Shiel to **Shiel Bridge**, on the way to Kyle of Lochalsh on the west coast (see page 243). About seven miles along the A87, past the turning for Kinloch Hourn (see below) is the Glen Garry viewpoint, from where you get one of the most stunning, and famous, of all Highland views. From this angle Loch Garry looks uncannily like a map of Scotland, so get out the camera for that classic holiday snap.

Glen Garry to Kinloch Hourn

A mile or so before the Glen Garry viewpoint, where the A87 begins to leave the shores of Loch Garry, is the turning left for the road through Glen Garry, described as the longest and most beautiful cul-de-sac in Britain. The little

Colour map 3, grid A5/6

North & Northwest Highlands

single-track road turns and twists for 22 glorious miles along the shores of **Loch Garry** and **Loch Quoich** all the way to **Kinloch Hourn**, at the head of Loch Hourn, a sea loch on the west coast.

Glen Garry is now virtually deserted but was once home to some 5,000 people who were driven out during the infamous Highland Clearances in the 19th century. The road passes the tiny hamlet of **Tomdoun**, once the junction of the main road to Skye, until the massive post-war hydroelectric schemes changed the landscape. Experienced hillwalkers can still follow the old route to Skye, through Glen Kingie, along Loch Hourn and then across the wild **Knoydart peninsula** till they reach the tiny settlement of **Inverie**. From here a little ferry runs twice a day on Mon-Wed and Fri to **Mallaig**.

Beyond Tomdoun the road passes a huge dam, built in the 1950s, which raised the waters of Loch Quoich by over 100 ft, flooding many of the old settlements. Also flooded was Glen Quoich Lodge, which can count Edward VII and Sir Edward Landseer among its notable guests. It was reputedly Glen Garry that gave Landseer the inspiration for his famous painting *The Monarch of the Glen*. The road then reaches its highest point, at 1,200 ft, before descending to **Kinloch Hourn**, once a thriving fishing village but now remote and isolated. Incredible as it may seem, you can actually stay here.

Sleeping **B** *Skiary*, T01809-511214, open May-Sep, phone ahead to arrange for a boat to meet you. This is perhaps the most remote guesthouse in the Highlands. It is accessible only by boat or foot and has no mains electricity. There are 3 rooms and prices are for full board, and include the boat trip both ways. The food is wonderful and the setting is simply magnificent.

Transport There's a **postbus** from Invergarry post office on Mon, Wed and Fri, which runs to Kingie, which is halfway to Kinloch Hourn. A 4-seater post car runs all the way to Kincloch Hourn from Invergarry on Tue, Wed, Thu and Sat. A more scenic return would be to take the **ferry** from Kinloch Hourn to **Arnisdale** (summer only; daily by arrangement) and then head to **Glenelg**, from where you can take a ferry across to **Kylerhea** on Skye (see page 306).

Spean Bridge

Phone code: 01397
Colour map 3, grid B6

The main A82 runs down the east shore of Loch Lochy to the village of Spean Bridge, at the head of Glen Spean, beneath the towering Lochaber mountains. The village gets its name from Thomas Telford's bridge across the river Spean. Two miles west are the remains of the old 'Highbridge', built in 1736 by General Wade, and the site of the first clash between Government troops and the Jacobites, three days before Prince Charles raised his standard at Glenfinnan.

Spean Bridge is only eight miles north of Fort William so gets busy in the summer, but it still makes a more peaceful and attractive alternative base for exploring this astoundingly beautiful part of the Highlands. There's a **Tourist Information Centre** just off the main road behind the post office. ■ *Easter-Oct. T712576, F712675.* Spean Bridge is also the starting point for the excellent **Grey Corries ridge walk** (OS Landranger Map No 41).

Sleeping There's no shortage of accommodation in Spean Bridge. Pick of the bunch has to be **A** *Old Pines Restaurant with Rooms*, T712324, F712433, www.lochaber. com/oldpines 8 rooms, just past the Commando Memorial, on the B8004, price includes dinner. This Scandinavian-style chalet is a great place to stay, especially if you have kids in tow, and is renowned for its exceptional, award-winning Scottish cuisine. Food is available to non-residents (the 5-course dinner is expensive but lunch is much cheaper). **A** *Corriegour Lodge Hotel*, 9 miles north of Spean Bridge on the A82, T712685, F712696. 9 rooms, open Feb-Dec. Lovely Victorian hunting lodge on the shores of Loch Lochy with fine views and an excellent restaurant (non-residents dinner only; expensive). Further south, on the shores of Loch Lochy, is a very good **B&B**, **D** *Invergloy House*, T712681. In the village itself is **E** *Smiddy House*, T712335, F712043. A comfortable guesthouse with a bistro attached, serving good, cheap meals. Also good is the **D** *Corriechoille Lodge*, T/F712002, www.corrie1.demon. co.uk Open Mar-Nov.

There are lots more guesthouses and B&Bs and a couple of **campsites**, north of the village at *Stronaba Caravan & Camping*, T712259, open Apr-Oct, and west towards Gairlochy at *Gairlochy Holiday Park*, T712711, F712712, open Apr-Oct.

There's also a wide choice of places to eat. As well as those listed above, there's the *Old Station Restaurant*, T712535, in a converted railway station. Has a very good reputation, dinner is expensive; lunch by prior arrangement only, open Apr-Oct, Tue-Sun 1800-2100. Also recommended is *The Coach House Restaurant*, T712680, crann_tara@bigfoot.com, which is about 3 miles north of town on the right-hand side, at Glenfintaig. It's a popular place and small, so you'll have to book ahead for lunch (cheap) or dinner (mid-range to expensive), open late Apr to late Oct, daily 1200-1500 and 1800-2100.

Eating

There are regular **buses** to and from Fort William and Inverness (£6 single). Spean Bridge is also on the Fort William-Glasgow **rail** line (see Fort William Transport below).

Transport

Loch Arkaig

A mile north of Spean Bridge on the A82 is the **Commando Memorial**, which commemorates the commandos who trained here during the Second World War. It's worth lingering for a few moments to appreciate the fantastic views all around. From here the B8004 branches west to **Gairlochy**, crossing the Caledonian Canal, then the B8005 heads north to Loch Arkaig, a long, deep and mysterious loch stretching west through the mountains. Bonnie Prince Charlie passed this way, before and after Culloden, through an area which has, for centuries, been the seat of the Camerons of Lochiel. The Camerons were fervent supporters of the Jacobite cause and when Prince Charles landed at Loch nan Uamh, on the road from Fort William to Mallaig, he called on Cameron of Lochiel to join him at Glenfinnan.

Phone code: 01397
Colour map 3,
grid A6

You can find out all about the Camerons and their involvement in the Jacobite rebellion of 1745 in the **Clan Cameron Museum**, in the tiny township of **Achnacarry**, nestled between the shores of Loch Lochy and **Loch Arkaig**. The museum is housed in an old cottage rebuilt after being burned by government troops in 1746. ■ *Daily Easter to mid-Oct 1330-1700; Jul-Aug 1100-1700. Adult £3, concession £1.50, children free. T712480.*

Beyond the turn-off to Achnacarry, the single-track road runs through the Clunes Forest and **The Dark Mile**, a long line of beech trees which completely cuts out daylight. At the east end of Loch Arkaig, a stone bridge crosses the Caig Burn. Beside the bridge is a car park, from where a path leads up to the spectacular **Cia-Aig Falls** which tumble into a deep, dark pool known as **The Witch's Cauldron**. It was here that an old hag was accused of casting her evil eye over Lochiel's cattle, causing them to fall ill and die. But when she fell into the pool and drowned, the cattle miraculously began to recover from their illness.

Beyond the falls is *Highland Icelandic Horse Trekking*, T/F712427, hihot@compuserve.com, which offers one-hour, two-hour and day rides in the surrounding hills. The road runs along the north shore of Loch Arkaig all the way to the head of the loch, from where experienced and well-equipped hill walkers can hike through the glens to Loch Nevis and Knoydart.

Transport There's no public transport beyond Achnacarry, and there's only 1 **bus** a day to Achnacarry from Lochaber High School in Fort William.

Glen Roy and Loch Laggan

Phone code: 01397 From Spean Bridge, the A86 runs east through Glen Spean to meet the A9 *Colour map 4,* Perth to Inverness road which leads to **Aviemore**, Scotland's main ski centre *grid A/B1* (see page 187). The road passes through **Roy Bridge**, which is the turn-off for **Glen Roy**, noted for its amazing 'parallel roads'. These are not in fact roads but three gravel ledges etched on to the mountains at different heights. The 'roads' marked the shorelines of a glacial lake formed during the last ice-age. Roy Bridge was also the site of the infamous Keppoch Murders (see page 216).

The road continues east towards Loch Laggan. After a couple of miles it passes **Cille Choirille**, an ancient church built by a 15th-century Cameron chief as penance for a life of violence. The church fell into disrepair but was restored and reopened in 1932 and now attracts people of all creeds as it's said to inspire peace and spiritual healing. Further east, at the eastern end of Loch Laggan, is the massive **Laggan Dam**, built in 1933 to provide water for the aluminium smelter at Fort William. The water is piped through tunnels up to 15 ft in diameter carved through the core of Ben Nevis. The road runs along the north shore of the loch, past the **Creag Meagaidh National Nature Reserve**, where you can see herds of red deer right by the reserve car park. A track leads from here up to **Lochan a' Choire** (about four hours).

Sleeping There are several hotels in **Roy Bridge**, including the **C** *Stronlossit Hotel*, T712253, **& eating** F712641, which serves good meals all day from 1100 (cheap lunch; mid-range dinner). There are also 3 independent **hostels**: the **F** *Grey Corrie Lodge*, T712236, F712241, is handy for shops and transport, serves cheap bar meals and also has laundry facilities. A mile and a half from the village is the cheaper **F** *Aite Cruinnichidh* hostel, at Achluachrach, T712315. Five miles east, at Tulloch train station, is **F** *Station Lodge*, T/F732333, which also serves meals (including vegetarian).

Aside from the places listed above, a good place to eat is the *Glenspean Lodge Hotel*, T712223. Lunch served 1230-1430 (cheap) and dinner 1830-2100 (expensive).

Sport **Fishing** *Fishing Scotland*, T/F712812, www.fishing-scotland.co.uk, runs fishing courses and trips on the surrounding lochs. Loch Arkaig in particular is renowned for its trout fishing. **Hiking and climbing** *Nevis Guides*, Bohuntin, Roy Bridge, T712356.

Transport There are **buses** from Fort William to Roy Bridge (3 times daily Mon-Fri; 1 on Sat). Roy Bridge is also on the Fort William-Glasgow **rail** line.

Fort William and around

Fort William is the gateway to the Western Highlands and one of the country's main tourist centres. It stands at the head of Loch Linnhe, with the snow-topped mass of Ben Nevis towering behind. You could be forgiven for assuming that it's quite an attractive place, but you'd be wrong. Despite its magnificent setting, Fort William has all the charm of a motorway service station. A dual carriageway runs along the lochside, over a litter-strewn pedestrian underpass and past dismal 1960s concrete boxes masquerading as hotels.

Phone code: 01397
Colour map 3, grid B6
Population: 10,774

Most of the good things about Fort William are outside the town. The surrounding mountains and glens are amongst the most stunning in the Highlands and attract hikers and climbers in their droves. **Ben Nevis** – Britain's highest peak at 4,406 ft – and also the very beautiful **Glen Nevis**, which many of you may recognize from movies such as Braveheart and Rob Roy, see page 226. There's also skiing and snowboarding at nearby **Aonach Mor**, one of Scotland's top ski areas, see page 225, and some good mountain biking around the **Leanachan Forest**, see page 225.

Though it's not a pretty sight, Fort William is the largest town hereabouts and has all the services and facilities you'd expect. There are banks with ATMs on the pedestrianized High Street, as well as a couple of good supermarkets and two well-stocked outdoor-equipment shops.

Ins and outs

Fort William is easily reached by **bus**, from Inverness, Glasgow and Oban, and by **train**, direct from Glasgow via the amazing and beautiful West Highland Railway. The train and bus stations are next to each other at the north end of the High St, on the other side of the dual carriageway. If you're driving, parking can be a problem. There's a big **car park** beside the loch at the south end of town, and another behind the tourist office. You can also walk to Fort William, if you have a week to spare, from just north of Glasgow, along the 95 mile-long **West Highland Way** (see page 52).

Getting there
For more details see 'Transport', on page 226

The town is strung out for several miles along the banks of Loch Linnhe. The centre is compact and easy to get around on foot. Many of the **guesthouses** and **B&Bs**, and a few youth hostels, are in **Corpach**, 1½ miles to the north, but there are frequent buses from the town centre. There are also buses to the youth hostel in **Glen Nevis**. For information on these and on **taxis** and **car hire** see under Transport, page 226.

Getting around

The busy TIC is on Cameron Square, just off the High St, T703781, F705184. They stock a good range of books, maps and leaflets covering local walks. They will also help arrange transport to more remote Highland parts. Open Apr-late May Mon-Sat 0900-1700, Sun 1000-1600; Jun-early Jul Mon-Sat 0900-1800, Sun 1000-1700; Jul-Aug Mon-Sat 0900-2030, Sun 0900-1800; Sep-late Oct Mon-Sat 0900-1800, Sun 1000-1700; Nov-Mar Mon-Fri 0900-1700, Sat 1000-1600, closed Sun.

Tourist Information Centre

Sights

There's little of real interest in the town, though the **West Highland Museum**, on Cameron Square by the tourist office, is a worthwhile exception. It contains excellent exhibits of Jacobite memorabilia, including a bed in which Prince

North & Northwest Highlands

Charles slept and a 'secret' portrait of the prince which is revealed only when reflected in a cylindrical mirror. There are also fine displays of Highland clans and tartans, wildlife and local history. ■ *Jun-Sep Mon-Sat 1000-1700; Oct-May 1000-1600; also Sun Jul-Aug 1400-1700. Adult £2, concession £1.50, children £0.50. T702169.* The **fort** from which the town gets its name was built in 1690 by order of William III to keep the rebellious Scottish clans in order. The garrison fought off attacks by Jacobites during the rebellions of 1715 and 1745 but was then demolished to make way for the railway line. The scant remains of the fort can be seen on the lochside, near the train station.

The **Ben Nevis Distillery** is at Lochy Bridge, at the junction of the A82 to Inverness and the A830 to Mallaig, about a mile north of the town centre. To get there take a Caol or Corpach bus (see below under Transport). ■ *Visitor Centre open Mon-Fri 0900-1700 (also Sat in Jul-Aug 1000-1600). Tours £2 per*

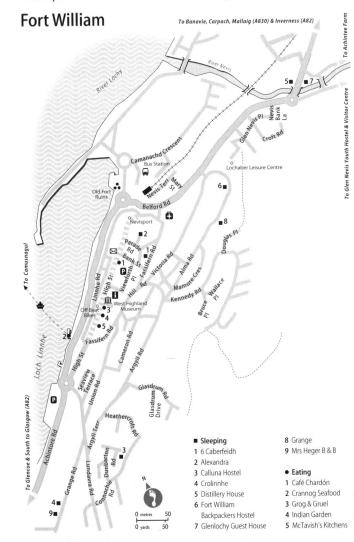

Fort William

To Banavie, Carpach, Mallaig (A830) & Inverness (A82)

To Achintee Farm

To Glen Nevis Youth Hostel & Visitor Centre

River Lochy

River Nevis

Glen Nevis Pl

Nevis Bank La

Croft Rd

Camanachd Crescent

Bus Station

Lochaber Leisure Centre

Old Fort Ruins

Nevis Terr

Mary St

Belford Rd

Nevisport

Parade Rd

Bank St

Linnhe Rd

High St

Viewforth

Hill Rd

Fassifern Rd

Victoria Rd

Alma Rd

Mamore Cres

Kennedy Rd

Bruce Pl

Wallace Pl

Douglas Pl

West Highland Museum

Off Beat Bikes

Fassifern Rd

To Camusnagul

To Glencoe & South to Glasgow (A82)

Loch Linnhe

Cameron Rd

Argyll Rd

Seaview Terrace

Union Rd

High St

Achintore Rd

Grange Rd

Argyll Terr

Lundavra Rd

Heathercroft Rd

Comochie Rd

Dunbarton Rd

Glasdrum Rd

Glasdrum Drive

N

0 metres 50
0 yards 50

North & Northwest Highlands

Tours from Fort William

*Top of the Pops as far as tours are concerned has to be the **Jacobite Steam Train** to Mallaig. The train runs through some of the West Highlands' most stunning scenery and crosses the historic Glenfinnan viaduct, with great views down Loch Shiel. The train runs from mid-June to September, daily except Saturday. It leaves Fort William at 1035*

and returns from Mallaig at 1410. For more details, T703791.

*There are several **cruises** which leave from the Town Pier, giving you the chance to spot local marine wildlife, including seals, otters and seabirds. One of the operators is **Seal Island Cruises** (T705589), who run trips of 1½ hours from April to September.*

---

person. T700200. Just before the distillery, on the left, are the 13th-century ruins of **Inverlochy Castle**.

Three miles from the town centre along the A830 to Mallaig, in the suburb of Banavie, is **Neptune's Staircase**, a series of eight linked locks on the Caledonian Canal. The locks lower the canal by 90 ft in less than two miles between Loch Lochy and Loch Eil and comprise the last section of the canal which links the North Sea with the Irish Sea. It's a pretty dramatic sight, with equally dramatic views of Ben Nevis and its neighbours behind Fort William. From here you can walk or cycle along the canal towpath. Further along the A830 to Mallaig, in the village of Corpach, is **Treasures of the Earth**, an exhibition of crystals, gemstones and fossils displayed in a huge simulated cave. ■ *Daily May-Sep 0930-1900, Oct-Apr 1000-1700. Adult £3, concession £2.75, children £1.50. T772283.*

Essentials

Fort William has plentiful accommodation, ranging from large luxury hotels to modest guesthouses and B&Bs. Many of the B&Bs are in **Corpach** and **Banavie** to the north of town (see 'Transport' below). As a main tourist centre, Fort William gets very busy in the high season and you'll need to book ahead at this time. The tourist office will book a room for you, for a small fee, or you can ask for their free *Fort William & Lochaber Visitor Guide* and phone around yourself.

Sleeping
■ *on map*
Price codes:
see inside front cover

L *Inverlochy Castle Hotel*, 3 miles north of town on the A82 to Inverness, T702177, F702953. 16 rooms. One of the best hotels in the country and everything you'd expect to find in a real castle, unsurpassed elegance, impeccable service and superb food, all set in 500 acres of beautiful grounds.

B *The Moorings Hotel*, 3 miles out of town in Banavie, on the road to Corpach and Mallaig, T772797, F772441. 21 rooms. Overlooks 'Neptune's Staircase', well situated and comfortable with an excellent restaurant.

C *Alexandra Hotel*, The Parade, T702241, F705554, sales@miltonhotels.com 97 rooms, large established hotel right in the centre of town, with restaurant. **C** *Glenloy Lodge Hotel*, about 6 miles from town on the B8004 north from Banavie, T/F712700. 9 rooms, open mid-Dec to late Oct. Friendly and comfortable little hotel tucked away in a quiet, secluded location, and with a good restaurant. **C-D** *Glenlochy Guesthouse*, Nevis Bridge, North Rd, T702909, is recommended. C Highland Hotel, Union Rd, T702291, F700133. Traditional Highland hotel overlooking the town with great views across Loch Linnhe. Good restaurant, comfortable, cheaper off-season.

D *Distillery House*, across the road from the *Glenorchy Guesthouse* (opposite the road into Glen Nevis), T700103, F702980. 6 rooms, comfortable, upmarket guesthouse.

North & Northwest Highlands

Riding the rails

*The spectacular **West Highland Railway** runs from Glasgow via Fort William to Mallaig. It is a magnificent feat of engineering and the most dramatic entrance possible to the West Highlands. The stretch before Fort William is particularly breathtaking as the train crosses the bleak and desolate Rannoch Moor, then skirts Loch Ossian, runs around Ben Nevis and enters Fort William from the northeast, through the Monessie Gorge and the most southerly part of the Great Glen. But this railway line saves the best for last. The final section is even more stunning and must rank as one of the most beautiful railway journeys in Europe.*

Achintore Rd, which runs south along the loch, is packed with B&Bs and hotels, many of which are large and characterless. More appealing than most is **D** *Lawriestone Guesthouse*, T/F700777.

Running parallel is **Grange Rd**, which is lined with B&B accommodation. Two of the best are **B** *Crolinnhe*, T702709, open Mar-Nov, and **B** *The Grange*, T705516, open Apr-Oct.

There are also plenty of B&Bs which are closer to the **bus and train stations**, mostly on and around Fassifern Rd and Alma Rd. These include **D-E** *Guisachan House*, T/F703797, and **E** *Mrs Heger*, 'Finnisaig', T702453, both on Alma Rd, and **D** *6 Caberfeidh*, Fassifern Rd, T703756.

There are several more places to stay in **Glen Nevis**, including **E** *Achintee Farm Guesthouse*, T702240, mcy@btinternet.com, by the start of the path to Ben Nevis. For details of how to get there, see Transport below.

There are also cheaper options, in the shape of several hostels and a couple of campsites. The popular **F** *Fort William Backpackers* is on Alma Rd, 500yd from the train station, T700711. 3 miles out of town in Glen Nevis, near the start of the path up Ben Nevis, is the large **F** *SYHA Youth Hostel*, T702336, which gets very busy in summer. A better bet is the independent **F** *Ben Nevis Bunkhouse*, at Achintee Farm, across the river from the visitor centre (see above). **F** *Calluna*, T700451, F700489, www.guide.u.net.com, is at Heathercroft, about a 15-min walk from the tourist office (see map). It's run by experienced mountain guide, Alan Kimber. There are 2 hostels in Corpach (see Transport below). **F** *The Smiddy Bunkhouse*, T772467, www.highland.mountain.guide.co.uk, is next to Corpach train station with the Snowgoose Mountain Centre attached. **F** *Scottish International Backpackers* is at Farr Cottage Activity Centre, T772315, F772247, www.fort-william.co.uk\farrcottage, which also organizes hill walking trips and rents out mountain bikes. Two miles up the Glen Nevis Rd is *Glen Nevis Caravan & Camping Park*, T702191, open mid-Mar to late Oct, which has excellent facilities. Five miles from town on the road to Mallaig, is Linnhe Caravan & Chalet Park, T772376, open Christmas to late Oct, also with full facilities.

Eating

Fort William isn't exactly the culinary capital of the Highlands, but there are some top quality restaurants and a decent choice across the range

Most of the hotels offer lunch and dinner, and the best of these are the Inverlochy Castle and The Moorings (see 'Sleeping' above). Otherwise, by far the best option is the excellent *Crannog Seafood Restaurant*, on the Town Pier, T705589, crannogallan@msn.com Housed in an old smokehouse, the seafood is as fresh as you can get and the surroundings are unpretentious. It gets very busy and service can be slow, so book ahead and take your time (lunch cheap to mid-range; dinner mid-range). Four miles from town is *An Crann*, T772077. Take the A830 to Mallaig, then turn right to Banavie on the B8004. This converted barn is a local favourite and offers good Scottish cooking in a friendly atmosphere. (Mid-range prices.) Lunch 1230-1500, dinner 1700-2100, closed Sun. Open late Mar to mid-Oct.

Nevis Range Ski Centre

*The Nevis Range Ski Centre, four miles northeast of Fort William, at Torlundy, is situated on the mountain of **Aonach Mhor** (4,006 ft). It's Scotland's highest skiing and snowboarding area and has the longest ski season, running from Christmas to May. It also boasts the country's only cable-car system, built in 1989. The 1½ mile gondola ride is a popular attraction not only with skiers and snowboarders in the winter but also during the summer off-season period, when it's used by hill walkers to gain easy access to the mountains. For most tourists,*

though, it's an easy way to climb to over 2,000 ft and enjoy the wonderful views from the terrace of the self-service restaurant at the top. There are ski and snowboarding schools and also a dry slope for summer skiing in July and August (open Sunday-Thursday 1100-1230, £18 including gondola).

The gondola is open all year, except early November to the week before Christmas, 1000-1700 (July-August 0930-1800, Thu & fri till 2100) and costs £6.75 return (children £4.15). T01397-705825, www.ski.scotland.net

A great place for baguettes, filled rolls and pastries to eat in or takeaway is *Café Chardón*, upstairs at Peter Maclennan's store, in a side lane off the High St, T772077. Fort William boasts a very fine curry house, the *Indian Garden Restaurant*, at 88 High St, T705011. It does a cheap lunch, takeaways and is open late. *The Grog & Gruel*, 66 High St, T705078, is a pub-cum-restaurant offering good value pizza, pasta and Tex Mex and a wide range of superb cask ales. Open till 2400/0100. Also on the High St is *McTavish's Kitchens*, T702406, serving steaks and seafood at mid-range prices. In summer it hosts nightly Scottish music shows, with dancing and bagpipes, from 2030.

In Glen Nevis, near the SYHA hostel, the *Glen Nevis Restaurant*, T705459, serves a cheap-mid-range 2-course lunch and mid-range 3-course dinner. Open 1200-2200, Apr-Oct. Nearby is *Café Beag*, T703601, a cosy place with log fire. Good vegetarian food.

Canoeing There are several good rivers around Fort William, ranging in difficulty from Grade 1 to 6. Canoe courses are run by *Snowgoose Mountain Centre*, which is attached to *The Smiddy Bunkhouse* (see 'Sleeping' above). A useful contact is the *Nevis Canoe Club*, T705388.

Sports

Fishing *Torlundy Trout Fishery*, at Torlundy Farm in Tomacharich, 3 miles north, off the A82, T703015, has 3 lakes filled with rainbow trout and hires out rods.

Hiking and climbing Fort William is a mecca for hikers and climbers. For information on the climb up Ben Nevis and walks around Glen Nevis, see page 226. If you want to hire a guide, try *Lochaber Walks*, 22 Zetland Av, T703828, *Fort William Mountain Guides*, T700451, *Alba Walking Holidays*, T704964 and *Snowgoose Mountain Centre* (see 'Sleeping' above). Fort William has 2 excellent outdoor activity equipment shops. *Nevisport*, T704921, is on the High St, and has a huge selection of books, maps and guides, a bureau de change and bar-restaurant. At the other end of the High St is *West Coast Outdoor Sports*, T705777. There's an indoor climbing wall at the *Lochaber Leisure Centre* (see below).

Mountain biking The Leanachan Forest, below Aonach Mhor, is 4 miles north of Fort William. Access is via the road to the Aonach Mhor ski development. The forest covers a huge area with 25 miles of mountain bike trails, ranging from easy to demanding. There is also the Great Glen Cycle Route, which is mainly off-road and runs all the way from Fort William to Inverness. For the hire, sale or repair of bikes, and good advice on local cycle routes, visit *Off Beat Bikes*, 117 High St and at the Nevis Range Ski Centre, T704008, www.offbeatbikes.co.uk, open only Jul-Aug.

Skiing The Nevis Range ski centre is at nearby Aonach Mhor. For details, see page 225, and for ski equipment, try *Nevisport* (see above).

North & Northwest Highlands

Swimming There's an indoor pool at the *Lochaber Leisure Centre*, off Belford Rd (see map), T704359.

Transport **Bus Local**: There are buses every 10-20 mins to and from **Caol** and **Corpach**, and every hour on Sun and in the evening. There is an hourly service to **Glen Nevis**, Mon-Sat from 0800-2300, Jun to Sep only (less frequent on Sun). There are 4 buses daily to **Aonach Mhor** during the ski season.

Bus Long distance: There are several daily *Citylink* buses to **Inverness** (1 hr); to **Oban** (1 hr 45 mins) via **Glencoe** (30 mins); and to **Uig** (3 ½ hrs), via **Portree** and **Kyle of Lochalsh** (1 hr 50 mins). *Citylink* buses also go several times daily to **Glasgow** (3 ¼ hrs), via Glencoe and Tyndrum, and to **Edinburgh** (4 hrs), via **Stirling** (3 hrs). There is a bus to **Mallaig** (1 ½ hrs) daily except Sun with *Shiel Buses*, T01967-431272. *Highland Country Buses*, T702373, run several times a day to **Kinlochleven** (50 mins) via Glencoe. There is also a *Postbus* service (Mon-Sat) to **Glen Etive**.

Car hire: *Easydrive*, at Lochy Bridge, T701616, *Volkswagen Rental*, at Nevis Garage, Argour Rd, Caol, T702432, *Budget*, at North Rd, T702500, or *Practical Car & Van Hire*, at Slipway Autos, Corpach, T772404. Prices start from around £35 per day. **Taxi:** You can call a taxi on T706070, or T704000.

Ferry: There is a passenger-only ferry service to **Camusnagaul**, on the opposite bank of Loch Linnhe, from the Town Pier. It sails several times daily (Mon-Sat) and takes 10 mins. For times etc contact Highland Council, T01463-702695, or ask at the tourist office.

Train: There are 2-3 trains daily from **Glasgow** to Fort William (3 ¾ hrs) via **Crianlarich**. These trains continue to **Mallaig** (a further 1 hr 20 mins) where they connect with ferries to Armadale on Skye (see page 292). There are no direct trains to Oban; you need to change at Crianlarich. There is a sleeper service from **London Euston** (see page 35), but you'll miss the views. For all rail enquiries, T0345-484950.

Glen Nevis

Colour map 3, grid B6

Only 10 minutes drive from Fort William is one of Scotland's great glens, the classic Glen Nevis. The sparkling Water of Nevis tumbles through a wooded gorge, closed in by steep, bracken-covered slopes, with the massive hulk of Ben Nevis watching over. The whole scene is both rugged and sylvan and the nearest you'll get to a Himalayan valley in the Scottish Highlands. It's not surprising, then, that this is a favourite with movie directors and has featured in films such as *Rob Roy* and *Braveheart*.

There are many walks in and around the glen, not least of which is the trek up to the summit of Britain's highest mountain. Aside from the walks described below, there are several easy, marked forest walks which start from the car park at Achriabhach. There are buses into Glen Nevis, as far as the youth hostel, from Fort William bus station (see 'Transport' above).

Walking up Ben Nevis

Advice & information
OS Landranger No 41

Every year many thousands of people make the relatively straightforward ascent of Ben Nevis, and every year a frighteningly high percentage end up injured, or lost, or dead. More people die annually on the 'Ben' than Everest, so this is a mountain that needs to be taken seriously. Though it may be in the 70s in the car park when you set off, the weather changes with alarming speed and you can

Steall Falls

A fairly easy low level walk is to the spectacular 300 ft-high Steall Falls at the head of the glen. It's a popular walk, especially in the summer when the trail can resemble the queue for the Ladies at a Tom Jones concert, but this doesn't detract from its stunning natural beauty.

The path starts at the end of the road, at the second car park. Before setting off, you might like to note the sign by the steep waterfall that cascades down to the edge of the car park. It reads 'Warning! This is not the path to Ben Nevis'. Now, if you need to be warned against attempting to climb up Ben Nevis through a waterfall, you probably shouldn't be left alone in possession of this book, never mind let loose on the Scottish mountains. Once you've shaken your head in disbelief at the apparent mind-numbing stupidity of some of your fellow travellers, follow the track alongside the Water of Nevis. The path climbs steadily through the woods

and becomes rocky, with the river thundering below through the steep gorge. It runs close to the river before emerging from the gorge and opening up into a wide, flower-filled meadow, with a high waterfall at the far end. It's a beautiful, tranquil place and ideal for a picnic. Follow the path across the valley floor till it crosses the river via a precarious bridge that consists of three ropes of thick wire in a V-shape. The path then leads to the bottom of the falls. You can also head left at the bridge and continue up the valley to some ruins. From here the path leads to **Corrour station**, 14 miles away, but it's for fit and experienced hillwalkers only. You can then catch a train back to Fort William. It's a very popular route, and there's even accommodation at the end of it, near the train station, at the **SYHA Loch Lochy Youth Hostel** (T01809-501239; open mid-March to late October).

OS Landranger No 41 covers the route.

North & Northwest Highlands

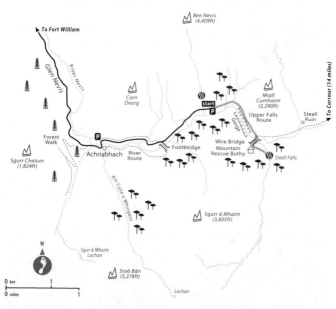

find yourself in a blizzard at the summit, or, as is usually the case, in a blanket of cloud or hill fog. It goes without saying that you need to be well prepared. You will need a good, strong pair of boots, warm clothing, waterproofs, food and drink. You should also take a map and a compass. Allow six to eight hours for the return trip. In the winter the top part of the mountain is covered in snow and you should not attempt the walk unless you are an experienced hill climber.

The route The main tourist path, built as a pony track to service the now-dilapidated observatory on the summit, starts from the car park at Achintee Farm, on the north side of the river, reached by the road through Claggan. It climbs gradually at first across the flank of Meal an t-Suidhe, before joining the alternative path from the youth hostel. This latter route is shorter but much steeper.

The trail continues to climb steadily as it begins to follow the **Red Burn**, until it reaches a junction, with Lochan Meal an t-Suidhe down to the left. Here, an alternative route down from the summit heads left under the north face of the mountain (see below). This is the halfway point of the main route. The path crosses the Red Burn and then climbs by a series of long and seemingly never-ending zig-zags up to a plateau. The path splits in two, but both paths take you up to the summit, marked by a cairn and emergency shelter, on ruins of the old observatory. Note that on the upper sloping palteau the path can 'disappear' in mist and snow, and some cairns and beacons have been removed by vandals masquerading as purists. If conditions deteriorate, a compass is a life-saver. There is a shelter on the summit and at least two others on the mountain.

To return simply retrace your steps all the way. If the weather is settled enough and you have time, you can follow the alternative route below the north face. This leads right round the mountain to the Charles Inglis Clark mountain hut, then heads down into the **Allt a' Mhuilinn** glen which leads all the way down to the distillery on the A82, a mile north of the town centre. Note that this route adds an extra three or four miles to the descent and should only be attempted by fit and experienced hillwalkers.

Ben Nevis

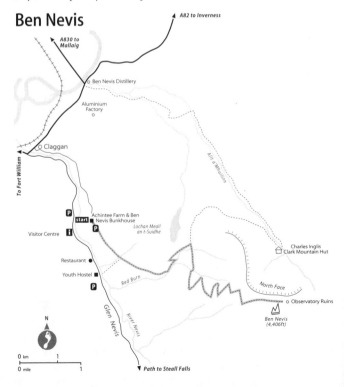

Fort William to Glen Coe

The main A82 south to Glasgow runs down the side of Loch Linnhe towards *Phone code: 01855* Glen Coe. About eight miles south of Fort William it passes the **Corran Ferry** *Colour map 3, grid B6* to **Ardgour** (see page 236). The ferry makes the five-minute crossing every 30 minutes. Foot passengers are free and cars cost £4.70. By the ferry is the **D** *Nether Lochaber Hotel*, T821235, which serves decent, cheap pub meals.

Less than half a mile south of the ferry is the turning to **Inchree**, where you'll find cheap lodging at the *Inchree Bunkhouse Hostel*, T821287. There's also a good restaurant nearby, the *Four Seasons Bistro and Bar*, T821393, a friendly and informal place that looks like a log cabin. It's open daily except Tuesdays, 1800-2130. Prices are mid-range.

There's an easy 40-minute circular walk up to **Inchree Waterfall**. It starts from the car park at the end of the road beyond the tiny hamlet and is clearly marked. The waterfall is impressive and divided into three sections. The views from the top, down the length of Loch Linnhe, are worth the walk alone. The path continues up past the waterfall to the forest road which leads back downhill to the car park.

Sleeping A mile south of the ferry are the villages of **Onich** and **North Ballachulish**. There's a wide selection of places to stay here, mostly with good views of the loch, which make an attractive alternative to Fort William. Overlooking the loch are **L** *Allt-nan-Ros Hotel*, T821210, allt-nan-ros@zetnet.co.uk, and **L** *The Lodge on the Loch Hotel*, T821237, laurence@mysteryworld.co.uk, open Feb-Dec. Both are high-quality hotels with great views and good restaurants (lunch mid-range; dinner expensive). A cheaper option is **B** *Onich Hotel*, T821214, which also has loch views and serves good meals (cheap-mid-range) in its busy bar. A good place to dine, but for residents only, is **B** *Cuilcheanna House*, T821226; open Easter-Oct, a comfortable guesthouse just off the main road.

Sport *Alfresco Adventure*, T821248, just to the east of North Ballachulish on the B863 to Kinlochleven, offers boat hire and various outdoor activities such as mountain biking and canoeing.

Kinlochleven

The B863 turns east off the A82 at North Ballachulish and heads to *Phone code: 01855* Kinlochleven, at the head of Loch Leven. It can also be reached on the same *Colour map 3, grid B6* road from Glencoe village, seven miles west. It's an unlikely place to find a huge aluminium factory, but it kept the village alive for many years. Now, though, it's threatened with closure and there's talk of Kinlochleven being developed as a major mountaineering centre.

You can find out all about the long, and often tragic, history of aluminium working in Lochaber at **The Aluminium Story**, in the Kinlochleven Visitor Centre and Library, on Linnhe Road. ■ *Apr-Oct, Tue-Fri 1030-1800, Sat/Sun 1100-1500. Free. T831663.*

The West Highland Way passes through the village and many walkers spend the night here before setting out on the last stretch before Fort William. There are also several good walks in the surrounding hills and glens, a few of which are described below.

North & Northwest Highlands

Sleeping & eating There's not a huge amount to choose from in the way of accommodation or eating out. The **D** *MacDonald Hotel*, on the Fort William Rd, T831539, open Mar-Dec, serves cheap bar lunches and moderately priced dinners, and the **E** *Tailrace Inn*, on Riverside Rd, T831777, does cheap bar meals all day. There are also several **B&Bs**, as well as an independent hostel, the *West Highland Lodge*, Hostel Brae, T831471.

Transport *Highland Country Buses*, T01397-702373, runs 6 times a day (Mon-Sat) between Fort William and Kinlochleven (50 mins).

Walks around Kinlochleven
OS Landranger No 41
There are some fairly easy short walks from Kinlochleven up the glen of the river Leven, including the one to the impressive **Grey Mare's Tail** waterfall. A fairly easy but rewarding half day walk is to follow the **West Highland Way** south from the village to the top of the **Devil's Staircase**, where it meets the A82 at the eastern end of Glen Coe.

The route starts from the British Aluminium Visitor Centre, runs around the side of the aluminium factory, then crosses a wooden bridge and climbs gradually on a dirt jeep-track up to Penstock House, at 1,000 ft. At the top, near the house, the track forks to the right and continues on a rough footpath to the **Devil's Staircase**. The path is marked with the West Highland Way thistle sign, so it's easy to follow, uphill to the top of the pass (1,804 ft), from

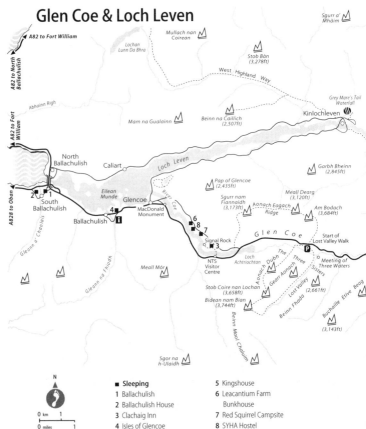

Glen Coe & Loch Leven

(Map showing the Glen Coe & Loch Leven area, including:)

A82 to Fort William
A82 to North Ballachulish
A82 to Fort William
A828 to Oban

Mullach nan Coirean
Lochan Lunn Da Bhra
Stob Bàn (3,278ft)
West Highland Way
Sgurr a' Mhàim
Grey Mare's Tail Waterfall
Kinlochleven
Abhainn Righ
Mam na Gualainn
Beinn na Caillich (2,507ft)
North Ballachulish
Caliart
Loch Leven
Garbh Bheinn (2,845ft)
Eilean Munde
Glencoe
South Ballachulish
Ballachulish
MacDonald Monument
River Coe
Pap of Glencoe (2,435ft)
Sgurr nam Fiannaidh (3,173ft)
Meall Dearg (3,120ft)
Aonach Eagach Ridge
Am Bodach (3,684ft)
Signal Rock
Glen Coe
Start of Lost Valley Walk
Loch Achtriochtan
The Three Sisters
Aonach Dubh
Gearr Aonach
Meeting of Three Waters
NTS Visitor Centre
Meall Mòr
Stob Coire nan Lochan (3,658ft)
Bidean nam Bian (3,744ft)
Lost Valley (2,661ft)
Beinn Fhada
Buachaille Etive Beag
(3,143ft)
Gleann a' Chaolais
Gleann na Fhiodh
Beinn Maol Chaluim
Sgor na h-Ulaidh

N
0 km 1
0 miles 1

■ Sleeping
1 Ballachulish
2 Ballachulish House
3 Clachaig Inn
4 Isles of Glencoe
5 Kingshouse
6 Leacantuim Farm Bunkhouse
7 Red Squirrel Campsite
8 SYHA Hostel

North & Northwest Highlands

where you get great views of Loch Eilde Mór and the Mamores to the north. The path then descends down the staircase to Glen Coe, with breathtaking Buachaille Etive Mór in front of you all the way.

You'll have to return to Kinlochleven by the same route, or you could carry on to the *Kingshouse Hotel* (see below). The return trip from Kinlochleven should take four to five hours, or you can start out from Glencoe (see below). This section of the West Highland Way was once part of the old military road which ran from Fort William to Stirling. The Devil's Staircase was named by the 400 soldiers who had to endure severe hardship while building it in the 17th century.

Another good hike, though more strenuous, is to **Beinn na Callich** (2,507 ft). You'll need to be fairly fit for this steep climb and allow around six to seven hours for the return trip. The route is well marked and starts from the West Highland Way footpath opposite the school, which is on the road heading out of the village towards Fort William.

The path climbs steeply at first, crosses the tarmac road to Mamore Lodge, then continues till it joins General Wade's old military road, which takes the West Highland Way on its final 11 miles to Fort William. From here, you'll see the path zig-zagging up the mountain. Continue along the old military road for about 400yd until you cross a wooden bridge. Then follow a path down to another wooden bridge, where the ground is quite boggy. Cross the bridge and the path begins to zig-zag uphill till it levels out onto a plateau, before continuing relentlessly upwards through a long series of zig-zags to the summit, marked by a couple of cairn and a commemorative plaque. The views from the top make the tiring climb worthwhile. You can see down onto Loch Leven, across to Glen Coe and the magnificent Mamores looming close by.

Fit and experienced hill walkers can access the Mamores from the Mamore Lodge road. Once you're up there you have the opportunity to bag several Munros, via a series of excellent ridge walks connecting **Am Bodach** (3,386 ft) with **Stob Coire a' Chairn** (3,219 ft), **Na Gruagaichean** (3,461 ft), **An Gearanach** (3,222 ft), **Sgor An Iubhair** (3,285 ft), **Sgurr a'Mhaim** (3,606 ft) and **Stob Ban** (3,278 ft). These peaks and ridges can also be reached from Glen Nevis (see page 226). As well as a good pair of lungs and the proper equipment, take a map and a compass.

Map showing Binnein Mór, Na Gruagaichean (3,461ft), Loch Eilde Mór, River Leven, Blackwater Reservoir, Dam, Devil's Staircase, West Highland Way, Altnafeadh, (3,032ft), Buachaille Etive Mór (Great Shepherd of Etive) (2,963ft), Glen Etive, River Etive, Museum of Scottish Skiing & Climbing, To Glencoe Ski Centre, Rannoch Moor, A82 To Crianlarich & Glasgow, 5

North & Northwest Highlands

Ballachulish

On the southern shore of Loch Leven, a mile or so west of Glencoe village, on the A82, is the old slate quarrying village of Ballachulish. There's a good range of accommodation here and many use the place as a base to visit Glencoe.

In the car park just off the main road is the **Tourist Information Centre**, T811296. As well as the usual accommodation booking service they have displays about the quarries. It's open April-May Monday-Saturday 0900-1700, Sunday 1200-1600; June-September Monday-Saturday 0900-1800, Sunday 1000-1700; September-October Monday-Saturday 1000-1700, Sunday 1000-1600.

Sleeping   **L** *The Isles of Glencoe Hotel*, T811602, F811770, reservations@mysteryworld.co.uk 39 rooms. A modern hotel and leisure complex next to Highland Mysteryworld, excellent location on the shores of the loch and facilities include heated pool, sauna and gym. The restaurant serves a mid-range to cheap 3-course lunch and expensive to mid-range 3-course dinner. **L** *Ballachulish Hotel*, in South Ballachulish by the bridge, T821582, F821463, reservations@mysteryworld.co.uk 54 rooms, grand old hotel, handily placed for Glen Coe, Fort William or Oban, restaurant serves meals all day (3-course lunch mid-range to cheap; 3-course dinner expensive). **L** *Ballachulish House*, T811266, F811498, open Mar-Oct. 7 rooms, 200 yd beyond the *Ballachulish Hotel* on the A828 to Oban. This comfortable and elegant hotel/guesthouse is steeped in history and said to be the most haunted house in Scotland. The seat of the Stewarts of Ballachulish since the 16th century, this was where the final order for the Glencoe Massacre was signed (see below). Hospitality is second-to-none and the food is superb, even if you're not staying you can enjoy the experience of dining here (expensive), but book ahead. There's also a wide selection of cheaper B&Bs and guesthouses in the village, including the very good **E** *Fern Villa*, T811393.

Glen Coe

There are many spectacular places in the Scottish Highlands, but few, if any, can compare to the truly awesome scenery of Glen Coe. No one could fail to be moved by its haunting beauty, with imposing mountains, their tops often wreathed in cloud, rising steeply on either side from the valley floor. The brooding atmosphere of the landscape is only enhanced by the glen's tragic history. Once you've heard of

Glen Coe

The Glen Coe Massacre

Glen Coe is probably best known as the scene of one of the most shameful and notorious incidents in Scottish history.

Following his succession to the throne, William III wanted all the clans to swear an oath of allegiance by 1 January 1692. After much hesitation, the Jacobite clans of the West Highlands agreed to do so. However, Maclain of Glencoe, chief of a small branch of the MacDonalds, was not only late in setting off on the journey, but mistakenly went to Fort William to sign, instead of Inveraray. By the time he reached Inveraray it was 6 January and the deadline had passed.

The government decided that the rebellious clan be punished, in order to set an example to other clans, some of whom had not taken the oath. A company of 120 soldiers, under the command of Cambell of Glenlyon, were sent to Glen Coe, and since their leader was related by marriage to Maclain, the troops were billeted in

MacDonald homes, in keeping with the long-standing Highland tradition of hospitality.

There they stayed for almost two weeks, until the cold-blooded order came through to '. . . put all to the sword under seventy'. And so, on a cold winter's night, in the early hours of 13 February 1692, the Campbells ruthlessly slaughtered their hosts. Maclain and 37 men, women and children were slain in their beds, while many others fled into the hills, only to die of hunger and exposure. It was a bloody incident which had deep repercussions and proved to be the beginning of the end of the Highland way of life.

There's a monument to the fallen MacDonalds in the village of Glencoe, where members of the clan still gather on 13 February each year. For a powerful and evocative account of the Massacre, you should read Glencoe *by John Prebble (Penguin).*

the Glen Coe Massacre it sends a shiver down the spine every time you pass this way. Scotland's most famous glen is also one of the most accessible, with the A82 Glasgow to Fort William road running through it. Much of the area is owned by the National Trust for Scotland and virtually uninhabited, leaving huge tracts of glen and mountain which provide outstanding climbing and walking. There's also skiing, at the Glencoe Ski Centre (see below), and canoeing on the River Coe and River Etive.

There's a small **National Trust for Scotland Visitor Centre** at the western end of the glen, about three miles south of Glencoe village. It shows a short video on the Glencoe Massacre and has a gift shop selling the usual stuff. ■ *Daily, early Apr to mid-May and early Sep to end Oct 1000-1700; mid-May to end Aug 0930-1730. 50p. T811307.*

Glencoe Village

At the western entrance to the glen, on the shores of Loch Leven, is Glencoe village, 16 miles south of Fort William, just off the A82. There are several places to stay in and around the village, as well as a general store, post office and the thatched **Glencoe Folk Museum**, which has collections of costumes, military memorabilia and domestic and farm tools and equipment. ■ *Late May to Sep 1000-1730. £1.50.*

Phone code: 01855
Colour map 3, grid B6

About 3 miles south of the village, on the old road which leads from the village to the NTS visitor centre is **D** *Clachaig Inn*, T811252, inn@glencoe-scotland.co.uk 19 rooms. Good-value accommodation and one of the great Highland pubs, it's a favourite haunt

Sleeping & eating

North & Northwest Highlands

Glencoe Ski Centre

The Glencoe Ski Centre is just over a mile from the Kingshouse Hotel, on the other side of the A82, on **Meall A'Bhuiridh** (3,636 ft). This is Scotland's oldest ski centre, established in 1956, and remains one of the best, with the longest single descent. At the base station is the **Museum of Scottish Skiing and Climbing** where you can see the ice axe used by Chris Bonnington, among other things. It's open daily May-September 0900-1700. There's also a restaurant and café. The chair lift operates daily 0930-1700. A full day pass, including lifts, costs £17 (children £9.50). There's also a combined five-day pass for Glencoe and Nevis Range. T851226, glencoe@sol.co.uk, www.ski.scotland.net

of climbers and there's a lively atmosphere as well as some fine real ales and decent cheap food. There are also 3 chalets which can be rented on a weekly basis (phone for details), and mountain bike hire (see below).

On the same road, about 2 miles from the village, is the excellent **F** *SYHA Youth Hostel*, T811219. It's open all year and is very popular with climbers, so you should book ahead. Nearby are the **F** *Leacantuim Farm Bunkhouses*, T811256, which offer cheap, basic accommodation in 2 bunkhouses and an alpine barn. It also runs the *Red Squirrel Campsite* further along the road, which charges £3.50 per person per night.

There are several B&Bs and guesthouses in the village itself, including **E** *Scorrybreac Guesthouse*, T/F811354, john@tajones.demon.co.uk, open Dec-Oct, and on the outskirts of the village, at Upper Carnoch, is **E** *The Glencoe Guesthouse*, T811244. To the east of the village, on the shores of Loch Leven, you can camp at *Invercoe Caravans*, T/F811210.

At the east end of the glen, almost opposite the turn-off to the Glencoe Ski Centre, is **D** *Kingshouse Hotel*, T851259. 22 rooms. This is Scotland's oldest established inn and such a landmark that it even appears on maps, marked as 'hotel', it's on the West Highland Way and is popular with hikers, climbers and skiers who frequently drop in for a refreshing drink in the bar and some good-value food.

Apart from the places listed above, you can eat in the village at **C** *The Glencoe Hotel*, T811245, which serves cheap bar lunches and moderately priced 3-course dinner.

Sports **Cycle hire** *Glencoe Mountain Bike Centre* at the *Clachaig Inn* (see above); £12 for a full day, £8 for a half day.

Transport *Highland Country Buses* run several times daily from **Fort William** to Glencoe village (30 mins). There are *Citylink* buses to **Glasgow** (2 ½ hrs) and **Fort William**. The daily *Postbus* service from **Fort William** to the *Kingshouse Hotel* and **Glen Etive** stops at the Glencoe crossroads.

Climbing and hiking in Glen Coe

OS Landranger No 41 Glen Coe offers some of Britain's most challenging climbing and hiking, with some notoriously treacherous routes and unpredictable weather conditions that claim lives every year. The routes described below are some of the least strenuous but you'll need a map, good boots, warm clothing, food and water, and you should take the usual precautions (see page 53).

One of the most popular walks is the relatively straightforward hike up to the **Lost Valley**, a secret glen where the ill-fated MacDonalds hid the cattle they'd stolen. Allow around three hours for the return trip. Start from the car park by the large boulder (see map, page 230), opposite the distinctive **Three**

Sisters. Head down to the valley floor and follow the gravel path which leads down to a wooden bridge across the river Coe. Cross the bridge and follow the path up and over the stile. From here there's a choice of two routes. The less obvious route heads right and offers an easier climb into the valley. This eventually meets the lower, well-worn track, which involves a bit of scrambling but is more exciting as it follows the rushing waters of the **Allt Coire Gabhail**. The upper and lower paths meet a few miles further up and here you cross the river by some stepping stones. Proceed up the steep scree slope till you reach the rim of the Lost Valley, where many of the MacDonalds fled on the night of the infamous massacre. Once in the valley there are great views of Bidean nam Bian, Gearr Aonach and Beinn Fhada and you can continue for a further 20-30 minutes to the head of the valley. From here it's possible to climb Bidean, but you'll need to be fit, experienced and well equipped.

Glen Coe also offers one of the world's classic ridge walks, the **Aonach Eagach**. It's not for the inexperienced or faint-hearted as there are some fairly exposed pinnacles. The ridge runs almost the entire length of the glen, starting at Am Bodach and ending at Sgor nam Fiannaidh. Don't make the mistake of descending from the last summit straight down to the Clachaig Inn. This is not the correct route.

Another difficult route is to the summit of **Buachaille Etive Mór**, one of the most photographed mountains in Scotland and one you'll probably recognize immediately the first time you see it from the A82 on the way to or from Glencoe. The mountain is best viewed from the *Kingshouse Hotel* and the route starts from Altnafeadh, a couple of miles west of the hotel. This is also the start or finish point for the fairly easy half-day walk over the **Devil's Staircase**, which is part of the **West Highland Way** (for a description of the route, see page 230).

Glen Etive runs southwest from the hotel. It's a very beautiful and little-visited place and great for wild camping. There's a postbus service once a day from Fort William.

Finally, there are some short, pleasant walks around **Glencoe Lochan**, an artificial loch created in the mid-19th century by Lord Strathcona for his homesick Canadian wife. Take the left turning off the minor road to the youth hostel just beyond the bridge over the river Coe. There's a choice of three walks of between 40 minutes and an hour, all detailed at the car park.

Mountain guides *Hadrian Mountaineering*, 19b Carnoch, T/F811472, www.glencoe-mountain-sport.co.uk *Glencoe Guides*, T811402. *Dave Hanna*, Ardarroch, Ballachulish, T811620.

Ardgour, Ardnamurchan and Morvern

*West of Fort William is one of the most remote parts of the Highland region, stretching south from **Loch Ailort** to the **Morvern Peninsula**, and west to the wild and beautiful **Ardnamurchan Peninsula**. This lonely, southwestern corner features a dramatic landscape of rugged mountains, desolate moorland and near-deserted glens, fringed by a coastline of sparkling white beaches and clear turquoise seas with wonderful views across to the isles of Mull and Skye. This is one of the least-populated areas in Britain, mainly due to the legacy of the*

Colour map 3, grid B4/5

Highland Clearances in the mid-19th century, when whole communities were evicted by landlords in favour of more profitable sheep.

With so few people around, this is an area noted for its wildlife, with a huge variety of birds and animals, such as deer, pine martens, wildcats and eagles. If you have both the time and the energy, it's worth exploring on foot. There's a series of footpaths throughout the area, particularly around Ardnamurchan.

Ins and outs

Getting there & getting around

30 walks in the area are listed in a local guide book available at tourist offices. You should also have OS Map numbers 40, 47 and 49, which cover the area

It's an area of few roads. Once you leave the A830 Fort William to Mallaig road, **buses** are few and far between, so it's not easy to get around quickly without your own transport. *Shiel Buses*, T01967-431272, run most of the bus services. There's a bus once a day on Tue, Thu and Sat from Fort William to Lochaline (2 hrs), via the **Corran Ferry**. There's a bus once a day (Mon-Sat) from Fort William to Acharacle (1 hr 30 mins, £4.25), via Lochailort. There's also a bus (Mon-Fri) to Acharacle from Mallaig (1 hr 30 mins). There's a bus once a day (Mon-Sat) from Fort William to Kilchoan (2 hrs 25 mins, £5), via Strontian (1 hr, £2.70), Salen and Glenborrodale.

For details of the **ferry** from Lochaline to Fishnish on Mull and from Kilchoan to Tobermory, see page 115. If you're travelling by **car**, access is via the A861, leaving the A830 before Glenfinnan or at Lochailort. You can also make the 5-min ferry crossing to Ardgour from the Corran Ferry, about 8 miles south of Fort William on the A82, see page 229.

Ardgour

The name Ardgour means 'height of the goats', and you can still see feral goats in this huge, sparsely populated wilderness bordered by Loch Shiel, Loch Eil, Loch Linnhe and Loch Sunart. Access is via the A861 south from Kinlocheil, or on the Corran Ferry to the tiny lochside villages of **Corran** and **Clovulin**. There's accommodation here at **D-E** *The Inn at Ardgour*, T01855-841225.

Strontian

Phone code: 01967
Colour map 3, grid B5

The attractive little village of Strontian on the shores of Loch Sunart gave its name to the element strontium, which was first discovered in the nearby lead mines in 1790. These now-abandoned mines also produced most of the lead shot used in the Napoleonic wars. Strontian is the largest settlement in these parts and has a couple of shops, a post office and a **Tourist Information Centre**; open April to October, Monday-Friday 0900-1700, Saturday 1000-1600 and Sunday 1000-1400. T402131.

About two miles north of the village is the **Ariundle Nature Reserve**, which offers a pleasant two-hour nature trail through the glen and a 40-minute forest walk.

Sleeping Strontian has a couple of good hotels. The luxurious **L-A** *Kilcamb Lodge Hotel*, T402257, F402041, open Mar-Nov, stands in its own grounds on the lochside and serves superb food. There are several B&Bs, including the very comfortable **E** *Kinloch House*, T402138, open Jan-Nov.

Morvern

Phone code: 01967

Just east of Strontian the A884 leads south through the bleak, desolate landscape of Morvern to the tiny remote community of **Lochaline** on the Sound of Mull, departure point for the *CalMac* ferry to **Fishnish**.

About three miles before Lochaline is the turning left for the track which leads down the side of Loch Aline to the 14th-century ruins of **Ardtornish Castle**. First you'll come to **Kinlochaline Castle** (keys available at the cottage) and **Ardtornish House**. This house stands on the site of the original house, which was visited on several occasions by Florence Nightingale, who was a family member of the original owners. The author John Buchan spent many summers here in the 1930s. There's a path which leads from the estate office and uphill across open moorland for an hour till it reaches **Loch Tearnait**. In the centre of the loch is a 1,500 year-old crannog, an artificial island built for defensive purposes. This walk is detailed in the tourist board's *Great Walks* leaflet, along with the Ariundle Nature Trail, available from local tourist offices. During the stalking season (1 July-20 October) check at the estate office before setting out.

If you want to stay in Lochaline, there are a couple of **B&Bs** and the **L** *Lochaline Hotel*, T421657, which serves decent bar meals. There's also a **scuba diving school** at the ferry pier, T421627.

Sleeping

Ardnamurchan Peninsula

The main places of interest in this area are to be found on the rugged Ardnamurchan peninsula, the end of which is the most westerly point on the British mainland.

The winding A861 runs west from Strontian along the north shore of Loch Sunart to **Salen**, where the single-track B8007 branches west and runs all the way out to the tip of the peninsula. The A861 meanwhile turns north to **Acharacle**. There's accommodation at Salen in the **E** *Salen Hotel*, T431661, salenhotel@aol.com, where you can also get food (cheap to mid-range) and information on local walks. A mile or so east of Salen, at **Resipole**, you can pitch a tent at the *Resipole Farm Caravan Park*, T431235. There's also a restaurant and bar on site.

The first settlement you reach heading west out to Ardnamurchan Point is Glenborrodale. Before you reach the tiny hamlet look out on the left for the castellated late-Victorian towers of Glenborrodale Castle, once the property of a certain Jesse Boot, who founded a chain of chemist shops which you may have heard of.

Just west of Glenborrodale is the excellent **Glenmore Natural History Centre**, local photographer Michael McGregor's interactive exhibition which features some of his most stunning photographs of local wildlife. The centre is designed to interact with the environment and there's live video action of the surrounding wildlife, including pine martens, birds and even fish in the nearby river. It's a great place for kids, and adults, too. There's also a café serving snacks and a bookshop. ■ *Apr-Oct 1030-1730 (1200-1730 on Sun). Adult £2.50, concession £2, children £1.50. T500254.*

A mile to the east is the **RSPB Reserve** where you can see golden eagles, otters and seals. You can take a two-hour wildlife trip to the **seal colonies** – or further afield to Tobermory on Mull or Staffa and the Treshnish Islands – with *Ardnamurchan Charters*, T500208 or T01967-431263.

A few miles west of the centre, the B8007 turns away from the coast. Here, you'll see the beautiful bay of **Camas nan Geall**. It's worth stopping at the car park to admire the fantastic views, or take the path down to the beach. A great place to stay in Glenborrodale is **C** *Feorag House*, T500248, F500285. Between Glenborrodale and Kilchoan, a road runs to the north coast of the peninsula and the beautiful beaches at **Fascadale**, **Kilmory** and **Ockle**.

Glenborrodale & Glenmore
Phone code: 01972
Colour map 3, grid B4

Kilchoan
Phone code: 01972
Colour map 3, grid B4

The straggling crofting village Kilchoan is the main settlement on Ardnamurchan. Shortly after passing the sign for the village, you can turn left to the scenic ruin of **Mingary Castle**, built around the 13th century. There's a **Tourist Information Centre** here which provides information on local scenic walks and will help with accommodation. It's open Easter-October Monday-Saturday 0900-1845, Sunday 1030-1715. T510222. A car and passenger **ferry** leaves Kilchoan for Tobermory on Mull. It sails mid-April to mid-October and the crossing takes 35 minutes (see page 115).

Sleeping There's a decent selection of accommodation. **B** *Far View Cottage*, T510357, www.ardnamurchan.com/farview Open Mar-Nov. Superior and friendly B&B with great views and excellent food (mid-range; also for non-residents but booking essential). **B** *Meall Mo Chridhe*, T/F510328. Open Apr-Oct. A beautiful 18th-century converted manse with great sea views and fine cooking. Full board also available (**A**). Dinner available for non-residents (expensive) but booking essential. A cheaper option is **E** *Doirlinn House*, T/F510209. A few miles beyond the village, on the road to Ardnamurchan Point, is **D** *Sonachan Hotel*, T/F510211, darie@sonachan.u-net.com You can get lunch (1200-1430; cheap) and dinner (1800-2000; mid-range) at the **C** *Kilchoan House Hotel*, T510200.

**Ardnamurchan Point &
Sanna Bay**
Phone code: 01972
*Colour map 3,
grid B3*

Beyond Kilchoan the road leads to the **lighthouse** at mainland Britain's most westerly point, with stunning views (on a clear day) across to the small isles of Rum, Eigg, Muck and Canna, with the Cuillins of Skye rising behind Rum. The former lighthouse was designed by Alan Stevenson, father of Robert Louis, and built in 1849. The buildings have been converted into the **Ardnamurchan Visitor Centre**, where you can learn about the history and workings of lighthouses. There's also self-catering accommodation, a café and gift shop. ■ *Daily 1 Apr- 31 Oct, from 1000-1800 (1700 in Oct). Adult £2.50, concession/children £1.50. T510210.*

A mile northwest of Kilchoan, a road branches to the right to the beautiful long, white beach at **Sanna Bay**. It's worth making the trip here just to walk on the beach, but this is also a good place to spot whales and dolphins. On the road to Sanna Bay is the tiny settlement of **Achnaha**, which is famed for its rare 'ring-dyke' system, a huge, natural rock formation which is the crater of an extinct volcano. You can stay in Achnaha, at **E-F** *Hillview*, T510322.

You'll need your own transport to reach Ardnamurchan Point and Sanna Bay as there are no buses beyond Kilchoan (see 'Getting around' above).

**Acharacle &
Castle Tioram**
Phone code: 01967
Colour map 3, grid B4

North of Salen on the A861 is the scattered crofting township of Acharacle, at the western end of Loch Shiel surrounded by rolling hills. A couple of miles to the west a road leads to beautiful **Kentra Bay**. Cross the wooden bridge, follow the footpath round the side of Kentra Bay and then follow the signs for Gortenfearn, where you'll find the famous '**singing sands**'. Not only is the beach music to the ears as you walk its length, but the view across to Skye and the small isles is a feast for the eyes.

Three miles north of Acharacle is **Loch Moidart**. Here, perched on a rocky promontory in the middle of the loch, is the 13th-century ruin of **Castle Tioram** (pronounced 'Cheerum'), one of Scotland's most romantic and atmospheric castles. This was the seat of the MacDonalds of Clanranald, until it was destroyed by their chief in 1715, to prevent it from falling into Hanoverian hands while he was away fighting for the Jacobites. There are plans to restore the castle, but you can visit it (free) via the sandy causeway that connects it to the mainland at low tide.

Sleeping The village has several shops, a post office, garage and plenty of places to stay. **C** *Loch Shiel House Hotel*, T431224, F431200. 10 rooms. Comfortable and decent bar meals (cheap lunch; mid-range to cheap dinner). Contact them for details of cruises on Loch Shiel. A couple of good B&Bs are **C** *Belmont House*, T431266, and **D-E** *Ardshealach House*, T431301; open Apr-Sep. Food is also available at the *Clanranald Hotel*, at Mingarry, T431202. About 5 miles east of the village, on a side road off the A861 north to Lochailort and Mallaig, is the very beautiful **D** *Dalilea House*, T431253; open Apr-Oct.

From Dalilea Pier you can cross to The *Achnanellan Centre*, T431265, an outdoor activi- **Sports** ties centre on the south shore of Loch Shiel, at the foot of **Beinn Resipol** (2,772 ft). They hire out mountain bikes, canoes, sail boats and camping equipment as well as providing cheap, basic bunkhouse accommodation (**F**). It was from Dalilea Pier that Bonnie Prince Charlie left to sail up Loch Shiel to raise his standard at Glenfinnan (see below).

The Road to the Isles

The 46-mile stretch of A830 from **Fort William** *to* **Mallaig** *is known as 'The Road to the Isles'. It's a very beautiful journey, particularly by train (see page 224), through a landscape that resonates with historical significance. This is Bonnie Prince Charlie country, where the ill-fated Jacobite Rising not only began, but also ended, with the Prince's flight to France.*

Glenfinnan

It all started on 19 August 1745, at Glenfinnan, 19 miles west of Fort William, *Phone code: 01397* at the head of Loch Shiel. Less than a month earlier, Prince Charles Edward *Colour map 3,* Stuart had landed on the Scottish mainland for the first time, on the shores of *grid B4* Loch nan Uamh, between Lochailort and Arisaig (see below). He had come to claim the British throne for his father, James, son of the exiled King James VII of Scotland and II of England.

The clan chiefs had expected French support, but when the Prince arrived with only a handful of men they were reluctant to join the cause. Unde-terred, the prince raised his standard and his faith was soon rewarded when he heard the sound of the pipes and Cameron of Lochiel, along with 800 men, came marching down the valley to join them. It must have been an incredible moment.

There's a powerful sense of history here. You don't have to be Scottish to feel a shiver run down the spine and a tear well in the eye as you gaze across stunning Loch Shiel stretching into the distance, veiled by steep mountains. You can almost hear the wail of the bagpipes in the distance. A commemora-tive **tower** stands proudly at the head of the loch, erected in 1815 by Alexander MacDonald of Glenaladale in memory of the clansmen who fought and died for the Prince. You can climb to the top of the tower (mind your head, though) for even better views down the loch. The Glenfinnan Games are held here in mid-August.

On the other side of the road is the National Trust for Scotland **visitor cen-tre**, which has displays and an audio programme of the Prince's campaign, from Glenfinnan to its grim conclusion at Culloden. There's also a café. ■ *Daily 1 Apr- 18 May and 1 Sep-31 Oct 1000-1700; 19 May to 31 Aug 0930-1800. Adult £1.50, concession £1. T722250.*

North & Northwest Highlands

A mile away, in Glenfinnan village, is the **Station Museum**, which is housed in the railway station, on the magnificent Fort-William to Mallaig railway line. It has displays of memorabilia from the line's 100-year history. ■ *T722295. Daily Apr-Oct 0930-1630. 50p.* You can also sleep and eat here (see below). The 1,000-ft span of the **Glenfinnan viaduct**, between the visitor centre and the village, is one of the most spectacular sections of the famous **West Highland Railway** (see page 224).

You can take a cruise down Loch Shiel, from Glenfinnan to Acharacle (see above) at its southern end. Contact *Loch Shiel Cruises* at the *Glenfinnan House Hotel* (see below). There are sailings most days from April to October.

Sleeping & eating On the main road, half a mile past the monument on the right, heading west, is **A** *The Prince's House*, T722246, F722307, princeshouse@ glenfinnan.co.uk 9 rooms, open Mar-Nov. Comfortable old coaching inn which offers good food (mid-range). Just off the main road is **B-C** *Glenfinnan House Hotel*, T/F722235. 17 rooms, open Apr-Oct. Wonderful historic house that oozes charm, dinner is served from 1930 (expensive to mid-range for 4 courses), you can also walk in the vast grounds or fish on the loch. A much cheaper option is the **F** *Glenfinnan Sleeping Car*, at the train station, T722400. Bunkhouse accommodation for 10 people, also mountain bike hire. You can eat here, too, in the *Glenfinnan Dining Car* (cheap 2-course lunch; mid-range 3-course dinner).

Lochailort
Phone code: 01687
Colour map 3, grid B5

About 10 miles west of Glenfinnan the road passes through the village of Lochailort, where the A861 branches south to the remote Ardnamurchan Peninsula (see above). There's accommodation and food here at the **D** *Lochailort Inn*, T470208, open March-October.

A couple of miles further on, is **Loch nan Uamh**, where Prince Charles first landed on the Scottish mainland and from where, a year later, he fled for France following the disastrous defeat at Culloden (see page 205). A path leads down from the car park to the **Prince's Cairn**, which marks the beginning and the end of the Jacobite cause.

Arisaig and Morar

Phone code: 01687
Colour map 3, grid A4

At the western end of the Morar Peninsula is the little village of Arisaig, scattered round a sandy bay. This was the birthplace of Long John Silver, who worked on the construction of the nearby lighthouse at Barrahead, which happened to be one of many such lighthouses designed by the father of Robert Louis Stevenson. Silver met Robert Louis on a few occasions, and so impressed the young writer that he immortalized him in his classic novel *Treasure Island*.

There are some nice beaches around and the road west from the village out to the **Rhue Peninsula** is great for seal spotting. You can also take a **cruise** from Arisaig to the islands of **Rùm, Eigg** and **Muck**. ■ *There are sailings daily Mon-Fri, and also Sat-Sun during the summer months. For details contact Murdo Grant, T450224. See also page 143.*

Between Arisaig and Morar is a string of glorious beaches of white sand backed by beautiful machair, washed by turquoise seas and enjoying magnificent views across to Rùm and the Cuillins of Skye. This is one of the most stunning stretches of coastline in Britain, despite the presence of too many ugly holiday bungalows and caravan sites. Eight miles north of Arisaig is **Morar**, where the famous beach scenes from the movie *Local Hero* were filmed – with not a caravan in sight.

This coastline gets very busy in summer, but like so much of the Highlands, it's easy to get away from it all. A single-track road leads up behind the village of Morar to dark, mysterious **Loch Morar**, the deepest inland loch in the country and home of Morag, Scotland's other, lesser-known monster. Two locals reported seeing her in August 1969 and a scientific investigation two years later uncovered a remarkable number of eye-witness accounts. You could always try to elicit further information from the locals over a wee dram in the bar of the *Morar Hotel*. The road runs along the north shore of the loch for three miles till it reaches the pretty little hamlets of **Bracora** and **Bracorina**. Here the road stops, but a footpath continues all the way to **Tarbet** on the shores of Loch Nevis, from where it's possible to catch a boat back to Mallaig (see below). It takes about three hours to walk to Tarbet (where there's now a bothy) and you'll need to get there by 1530 for the boat.

Arisaig has plenty of accommodation and a decent range of services. There are several hotels, including **B** *Arisaig Hotel*, T450210, arisaighotel@dial.pipex.com They serve moderately priced food 1200-1400 and 1800-2100. A good restaurant is *The Old Library Lodge*, T450651, open Apr-Oct, which also has rooms (**B**).

Sleeping & eating

Mallaig

The end of the road is Mallaig, a busy fishing port and main departure point for the ferry to Skye. It's not a particularly appealing place, but it's always busy with people waiting for the ferry to Skye or the train to Fort William.

*Phone code: 01687
Colour map 3, grid A4*

Mallaig is a small place, huddled round its harbour, and the train and bus stations and *CalMac* ferry office are all within a few yards of each other. Also close by are banks with ATMs and the post office. The **Tourist Information Centre** is also by the harbour. Open Monday-Saturday 0900-2000, Sunday 1000-1700. T462170.

If you have some time to kill you could visit **Mallaig Marine World**, an aquarium with indigenous marine creatures as well as displays on the history of the local fishing industry. ■ *T462292. Jun-Sep Mon-Sat 0900-2100, Sun 1000-1800; Oct-May Mon-Sat 0900-1700. Adult £2.75, children £1.35.* Beside the train station is the **Mallaig Heritage Centre**, with interesting descriptions of the local Clearances, the railway line and the fishing industry. ■ *May-Sep Mon-Sat 0930-1700, Sun 1300-1700. Adult £1.80, children £1.*

Sights

For something a bit more energetic, there are a couple of good walks around the village. An easy one which should take around 45 minutes goes to the little village of **Mallaig Bheag** (Mallaigviag), further east along the coast. Just before the car park at the eastern end of the harbour you'll see a sign, on the right as you head east, which points you towards the old road to Mallaig Bheag. Follow the path up behind the houses and continue into a small glen behind the hill that overlooks the port. The path then rises gradually till you're rewarded with great views Loch Nevis. It continues through Mallaig Bheag then joins up with the main road back to Mallaig. Follow this till the end of the row of houses on your right, turn right and then left and back down to Mallaig bay and the start of the walk.

C *Marine Hotel*, T462217, Marinehotel@btinternet Next to the train station and much nicer inside than it appears. Their restaurant also serves the best food in the town (mid-range). Follow the road round the harbour to East Bay, where you'll find the excellent value **E-F** *Western Isles Guesthouse*, T/F462320, open Jan-Nov, which serves dinner to guests. Nearby is **E** *Glencairn*, T462412; open Apr-Sep. There are lots of other **B&Bs** to choose from. The cheapest place to stay is **F** *Sheena's Backapackers Lodge*,

Sleeping & eating

North & Northwest Highlands

T462764, a friendly, easy-going independent hostel, with dorm beds, double rooms and kitchen facilities.

The *Cabin Seafood Restaurant* serves cheap to mid-range main courses and a great value 'teatime special'. The *Cornerstone Café* also does cheap meals and snacks, but cheapest of the lot is the cafetería in the *Fisherman's Mission* at the pier.

Transport **Bus** *Shiel Buses*, T01967-431272 run 2 buses daily Mon-Sat from Mallaig to **Fort William** (1 hr 30 mins, £4.50) from Jul-Sep, and on Mon, Thu-Fri the rest of the year.

Ferry *CalMac*, T462403, ferries run throughout the year to **Armadale** on Skye (see page 292), to **Lochboisdale** and **Castlebay** (see page 318) and to the *Small Isles* (see page 242). *Bruce Watt Sea Cruises* , T462320, have trips to the remote village of **Inverie**, on the Knoydart Peninsula (see below), and **Tarbet** on Loch Nevis (see above). They sail on Mon, Wed and Fri throughout the year, departing at 1015 (to Inverie only) and 1415, and returning at 1155 and 1745. They also sail on Sat during Jun-Aug to Inverie, departing at 1030 and returning at 1215.

Train The best way to arrive in Mallaig is by train. There are several services daily (1 on Sun) to and from **Fort William**, with connections to **Glasgow** (see page 226). There's also a steam train which runs in the summer months (see page 224).

Knoydart Peninsula

Colour map 3,
grid A5

Knoydart Peninsula, the most remote and unspoilt region in Britain and one of Europe's last great wildernesses, literally lies between Heaven and Hell, for it is bordered to the north by **Loch Hourn** ('Loch of Hell') and to the south by **Loch Nevis** ('Loch of Heaven'). It can only be reached on foot or by boat and consequently attracts walkers, who can wander for days around a network of trails without seeing another soul.

Ins & outs
As mentioned above,
the only way in is by
boat or on foot

A 2-day **hiking** route starts from Kinloch Hourn, reached by bus from Invergarry (see page 216). The trail winds its way around the coast to Barrisdale and on to Inverie. Another route into Knoydart starts from the west end of Loch Arkaig (see page 219) and runs through Glen Dessarry. Both are tough hikes and only for fit, experienced and well-equipped hill walkers.

An easier way in is by **boat**. *Bruce Watt Sea Cruises* sail from Mallaig to Inverie (see above). There's also a ferry service from **Arnisdale** on the north shore of Loch Hourn, to Barrisdale. To arrange a crossing, contact Len Morrison, Croftfoot, Arnisdale, T01599-522352. It's a small open boat which takes 5 passengers and all sailings are subject to weather.

Inverie
Phone code: 01867

The peninsula's only settlement of any size is tiny Inverie, with just 60 inhabitants. It's the only village in Scotland which can't be reached by road, but still has a post office, a shop, a few places to stay and Britain's most remote pub.

The only **guesthouse** is **C** *Pier House*, T462347, which offers good, old-fashioned hospitality and wonderful local seafood (mid-range prices). A cheaper option is **F** *Torrie Shieling*, T462669. It's a bit more expensive than most other hostels, but is very comfortable and popular with hikers. They also have their own transport for trips around the peninsula and will collect guests from Mallaig by arrangement. The only alternative is the much cheaper, but less appealing **F** *Knoydart Hostel*, T462242, near Inverie House.

Another place to eat is *The Old Forge*, T462267, the most remote pub on mainland Britain. You can enjoy some tasty local seafood and a pint of real ale in front of an open fire. There's even the occasional impromptu ceilidh.

Three or four miles up the peninsula's only road is the highly recommended **B** *Doune Stone Lodge*, T462667, standing in splendid isolation. The minimum is 3 nights as guests are picked up from Mallaig by boat.

The Great Glen to Kyle of Lochalsh

The A87 is one of the main Highland tourist routes, connecting the Great Glen with the west coast and the Isle of Skye. It runs west from Invergarry, between Fort Augustus and Fort William, through Glen Moriston and Glen Shiel to Shiel Bridge, at the head of Loch Duich, and on to Kyle. At Shiel Bridge, a road branches off to Glenelg, from where you can sail across to Skye. It's a beautiful journey and by far the best way to reach the island.

Glen Shiel

The journey from Invergarry to **Shiel Bridge** is worth it for the views alone. Glen Shiel is a spectacular sight, with 3,000 ft-high peaks soaring up on either side. This is one of the most popular hiking areas in Scotland, with the magnificent and much-photographed **Five Sisters of Kintail** on the north side of the glen, and the equally beautiful **South Glen Shiel Ridge** on the other. There's a **Tourist Information Centre** in Shiel Bridge; open from April-October.

Colour map 3, grid A5

There are several excellent hiking routes in Glen Shiel but these mountains are to be treated with great respect. They require fitness, experience and proper equipment and planning. None of the routes should be attempted without a map, compass and detailed route instructions. You should be aware of the notoriously unpredictable weather conditions and also check locally about deer stalking. The season runs from August to October, but for more details contact the local stalkers (T01599-511282 or 01320-340262). A good trekking guide is the SMC's *Hill Walks in Northwest Scotland*.

OS Landranger No 33

The **Five Sisters Traverse** is a classic ridge route. It starts at the first fire break on the left as you head southeast down the glen from Shiel Bridge and finishes at Morvich, on the other side of the ridge. Allow a full day (eight to 10 hours). You can also hike from Morvich to *Glen Affric Youth Hostel* at Cannich. It's a strenuous 20-mile walk, but you can stop off midway at the remote *Allt Beithe Youth Hostel* (see page 210).

The magnificent **South Glen Shiel Ridge** is one of the world's great hikes. It starts from above the *Cluanie Inn* (see below). From here, follow the old public road to Tomdoun which meets up with a good stalking path which climbs to the summit of the first Munro, **Creag a' Mhaim** (3,108 ft). The ridge then runs west for almost nine miles and gives you the chance to pick off no fewer than seven Munros. Allow a full day for the walk (nine to 10 hours), and you'll need to set off early.

About 9 miles east of Shiel Bridge is one of the Highlands' classic hotels, the **C** *Cluanie Inn*, T0320-340238. It's a firm favourite with hikers and climbers and it's easy to see

Sleeping

why. After a hard day's ridge walking, what could be better than jumping into the jacuzzi, then having a hot dinner and a good pint beside a log fire. You can also camp nearby, but why deny yourself the pleasure if you can afford it?

A less salubrious option is the **F** *Ratagan Youth Hostel*, T01599-511243, just outside Shiel Bridge. It's also popular with hikers and is open all year, except Jan. You can **camp** at *Morvich Caravan Club Site*, T01599-511354, open late Mar to late Oct, or at Shiel Bridge, T01599-511211.

Transport   *Citylink* buses between Fort William, Inverness and Skye pass through Glen Shiel several times daily in each direction. There's a *Postbus* service between Kyle and Glenelg (see below) and *Highland Country Buses* run from *Ratagan Youth Hostel* to Kyle (30 mins) and on to Plockton (50 mins), on schooldays only, departing at 0755 and returning at 1640.

Glenelg

Phone code: 01599
Colour map 3,
grid A5

One of the most beautiful journeys in Scotland is the road from Shiel Bridge to the picturesque little village of Glenelg on the Sound of Sleat, only a short distance opposite Kylerhea on Skye.

The unclassified single-track road turns off the A87 and climbs steeply and dramatically through a series of sharp switchbacks to the top of the **Mam Ratagan Pass** (1,115 ft). From here the view back across Loch Duich to the Five Sisters of Kintail is simply amazing and the all-time classic calendar shot.

The road then drops down through Glen More to Glenelg, the main settlement on the peninsula, which lies on the old drover's route which ran from Skye to the cattle markets in the south. This little-known corner of the Western Highlands is Gavin Maxwell country and was featured in *Ring of Bright Water*, his novel about otters. He disguised the identity of this beautiful, unspoiled stretch of coastline, calling it Camusfearna, and today it remains a quiet backwater.

You can see the famous otters at **Sandaig**, on the road running from Glenelg, where Gavin Maxwell lived. The site of his cottage is now marked with a cairn. As well as otters, you can see numerous seabirds, seals and porpoises in the Sound of Sleat, and around the peninsula you may be lucky enough to catch a glimpse of wildcats, pine martens, golden eagles and the recently reintroduced sea eagles.

The village itself consists of a row of whitewashed cottages surrounded by trees and overlooked by the ruins of the 18th-century Bernera Barracks. It's worth stopping in Glenelg, if you've got the time, to experience a night in the wonderfully cosy **E** *Glenelg Inn*, T522273. Even if you can't spend the night, at least spend an hour or two enjoying the atmosphere, good ale and fine seafood. It's one of those places that almost makes you glad it's raining.

Just before the village the road forks. The right turning leads to the **Glenelg-Kylerhea ferry**, which makes the five-minute crossing to Skye. The tiny six-car ferry runs from April to October and is the most scenic and romantic route to the misty isle. For more details, see the Skye chapter (page 292).

A road runs south from Glenelg to Arnisdale. About a mile and a half along this road, a branch left leads to the **Glenelg Brochs** – Dun Telve and Dun Dun Troddan – two of the best-preserved Iron Age buildings in the country. Dun Telve stands to a height of over 30 ft and the internal passages are almost intact.

The road south from Glenelg continues past Sandaig Bay and runs along the north shore of unearthly Loch Hourn with great views across the mountains of Knoydart. The road ends at the impossibly cute little fishing hamlet of **Arnsidale**, from where you can take a boat across the loch to Barrisdale on the Knoydart peninsula. For details, see page 242. A bit further along the coast, the road ends at the even tinier hamlet of **Corran**, where there's B&B accommodation at **E-F** *Mrs Nash*.

There's a *Postbus* service from **Kyle of Lochalsh** to **Arnisdale** and **Corran** via Glenelg at **Transport**
0945 Mon-Sat. It takes 3 ¾ hrs. The return bus from Corran departs at 0725.

Eilean Donan Castle

One of Scotland's most photographed sights is the stunningly located Eilean   *Phone code: 01599*
Donan, 10 miles west of Shiel Bridge on the A87. It stands on a tiny islet at the   *Colour map 3, grid A5*
confluence of Loch Duich and Loch Alsh, joined to the shore by a narrow stone bridge and backed by high mountains. This great calendar favourite has also featured in several movies, including *Highlander*, which starred Sean Connery.

The original castle dates from 1230 when Alexander III had it built to protect the area from marauding Vikings. It was destroyed by King George in 1719 during its occupation by Spanish Jacobite forces sent to help the 'Old Pretender', James Stuart. It then lay in ruins, until one of the Macraes had it rebuilt between 1912 and 1932. Inside, the Banqueting Hall with its Pipers' Gallery is most impressive and there's an exhibition of military regalia and interesting displays of the castle's history. The views from the battlements are also worthwhile. ■ *Daily Apr-Oct 0900-1700. Adult £3.95, concession £3.20, group rates £2.95. T555202.*

There are several places to stay in the nearby village of **Dornie**. **D** *Dornie Hotel*,   **Sleeping**
T555205, is a good option and serves very good food (mid-range). Just across the   **& eating**
bridge is **D** *Loch Duich Hotel*, T555213. It offers comfortable accommodation, meals and live music in the bar on a Sun evening. There are several good **B&Bs**, including **E** *Tigh Tasgaidh*, T555242, and **F** *Fasgadale*, T588238. A cheaper place to stay is the 6-bed **F** *Silver Fir Bunkhouse*, Carndubh, T555264.

Aside from the hotels listed above, there are a couple of places in Dornie serving decent food. Across the bridge is *Jenny Js*, T555362, which is moderately priced but can be variable. There's also the *Clachan Pub* where you can enjoy a good value 3-course evening meal.

Across the bridge is the turning right for Killilan, a tiny hamlet at the head of Loch Long. About ¾ of a mile up this road is the **B** *Conchra House Hotel*, T555233, conchra@aol.com 6 rooms, this historic 18th-century hunting lodge is peaceful, has lovely views and boasts a reputation for good food. At the end of this road, at Camas-luinie, is **F** *Tigh Iseabeal*, T588205, a 10-bed independent hostel.

Citylink buses between **Fort William** and **Inverness** and **Skye** stop by the castle.   **Transport**

Kyle of Lochalsh

Before the coming of the controversial Skye Bridge a mile to the north (see   *Phone code: 01599*
page 292), the little town of Kyle, as it is known, was the main ferry crossing to   *Colour map 3, grid A5*
Skye and consequently a place which attracted a busy tourist trade. Now, though, the tourist traffic bypasses Kyle, which is probably the most sensible thing to do as it's not the most attractive of places.

There are a couple of interesting boat trips which you can take from Kyle. One is on board the *Seaprobe Atlantis*, which is fitted with underwater windows allowing you to watch 'the world beneath the waves'. Check sailing times at the pier, or at the **Tourist Information Centre**, which is at the main seafront car park, T534276. It's open April, May and mid-September-late October Monday-Saturday 0930-1730; June-mid-July and late August-mid-September Monday-Saturday 0930-1900; mid-July-late August Monday-Saturday 0930-2100, Sunday 1230-1630. If you prefer, you could take a **seafood cruise** – a 2½-hour wildlife-spotting and seafood-eating boat trip. Contact Neil MacRae, T577230.

Sleeping It's a good idea to get the tourist office to book a room for you, as there's not a lot to choose from. There are a couple of hotels, most luxurious of which is the **B** *Lochalsh Hotel*, T534202, with great views across to Skye and good food. Three miles north, at Erbusaig, is the very comfortable **D** *Old Schoolhouse*, T534369, a B&B with a highly rated restaurant. A mile and a half north of Kyle is **E** *Crowlin View*, T534286. There's also cheap hostel accommodation at **F** *Cuchulainn's*, T534492, on Station Rd. 4 miles east of Kyle, at **Balmacara**, you can camp at *Reraig Caravan Site*, T566215.

Eating Just outside the village, on the road to Plockton, is the *Seagreen Restaurant & Bookshop*, T534388, a bistro-cum-bookshop and gallery serving wholefood and local seafood throughout the day (mid-range to expensive). At the railway station is *The Seafood Restaurant*, T534813, which has a good reputation for seafood (mid-range to expensive), it's open Easter-Oct 1000-1500 and 1830-2100. Another option is the *Lochalsh Hotel*, which does very good bar lunches.

Transport **Bus** *Scottish Citylink* buses, T0990-505050, run to Kyle from **Inverness** (3 daily, 2 hrs); **Glasgow** via **Fort William** (4 daily, 5 hrs); and **Edinburgh** via **Fort William** (1 daily, 6 ½ hrs). These buses continue to **Portree** (a further hour) and **Uig** (1½ hrs), for ferries to Tarbert on Harris and Lochmaddy on North Uist. There's also a regular shuttle service across the bridge to **Kyleakin** (every 30 mins).

Train The train journey from Inverness to Kyle, though not as spectacular as the West Highland line, is very scenic. It runs 3-4 times Mon-Sat (2 ½ hrs) and once or twice on Sun from May to Sep. There's also an observation car and dining car in the summer.

Directory There are a couple of banks with ATMs, 2 small supermarkets and a post office in the village.

Plockton

Phone code: 01599
Colour map 3, grid A4

If there were a poll taken of visitors' favourite Highland villages then you can bet your bottom dollar that Plockton would come top with most folk. If you look for a definition of picturesque in your dictionary, it'll say "see Plockton". Well, maybe not – but it should.

Plockton's neat little painted cottages are ranged around the curve of a wooded bay, with flowering gardens and palm trees. Yachts bob up and down in the harbour and there are views across the island-studded waters of Loch Carron to the hills beyond. Even on the telly Plockton's charms proved irresistible and millions of viewers tuned in each week to watch the TV series *Hamish Macbeth*, which featured Robert Carlyle as the local bobby.

There are lots of good walks around the village. One of the best ways to appreciate it is to head up to Frithard Hill, from where there are great views of the bay. Another good walk is along the beach, starting from the High School playing fields at the top of the village.

Plockton's a popular place with artists who are drawn by the village's setting and the wonderful light. A good place to find some of their work, as well as other souvenirs, is *The Studio Craft Shop*, on the corner of the seafront and the road leading out of town.

The best place to stay, and eat, is **C** *The Haven Hotel*, T544223, on Innes St. 15 rooms, open Feb-Dec. Good value and the food in the restaurant is quite superb (5-course dinner; expensive). Nearby is the cosy and comfortable **D** *Plockton Inn*, T544222. There are quite a few places on Harbour St along the waterfront, including the **D** *Plockton Hotel*, T544274. It also serves decent (and cheap) pub food and has a great little beer garden at the front where you can sit and enjoy a drink on a balmy summer evening.

    There are lots of **B&Bs** to choose from and one of the nicest is the **E** *Shieling*, T544282, at the far end of the harbour. Also on the seafront is **E** *An Caladh*, T544356. There's cheaper accommodation at the **F** *Plockton Station Bunkhouse*, Nessun Dorma, Burnside, T544235.

    A few miles out of Plockton, on the road to Achmore, is the **E** *Craig Highland Farm*, T544205, which offers B&B accommodation and self-catering cottages from £235 per week. The farm is also a conservation centre, where you can see, and feed, rare and ancient breeds of domestic animals.

    Apart from the hotels listed above, a good place to eat in Plockton is *Off the Rails*, T544423, at the railway station. It's open from 0830 for breakfast, snacks, lunch and evening meals (cheap to mid-range).

Sleeping & eating

A good way to see the local wildlife is to take a boat trip. *Leisure Marine*, T544306, runs one-hour seal and otter-watching cruises in the summer for £3.50 per person. They also hire out boats. Similar trips are run by *Sea Trek Marine*, T544346.

Tours

Wester Ross

From Loch Carron north to Ullapool, is the region of Wester Ross, an area of dramatic mountain massifs, fjord-like sea lochs and remote coastal villages. Here lies some of Europe's most spectacular scenery, from the isolated peninsular of **Applecross** *to the mighty peaks of* **Torridon**, *which offer some of Scotland's best climbing and hillwalking. There are also gentler attractions such as the magnificent gardens at* **Inverewe** *and the beautiful pink sands of* **Gruinard Bay**.

East of Plockton, just before the road meets the A890, at **Achmore** , is the **West Highland Dairy**, where you can pick up some good local cheese for a picnic (if the weather's fine). The road passes the turn-off for **Stromeferry**continues along the east shore of Loch Carron to **Strathcarron**, at its northeastern end, on the Inverness to Kyle of Lochalsh rail line.

East from Plockton

Sleeping There's **B&B** accommodation at **E** *The Shieling*, T01520-722364, open April-October, by the rail station, and at **F** *Achnashellach Hostel*, T01520-766232.

Transport There's a **postbus** service from Strathcarron to **Shieldaig** and **Torridon** twice a day Mon-Sat.

About a mile further on you come to a road junction. The A890 heads right (east) through Glen Carron to **Achnasheen**, where it meets the A832, nine miles east of **Kinlochewe**. The A832 then continues east till it meets the main A835 which connects **Ullapool** with the A9 north of **Inverness**. The A896 meanwhile heads left (west) to Lochcarron.

Lochcarron

Lochcarron village consists of little more than a main street along the shore of the loch, but it has more facilities and services than most other places in these parts. Here you should take the opportunity to withdraw cash at the *Bank of Scotland* ATM, fill up with petrol and buy some supplies at the small self-service store. There's also a **Tourist Information Centre**, T722357, which will provide details of the many excellent walks in the surrounding hills; it's open April-October. For guided walks around Lochcarron, contact *Island Horizons*, Kirkton Road, T722238.

Two miles south of the village, on the road to the 15th-century ruins of **Strome Castle** is *Lochcarron Weavers*, where you can see tartan being made and also buy from a vast range of woven goods.

There's a wide range of accommodation and several places to eat. Best of the bunch is the **D** *Rockvilla Hotel & Restaurant*, T722379, rockvilla@btinternet.com This small, family-run hotel offers very good food at cheap-mid-range prices. There are lots of B&Bs including **E** *Bank House*, T722332, in the same building as the Bank of Scotland.

About 5 mins drive from the village, across the loch on the A890, is the excellent *Carron Restaurant*, T722488, mid-range prices.

Applecross

West of Lochcarron, at Loch Kishorn, a side road leaves the A896 and heads to Applecross. There are many scenic routes in the Highlands but this one beats them all. The **Bealach na Ba** ('Pass of the Cattle') is the highest road in Scotland and is often closed during the winter snows. It climbs relentlessly and dramatically through a series of tortuous switchbacks – both spectacular and terrifying in equal measure. The high plateau, at 2,053 ft, is cold and desolate but from here you have the most stunning views; from Ardnamurchan Peninsula to Loch Torridon and taking in Eigg, Rum, the Cuillins of Skye, the Old Man of Storr and the Quirang.

The narrow, single-track road then begins its gradual descent to the isolated little village of Applecross, site of one Scotland's first Christian monasteries, in 673 AD. The village consists of a row of whitewashed fishermen's cottages looking across to the island of Raasay and backed by wooded slopes. It's a beautifully tranquil place where you can explore beaches and rock pools or enjoy a stroll along sylvan lanes.

The reason many people make the long detour is to savour the delights of the venerable **E** *Applecross Inn*, T744262. There are, sadly, too few authentic Highland hostelries where you could quite happily while away a few hours, or even an entire afternoon, but if you have to be holed up somewhere to escape the rotten weather, then this place is as good as any and better than most. The welcome is warm, the crack is good and the seafood is so fresh you can almost see it swimming past as you order (try a half pint of prawns for a fiver or scallops for £7.50). The rooms upstairs are nothing fancy but comfortable, with sea views. If there's no room at he *Inn* there are a few B&Bs a mile to the south in the village of **Camusteel**: **E** *Mrs Cross*, 'Seawinds', T744373; **F** *Mrs Thompson*, 'Raon-Mor', T744260, open Apr-Oct. Just before Applecross is a bakery with a poly-tunnel sheltered restaurant which serves good cheap light meals.

It's possible to reach Applecross by public transport, but only just. A *Postbus* service leaves Strathcarron train station daily (except Sun) at 0955, arriving in **Shieldaig** at

1040. Another *Postbus* then leaves Shieldaig at 1130 and arrives in Applecross at 1300, via the beautiful and winding coast road. No buses run over the Bealach na Ba. A *Postbus* leaves Applecross at 0915 and arrives in Shieldaig at 1010. It continues to **Torridon** (see below) and arrives at 1030. Another *Postbus* leaves Shieldaig at 1045 and arrives at Strathcarron train station at 1130. There are train connections from Strathcarron to Inverness and Kyle (for times T0345-484950).

Torridon

Torridon is perhaps the most striking skyline in the Scottish Highlands. The multi-peaked mountains of **Beinn Alligin**, **Liathach** (pronounced '*Lee*-ahakh') and **Beinn Eighe** ('Ben-*eay*') form a massive fortress of turrets, spires and pinnacles that provides an awesome backdrop to Loch Torridon as well as the most exhilarating walking and climbing on the Scottish mainland (see below).

Phone code: 01445
Colour map 1,
grid C4/5

The coast road from Applecross meets the A896 from Lochcarron at the lovely little village of **Shieldaig**, on the southern shore of **Loch Torridon**. There's a shop, a post office, a campsite, a couple of B&Bs and the **B** *Tigh-an-Eilean Hotel*, T01520-755251, where you can get reasonable meals.

Several miles east, a side road turns off the A896 by **Torridon** village and winds its way along the northern shore of the loch, then climbs through dramatic scenery before dropping to the beautiful little village of **Diabaig** (pronounced 'Jee-a-beg'), 10 miles from Torridon village. It's a worthwhile side trip, as the views across to the Applecross peninsula and Raasay are fantastic. There's also a great seven-mile coastal walk from Diabaig to Redpoint (see 'Walks around Torridon' below).

Much of the Torridon massif is in the care of the National Trust for Scotland and just before Torridon village is the **NTS countryside centre**, T791221, where you can get information and advice on walks in the area, as well as books and maps. About 400 yards past the centre is the **Deer Museum**, which has a small display describing the management of red deer in the Highlands and some live specimens outside.

About a mile south of the turn-off to Torridon village is the magnificent **L** *Loch Torridon Hotel*, T791242, F791296, www.lochtorridonhotel.com 22 rooms. This elegant former hunting lodge sits on the lochside surrounded by majestic mountains and offers the ultimate in style and comfort, it also boasts one of the finest restaurants in the area (expensive). There are several B&Bs, including the excellent **E** *Upper Diabaig Farm*, T790227, open Apr-Sep, in Upper Diabaig. There are also a couple of **F** *SYHA hostels*. One is in Torridon village, T791284, open 29 Jan-31 Oct, with an adjacent campsite. The other is much smaller and more basic, 4 miles north of Diabaig, on the trail to Redpoint, at the disused crofting township of Craig (no phone; open 14 May-3 Oct).

Sleeping

The *Postbus* from Applecross to Shieldaig continues to Torridon village (see above). There's a postbus from Strathcarron station at 0955 which arrives in Shieldaig at 1040. *Duncan Maclennan* buses (T01520-755239) have a service which leaves Strathcarron at 1230 and arrives in Torridon at 1330 (daily except Sun). There's also a daily (Mon-Sat) *Postbus* service from Diabaig to Kinlochewe and Achnasheen, via Torridon, at 0955. There are also *Duncan Maclennan* buses between Torridon and Shieldaig and Strathcarron.

Transport

North & Northwest Highlands

Walking around Torridon

OS Outdoor Leisure
series No 8 Torridon offers some of the most spectacular walking on the Scottish mainland but also presents some of the most serious challenges. You need to be fit, experienced and well prepared and also be aware of the notoriously unpredictable weather (see page 53). You should have a compass and the relevant map. **Beinn Eighe** (3,309 ft) has nine peaks and is the largest of the Torridon mountains. To traverse its ridge is a mighty undertaking and can take two days. A much shorter and easier walk around the base of the mountain is described below, under **Beinn Eighe National Nature Reserve**.

For those who are not experienced hill walkers, there's a Ranger Service for visitors. During July and August the ranger, Seamus McNally, takes guided walks up into the mountains three times a week. For more details call T791221. A recommended local mountain guide is Steve Chadwick, T712455.

Beinn Alligin Beinn Alligin (3,232 ft) is the most westerly of the Torridon peaks and probably the least demanding. The **Allt a'Bhealaich Walk** is a steep but short walk of about two hours. It starts from the car park just beyond the stone bridge that crosses the Abhainn Coire Mhic Nobuil. Follow the path that runs beside the river gorge until you reach the first bridge, cross it and follow the east bank of the Allt a' Bhealaich burn. Higher up, cross the second bridge and continue to follow the track up to the 380-m contour line, then turn back retracing your steps. This walk doesn't include the ascent of peak but the views are magnificent.

Those who wish to climb the three Horns of Beinn Alligin can continue from the 380-m contour line above the second bridge. The track that follows their ridge is exposed and requires rock scrambling experience.

Liathach Seven-peaked Liathach (3,460 ft) stretches over five miles and the magnificent **ridge walk** is considered by many to be the most impressive in Britain. This walk requires a high level of stamina and will take at least seven to eight hours. It also helps of you have a car waiting at the end.

A good place to start this long and strenuous challenge is about half a mile or so east of Glen Cottage, which is just over two miles east of the Countryside Centre. A steep climb takes you to a point just west of Stuc a'Choire Dhuibh Bhig (3,000 ft). Then retrace your route to climb the twin tops of Bidein Toll a'Mhuic (3,200 ft), linked by a narrow ridge. The path from here descends to the head of a deep ravine and keeps to the crest of the ridge around the rim of Coireag Dubh Beag which plunges steeply to the north. The ridge then rises across a field of huge and unstable boulders to the highest peak – Spidean a'Choire Leith. The view from this point is stunning, with Coire na Caime before you, surrounded by 2,000 ft sheer cliffs. From here, the path follows a narrow exposed ridge for over a mile towards Mullach an Rathain (3,358 ft). Unless you are an experienced scrambler with a good head for heights, the best way from here is to take the path to the south, below the sharp pinnacles. Beyond the pinnacles the climb to Mullach an Rathain is straightforward. The track from here to Sgorr a'Chadail is a long but fairly easy walk and ends on the path in Coire Mhic Nobuil (see Beinn Alligin above).

Coire Walk A less difficult walk, but still requiring a fair degree of fitness and taking most of the day, is the Coire Walk. It follows the river Coire Mhic Nobuil to its watershed and down again by the Allt a'Choire Dhuibh Mhoir to the main road in Glen Torridon. Again, two cars will shorten the distance considerably.

The walk starts at the same point as the Beinn Alligin walk above. It follows the path up to the first bridge then branches east and continues on the path that runs north of the river, all the way to its source in the pass between Liathach and Beinn Dearg. Here the ground is boggy between the string of pools and lochans and the path is less distinct, but it becomes clear again in the upper reaches of the Coire Dubh Mor, a huge gully that separates Liathach from Beinn Eighe. A little further on, the track joins a stalker's path which curves round Sail Mhor to the famous Coire Mhic Fhearchair, considered to be the most spectacular corrie in Scotland (see Beinn Eighe below). The Coire path leads to a ford, which is crossed by stepping stones, then descends following the west side of the burn down to the car park on the Torridon road, from where it's about 4½ miles to Torridon village.

An excellent low-level coastal walk is from Diabaig to Redpoint. It is far less strenuous or daunting than the others described above and there is a clear path. It starts at the wooden gate to the right of the post office in Diabaig and ends at Red Point Farm, seven miles away.

Diabaig to Red Point Walk
OS Landranger No 19

After four miles, the coastal path reaches the derelict croft houses in the Craig valley. One of these has been converted into a *SYHA* Hostel (see 'Sleeping' above). There are two possible routes from here. You can follow the footpath above the coastline, or leave the footpath after crossing the wooden bridge over the Craig River and climb through an area of woodland. Take a reference from your OS map and you'll reach the highest point, Meall na h-Uamha, from where there are superb views. You can then descend to rejoin the coastal path and continue till you reach the glorious golden sands of Red Point, with wonderful views across to Skye and Raasay. Keep to the path through the farm till you reach the car park. Unless you've arranged your own transport here, you'll have to walk back the way you came, or catch the schoolbus to Gairloch (see page 254).

Loch Maree

On the north side of the Torridon mountains is beautiful Loch Maree, dotted with islands and bordered by the mass of **Slioch** (3,215 ft) to the north and ancient Caledonian pine forest to the south. Running along its northern shore, from Slioch almost as far as Poolewe, is the remote Letterewe Estate, one of Scotland's great deer forests. The A832 skirts the south shore of the loch, running northwest from **Kinlochewe**, and passes the **Victoria Falls**, a mile or so beyond **Talladale**. The falls commemorate Queen Victoria's visit in 1877. To find them, look for the 'Hydro Power' signs.

Phone code: 01445
Colour map 1, grid C5

The village of **Kinlochewe** is a good base for walking in this area. It has a post office, shop, garage and accommodation. The **E** *Kinlochewe Hotel*, T760253, offers B&B as well as cheaper bunkhouse beds and cheap bar meals. There's also **B&B** at **D** *Cromasaig*, on the Torridon road, T760234, cromasaig@msn.com, and a basic campsite a few miles northwest, at *Taangan Farm*, at the head of Loch Maree.

Sleeping

The best accommodation, though, is at **Talladale**, halfway between Kinlochewe and Gairloch. **B** *The Old Mill Highland Lodge*, T760271, open mid-Dec to mid-Oct, is a converted mill set in its own gardens. It's friendly and comfortable, offers great food (price includes dinner), seclusion and great views. **B-C** *Loch Maree Hotel*, T760288, lochmaree@easynet.co.uk This beautifully located hotel is being returned to its former glory. Queen Victoria was here! It also offers superb cuisine (**A** including dinner).

North & Northwest Highlands

Transport   Kinlochewe is 9 miles west of **Achnasheen** rail station which is on the Inverness-Kyle line. There's a daily (except Sun) *Postbus* service. There's also a *Postbus* (Mon-Sat) from Kinlochewe to **Torridon** and **Diabaig** and a bus to Torridon and **Shieldaig**, T01520-755239. Buses between Gairloch and Inverness (see below) stop in Kinlochewe.

Beinn Eighe National Nature Reserve

While most of the Torridon massif is managed by the NTS, Beinn Eighe (which means 'File Peak' in Gaelic) is under the control of Scottish Natural Heritage. It is Britain's oldest National Nature Reserve, set up in 1951 to protect the ancient Caledonain pine forest west of Kinlochewe. It has since been designated an International Biosphere Reserve and extended to cover 30 square miles. The reserve is the home of a great variety of rare Highland wildlife, including pine martens, wildcats, buzzards, Scottish crossbills and golden eagles. There's also a wide range of flora which can best be appreciated on the excellent mountain trail described below. The trail climbs from the ancient pine woods through alpine vegetation to the tundra-like upper slopes.

About half a mile northwest of Kinlochewe on the A832, is the **Beinn Eighe Visitor Centre**, which has information on the flora and fauna in the reserve and sells pamphlets on the trails described below. Note that camping is restricted to the official campsite at Taangan Farm (see 'Sleeping' above).

The mountain & woodland trails   Both trails start and end in the car park at the side of Loch Maree, about two miles beyond the visitor centre. The **woodland trail** heads west along the lochside then crosses the road and climbs for about a mile up to the Conservation cabin before descending back to the starting point. It should take about an hour and is easy to follow, though quite steep in parts, and you'll need a good pair of walking boots.

The **mountain trail** is four miles long and rough and steep in parts. You should be well equipped with good walking boots, waterproofs, food and warm clothing. It should take around three to four hours. The route is well marked with cairns and you should not stray from the path.

The trail heads south from the car park and begins a gentle ascent through woodland to a boggy area and then begins to zigzag up a very steep and rugged section, climbing to over 1,000 ft in less than half a mile. This is the steepest section of the trail but the views back across Loch Maree to Slioch are fabulous. The summit of the mountain trail is **Conservation cairn** (1,800 ft) from where you can see the tops of 31 Munros on a clear day and enjoy a close-up view of the impressive Beinn Eighe ridge a few miles to the south.

The trail now begins to descend as it heads northwest towards An t-Allt (1,000 ft), turns northwards down to a small enclosure, then heads east to the deep Allt na h-Airidhe gorge. From here the trail continues down to the treeline and runs through woodland to join up with the top of the Woodland Trail. Follow the path to the right and this takes you back to the car park.

Gairloch and around

Phone code: 01445
Colour map 1, grid C4
Gairloch consists of a string of tiny crofting townships scattered around the northeastern shore of the loch of the same name. It's a great place which attracts a large number of visitors who come for the many beautiful beaches, excellent walks, golf and fishing and the chance of seeing seals, porpoises, dolphins and whales in the surrounding waters.

Ins & outs

There are buses to and from Inverness 3 times a week, also buses to Kinlochewe and a local postbus service (see Transport on next page).

The TIC, T712130, is at the car park in Auchtercairn, where the road branches off to Strath. They will book accommodation for you and sell a wide range of books and maps. Jan-Mar, Nov and Dec Mon-Thu 0900-1230 and 1300-1700, Fri 0900-1230 and 1300-1630; Apr and May, Sep and Oct Mon-Sat 0900-1730, Sun 1300-1800; Jun-Aug Mon-Fri 0900-1800, Sat 1000-1800, Sun 1300-1800

Sights

If the weather's bad (as it sometimes can be) or if you're interested in local history, then visit the **Gairloch Heritage Museum**, which is beside the tourist office, on the A832 to Poolewe, a few yards beyond the turn-off to Strath. Included are archaeological finds, a mock-up of a crofthouse room, schoolroom and shop, the interior of the local lighthouse and an archive of old photographs. ■ *Apr-mid-Oct Mon-Sat 1000-1700. Adult £2.50, concession £2, children £0.50. T712287.*

The waters around Gairloch are home to a wide variety of marine mammals such as seals, otters, porpoises, dolphins, minke whales and even killer whales. You can take a wildlife-spotting cruise with *Sail Gairloch*, T712636. The cruise lasts two hours and leaves daily from Gairloch Pier (subject to weather conditions). It can be booked at the Gairloch Marine Life Centre by the pier. For information on **sea angling trips**, contact the chandlery shop at the harbour, T712458. For those who prefer dry land, try a **quad bike tour** of the Flowerdale Deer Forest with *Highland Trails*. Book at *The Anchorage* post office/craft shop at the harbour or at Flowerdale estate office, T712378.

Essentials

B-C *Myrtle Bank Hotel*, T712004, F712214, MyrtleBank@email.msn.com 12 rooms. Modern hotel in the centre of Gairloch overlooking the loch, very good food and service in the restaurant (expensive dinner and cheap bar meals). There are numerous cheaper B&Bs scattered throughout the area. Most of the owners will provide maps and information on local walks. On the main street in **Strath**, near the shops, is **F** *Bains House*, T712472, which is friendly and great value. On the road that turns off to the right by the *Millcroft Hotel*, beyond the fire station, is **E-F** *Duisary*, T712252, open Apr-Oct. In **Charleston**, by the harbour, is **E** *Mrs A MacIver*, T712388, open Feb-Nov.

Further afield, at **Badachro**, south of Gairloch on the road to Red Point, is **E** *Lochside*, T741295. Also at Badachro is **F** *Badachro Bunkhouse*, T07760-344008. 13 miles north of Gairloch, at the end of the road, is the **F** *Rubha Reidh Lighthouse*, T/F771263, ruareidh@netcomuk.co.uk, which offers comfortable B&B (**D** including dinner) and hostel accommodation. It's best to book ahead in the high season. They also have a tearoom serving home baking, snacks and light lunches; open Sun, Tue and Thu 1100-1700, Easter-Oct. Self-catering is also available for private rooms or the hostel. There are buses from Gairloch as far as Melvaig (see below), then it's a 3-mile hike along the road to the lighthouse.

There are a couple of hostels in Gairloch: **F** *Auchtercairn Hostel*, T712131, open Mar-Nov, is at Gairloch Sands Apartments, just before the turn-off to Strath; 3 miles beyond Gairloch, on the road to Melvaig, is **F** *Carn Dearg Youth Hostel*, T712219, open 15 May-3 Oct.

There are a couple of **campsites**: *Gairloch Caravan & Camping Park*, T712373, is at Strath, with full facilities and close to all amenities; *Sands Holiday Centre*, T712152, open Easter-Oct, is at Big Sand, about a mile beyond Strath.

Eating The *Myrtle Bank Hotel* (see above) serves very good, expensive, meals, though its bar lunches are good value. The *Scottish Seafood Restaurant*, T712137, next to Gairloch filling station, is good for seafood at mid-range prices (unlicensed). The *Mountain Restaurant*, Strath Sq, T712316, has a terrace overlooking Gair Loch. It is run by mountaineers and offers an interesting menu, as well as accommodation in several themed rooms. There's also *The Steading Restaurant*, T712449, next to the Heritage Museum, which is open daily 0930-2100. For a lite bite, or tea and scones, try the *Conservatory Coffee Shop*, on the square in Strath. For cheap pasta, there's *Gino's Italian Restaurant* at the friendly *Millcroft Hotel* in Strath, T712376. The best place for a good pint of real ale and some hearty pub grub is *The Old Inn*, T712006, near the harbour.

Transport There's a **bus** from **Inverness** to Gairloch 3 times a week (Mon, Wed and Sat) at 1705 with *Westerbus*, T712255. The return bus is at 0805. *Westerbus* also have services to **Kinlochewe** (Mon-Sat at 0730) and to **Mellon Charles/Laide**, via **Poolewe** (Mon-Sat). There's a **Melvaig-Gairloch-Red Point** *postbus* service Mon-Sat which leaves Gairloch at 0820 heading north to Melvaig and leaves Gairloch heading south to **Red Point** at 1035. On Fri only there's a subsidized taxi service between Gairloch and Melvaig 1030-1230 (to book T712559/712497).

Directory There are shops and takeaways in Strath and Auchtercairn, a petrol station in Auchtercairn and a bank with ATM near the harbour at Charleston.

Around Gairloch

The beach at Gairloch, by the golf course, is nice but the beach at **Big Sand**, a few miles northwest of Strath, is better, and quieter. Further north is Melvaig, from where you can walk to **Rubha Reidh Lighthouse** (see 'Sleeping' below). Around the headland from the lighthouse is the beautiful, secluded beach at **Camas Mor**. This is a good place for spotting sea birds, and there's a great walk from here, on a marked footpath, to **Midtown**, four miles northwest of Poolewe. You'll have to walk or hitch from here as there's no public transport to Poolewe.

Many of the roads in the area were built during the Potato Famine of 1840 in order to give men work, with funds supplied by Dowager Lady Mackenzie of Gairloch. These became know as the 'Destitution Roads', and one of these is the narrow B8056 which runs west for nine miles to **Red Point** from the junction three miles south of Gairloch, at Kerrysdale. This is a lovely little side trip and well worth it, especially on a clear evening to enjoy the magnificent sunsets at Red Point beach. The beach itself is extremely beautiful, backed by steep dunes and looking across to the Trotternish peninsula on Skye. So romantic is this spot that some people (naming no names) have been known to plight their troth here. Red Point is also the start or finish point for the excellent coastal walk to or from **Diabaig** (see page 251). On the road to Red Point is the picturesque little hamlet of **Badachro**, tucked away in a wooded, sheltered bay with fishing boats moored in its natural harbour. It's worth stopping off here on the way back from Red Point for a wee dram at the *Badachro Inn*. What finer way could there be to end the day?

There are lots of other good walks in the area, including to **Flowerdale Falls** and the **Fairy Lochs** and the **USAAF Liberator**. The TIC (see previous page) has a selection of walking guides and OS maps.

Walk around Loch Kernsary

This straightforward but rewarding walk covers six miles and should take around 2½ to three hours. The track is very boggy underfoot in places, especially after rain, so you'll need good boots.

Start in Poolewe, from the car park by the school near the bridge over the Ewe. Head up the single-track road with the river on your right. Go through the gate, then the track heads away from the river and up into woodland. At the Letterewe Estate gate cross the stile and continue to the next fork. Turn left here to Kernsary Estate, with views of Loch Maree and Beinn Eighe to the south. Follow the track to the next gate, go through and cross the wooden bridge. Continue along the track and you'll see Loch Kernsary on your left. At the next fork, turn left over the bridge and pass Kernsary Cottage on the right. Beyond the cottage, go through the gate and immediately head left down towards the burn where the ground may be

boggy. There's no path here, but cross the wooden footbridge and continue straight on, past the piles of stones on your left. Cross the stile, and the path follows the length of Loch Kernsary. At the head of the loch, the path climbs to give you views down to Poolewe. Follow the path down till it eventually takes you to the main road. Turn left and follow the road back to the car park. OS Landranger Map No 19 covers the

Poolewe

Five miles east of Gairloch on the other side of the peninsula is the neat little village of Poolewe, beautifully set at the mouth of the river Ewe, where it cascades into sheltered Loch Ewe.

Phone code: 01445
Colour map 1,
grid B4

There are some good walks around Poolewe, including the one around **Loch Kernsary** described below. There's also a nice little drive up the side road running along the west shore of Loch Ewe to **Cove**. You can walk from **Midtown**, midway along the road, to **Rubha Reidh**, north of Gairloch (see above).

There are several places to stay in and around **Poolewe** and the TIC in Gairloch will help you find accommodation. On the Cove road by the lochside is the former home of Osgood Mackenzie, the **L** *Pool House Hotel*, T781272, poolhouse@inverewe.co.uk, open Mar- Dec. It enjoys great views and serves good food. At **Inverasdale**, a few miles up the Cove road, is **E** *Bruach Ard*, T781214, open Apr-Oct. Further up this road, near Cove, is **E** *Mrs MacDonald*, T781354, open Apr-Oct. Above Poolewe, reached by a path that leads from the road beside the campsite, is **E** *Mrs MacIver*, T781389, open Apr-Oct. The excellent *Camping and Caravan Club Site*, T781249, is between Poolewe village and Inverewe Garden.

Sleeping & eating

The best place to eat in Poolewe is probably the licensed restaurant at Inverewe Garden which is open daily 1000-1700 (see below). If you need to grab a quick snack, or fancy a coffee, try the *Bridge Cottage Café*, which is on the left at the turn-off to Cove.

Inverewe Garden

The reason most people come here is to visit Inverewe Garden where you'll find an astonishing collection of exotic subtropical plants growing on the same latitude as Siberia, thanks to the mild climate created by the North Atlantic Drift. This wonderful 50-acre oasis of colour is a mecca for garden lovers, but even those who flinch at the mere sight of a lawn-mower will be bowled over the sheer scale and diversity of plants and flowers on view.

The garden was created from a treeless wilderness by Osgood Mackenzie, starting in 1862. By the time of his death, in 1922, he had produced an internationally renowned walled and woodland garden. His work was continued by his daughter, who then gave the garden to the National Trust for Scotland in 1952. Since then, the plant collection has diversified even more and an intricate maze of paths leads you through ever-changing displays of Himalayan rhododendrons, Tasmanian eucalyptus, many Chilean and South African species, together with a large collection of New Zealand plants.

The garden is well worth visiting, in any weather, but especially from the end of April through the summer when the rhododendrons are in bloom. You should allow at least a couple of hours to do it justice. The garden is about a mile north of Poolewe, on the main A832. There's a visitor centre and gift shop and a good restaurant, which serves snacks and hot meals. ■ *Garden open 15 Mar-31 Oct daily 0930-2100; 1 Nov-14 Mar daily 0930-1700. Visitor Centre open 15 Mar to 31 Oct 0930-1730. Guided garden walks 15 Apr to 15 Sep Mon-Thu at 1330. Adult £5, concession £4, children £1. T781200.*

Gruinard Bay to Loch Broom

Around Laide
Phone code: 01445
Colour map 1,
grid B5

North of Poolewe, the A832 passes **Aultbea** on its way to **Laide**, where it then skirts the shores of Gruinard Bay, with its lovely coves of pink sand. From Laide Post Office a side road branches north to **Mellon Udrigle** and **Opinan**, both with great beaches. Between Laide and Mellon Udrigle, at **Achgarve**, a road branches left for about half a mile. From the end of this road you can walk all the way to **Slaggan**, a ruined village on the other side of the peninsula. It's a nice spot for a picnic but don't be tempted to swim in the sea as the tidal race makes it dangerous.

Gruinard Bay is a very beautiful part of the northwest coast but will always be synonymous with **Gruinard Island**, standing ominously in the middle of the bay. The island was used as a testing ground for biological warfare during the Second World War and was contaminated with anthrax spores. The Ministry of Defence finally agreed to decontaminate it in 1990 and it has now been declared 'safe'.

Sleeping There are a couple of really good places to stay around here. In the village of **Laide** is the **D** *Old Smiddy Guest House*, T731425, oldsmiddy@aol.com, open Apr-Oct. Its excellent restaurant is also open to non-residents, but it's best to book well in advance (expensive). There's also a **campsite** in Laide, the *Gruinard Bay Caravan Park*, T731225, open Apr-Oct.

Transport There are daily **buses** to Laide from **Gairloch** with *Westerbus*, T712255. Some of them continue to Mellon Udrigle. There are buses between Laide and **Inverness** 3 times a week (Tue, Thu and Fri), leaving at 0805 and returning at 1705. There are also buses on other days between **Gairloch** and **Inverness** which stop at Laide (see above under Gairloch).

Dundonnell
Phone code: 01854
Colour map 1, grid B5

The road heads inland then runs along the southern shore of **Little Loch Broom** to **Dundonnell**, from where there are spectacular views of awesome **An Teallach** (3,483 ft), a mountain of almost mythical status amongst

£4000 worth of holiday vouchers to be won!

... that can be claimed against any exodus, Peregrine or Gecko's holiday, a choice of around 570 holidays that set industry standards for responsible tourism in 90 countries across seven continents.

exodus

The UK's leading adventurous travel company, with over 25 years' experience in running the most exciting holidays in 80 different countries. We have an unrivalled choice of trips, from a week exploring the hidden corners of Tuscany to a high altitude trek to Everest Base Camp or 3 months travelling across South America. If you want to do something a little different, chances are you'll find it in one of our brochures.

Peregrine

Australia's leading quality adventure travel company, Peregrine aims to explore some of the world's most interesting and inaccessible places. Providing exciting and enjoyable holidays that focus in some depth on the lifestyle, culture, history, wildlife, wilderness and landscapes of areas that are usually quite different to our own. There is an emphasis on the outdoors, using a variety of transport and staying in a range of accommodation, from comfortable hotels to tribal huts.

Gecko's

Gecko's holidays will get you to the best places with the minimum of hassle. They are designed for younger people who like independent travel but don't have the time to organise everything themselves. Be prepared to take the rough with the smooth, these holidays are for active people with a flexible approach to travel.

To enter the competition, simply tear out the postcard and return it to Exodus Travels, 9 Weir Road, London SW12 OLT. Or go to the competition page on www.exodus.co.uk and register online. Two draws will be made, Easter 2001 and Easter 2002, and the winner of each draw will receive £2000 in travel vouchers. The closing date for entry will be 1st March 2002. If you do not wish to receive further information about these holidays, please tick here. ☐ No purchase necessary. Plain paper entries should be sent to the above address. The prize value is non-transferable and there is no cash alternative. Winners must be over 18 years of age and must sign and adhere to operators' standard booking conditions. A list of prizewinners will be available for a period of one month from the draw by writing to the above address. For a full list of terms and conditions please write to the above address or visit our website.

To receive a brochure, please tick the relevant boxes below (maximum number of brochures 2) or telephone (44) 20 8772 3822.

exodus	Peregrine	Gecko's
☐ Walking & Trekking	☐ Himalaya	☐ Egypt, Jordan & Israel
☐ Discovery & Adventure	☐ China	☐ South America
☐ European Destinations	☐ South East Asia	☐ Africa
☐ Overland Journeys	☐ Antarctica	☐ South East Asia
☐ Biking Adventures	☐ Africa	☐ India
☐ Multi Activity	☐ Arctic	

Please give us your details:

Name: --

Address: ---

Postcode: --

e-mail: ---

Which footprint guide did you take this from?

----

getaway tonight on www.exodus.co.uk

The Different Holiday

exodus
The Different Holiday

getaway tonight on

www.exodus.co.uk

exodus
The Different Holiday

2
1

exodus
9 Weir Road
LONDON
SW12 0BR

BUSINESS REPLY SERVICE
Licence No SW4909

Scottish climbers and spoken of in hushed, reverential tones. The path to the highest of its summits is clear and begins southeast of the *Dundonell Hotel*. It will take a full day and you'll need to be well prepared (OS map No 19) and heed the usual advice. You can stay at the **B** *Dundonnell Hotel*, T633204, selbie@ dundonnellhotel.co.uk, open February-December, which does good meals (cheap to mid-range bar meals; expensive three-course dinner). Alternatively there's B&B at **E** *Mrs Ross*, T633237, in Camusnagaul, a few miles back up the loch. Also in Camusnagaul is the *Sail Mhor Croft Independent Hostel*, T633224, sailmhor@btinternet.com, but you should call before arriving.

A few miles beyond Dundonnell, a side road branches left and runs for seven miles to the tiny, remote hamlet of **Badrallach**, where you can stay at the *Badrallach Bothy & Camp Site*, T633281.

The A832 coastal road from Gairloch and Poolewe meets the A835 Ullapool-Inverness main road at **Braemore junction**, 12 miles south of Ullapool. Before heading on to Ullapool it's worth stopping at the very impressive Falls of Measach, just by the junction. The falls plunge 150 ft into the spectacular **Corrieshalloch Gorge** (or 'ugly/fearsome gorge' in Gaelic) and can be crossed by a distinctly wobbly suspension bridge (not for vertigo sufferers). The falls can be reached from the A835 but the most dramatic approach is from the A832 Gairloch road. | **Falls of Measach**

North & Northwest Highlands

Ullapool

The attractive little fishing port of Ullapool, on the shores of Loch Broom, is the largest settlement in Wester Ross. The grid-pattern village, created in 1788 at the height of the herring boom by the British Fisheries Society, is still an important fishing centre as well as being the major tourist centre in the northwest of Scotland and one of the main ferry terminals for the Outer Hebrides. At the height of the busy summer season the town is swamped by visitors passing through on their way to or from Stornoway on Lewis, heading north into the wilds, or south to Inverness. It has excellent tourist amenities and services and relatively good transport links, making it the ideal base for those exploring the northwest coast and a good place to be if the weather is bad. | Phone code: 01854 Colour map 1, grid B5 Population: 1,800

Ins and outs

Ullapool is the mainland terminal for **ferries** to Stornoway (Lewis). *Scottish Citylink* **buses**, T08705-505050, to and from Inverness (twice daily Mon-Sat, 1 hr 20 mins; £6 single) connect with the ferry to and from Stornoway. For further details of ferries, see the Outer Hebrides chapter (page 318), or contact the local *CalMac* office on Shore St, opposite the pier, T612358. There are also buses to places further north, and south along the coast. Buses stop at the pier near the ferry dock. | **Getting there** *See also page 261*

The TIC is at 6 Argyle St, T612135. It is well run and provides an accommodation booking service as well as information on local walks and trips and has a good stock of books and maps. Easter-Jun and Sep-Nov, Mon-Sat 0900-1800, Sun 1300-1800; Jul and Aug, Mon-Sat 0900-1900, Sun 1300-1800. | **Tourist Information Centre**

Sights

Ullapool's attractions are very much of the outdoor variety and include the **Falls of Measach**, **Achiltibuie** and **Stac Pollaidh**. There are also many good local walks and cruises to the **Summer Isles** (see 'Tours' below). It's worth taking a stroll around the **harbour** to watch the comings and goings of the fishing fleet and you might even see the occasional seal or otter swimming close to the shore.

The only real 'sight' as such is the **Ullapool Museum and Visitor Centre** in a converted church in West Argyle Street. It has some interesting displays on local history, including the story of those who set sail from here, in 1773, on board *The Hector*, the first ship to carry emigrants from the Highlands to Nova Scotia in Canada. ■ *Apr-Oct Mon-Sat 0930-1730; Jul and Aug also 1930-2130; Nov-Mar 1200-1600. Adult £2, concession £1.50, children free. T612987.*

Essentials

Sleeping
■ *on map*
Price codes:
see inside
front cover

There is no shortage of places to stay in Ullapool, ranging from one of the very finest hotels in the UK to numerous guesthouses and B&Bs, a couple of good youth hostels and a campsite.

L *Altnaharrie Inn*, T633230. 8 rooms, open Apr-Oct, this world-renowned hotel is on the other side of Loch Broom and you'll be picked up from town in their own launch. The ultimate Highland retreat, if you can afford it, and unique in every sense, their restaurant is one of most highly acclaimed in the UK. The hotel is closed for the 2001 season; check if it will re-open in 2002.

B *The Ceilidh Place*, 14 West Argyle Pl, T612103, F612886, reservations@ ceilidh.demon.co.uk 23 rooms. This former boat-shed has grown over the years to become one of the most refreshingly different hotels in the country with comfortable bedrooms, cosy lounge, bookshop, restaurant, bar and coffee shop. They also host a varied programme of arts events such as live music, plays, poetry readings, exhibitions and ceilidhs (see below), a great place to relax and soak up some local culture. Across the road is their clubhouse, with basic but comfortable dorms (**E-F**).

D-C *Harbour Lights Hotel*, Garve Rd (on the left, heading into Ullapool on the A835), T612222, harbour@vacations-scotland.co.uk 22 rooms, open 1 Mar-31 Oct. Modern hotel offering good service and very good food available all day (mid-range). **D** *Ferry Boat Inn*, Shore St, T612366, www.ferryboat-inn.com On the lochside, decent accommodation and food and the best pub in town. **C-D** *Morefield Hotel*, North Rd, T612161. Open May-Oct. On the edge of town heading north, in the middle of a housing estate, motel-style accommodation and a superb seafood restaurant. On the other side of Loch Broom, 12 miles from Ullapool, is **C-D** *Tigh-na-Mara*, T655282. Price includes dinner, completely remote and acclaimed vegetarian guesthouse. An absolute must for nature lovers.

D *Point Cottage Guest House*, 22 West Shore St, T612494, www.pointcottage.co.uk Lovely old fishing cottage at the quieter end of the loch-front.

E *Brae Guest House*, Shore St, T612421. 8 rooms, open May-Oct, comfortable guesthouse on the loch-front. **E** *Eilean Donan Guest House*, 14 Market St, T612524. Friendly and central. **E** *Strathmore House*, Strathmore, Morefield (1 mile north of town),

T612423, murdo@strathmore.fsnet.co.uk Open Apr-Oct, friendly, comfortable and good value. There are more **guesthouses** on Garve Rd, heading south out of town, and lots of B&Bs along Seaforth Rd and Pulteney St.

Ullapool has a very good **F** *SYHA* youth hostel on Shore St, T612254, open Feb-Dec, where you can pick up some good information on local walks. There's an independent hostel, **F** *West House*, on West Argyle St, T613126, which has the full range of facilities and hires out mountain bikes. The only **campsite** is at *Broomfield Holiday Park*, T6120020, on Shore St, at the west end of the village with great views across to the Summer Isles and a laundrette on site. It's open Easter-Sep.

Ullapool

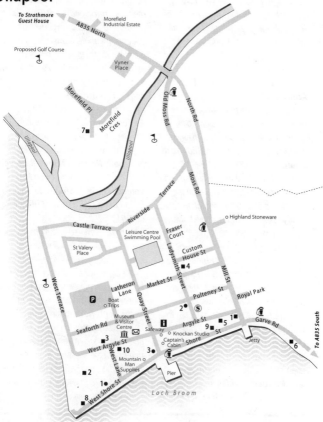

North & Northwest Highlands

■ **Sleeping**
1 Brae Guest House
2 Broomfield Holiday Park
3 The Ceilidh Place
4 Eilean Donan Guest House
5 Ferry Boat Inn
6 Harbour Lights
7 Morefield Hotel & Mariner's Restaurant
8 Point Cottage Guest House
9 SYHA Youth Hostel
10 West House Hostel

● **Eating**
1 Arch Inn
2 Scottish Larder
3 Seaforth Inn

N

0 metres   100
0 yards   100

Walks around Ullapool

There are several good walking trails which start in Ullapool. One of these is to the top of **Ullapool Hill**, or Meall Mhor (886 ft). Starting from the tourist office, head to the end of Argyle Street, turn left onto North Road and then cross the road at the Far Isles Restaurant. Walk down the lane between Broom Court and the Hydro sub-station and then follow the path which zig-zags up the hillside. There's a good cairned path up to the top of the hill. The views from the top over Glen Achall and, on a clear day, the mountains of Sutherland, are superb. You can return by traversing the hillside to the top of the Braes, or take a track leading to **Loch Achall** and follow the Ullapool River through the quarry road back to the village. The return trip takes one to two hours. A relatively easy, but much longer walk, of five to six hours, is to **Rhidorroch Estate**. Take the A835 north out of Ullapool. Opposite the petrol station and before the bridge, take the road on the right signed 'Quarry'. Go through the quarry keeping to the left, and follow the Ullapool River till you see Loch Achall. Continue along the north bank of the loch for another six miles. **East Rhidorroch Lodge** is on the right; cross the bridge to get there, then skirt the lodge fences and cross to the track which leads up the southwestern hill. This brings you out to **Leckmelm**, about four miles south of Ullapool on the A835. This last section offers wonderful views across Loch Broom to An Teallach. From Leckmelm you can also climb **Beinn Eilideach** (1,837 ft). A good coastal walk is to **Rhue Lighthouse**

and back. From the north end of Quay Street go down the steps to the river. Cross the bridges and head left by the football field. Follow the path to the left by the duck pond and cross in front of the bungalow. Then follow the shoreline north for about two miles, climbing up the hillside when the tide is high. Follow the path till you reach the little white lighthouse at Rhue Point. To return, take the single-track road out of Rhue back to the main road and up over the hill to Ullapool. It's about six miles in total. There are many more strenuous hiking routes around Ullapool. The A835 south of town gives access to **Beinn Dearg** (3,556 ft) and the **Fannichs**, a range of hills on the southern side of Dirrie More. There's also **An Teallach**, a favourite with Scottish climbers (see page 256). North of Ullapool are the mountains within the **Inverpolly National Nature Reserve** (see below). These include **Ben Mór Coigach** (2,438 ft), **Stac Pollaidh** (2,011 ft), **Cul Beag** (2,523 ft) and **Cul Mór** (2,786 ft).

All routes are covered by OS Maps Nos 15, 19 and 20. They all require hillwalking experience and you should be well prepared for the unpredictable weather conditions. A good climbing guidebook is The Northern Highlands, SMC District Guide, by Tom Strang. North West Frontiers is an Ullapool-based tour company offering guided walking tours around Ullapool and throughout the Northwest Highlands. Contact them at: 18A Braes, Ullapool, IV26 2SZ, T/F612628, NWF@compuserve.com, ourworld.compuserve.com/

Eating

There's plenty of choice across the range, from one of the UK's top hotel/ restaurants to the humble seafront chippie

The *Altnaharrie Inn* (see above) is considered perhaps the finest in the country and Gunn Erikson's cooking is of world renown. Expensive, and non-residents will need to book well in advance. *Mariner's Restaurant* is part of the *Morefield Hotel* (see above). The setting may be a little incongruous but there's nothing wrong with the food. The seafood is sensational, which is why people travel from miles around and it's always busy. Mid-range prices and excellent value.

The Ceilidh Place (see above) is one of those places that tourists seem to hang around for hours or even days. It exudes a laid-back, cultured ambience. The self-service coffee shop does cheap wholefood all day during the summer while the restaurant serves more expensive full meals, with an emphasis on vegetarian and seafood, at night. There's even outdoor seating. Open 1100-2300. Also live music and various other events (see below). *Scottish Larder*, Ladysmith St, T612185. Should be called 'Pies-R-Us'. They have a huge selection, as well as vegetarian options and local seafood. Great value. You can also get decent, cheap pub food at lunchtime and early evening in the *Ferry Boat Inn*, the *Seaforth Inn* and the *Arch Inn* (see below).

Ullapool's favourite pub has to be the *Ferry Boat Inn* (or 'FBI' as it's known locally), on Shore St. It has regular live music sessions through the week and during the summer you sit outside on the sea wall and watch the sun go down as you drain your glass. Another good place for a drink is the *Arch Inn*, at the other end of Shore St. The bar of the *Seaforth Inn* has live music at weekends, which has been described by one local as 'raucous'. For something a wee bit more sedate and civilized, head for *The Ceilidh Place*, where you can enjoy a quiet drink in the cosy *Parlour Bar* or take advantage of their varied programme of events. There's live music nightly (except Sun) throughout the summer, ceilidhs and poetry readings, and the clubhouse opposite stages plays.

Entertainment

The town is well supplied with shops. *Boots* the chemist is on Shore St by the pier, and there's a *Safeway* supermarket next to the car park north of Seafield Rd. A good outdoor equipment shop is *Mountain Man Supplies*, opposite the museum, on West Argyle St.

The best **bookshop** in the northwest is the one at *The Ceilidh Place* (see above). The *Captain's Cabin*, on the corner of Quay St and Shore St, also sells books, as well as crafts and souvenirs.

An excellent **jewellers** is the *Knockan Studio*, opposite the TIC on Argyle St, T613365, open Mar-Oct, Mon-Sat 0900-1800. For **pottery**, look no further than *Highland Stoneware*, T612980, on Mill St heading north towards Morefield. You can wander round the studios before browsing in their gift shop, which is pricey but you may have luck in their bargain baskets. They also have a factory in Lochinver (see page 263). Open Mon-Fri 0900-1800 (also Sat 0900-1700 Easter-Oct).

Shopping

During the summer the *MV Summer Queen* runs 4-hour cruises to the **Summer Isles**, with a 45-min landing on Tanera Mór. These leave Mon-Sat at 1000 from the pier and cost £14 per person. There are also 2-hr wildlife cruises around **Loch Broom**, **Annat Bay** and **Isle Martin**, which leave daily at 1415 and also on Sun at 1100, and cost £8 per person. Cruises can be booked at the booth by the pier or by calling T612472.

Tours

Scottish Citylink **buses** run 2-3 times daily (except Sun) between Ullapool and **Inverness**, connecting with the ferry to Stornoway. There are also buses daily (except Sun) to and from Inverness with *Rapson's Coaches*, T01463-710555, and *Spa Coaches*, T01997-421311. There's a service to **Lochinver** (1-2 times daily except Sun, 1 hr) with *Spa Coaches* and *Rapson's of Brora*, T01408-621245, and to **Achilitibuie** (twice daily Mon-Thu, once on Sat, 1 hr) with *Spa Coaches*. There's also a daily bus to and from **Gairloch**, which continues to Inverness, during the summer only. **Cycle hire** At *West House* independent hostel (see 'Sleeping' above); £10 per day.

Transport

Banks The only bank is the *Royal Bank of Scotland* in Ladysmith St.

Directory

North & Northwest Highlands

North of Ullapool

Colour map 1,
grid B5/6

North of Ullapool you enter a different world. The landscape becomes ever more dramatic and unreal – a huge emptiness of bleak moorland punctuated by isolated peaks and shimmering lochs. A narrow and tortuously twisting road winds its way up the coast, past deserted beaches of sparkling white sand washed by turquoise sea. There's not much tourist traffic this far north and once you get off the main road and on to the backroads, you can enjoy the wonderful sensation of having all this astonishingly beautiful scenery to yourself.

The region immediately north of Ullapool is called **Assynt** *and is heaven for serious hill walkers and climbers. Though most are not Munros, and not particularly difficult by Scottish standards, they can attract some of the worst weather imaginable, even in the height of summer. Also remember to check locally regarding access during the deer-stalking season which runs from mid-August to mid-October. (See also 'Safety in the Scottish Mountains', page 53.) Amongst the most spectacular of Assynt's distinctive 'island peaks' are* **Suilven** *(2,398 ft),* **Ben More Assynt** *(3,275 ft),* **Quinag** *(2,650 ft) and* **Canisp** *(2,775 ft). Much of this region is protected in the* **Inverpolly** *and* **Inchnadamph National Nature Reserves***, home to an extremely rich and diverse wildlife.*

Inverpolly National Nature Reserve

Phone code: 01854
Colour map 1,
grid B5

About 12 miles north of Ullapool, on the main A835, is the SNH visitor centre at **Knockan Crag**, which gives a good introduction to the diverse flora and fauna in the area. ■ *Mid-May to mid-Sep daily 1000-1700. T666234.* From the visitor centre there's a marked trail which leads up to the Crag and the views from the clifftop are excellent, across to Inverpolly's 'island' peaks of **Cul Mór**, **Cul Beag** and **Stac Pollaidh**.

A few miles north of here is the village of **Knockan**, with accommodation at **E** *Assynt Guided Holidays*, T666215, open mid-May to mid-Oct. Nearby, at **Elphin**, is the **Highland and Rare Breeds Farm** (open mid-May to end of September, daily 1000-1700). Beyond Elphin is **Ledmore**, where the A837 branches east towards **Lairg** and **Bonar Bridge**. There's a good craft shop at Ledmore where you can buy hand-knitted sweaters.

Stac Pollaidh
OS Landrayer No 15

Between Ullapool and Knockan Crag is the turn-off west (left) to the distinctive craggy peak of Stac Pollaidh. The climb up and down takes around four hours. The well-worn path starts from the car park beside Loch Lurgainn and leads to the lowest point on the ridge. The summit lies to the west and the huge buttress which bars the way should be turned on the right when the track along the ridge can be taken. You'll need a head for heights to reach the summit as much of the route is exposed. The summit lies beyond a little tower of rock which requires great care. The descent can be made by way of the big scree gully on the south side, but great care and sure-footedness is needed.

Stac Pollaidh is a very rewarding climb, hence its enduring popularity, but please consider the damage inflicted by tens of thousands of pairs of boots every year. The damage caused has resulted in serious erosion on the south face.

Achiltibuie

The unclassified single-track road winds its way west past Stac Pollaidh to the turn-off for Achiltibuie. This old crofting village, with whitewashed cottages set back from the sea views across to the beautiful **Summer Isles**, is home to one of the northwest's main tourist attractions. The **Hydroponicum**, or 'Garden of the Future', is a gigantic greenhouse which is pioneering the system of hydroponics to grow plants from all over the world. Hydroponics uses water instead of soil to carry nutrients to the plants and can be carried out anywhere. Here you can see an incredible variety of subtropical trees, orchids, flowers, vegetables, herbs and fruits. A guided tour takes you through the different climatic zones and you can taste their produce, including the famous strawberries, in the *Lilypond Café*, which serves meals and snacks. ■ *Daily Easter to end of Sep 1000-1800. Guided tours every hour on the hour. Adult £4.75, concession £3.50, children £2.75. T622202, www.race.co.uk/hydroponicum*

Phone code: 01854
Colour map 1, grid B5

Another worthwhile attraction is the **Achiltibuie Smokehouse**, five miles to the north, at Altandhu. Here, you can watch the salmon, herring, trout and other fish being cured before buying some afterwards. ■ *May-Sep Mon-Sat 0930-1700. Free. T622353.*

Near the Hydroponicum is the **L** *Summer Isles Hotel*, T622282, F622251, summerislesyhotel@aol.com Open Easter-Oct, which enjoys magnificent views across to the Summer Isles. It also boasts an excellent restaurant (expensive). Even if you're not staying or eating here, it's worth stopping to have a drink on the terrace and watch the sun set over the islands. The basic but very cheap **F** *SYHA Youth Hostel* is a few miles south at Achininver, T622254; open mid-May to early Oct. There are also several B&Bs in Achiltibuie.

Sleeping & eating

Those inviting **Summer Isles** lying offshore can be visited from Achiltibuie pier on board the *Hectoria*. **Cruises** leave Mon-Sat at 1030 and 1415 and last 3½ hrs, with 1 hr ashore on the islands. To book, contact *I Macleod* at Achiltibuie Post Office, T622200, or at home, T622315. Cruises cost £12 per person (half price for children). There are also deep-sea angling trips (1800-2100) which cost £6 per person and £15 per rod.

Tours

There are 2 **buses** daily (Mon-Thu) to **Ullapool** with *Spa Coaches*, T01997-421311, leaving Achiltibuie Post Office at 0800 and 1300. The early bus starts in Reiff (at 0740) and the other one leaves from Badenscallie. The journey takes an hour. There's also a bus on Sat, leaving at 0750.

Transport

Lochinver

The road from Achiltibuie north to Lochinver is known locally as the 'wee mad road' and you'd be mad to miss this thrilling route which twists and winds its way through some the northwest's most stunning scenery. The village of Lochinver is a working fishing port and the last sizeable village before Thurso. It has a good tourist office (see below), lots of accommodation, a bank with ATM, post office and petrol station.

Phone code: 01571
Colour map 1, grid B5

The best place to start is the **Assynt Visitor Centre**, which houses the **Tourist Information Centre**. It has displays on the local geology, history and wildlife and there's also a ranger service with guided walks throughout the summer. ■ *The centre is open Apr-Oct, Mon-Fri 1000-1700 and Sun 1000-1600. T844330.* Those looking for local souvenirs should head for **Highland Stoneware**, T844376, www.highlandtrail.co.uk/stoneware.html, a local pottery factory just outside the village on the road north.

North & Northwest Highlands

A few miles south of Lochinver, beyond **Inverkirkaig**, is the trail along the river to the **Kirkaig Falls**. The path starts near the *Achins Bookshop*, T844262, which has a good stock of Scottish titles and a café. Follow the path for about two miles till it branches right to the falls in the gorge below. Continue along the main path for about another ¾ mile till you reach Fionn Loch with superb views of mighty **Suilven**. The walk up to the falls and back should take around 1½ hours. This is one of the main approaches to the foot of the mountain.

Sleeping & eating **L** *Inver Lodge Hotel*, Iolaire Rd, T844496, F844395, inverlodge@compuserve.com 20 rooms, open Apr-Oct, a modern luxury hotel standing above the village with great views and excellent restaurant (lunch mid-range; dinner expensive). **L** *The Albannach Hotel*, at Baddidaroch, T844407, F844285. This wonderful 18th-century house overlooking Loch Inver is one of the very best places to stay in the northwest and the food offered in the award-winning restaurant is sublime, the price includes dinner, non-residents are also welcome but booking is essential. There are many comfortable guesthouses and B&Bs, including **E** *Ardglas Guest House*, T844257, ardglass@btinternet.com, and **E** *Polcraig*, T844429, cathelmac@aol.com, **E** *Davar*, T844501, open Mar-Oct, and **E** *Tigh-Na-Sith*, T844740; open Apr-Sep.

Apart from the hotels listed above, the best food can be found at *Lochinver's Larder Riverside Bistro*, T844356, on the way into town on the A837. You can eat in or takeaway and prices are mid-range. Nearby is the cheap and cheerful *Caberfeidh*, T844321.

Transport There's a *Postbus* service from Lochinver to and from **Drumbeg**, via the coast road, which continues to **Lairg**. It runs once a day, Mon-Sat. There are also buses to and from Drumbeg and on to **Ullapool**, once or twice daily except Sun, with *Rapsons of Brora*, T01408-621245, and *Spa Coaches*, T01997-421311.

Loch Assynt and Inchnadamph

Phone code: 01571
Colour map 1, grid B5/6

The area east of Lochinver is a remote wilderness of mountains and moorland dotted with lochs and lochans. As well as being a favourite haunt of hardy climbers and walkers, Assynt is a paradise for anglers. Most of the lochs are teeming with brown trout, and fishing permits are readily available throughout the area from the TIC in Lochinver or at local hotels, guesthouses and B&Bs. There's also salmon fishing on the River Kirkaig, available through the *Inver Lodge Hotel* (see above), and on Loch Assynt through the *Inchnadamph Hotel* (see below).

The A837 Lochinver-Lairg road meets the A894 to Durness 10 miles east of Lochinver at **Skiag Bridge** by Loch Assynt. Half a mile south of here, by the loch, are the ruins of **Ardvreck Castle**. The castle dates from 1597 and was the stronghold of the Macleods of Assynt until a siege of the castle in 1691, when it was taken by the Seaforth Mackenzies. Before that, the Marquis of Montrose had been imprisoned here following his defeat at Carbisdale in 1650. Access to the castle is free but the ruins are in a dangerous state and should be approached with care.

To the east of the road lies the **Inchnadamph National Nature Reserve**, dominated by the massive peaks of **Ben More Assynt** and **Conival**, which should only be attempted by experienced hill walkers. A few miles south of the village of **Inchnadamph**, at the fish farm, is a steep, but well-marked footpath up to the **Bone Caves**. This is one of Scotland's oldest historical sites, where the bones of humans and animals such as lynx and bear were found together with sawn-off deer antlers dating from over 8,000 years ago.

C *Inchnadamph Hotel*, T822202, inchnadamphhotel@assynt99.freeserve.co.uk is an old-fashioned Highland hotel on the shores of Loch Assynt catering for the hunting and fishing fraternity (see above). Nearby is the **F** *Inchnadamph Lodge*, T822218, assynt@presence.co.uk, or *Assynt Field Centre*, which offers basic hostel accommodation in bunk rooms, as well as twin, double and family rooms. Continental breakfast is included. It's open all year but phone ahead between Nov and Mar. It's ideally situated for climbing Ben More Assynt and guides are available.

Lochinver to Kylesku: the coast road

The quickest way north from Lochinver is the A837 east to the junction with *Phone code: 01571* the A894 which heads to Kylesku. But by far the most scenic route is the B869 *Colour map 1, grid B5* coast road that passes moorland, lochs and beautiful sandy bays. It's best travelled from north to south, giving you the most fantastic views of Suilven. Untypically, most of the land in this part of Assynt is owned by local crofters, who under the aegis of the *Assynt Crofters' Trust*, bought 21,000 acres of the North Assynt Estate, thus setting a precedent for change in the history of land ownership in the Highlands.

The trust now owns the fishing rights to the area and sells permits through local post offices and the tourist office in Lochinver. It has also undertaken a number of conservation projects, including one at **Achmelvich**, a few miles north of Lochinver, at the end of a side road which branches off the coast road. It's worth a detour to see one of the loveliest beaches on the west coast, with sparkling white sand and clear turquoise sea straight out of a Caribbean tourist brochure. You can stay here, at the *SYHA Hostel*, T844480, open mid-May to early October, or camp at the *Shore Caravan Site*, T844393, open April-September.

From the beach car park below the hostel a path leads northwest along the coast. Bear left off the sandy path shortly after the white cottage on the hill ahead comes into view and follow the footpath until the road is reached at **Alltan na Bradhan**, where there are remains of an old meal mill. Continue north from here along the coast for about a mile till you reach a small bay just before **Clachtoll**, the Split Rock. Close by are the remains of an Iron Age Broch, but don't cause further damage by clambering over the ruins. Return to the beach by the same path. The walk there and back should take about 1½ hours.

Kylesku

The road runs east from Drumbeg, under the shadow of towering **Quinag** *Phone code: 01971* (2,654 ft), to meet the A894 heading north to **Kylesku**, site of the sweeping *Colour map 1, grid B5* modern road bridge over Loch a'Cháirn Bháin. From Kylesku you can visit Britain's highest waterfall, the 650-ft high **Eas a'Chùal Aluinn**, near the head of Loch Glencoul. **Cruises** leave from the old ferry jetty below the *Kylesku Hotel* to the falls on board the *MV Statesman*, T01571-844446. You can also see porpoises, seals and minke whales *en route*. You may be able to get closer to the falls by getting off the boat and walking to the bottom, then getting on the next boat. ■ *The 2-hr round trip runs daily Apr- Sep at 1100 and 1400 (also at 1600 in Jul and Aug), and costs £9, £3 children.*

There's also a trail to the top of the falls. It starts at the south end of Loch na Gainmhich, about three miles north of Skiag Bridge. Skirting the loch follow the track in a southeasterly direction up to the head of the **Bealach a Bhuirich** (the Roaring Pass). Continue until you meet a stream, with several small lochans on your right. Follow this stream until it plunges over the **Cliffs of**

Old Man of Stoer

A side road turns left off the B869 north of Stoer and runs out to Stoer lighthouse. From here you can walk across the Stoer Peninsula to the Old Man of Stoer, a dramatic rock pillar standing offshore, surrounded by sheer cliffs. Allow about three hours for the circular walk which starts and ends in the lighthouse car park. There is no public transport to the lighthouse, but the Lochinver-Drumbeg postbus runs to Raffin, one mile away.

A clear path runs from the car park to the cliffs then follows the line of the cliffs northwards. The path heads inland for a short distance as it bypasses a deep gully then meets the clifftop again and after a mile or so you can see the Old Man tucked away in a shallow bay, battered by huge waves.

Beyond the Old Man the path continues to the headland, the Point of Stoer, from where it turns back on itself and climbs Sidhean Mór (532 ft). The views from here are fantastic, across to Harris and Lewis and south to the mountains of Assynt. From here, follow the faint path south, back towards the lighthouse, passing a small loch below Sidhean Beag on your left and an obvious cairn on your right. Then you pass a radio mast and follow the

clear track back to the lighthouse car park. Nine miles further on, in beautiful Eddrachillis Bay, is Drumbeg, a popular place for anglers who come to fish in the many lochs of North Assynt. There's not much accommodation around here other than self-catering cottages, but you can spend the night at D Taigh Druimbeag, T833209; open Easter to the end of October. OS Landranger Map No 15 covers the route.

North & Northwest Highlands

Dubh (the Dark Cliffs). You can get a better view of the falls by walking to the right about 100 yards and descending a heather slope for a short distance. Allow about three to four hours for the round trip.

Sleeping & eating Before you leave on the boat trip, pop into the **B** *Kylesku Hotel*, T502231, kylesku.hotel@excite.co.uk, for some delicious and great-value pub seafood or for B&B, open Mar-Oct. There's also a more formal and expensive restaurant next door. If you want to spend the night here, a cheaper option is the **D** *Newton Lodge*, T/F502070, newtonlge@aol.com, open mid-Mar to mid-Oct. There's also a small hostel at **F** *Kylesku Lodges*, T502003, open Easter-Oct.

Scourie and Handa Island

Phone code: 01971
Colour map 1, grid A5

Ten miles north of Kylesku is the little crofting community of Scourie, sitting above a sandy bay. Anyone remotely interested in wildlife is strongly advised to make a stop here to visit Handa Island, a sea bird reserve run by the Scottish Wildlife Trust, and one of the best places in the country for bird life. The island is now deserted, except for the warden, but once supported a thriving community of crofters, until the potato famine of 1846 forced them to leave, most emigrating to Canada's Cape Breton. Now it's home to huge colonies of shags, fulmars, razorbills, guillemots and puffins. The best time to visit is during the summer breeding season, from late May to August. There's a footpath right round the island, which is detailed in the free SWT leaflet available at the warden's office when you arrive. You should allow three to four hours.

There's a **ferry service** to the island from **Tarbet Beach**, three miles northwest off the A894, about three miles north of Scourie. It sails continuously, depending on demand. ■ *From 0930 to 1700 Mon-Sat during Apr-Sep. The 15-min crossing costs £7.50 return. T502077.*

Another excellent wildlife boat trip leaves from **Fanagmore**, a mile from Tarbet on the other side of the peninsula, with *Laxford Cruises*, T502251. They sail around beautiful Loch Laxford, where you can see lots of birds from nearby Handa Island, as well as seals, porpoises and otters. ■ *Trips leave at 1000, 1200 and 1400 daily except Sun from Easter till the end of Sep (also at 1600 in Jul and Aug). The trips last 1 hr 45 mins and cost £10 for adults, £5 for children.*

For bookings contact Julian Pearce, who also runs the wonderful *Seafood Restaurant* (mid-range) just above the jetty at Tarbet. If you're up this way, don't miss a visit to this restaurant which serves seafood caught by Julian during his boat trips! It's a great place and you can even stay here, in the self-catering caravan next door, which sleeps up to six.

Sleeping & eating There is lots of accommodation in and around Scourie. Best of all is the **C** *Eddrachilles Hotel*, a few miles south in Badcall Bay, T502080, F502477, eddrachilles@ compuserve.com 11 rooms, open Mar-Oct, this is one of the most magnificently situated hotels in the country, the 200 year-old building stands in 300 acres of grounds overlooking the bay, the food on offer is superb, though the atmosphere is a little stuffy (their Eddrachilles heel, you might say). Another excellent place to eat is the **B** *Scourie Hotel*, T502396, www.scourie-hotel.co.uk, open 1 Apr-mid-Oct, a 17th-century former coaching inn popular with anglers (lunch mid-range; dinner expensive). There are several **B&Bs** in the village, but none better than the welcoming **C** *Scourie Lodge*, T502248, open Mar-Oct, which also does good evening meals. There's also a **campsite**, T502060, on Harbour Rd.

Transport There's a *Postbus* service to Scourie from Durness and Lairg once a day, Mon-Sat. It leaves Durness at 0820 and arrives at 0935 and continues to Lairg. It returns at 1245 and arrives at 1420. There's also a *Postbus* service between Scourie and **Elphin**, with connections to **Lochinver**.

Kinlochbervie and around

Phone code: 01971
Colour map 1, grid A5

The road north from Scourie passes **Laxford Bridge**, where it meets the A838 running southeast to **Lairg** (see page 281). The A838 also runs north to Durness, on the north coast (see below). At **Rhiconich**, the B801 branches northwest to Kinlochbervie, a small village with a very big fish market. This is one of the west coast's major fishing ports and huge container lorries thunder along the narrow single-track roads carrying frozen fish and seafood to all corners of Europe. It's worth heading down to the fish market in the evenings to see the day's catch being landed and sold.

A few miles beyond Kinlochbervie is **Oldshoremore**, a tiny crofters' village scattered around a stunning white beach and a great place to swim. The less hardy can instead explore the hidden rocky coves nearby.

At the end of the road is **Blairmore**, from where a footpath leads to **Sandwood Bay**, the most stunning and beautiful beach on the west coast. It's a long walk but because of its isolation you'll probably have this glorious mile-long stretch of white sand all to yourself. The beach is flanked at one end by a spectacular rock pinnacle and is said to be haunted by the ghost of an ancient shipwrecked mariner. Allow three hours for the walk there and back, plus time at the beach. You could take a tent and watch the sunset. Sandwood Bay can also be reached from **Cape Wrath**, a day's hike to the north (see page 269).

Sleeping In Kinlochbervie village is **B** *The Kinlochbervie Hotel*, T521275, F521438, klbhotel@ aol.com A nicer place to stay is the **D** *Old School Hotel*, T/F521383, www.host.co.uk, halfway between Kinlochbervie and the A838 at Rhiconich. It used to be a school, as the name implies, and this only adds to the charm. They also serve great food at mid-range prices, daily 1200-1400 and 1800-2000. In Rhiconich is the **A** *Rhiconich Hotel*, T521224, rhiconichhotel@ compuserve.com, and also **B&B** at **E** *Benview*, T521242, open Apr-Sep. There's a good **campsite** at Oldshoremore, T521281.

Transport A *Postbus* leaves Kinlochbervie harbour at 0900 and goes to **Scourie** (35 mins) and on to **Lairg** (1 hr 50 mins) from where there are connections to **Inverness**. The same postbus returns from Lairg at 1245, arrives in Kinlochbervie at 1448, then continues to **Durness** (35 mins).

The North Coast

*Scotland's rugged north coast attracts few visitors, but those who do venture this far find that's there's plenty to write home about. This is some of Britain's most spectacular and undisturbed coastline, from the wild and remote **Cape Wrath** in the far northwest, to **John O'Groats**, that perennial favourite of sponsored walkers, in the far northeast. In between lies over 100 miles of storm-lashed cliffs, sheer rocky headlands and deserted sandy coves, all waiting to be explored. It's also great place for birdwatching, with vast colonies of seabirds, and there's a good chance of seeing seals, porpoises and minke whales in the more sheltered estuaries.*

Ins & outs Getting around the far north without your own transport can be a slow process. Getting to **Thurso**, the main town, by bus or train is easy, but beyond that things get more difficult. Details of what little public transport there is are given under the relevant destination.

Durness and around

Phone code: 01971 Durness is not only the most northwesterly village on the British mainland but
Colour map 1, grid A6 also one of the most attractively located, surrounded by sheltered coves of sparkling white sand and machair-covered limestone cliffs. It's worth stopping here for a few days to explore the area. The **Tourist Information Centre**, T511259, arranges guided walks and has a small visitor centre with displays on local history, flora and fauna and geology. Open April-October Monday-Saturday 0900-1800; also Sunday 1100-1900 in July and August.

Around A mile east of the village is the vast 200 ft-long **Smoo Cave**. A path from near
Durness the youth hostel leads down to the cave entrance which is hidden away at the end of a steep, narrow inlet. Plunging through the roof of the cathedral-like cavern is an 80-ft waterfall which can be seen from the entrance, but the more adventurous can take a boat trip into the floodlit interior.

A few miles east of the Smoo Cave are a couple of excellent beaches, at **Sangobeg** and **Rispond**, where the road leaves the coast and heads south along the west shore of stunning **Loch Eriboll**, Britain's deepest sea loch, which was used by the Royal Navy during the Second World War as a base for protecting Russian convoys.

About a mile northwest of Durness is the tiny hamlet of **Balnakeil**, overlooked by a ruined 17th-century church. In the south wall is a graveslab with carved skull-and-crossbones marking the grave of the notorious highwayman Donald MacMurchow. If you're looking for souvenirs, or an escape from the rat race, then head for the **Balnakeil Craft Village**, an alternative artists' community set up in the 1960s, in a former RAF radar station. Here you can buy weavings, pottery, paintings, leatherwork and woodwork in the little prefab huts. There's also a café. ■ *Apr-Oct daily 1000-1800*. Balnakeil has also become well-known in golfing circles. The nine-hole course, T511364, is the most northerly in mainland Britain and its famous ninth hole involves a drive over the Atlantic Ocean. The beach here is glorious, especially in fine weather when the sea turns a brilliant shade of turquoise. Even better, walk north along the bay to **Faraid Head**, where you can see puffin colonies in early summer. The views from here, across to Cape Wrath in the west and Loch Eriboll in the east, are stupendous.

There are several excellent trips around Durness, but the most spectacular is to Cape Wrath, Britain's most northwesterly point. It's a wild place and the name seems entirely appropriate, though it actually derives from the Norse word *hwarf*, meaning 'turning place'. Viking ships used it as a navigation point during their raids on the Scottish west coast. Now, a lighthouse stands on the cape, above the 1,000 ft-high **Clo Mor Cliffs**, the highest on the mainland and breeding ground for huge colonies of seabirds. **Cape Wrath**

You can walk south from here to Sandwood Bay (see page 267). It's an exhilarating, but long coastal walk, and will take around eight hours. It's safer doing this walk from north to south as the area around the headland is a military firing range and access may be restricted, which could leave you stranded.

A good place to stay is the **C** *Cape Wrath Hotel*, T511212, jack@capewrathhotel.co.uk, which is just off the A838 on the road to the ferry at Keoldale. It overlooks the loch and is popular with fishermen and passing tourists who stop here to enjoy the great food and superb views. The best value around Durness has to be the **B-C** *Port-Na-Con Guest House*, T511367, portnacon70@hotmail.com, on the west shore of Loch Eriboll, 7 miles from Durness. It's popular with anglers and divers so you'll need to book ahead to take advantage of such comfort amidst all this great scenery. The food in the adjoining restaurant is superb and also great value, especially the seafood. Non-residents are welcome but should book. There are also several B&Bs in Durness, best of which is **E** *Puffin Cottage*, T511208, puffincottage@aol.com, open Apr-Sep. There's a basic **F** *SYHA Youth Hostel*, at Smoo, to the east of the village, T511244; open mid-Mar to early Oct. There's also **camping** at *Salgo Sands Caravan Park*, T511222. **Sleeping & eating**

A daily **bus** runs to and from **Thurso**, via Tongue and Bettyhill (Jun-Aug, Mon-Sat) with *Highland Country Buses*, T01847-893123, leaving Thurso at 1130 and Durness at 1500. There's also a daily bus service (May to early Oct) to and from **Inverness** via Ullapool and Lochinver, with *Bluebird/Inverness Traction*, T01463-239292. There's a *Postbus* service to **Lairg** via **Tongue** and **Altnaharra**, daily Mon-Sat at 1115; also via **Kinlochbervie** and **Scourie** daily Mon-Sat at 0820. To get to **Cape Wrath**, first take the passenger **ferry** across the Kyle of Durness from Keoldale, 3 miles south of Durness, **Transport**

North & Northwest Highlands

T511376. It runs from May-Sep, hourly 0930-1630. The ferry connects with a minibus, T511287, for the 11 miles to the cape (40 mins).

Durness to Thurso

Tongue
Phone code: 01847
Colour map 2, grid A1

The road east from Durness runs around Loch Eriboll on its way to the lovely little village of Tongue. A causeway runs across the beautiful **Kyle of Tongue**, but a much more scenic route is the single-track road around its southern side, with great views of **Ben Hope** (3,041 ft) looming to the southwest. The village of Tongue is overlooked by the 14th-century ruins of **Varick Castle** and there's a great beach at **Coldbackie**, two miles northeast.

Sleeping and eating There are several places to stay in Tongue. The **B-C** *Tongue Hotel*, T611206, is a former hunting lodge of the Duke of Sutherland. It overlooks the Kyle of Tongue and does good food. Also recommended for its food is the excellent **C** *Ben Loyal Hotel*, T611216, Thebenloyalhotel@byinternet.com There are cheaper options, such as the excellent-value **E** *Rhian Cottage*, T611257, jenny.anderson@ tesco.net There's also a good **F** *SYHA Youth Hostel*, T611301, open mid-Mar to late Oct, beautifully situated at the east end of the causeway, and a couple of **campsites**; one is at Talmine, T601225, 5 miles north of Tongue by the beach, and the other is *Kincraig Camping and Caravan Site*, T611218, just to the south of the village. Also at Talmine is the lovely 19th-century **E** *Cloisters*, T601286, reception@ cloisteral.demon.co.uk

Bettyhill
Phone code: 01641
Colour map 2, grid A2

The A836 runs south from Tongue, through **Altnaharra**, to **Lairg** (see page 281). It also continues east to the crofting community of **Bettyhill**, named after the Countess of Sutherland who ruthlessly evicted her tenants from their homes in Strathnaver to make way for more profitable sheep. The whole sorry saga is told in the interesting **Strathnaver Museum**, housed in an old church in the village. There are also Pictish stones in the churchyard behind the museum. ■ *Apr-Oct Mon-Sat 1000-1300 and 1400-1700. Adult £1.90, concession £1.20, children £0.50. T521418.*

The museum sells a leaflet detailing the many prehistoric sites in the Strathnaver valley which runs due south from Bettyhill. The B871 then branches southeast to meet the A897 to Helmsdale. There are a couple of great beaches around Bettyhill, at **Farr Bay** and at **Torrisdale Bay**, which is the more impressive of the two and forms part of the **Invernaver Nature Reserve**.

There's a small **Tourist Information Centre** in Bettyhill, T521342, open Easter-September, Monday-Saturday.

Sleeping and eating The **E** *Farr Bay Inn*, T521230, www.bettyhill.com, does decent bar food. A good value B&B is **F** *Bruachmor*, T521265, open Apr-Oct.

Melvich &
Dournreay
Colour map 2, grid 2/3

East from Bettyhill the hills of Sutherland begin to give way to the fields of Caithness. The road passes the turn-off to **Strathy Point** before reaching **Melvich**, another wee crofting settlement overlooking a lovely sandy bay.

South from Melvich the A897 heads to Helmsdale (see page 284) through the **Flow Country**, a vast expanse of bleak bog of major ecological importance. About 15 miles south of Melvich, at **Forsinard**, is an **RSPB Visitor Centre**. The peatlands here are a breeding ground for black and red throated divers, golden plovers and merlins as well as other species. Otters and roe deer can also be spotted. ■ *Easter-Oct daily 0900-1800. Guided walks through the nature reserve leave from the visitor centre. T01641-571225.*

Strathmore to Braemore walk

This walk gives a flavour of the bleak but beautiful landscape of the Caithness hinterland. The 16-mile linear route starts from Strathmore Lodge. To get there, head south from Thurso on the B874. After a short distance turn onto the B870 and follow it for 10 miles to the little hamlet of Westerdale, which stands on the River Thurso. Turn right here onto an unnumbered road and follow this road for about five miles. Just past the white Strathmore Lodge the road splits. Follow the right-hand track which runs through commercial forestry, before emrging onto open moor with Loch More on the left. Where the forestry begins again on the right, the track swings left across an arm of the loch and heads southwards. At the southern end of the loch a track runs left to Dalnaha, but keep going straight ahead, along the valley of the River Thurso. You then reach a cluster of buildings at Dalnawillan Lodge. Ignore the track which heads off to the right and carry straight on, past the house at Dalganachan, over Rumsdale Water and on to the junction before The Glutt, which is a series of

buildings. Turn left here and follow the track for a further four miles till you reach the junction beside Lochan nan Bò Riabach. Continue down the valley of Berriedale Water to Braemore.

There is no public transport from here, so you'll have to arrange your own transport if you don't want to retrace your steps. OS sheet No 11 covers the route.

The north coast of Scotland is ideally suited to the more active type of tourist, and 10 miles west of Thurso you might say that the radioactive tourist is catered for at the **Dounreay Nuclear Power Station**. Though its fast breeder reactors were decommissioned in 1994, the plant is still a major local employer and now reprocesses spent nuclear fuel. There's a permanent exhibition at the **visitor centre**, where you learn all about the 'benefits' of nuclear power. ■ *Easter-Sep daily 1000-1700. Free. T01847-802572.*

Sleeping and eating There's some excellent accommodation in **Melvich**, including **D** *Bighouse Lodge*, T01641-531207, open May-Oct, an 18th-century mansion sitting at the mouth of the Halladale River in 4 acres of its own grounds. Also recommended is **E** *Shieling Guest House*, T/F01641-531256, theshieling@btinternet.com, open Apr-Oct.

Thurso

Thurso is the most northerly town on the British mainland and by far the largest settlement on the north coast. In medieval times it was Scotland's chief port for trade with Scandinavia, though most of the town dates from the late 18th century when Sir John Sinclair built the 'new' extension to the old fishing port. The town increased in size to accommodate the workforce of the new nuclear power plant at nearby **Dounreay**, but the plant's demise has

Phone code: 01847
Colour map 2, grid A3
Population: 9,000

threatened the local economy. Today, Thurso is a fairly nondescript place, mostly visited by people catching the ferry to Stromness in Orkney.

Ins & outs **Getting there** There are daily buses to and from **Inverness** which connect with buses to **Edinburgh**. There are regular daily buses to and from **Wick airport** (see page 287). **Ferries** to Stromness in Orkney leave from Scrabster, 2 miles north of Thurso (see page 356), and a bus service runs between **Thurso train station** and **Scrabster ferry pier**. The **train station** is at the south end of Princes St, 500 yds from the TIC (see below). There are daily trains from **Inverness**.

The **Tourist Information Centre** is on Riverside Rd, T892371. Open Apr-Oct Mon-Sat 0900-1800, also Sun 1000-1800 in Jul and Aug. They have a leaflet on local surfing beaches.

Sights There's little of real interest in the town centre. Near the harbour are the 17th-century ruins of **Old St Peter's Church**, which stand on the site of the original 13th-century church founded by the Bishop of Caithness. In the town hall on the High Street is the **Heritage Museum**, which features some Pictish carved stones. ■ *Jun-Sep Mon-Sat 1000-1300 and 1400-1700. £0.50. T892459.*

Thurso is also known to keen surfers who come here for the unbeatable surf. To the east of town, at **Dunnet Bay**, is a three-mile-long beach with an excellent reef break and there's another good reef break at **Brims Ness** to the west. Further west, at **Strathy Bay** (see above) you'll find rollers that can match anything in Hawaii (though the water's a lot colder).

Thurso

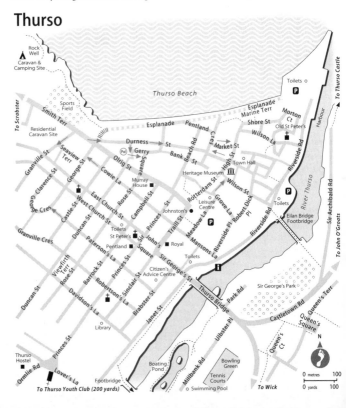

A reasonable bet is the huge **B** *Royal Hotel*, Traill St, T893191. 102 rooms. Upgraded to include indoor pool and leisure facilities and central. The nicest place to stay, though, is the **A** *Forss Country House Hotel*, T861201, jamie@forsshouse.freeserve.co.uk, 4 miles out of town at Bridge of Forss. This small family-run hotel is set in 20 acres of lovely woodland and has an excellent restaurant, open to non-residents (mid-range to expensive). There are lots of cheap B&Bs, including: **E** *Murray House*, 1 Campbell St, T895759, murrayhouse.thurso@bigfoot.com; **E** *Annandale*, 2 Rendel Govan Rd, T893942, thomson@annandale2.freeserve.co.ul; and **E** *Mrs C Murray*, 1 Granville Cresent, T892993. Thurso also has 3 independent hostels: **F** *Sandra's Backpackers*, 24-26 Princes St, T894575; **F** *Thurso Hostel*, Ormlie Lodge, Ormlie Rd, T/F896888; and **F** *Thurso Youth Club*, Old Mill, Millbank, T892964, open 1 Jul-30 Aug. The nearest **campsite** is *Thurso Camping Site*, T607771, north of town on the road to Scrabster.

Sleeping
Thurso boasts a wide variety of accommodation, most of it fairly average

The best place to eat in town is *The Upper Deck* in Scrabster, T892814, by the harbour. It has a mid-range surf'n'turf menu. Other than that, your best bet is a bar meal at the *Pentland Hotel*, T893202. A decent café is *Johnston's* on Traill St. There are also the ubiquitous Indian and Chinese restaurants and fish and chip shops. Out of town is the *Forss Country House Hotel* (see above) and *The Bower Inn*, T01955-661292, between Thurso and Wick. To get there, turn off the coast road at Castletown and follow the B876 till you see the sign for Gillock.

Eating

Cinema At *Viking Bowl*. **Bowling** *Viking Bowl*, Ormlie Rd, T895050. **Swimming** Millbank Rd, T893260.

Entertainment

Bus *Citylink* buses run to and from **Inverness** (3 ½ hrs) 4 times daily, T0870-5505050, continuing to Scrabster to connect with the ferries to and from Stromness in Orkney. *Citylink* buses to Inverness connect with buses to **Edinburgh**. *Highland Country Buses*, T01847-893123, run local services to **Bettyhill** (3 times daily Mon-Thu, twice on Sat; 1 hr 10 mins) and to **Reay** (4 times daily Mon-Thu, 3 times on Sat). There are regular daily buses to and from **Wick** via **Halkirk** or Castletown. *Highland Country Buses* also run the service between **Thurso train station** and **Scrabster ferry pier** (5-10 mins). *Harrold Coaches*, T01955-631295, runs a service to and from **John O'Groats** (4 times daily Mon-Thu, twice on Sat; 1 hr). There's also a *Postbus* service to **Wick airport**, leaving Riverside Rd at 0920 and arriving at 1000.

Transport
Buses arrive at Sir George's St Port Office and depart from Sir George's St Church

Car hire *William Dunnett & Co*, T893101. **Cycle hire** *The Bike & Camping Shop*, the Arcade, 34 High St, T896124, rents mountain bikes for £8 per day.

Ferry To **Stromness** in Orkney leave from Scrabster, 2 miles north of Thurso. For details, see page 356).

Train Three trains leave daily from **Inverness** (3 ½ hrs), 2 of them connecting with the ferries from Scrabster to **Stromness** in Orkney. Trains continue to **Wick** (30 mins) and return trains to Inverness leave from Wick.

Dunnett Head and John O'Groats

About 10 miles northeast of Thurso is the most northerly point on the British mainland. No, not John O'Groats, but Dunnet Head. It's reached by turning off the Thurso-John O'Groats road at Dunnett, at the east end of **Dunnett Bay**, a three-mile-long sandy beach that's popular with surfers who come to tackle the gigantic waves of the **Pentland Firth**, the wild and treacherous strait between the mainland and Orkney.

Dunnett
*Phone code: 01847
Colour map 2, grid A3/4*

North & Northwest Highlands

It's a much nicer place than John O'Groats, with marvellous views across to Orkney and along the entire north coast (on a clear day). There's a Victorian lighthouse out at the point and the dramatic seacliffs are teeming with seabirds. There's also a great little café, the *Dunnett Head Tearoom*, T851774, a few miles from the lighthouse, which serves cheap snacks and meals (open daily April-October 1500-2000).

John O'Groats
Phone code: 01955
Colour map 2, grid A4

If you still feel inclined to visit this dreary tourist trap, then that's your prerogative, but don't say we didn't warn you. It's boring at best and pretty miserable most of the time. It gets its name from the Dutchman Jan de Groot, who was commissioned by King James IV to run a ferry service to Orkney in 1496. Ferries still operate from here to Burwick in Orkney (see Transport below). There's a **Tourist Information Centre** here (T611373, open April-October Monday-Saturday 0900-1700), as well as a post office, craft shops and a chippie.

Two miles east of John O'Groats is **Duncansby Head**, which is far more rewarding. South of the headland a path leads to the spectacular **Duncansby Stacks**, a series of dramatic rock formations. The 200-ft cliffs are home to countless seabirds and you can see the narrow, sheer-sided inlets known locally as *geos*.

Sleeping and eating **C** *John O'Groats House Hotel*, T611203, which has a restaurant. There are also several B&Bs, including the very decent **E** *Bencorragh House*, at Upper Gills in Canisbay, a few miles west, T611449, bartonsandy@hotmail.com, open Mar-Oct. Also in Canisbay is the **F** *SYHA Youth Hostel*, T611424, open 19 Mar-31 Oct. There are a couple of **campsites**, at John O'Groats and further west by the beach at Huna. The tourist office will help you find accommodation.

Tours There are also **Orkney Islands Day Tours**, which leave daily 1 May-30 Sep at 0900, and return at 1945 (£33 per person, under 16 half price). A shorter day tour departs daily from 1 Jun-2 Sep 1030, and returns at 1800 (£30 per person, under 16 £8). There's also a wildlife cruise 20 Jun-31 Aug, which departs at 1430; £12 per person. Contact: *John O'Groats Ferries*, Ferry Office, John O'Groats, T611353, F611301, www.jogferry.co.uk Tours also leave from Inverness.

Transport There are **buses** to John O'Groats from Thurso (see above under Thurso), and from **Wick** (5 daily Mon-Fri, 4 on Sat) with *Highland Country Buses*.

Ferries to Burwick (Orkney) sail twice daily from May to September (45 mins, £16 one way). A connecting bus takes passengers on to Kirkwall (40 mins; £25 off-peak return).

The East Coast

*The east coast of the Highlands, from Inverness north to Wick, doesn't have the same draw as the west coast and attracts far fewer visitors, but it has its own, gentler appeal, and there are many lovely little seaside towns to explore. The sea lochs and estuaries of the inner **Moray Firth** are fringed with fields and woods, a fertile lowland landscape dotted with farms and crofts. Fast-flowing rivers drop from the hills through deep, wooded straths. The bulk of **Ben Wyvis** dominates the horizon northwest of Dingwall.*

Across the **Dornoch Firth** is Sutherland – the south land of the Norsemen – where the coastal strip of fertile land narrows towards Helmsdale, backed by heather-clad hills deep blue in the reflective sea light. Prehistoric sites are abundant throughout East Sutherland as are Pictish sculptured stones in Easter Ross. The seagoing Norsemen of Orkney used the firths to extend Viking influence into the Pictish lands, lured by good land and timber for shipbuilding. Dingwall was their *Thingvallr* – or place of assembly. Many existing villages grew up around Celtic Christian missions of the seventh or eighth centuries. From the 11th-century **Tain** was an important place of pilgrimage, and the cathedrals at **Dornoch** and **Fortrose**, and **Fearn Abbey**, date from the 13th century.

Few roads existed before the late 18th century. Land routes, like the road over Struie, were drove roads on which cattle, the mainstay of the Highland economy, were walked to market. Travel by sea was easier and firths were crossed by ferry. The fast track across bridges and causeways is a recent phenomenon, although the building of the **Kessock Bridge**, linking Inverness and the Black Isle, was foreseen in the 17th century by the Brahan Seer, a local prophet (see below).

Diverse sea life flourishes in an offshoot of the Gulf Stream, attracting seals, whales, porpoises and a diminishing colony of dolphins, which is carefully monitored and researched. The sea has long provided a living from salmon netting around the river mouths, fishing for herring and cod, shipping and, most recently, oil.

The Black Isle

Across the Kessock Bridge from Inverness is the Black Isle, which is neither an island nor black. It shares with the Moray coast long hours of sunshine and low rainfall, rolling acres of barley and stately woods of oak and beech dropping down to the shores. It also has a compelling atmosphere – a combination perhaps of its soft microclimate, lush vegetation and attractive architecture. Its main attractions are the picturesque town of **Cromarty** and **Chanonry Point**, on the southern side near Rosemarkie, which is one of the best **dolphin-spotting** sites in Europe.

Phone code: 01381
Colour map 2,
grid C2

On the north side of the Kessock Bridge is the **North Kessock Tourist Information Centre**, T01463-731505; open daily from Easter to October. Next door is the **Dolphin and Seal Visitor Centre**, which gives details of accredited dolphin cruises. You can see dolphins from the village of **North Kessock** just to the south.

One of the many sacred wells (and caves) in the area is the unmissable **Clootie Well**, on the verge of the main road between Tore and Munlochy Bay Nature Reserve. It was once blessed by St Curitan (see below under Rosemarkie) and is thought to cure sick children. Thousands of rags still flutter from the surrounding trees, though well-worshippers are in danger of being mown down by traffic. Despite the presence of traffic, it's an eerie place. Go at night, if you dare.

Clootie Well

Further east on this road, beyond **Munlochy** and **Avoch** (pronounced 'Och') is the village of **Fortrose**, on the east shore. The magnificent **cathedral** at Fortrose is now largely a ruin where rainwashed carved faces of rose-coloured sandstone peer down from roof bosses, and snapped-off stumps of window tracery are redolent of Reformation vandalism. On the golf course at **Chanonry Point**, overlooking the Moray Firth, a plaque marks the spot where the **Brahan Seer** was boiled in a barrel of tar (see box). Chanonry Point is also a great place for seeing **dolphins**. They come close to shore at high tide and there's a good chance of seeing them leaping above the waves.

Fortrose & Chanonry Point

North & Northwest Highlands

A seerious crime

The Brahan Seer was boiled in a barrel of tar in 1660 but not before he had foretold the building of the Caledonian Canal and Kessock Bridge, the Highland Clearances and the Second World War. He also predicted the demise of the local lairds and the Seaforths. It was Lady Seaforth who ordered his execution, after the seer had a vision of her husband in the arms of another woman. Apparently the precise spot where he met his end is now the 13th hole of the golf course at Chanonry Point, which just goes to prove that it is indeed unlucky for some.

Rosemarkie A few miles from Fortrose on the north side of Chanonry Point is the tiny village of **Rosemarkie**. Celtic saints Curitan and Boniface selected this sheltered spot on the southern shore for their Christian mission in the seventh century. St Boniface is remembered at nearby St Bennet's Well. **Groam Museum** houses a superb collection of Pictish sculptured stones found locally, imaginatively displayed alongside contemporary artwork inspired by them. A year-round programme of events and lectures is devoted to the study of Pictish culture. ■ *Easter-Sep Mon-Sat 1000-1700, Sun 1400-1630; Oct-Apr Sat and Sun 1400-1600. Adult £1.50, concession £1, children £0.50 . T620961.*

Beware of fairies, last sighted in the 1970's in **Fairy Glen**, now a nature reserve. A lovely marked trail leads into the glen from the top end of the High Street, through a wooded gorge where you may spot woodpeckers and treecreepers. A couple of places to eat in Rosemarkie are *Crofters*, T620844, on the seafront, which does cheap bar meals, and the *Plough Inn*, near the museum.

Cromarty

Phone code: 01381
Cromarty has its own website: www.cali.co.uk/ highexp/Cromarty

On the northeastern tip of the Black Isle Peninsula, at the mouth of the Cromarty Firth, is the gorgeous village of Cromarty, one of the east coast's major attractions. Its neat white-harled houses interspersed with gracious merchants' residences are almost unchanged since the 18th century when it was a sea port thriving on trade as far afield as Russia and the Baltic. Many emigrants bound for the New World embarked here. A prosperity based on textiles and fishing led to decline and dereliction.

Ins & outs There are regular daily **buses** from **Inverness** and a bus service twice a week to and from **Dingwall**.

Sights Although restored and much inhabited, Cromarty now has the atmosphere of a backwater, but a very attractive one at that, where you feel as if you're stepping back in time, in stark contrast to the numerous oil rigs moored on the opposite shore in **Nigg Bay** (see below).

For a fascinating insight into the history of the area, visit the 18th-century **Cromarty Courthouse**, in Church Street, which houses the town's museum. ■ *Apr-Oct daily 1000-1700; Nov, Dec and Mar daily 1200-1600. Adult £3, concession/children £2; includes loan of headset for recorded tour of the town's other historic buildings. T600418.*

Next to the courthouse is the thatch-roofed **Hugh Miller's Cottage**, birthplace of the eminent local geologist and author. ■ *1 May-30 Sep daily 1100-1300 and 1400-1700 (Sun afternoon only). Aqdult £2.50, concession £1.70, family ticket £7. T600245.* Also worth seeing is the elegant 17th-century **East Church**.

There's a good walk along a coastal path from the east end of the village through woodland to the top of the South Sutor headland, one of the two steep headlands guarding the narrow entrance to the Cromarty Firth. There are excellent views from here across the Moray Firth. Leaflets describing this and other local walks are available at the Cromarty Courthouse.

One of Cromarty's main attractions is its **dolphins**. They can be seen from the shore, or with a **boat trip**, but make sure you go with an accredited operator, such as *Dolphin Ecosse*, T600323. Full-day or half-day trips leave from the harbour and you can see porpoises and seals as well as dolphins, and perhaps even killer whales further out.

To the west, the mudflats of **Udale Bay**, are an RSPB reserve and a haven for wading birds and wintering duck and geese which can be viewed from a hide. In the winter other birds such as pinkfooted geese and whooper swans use the bay as a roost. **Poyntzfield Herb Garden** is an organic plant nursery specializing in rare and native medicinal herbs. Worth visiting if only for a glimpse of the house and the view from the car park over the Cromarty Firth through massive beech trees.

For such an appealing place, there's precious little accommodation. The best place to stay is the **C** *Royal Hotel*, on Marine Terr, T600217, royalcrom@cali.co.uk It has a good restaurant and cheaper meals are available in the bar. There are a couple of B&Bs, including the very good **E** *Beechfield House* at 4 Urquhart Court, T600308, beechfield@cali.co.uk Another good place to eat is *Thistle's Restaurant* on Church St, T600471, which has a moderately priced and imaginative menu, including interesting vegetarian dishes. A great place for tea and scones is *Binnie's Tearoom* on Church St. For cheap bar food try the *Cromarty Arms*, opposite the Cromarty Courthouse, which also has live music some nights.

Sleeping & eating
It's advisable to book ahead during the summer

A 2-car **ferry** crosses to **Nigg** every half hour from Apr to Oct, 0900-1800. *Highland Bus & Coach*, T01463-233371, runs a **bus** service from **Inverness** to Fortrose and Cromarty (4-7 times daily Mon-Sat). There is also a bus service to and from **Dingwall** on Wed and Thu.

Transport

Strathpeffer

Strathpeffer gets busy in the summer with coach parties but it's a pleasant place and there are some excellent walks in the surrounding hills. The little village gained recognition in 1819 when Dr Morrison, a physician from Aberdeen bathed in its sulphur springs and cured himself of rheumatoid arthritis. He quickly spread the word and Strathpeffer became a fashionable spa resort attracting thousands of visitors. Two world wars intervened and the town's popularity declined. Today the only reminder of its past is the **Water Sampling Pavilion** in the square where you can test the waters.

Phone code: 01997
Colour map 2, grid C1
Population: 1,384

There are regular **buses** between Strathpeffer and **Dingwall** (see below). There's a seasonal Tourist Information Centre, on the main square, T421415; open Easter-Nov Mon-Sat 1000-1700.

Ins & outs

Just outside Strathpeffer on the road to Dingwall is the **Highland Museum of Childhood** which has many historical displays on childhood in the highlands, as well as collections of dolls, toys and games. ■ *Mar-Oct Mon-Sat 1000-1700, Sun 1400-1700; Jul and Aug Mon-Thu 1000-1700 and 1900-2100, Sat 1000-1700, Sun 1400-1700. Adult £1.50, concession £1, family ticket £3.50. T421031.*

North & Northwest Highlands

Walks around
Strathpeffer
OS Landranger No 26

A fine walk is to **Knock Farrel and the Touchstone Maze**, site of an Iron Age vitrified fort which lies at the north end of a ridge known locally as the **Cat's Back**. A marked trail starts from Blackmuir Wood car park. Head up the hill from town, turn left up a road immediately before the youth hostel, and the car park is on the left. The walk is six miles in total and takes about three hours. Aside from OS Landranger sheet 26, the route is also described in a Forestry Commission leaflet *Forests of Easter Ross*, available from tourist offices.

Another excellent side trip is to **Rogie Falls**, near Contin, which is three miles southwest of Strathpeffer on the main A835 Inverness-Ullapool road. The short walk up to the falls starts from the car park three miles north of Contin on the A835. There are also some pleasant woodland walks around here. Experienced hikers can tackle magnificent **Ben Wyvis** (3,432 ft). The route to the summit starts four miles north of **Garve**, seven miles northwest of Contin.

Sleeping

The best accommodation is in **Contin**, 3 miles southwest of Strathpeffer. Top of the list is the excellent **B** *Coull House Hotel*, T421487, www.milford.co.uk/go/coulhouse.html, an elegant 19th-century country house offering fine food. There are several **B&Bs** in Contin, including the very grand-looking **E** *Taigh an Eilein*, T421009, lorna.mac@talk21.com, open Apr-Sep. In Strathpeffer itself is the **C** *Brunstane Lodge Hotel*, on Golf Course Rd, T421261, open Mar-Dec, which serves decent cheap bar meals. There are many good value B&Bs in Strathpeffer, including: **D** *Inver Lodge*, T421392, open Mar-Dec, **E** *White Lodge*, T421730, walter_fleming@lineone.net, open Apr-Oct, and the elegant **D-E** *Craigvar*, on the Square, T421622, www.craigvar.com

Dingwall and the Cromarty Firth

Phone code: 01349
Colour map 2,
grid C1

Dingwall, at the head of the Cromarty Firth, has two major claims to fame. Not only is it believed to be the birthplace of Macbeth, it was also the home for many years of **Neil Gunn** (1891-1973), perhaps the Highlands' greatest literary figure (see also page 285). It's a fairly dull, though functional town, with good shops and banks (with ATMs) lining its long main street. The **Dingwall Museum** tells the history of this Royal Burgh. ■ *May-Sep Mon-Sat 1000-1700. Adult £1.50, concession £1, children £0.50. T865366.*

East of Dingwall, before **Evanton**, is **Clanland and Sealpoint**, which has history and wildlife exhibitions and offers the chance to see the local seal population. ■ *Daily all year 0930-1730. T830033.* Standing on a hill above Evanton is the **Fyrish Monument**, a replica of the Gate of Negapatam in India, built by local men and funded by local military hero, Sir Hector Munro, to commemorate his capture of the Indian town, in 1781. To get there, turn off the B9176 towards Boath. It's a stiff two-hour climb up to the top.

The Cromarty Firth is a centre for repairing North Sea oil rigs and many of the villages along its north shore have benefited from the oil industry. One of these is **Invergordon**, just west of Nigg Bay, which has suffered in recent years due to the closure of the local aluminium factory.

Beyond Invergordon, a road branches south to **Nigg Ferry**. The ferry from Cromarty to Nigg was once a major thoroughfare, and now a tiny two-car ferry makes the 20-minute crossing in the summer months (see **Cromarty** above). From the ferry you get a good view of **Nigg Bay**, a vast natural harbour used in both world wars by the Royal Navy. Its entry is guarded by the dramatic headlands of the Sutors, identified in folklore as friendly giants. Also gigantic are the oil rigs ranged along the firth and the oil terminal at Nigg, a dramatic and not unpleasant contrast with Lilliputian Cromarty. Away from the shore, in **Nigg Old Church** (1626) is an old Pictish cross slab. ■ *Daily Easter-Oct 1000-1630.*

If you need to stay in **Dingwall**, the smartest place around is **B** *Tulloch Castle Hotel*, **Sleeping**
T861325, a castle dating from the 12th century. There's hostel accommodation in
Evanton at the *Blackrock Bunkhouse*, T830917, open 1 Apr-31 Oct.

Dingwall is on the rail line between **Inverness** and **Kyle of Lochalsh** and **Thurso**. There **Transport**
are several **trains** daily in each direction (30 mins to Inverness). There are hourly **buses**
between **Inverness** and **Invergordon**, via Dingwall. There are also hourly buses
between Inverness and Dingwall via **Muir of Ord**. There are buses between Dingwall
and **Rosemarkie** (twice a day Mon-Thu) and between Dingwall and **Cromarty** (Wed
and Thu).

Tain

Squeezed between the Cromarty Firth to the south and the Dornoch Firth to   *Phone code: 01862*
the north is the **Tain Peninsula**, whose largest town is Tain. It has an impres-   *Colour map 2, grid B2*
sive historical portfolio. Its backstreets are an intriguing jigsaw of imposing   *Population: 4,110*
merchants' houses, steep vennels, secret gardens and dormer windows.

Tain is on the **Inverness-Thurso** rail line and there are **trains** daily in each direction.   **Ins & outs**
There are also daily **buses** between to and from Inverness and Thurso.

Tain was the birthplace of the 11th-century missionary **St Duthac**. Pilgrims   **Sights**
flocked here in the Middle Ages to his shrine and a ruin near the links is   *Tain is a place*
thought to be the original **chapel**. His head and heart, encapsulated in gold   *with a 1950's*
and silver reliquaries, were later kept in the still extant medieval **Collegiate**   *time-warp feel*
church until their disappearance during the Reformation. The shrine was
much favoured by the Stewart kings, notably James IV who on one of his frequent pilgrimages reputedly approached walking penitentially barefoot along
the King's Causeway. Tain's status as a place of sanctuary probably explains
why Bruce's family fled here during the Wars of Independence.

The Collegiate church is on Castle Brae, just off the High Street, and inside
is a 17th-century panel painted with the badges of the trade guilds, a reminder
of the town's busy international trade. Another reminder is the imposing
16th-century **Tolbooth** in the High Street. Next to the church is a **museum**
housed in the Pilgrimage which charts the town's medieval history in the **Tain**
through Time exhibition. ■ *Apr-Oct daily 1000-1800; Nov, Dec and Mar*
1200-1600. Adult £3.50, concession £2.50. T894089.

One of Tain's main attractions is the **Glenmorangie whisky distillery**, just
off the A9 to the north of town, where you can see how the world-famous
whisky is made and try a sample. ■ *All year Mon-Thu 0900-1700; Jun-Aug also*
Sat 1000-1600 and Sun 1200-1600. Tours from 1030-1530. Adult £2. T892477.

Also out of town, just to the south off the A9, is the **Aldie Water Mill**, a
restored 16th-century mill in working order, with various high-quality craft
shops attached. Nearby is **The Tain Pottery**, which you can also visit. ■ *Daily*
1000-1700. T893786.

There are several grand hotels in and around Tain. **L** *Mansfield House Hotel*, Scotsburn   **Sleeping**
Rd, T892052, www.mansfield-house.co.uk 19th-century baronial splendour and   **& eating**
superb cuisine. Restaurant also open to non-residents (mid-range to expensive).
There's the excellent value **C** *Morangie House Hotel*, on Morangie Rd, T892281. It's
popular locally for its food (mid-range) and is open for lunch and dinner. There are also
more modest B&B options, such as **E** *Golf View House*, at 13 Knockbreck Rd, T892856,
www.golfview.co.uk

North & Northwest Highlands

Shopping *Brown's Gallery*, Castle Brae. Showcases work by Highland artists. Local mussels can be bought from *Bannerman's*, a fish and seafood wholesalers.

Transport Tain is on the **Inverness-Thurso** rail line and there are 3 **trains** daily in each direction. *Citylink* **buses** between Inverness and Thurso pass through Tain 4 times a day. There are also buses to **Portmahomack** (4 times daily Mon-Thu), **Balintore** (5-6 times daily Mon-Sat), **Lairg** via **Bonar Bridge** (3 times daily Mon-Sat) and **Dornoch** via **Bonar Bridge** (once a day Mon-Thu) with *Inverness Traction*, T01463-239292, and *Rapson's of Brora*, T01408-621245.

Around Tain

The town of Tain serves a vast hinterland. Inland the hills are little-visited backwoods and farm towns, narrow valleys lined with crofts where cattle graze in boggy haughs and, to the west, glens and moorland. Along the seaboard are the windswept fields of the **Tarbat Peninsula**. Good sea angling is to be had from the harbours of the otherwise dull coastal villages such as **Balintore**, and at **Shandwick** is a massive Pictish stone. It is said that unbaptized children were buried near the stone which is now in the Museum of Scotland in Edinburgh.

Portmahomack The seaside village of Portmahomack, or 'port of Colman', is named after the
Colour map 2, missionary who was keen as mustard to found a religious settlement here.
grid B2 Archaeological work is revealing the importance of this area in Pictish times. The **Tarbat Discovery Centre**, T871790, in Tarbat Old Church displays recently discovered Pictish stonecarving. From the harbour, with its 18th-century girnals (grain warehouses) and sheltered sandy beach, you can see a huge stretch of the Sutherland coast, and the great sandbanks – the 'gizzen brigs' – at the mouth of the Dornoch Firth. Boat trips are available from the harbour for sea angling. A worthwhile trip is out to **Tarbat Ness lighthouse**, about three miles north.

Eating A great place to eat out here is *The Oyster Catcher*, T871560, small café-restaurant serving snacks and lunches and dinner from 1930 (if booked). Crêpes are a speciality, but it also does pasta, seafood and fish.

Hill of Fearn South from Portmahomack, just west of the junction of the B9165 and the B9166,
Colour map 2, is Hill of Fearn. **Fearn Abbey** was moved here around 1250 from its original site
grid C2 near Edderton, where it was too vulnerable to sea raiders. It later became the parish church, but in 1742 lightning struck the roof which fell in, killing 38 Sunday worshippers. A tragedy was preceded by a fairy harbinger sighted at nearby Loch Eye. In Hill of Fearn is the excellent **Anta Factory Shop**, one of the very best places in the country for classy tartan furnishing fabrics, as well as tartan rugs and throws, and pottery. ■ *Mon-Sat 1000-1700 (also Sun 1000-1600 Jun-Sep).*

The Dornoch Firth

Colour map 2, Fairies were said to cross the Dornoch Firth on cockle shells and were once
grid B2 seen building a bridge of fairy gold, perhaps a forerunner of the Dornoch Bridge which carries the A9 across the firth just north of Tain. A more pleasant and interesting route is to follow the A836 along the south shore. From **The Struie**, reached by the B9176 which branches south at Easter Fearn, there's a panoramic view over the Dornoch Firth and the Sutherland hills. In the

churches of **Edderton** and **Kincardine** are Pictish stones. Another stands in a field northwest of Edderton, but don't disturb the crops or livestock. A quartz boulder at **Ardgay**, the 'Clach Eiteag', commemorates the cattle tryst and fair which once took place locally.

Ten miles from Ardgay, at the end of lovely **Strathcarron**, is the isolated **Croick church**, one of most poignant reminders of the infamous Clearances. Here, in 1845, 90 local folk took refuge in the churchyard after they had been evicted from their homes in Glencalvie by the Duke of Sutherland to make way for flocks of sheep. A reporter from *The Times* described the 'wretched spectacle' as men, women and children were carted off, many never to return. The report is there to read. Far more evocative and harrowing, though, are the names and messages the people scratched in spidery copperplate in the window panes.

Croik Church

North of Ardgay is the **Kyle of Sutherland**, where several rivers converge to flood into the sea through lush water meadows. Montrose was defeated here, at **Carbisdale**, in 1651. Overlooking the Kyle, at **Culrain**, is the 19th-century **Carbisdale Castle**, once home of the exiled King of Norway, which now houses the largest and most sumptuous **F** *Youth Hostel* in Scotland, and possibly anywhere else, T01549-421232. It's open 26 February-31 October (except the first two weeks in May). Trains between Inverness and Thurso stop at Ardgay and Culrain. The youth hostel is half a mile up a steep hill from the station. Buses between Inverness and Lairg (see below) stop in Ardgay and Bonar Bridge.

Culrain

After the Dornoch Ferry disaster of 1809, a bridge was built over the Kyle at **Bonar Bridge**, from where the A949 runs eastwards to join the main A9 just before Dornoch, while the A836 continues north to Lairg (see below). A few miles north of **Invershin** are the **Falls of Shin**, an excellent place to watch salmon battling upstream on their way to spawning grounds (best seen June to September). A visitor centre and café/restaurant/shop, has information about six easy walks in the immediate area; all under an hour long. The café/restaurant serves good, cheap food daily till 1730.

Bonar Bridge
& Invershin

Lairg

Eleven miles north of Bonar Bridge is the uninspiring village of Lairg, the region's main transport hub. Lairg is best known for its annual lamb sale, when young sheep from all over the north of Scotland are bought and sold.

Phone code: 01549
Colour map 2, grid B1

It is said that all roads meet at Lairg and it's certainly a hard place to avoid. From here, the A839 heads east to meet the A9 between Dornoch and Golspie, and west to meet the A837 which runs out to Lochinver. The A836 heads north to Tongue, and south to Bonar Bridge. The A838 meanwhile heads northwest to Laxford Bridge and on to Durness, near Cape Wrath. **Trains** between **Inverness** and **Thurso** stop at Lairg and **buses** run from here to **Ullapool**.

There's a **Tourist Information Centre**, T402160, which is open Mon-Sat 0900-1700 and Sun 1300-1700.

Ins & outs

There are several interesting walks around the village, some of which lead to prehistoric sites such as the Neolithic hut circles at nearby **Ord Hill**. These walks, and many others in the region, are described, with maps, in the Forestry Commission's leaflet *Forests of the Far North* (50p), which is available at the Ferrycroft Countryside Centre and the TIC.

North & Northwest Highlands

North & Northwest Highlands

Sleeping & eating There's a bank with ATM in the village and several places to stay, including **D-E** *The Nip Inn*, on the main street, T402243, info@nipinn.co.uk, which also does bar meals. There are several **B&Bs** and a **campsite** too, but the most interesting place to stay is 9 miles east at **Rogart** train station, where you can get cheap hostel accommodation at the *Rogart Railway Carriages*, T01408-641343, rogmail@globalnet.co.uk Two old rail carriages have been converted to sleep 16 people and there's a 10% discount for bike or train users.

Transport **Trains** between **Inverness** and **Thurso** stop at Lairg and Rogart stations 3 times daily. *Inverness Traction* **buses**, T01463-239292, run from here to **Ullapool**, with connections to **Lochinver** and **Durness**, from May to early Oct (Mon-Sat). Lairg is also the central point for several *postbus* routes, T01463-256228.

Dornoch

Phone code: 01862
Colour map 2, grid B2

Dornoch is another architectural gem with its deep, golden sandstone houses and leafy cathedral square. Bishop Gilbert of Moravia (Moray) built the cathedral circa 1245. His family's success in gaining a foothold in Northeast Scotland against the Norsemen was rewarded with the Earldom of Sutherland. It was trouble with the Jarls which prompted Gilbert to move his power base here from Caithness, mindful that his predecessor had been boiled in butter by the locals.

Ins & outs Getting there There are **buses** to and from **Inverness** (hourly Mon-Sat, 5 times on Sun). *Citylink buses* between Inverness and **Thurso** also stop in Dornoch 4 daily.
The **Tourist Information Centre**, T810400, is on the main square. Open Mon-Sat 0900-1300 and 1400-1700.

Sights The 13th-century **cathedral** was badly damaged in 1570, then subjected to an ill-conceived 'restoration' by the Countess of Sutherland in 1835. Among the few surviving features is a series of gargoyles, including a green man, and the effigy of an unknown knight. ■ *Mon-Fri 0730-2000. You can climb the cathedral tower during Jul and Aug.* Opposite the cathedral is the 16th-century **Bishop's Palace**, now a hotel (see below).

Nowadays, Dornoch is famous for its links **golf course**, rated as one of the world's finest and relatively easy to get on. It overlooks miles of dunes and pristine sandy beach. A stone near the links marks the spot where the last **witch** in Scotland was burned, in 1722. Folklore recounts a bloody battle on the beach at **Embo**, just to the north, against raiding Vikings in 1259 in which Sir Richard Murray was killed. The battle is commemorated at the **Earl's Cross**. Trout fishing is available on Dornoch Lochans; enquire locally.

Straggling crofting townships such as **Rogart** (see above) are scattered through the glens and around the coast, all occupied and worked vigorously. The coastal population was swollen in the 19th century by tenants evicted from the inland glens, resettled here and encouraged to try fishing at such villages as **Embo**. Others joined the eager flood of emigrants to the New World already under way. Crofting tenancies still exist but crofters now enjoy more protection (see page 328).

North of Dornoch is **Loch Fleet**, a river estuary with a ferocious tide race at its mouth and an SNH reserve protecting rare birds and plants. The rotting skeletons of the fishing fleet abandoned in the First World War lie in the sand on the south shore west of the car park. Nearby **Skibo Castle** is where Madonna and Guy Ritchie tied the knot, in relative secrecy. It is an exclusive club, but details of accommodation are available from the Dornoch tourist office. There are several walks in the forestry plantations in the area.

There's plenty of accommodation in Dornoch, which can be booked at the tourist **Sleeping** office. **B-D** *Dornoch Castle Hotel*, T810216, www.dornochcastle.com, open Apr-Oct. Formerly the Bishop's Palace, this 16th-century building is full of character and boasts excellent food (expensive). Another fine hotel is **L** *The Royal Golf Hotel*, T/F810283, scotland@morton-hotels.demon.co.uk, next to the first tee. There are also lots of good B&Bs and a **campsite**.

Apart from the hotels listed above, a good place to dine is *The Two Quails*, on Castle St, **Eating** where you can enjoy an expensive but top-class dinner cooked by a chef trained at the *Ritz*. Next door is *Luigi's*, for excellent coffee and a range of exotic ice creams.

Bookshops *The Dornoch Bookshop* on the High St, T810165, is the only bookshop in **Shopping** the area and stocks local books.

Golspie

There is little to recommend the dull little town of Golspie, though it does have a couple of banks and supermarkets. There's an 18-hole golf course and the *Orcadian Stone Company* has a large display of fossils and geological specimens from the Highlands and beyond.

Phone code: 01408
Colour map 2, grid B2
Population: 1,650

The town lives in the dark shadow of the Sutherlands. On **Beinn a'Bhraggaidh** (1,293 ft), to the southwest, is a huge, 100 ft-high **monument** to the Duke of Sutherland. Those who make it up to the monument and who know something of the Duke's many despicable acts may find the inscription risible, as it describes him as "a judicious, kind and liberal landlord". There's no reference to the fact that he forcibly evicted 15,000 tenants from his estate. Not surprisingly, locals would like to see this eyesore removed from the landscape, broken into tiny pieces and then scattered far and wide. Unfortunately, they have thus far been unsuccessful.

The aptly named Dunrobin Castle, one mile north of the village, is the ancient **Dunrobin** seat of the Dukes of Sutherland, who once owned more land than anyone else **Castle** in the British Empire. Much enlarged and aggrandized in the 19th century with fairy-tale turrets, the enormous 189-room castle, the largest house in the Highlands, is stuffed full of fine furniture, paintings, tapestries and *objets d'art* and bears witness to their obscene wealth. The castle overlooks beautiful gardens laid out with box hedges, ornamental trees and fountains. In stormy weather you should listen to the sea crashing on the beach beyond the walls. The **museum** is an animal-lover's nightmare and almost a caricature of the aristocracy, with a spectacular Victorian taxidermy collection. There are also local antiquities, some from ancient brochs, and Pictish stonecarvings. ■ *1 Apr-31 May and 1-15 Oct Mon-Sat 1030-1630, Sun 1200-1630; 1 Jun-30 Sep Mon-Sat 1030-1730, Sun 1200-1730. Adult £6, students £5, OAPs & children £4.50. T633177.*

Brora

Brora sits at the mouth of the River Brora, which as everywhere on this coast, is the site of a once lucrative salmon netting industry. At the harbour, the ice house is a relic of the herring boom. Coal mines, opened in the 16th century, salt pans and a brickworks are all defunct. Still very much alive, however, is *Hunter's*, the local weavers of heavyweight traditional tweeds and a good place to invest in some natty headwear. A mile or so north of town is the **Clynelish**

Phone code: 01408
Colour map 2, grid B2
Population: 1,860

North & Northwest Highlands

After the Gold Rush

*A short drive from Helmsdale, up the **Strath of Kildonan** (or Strath Ullie), is **Baile an Or** (Gaelic for 'goldfield'), site of the great Sutherland Gold Rush of 1869. It all started after local man Robert Gilchrist returned home from the Australian gold fields only to discover gold here, on his doorstep. His success brought others rushing to Kildonan and soon a shanty town had sprung up to accommodate them.*

Within a year the gold rush was over, but small amounts are still found today. Anyone who fancies their luck can try a bit of gold panning in the Kildonan Burn at Baile an Or, about a mile from Kildonan train station. You can rent out gold panning kits at Strath Ullie Crafts & Fishing Tackle, T821343, opposite the Timespan Heritage Centre in Helmsdale, for £2.50 per day, and licences are free.

distillery. ■ *Tours all year Mon-Thu 0930-1630. £3 per person. T623000.*

Castle Cole in lovely **Strath Brora**, eight miles northwest, is one of several ruined brochs. Another, **Carn Liath** (signposted) is by the main road, three miles south of Brora.

Sleeping & eating Next to each other, overlooking Brora's golf course are **L-A** *The Links & Royal Marine Hotels*, T621252, highlandescape@btinternet.com Among the many B&Bs is **D** *Glenaveron*, on Golf Rd, T/F621601, glenaveron@hotmail.com If you're staying or just passing through don't miss *Capaldi's*, on the High St, for exquisite home-made Italian ice cream.

Helmsdale

Phone code: 01431
Colour map 2,
grid B2

North of Brora is the former herring port of Helmsdale, which gets busy in the summer. The village is most notable for its excellent **Timespan Heritage Centre**, which brings the history of the Highlands to life through a series of high-tech displays, sound effects and an audiovisual programme. ■ *Easter-Oct Mon-Sat 0930-1700, Sun 1400-1700. Adult £3.50, concession £2.80, children £1.75. T821327.*

The centre also includes a model of Barbara Cartland, which may seem incongruous, until you venture across the road to the *La Mirage* tearoom and see the lady herself in the flesh (pink, of course) – or so it seems. The proprietrix is the inimitable Nancy Sinclair, who has modelled herself, and her tearoom, on the queen of romantic novels. The whole effect is pure kitsch and you never know who might pop in for a plate of fish and chips. Barabara Cartland has been holidaying in Helmsdale for over 60 years. ■ *Daily 1200-2045 (till 1900 Dec-Apr).*

Sleeping & eating Another good place to eat is the **B-C** *Navidale House Hotel*, T821258, open Feb-Nov. There are also several **B&Bs**, including **D** *Broomhill House*, T821259, with its distinctive turret, and **E** *Torbuie*, T821424, in Navidale, about a mile south. There's also an *SYHA Youth Hostel*, T821577, open mid-May to early Oct.

Tourist office The tourist office, T821640, is on the south side of the village, by the A9. Apr-Sep Mon-Sat 1000-1700.

Transport Helmsdale is on the Inverness-Wick/Thurso rail line. Buses and trains are the same as for Wick (see below).

Helmsdale to Wick

North from Helmsdale the A9 climbs spectacularly up the **Ord of Caithness** and over the pass enters a desolate, treeless landscape; an area devastated during the Clearances. To get some idea of the hardships people had to endure, stop at the ruined crofting village of **Badbea**, just beyond **Ousdale**. At **Berriedale**, a farm track leads west to the **Wag**, from where you can climb **Morven** (2,313 ft), the highest hill in Caithness, with amazing views across the whole county.

The A9 coast road then drops down into **Dunbeath**, a pleasant little village at the mouth of a small strath (or glen). This was the birthplace of one of Scotland's foremost writers, **Neil Gunn** (1891-1973). His finest works such as *The Silver Darlings* and *Highland River* reflect his experiences of growing up in the northeast and are fascinating accounts of life here during the days of the herring boom, though the sleepy harbour of today is barely recognizable as the erstwhile bustling fishing port. The villages of Dunbeath, and **Latheron** to the north, are included on the *Neil Gunn Trail*, as is the beautiful walk up the glen, described in the leaflet available at the **Dunbeath Heritage Centre**. Here, you can learn all about the life and works of the famous novelist as well as the history of Caithness. ■ *Apr-Sep daily 1100-1700. Adult £1.50, concession £0.50, children free. T731233.* If you fancy something to eat, the D *Dunbeath Hotel*, T731208, does good, cheap bar meals.

Just outside the village is the **Laidhay Croft Museum**, a restored traditional longhouse with stable, house and byre all under the same roof. ■ *Daily Apr-Oct 1000-1800. Adult £1, children £0.50. T 731370.*

Dunbeath
Phone code: 01593

Wick

A century ago Wick was Europe's busiest herring port, its harbour jam-packed with fishing boats and larger ships exporting tons of salted fish to Russia, Scandinavia and the West Indian slave plantations. The fishing industry has long since gone and the demise of the nearby nuclear power station at Douneray has only added to the sense of a place that's past its best. However, there are some interesting archaeological sites in Caithness, as well as the dramatic landscapes, and Wick makes a useful base for exploring the area.

Phone code: 01955
Colour map 2,
grid A4
Population: 8,000

Wick has an **airport**, a few miles north of town, with daily direct flights to and from **Kirkwall** (Orkney), **Sumburgh** (Shetland), **Aberdeen** and **Newcastle**. The train and bus stations are next to each other behind the hospital. There are buses to and from **Inverness** and **Thurso**, and trains to **Inverness**.

The **Tourist Information Centre** is on Whitechapel Rd (just off the High St), T602596. Open all year Mon-Fri 0900-1700, Sun 0900-1300.

Ins & outs
See also Transport on next page

Wick is actually two towns. On one side of the river is Wick proper and on the other is **Pulteneytown**, the model town planned by Thomas Telford for the British Fisheries Society in 1806 to house evicted crofters who came to work here. Now it's one great living museum of fishermen's cottages and derelict sheds and stores around the near-deserted quays. It gives a good idea of the scale of the herring trade during its heyday in the mid-19th century, when over 1,000 boats set sail to catch the 'silver darlings'. Here, on Bank Row is the superb **Wick Heritage Centre**. The highlight of the centre is its massive photographic collection dating from the late 19th century. ■ *May-Sep Mon-Sat 1000-1700. Adult £2, children £0.50. T605393.*

Sights

North & Northwest Highlands

Archaeological sites in Caithness

Caithness is home to some of the most fascinating archaeological sites in the north. Though first occupied some 6000 years ago, the earliest significant remains in Caithness are the chambered cairns dating from the third and fourth millenia BC. These are burial mounds of stone raised around carefully structured circular chambers with narrow entrances passages. The best preserved of these are the **Grey Cairns of Camster**. To get there, head a mile east of **Lybster** on the A9, then turn left onto the minor road leading north to Watten. The cairns are five miles along this road, on the left-hand side. They comprise two enormous prehistoric burial chambers dating from 2500 BC. They are amazingly complete, with corbelled ceilings, and can be entered on hands and knees through narrow passageways. Caithness may lack the impressive henges of other parts of the UK but it does boast a number of stone rows: areas covered by large numbers of small stones arranged in geometric patterns. These are thought to date from circa 2000 BC. The best and most easily accessible is the **Hill o' Many Stones**. To get there, drive nine miles south of Wick. On the A9 and turn right onto a minor road where you see the signpost. A short way up this road is a signposted gate into the field, on the left-hand side. A path leads to the curious fan-shaped configuration of Bronze Age standing stones; 200 of them in 22 rows. No one yet knows their precise purpose but studies have shown that there were once 600 stones here.

There are also a couple of **Pictish Brochs** in Caithness. These were almost entirely unique to the north and northwest of Scotland and were windowless, dry-stone towers, between 3-15 m in height, with a circular ground plan. The walls were hollow in places to allow staircases and small chambers. These were built between 2000 BC and 200 AD, though they continued in use after that time, and were used for both domestic and defensive purposes. There are remains of a broch at **Nybster**, seven miles south of John o' Groats on the A9. Look out for the sign for the harbour and broch on the right heading north. Turn onto the minor road which leads down to a small car park. Follow the path along the cliff-top to the broch, which stands on a headland surrounded by steep cliffs on three sides. Just to the south of here, at **Keiss**, are the remains of another broch.

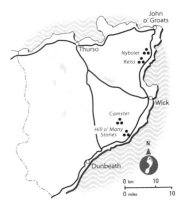

Three miles north of Wick are the impressive 15th-century clifftop ruins of **Sinclair and Girnigoe Castle**. On the A99 heading north out of town is the **Caithness Glass Visitors Centre**, where you can watch the famous glass being blown. ■ *Mon-Thu 0900-1630. The shop is open till 1700. T602286.*

There is a good **walk** along the rocky shore east of town to **The Trinkie**, and about a mile further on to the **Brig o' Trams**. Ask for details at the TIC. Before Wick, at Ulbster, is another archaeological site, the **Cairn o' Get**. Opposite the sign, are the precipitous **Whaligoe Steps**, which lead down to a tiny, picturesque harbour.

Sleeping If you wish to stay in Wick, there's a reasonable selection of hotels such as C *Mackay's Hotel*, Union St, T602323, www.mackayshotel.co.uk, by the roundabout just across the

North & Northwest Highlands

bridge from the town centre. But you're better off going for the excellent **A-B** *Portland Arms Hotel*, about 15 miles south, in Lybster, T01593-721208, www.portlandarms.co.uk A 19th-century coaching inn, full of character and offering great food (mid-range to expensive). The best of the guesthouses and B&Bs are **E** *Wellington Guest House*, 41-43 High St, T603287, open Mar-Oct, and **E** *The Clachan*, on South Rd, T605384. Also good value is **E** *Greenvoe*, George St, near the town centre, T603942.

The best places to eat are also out of town. These include *The Bower Inn* (see page 273), and the *Old Smiddy Inn*, in Thrumster, 5 miles south of Wick, T651256, open daily 1200-2100. Probably the best place in town is the *Queen's Hotel*, on Francis St, T602992, which has a varied menu (mid-range). Alternatively, try *Cabrelli's*, 134 High St, a great caff serving pizza and fish and chips. A few yards away is *Carter's Bar*, which does pub food and is an okay place for a drink at night. **Eating**

Air Wick has an **airport** (T602215), a few miles north of town, with daily direct flights to and from **Kirkwall** (Orkney), **Sumburgh** (Shetland), **Aberdeen** and **Edinburgh** with connections south. Flights are with *Gill Airways*, T0191-214 6666, www.gill-airways.com, and *British Airways Express*, T0845-7222111. There's a *Postbus* service to **Wick** airport Mon-Sat at 1015. **Transport**

    Bus *Scottish Citylink*, T0870-5505050, buses between **Inverness** and **Thurso** stop en route in Wick (3 daily). There are also regular local buses to Thurso, via Halkirk or Castletown, and buses to **Helmsdale** (2-6 times daily Mon-Sat, 1-4 on Sun) and **John O'Groats** (5 daily Mon-Sat, 4 on Sun).

    Car/bike hire *Richard's Garage*, Francis St, T604123.

    Train The train and bus stations are next to each other behind the hospital. Trains leave for **Inverness** (3 daily Mon-Sat, 2 on Sun; 3 ¾ hrs) via **Thurso**, **Helmsdale**, **Gols-pie**, **Lairg** and **Dingwall**.

North & Northwest Highlands

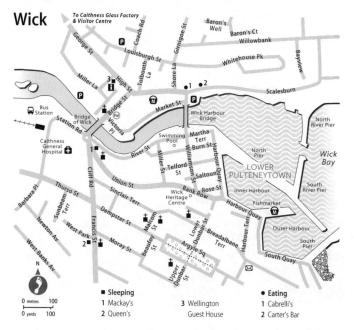

Wick

■ Sleeping		● Eating
1 Mackay's	3 Wellington	1 Cabrelli's
2 Queen's	Guest House	2 Carter's Bar

0 metres 100
0 yards 100

Skye

7

Skye

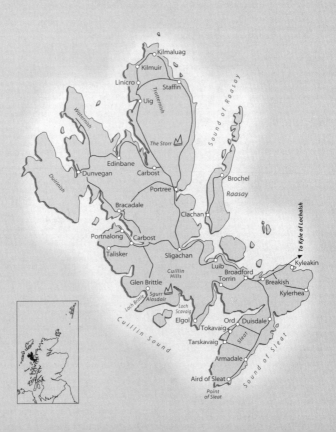

The Isle of Skye (An t-Eilean Sgitheanach), the most scenically spectacular of all the Scottish islands, gets its name from the Norse word for cloud (skuy) and it is commonly known as Eilean a Cheo (the Misty Isle), so it obviously rains a lot here. But when the rain and mist clear, the views make the heart soar.

Despite the unpredictable weather, tourism is an important part of the island's economy, and has been since Victorian times when climbers returned home extolling its beauty. In the busy summer months, the main roads become choked with coach tours and caravans, but the island is large enough to escape the worst of the crowds if you take the time to explore it.

The most popular destination is the **Cuillins**, the greatest concentration of peaks in Britain. They provide Scotland's best climbing and have become a mecca for all serious and experienced walkers. Equally spectacular are the bizarre rock formations of the **Trotternish** Peninsula, in the north.

Trotternish is also inextricably linked with one of the most significant characters from the island's colourful past, Flora MacDonald, who is buried at **Kilmuir**. More of the island's fascinating history can be discovered at **Dunvegan Castle**, ancient seat of the Macleods and a major tourist landmark.

The island's main settlement, **Portree**, is a pleasant base from which to explore most of the island, though **Broadford** is ideally situated for the south of the island. If you really want to get away from it all, then you should head for the island of **Raasay**, just off the east coast, or the remote **Duirinish** and **Waternish** peninsulas.

Ins and outs

Getting there The most popular, and quickest, route to Skye is across the new **bridge** (£5 toll), from Kyle of Lochalsh to Kyleakin. **Coach** services run to Skye from Glasgow and Inverness, with connections to all main cities in the UK (*Citylink*, T0870-5505050; *National Express*, T0870-580 8080). There is also a **train** service from Kyle of Lochalsh to Inverness (see page 245).

A more scenic approach is by **ferry** from Mallaig **to Armadale**, on the southern Sleat Peninsula. The car and passenger ferry makes the 30-min crossing 7 times daily each way (first one leaves Mallaig at 0840, Armadale at 0925; the last one at 1845 and 1920) Mon-Sat from Mar to Oct, and Sun end of May to mid-Sep. The ferry is passenger only during the winter; for details contact Mallaig, T01687-462403, or Armadale, T01471-844248. Booking is recommended during the summer months, T08705- 650000. The one-way trip costs £2.80 per passenger and £15.65 per car. Trains to and from Fort William and Glasgow Queen St connect with some of the ferries (see page 241).

The best way to Skye is from Glenelg **to Kylerhea**, south of Kyleakin. The tiny private car ferry makes the 10-minute crossing when required, from Easter to Oct (Mon-Sat 0900-1800 till mid-May; Mon-Sat 0900-2000, Sun 1000-1800 from mid-May to end-Aug; Mon-Sat 0900-1800, Sun 1000-1800 end-Aug to end Oct). Cost per car with up to 4 passengers, £6; day return £10. T01599-511302.

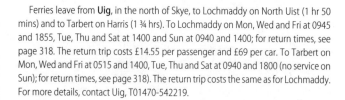

Things to do on Skye

- Walk the mighty **Quiraing** and, if you're still in one piece, tackle the **Old Man of Storr**.
- Walk out to the lighthouse at **Neist Point**.
- Take a boat trip into the gaping mouth

of **Loch Coruisk**.
- Visit the Otter Haven at **Kylerhea** and try to spot these elusive little creatures.
- Visit the beautiful island of **Raasay** and climb to the top of Dun Caan.

Ferries leave from **Uig**, in the north of Skye, to Lochmaddy on North Uist (1 hr 50 mins) and to Tarbert on Harris (1 ¾ hrs). To Lochmaddy on Mon, Wed and Fri at 0945 and 1855, Tue, Thu and Sat at 1400 and Sun at 0940 and 1400; for return times, see page 318. The return trip costs £14.55 per passenger and £69 per car. To Tarbert on Mon, Wed and Fri at 0515 and 1400, Tue, Thu and Sat at 0940 and 1800 (no service on Sun); for return times, see page 318). The return trip costs the same as for Lochmaddy. For more details, contact Uig, T01470-542219.

Getting around

Skye is the largest of the Hebridean islands at almost 50 miles long, and between 7 and 25 miles wide. It is possible to run up a hefty mileage as the extensive road system penetrates to all but the most remote corners of its many peninsulas. It is possible to get around by public transport midweek, with *postbuses* supplementing the normal services, but as everywhere in the Highlands and Islands, buses are few and far between at weekends, especially Sun, and during the winter months. **Buses** run between Portree, Broadford, Uig (for ferries to the Western Isles), Kyleakin, Armadale (for ferries to Mallaig), Dunvegan and Carbost, and a more limited service runs from Broadford to Elgol and Portree to Glen Brittle. For full details, contact the local TIC.

Information

Skye is well served by all types of accommodation: B&Bs, guesthouses, hostels, bunkhouses, campsites and some very fine hotels. During the peak summer months advance bookings are recommended. These can be made directly or through the island's **Tourist Information Centres**; in Portree (open all year), Broadford, Uig and Dunvegan (see relevant section).

Skye

Portree

Portree is the island's capital and main settlement. It's a fairly attractive little fishing port, built around a natural harbour, with a row of brightly-painted houses along the shorefront and the rest of the town rising steeply up to the central Somerled Square.

Phone code: 01478
Colour map 1, grid C3

Ins and outs

Portree is ideally placed for trips to all parts of the island. **Buses** leave from the bus station in Somerled Square to Dunvegan, Uig, Broadford, Kyleakin, Armadale, the Talisker Distillery and Glenbrittle. There are also services to the mainland. The *Calmac* **ferry** office is on Park Rd, just off Somerled Sq, T612075, F613090. The town is compact enough to get around easily on foot, though there is a regular town bus service for those needing to get into the centre from the outskirts.

Getting there & around
See page 297 for further details

The TIC is just off Bridge St, T612137. They have bus timetables and a good selection of books and maps. It's open Apr to mid-May Mon-Sat 0900-1730; mid-May to Jul Mon-Sat 0900-1800, Sun 1000-1600; mid-Jul to mid-Aug Mon-Sat 0900-2000, Sun 1000-1600; mid-Aug to Sep Mon-Sat 0900-1800; Oct-Mar Mon-Fri 0900-1700, Sat 1000-1600.

Tourist Information Centre

Gaelic culture

Outside of the Outer Hebrides, Skye is the most important centre of Gaelic culture, with a large proportion of the island's population speaking the Gaelic language in everyday life. This in itself is remarkable given the significant drop in population during the Clearances and the continued undermining of the Gaelic culture ever since, especially through the State education system.

Today, as in other parts of the Hebrides, the native culture is again under threat, this time from the huge influx of 'white settlers' from the south, but there is also a new-found pride and interest in the Gaelic language. This has been helped by the existence of the Gaelic college on Sleat, through Gaelic writers such as the late Sorley Maclean, a radical local newspaper (The West Highland Free Press), economic support from Highlands and Islands Enterprise and spiritual underpinning from the Sabbatarian Free Church. Gaelic is being taught again in schools and can be heard on television. The ancient heritage of the Highlands and Islands is fighting back and reasserting itself as a major European culture.

History

The town was so named (*Port Righ* means 'King's Harbour' in Gaelic) to commemorate a visit by King James V in 1540. He came with his fleet to quell a long-standing and bitter feud between the island's main clans, the Macleods and the MacDonalds. The town's other notable royal occasion, in 1746, one of the most poignant moments in Scottish history, was when Prince Charlie bade farewell to Flora MacDonald in MacNab's hostelry, now the *Royal Hotel*.

Almost a quarter of a century later, the town was visited by Dr Johnson and Boswell, who dined in MacNab's, believing it to be 'the only inn on the island'. That may or may not have been the case in those days, but today Portree offers a wide range of places to eat, hotels, B&Bs, pubs, shops and banks to cater for the huge numbers of tourists that come here in the summer.

Sights

The Aros Experience, on Viewfield Road, half a mile from the town centre on the road to Broadford, is an exhibition and audio-visual display of the island's history and cultural heritage. The island's only theatre is housed here and features a varied programme of events, including drama, traditional music and movies (see 'Entertainment' below). There's also a restaurant serving good value snacks and main meals, a gift shop and a network of forest trails to explore. ■ *Daily 0900-2100 (off season 0900-1800). Adult £3, concession £2, children £1, under 12 free, T613649, aros@ demon.co.uk*

The **An Tuireann Arts Centre**, on Struan Road, hosts contemporary exhibitions of contemporary visual arts and crafts. It has a fine café (see 'Eating' below). ■ *Mon-Sat 1000- 1800. Free, T613306. norahcampbell@antuireann.demon.co.uk*

If the weather's good, Portree offers many opportunities for a wide variety of outdoor activities. **Boat trips** can be made to the island of Rona, north of Raasay, with the *MV Brigadoon*. ■ *Trips leave from the pier and cost from £5-15 per person. Full-day charters are also available for £75-150 (12 passengers). T613718, or ask for Peter Urquhart at the pier. For* **horse riding**, *Portree Riding and Trekking Stables are a couple of miles from the town centre.* ■ *T612945. Follow the Struan Road (B885) for 2 miles, then bear right at the fork towards Peiness.* Four miles north of Portree, at Borve, on the road to Uig is the *Skye*

Things to do on Skye when it's raining ★

- Just in case you didn't know, it can rain quite often on Skye and unless you're one of those hardy souls who's prepared to brave the elements, you'll need to know about the island's main indoor attractions. There are numerous opportunities to shelter from the rain, but most of them cost money, and many will leave you regretting it, so here's our list of top ten things to do. Details of opening times and admission prices are given under each relevant destination.

- Beginning in **Portree**, there's the **Aros Experience**, which gives a good introduction to the island's history. North of Uig, at **Kilmuir** on the **Trotternish** Peninsula, is the **Skye Museum of Island Life**, which pretty much does what it says on the sign. Northwest from Portree is **Dunvegan Castle**, home of the Clan Maclead and top of most visitors' itineraries. On the road to Dunvegan, is **Edinbane Pottery**, where you can buy pots of every shape and size and watch them being made.

- Travelling south from Dunvegan, you'll reach the turn-off to the **Talisker Distillery**, the island's only whisky distillery, where you can sample the distinctive peaty taste. While you're there you can visit nearby **Carbostcraft Pottery**, in the village of **Carbost**, and indulge in some more gift buying. If you're in need of some refreshment after all that culture and shopping, you could do a lot worse than the bar at the **Sligachan Hotel**, which boasts an impressive array of whiskies and climbers' beards. In the southern peninsular of **Sleat**, near the Armadale ferry terminal, is the **Clan Donald Visitor Centre**, a visitor centre that is actually worth visiting. Nearby is one of the branches of **Skye Batiks**, with a huge selection of these 'new age' style fabrics in a range of original Celtic designs (the other branch is in Portree). And for that final drink before boarding the ferry to Mallaig, why not pop in to the cosy bar of the **Hotel Eilean Iarmain**, which also happens to serve wonderful food.

Riding Centre, T01470-532439. **Mountain bikes** can be hired at *Island Cycles*, on The Green. ■ *Mon-Sat 1000-1700, T613121.*

Essentials

There are numerous hotels, guesthouses and B&Bs in Portree, but accommodation can be hard to find in the busy summer season. For a small fee the tourist office will book accommodation for you. Prices tend to be slightly higher in Portree than the rest of the island, though B&Bs on the outskirts of town are usually cheaper.

Sleeping
■ on map page 296
Price codes:
see inside front cover

B *Rosedale Hotel*, Beaumont Cres, T613131. 23 rooms, Open May-Sep. Cosy little hotel by the harbour, converted from fishermen's houses.

C *Bosville Hotel*, Bosville Terr, T612846, F613434, www.macleodhotels.co.uk/bosville 18 rooms. Comfortable and stylish accommodation with friendly service. Boasts 2 award-winning restaurants (see 'Eating' below). **C** *Viewfield House Hotel*, on the road into Portree from the south, T612217, F613517, www.skye.co.uk/viewfield 9 rooms. Open mid-Apr to mid-Oct. Grand old country house full of antiques set in 20 acres of woodland garden. Log fire adds to the welcoming atmosphere, great value.

There are also several **guesthouses** on Bosville Terr and many **B&Bs** on Stormyhill Rd and the streets running off it. There are also lots of places to stay on Viewfield Rd heading south out of town. These include: **E** *Mrs Macphie*, 'Balloch', Viewfield Rd, T612093; and particularly good value is **E** *Mr & Mrs Mathieson*, 'Grenitote', 9 Martin Cres, T612808.

There are a couple of options for budget travellers. **F** *Portree Independent Hostel*, Old Post Office, The Green, T613737. 60 beds. Right in the centre of town, with laundrette (£5 per wash) and email facilities (£5 per hour). **F** *Portree Backpackers Hostel*, 6 Woodpark, Dunvegan Rd, T613641, F613643. 26 beds. There's a **campsite** at Torvaig, just outside the town, T612209, open Apr-Oct.

Eating **Expensive** *Chandlery Seafood Restaurant*, next door to the *Bosville Hotel* (see under 'Sleeping' for details). Superb French/Scottish cuisine using local produce. Seafood a speciality. *Lower Deck Seafood Restaurant*, on the harbour front at the foot of Quay Brae, T613611. Freshest of seafood and a contender with the *Chandlery* for the best food in town. Open daily Apr-Oct, 1100-2200. For a budget treat try the excellent fish and chips from their takeaway next door. *Skeabost House Hotel*, 4 miles north of Portree on the Dunvegan road, T01470-532202, F532454, skeabost@sol.co.uk This peaceful country house in lovely grounds on the shores of Loch Snizort has a reputation for fine food using the best local produce.

Mid-range *Ben Tianavaig*, 5 Bosville Terr, T612152. Excellent vegetarian bistro. Seating is limited so you'll need to book. Open lunchtimes at weekends and Tue-Sun

Portree

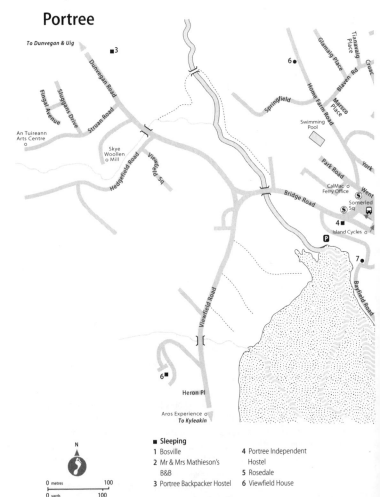

Skye

■ **Sleeping**
1 Bosville
2 Mr & Mrs Mathieson's B&B
3 Portree Backpacker Hostel
4 Portree Independent Hostel
5 Rosedale
6 Viewfield House

1800-2130. *Bosville Restaurant*, in the *Bosville Hotel* (see 'Sleeping' above). Also recommended. They offer a lunchtime special (soup, sandwich and coffee for £5) which is great value.

Cheap *Tuireann Café*, part of the arts centre (see 'Sights' above). Natural whole-foods and organic produce, home-made bread, cakes and pastries. Excellent quality and value. Open Mon-Tue 1000-1800, Wed-Sat 1000-2300, Sun 1200-1700 (in the summer). *Spicehut*, Bayfield Rd, T612681. Indian restaurant and takeaway. Open daily 1200-1430 and 1700-2400. For cheap Chinese takeaway food, there's *Steve's Kitchen Takeaway*, on Bayfield Rd, opposite the library. For cheap bar lunches try the *Portree House*, Home Farm Rd, T613713 (1200-1545).

The town's nightlife is mainly confined to eating and drinking. The bar of the *Pier Hotel* by the harbour is a real fishermen's drinking den. Also popular is the *Royal Hotel*. If you fancy a wild Fri night ceilidh, try the *Portree Community Centre*, Camanachd Square, T613736. The *Aros Experience* (see 'Sights' above) has a theatre which shows drama, movies and live music. Call the box office for details of their monthly programme; T613750. The **swimming pool** is at Camanachd Square, T612655.

Entertainment

The island's annual **Highland Games** are a 1-day event held in Portree in early **Aug**.

Festivals

There's a *Safeway* supermarket diagonally opposite the *Bosville Hotel* and a wholefood store, *Jackson's Wholefoods*, at Park Pl, opposite the council offices. *Skye Batiks*, The Green (near the tourist office), T613331. Sells handmade 'batiks' (colourful cotton fabrics), which are pricey but unique souvenirs of Skye (see also under Armadale, page 311). A good pottery is *Carbostcraft Pottery*, on Bayfield Rd, which sells a huge variety of designs (they also have a shop near the Talisker Distillery, see page 306). A good place to buy woollens is *Over the Rainbow*, at the top of Quay Brae, T612555. Open 0900-2200 in the high season. Knitwear and tartan souvenirs can be found at the *Skye Woollen Mill*, Dunvegan Rd, T612889.

Shopping
Most of the shops are within a few streets of Somerled Square

Skye

There are 4 **buses** daily Mon-Fri (2 on Sat) around the **Trotternish Peninsula**, in each direction, via **Uig**. There are daily buses (4 Mon-Sat, 3 on Sun) to **Kyleakin**, and 3 buses daily Mon-Sat to **Armadale** via **Broadford**. There are 2 daily buses to **Carbost** (for the Talisker Distillery) and **Fiskavaig** Mon-Fri (1 on Sat), and 2 daily buses to **Glenbrittle** (in the summer

Transport

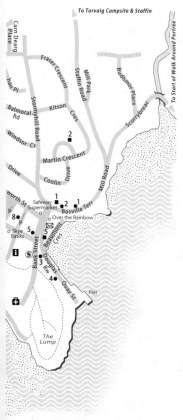

• **Eating**
1 Ben Tianavaig
2 Chandlery Seafood
3 Lower Deck Seafood
4 Pier Hotel
5 Royal Hotel
6 Portree House
7 Spicehut
8 Steve's Kitchen
 Takeaway

only). There are 3 buses daily Mon-Fri to **Glendale** via **Dunvegan** (1 on Sat), and 3 buses to **Waternish** via **Dunvegan** (Mon-Sat). There's a Scottish Citylink service from **Inverness** (3 Mon-Sat, 2 on Sun, 3 hrs) and also from **Glasgow** via **Fort William** to **Kyleakin**, **Portree** and **Uig** 3-4 times daily (3 hrs from Fort William to Portree).

Taxis: *Ace Taxis*, T613600; *A2B Taxis*, T613456.

Directory **Banks** *Bank of Scotland* and *Clydesdale Bank*, both on Somerled Sq. The *Royal Bank of Scotland* is on Bank St. All have ATMs. **Communications** Internet: At the *Portree Independent Hostel* (see 'Sleeping' above). **Post office**: At the top of Quay Brae. **Laundry** At the *Portree Independent Hostel*.

Trotternish Peninsula

Colour map 1, grid C3 *North from Portree is the 30-mile long Trotternish Peninsula, sticking out like a giant thumb. The interior of the peninsular is a basaltic lava wilderness full of bizarre rock formations. A 20-mile long escarpment of sheer cliffs and towering pinnacles dominates the landscape. The best known of these strange formations, the* **Quiraing** *and* **Old Man of Storr**, *can be explored on foot. The A855 and A87 roads follow the coast around the peninsula and a spectacular minor road bisects the ridge from Staffin Bay to Uig. Trotternish is best explored with your own transport, but there a few daily buses covering the circular route from Portree (see Portree Transport).*

Uig

Phone code: 01470 The A87 runs northwest from Portree to the tiny ferry port of Uig, dramati-
Colour map 1, grid C3 cally set in a horseshoe bay and the departure point for ferries to **Tarbert** (Harris) and **Lochmaddy** (North Uist). Everything in the village revolves around the ferry timetables and the regular bus service to and from Portree coincides with the arrival and departure of the ferries (for ferry times, see page 292). *Scottish Citylink* runs a service to/from Inverness, Fort William and Glasgow.

The **Tourist Information Centre** is inside the *CalMac* office at the ferry pier, T542404, and will book accommodation anywhere on the island; open 1 April-31 October, Monday-Saturday 0845-1830, also Sunday 0845-1400 July-September.

Just outside the village is the magical **Fairy Glen**. Turn right just before the *Uig Hotel* coming down the hill from the Portree direction. About a mile up the single track road you enter an eerie, mysterious world of perfect conical hills, some up to 60-ft high. It's almost inconceivable that these are natural formations and the inevitable mist only adds to the spooky strangeness of the place.

Sleeping **B** *Uig Hotel*, on the right of the road into the village from Portree, beside a white church and opposite a round tower, T542205, F542308 17 rooms, open Apr-Oct. Classy accommodation with great views across the bay, good food and a friendly island welcome. Offers a wide range of outdoor activities including nature walks and fly fishing. A cheaper option is **D** *The Ferry Inn*, T542242, F542377, joycemary@ supanet.com Amongst the good value **B&Bs** is **E** *Idrigill House*, T542398, F542447, s.watkins@lineone.net The **F** *SYHA Youth Hostel*, T542211, is high above the port on the south side of the village and is open mid-Mar to Oct.

Flora MacDonald

In Kilmuir graveyard is the memorial which marks the grave of Flora MacDonald, one of the most famous characters in Skye's long history. The memorial bears Dr Johnson's fitting epitaph: "A name that will be mentioned in history, and if courage and fidelity be virtues, mentioned with honour".

It was Flora Macdonald who helped Bonnie Prince Charlie to escape capture following the Jacobite defeat at Culloden in 1746. Pursued by government troops, the prince fled from South Uist 'over the sea to Skye' aboard Flora's boat, disguised as an Irish servant girl by the name of Betty Burke. He then made his way to Portree, where he bade his farewell to the young woman who had risked her own life to protect his.

When Flora's part in the prince's escape became known, she was immediately arrested and sent to the Tower of London. She was released a year later, married a Skye man and then emigrated to North Carolina where she spent the next 12 years of her life. They returned to her husband's house in Kingsburgh in 1786. Flora died in Skye in 1790, and it is said that her funeral was the largest ever witnessed in the Highlands.

The **Pub on the Pier** (open till 2300) serves cheap bar meals and the famous Cuillin ales are brewed at the nearby Skye Brewery (tours by appointment, T542477). You can also change foreign currency here. **The Ferry Inn** serves bar meals and there's also **The Norseman**, a self-service café next to the CalMac office (open Mon-Sat 0800-2200, Sun 1000-2200). **Eating**

Uig to Duntulm

A few miles north of Uig, on the A855, at **Linicro**, is Whitewave Activities, where you can try windsurfing and sea kayaking. There's also B&B and a café. T542414, activities@whiteact.demon.co.uk **Phone code: 01470**

Further north, at **Kilmuir**, is **The Skye Museum of Island Life**. The group of thatched houses give a fascinating insight into the way of life of a crofting community at the end of the last century and is the most authentic of several such museums on Skye. ■ Easter to Oct Mon-Sat 0930-1700. Adult £2, children £1.

Behind the museum, at the end of the road is **Flora MacDonald's Monument**, which marks the grave of Skye's most famous daughter, with her husband buried alongside. The rather austere memorial is inscribed with Dr Johnson's poignant tribute.

At the northwest tip of the peninsula, 15 minutes' drive from Uig, is **Duntulm Castle**, a fairy-tale ruin dramatically perched on a steep cliff. This 15th-century structure, built on the site of an ancient Norse stronghold, became the chief Skye residence of the powerful MacDonalds and was the most imposing castle in the Hebrides. According to local legend, the castle was abandoned around 1732 when a nursemaid accidentally let the baby heir fall from a window onto the cliffs below.

Sleeping and eating Near the castle is **C** Duntulm Castle Hotel, T552213, F552292, www.duntulmcastle.co.uk Open Mar-Nov. Friendly and homely with great views across the Minch to the Outer Hebrides. Idyllic and good value. Restaurant is open to non-residents.

Skye

Duntulm to Portree

For full details of the routes for the Quiraing and Old Man of Storr walks, see page 312.

Beyond Duntulm the A855 heads across the tip of the peninsula to the east coast, where the famous bizarre rock scenery is found. Here, a few miles north of Staffin and 20 miles north of Portree, is **A** *Flodigarry Country House Hotel*, T01470-552203, F552301. Beautifully located at the foot of the mighty **Quiraing** and with stunning views across Staffin Bay, this is one of the great country house hotels, with a relaxing old-world atmosphere and excellent restaurant. Flora MacDonald's actual cottage is in the grounds and has been tastefully refurbished, giving the chance to stay in a place steeped in the island's history. The lively bar is a good place to enjoy a laugh and a jig.

Those that can't afford such luxury can always opt for the more modest **F** *Dun Flodigarry Backpackers Hostel*, T/F552212. 66 beds. Laundry facilities, breakfast available and only 100 yards from the bar of the *Flodigarry Country House Hotel*.

At the north end of **Staffin Bay**, a minor road cuts across the peninsula to Uig. This road is the access point for the **Quiraing**, the famous jumble of strangely-shaped hills and rocks that is one of the island's classic walks. Even if you don't attempt the walk, the road over the back of the Trotternish ridge from Uig makes a worthwhile detour.

A few miles south of Staffin Bay is **Kilt Rock**, an impressive sea cliff which gets its name from the vertical columnar basalt strata overlying horizontal ones beneath. A rather tenuous comparison perhaps, but the cliffs south of Staffin are particularly spectacular, as are the **Lealt Falls**, a torrent of mountain water at the head of a gorge, a few miles south of Kilt Rock. The falls are signposted by the road, so all you have to do is park the car and peer over.

There's a **campsite** south of Staffin Bay, T562213, open mid-April-end September. A good place for food is the *Oystercatcher Restaurant* in the village of Staffin, T562384, closed Sunday. At **Culnacnoc**, just north of the Lealt Falls, is **D** *Glenview Inn and Restaurant*, T562248, F562211. Five rooms. Cosy and relaxed accommodation with a very fine restaurant.

A few miles further south, and 7 miles north of Portree, is a car park which is the starting point for another of Skye's famous walks; up to the **Old Man of Storr**, the distinctive pinnacle of rock which has detached itself from the cliffs of the Storr behind. For a description of the route, see page 312.

Old Man of Storr

Skye

Clan warfare

Violent conflict between neighbouring clan chiefs was so commonplace on Skye and the rest of the Western Highlands that it was almost accepted as part of the very fabric of society. One particular gruesome example took place on Eigg, in 1577. The Macleod's had taken refuge in a cave but their presence was discovered by the MacDonalds, who piled brushwood at the entrance and set fire to it, burning alive the 395 people sheltering inside, almost the entire population of the island. Revenge came the following year, at Trumpan church in Ardmore Bay. The Macleods landed under cover of the early morning fog and set light to the church, burning the congregation inside.

Dunvegan, Waternish and Duirinish

In the northwest of Skye the peninsulas of Waternish (or Vaternish) and Duirinish point out into the Minch towards the Western Isles. The larger Duirinish peninsula holds more interest for the visitor, featuring the beautiful green valley of **Glendale***, an area brimming with history, the dramatic walk to* **Neist Point** *and* **Dunvegan Castle***, Skye's most famous landmark.*

Phone code: 01470

The turn-off to this much-visited part of the island is four miles northwest of Portree. The A850 swings west towards Dunvegan, by-passing the tiny village of Edinbane. There's a campsite, two hotels, several B&Bs, petrol station, Land Rover tours with *Skyetrak Safari*, T582224, and the renowned *Edinbane Pottery* workshop and showroom, which is a must for souvenir hunters. ■ *Daily Easter-Oct 0900-1800. T582234.*

Edinbane

Waternish Peninsula

The A850 continues west and those with their own transport and time on their hands might wish to make an interesting little detour at the **Fairy Bridge**, where the B886 runs north to **Trumpan**, near the tip of the Waternish Peninsula. If the weather's good (and it is, occasionally) this is the best place to watch the sun set, in a blaze of red over the Outer Hebrides. If there's no sunset, then you could always visit *Skyeskins*, the country's only traditional exhibition tannery, at Loch Bay, T592237, or pop into the island's oldest pub, at **Stein**. Either way, you should finish off the day with a meal at the wonderful *Lochbay Seafood*, T592235 for reservations, where you can almost see your dinner being landed. Mid-range prices, open April-October for lunch and till 2030 (closed Saturday).

Colour map 1, grid C2/3

The ruined church at Trumpan, at the end of the road, has some grisly skeletons in its cupboard (see box above). In the graveyard is the 'trial stone'. A hole in the stone was used to test whether or not an accused person was telling the truth. If they could quickly find the hole and stick their arm through it while blindfolded, they were found innocent, but if not, they were guilty. The church is also the starting point for the strenuous eight-mile **walk** out to **Waternish point** and back.

Dunvegan

**Dunvegan
Castle**
Colour map 1, grid C2

A few miles further on from the turn-off to Waternish is the little village of Dunvegan. Just to the north of the village is proud Dunvegan Castle, the island's most important tourist attraction. This is the home of the chiefs of the Clan Macleod who have lived here for over seven centuries, making it the oldest inhabited castle in Britain. The present structure dates from the 15th and 16th centuries, and though the Victorian restoration has left it looking more like a baronial house, a look inside reveals its true age. Among the many relics on display is Rory Mor's horn, a huge drinking vessel which the chief's heir must drain 'without setting down or falling down', when filled with claret (about 1½ bottles). There's also a lock of Bonnie Prince Charlie's hair, clipped from his head by Flora MacDonald as a keepsake, but pride of place goes to the **Fairy Flag**. The flag has been dated to between the fourth and seventh centuries and is made of Middle Eastern silk. It is said to have been given to the clan chief by a fairy and has the power to ensure victory in battle for the clan, on three occasions. It has so far been used twice. The lovely castle gardens lead down to the lochside jetty, from where you can take seal-spotting cruise or a boat trip around the loch. There's also a busy restaurant and gift shop by the castle gates. A bus leaves Portree at 1000, arrives at the castle at 1048 and returns at 1252. ■ *Mid-Mar-Oct daily 1000-1730. Castle: adult £5.50, children £3. Seal-spotting cruise: adult £4, children £2.50. Boat trip: adult £3.80, children £2. T521206.*

In the village itself is the **Giant Angus MacAskill Museum**, housed in thatched whitewashed cottage, which relates the life story of the tallest ever Scotsman, Angus MacAskill, who grew to 7 ft and 9 ins tall. He emigrated to Novia Scotia and toured the United States with the midget General Tom Thumb, who is said to have danced on his outstretched hand. More interesting than the museum, though, are the stories of its owner, Peter MacAskill, in particular the one about the replica coffin, which is worth the admission fee alone. Peter is a descendent of Angus and also runs the museum at Colbost (see below). ■ *Daily 0930-1830. £1. T521296.*

**Sleeping
& eating**

There are numerous places to stay in and around Dunvegan, and the **Tourist Information Centre** in the village will arrange accommodation for you, T521581. There are several hotels including the very comfortable **B** *Atholl House Hotel*, T521219, F521481, reservations@athollhotel.demon.co.uk A recommended guesthouse is **D** *Roskhill House*, 3 miles south of Dunvegan Castle on the A863, T521317, F521761, stay@roskhill.demon.co.uk 5 cosy rooms, peaceful setting, great food. Just beyond Roskhill is a turning south off the A863 to **B** *Harlosh House Hotel*, T/F521367, harlosh.house@virgin.net 6 rooms. Open Easter to mid-Oct. Cosy, comfortable, great views and a reputation for superb food (evenings only). There are also over a dozen **B&Bs**, mostly in the **E** price range.

Duirinish Peninsula

Colour map 1, grid C2

West of Dunvegan is the Duirinish Peninsula. The northern half is populated along the western shores of **Loch Dunvegan** and in the beautiful and green **Glendale**, an area brimming with history but with hardly an island family left. Glendale is now dubbed 'Little England', owing to the large number of incoming settlers from the south. The area is famed throughout the Highlands and Islands, for it was here in 1882 that local crofters, spurred on by the 'Battle of the Braes' (see page 308), resisted the cruel and petty tyranny of their estate manager. The authorities sent a gunboat to deal with the uprising and arrested the ringleaders, some of whom were imprisoned in Edinburgh and became known as 'the Glendale Martyrs'. This episode sparked a radical movement throughout the Highlands and led to the Crofter's Holdings Act of 1886 which gave the crofters a more secure tenure and fair rent (see page 414). The uninhabited southern half of the peninsula is dominated by the flat-topped hills, Healabhal Bheag (1,601 ft) and Healabhal Mhor (1,538 ft), known as **Macleod's Tables**.

The **Glendale Visitor Route** is sign posted from just before Dunvegan village and leads westwards along the shores of the loch and across the peninsular. There are several interesting little sights along the way. Those interested in finding out more about crofting on the island should head for **Colbost Croft Museum**, housed in a restored 'black house' and with a peat fire burning and an illicit still out the back. The museum is 4 miles from Dunvegan on the B884 to Glendale. ■ *Daily 1000-1830. Adult £1, children free. T521296.* A little further on is *Skye Silver*, where you can buy silver jewellery in traditional Celtic designs. ■ *Daily 1000-1800. T511263, www.skyesilver.com* Further north is the **Borreraig Park Exhibition Croft**, which features a huge display of farm equipment from days gone by. ■ *Daily 0900-1800. Adult £1.50.*

At **Borreraig** is the **MacCrimmon Piping Heritage Centre**, a fascinating place which is more of a shrine to the famous MacCrimmons, who were hereditary pipers to the Macleod Chiefs and the first composers, players and teachers of *piobaireachd* (pibroch), which can be heard in the museum (there's an annual recital at Dunvegan Castle in early August). Opposite are the ruins of the ancient piping college. ■ *Easter to late May daily (except Mon) 1100-1730; late May to end Aug daily 1100-1730; Sep to early Oct daily (except Mon) 1100-1730. £1.50. T511369.*

Moving from the sublime to the ridiculous, in the village of **Glendale** is a **Toy Museum**, which should appeal to kids of all ages. ■ *Mon-Sat 1000-1800. Adult £2.50, children £1. T511240.*

The B884 continues west, then a road turns off left for Waterstein. At the end of this road (just over 2 miles) is a car park which is the starting point for the walk out to the lighthouse at **Neist Point**, the most westerly point on Skye and one of the most pleasant walks on the island. It's about 1½ miles there and back and well worth the effort. The path is easy to follow and the views of the sea cliffs are wonderful. There are lots of nesting seabirds around and you might even spot whales offshore. The **lighthouse**, built in 1909, is now unmanned, and you can stay in one of the self-catering cottages, T/F511200. You can also join a guided walk to the lighthouse with a local naturalist. ■ *Walks leave from the road-end at 1400, 1515 and 1630 most days. T511265.* The graveyard at the lighthouse looks real enough but take a closer look and you'll see the names of the film crew who worked on the superb 1997 film, *Breaking the Waves*.

Skye

Sleeping & eating
Next to the Colbost Croft Museum is *The Three Chimneys*, T01470-511258, www.threechimneys.co.uk, considered by many to be the best restaurant in the north of Scotland and, judging by the numerous awards they've won, that judgement can't be far wrong. Local seafood, meat, veg and dairy produce and a great wine list. Open daily 1230-1400 (except Sun) and 1830-2130; expensive. They also now have accommodation a few yards away at **A** *The House Over-By* (6 rooms).

Transport
There are 3 **buses** daily (Mon-Fri) from Glendale to and from Portree via Dunvegan (see above), and 1 bus on Sat and a daily bus from Dunvegan to Glendale (not Sun).

The Cuillins and Minginish

Colour map 3,   *The district of Minginish is the wildest and least populated part of the island but*
grid A3/4   *for many it is the greatest attraction, for this is where the Cuillins are to be found.*
This hugely impressive mountain range, often shrouded in rain or cloud, is the
spiritual heartland of the island, and when it's clear their heart-aching grandeur
can be appreciated from every other peninsula on Skye.

Walking and climbing

OS Landranger No 32   Though officially called the Cuillin 'Hills', these are the most untamed moun-
OS Outdoor Leisure   tains in Britain. The magnificent scenery and vast range of walks and scram-
No 8   bles have attracted climbers and walkers for centuries but have also claimed
many lives. It cannot be stressed too strongly that the Cuillins are the most
dangerous mountains in Britain and only for experienced climbers (for more
on safety, see page 53).

There are three routes into the Cuillins: from the *Sligachan Hotel* (see
below); from Glen Brittle (see below); and from Elgol (see below). The eastern
part of the range is known as the **Red Cuillins**. Their smoother, conical granite peaks contrast sharply with the older, darker gabbro of the jagged-edged
Black Cuillins to the west. The latter are particularly suitable for rock climbing and best approached from Glen Brittle, while the former are accessed from
the *Sligachan Hotel*. There are 20 'Munros' (mountains over 3,000 ft in
height) in the Cuillins, with the highest being Sgurr Alasdair, at 3,251 ft.
Though the sheer majesty of the mountains can only be appreciated at close
quarters by the climber, there are impressive views from Elgol, from the road
into Glen Brittle and, more distantly, from the west coast of Sleat.

Glen Sligachan is one of the most popular routes into the Cuillin range and
the main access point for the more forgiving Red Cuillins, the walk to **Loch
Coruisk**, or the ascent of **Marsco**. Every year there's a hill race up nearby
Glamaig, which was climbed in 55 minutes (up and down) in 1899 by a
Gurkha soldier – in bare feet! The legendary rallying point for climbers who
come to Skye for the Cuillins is **C** *Sligachan Hotel*, seven miles south of
Portree, where the A87 Kyleakin-Portree road meets the A863 to Dunvegan,
T01471-8650204, F650207. The hotel's *Seamus* bar stocks an impressive
selection of malts and also serves the island's real ales and meals. The **camp-
site** opposite is the most popular place to stay in the area.

Guides &   The following guides have all been recommended. *Skye Highs*, Mike Lates, 3 Luib, Broad-
equipment   ford, T01471-822116. *Cuillin Guides*, Gerry Achroyd, Stac Lee, Glen Brittle,
T01478-640289. *Hugh Evans*, 4d Wentworth St, Portree, T01478-612682. *Richard
MacGuire*, 4 Matheson Place, Portree, T01478-613180. *Colin Threlfall*, at *Outdoor Sports*
(see below). Two good shops for mountain gear are *Cioch Direct*, 4 Ullinish, Struan,
T01470-572307, and *Outdoor Sports*, on Bridge Road (next to *Skye Batiks*), Portree.

Elgol

Phone code: 01471   One of the most rewarding drives on Skye is the 14-mile single-track road from
Colour map 3, grid A4   Broadford to Elgol (Ealaghol), a tiny settlement near the tip of the Strathaird
Peninsula, from where you can enjoy the classic view of the Cuillins from across
Loch Scavaig and of the islands of Soay, Rum and Canna. It was from here, on 4
July 1746, that the Young Pretender finally left the Hebrides. Before leaving, he

was given a farewell banquet by the MacKinnons in what is now called **Prince Charlie's Cave**. There's also the added attraction of a dramatic boat trip to the mouth of **Loch Coruisk**, in the heart of the Black Cuillin. The glacial sea loch, romanticized by Walter Scott and painted by Turner, is over two miles long but only a few hundred yards wide, closed in by the sheer cliffs on either side and overshadowed by the towering mountains of black basalt and gabbro. Elgol is also the starting point for the walk to Camasunary (see page 313). The road to Elgol also gives great views of Bla Bheinn (pronounced *Blaven*), best seen from Torrin, at the head of Loch Slapin.

■ *For details of sailing times on the Bella Jane, T866244, to book T0800-7313089 (freephone). Return boat trips take 3 hours, including about 1½ hours ashore, and cost £12.50, £6 child. You should be able to see seals and porpoises en route. There's also a one-way trip for experienced walkers/climbers who wish to make the return journey on foot or to explore the Cuillins (costs £9). There are also trips on the Nicola, T866236.*

There are several B&Bs in Elgol, but a more attractive option is **E** *Rowan Cottage*, **Sleeping**
T/F866287, www.rowncott.demon.co.uk Open Apr-Nov, a mile east at Glasnakille.

The only public transport is the *Postbus* from Broadford, which runs twice Mon-Sat and **Transport**
once on Sun and takes 2 hrs.

Glen Brittle

Six miles along the A863 to Dunvegan from Sligachan is a turning left to *Phone code: 01478*
Portnalong, Carbost and the Talisker Distillery (B8009), which soon leads to *Colour map 3, grid A3*
the entrance to Glen Brittle. The road down Glen Brittle affords great views of
the western side of the imposing Black Cuillins, until it ends at the campsite
and shore at the foot of the glen.

From Glen Brittle there are numerous paths leading up to the corries of the
Black Cuillins. There are many alternative options for those wishing to continue up to upper corries or to the Main Ridge. One of the finest of the Cuillin
corries is **Coire Lagan**. This walk starts from the beach at Glen Brittle village
and takes you up to the lochan in the upper coire, with Sgurr Alasdair, the
most difficult of the Munros, towering overhead. A fine Cuillin sampler is the
short walk to the spectacular **Eas Mor** waterfall.

Apart from the campsite by the shore, T640404, the only accommodation is at the **F** **Sleeping**
SYHA Hostel, T640278, in the village. It's open mid-Mar to end of Oct and has 39 beds.

There are 2 daily **buses** from Portree to Glen Brittle Mon-Sat during the summer only. **Transport**
Otherwise, take the Portree-Carbost-Fiscavaig bus, which leaves twice Mon-Fri and
once on Sat, and get off at the turn-off, then walk the remaining 7 miles, or hitch,
though it can be slow.

Talisker

A recommended trip for whisky drinkers, or if it's raining, is to the **Talisker** *Phone code: 01478*
Distillery, at **Carbost** on the shores of Loch Harport, on the B8009 (not in the *Colour map 3, grid A3*
village of Talisker itself, which is on the west coast). This is Skye's only whisky
distillery and produces a very smoky, peaty single malt. The informative tours
last around 20-30 minutes and begin with a complimentary dram. ■ *Apr-Jun
Mon-Fri 0900-1630; Jul-Sep Mon-Sat 0900-1630; Oct Mon-Fri 0900-1630;*

Nov-Mar Mon-Fri 1400-1630. Tours £3.50 (includes discount voucher). T640314, F640401, large groups need to book in advance.

Near the distillery is *Carbostcraft Pottery*, which produces a wide range of traditional and original pottery, including the famous 'torn pots'. It's open Monday-Saturday 0900-1700 from February-December (also Sunday in summer). T640259. They also have a shop in Portree.

Sleeping There are a few places to stay in and around **Carbost**. Further west, in the village of **Talisker**, is **C** *Talisker House*, T640245, F640214, jon_and_ros.wathen@virgin.net 4 rooms. This excellent guesthouse makes an ideal retreat from the summer hordes and serves fine food. North of Carbost, near **Portnalong**, are 2 hostels. **F** *Croft Bunkhouse & Bothies*, T/F640254, pete@skyehostel.free-online.co.uk Sleeps 26. Also room for camping, transport from Sligachan or Portree, rents mountain bikes, pub and shop nearby. *Skyewalker Independent Hostel*, T640250, F640420, skyewalker@ easynet.co.uk In a converted school beyond Portnalong on the road to Fiscavaig. 32 beds.

Transport There's a regular bus service (weekdays only) from Portree and Sligachan to Portnalong, T01470-532240.

Kyleakin to Portree

Kyleakin

Phone code: 01599
Colour map 3, grid A5
The opening of the Skye Bridge, linking the island with the Kyle of Lochalsh (see page 245), has turned the former ferry terminal of Kyleakin (Caol Acain) into something of a backwater, as well as infuriating the locals with its £5 per car toll. The absence of road traffic, though, makes it a quiet place to stay and it's now a favourite with backpackers, judging by the number of hostels. There's precious little to do here, other than look at the small ruin of **Castle Moil**, but you could take one of the seal cruises organized by *Castle Moil Seal Cruises*, which leave from the ferry pier, taking you to see the seal colony on **Eilean Mahl**. ■ *Cruises last 1¼ hours and cost £5.50. T544235.*

Sleeping The large, modern **F** *SYHA Hostel*, T534585) is a few hundred yards from the pier, is open all year. Nearby is the **F** *Skye Backpackers Hostel*, T/F534510, open all year, and offers breakfast for £1.40. There's also the **F** *Dun Caan Hostel*, T534087, T/F534795, near the old ferry quay, which is open all year and also hires bikes for £5 per day. There are also several **B&Bs**.

Eating The backpacker's pub, *Saucy Mary's* serves cheap meals, but the best place to eat is *The Crofter's Kitchen*, outside the village on the road to Broadford, T534134. It serves 3-course meals and snacks (mid-range). Open Mon-Sat 1000-2100, Sun 1230-2100.

Transport There are **buses** from Kyleakin to **Portree** via Broadford (4 daily), to **Armadale** and **Ardvasar** via Broadford (3 daily Mon-Sat) and half hourly to **Kyle** via the Skye Bridge. *Kyleakin Private Hire* (T534452) run a **taxi** service and guided tours of the island.

Kylerhea About four miles out of Kyleakin a road turns left off the A87 and heads southeast to Kylerhea (pronounced Kile-ray). The bridge may be the most convenient route to Skye but the best way to cross is on the small car and passenger ferry that makes the 10-minute crossing to Kylerhea from Glenelg (see page 244). For full details of times and prices, see page 292. Near

Kylerhea is the Forestry Commission **Otter Haven**. An hour long nature trail takes you to an observation hide where you can look out for these elusive creatures. ■ *Daily 0900 till 1 hr before dusk. Free. T01320-366322.*

Broadford

Eight miles west of Kyleakin is Broadford (An t-Ath Leathann), Skye's second largest village, which basically consists of a mile-long main street strung out along a wide bay. Broadford may be low on charm but it's high on tourist facilities, with plenty accommodation and places to eat, a tourist office, garage, supermarket and bank (with ATM). There are also a few interesting, and unusual, things to do when it rains, which is always a bonus.

Phone code: 01471
Colour map 3, grid A4

Getting there Buses between Portree, Inverness and Fort William pass through daily. There are also daily buses to and from Kyleakin, Portree and Armadale/Ardvasar. See Transport on next page.

Ins & outs

The **Tourist Information Centre** is by the Esso petrol station, T822361. Open Apr-Oct Mon-Sat 0930-1730, Mon-Sat 0900-1900, Sun 1000-1700 in Jul/Aug.

One of the most incongruous attractions on the island, or elsewhere in the Highlands, is the **Skye Serpentarium**, where you can see, and touch, all kinds of snakes, lizards and other reptiles. ■ *Easter-Oct, Mon-Sat 1000-1700 (also Sun in Jul/Aug). Adult £2.50, children 1.50. T822209.* More familiar but also interesting is the **International Otter Survival Fund** visitor centre. ■ *Daily Mar-Oct 0930-1700. £1.50.* At the north end of the village, near the post office, is **World of Wood**, where you can find out everything you ever wanted to know about wood and buy all sorts of souvenirs.

Sights

When the weather's clear you can take a boat trip to the island of **Pabay** with *Family's Pride II*. ■ *Trips last 1½ hours, cost £9 and leave daily from the main pier. T822037.*

Skye

Two notable places are **D** *Lime Stone Cottage*, 4 Lime Park (behind the Serpentarium), T822142, kathielimepark@btinternet.com, which is full of rustic charm, and **D** *Ptarmigan*, overlooking the bay, T822744, F822745, www.ptarmigan-cottage.com The **F** *SYHA Hostel* is by the new pier, T822422. Open all year. A mile or so south of the village, at Lower Breakish, off the A87 to Kyleakin, is the **F** *Fossil Bothy*, T822297, which has 8 beds and is open Easter-Oct, book in advance.

Sleeping
Finding a room shouldn't be a problem, except maybe in the peak months

The best place to eat is the *Seagull Restaurant*, at Breakish, south of Broadford on the main road to Kyleakin, T822001. It serves excellent local food with a European twist. Mid-range. For cheap to mid-range bar meals, try the *Claymore Bar-Restaurant*, at the south end of the village, T822333.

Eating

Daily Citylink **buses** run to and from Portree, Inverness and Fort William. *Waterloo* buses run daily to and from Kyleakin, Portree (£6 return) and Armadale/Ardvasar. For **car hire** try *Sutherlands* at the Esso Garage, T822225, F822759, they charge from £30 per day. You can rent **mountain bikes** from *Fairwinds Bicycle Hire*, just past the *Broadford Hotel*, T822270, for £7 per day.

Transport

Bank of Scotland with ATM by the shops opposite the road to the new pier. Next to the Esso station is a Co-op **supermarket**, and there's a **laundrette** in the petrol station shop (open 24 hrs).

Directory

The Battle of the Braes

One of the most significant incidents in the island's history took place in April, 1882, when a group of around 100 local crofters and their families fought a pitched battle against a force of 60 police sent by the government from Glasgow. The 'Battle of the Braes', as it became known, was caused, like many other such uprisings throughout the Highlands and Islands (see page 302), by threatened evictions. The local crofters were so incensed by the *injustice of the eviction notices served on them that they destroyed the offending documents, leading the government to dispatch its police force. The defeat of the government forces of law and order by a bunch of men, women and children with sticks and stones, is often described as the last battle fought on British soil, and led eventually to the setting up of a Royal Commission to look into the crofters' grievances.*

Broadford to Portree

Colour map 3, grid A4

The road north to Portree runs between the fringes of the Red Cuillins and the coast, giving good views across to the **Isle of Scalpay**. The road then turns west along the shores of Loch Ainort to the turn-off for the **Luib Folk Museum**, another of Peter MacAskill's island museum's. The restored croft house has a smoky atmosphere and has old newspaper cuttings telling of the 'Battle of the Braes' and the 'Glendale Martyrs'. ■ *Daily 0900-1800. Adult £1.*

The road runs north to **Sconser**, departure point for the ferry to Raasay (see below), then runs around Loch Sligachan and heads north to Portree. On the opposite side of the loch from Sconser are the crofting communities known as **The Braes**, who successfully opposed their landlords' eviction notices and brought the crofters' cause to the public's attention.

Isle of Raasay

Phone code: 01478
Colour map 1,
grid C3/4
OS Landranger No 24
The island is a nature conservancy, and you may see seals, eagles and otters

The lush and beautiful island of Raasay lies only a few miles off the east coast of Skye yet remains well and truly off the tourist trail. Its hilly terrain and superb cliff scenery offer numerous walking opportunities and the views from the highest point, **Dun Caan** (1,456 ft), with the Cuillins on one side and Torridon on the other, are, quite simply, beyond compare. The walk to the distinctive flat-topped summit of this extinct volcano, via an old iron mine, is relatively straightforward and one of the most rewarding anywhere in the islands. So much so, in fact, that Boswell was inspired to dance a Highland jig on reaching the top, in 1773, during his grand tour with Dr Johnson. Another excellent walk starts from North Fearns, at the end of a road running east from **Inverarish**, to the deserted township of **Hallaig**, down the side of Beinn na Leac and back to North Fearns. The circular route is five miles long.

Raasay was for much of its history the property of the Macleods of Lewis, whose chief residence was the ruined **Brochel Castle**, before moving to **Clachan**, where **Raasay House** is now located (see below). The original Raasay House was torched by government troops after Culloden, along with all the island's houses and its boats, as punishment for the Macleods giving refuge to Bonnie Prince Charlie. After the Macleods sold the island, in 1843, the Clearances began in earnest and Raasay suffered a long period of emigration, depopulation and poverty. It is not surprising, then, that the island's most famous son, the great poet **Sorley Maclean**, writes so passionately about this lost society. Born in Oskaig in 1911, he writes in his native Gaelic, as well as in

Skye

English, and is highly regarded internationally. Raasay's population now numbers around 150 and the island is a bastion of the Free Church, whose strict Sabbatarian beliefs should be respected by visitors.

Those who make it to the north of the island may wish to note that the two miles of road linking **Brochel** to **Arnish** was the work of one man, Calum Macleod. He decided to build the road himself after the council turned down his requests for proper access to his home. He spent between 10 and 15 years building it with the aid of a pick, a shovel and a wheelbarrow and a road-making manual which cost him three shillings. He died in 1988, soon after its completion, and to this day it is known as 'Calum's Road'.

Sleeping The main settlement on the island is **Inverarish**, a 15-min walk from the ferry dock. Half a mile further on is the *Raasay Outdoor Centre*, housed in the huge Georgian mansion that was Raasay House, which runs many and various adventure courses, from climbing to windsurfing, as well as offering basic accommodation from Mar to mid-Oct and a **campsite**, T660266. Nearby are **E** *Isle of Raasay Hotel*, T/F660222, and **E** *Churchton House*, T660260, both of which are open all year.

Further north along the coast, at **Oskaig**, B&B is available at **E** *Mrs Mackay*, T660207, including dinner. A rough track leads up a steep hill from the tiny village to the island's **F** *SYHA Hostel*, T660240, open mid-Mar to end-Oct.

Transport The *CalMac* car and passenger ferry runs from Sconser daily Mon-Sat every hour from 0830 till 1800 (2130 in Jul/Aug). Last return is at 1735 (2100 in Jul/Aug). It takes 15 mins and costs £3.65 per person return, plus £15.70 per car and £1 per bicycle (so leave the car behind!).

Sleat Peninsula

East of Broadford is the turn-off to peninsula of Sleat (pronouned 'slate'), a part of the island so uncharacteristically green and fertile that it's known as 'The Garden of Skye'. Sleat is another entry point to the island. Ferries cross from Mallaig on the mainland to **Armadale** *on the southeastern shore of the peninsula. While the rest of the island is the preserve of the Macleods, Sleat is* **MacDonald country***. The MacDonalds of Sleat are one of the major surviving branches of Clan Donald and have the right to use the title Lord MacDonald (but not Lord of the Isles, which is now used by the heir to the throne).*

Phone code: 01471
Colour map 3, grid A4

Broadford to Duisdale **Sleeping and eating** The clan seat is Armadale Castle, which now houses the Clan Donald Visitor Centre (see below), but the home of the present Lord MacDonald is *Kinloch Lodge*, T833214, F833277, www.kinloch-lodge.com, at the head of **Loch na Dal**. Lord and Lady MacDonald's family home is also an award-winning restaurant, offering the rare chance to enjoy superb food in the grandest of settings. The track that leads to the 19th-century Sporting Lodge turns off the A851 about 8 miles south of Broadford. Lady Claire MacDonald is one of the best known cooks in Scotland and author of several cookbooks, and if you do decide to treat yourself make sure you leave enough room for their exquisite puddings. The 5 course fixed menu is in our expensive range, but well worth it. Accommodation (in our **L** range) is also available in 10 en suite rooms. Open Mar-Nov.

A little further on is **B** *Duisdale Hotel*, T833202, F833404, www.duisdale.com 19 rooms (2 with 4-poster beds). Country house hotel set in lovely grounds with great views across the Sound of Sleat. The restaurant serves good traditional Scottish cooking, and a 5-course meal is in our expensive range.

Skye

Isle Ornsay South of Duisdale is the signed turning for Isle Ornsay, or **Eilean Iarmain** (pronounced eelan yarman) in Gaelic, a very beautiful place in a small rocky bay overlooking the tidal Isle of Ornsay with the mountains of Knoydart in the background. This was once Skye's main fishing port and the neat white-washed cottages and tiny harbour are still there. It is also largely Gaelic-speaking, thanks mainly to the efforts of its landlord, Sir Iain Noble, who owns the hotel and his own local Gaelic whisky company as well as the northern half of the peninsula, which is known as *Fearan Eilean Iarmain*.

Sleeping and eating L *Hotel Eilean Iarmain*, T833332, F833275, www.eileanarmain.co.uk 12 rooms. Award-winning Victorian hotel full of charm and old-world character, with wonderful views. It is utterly lovely and romantic and an absolute must if you're in the area and can afford it. Award-winning restaurant features local shellfish landed only yards away (open to non-restaurants). A cheaper option is to eat in the cosy **bar** next door, which serves pub grub of an impossibly high standard in a more informal atmosphere. The hotel also offers winter shooting on the local estate and you can enjoy a tasting of the local whisky, T833266.

West Sleat

A few miles further on is a turn-off to the left to the villages of **Ord**, **Tokavaig** and **Tarskavaig**, on the west coast of the peninsula and from where, on a clear day, the views across to the Cuillins. Near Tokavaig is the ruin of **Dunsgaith Castle**, home of the MacDonalds of Sleat until the 17th century. Tarskavaig is a typical crofting township. In the early 19th century the MacDonalds wanted the more fertile glens inland for their sheep farms and so evicted the people to coastal townships like Tarskavaig. Just beyond the turn-off to Ord are the remains of **Knock Castle**, yet another MacDonald stronghold.

Nearby, in Toravaig House, is the **F** *Hairy Coo Backpacker Hotel*, T833231, F833393, stotty@hairycooskye.freeserve.co.uk 30 beds, open all year, breakfast on request, also serves bar meals. A few miles further on, at Kilmore, is the **F** *Sleat Independent Hostel*, T844440, F844272. Newly-refurbished with all facilities, 24 beds, open all year, free transport to and from Armadale Pier.

At **Ostaig** is the Gaelic College, *Sabhal Mor Ostaig*, where all subjects are taught in Gaelic, including full-time courses in business studies and media, as well as short courses in Gaelic music and culture during the summer months, T844373. The bookshop has a good selection of books and tapes for those wishing to learn the language. The college was founded by Sir Iain Noble (see above). Ostaig is also the beginning or end (depending on which direction you're heading) of the detour to Tarskavaig, Tokavaig and Ord.

Clan Donald Visitor Centre Just before the ferry pier at Armadale is the Clan Donald Visitor Centre, housed in Armadale Castle which was built in 1815 as the main residence of the MacDonalds of Sleat. Most of the castle is now a roofless ruin but the servants' quarters now contain an excellent exhibition and accompanying video explaining the history of the Lordship of the Isles. The Clan Donald Lords of the Isles took over from their Norse predecessors in ruling the Hebrides, until their power was broken in 1493. The former stables at the entrance comprise offices, a restaurant and bookshop, while the estate manager's house has been converted to accommodate an extensive library and archives. The castle is surrounded by 40 acres of handsome gardens and woodland and there are ranger-led walks along nature trails with fine views across to the mainland.

Skye

■ *Daily Apr to end-Oct 0930-1730. Adult £3.95, concession/children £2.85. T844305, 844275, office@cland.demon.co.uk*

Just beyond the Clan Donald Centre is the tiny village of **Armadale** which is strung out along the wooded shoreline and merges into the neighbouring village of **Ardvasar** (pronounced Ard-*vaa*-sar), which has a post office, general store. Armadale's *raison d'être* is the ferry pier and there's not a huge amount to keep you occupied, but there are a couple of good handicraft shops. At the turn-off to the pier is *Skye Batiks* , which also has a shop in Portree (see page 297). Here you'll find the colourful cotton garments which make a unique souvenir of the island, T844396. They also now have B&B accommodation. On the ferry pier is *Ragamuffin*, T844217, which sells a wide range of knitwear and is open daily 0900-1800.

Armadale & Ardvasar

Sleeping and eating Just before the turn-off to the ferry pier is **F** *SYHA Hostel*, T844260. 42 beds. Open mid-Mar to end Oct, rents bikes. There's also **B&B** accommodation in Arvasar, at the lovely **C** *Ardvasar Hotel*, T844223, F844495, www.ardvasar.com, a traditional whitewashed coaching in with 9 rooms, an excellent restaurant and the liveliest pub in the vicinity. Alternative eating options are *Pasta Shed*, on the ferry pier, which does good eat-in or takeaway pizzas. A few hundred yards away is the *Gallery* café/restaurant which serves cheap fish and seafood dishes.

For full details of **ferry crossings to Mallaig**, see page 292. There are 3 **buses** daily, except Sun, from Armadale Pier to **Portree** (1 hr 20 min) and **Kyleakin** (1 hr) via **Broadford** (40 min). The first bus leaves at 0935.

Transport

Skye

About four or five miles past the ferry port, at the end of the road, is **Aird of Sleat**, a crofting township, from where you walk out to the lighthouse at the **Point of Sleat**. It's a five mile walk on a clear path across moorland with fine coastal scenery.

Walks on Skye

Skye is one of the best places in Scotland for walking. The walks described below range from easy low-level routes to harder walks requiring a reasonably good level of fitness and a detailed map. As in the rest of the Highlands, you should be prepared for the worst and be properly equipped to cope with the wind and rain, even in the height of summer. Good hiking boots are also essential as the ground underfoot is likely to be boggy once off roads and tracks. See also the safety precautions outlined on page 53.

OS Landranger Nos 23 and 32

For the Cuillin Ridge, a good book is *Black Cuillin Ridge – A Scrambler's Guide*, by SP Bull (Scottish Mountaineering Trust). Also good are the Charles Rhodes books, such as *Introductory Scrambles from Glen Brittle*. For less strenuous walks, try *Selected Walks on North (and South) Skye*, at £3.75. All these books are available in local bookshops and the tourist office in Portree.

Recommended reading

Around Portree

A nice, gentle introduction to walking in the area, and an opportunity to stretch your legs before tackling more strenuous routes such as the Old Man of Storr or the Quiraing, starts out from Bosville Terrace. Follow the street as it curves round then take the right fork at the first junction, down towards the shore. Just after the car park to the right the road splits: follow the path to the right along the northern shore of the bay. The path follows the shore and passes a viewpoint and flagpole. It then becomes rougher as it swings round the headland and reaches a gate in a dyke. Go through the gate and cross the muddy field, then follow the fence up to the left till you reach another gate. Go over the gate and continue along the edge of the next field, then cross a stile at the top of the field. Climb up the slope to the clear track and follow this left as it heads uphill. You'll then see some houses; take the track beyond the house on the left and follow it down between two large farm buildings. The path heads down across rough moorland towards Portree. Cross the stile and continue downhill through some woods, then you'll see a hotel on your left before rejoining the original road near the car park. It's about 2½ miles in total and takes about an hour and a half at an easy pace. The path can get very muddy in places.

The Old Man of Storr

For transport details, see page 297

This dramatic basalt finger of rock, 165 ft high, stands beneath the steep cliffs of The Storr (2,360 ft) and is visible from the A855. The starting point for the 3½ mile walk up and back (1½ hours) is the car park on the left, just over six miles north of Portree, near the northern end of Loch Leathan, which can be reached by bus from Portree.

Cross the stile over the wall by the Forestry Commission sign and follow the clear track up through the conifer plantation. The track is a gradual uphill climb until you come out into open grassland. Go through the gate in the fence and then it's a steep climb up the grassy slope with the massive pinnacle towering overhead. Once at the top you enter an area of weird and impressive rock formations. You can follow any of the dozens of paths that lead between the rocks, or just enjoy the fantastic views across to Raasay and the mainland beyond. You can follow the same path back down to the car park.

The Quiraing

This four mile walk is quite demanding but the dramatic scenery more than compensates. To get to the starting point, drive 19 miles north from Portree on the A855. At Brogaig, just north of Staffin, take the single-track road to Uig. Follow this for about 2½ miles and, just after the road has zig-zagged its way up the face of the ridge, park in the car park to the left.

Cross the road and follow the well-defined path along the base of the cliffs, with a steep grassy slope down to the right. After about one mile you'll start to see some of the well-known rocky features on the far side of a rough valley. The most imposing of these is **The Prison**, a huge, tilted square block. On the left, among the towering cliffs, is **The Needle**, a shaft of rock about 120-ft high. Scramble up the narrow gully to the left of The Needle to reach **The Table**, an area of flat grassland surrounded by high cliffs (local shinty teams used to play here!). From The Table continue along the path at the foot of the cliffs, past a small lochan on the right and through a stone dyke, until you reach the lowest point of the ridge on your left. Scramble up onto the ridge and make your way back along the tops of the cliffs (take care at this point). There's a hard climb up the slopes of Meall na Suirmamach, but the views from the top are spectacular. Continue along the top of the cliffs for just over a mile and you'll see the car park.

Elgol to Camasunary Bay

This nine mile coastal walk is quite demanding but on a clear day the views of the Cuillins make it well worth the effort. It starts from the car park in Elgol. From the car park, walk back up the road for a short distance, then turn left along a track behind some houses, signposted for 'Garsbheinn'. Beside the last of these houses is a sign for the path to Coruisk. Follow this path along a steep grassy slope. The views across Loch Scavaig to the island of Soay and the Cuillins behind are marvellous. The slope get seven steeper beneath Ben Cleat, then comes the point where vertigo sufferers may wish they hadn't started. This is the notorious 'bad step', an overhanging rock with a 30 ft drop to the sea below. Once you negotiate this, you then continue along the foot of Glen Scaladal and cross a burn, which can be tricky if its in spate. Then it's on along the path beyond Beinn Leacach to Camasunary Bay. The shortest way back to Elgol is to retrace your steps (including bad ones), but as an alternative, follow the clear track from Camasunary up the right side of Abhainn nan Lean over the hills to the east until it joins the B8083 from Broadford. From here it's about 3½ miles back along the road to Elgol.

For transport to and from Elgol, see page 305

Outer Hebrides

Outer Hebrides

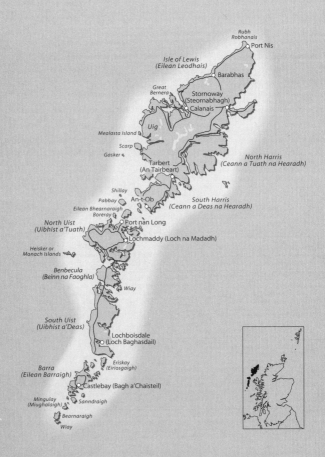

The Outer Hebrides – or Long Island as they are also known – consist of a narrow 130-mile long chain of islands, lying 40 miles off the northwest coast of the Scottish mainland. Relentlessly battered by fierce Atlantic winds the islands can seem a hostile environment and an unappealing proposition, particularly if you happen to be stuck there on a wet Sunday without your own means of transport. Much of the interior is bleak peat bog, rocks and endless tiny lochs, and the long, straggling crofting communities only add to the feeling of desolation. But there are also miles of superb beaches, wild mountain scenery, numerous archaeological treasures and long hours of summer daylight in which to appreciate it all.

Despite the frequency of transport connections with the mainland, the Outer Hebrides remain remote in every sense. Unlike Skye and the Inner Hebrides, tourism is of far less importance to the local economy. In many ways, the islands are the last bastion of the old Highland life. Though newer industries such as fish farming have been introduced, the traditional occupations of crofting, fishing and weaving still dominate, and outside Stornoway on Lewis (the only decent-sized town in the islands) life is very much a traditional one, revolving around the seasons and the tides. Almost every islander has more than one occupation, so don't be surprised if the landlady of your guesthouse also weaves Harris Tweed, or if her husband drives the Postbus as well as doing a bit of fishing on the side. This creates a network of relationships where everyone knows everyone else.

Ins and outs

Getting there **By air** *British Airways*, T08457-733377, flies daily, except Sun, from Glasgow to Stornoway on Lewis (1 hr), Barra (1 hr 5 mins) and Benbecula on North Uist (1 hr). There are also flights from Edinburgh to Stornoway (1hr 10 mins), Inverness to Stornoway (40 mins) daily except Sun, and to Benbecula (2 hrs 40 mins) Mon-Fri. Note that weather conditions are so changeable that flights are prone to delay and can be very bumpy. Flights to Barra have an added complication in that they land on the beach, meaning that the runway disappears twice a day under the incoming tide.

By boat *CalMac* car and passenger ferries sail to and from Stornoway (Lewis), Tarbert (Harris), Lochmaddy (North Uist), Lochboisdale (South Uist) and Castlebay (Barra). Ferry times change according to the day of the week and time of the year, so they aren't listed in full below. For full details see the *CalMac Ferry Guide* or call *CalMac*, T0990-650000, reservations@calmac.co.uk, for reservations and T01475-650100, www.calmac.co.uk, for general enquiries. See also 'Essentials', page 45. Car space is limited during the summer months, so it's advisable to book ahead. For details of bus connections on Skye and on the mainland, contact Scottish Citylink, T0990-505050.

Lewis & Harris

Things to do in the Outer Hebrides

- Visit the standing stones at **Callanais**, preferably at night when there's a spooky atmosphere.
- Take a stroll along the wonderful **Uig sands**, the loveliest beach on Lewis.
- Hire a car and drive along the amazing **Golden Road**, on the east coast of Harris.
- Fly to the island of **Barra**, where the planes land on the beach.
- Take a trip to **St Kilda**, home to some of the largest seabird colonies in Europe.

To Lewis: *CalMac* ferry from Ullapool to Stornoway (2 hrs 40 minutes) 2-3 times daily Mon-Sat in the summer (Jun-Sep) and twice daily Mon-Sat in the winter. One-way ticket costs £13 per passenger and £62 per car. CalMac offices: Ullapool (T01854-612358) and Stornoway (T01851-702361).

To Harris: from Uig (Skye) to Tarbert (1 hr 35 mins) twice daily Mon-Sat. One-way ticket £8.50 per passenger, £40 per car. Contact Uig (T01470-542219) or Tarbert (T01859-502444).

To North Uist: from Uig to Lochmaddy (1 hr 40 mins) 1-2 times daily. One-way ticket £8.50 per passenger, £40 per car. Contact Lochmaddy (T5000337).

To Barra and South Uist: from Oban to Castlebay (5 hrs) and Lochboisdale (6 hrs 40 mins) once daily except Tue and Sun. One-way ticket £18.75 per passenger, £67 per car. From Mallaig to Castlebay (3 hrs 45 mins) on Sun only, and to Lochboisdale (3 hrs 30 mins) on Tue only. One-way ticket £13.85 per passenger, £49.50 per car. From Castlebay to Lochboisdale (1 hr 50 mins) on Mon, Wed, Thu and Sat, and from Lochboisdale to Castlebay on Tue, Thu, Fri and Sun. One-way ticket £5.30 per passenger, £30.50 per car.

To North Uist and Harris: a ferry sails to Otternish (North Uist) from Leverburgh (Harris) 3 or 4 times daily. The trip takes 1 hr 10 mins and a one-way ticket costs £4.75 per passenger, £21.90 per car.

Island Hopscotch Tickets: a much cheaper way to get around the islands with a car is with one of *CalMac's* Island Hopscotch tickets. There are various route options and tickets give you 30 days unlimited travel on each route. For example, a ticket for the Oban-Castlebay- Lochboisdale- Otternish- Leverburgh- Stornoway- Ullapool route, allows you to visit all the main islands and costs £38 per passenger and £164 per car. See the *CalMac* guide or call the numbers above for full details of the Island Hopscotch Tickets, and the **Island Rover Ticket**, which gives unlimited travel on most CalMac routes for 8 or 15 days.

You should allow plenty of time to fully explore the islands. With your own transport and travelling from top to bottom, a week would be enough time for a whistle-stop tour but not enough to explore in any depth or scratch beneath the surface. You will need to allow for the lack of public transport on Sun on most islands and for the fact that weather conditions frequently affect ferry and flight timetables.

Getting around

By air *Loganair* (operating as *British Airways*) fly between Barra, Benbecula and Stornoway Mon-Fri. For full details, T08457-733377.

By boat Passenger ferries run regularly between Ludag in South Uist to both Eoligarry in Barra and to the island of Eriskay, T01878-720238/265. **Car ferries** also connect Eriskay with South Uist, T08178-720261. There are also *CalMac* ferries between Harris and North Uist, and South Uist and Barra (see above for details).

The car ferry to Eriskay from South Uist will close after the opening of the new causeway in Aug 2001

Outer Hebrides

Festivals in the Outer Hebrides

As the heartland of Gaelic culture, the Outer Hebrides are host to many music events throughout the year, ranging from a spontaneous ceilidh to one of the three local mods. Mods usually consist of three days of competition in piping, singing, instrumental music, drama and poetry and are an opportunity to see the best of the local talent. More information can be obtained from An Comunn Gaidhealach, T01851-703487. Also listed below are the various Highland Games and agricultural shows, where you can also see piping competitions and highland dancing.

Late March: Feis nan Coisir, *Stornoway, Lewis*.

1st Friday in April: Donald Macleod Memorial Piping Competition, *Stornoway, Lewis*.

May-June: Highland Festival, *held in various locations*.

Early June: Harris Mod, *Tarbert, Harris*.

2nd week in June: Lewis Mod, *Stornoway, Lewis*.

Mid June: Uist Mod, *Iochdar, South Uist*.

May-June: Lochmaddy Boat Festival, *Lochmaddy, North Uist*.

Mid July: Berneray Week, *Bearnaraigh (Berneray), North Uist*.

July: Ceolas Music School, *South Uist*.

Early July (2 weeks): Barra Festival.

Early/mid July (1 week): Feis Tir an Eorna, *Paibeil, North Uist*; Barra Highland Games, *Borgh (Borve), Barra*.

11-14 July: Hebridean Celtic Music Festival, *Stornoway, Lewis*.

Mid July: North Uist Highland Games, *Hosta, North Uist*.

Mid/late July: Harris Gala; South Uist Highland Games, *Aisgeirnis (Askernish), South Uist*; Lewis Highland Games, *Tong, Lewis*.

Mid July: Barra Highland Games.

3rd week July: Harris Festival

Late July: Barra Live, *Barra;* West Side Agricultural Show, *Barabhas (Barvas), Lewis*; South Uist Agricultural Show, *Iochdar, South Uist;* South Harris Agricultural Show, *Leverburgh, Harris*.

July: Feis Eilean an Fhraoich, *Stornoway, Lewis*.

Late July/early August: North Uist Agricultural Show, *Hosta, North Uist*.

Early August: Carloway Agricultural Show, *Càrlabhagh (Carloway), Lewis;* Fies Tir a Mhurain, *Lionacleit, Benbecula;* Lewis Carnival, *Stornoway;* Fish Festival, *Stornoway;* Twin Peaks Hill Race, *North Uist*.

2nd week August: Harris Arts Festival, *Tarbert*.

By bus Bus services have improved and now run regularly to most main towns and villages on the islands. Details of local services are given under each destination. You should also invest in a copy of the *Highlands & Islands Travel Guide* (£1) which is available from the local Tourist Information Centres.

Note that you cannot take a rented car off the islands

By car Most of the islands' roads are single track but in good condition and, unlike other parts of the Highlands and Islands, not too busy. On Sun you'll barely meet another soul, save for the occasional perplexed tourist looking in vain for somewhere to go. Drivers should note that petrol stations are few and far between, expensive and closed on Sun. The normal rules for single track roads apply and, as elsewhere in the Highlands, you need to look out for wandering sheep. Also note that distances are greater than most people imagine. For example, the distance from Nis (Ness), at the northern tip of Lewis, to Leverburgh in the south of Harris, is 85 miles. From Stornoway to Tarbert is 37 miles. And the distance from Otternish, in the north of North Uist, to Lochboisdale, the main ferry port on South Uist, is 50 miles. Several local **car hire** agencies offer reasonable rental deals. Expect to pay around £15-25 per day, depending on the size of engine and age of the car.

Keeping with tradition

The islands are the 'Gaidhealtachd', the land of the Gael. Gaelic culture has remained more prominent here than in any other part of Scotland and the way of life and philosophy of the islanders will seem totally alien and fascinating to many visitors. Gaelic is the first language for the majority of the islanders – and the only one for the older generation – but the all-pervading influence of the English media has taken its toll and the language is under threat. Though Gaelic is still taught in schools, the younger generation tend to speak to each other in English. Visitors will not have any language problems, as the Gaelic-speaking inhabitants are so polite they will always change to English when visitors are present, though place names and signposts are in Gaelic.

The church is also an important factor in preserving the language, and services are usually held in Gaelic. In fact, religion is one of the most pervasive influences of Hebridean life and the islanders' faith is as strong as the winds that pound their shores. The islands are split between the Presbyterian Lewis, Harris and North Uist, and the predominantly Roman Catholic South Uist and Barra. Benbecula, meanwhile, has a foot in either camp. On Lewis and Harris, the Free Church is immensely powerful and the Sabbath is strictly observed. Don't expect to travel anywhere by public transport, shops and petrol stations will be closed and you'll be hard pressed to find a place to eat. Even the swings in the playgrounds are padlocked! On the Roman Catholic islands, however, things are a bit more relaxed.

By bicycle Cycling is a great way to explore the islands. You can fully appreciate the amazing scenery around you without the risk of driving over the edge of a cliff, and it only costs a few pounds to transport a bike by ferry. There is, of course, the major problem of strong winds, which can leave you frustrated and exhausted, especially when cycling into the prevailing easterly wind. **Bike hire** agencies are also given under the relevant town.

Orientation & information

The Outer Hebrides is made up of more than 200 islands, only 10 of which are populated: Lewis and Harris; Scalpay; Berneray; North Uist; Benbecula; South Uist; Eriskay; Barra; and Vatersay, giving a total population of just under 30,000. The main population centre is Stornoway on Lewis, the only major town in the islands. The rest of the population is scattered throughout the islands in much smaller villages, mostly strung out along the coast.

Lewis and Harris are actually one island, divided by history and a line of high hills that runs between them. The northern part of Lewis is mostly bleak, flat peat moor, while the south and Harris are more rugged, with rocky peaks and superb beaches. The more southerly islands of North Uist, Benbecula and South Uist, joined together by bridges and causeways, are mostly low and flat and peppered with so many lochs they resemble a giant sieve. Toll-free road bridges connect the island of Scalpay with Harris and Great Bernera with Lewis and a causeway connects Berneray with North Uist. A new causeway will connect Eriskay to South Uist in 2001.

There are **tourist information centres** in Stornoway and Tarbert which are open all year round, and also in Lochmaddy, Lochboisdale and Castlebay which are open early Apr to mid Oct. Full details are given under each destination.

The **Western Isles Tourist Board** produces an accommodation brochure as well as the essential *Western Isles Official Tourist Map* (Estate Publications; £3.95), which gives place names in English and Gaelic. They also have their own website (www.witb.co.uk)

Outer Hebrides

Things to do when it's raining

- The climate is mild due to the effect of the Gulf Stream, but also moist. You can expect it to rain on an average of two out of every three days, even in summer. The wind is constant and weather fronts come and go with such speed that there's little chance for mist or fog to settle and few problems with that scourge of many a Scottish holiday, the midge.
- So what is there to do in the Outer Hebrides when it's raining? That's easy –

there ain't much. There are a few museums and heritage centres dotted around, but you can only look at old black and white photographs for so long. The delights of the islands are very much of the outdoor variety, so unless you're fortunate with the weather, get out there and brave the elements. And if it's a Sunday on one of the northerly Presbyterian islands, you'll have no choice, as everything will be closed.

which provides lots of information on the islands, including up and coming events such as The Royal National Mod, to be held in 2001. Information about the islands can also be obtained at www.hebrides.com and www.gatliff.ic24.net The *Outer Hebrides Handbook and Guide* (£7.95) is written by local experts and is useful on history, culture, and flora and fauna.

Sleeping Accommodation on the islands is generally not difficult to find, except perhaps at the height of the summer, when you should book in advance, either directly or through the local tourist office. There are plenty of **B&Bs** and **guesthouses** scattered throughout the islands, many of which offer better value than the hotels. Most don't have private bathrooms, but they're comfortable, very welcoming and will offer evening meals. It's a good idea to book ahead if you're staying on a Sun. If you're staying in the countryside, you should check if there's a convenient pub or hotel to eat in, and if not, make arrangements to eat at your B&B.

There are numerous self-catering style cottages across the islands, many of which are advertised in the Western Isles brochure published annually by the Western Isles Tourist Board. There are also several official **youth hostels**, in converted crofts scattered around the islands in isolated locations. Some are difficult to get to without your own transport, but you can always hitchhike. They are run by the **SYHA** or the **Gatliff Hebridean Hostels Trust** (see next page). They are basic and adequate, but take a sleeping bag and food. Most of them don't have phones, so you can't book in advance, and try not to arrive or leave on a Sun. The Gatliff Trust has 4 hostels throughout the islands. Contact them at 71-77 Cromwell Street, Stornoway, or visit their website: www.gatliff.ic24.net There are also several new independent private hostels, which are clean and modern and more expensive.

Leodhas (Lewis)

Phone code: 01851
Colour map 1, grid A3

Lewis constitutes the northern two thirds of the most northerly island in the Outer Hebrides (which includes Harris to the south). It is by far the most populous of the Outer Hebridean islands, and with over 20,000 inhabitants, makes up two thirds of the total population. Just over 8,000 people live in Stornoway, the largest town in the Hebrides and the administrative capital of the Western Isles.

The majority of the rest of the population live in the long line of crofting townships strung out along the west coast between Port Nis (Ness) and Càrlabhagh (Carloway). The west coast is also where you'll find the island's most interesting sites, the prehistoric remains of Dùn Chàrlabhaigh (Carloway) Broch and the impressive Calanais (Callanish) Standing Stones, the restored blackhouse village of Garenin and the Arnol Blackhouse. These can all be visited as a day trip from Stornoway, either as an organized tour or on the 'West Side Circular' bus service.

The interior of the northern half is flat peat bog, hence the island's name which means 'marshy' in Gaelic. Further south, where Lewis becomes Harris, the scenery is more dramatic as the relentlessly flat landscape gives way to rocky hills, providing the backdrop to the sea-lochs that cut deep into the coast and the beautiful beaches around Uig.

History

Lewis was dominated by the Vikings, and the Norse influence can be seen in many of the place names, such as Uig (which is Norse for 'a bay'). After the end of Norwegian sovereignty in 1266, the island was ruled by the Macleods, said to be descendants of early settlers from Iceland. Control of the island was wrested from them by the Mackenzies, who then proceeded to sell it, in 1844, to Sir James Matheson. The new owner built Lews Castle in Stornoway and began to develop the infrastructure of the island as well as investing in new industries. Though many crofts were cleared and families sent to Canada, the people of Lewis fared well and certainly much better than their counterparts in the Southern Isles.

The next proprietor was Lord Leverhulme, founder of Lever Brothers, who bought the island (along with Harris) in 1918. He planned to turn Lewis into a major fishing centre and ploughed money into developing the infrastructure. He was forced to abandon his plans, however, partly because of the decline of the fishing industry, and partly owing to the growing conflict between him and the islanders returning from the war who wanted land of their own to farm. As a final benevolent gesture, Lord Leverhulme offered Lewis to the islanders, but only Stornoway Council accepted. The island was then divided into estates and sold, and hundreds emigrated.

Today, the economy of Lewis is still based on the traditional industries of crofting, fishing and weaving, though there are other economic activities such as fish farming, which is now a major employer, service industries, tourism, construction and the onshore oil yard at Stornoway.

Steòrnabhagh (Stornoway)

The fishing port of Stornoway, the only town in the Outer Hebrides, is the islands' commercial capital and as such boasts more services and facilities than you might expect in any town of comparable size. It has the full range of banks, shops, hotels, guesthouses, pubs and restaurants, garages, car hire firms, sports facilities, an airport and ferry terminal, and for the visiting tourist it presents a rare opportunity to stock up on supplies.

Phone code: 01851 Colour map B1, grid B3 Population: 8,132

Stornoway is also the administrative capital and home to the *Comhairle nan Eilean* (The Western Isles Council), which has done much to broaden the local economy and to promote and protect Gaelic language and culture, but is probably best known for its disastrous financial dealings with the Bank of Credit and Commerce International (BCCI), which collapsed in 1991, losing the islands a cool £23 million.

The **tourist information centre** is at 26 Cromwell St. They stock maps, bus timetables and various books and brochures and sell tickets for minibus tours to Calanais and for wildlife trips round Lewis and Harris. ■ *T703088.*

Outer Hebrides

The Gatliff Trust

The Gatliff Hebridean Hostels Trust (GHHT) is a non-profit making charitable organisation run entirely by volunteers, working with the island community to establish, maintain and develop a chain of 'value-for-money' hostels offering clean, cheap, simple, safe, welcoming and traditional croft-style accommodation in dramatic and beautiful locations for visitors to the Outer Hebrides.

The GHHT is independent of the SYHA but has adopted status. Visitors do not have to be members of either organisation to use and stay in the hostels. First established as the Gatliff Trust in 1961 by Herbert Gatliff, the Trust was originally intended to provide young persons of limited means with the opportunity to meet local people and enjoy the unique natural environment and cultural heritage of the islands. However, in recent years visitors of all incomes, ages, nationalities and interests have been encouraged to use the facilities.

The Trust is currently involved in the operation of four hostels situated at Garenin (Isle of Lewis), Rhenigidale (Isle of Harris), Berneray (Isle of North Uist) and Howmore (South Uist). Further hostels may be opened on other islands in the future.

The hostels are open all year and looked after by non-resident wardens who live and practice crofting nearby. No advance bookings are accepted but it is very unlikely that visitors will find themselves turned away and without a bed for the night. There is also limited space for camping at the hostels. Hostels provide bunk/camp beds, cooking facilities and cutlery, piped water, toilets and coal/wood fires but visitors should bring their own food and a sleeping bag is recommended.

Charges for 2001: (18 and over- £6.50, 17 and under- £5.00, Camping- £3.25, Day Visitors- £0.90). Annual Membership: £5.00.

Further information including membership and contact details, hostel locations and photographs, a reading list and places of interest to visit in the surrounding area can be found at the GHHT website: www.gatliff.ic24.net

Apr-May and Sep-Oct, Mon-Fri 0900-1800, Sat 0900-1700; Jun-Aug, Mon-Fri 0900-2000; Oct-Mar Mon-Fri 0900-1700.

Getting there & around Stornoway is the island's transport hub. The **airport** is 4 miles east of the town centre, a £5 taxi ride away. For details of flights to the other islands and the mainland, see Ins and outs (page 318). The *CalMac* **ferry terminal** is just beyond the **bus station**, which is on South Beach, a short walk from the town centre. Full ferry details are also given in Ins and outs. Buses leave from Stornoway to all parts of the island and also to Tarbert and Levenburgh on Harris. Bus timetables are available from the **tourist office**. See also Transport on page 327.

The town is compact and most of what you need is within easy walking distance of the tourist office. Some of the B&Bs in the residential areas are a quite a distance from the centre, but there's an hourly town bus service, or hire a **taxi** from *Central Cabs* (T706900).

Sights Stornoway is short on conventional tourist sights and once you've been to the tourist office and bought the necessities from the local supermarkets, there's not much else to do. The focal point of the town has always been its sheltered deep-water **harbour**, and though the fishing industry has declined since its peak at the end of the last century, there's still a fair amount of activity, especially at the fish market on North Beach on Tuesday and Thursday evenings. The harbour is usually full of seals, giving the town its nickname of Portrona (port of seals). There's a good view across the harbour to **Lews Castle**, a 19th-century edifice built by Sir James Matheson with money earned from opium and tea. The castle now houses a college and its real attraction is the wooded grounds, the only place you'll see trees on the islands.

The **Museum nan Eilean**, on Francis Street, features a range of temporary exhibitions on island life and history. ■ *Mon-Sat 1000-1730 Apr to Sep; Tue 1000-1700 and Sat 1000-1300 Oct-Mar. Free. T703773.*

Anyone remotely interested in Harris Tweed should visit the **Lewis Loom Centre**, housed in the Old Grainstore at the northern end of Cromwell Street, just off Bayhead. The 40-minute guided tour includes demonstrations of traditional methods of warping, dyeing and spinning and a detailed lecture on the history of Harris Tweed. There's also a craft shop. ■ *Mon-Sat 1000-1700. Adult £2. T703117.*

The impressive baronial Town Hall on South Beach currently houses the **An Lanntair Art Gallery**, though plans are afoot to move the gallery into a new arts centre. The gallery features the work of local, national and international artists and also stages various musical events. The coffee shop serves home baking and tasty snacks. ■ *Mon-Sat 1000-1730. Free. T703307, lanntair@sol.co.uk*

Sleeping

As the largest settlement on the islands, Stornoway has a good selection of accommodation from which to choose, though you should book in advance in the peak summer season. The tourist information centre will do this for you, for a small fee.

There are several centrally-located hotels, the best of which is **B** *Royal Hotel*, Cromwell St, T702109, F702142. 24 rooms, good value and good food in its restaurant and bistro (see 'Eating' below). On the outskirts of town is **B** *Cabarfeidh Hotel*, Manor Park, T702604, F705572. 46 rooms, not as convenient as the *Royal* but with the full range of facilities and a decent restaurant. **B** *Park Guest House*, 30 James St, T702485, F703482. 10 rooms, this Victorian town house is comfortable, only 500yd from the ferry terminal, and the best of the guesthouses. It also has an excellent restaurant which is recommended even if you're not staying.

There are many **B&Bs** in and around the town centre, most of which offer a 'room only' rate for those requiring an early start to catch the first ferry. There are several along Matheson Rd, which is close to the town centre and the ferry terminal, including, **E** *Mrs Anne Maclead*, at No 12, T702673, and **E** (**F** room only) *Mrs M MacMillan*, 'Fernlea' No 9, T702125. Another option is **F** *Fairhaven*, 17 Keith St, T705862, which can also do meals.

The basic **F** *Stornoway Backpackers Hostel* is at 47 Keith St, T703628. Includes breakfast, open all year. There's also a Bunkhouse Hostel at **F** *Laxdale Holiday Park*, on Laxdale Lane, about a mile out of town on the road to Barabhas, T703234. It has 16 beds, basic facilities and is open all year.

Eating

Note that pubs are closed on Sun and hotels cater only for residents

The pubs and hotels serve the usual range of bar meals. Probably the best restaurant in town is at the *Park Guest House* (see 'Sleeping' above), which offers top class modern Scottish cooking using local fish, lamb and venison. It also caters for vegetarians and is open Tue-Sat. Mid-range to expensive. Also recommended is *The Boatshed*, in the *Royal Hotel* (see 'Sleeping' above), which specializes in seafood. Expensive. Less upmarket and cheaper is their *Barnacle Bistro*.

A good place cheap for snacks and light lunches is the café at the *Ann Lantair Gallery* (see 'Sights' above). For a touch of non-Scottish fare, try the *Stornoway Balti House*, near the bus station on South Beach, the *Golden Ocean Restaurant*, on Cromwell St, or the *Thai Café* on Church St. There are several other takeaways offering the standard fare of pizza, kebabs, fish and chips etc. The cheapest option is the all-day breakfast served in the *Co-op* supermarket (see map). For a cheap lunch try the *cafeteria* in the *Deep Sea Fishermen's Mission* on North Beach.

Outer Hebrides

Stornoway

To Port of Ness, Barras & Laxdale Holiday Park (A857)

To Tarbert (A858)

Guershader

Maclean Terr

Urquart

Stewart Dr

Cabarfeidh ■

Perceval Rd

Morrison Av

MacAulay Rd

Portrona Dr

Torquil Terr

River Bayhead

○ Co-op
Supermarket

Westview Terr

Kennedy Terr

Stag Rd

Leverhulme Dr

Bayhead St

MacKenzie St

Matheson Rd

Robertson

Plantation Rd

△ Lews

Mrs Anne Macleod's
Bed & Breakfast ■

Goathill Rd

○ Lewis
Loom Centre

Scotland St

Cromwell St

○ Cycle
Hire

Stornoway
Backpackers Hostel ■

Fernlea Bed & Breakfast ■

Royal ■

Kenneth St

(Pol)

Church St

Thai Café ●

Lewis St

Museum nan
Eilean
🏛

ⓘ
P

$

North Beach

Keith St

Francis St

Golden Ocean ●

✉
Public Library

Garden

Park Guest
House ■

Sandwick Rd

Quay St

Castle St

An Lanntair
Art Gallery

○

● Stornoway
Balti House

South Beach

Bus Station
🚌

James St

Esplanade
Quay

Safeway
○ Supermarket

Shell St

Bells Rd

Rigs Rd

Calmac Ferry
Terminal

Stornoway Harbour

Inaclete Rd

Newton St

To Airport (A866)

Outer Hebrides

N

0 metres 100
0 yards 100

There are 2 large supermarkets in town. *Safeway* is beside the ferry terminal and the *Co-op* is by the first roundabout on the road out to Barabhas. There's also a smaller supermarket opposite the tourist information centre.

Buses leave from Stornoway to all parts of the island. Note that buses do not run on Sun. To **Port Niss (Ness)** via **Barabhas (Barvas)** 4-6 times per day; to **Arnol**, **Siabost (Shawbost)**, **Càrlabhagh (Carloway)** , **Calanais (Callanish)**, and back to Stornoway ('West Side Circular') 4-6 times per day; to **Bearnaraigh (Great Bernera)** via **Gearraidh na h-Aibhne (Garynahine)** 4 per day; to **Uig District** 3-4 per day; to **Ranais (Ranish)** 6-8 times per day. For full details, T840269. There are also buses from Stornoway to **Tarbert** and on to **Leverburgh** (for the ferry to North Uist) 4-5 times per day (T01859-502441). 〔**Transport**〕

Car rental is available at good rates from *Lewis Car Rentals,* 52 Bayhead St, T703760, F705860. Also *Arnol Motors*, in Arnol (see page 327), T01851-710548 (0831-823318 mobile), F710248. You can **rent bikes** at *Alex Dan's Cycle Centre*, 67 Kenneth St, T704025, F701712.

Banks The *Bank of Scotland* is directly opposite the tourist office and has an ATM. The other major banks are also in the centre of town and also have ATMs. **Internet** *Captions*, 27 Church St, T702238, F706782, bayble@captions.co.uk, www.captions.co.uk Open Mon-Sat till late in the summer months. Internet facilities also available at the public library on Cromwell St. **Post office** On Francis St. **Tour companies** *MacDonald's Coaches*, at the Ferry Terminal, T706267. Coach tours. *Hebridean Exploration*, 19 Westview Tce, T705655 (T0374-292746 mobile). Sea kayak tours. *Elena C*, 5a Knock, Point, T870537, F706384. Wildlife trips from Stornoway harbour. 〔**Directory**〕

The West Coast

The west coast of Lewis contains most of what you'll want to see and can be covered in a day trip from Stornoway, either with your own transport, by public bus or as part of a minibus tour.

Phone code: 01851
Colour map 1,
grid A3

Outer Hebrides

At **Barabhas (Barvas)** the road forks. The A857 bears right (north) and continues all the way to **Nis (Ness)** and the Butt of Lewis (see page 331), but the road you want to take is the A858, which bears left (west). A few miles along this road is the turn-off for **Arnol**. At the end of the village is the **Blackhouse Museum**, one of the best surviving examples of an original blackhouse in Scotland and well worth visiting. These traditional thatched houses were once common throughout the Highlands and Islands and inhabited until the 1960s. They were built in the tradition of 'longhouses' which can be traced back 1,000 years to the time of the Viking invaders. The name 'blackhouses' dates back to the 1850s when modern buildings were introduced. These were known as 'white houses' and the older style houses were called 'blackhouses'. The blackhouses were well adapted to the harsh local climate. They had no windows or chimney and were built with local materials – stone, turf and thatch of oat, barley or marram grass, and with a peat fire burning continually in the central hearth – and attached to the living quarters was the cattle byre. This particular blackhouse was built in 1885 and lived in until 1964. ■ *T710395. Apr-Sep Mon-Sat 0930-1830; Oct-Mar Mon-Sat 0930-1630, Sun 1400-1630. Adult £2.80, concession £2, children £1.*

Hebridean Replicas (T710562) in the village offers quality handmade Lewis chess sets from local stone and provides a welcome alternative to much of the tacky tourist paraphenalia tp be found in Stornnoway.

Crofting

The word 'croft' is derived from the Gaelic croit, meaning a small area of land, and crofting has been the traditional way of life in the Scottish Highlands for many centuries. Its emotive hold on the psyche of the Highlander comes from the long, hard struggle for security of tenure (see page 414).

A croft is aptly described as a parcel of land entirely surrounded by regulations. Most crofts consist of a few acres of arable land with a proportion of grazing land shared with other crofts. Each crofter is, in effect, a kind of small tenant-farmer, the distinction being that he has almost absolute security of tenure and has the right to assign the croft to a member of his family whether the landlord agrees or not. In fact, over the years, the crofter has managed to acquire most of the rights of ownership with few of the disadvantages.

The croft is the area of land involved and not the house which is called the 'croft house'. Crofts can vary in size, from a quarter of an acre upwards. Those on

Lewis are small and relatively unproductive, with an average size of only about five acres, while on the Uists, where the land is more fertile, crofts are up to 50 acres or more.

As well as having the sole tenancy of the croft, the crofter usually also has a share in a huge area of 'common grazing' along with the other members of the crofting community – commonly called a township. They also work together in such activities as fencing, sheep dipping or cutting peat.

In reality, crofting does not provide a viable means of living. Very few crofters rely solely on their smallholding for an income and most need to have several occupations (including running a Bed & Breakfast establishment) to make ends meet. But without the family croft, whole communities would just pack up and leave, and so crofting functions as a means of preventing the depopulation of remote rural areas.

Two miles south of the Arnol turn-off, at **Bragar**, look out for an archway, formed from the jawbone of a blue whale which was washed up on the coast nearby, in 1920. A few miles further on is the township of **Siabost (Shawbost)**, where the charmingly ramshackle **folk museum**, which was started originally as a project by local schoolchildren, now contains an interesting collection of Hebridean artefacts. ■ *Mon-Sat 0900-1800, free.* Behind the museum is a **campsite**, T710504, March-October.

Just south of Siabost, beside a small loch, is the sign for the recently-restored **Norse Mill and Kiln**, which are a half-mile walk over the hill from the car park. There's not much to see as yet, but it's worth getting out of the car if you want to stretch your legs. A little further on is the turning for **Dail Beag (Dalbeg)**, a lovely secluded beach.

Eating Overlooking a small lochan surrounded by hills beside the car park is the *Copper Kettle*, T710592, an unassuming little house which is actually a superb restaurant. Meals must be booked at least 24 hrs in advance and are moderately priced (last booking 2000). Open 1030 till 1730 for tea, coffee, snacks and home baking (all year, Mon-Sat). Next door is a self-catering bungalow for rent (same phone number).

The landscape gradually becomes more undulating and scenically interesting as the road then passes through the village of **Càrlabhagh (Carloway)**, Lord Leverhulme's proposed fishing port. Here, a branch road leads to the ruined and deserted 'blackhouse' village of **Gearrannan (Garenin)**. The old village has been undergoing extensive renovation in recent years with the aid of EU funding and several derelict crofts have now been painstakingly restored to their original style of stone walls and thatched roofs. An old cart track leads down to the bay and wonderful sunsets out at sea. The village now boasts a Gatliff Trust hostel, heritage centre, café, and holiday dwellings. Above the village a footpath can be followed through the lazybeds and above the sea cliffs to reveal a stunning view of beautiful **Dal More Bay**. The Atlantic waves seem to break relentlessly onto golden sands and the beach is, not surprisingly, the favourite haunt of the surfing jet-set from Stornoway. Swimmers and bathers should be careful however because as with many of the west coast beaches there can be a fierce rip-current carrying the unwary into deeper water out at sea.

A little further on, standing a few hundred yards from the main road, is the **Dùn Chàrlabhaigh (Doune Carloway) Broch**, the best preserved building of its type in the Outer Hebrides. The impressive 2,000 year-old drystone habitation is beautifully situated on a rocky outcrop, commanding great views across Loch Carloway to the sea beyond. The remaining outer wall is 30 ft high and slopes inwards, with an inner wall which rises vertically, leaving chambers between the walls. Parts of the inner wall have collapsed, revealing the interior stairs and galleries. There's also the **Doune Broch Visitor Centre** by the car park, which tastefully complements the architectural style of the site, and which gives a good audio-visual description of how life must have been in one of these structures around 50 BC. ■ *T643338. Doune Broch Centre Apr-Oct, Mon-Sat 1000-1800. Free.*

Calanais (Callanish)

Five miles south of Dun Chàrlabhaigh is the jewel in the islands' prehistoric crown, the **Calanais Standing Stones**, which are unique in Scotland and the equal of Stonehenge in historical value. The stones are in a beautiful setting overlooking Loch Roag and are very atmospheric, especially at sunset or at night, when no one's around. They are in the form of a Celtic cross and in the centre is a circle of 13 stones with a central monolith over 12 ft tall, and a chambered burial cairn. The oldest part of this great ceremonial site – probably the stone circle – dates from around 3,000 BC (older than Stonehenge) and continued in use until about 800 BC. The full significance of the site is not yet known, though it probably is connected to the seasonal cycle as many of the stones are aligned with the rising and setting moon. There are also a number of smaller and more isolated stone circles a few miles south of Calanais, on the road to Gearraidh na h-Aibhne (Garynahine).

Next to the stones is the Calanais Visitor Centre, which features 'The Story of the Stones' exhibition, a restaurant and gift shop. On the other side of the stones is the *Blackhouse tearoom and craft shop*, run by the MacBears and better value if you fancy a bite to eat. ■ *Site open daily all year. Apr-Sep 1000-1900; Oct-Mar 1000-1600. Free. Visitor Centre closed Sun. Exhibition: adult £1.75, concession £1.25, children £0.75. Visitor Centre, T621422, calanais.centre@btinternet.com*

Phone code: 01851
Colour map 1,
grid B2

Outer Hebrides

If you want to stay near the stones and visit them after dark, there are several inexpensive B&Bs in the village of Calanais, including the friendly **E-F** *Mrs Morrison*, 27 Callanish (200 yd from the site), T621392 (open Mar-Sep). A few miles north, in Tolastadh a' Chaolais (Tolsta Chalois) is the recommended vegetarian B&B , **E**, run by *Debbie Nash*, 19 Tolsta Chaolais, T621321. There's also **E** *Aros*, T621266, kateblue@yahoo.com, owned by Kate Kirby.

Sleeping & eating

Outer Hebrides

Calanais
Standing Stones

Aside from the Calanais Visitor Centre or Blackhouse tearoom, places to eat are few and far between, but try *Tigh Mealros*, a few miles south, at Gearraidh na h-Aibhne, T621333. They serve good local grub in a cosy, relaxed atmosphere, with scallops a speciality (closes at 2100).

Transport Local **buses** travel from Stornoway. Contact the tourist office, T703088, in Stornoway, or the bus station, T704327, for details. There are also day trips to Calanais with *Galson Motors*, T840269, leaving from Stornoway bus station, and *W. MacDonald*, T706267, leaving from the pier.

The Uig peninsula

Phone code: 01851
Colour map 1, grid B2

From Gearraidh na h-Aibhne the main A858 runs back to Stornoway, while the B8011 forks west to the remote Uig peninsula in the southwest of the island. Four miles down this road is a turning to the right onto the B8059, which leads to the island of **Bearnaraigh (Great Bernera)**, now connected to the mainland of Lewis by a single-track road bridge. The main settlement on the island is **Breacleit (Breaclete)**, where you can find out about the island's history in the Bernera Museum. ■ *Apr-Sep, Mon-Sat 1100-1800.* The rest of the island is fairly interesting with tiny fishing villages and one or two brochs and some standing stones. The nicest part, though, is on the north coast, near the tiny hamlet of **Bostadh (Bosta)**, where a lovely little sandy bay looks out to the nearby island of **Bearnaraigh Beag (Little Bernera)**. There are a couple of good B&Bs on the island which both offer evening meals, one in **Tobson**, on the west coast (**E**, *Mrs MacDonald*, T612347), and the other in **Circebost** (**Kirkibost**), on the east coast (**E**, *Mrs Macauley*, T612341).

The B8011 continues across bleak moorland, then cuts north to **West Loch Roag**, which is fringed by some fine sandy beaches and backed by a much hillier landscape. Just beyond **Miabhag (Miavaig)** is the turn-off right to **Cliobh (Cliff)**, with its picturesque beach which is unsafe for swimming. A mile further on is the little village of **Cnip (Kneep)**, to the east of which is the beautiful **Traigh na Berie**, a long sandy beach backed by flat machair which is ideal for camping.

Beyond Miabhag, the eerie peninsula of Gallan Head provides a setting befitting of a science fiction drama or Cold War Orwellian novel with empty, decaying Ministry of Defence buildings battered by the Atlantic storms. Wandering around the abandoned site it is easy to form ideas of bizarre, top-secret government experiments and early warning missile tracking in this seemingly edge-of-the-world place far removed from the unwanted prying eyes of everyday society.

Gallan Head

Beyond Ardroil the road continues to **Mangersta** where at Aird Fenish is some of the most spectacular and photogenic coastal scenery in the Outer Hebrides. The cliffs plunge dramatically beyond the road to the inaccessible beach below with a series of crumbling sea stacks battered by the fierceome waves and seabirds riding the updraughts adding to the sense of natural beauty, energy and power. Further south at **Brenish** and about a 10-minute walk from the road is a menacing blowhole connected to the sea by an underground passage.

Mangersta

Far out into the Atlantic are the haunting **Flannan Islands**, scene of an unsolved mystery in 1900 following the disappearance of three lighthouse keepers. Various explanations have been put forward over the years ranging from a freak-wave in stormy weather, to a monster sea serpent or even a dispute and fight between the men but whatever the real reason the legend continues. For possible boat trips to the Flannan Islands contact Island Cruising in Uig, T01851 672381.

Outer Hebrides

At **Timsgearraidh (Timsgarry)** and the **Traigh Chapadail (Uig sands)** at the village of **Eadar Dha Fhadhail (Adroil)**. This is the loveliest of all the beaches on Lewis, with miles of sand dunes and machair, but it is famous for an entirely different reason. It was here, in 1831, that a crofter dug up the 'Lewis Chessmen', 78 pieces carved from walrus ivory and belonging to at least eight incomplete chess sets from 12th century Scandinavia. Some are now in the Museum of Scotland in Edinburgh but most can be found in the British Museum in London.

Timsgearraidh (Timsgarry)

There are a few places to stay around the Uig bay, the best of which is the beautifully-located **D** *Baile Na Cille Guest House*, in Timsgarry, T672242, F672241, RandJGollin @compuserve.com It's open Apr-Sep, offers dinner for residents and non-residents alike and one of the warmest welcomes in the islands. North of Timsgarry, at Aird Uig, is the *Bonaventure* restaurant and B&B, T672474, which serves lunches and dinners of a Franch/Scottish style.

Sleeping & eating
For details of public transport from Stornoway, see page 327

North to Nis (Ness)

The A857 leaves Stornoway and runs northwest through barren, treeless and relentlessly bleak moorland to **Barabhas (Barvas)**. The landscape is scarred by deep gashes caused by peat digging and the unfamiliar smell you detect in

Colour map 1, grid A3

your nostrils is peat burning – a strange mixture of burning grass, whisky and coffee. Peat is the main source of domestic fuel used on the islands and outside most houses, you'll see large stacks of peat, or 'cruachs'.

The road from Barabhas northeast to Nis runs through a series of forlorn-looking, scrawny settlements that all look identical and merge into one. They consist of modern, characterless grey pebble-dash cottages with the ubiquitous piles of peat in the gardens, and the abandoned cars and vans scattered around everywhere only adds to the ugly and depressing scene.

Just beyond Barabhas a sign points left to the **Morvern Art Gallery**, which has a café, making it a welcome refuge in bad weather. A few miles further on is a turning right to **Baile an Trùiseil (Ballantrushel)**, site of the huge **Clach an Trùiseil**, a 20-ft monolith (the largest in Europe), which was the scene of the last major battle on the island, fought between the Morrisons of Nis and the MacAuleys of Uig. This is the first of a number of prehistoric sights between here and **Siadar (Shader)**, which may be of interest to the keen archaeologist, but otherwise there's little of note on the road north to Nis as it passes through the typical crofting townships of **Coig Peighinnean Buirgh (Five Penny Borve), Gàbhsann bho Dheas (South Galson), Dail (Dell), Suainebost (Swainbost), Tàbost (Habost)** and **Lìonal (Lionel)**. In saying that, those interested in buying souvenirs should look in at the *Borgh Pottery*, by the bridge at Coig Peighinnean. Here you'll find a wide range of beautiful and original domestic and decorative ware. ■ *T850345. Mon-Sat 0930-1800.*

The road continues north, passing through a number of straggling villages that collectively make up **Nis (Ness)**, until it ends at the fishing village of **Port Nis (Port of Ness)**. It's a lovely spot, with a picturesque little harbour and golden sweep of beach enclosed by steep cliffs. Each September the locals head out to the island of **Sula Sgeir**, 30 miles to the north, for the annual cull of young gannets (or *gugas*), which are considered something of a delicacy by the people of Lewis. A few minutes to the northwest, the Butt of Lewis lighthouse forms the most northerly tip of the Outer Hebrides.

Just before Port Nis, is Lìonal, where the B8015 turns off right and leads to the start of the 10 mile **coastal trail** that works it way round to **Tòlstadh (Tolsta North)** and the beautiful beaches of Traigh Mhor and Garry. Numerous shielings pepper the landscape from an earlier era when local crofters drove their cattle to the summer pastures in the island's interior. The beaches can be reached much more easily by road north from Stornoway. For details of the coastal walk, see the tourist information centre in Stornoway.

Another minor road heads northwest to the tiny hamlet of **Eòropaidh (Eoropie)** (pronounced 'Yor-erpee'). By the road junction that leads to Rubha Robhanais is the ancient **Teampull Mholuaidh (St Moluag's Church)**, thought to date from the 12th century and restored to its present state in 1912. It is now used on certain Sundays by Stornoway's Episcopal Church. From Eòropaidh a narrow road runs to the lighthouse at **Rubha Robhanais (Butt of Lewis)**, which marks the nothernmost tip of the Outer Hebrides. It's a great place for spotting seabirds or whales and dolphins, but also very wild and windy. Half a mile back down the road, a path leads down to the tiny beach of **Port Sto**, which is more sheltered.

Sleeping There are several options should you wish to stay in this part of the island. There's the *Harbour View Gallery & Café*, T810735, which also offers B&B accommodation. At Gàbhsann bho Deas (South Galson), halfway between Barabhas and Port Nis, is the friendly and beautifully-restored 18th-century **D** *Galson Farm Guest House*, T850492.

Cheaper, more basic accommodation is available in the *Galson Farm Bunkhouse* (same phone number). At Coig Peighinnean Buirgh (Five Penny Borve) there's B&B with **D** *Ms Catriona Macleod*, T810240.

Na Hearadh (Harris)

Harris is not an island, but together with Lewis forms the largest of the Outer Hebrides, with Harris taking up the southern third. The two parts are divided by the long sea lochs of Loch Seaforth in the east and Loch Resort in the west, though this division is rarely shown on maps. Though joined, the two are very different in terms of geography. Harris is largely mountain and rock whereas Lewis is flat moorland.

Harris itself is almost split in two by the sea, at An Tairbeart (Tarbert), the largest town and ferry terminal. To the north are the highest peaks in the Outer Hebrides, surrounded by some of the finest unspoilt wilderness in the whole country, while to the south are miles of wonderful sandy beaches and, on the east coast, an almost indescribably strange lunar landscape straight out of a science fiction film.

With your own transport you could 'do' Harris in a day quite comfortably, but if the weather's good enough you'll want to spend more time and appreciate its precious natural beauty. There's a regular bus service between Tarbert and Stornoway, and a less frequent one that travels right round South Harris (see transport, Tarbert, on page 334).

Phone code: 01859
Colour map 1, grid B2

History

The separation of Harris and Lewis dates back to Norse times, when the island was divided between the two sons of Leod, progenitor of the Macleods. Harris remained in Macleod hands until 1834. The recent history of Harris is closely bound up with that of Lewis. Both were bought by the soap magnate, Lord Leverhulme (see page 323), whose grandiose schemes for Lewis came to nothing. Leverhulme then turned his attentions to Harris, where the peaceful little village of An t-Ob (Obbe) was renamed Leverburgh and transformed into a bustling port with all manner of public works programmes under development. His death in 1925 brought an end to all his plans for Harris and instead of becoming a town with a projected population of 10,000, Leverburgh reverted to being a sleepy village, with only the harbour, the roads and the change of name to show for it all.

Since the Leverhulme era there has been no main source of employment for the population of 2,400 on Harris, though a successful fishing industry continues on Scalpaigh (Scalpay). There is still some crofting supplemented by the Harris Tweed industry, though most production is now in Lewis, and whatever employment can be found: road-works, crafts and tourism. The most recent project proposed for Harris, to create one of Europe's largest superquarries, is highly controversial and would involve destroying an area of outstanding natural beauty for the sake of perhaps only a few dozen jobs (see page 339), with potentially disastrous consequences for the island's fragile tourist economy.

Outer Hebrides

An Tairbeart (Tarbert)

Tarbert, the largest settlement on Harris, lies in a sheltered bay on the narrow isthmus that joins North and South Harris. It's a tiny place and there's not much to do, but as it's the main ferry port for Harris, it has more facilities than

Phone code: 01859
Colour map 1, grid B2
Population: 500

anywhere else, such as shops, a bank, post office and tourist information centre. Tarbert's relatively wide range of accommodation and location make it the ideal base from which to explore the delights on offer.

The **tourist information centre** is close to the ferry terminal. They can arrange accommodation and are a good source of information on local walks. ■ *T502011. Apr-Oct Mon-Sat 0900-1700. It also opens in the winter (check times) and when the ferry arrives.*

Sleeping **C** *Harris Hotel*, on the main road from Stornoway on the left before the turning for the ferry, T502154, F502281. An old established favourite, but more importantly, the only place serving food on a Sun (see below). The bar next door also serves meals and is the social hub of the village. During the BBC television series *Castaway*, the hotel became a popular retreat for homesick 'castaways' craving the creature comforts of civilization. **C** *Leachin House*, 1 mile out of Tarbert on the Stornoway road, T/F502157. **B** including dinner. Luxurious Victorian home with great views and superb home cooking (for residents only), only 2 rooms so book ahead. **D** *Allan Cottage Guest House*, on the left after the turning into the village, T502146. Open Apr-Sep. Close to the ferry, very comfortable rooms and exceptional food. **B** including dinner. Book ahead. **E** *Macleod Motel*, right beside the ferry pier, T502364. Very handy for the early morning ferry, also has room-only rate.

There are also several B&Bs within 5 mins walk of the ferry pier, including the very friendly and welcoming **E-F** *Mrs Flora Morrison*, Tigh na Mara, T502270. Others to try are: **E**, *Mrs Morrison*, T502334; **E** *Mrs Mackinnon*, T502095; and **E**, *Mrs Miller*, T502140. A cheaper option is the new **F** *Rockview Bunkhouse*, on the main street, T/F5022211/502626. Open all year.

Eating Options on places to eat are limited. Most guesthouses and B&Bs will provide dinner on request but check in advance if they do so on a Sun. Aside from those guesthouses mentioned above, probably the best food in the village is the *Firstfruits Tearoom*, T502349, a cosy joint down by the ferry pier. Open Mon-Sat 1030-1630 Apr, May and Sep and till 1830 in Jun, Jul and Aug. Otherwise it's the *Harris Hotel* (see above) which serves food every day till around 2030. They do a 3-course fixed menu (mid-range) or basic and cheap bar meals, as does the bar next door Mon-Sat. The only other option is the chippy next door to the *Rockview Bunkhouse*, where you can get a decent carry out for £2-3. It's open for lunch and in the evening.

Transport **Ferry** details are given in the Ins and outs section on page 318. There's a **bus** service 4-5 times per day from **Stornoway** to Tarbert (1 hr 15 mins), which continues to **Leverburgh** (for the ferry to North Uist) via the west coast of South Harris. There's also a service 3-4 times per day from Tarbert to Leverburgh via the east coast (45 mins), along the so-called 'Golden Road'. There are also services to **Huisinis** (2-4 per day on schooldays, 45 mins), to **Reinigeadal** (2 per day on schooldays) and to **Scalpaigh** (2-5 per day, 10 mins). Bus timetables are available at the tourist office (see above).

Ceann a Tuath na Hearadh (North Harris)

Phone code: 01859
Colour map 1, grid B2

North Harris is the most mountainous part of the Outer Hebrides and its wild, rugged peaks are ideal for hill walking. The A859 south from Lewis gets progressively more scenic as it skirts **Loch Siophort (Seaforth)** and the mountains rise before you like a giant barrier. The road then climbs past **Bogha Glas (Bowglass)** and **Aird a Mhulaidh (Ardvourlie)** with **Clisham** (2,619 ft), the highest peak in the Outer Hebrides, and **Sgaoth Aird** (1,829 ft) towering overhead on either side. Just off the A859 near Ardvourlie is

Harris Tweed

Few visitors to Harris will not have heard of its most famous export, Harris Tweed. But how did it emerge from its humble origins to become a product synonymous with high quality craftsmanship and a de rigeur item of clothing for any self-respecting aristocrat?

Traditionally the tweed was made by fishermen's wives to clothe their own families using wool from their own sheep. They carried out the whole process themselves by hand. First the wool was washed, then dyed using native plants and bushes, tree bark and lichen, then carded, spun, warped, woven and finally waulked, or made soft, by beating it on a table. Many women could produce more than they needed and the surplus was available for sale or barter. The cloth was made throughout the Outer Hebrides and originally was not known as Harris Tweed, but simply as clo mòr (or big cloth).

All that changed in 1842 when the Countess of Dunmore, who owned a large part of Harris, took great interest and introduced many of her aristocratic friends to Harris Tweed. Very soon, much of the surplus tweed was being sold and becoming quite a fashion statement in high places. By the beginning of the 20th century demand was exceeding supply, stimulated by Royal patronage, and faster and more efficient ways of carrying out the ancillary processes were being developed by some of the larger producers. This led, in 1909, to the setting up of the Harris Tweed Association Ltd, to ensure quality control and to protect the interests of the independent crofter/ weavers. So Harris Tweed came officially into being, with its famous Orb trademark, originating from the Coat of Arms of the Countess of Dunmore.

To earn this official stamp of authenticity Harris Tweed must be made from pure Scottish wool, dyed, spun and finished in the Outer Hebrides and hand woven by the islanders in their own homes. There are now about 750 independent weavers and about 400 millworkers employed in the islands, and each weaver can produce three webs of tweed a week (a web measures 80-90 yds in length). In total the industry produces around 5,000,000 yds of tweed annually, depending on demand. The main production centre is now Lewis but all over the island you can see the woven tweed lying at the gates of crofts waiting to be collected and sent all over the world.

B *Ardvourlie Castle Guest House*, T502307, F508348. 4 rooms. Open April-October. This lovingly-restored Victorian hunting lodge on the shores of Loch Seaforth just oozes charm and elegance and can't be recommended highly enough. As if that weren't enough, they also happen to serve excellent food. There can be no better end to a day spent walking in the surrounding mountains.

If you can't afford such luxury but still crave the isolation, then carry on south until you reach the turn-off to **Reinigeadal (Rhenigidale)**, which was the most remote community on Harris and accessible only by sea or by a rough hill track until the access road was built. Here you'll find a Gatliff Trust **youth hostel**, a converted croft house (no phone) which sleeps 11 and is open all year (for details on how to get there on foot, see below). From Reinigeadal an ascent of shapely **Toddun** (528m) provides exhilarating exercise rewarded with fine views east across the Minch to the mainland and in the other direction to the mountain wilderness of North Harris.

Reinigeadal (Rhenigidale)

Outer Hebrides

Bun Abhainn Eadarra (Bunavoneader) to Hushinish (Huisinis) The A859 continues west across the crest of the craggy hills then drops down to the turn-off for the single-track B887 which winds its way all the way out to Huisinis (Hushinish) between the impressive mountains of the Forest of Harris on one side and the northern shore of West Loch Tarbert on the other, with views across to the Sound of Taransay and the beaches of South Harris.

Immediately beyond the turn-off you pass through **Bun Abhainn Eadarra (Bunavoneadar)**, which was a thriving whaling station until 1930 and one of Lord Leverhulme's many schemes for the island. The old whaling station is worth a visit even though the site has not been developed as a tourist attraction.

Just before the village of **Miabhag (Meavaig)** a defined footpath heads north into the hills up Glen Meavaig to Loch Voshimid. Further on, though, is a better opportunity for walking. Just before the gates of **Amhuinnsuidhe Castle** (pronounced 'Avan-soo-ee') is a signpost for Chliostair Power Station. From here you can walk two miles up to the dam, then follow the right-hand track round the reservoir and the left-hand track round the upper loch, before you arrive in wild and remote glen.

Just beyond the castle gates you'll see a beautiful waterfall spilling straight into the sea. The road then runs right past the front door of the castle, built in 1868 by the Earl of Dunmore, and which is still a private residence, before passing through an archway and continuing to the tiny crofting township of **Huisinis (Hushinish)**, beautifully situated in a sandy bay. This is where the road ends; next stop the USA! Follow the track to the right across the machair where a footpath above the jetty and rocky beach can be followed to the old fishing lodge at **Cravadale** and Loch Cravadale beyond. Make a detour to the golden sands and turquoise waters of **Traigh Mheilein** overlooking Scarp. From the coast strong walkers can follow Glen Cravadale inland eventually rejoining the main road near Amhuinnsuidhe Castle.

The rocky island of **Scarp** supported a population of more than 100 as late as the 1940s but was abandoned in 1971 and now the crofters' cottages are used as holiday homes. The island was the scene of a bizarre experiment in 1934, when a German rocket scientist, Gerhard Zucher, tried to prove that rockets could be used to transport mail and medical supplies to remote communities. His theory went up in smoke, however, when the rocket exploded before it even got off the ground, with 30,000 letters on board.

Tarbert to Carnach An interesting little excursion from Tarbert is the 10 mile return route that runs east through the tiny villages of **Urgha** and **Caolas Scalpaigh** to **Carnach** at the end of the road. Just beyond Urgha, on the north side of the road, is a path which leads across the hills to the **Reinigeadal**. It was originally used by the community in Reinigeadal and the children would make the daily journey across the hills to Tarbert bfore the village was connected to the A859 by the new road. The wonderfully engineered zigzag path passes through enchanting scenery above **Loch Trollamarig** in a setting more reminiscent of Scandinavia's Fjordland. A visit can easily be made to the deserted village of **Molinginish** nestled snugly in a small valley above the loch.

Scalpaigh (Scalpay) The island of **Scalpaigh (Scalpay)**, now connected to Harris by a road bridge opened by Prime Minister Tony Blair in 1998, is a thriving fishing community with a population of over 400. It's a pleasant three-mile walk across the island to Eilean Glas Lighthouse, built by the Stevensons and the first ever on the Outer Hebrides. Those who wish to stay on Scalpay can do so at **E** *Hirta*

The Forest Of Harris

The Forest of Harris is a vast tract of mountain wilderness extending north from West Loch Tarbert to Loch Resort that forms the de facto boundary with Lewis. Known as the North Harris Estate and owned and managed by the family of the Bulmer cider empire it is one of the most isolated and unspoilt upland landscapes in Scotland and because of its remoteness receives very few visitors. For experienced hillwalkers however it is a paradise offering rugged mountains, dramatic escarpments, airy ridges and desolate glens. There are endless walking possibilities including a horsehoe walk around Clisham and a long walk through Glen Ulladale to Kinlochresort, a former crofting community now abandoned, but once described as the remotest habitation in Britain. Apart from hillwalking the only other human activities now occurring in this wilderness are fishing, sheep and deer farming. As much of the area is in private ownership it is advisable to seek permission for access from Amhuinnsuidhe Castle (T01859-560262) or get further advice from TIC in Tarbert (T01859-502011).

House, T540394, **F** *New Haven*, T540325, or **F** *Seafield*, T540250. If you'd like to do some diving, contact *Scalpay Diving Services*, T540328.

Ceann a Deas na Hearadh (South Harris)

An absolute must while you're in the Outer Hebrides is the 45-mile circular route around South Harris. If you only do one thing while you're here, then make sure this is it, for the change in scenery from the west coast to the east is utterly fascinating. One thing you're sure to puzzle over as you travel round is the fact that most people live on the harsh and inhospitable east coast, known as **Na Baigh (Bays)**, while the beautiful west coast with its miles of glorious golden sands is scarcely populated. This is not through choice. The fertile west coast once housed most of the population until the end of the 18th century when they were cleared to make way for sheep farms. Some emigrated to Cape Breton, while others chose instead to stay in Harris and moved to the east side.

The main road from Tarbert runs south, skirting East Loch Tarbert, then cuts inland and heads west through a dramatic lunar landscape of rocks dotted with tiny lochans. It then begins to descend towards the sea and you can see the vast expanse of **Losgaintir (Luskentyre)** beach directly ahead. A single-track road turns off to the right and runs out to the tiny settlement of Losgaintir. The road cuts through the rich machair as it follows the magnificent stretch of bleached white sand that fills the entire bay, washed by turquoise sea and backed by steep dunes. All this set against the backdrop of the mountains to the north. Paradise! **The west coast**

A short distance offshore is the island of **Tarasaigh (Taransay)**, which was well populated at the beginning of the 1900s but was recently abandoned. The island has now gained national prominence as the setting for the popular BBC television series 'Castaway' where an assortment of supposedly normal people from a variety of backgrounds were challenged to pit their wits against the elements and themselves for a period of a full year in 2000. Some participants were more committed than others and rumour has it that the bar in the *Harris Hotel* in Tarbert had never seen such good business.

Outer Hebrides

Sleeping You can **camp** on the machair, but ask for permission at the first house. There are a couple of B&Bs **E-F** *Moravia*, T550262, open Mar-Oct, and **E-F** *Seaview*, T550263, open Apr-Oct.

The road follows the coast, passing through the tiny settlements of **Seilebost**, **Horgabost** and **Burgh (Borve)**. There's B&B accommodation at Seilebost and Horgabost, but a few miles further on is another beautiful stretch of white sands at **Sgarasta Bheag (Scaristabeg)**.

Sleeping Overlooking the beach in a wonderful setting is **B** *Scarista House*, T550238, F550277, tnpmartin@ukgateway.net 5 rooms, open May-Sep. To add to the peace and quiet, there's no TV, only an extensive library and drawing room with open fires. The food on offer is amongst the best on the islands, particularly the seafood. Even if you're not staying, you should treat yourself to dinner here. Expensive but well worth it. There are also self-catering cottages in the grounds. The golf course over the road is so scenic the views may put you off your swing.

Toe Head Beyond Sgarasta Bheag, the village of **Taobh Tuath** (Northton) provides access to the scenic promontory of **Toe Head**, almost cut off from the rest of Harris by the huge expanse of the golden sands of Sgarasta. At the MacGillivary Machair Centre you can learn about the ecology of the local machair which forms such a distinctive and attractive element of the landscape of the west coast of the Hebrides. A ruined chapel of 16th century origin is situated on the machair below **Chaipaval** (365m) whose heathery slopes can be climbed for one of the best views out to sea towards St Kilda some 40 miles distant.

Ant-Ob (Leverburgh)
For buses to Leverburgh see under Tarbert

The road then runs along the south shore till it reaches the sprawling village of **An t-Ob (Leverburgh)**, site of Lord Leverhulme's ambitious plan to turn a sleepy crofting township into a major fishing port (see page 333). A few of the original buildings can be seen near the pier, which is the departure point for *CalMac's* **car ferry** to Otternish on North Uist (for details, see Ins and outs, page 318).

Sleeping and eating The present village consists of little more than a row of incongruous Scandinavian-style wooden houses, but there are several B&Bs within a couple of miles of the ferry port. One of the best is **E-F** *Caberfeidh House*, T520276, which is close to the ferry and offers room only (**F**). More secluded is **E** *Shieldaig House*, T520378, kwhettall@aol.com, with free cycle hire. Also **E** *Mrs Paula Williams*, T520319, F520146, who caters for vegetarians, and **E** *Mrs Catherine Mackenzie*, T520246, aituated on Ferry Rd, a few mins from the ferry terminal. A cheaper option is **F** *Am Bothan Bunkhouse*, T520251, which is close to the ferry, has full facilities, space for tents and is open all year. The *An Clachan* café/restaurant (T520370) and shop is not far from the bunkhouse.

Ròghadal (Rodel) Three miles east of Leverburgh, at the southeastern tip of Harris, is **Ròghadal (Rodel)**, dominated by the beautiful 12th century **St Clement's Church**, something of an unusual sight in such a remote spot and one of the most impressive religious building in the Hebrides (only the Benedictine abbey on Iona is larger). The church stands on a site which goes back 1,500 years and was built by Alastair Crotach (Hunchback) Macleod of Harris in the 1520s. Though impressive from the outside, particularly the huge tower, the real interest lies inside, with a collection of remarkable carved wall tombs. There

Outer Hebrides

are three tombs, the most notable of which is that of the founder, Alastair Crotach. The one in the south wall of the choir is also worth a close look.

Running north from Roghadal up the east coast of South Harris is the **Golden Road**, so named by the locals because the of the huge expense of building it. This twisting, tortuous single-track road runs through a bizarre and striking moonscape and driving through it is a unique experience (but keep your eyes on the road or you'll end up in one of the many narrow sea lochs). It seems inconceivable that anyone could survive in such an environment, but the road passes through a string of townships created last century by the people evicted from the west coast (see page 337). People here have spent years eking a meagre living from the thin soil by building 'lazy beds' (thin strips of piled-up earth between the rocks) for planting potatoes. Weaving and fishing also provide much-needed income.

Na Baigh (Bays)

At **Lingreabhagh (Lingarabay)** the road skirts the foot **Roinebhal**, the proposed site of one of the largest superquarries in Europe, which would demolish virtually the entire mountain over many decades. Local people and environmentalists are up in arms at the prospect of losing precious fishing grounds not to mention a unique and precious natural asset.

The road passes through a succession of tiny settlements before joining the A859 just south of Tarbert.

Sleeping Accommodation on this coast is limited. There's also the independent *Drinishader Bunkhouse*, at Drinisiader (Drinishader), 3 miles south of Tarbert, T511255, open all year. Or there's **B&B** at **E-F** *Hillhead*, T511226, at Scadabhagh (Scadabay), between Stocinis and Drinisiadar.

Uibhist a Tuath (North Uist)

North Uist is the largest of the southern chain of the Outer Hebrides, about 13 miles from north to south and 18 miles east to west at its widest point. At first sight it comes as something of a disappointment after the dramatic landscapes of Harris. In fact, it's barely a landscape at all, as over a third of the island's surface is covered by water. The east coast around Lochmaddy, the main settlement, is so peppered with lochs it resembles a giant sieve. But heading west from Lochmaddy the island's attractions become apparent, particularly the magnificent beaches on the north and west coast. Also on the west coast, the Balranald Nature Reserve is the ideal place for bird watching. You're also likely to see otters. There are numerous prehistoric sites scattered across the island, and with all that water around there's obviously plenty of good fishing to be had.

Phone code: 01876
Colour map 1,
grid C1
Population: 1,815

Ins and outs

There are 3 **car ferry** services to North Uist. One is to Otternish from Leverburgh on South Harris, the others are to Lochmaddy, from Uig on Skye, and from Tarbert on Harris. For more details, see page 318. North Uist is joined to the islands of Benbecula and South Uist to the south by causeway and bridge. There are several **buses** daily (Mon-Sat) from Otternish to Lochmaddy and on to Lochboisdale on South Uist.

Getting there

There are 4-6 **buses** per day (not Sun) from Otternish to Lochmaddy. These buses continue to Baile a Mhanaich (Balivanich) on Benbecula, where there is an airport (see page 344) and Lochboisdale and Ludag on South Uist (see page 345). There are 4-7 buses per

Getting around

Outer Hebrides

The Uists, Benbecula & Barra

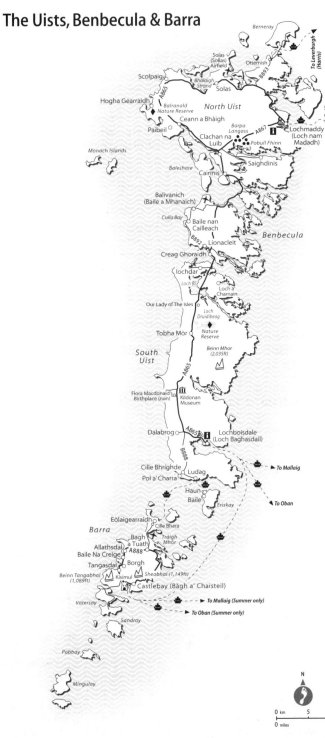

Rock 'n' roll suicide

Like Newbury Bypass in England, the proposed Lingerabay superquarry represents a cause célebre in the classic debate between the clashing interests of environment and development. Redland Aggregates originally proposed to develop the east face of Roineabhal (460 m) as a huge quarry providing a vast source of aggregate material for the construction industry in an economically impoverished part of Scotland perceived to be far removed from the mass tourism market. However, the proposal provoked a local, national and international outcry as environmental groups objected to the likely visual, landscape and ecological impacts in a unique and essentially unspoilt mountain environment designated a National Scenic Area and representative of some of the oldest rock in the world. A Public Enquiry followed in 1994-95 at which Redland presented the case for long-term local employment and the preference of one large quarry in a remote area rather than many smaller projects on the highly populated mainland. Objectors set out the concerns for the damage to a resource of national importance and the precedent it would set for environmental protection both within the industry and outside in the future if planning legislation were to be overcome. Following a lengthy follow up the Secretary of State rejected the proposal in 2000. Redland Aggregates who have now been taken over by French company, Lafarge, are now appealing against the decision. In the latest twist in the saga Scottish Natural Heritage and other action groups are now believed to be lobbying the UK government and European Parliament to reinforce the environmental value of the site by designation as a Special Area for Conservation under the EC Habitats Directive thereby making it illegal to develop the site for industrial purposes. In a case where each side attempts to out manoeuvre the other the outcome is still far from clear and the saga continues.

Outer Hebrides

day from Lochmaddy to Otternish. These continue via the new causeway to the island of Bearnaraigh (Berneray) just off the north coast in the sound of Harris. There are 3 buses per day from Lochmaddy to Clachan na Luib (Clachan-a-Luib) which run in an anti-clockwise direction around the north and west coasts. Two buses per day connect Clachan-a-Luib with Baile Sear (Baleshare) and also with Saighdinis (Sidinish). There are also Royal Mail post buses linking the main settlements. Local bus timetables are available at the tourist office in Lochmaddy (see below).

Loch nam Madadh (Lochmaddy)

Lochmaddy, the island's main village and ferry port, is a tiny place, so small you're almost through it before you realize. Though it's on the east coast and not close to the beaches, it is the best base for exploring the island as it boasts most facilities. It has a bank (next to the tourist office), a hotel and pub, a tourist office, a few shops, post office, hospital (T500325) and petrol station. If you have time the **Taigh Chearsabhagh Museum and Arts Centre** (T/F500293, www.taigh- chearsabhagh.com) is worth visiting and has a café.

Colour map 1, grid C1

The **tourist information centre** is near the ferry pier. *T500321. Mid-Apr to mid-Oct, Mon-Sat 0900-1700, and for the arrival of the evening ferry). They'll provide transport timetables.*

C *Lochmaddy Hotel*, T500332, F500210. Right by the ferry terminal. Open all year. Their restaurant serves great seafood and the lively bar serves snacks. This is also the place to ask about fishing, as they rent out boats and sells permits for trout and salmon fishing.

Sleeping & eating

A Fishy Tale

In the 1820s, a dead body was washed up in Culla Bay, near Griminish on Benbecula. It was said to have had the upper body of a well-developed four-year-old child, with long, dark glossy hair, and the lower half was like a salmon, but without scales. Many people came from all around to look at the bizarre creature, before the landlord of the estate ordered a coffin and shroud and it was given a decent burial on the shore of Culla Bay. What exactly this creature was has remained a mystery to this day.

There are a couple of good B&Bs: **D-E** *The Old Courthouse*, T500358, and **E** *The Old Bank House*, T500275/324, both of which are open all year. Half a mile from the ferry pier is an independent hostel, the *Lochmaddy Uist Outdoor Centre*, T500480. It is open all year and offers a wide range of outdoor activities including kayaking, windsurfing and rock climbing. *The Stag Lodge restaurant*, T500364, F500417, also does B&B (**D-E**).

Around the island

There are a number of interesting archaeological sites of different periods dotted around the island. The most notable is **Barpa Langass**, seven miles southwest of Lochmaddy, on the slope of Ben Langass, just off the A867 which cuts across the bleak peaty hinterland of North Uist. This is a huge chambered burial cairn dating from around 3,000 BC. Unfortunately, it is now too dangerous to enter. About a mile away, on the southern side of Ben Langass, is the small stone circle known as **Pobull Fhinn**, standing on the edge of Loch Langass. Nearby is **B** *Langass Lodge* (T580285, F580385, langars@btinternet.com), whose restaurant specialises in local seafood and game. Three miles northwest of Lochmaddy on the A865 are three bronze age standing stones called **Na Fir Bhreige** (The False Men), said to be the graves of three spies who were buried alive.

Bearnaraigh (Berneray)

Phone code: 01876
Colour map 1, grid B1

The low-lying island of Bearnaraigh, now connected by a new causeway, is famous as the place where Prince Charles spent a holiday helping out on a croft. It's also the birthplace of the giant Angus MacAskill (see 'Skye', page 302). Its real attraction, though, apart from the splendid isolation, is the three-mile-long sandy beach along its north and west coast.

A Western Isles Walks booklet for Bearnaraigh available from Lochmaddy TIC describes an enjoyable eight-mile walk around the island visiting all the main places of interest including the 16th Century gunnery at **Baile**, the beaches and machair of the north and west coast and archaeological sites dating from the Viking period near **Borgh**.

Sleeping
There are a couple of options for those wishing to stay. You can share the prince's crofting experience with Donald (Splash) MacKillop at **E** *Burnside Croft*, T540235, splashmackilloop@burnsidecroft.fsnet.co.uk which also offers cycle hire and stories round the fire for evening entertainment. There's also a *Gatliff Trust Hostel* (12 beds, no phone, open all year) in two restored blackhouses overlooking a lovely sandy beach and old Viking pier about a mile up the east coast from the old ferry pier.

Out to lunch

Travelling in the Outer Hebrides can be a very different experience from visiting other parts of Scotland. The pace of life is very different here and the needs of tourists have to come second to the ways of local people. Take the example of a passenger flight from Glasgow to Benbecula, which was delayed for 30 minutes when the plane had to circle because the air traffic controller was out to lunch!

Around the island

The real charms of North Uist are its fabulous beaches on the north and west coasts. Heading anti-clockwise from Lochmaddy, the A865 runs northwest, passing the turning for Otternish and **Bearnaraigh** (see above) which is now connected to North Uist by a causeway. It continues west through the township of **Sollas (Solas)**, where there are a couple of **B&Bs**, and then past the beautiful sands of **Bhalaigh (Vallay) Strand**. Near the northwestern tip of the island is **Scolpaig Tower**, standing on an islet in Loch Scolpaig, a 'folly' built for famine relief in the 19th century.

Three miles south of here is the turning to Balranald RSPB Reserve, an area of rocky coast, sandy beaches and dunes, machair and lochs. The reserve is ideal for bird watching, especially waders. A two-hour guided walk along the headland allows you to see Manx shearwaters, gannets, skuas, storm petrels and during the summer you can listen out for the distinctive rasping call of the corncrake, one of the rarest birds in Britain. There's a basic visitor centre, which is open April-September. **Balranald RSPB Reserve**

Sleeping There are a couple of places to stay near Balranald: in **Hogha Gearraidh (Houghgarry)**, overlooking the beautiful beach, is **E** *Mrs Kathy Simpson*, T510312; and in **Ceann a Bhaigh (Bayhead)**, a few miles to the south, is **E-F** *Mrs Morag Nicholson*, T510395.

Also in Ceann a Bhaigh is the **Uist Animal Visitors Centre**, where you can see Highland cattle and other rare native breeds as well as more exotic species such as llamas. ■ *Mon-Sat 1000-2200. Adult £2.*

The road continues south to Clachan na Luib, at the crossroads of the A865 and A867 which heads east back to Lochmaddy. There's a post office and general store, and a few miles south, at **Cladach a Bhaile Shear (Claddach-baleshare)** is **F** *Taigh Mo Sheannair*, T580246, a renovated crofthouse on a working farm which offers good hostel accommodation all year round, rents out bicycles and has space for camping **Clachan na Luib**

Offshore is the tidal island of **Baile Sear (Baleshare)**, now connected by a causeway to North Uist, with its three-mile long beach on the west coast. A further five miles west are the **Monach Isles** (also known by their old Norse name of Heisker), which were once connected to North Uist at low tide, until the 16th century when a huge tidal wave swept away the sand bridge, thus isolating them. Even so, the islands were still populated until as recently as the 1930s. Now they are populated by the largest breeding colony of grey seals in Europe.

South of Clachan, the road runs past **Cairinis (Carinish)** over a series of causeways to the little-visited lobster-fishing island of **Griomasaigh (Grimsay)** before heading across another causeway to Benbecula. There's **South of Clachan na Luib**

Machair

Machair is the name given to the strips of land that lie behind the many wonderful beaches of northwest Scotland and the islands. Machair is notable for its fertility, in sharp contrast to the poor, acid peat of the interior. In summer these strips are transformed into a blaze of colour when a multitude of wild flowers bloom – primroses, buttercups, orchids, gentian and wild iris – and this provides good grazing for sheep. The fertility of the machair comes from the calcium-rich shell sand which is blown inshore from the beaches and neutralises the acidity of the peaty soil.

accommodation at **C** *Temple View Hotel*, T580676, and B&B at **E** *Bonnieview*, T580211,

Near Cairinis is *Feith na Fala*, or Field of Blood, site of the last battle fought in Scotland solely with swords and bows and arrows, in 1601, between the MacDonalds of Sleat and Macleods of Harris. The bloodshed was provoked by one of the MacDonalds divorcing his Macleod wife. When 60 Skye Macleods set off to North Uist to wreak revenge, they were met by 16 MacDonalds who literally chopped them to pieces, proving that divorce was a messy affair even then.

Beinn na Faoghla (Benbecula)

Phone code: 01870
Colour map 1, grid C1
Population: 1,803

Tiny Benbecula may be suffering from delusions of stature. Its Gaelic name means 'mountain of the fords' but the highest point is a mere 407 ft, with the rest of the island as flat as a pancake. It lies between Protestant North Uist and Catholic South Uist and most visitors use it solely as a means of getting from one to the other via the A865 which cuts straight through the middle.

Getting there & around
Benbecula's **airport** is at Balivanich (see below) and there are direct flights to Glasgow, Barra and Stornoway (see page 318). The island is connected by causeways to both North and South Uist and **buses** travelling to and from Lochmaddy and Lochboisdale pass through the villages of Balivanich, Lionacleit (Liniclate) and Creag Ghoraidh (Creagorry). There are also regular island buses which run between these settlements.

Baile a Mhanaich (Balivanich)
Like North Uist, the east of the island is so pitted with lochs that most people live on the west coast. A large percentage of the population are Royal Artillery personnel and their families stationed at **Baile a Mhanaich (Balivanich)**, a sprawling army base of utilitarian buildings in the northwest of the island. The influx of so many English-speakers has had a less than positive impact on Gaelic culture and the military facilities have blighted much of the island's natural beauty, but Benbecula has benefited economically from the army's presence. Not only is there an airport here but also a relatively large number of shops and amenities, including the only NAAFI supermarket in the UK that's open to the public, a Bank of Scotland (with ATM) and post office. There are worries, however, that the base may be run down or closed, which would have a devastating effect on the local economy.

South to Lionacleit (Liniclate)
South of Balivanich the B892 runs around the west coast before joining the main A865 at the southern end of the island. It runs past **Culla Bay**, overlooked by **Baille nan Cailleach (Nunton)**. It was from here in 1746 that Bonnie Prince Charlie set off with Flora MacDonald over the sea to Skye, disguised as her maid

(see also page 299). To the south is **Poll-na-Crann**, better known as 'stinky bay' because of the piles of seaweed deposited there by fierce Atlantic storms. From the mid-18th century this kelp was used extensively in making glass and provided a source of income for many communities. By 1820, the so-called kelp boom was over, though it is still gathered today and used for fertilizer.

The B892 ends at **Lionacleit (Liniclate)**, where the new community school serves the Uists and Benbecula. It has extensive facilities, including internet, a swimming pool, library, theatre and even a small local history **museum**. ■ *Mon, Tue and Thu 0900-1600, Wed 0900-1230 and 1330-1600, Fri 0900-2000, Sat 1100-1300 and 1400-1600. Free.*

Most accommodation is in **Lioncleit**, including the functional **A** *Dark Island Hotel*, T603030, F602347, which is a lot nicer inside than its name may suggest and has a good restaurant. There's also **D** *Inchyra Guest House*, T602176, as well as a couple of **B&Bs** (both **E**) and the *Shellbay Caravan and Camping Park*, T602447; open Apr-Oct. In **Balinavich** is a new hostel, **F** *Tigh-na-Cille Bunkhouse*, T602522, which is open all year and sleeps 10 in 2 dorms and 2 twin rooms.

By far the best place to eat on the island is the *Stepping Stone Restaurant* in Balivanich, T603377, F603121, which offers good wholesome Scottish food every day from 1000 till 2100. Snacks, sandwiches, takeaways and home baking are all available, as well as 3- or 5-course meals (mid-range to expensive).

Sleeping & eating

Car hire *Maclennan Self Drive*, Balivanich (T602191, F603191); *Ask Car Hire*, Lionacleit (T602818, F602933).

Directory

Uibhist a Deas (South Uist)

Outer Hebrides

South Uist is the largest of the southern chain of Outer Hebridean islands and the most scenically attractive. Like its southern neighbour, Barra, South Uist is Roman Catholic and generally more relaxed about Sunday openings.

*Phone code: 01870
Colour map 3,
grid A1
Population: 2,285*

Its 20 miles of west coast is one long sandy beach, backed by dunes with a mile or two of beautiful, flowering machair behind. To the east of the main A865 that runs the length of the island rises a central mountainous spine of rock and peat dotted with numerous lochs. Its two highest peaks, Beinn Mhor (2,034 ft) and Hecla (1,988 ft), tower over the rocky cliffs of an inaccessible eastern coastline indented by sea lochs.

Ins and outs

The island's main **ferry port** is Loch Baghasdail (Lochboisdale), which is reached from Oban and Mallaig via Castlebay on Barra (it arrives late at night). There are also inter-island ferries from Ludag, at the southern tip of South Uist: a **car ferry** sails the short distance across to the island of Eriskay; and a private **passenger-only** ferry sails to Barra. There are passenger ferry sailings on Sun to and from Barra and a car ferry to Castlebay and Oban, but no ferry arrival from Oban, Mallaig or Castlebay and no bus services. For more details, see page 318.

Getting there
*The ferry to Eriskay
will be replaced by
a causeway in 2001*

A causeway connects South Uist to Benbecula by road and regular **buses** (4-6 per day Mon-Sat) run between Lochboisdale and Lochmaddy on North Uist, stopping en route at Dalabrog (Daliburgh), Tobha Mòr (Howmore) and Lionacleit and Balinavich on Benbecula. There is also a regular bus service between Lochboisdale and Ludag (for ferries to Eriskay and Barra). For **car hire**, there's *Laing Motors* in Lochboisdale (T700267) and you can **rent bikes** at *Rothan Cycles* (T01870-620283) .

Getting around

History

The dominant family in South Uist was Clan Ranald, who also owned Benbecula. They were descendants of the first Lord of the Isles, who was a MacDonald. The island's connections with Clanranald came to a sorry end, however, in 1837 when it was sold, along with Benbecula, to pay off bad debts, and became the property of the infamous Lieutenant-Colonel John Gordon Cluny. Though all the southern isles suffered during the brutal clearances of the 19th century, the experiences of people on South Uist were particularly cruel and inhumane. Between 1849 and 1851, over 2,000 were forcibly shipped to Quebec in Canada. Those who refused to board the transport ships were hunted down by dogs and bound before being thrown on board and shipped to Canada, where they were left to starve.

Around the island

At the north of the island a causeway leads across **Loch Bi** (pronounced 'Bee') to the distinctive modern statue of Our Lady of the Isles, standing by the main road on the lower slopes of **Rueval** hill. Further up the hill is the Royal Artillery control centre, known by the locals as 'Space City', due to its forest of aerials and 'golf balls', which tracks the missiles fired from a range on the northwestern corner of the island out into the Atlantic. Near here, at **Loch a' Chairnain (Lochcarnan)**, is the small, modern D *Orosay Inn* (T01870-610298, F610390, orosayinn@btinternet.com), which is open all year and offers fine Scottish cooking (cheap to mid-range).

Just to the south of here is **Loch Druidibeag Nature Reserve**, on the site of the large freshwater loch, one of the largest breeding grounds in the British Isles for greylag geese and also a favourite haunt for mute swans (there's a warden nearby at Groigearraidh (Grogarry) Lodge). From here the main road runs down the spine of the island, and all along the way little tracks branch off to the west, leading down to lovely beaches. Not far south of Loch Druidibeag is the turning to the tiny village of **Tobha Mòr (Howmore)**, where you can see a collection of the old traditional thatched 'blackhouses' beside the seemingly-endless stretch of golden sand. One of the houses has been converted into a *Gatliff Trust Youth Hostel* (13 beds, open all year, no phone) which overlooks the ruins of an ancient church and graveyard. The warden lives at Ben More House, at the junction with the main road. From the hostel it's a five minute walk across the machair to the sandy beach which stretches almost the entire length of South Uist.

From Tobha Mòr, there are superb walks through the lonely hills of **Beinn Mhor** (620 m), **Beinn Corodale** (527 m) and **Hecla** (606 m) to the picturesque and dramatic valleys of Glen Hellisdale, Glen Corodale and Glen Usinish on the east coast. In 1746, Bonnie Prince Charlie is reputed to have taken refuge in a cave above **Corodale Bay** for three weeks following his defeat and escape from Culloden.

Near **Bornais (Bornish)** another minor road can be followed east of the A865 to **Loch Eynort** that penetrates far inland from the Minch. An old stalkers path can be followed along the north shore of the loch towards the sea with views of numerous seals and the occasional otter and the steep upper slopes of Beinn Mhor towering above to the north.

A few miles south, at **Gearraidh Bhailteas (Milton)**, a cairn marks the birthplace of that famous Heridean lass, **Flora MacDonald** (see page 299). Nearby is the **Kildonan Museum** (T01878-710343) which has a tearoom.

The A865 continues south for a few miles to the village of **Dalabrog (Daliburgh)**, then heads east to the island's main ferry port, **Lochboisdale**.

Loch Baghasdail (Lochboisdale)

South Uists's largest settlement is set on a rocky promontory in a beautiful island-dotted sea loch. The imposing entrance is guarded by Calvay island with its 13th century castle ruin. Lochboisdale is a tiny place, with little in the way of tourist sights, though it does have a hotel, bank, post office and **tourist information**, at Pier Road. ■ *T700286. Open early Apr to mid-Oct.*

Phone code: 01878
Colour map 3, grid A1
Population: 300

You should book accommodation in advance, as the ferry arrives in Lochboisdale late in the evening. **C** *Lochboisdale Hotel*, T700332, F700367. This fishing hotel is right by the ferry terminal and the best place to stay and the only place to have a drink or a meal. There's also **B&B** accommodation by the terminal at **E** *Bayview*, T700329, and **F-E** *Lochside Cottage*, T700472. About a mile from the terminal is **D** *Brae Lea Guest House*, T/F700497, who will collect you from the ferry, and **E** *Kilchoan Bay*, T700517.

Sleeping

About 10 miles south of Lochboisdale, on the southern coast of the island, is **Ludag jetty**, the departure point for the small private passenger ferry to **Eòlaigearraidh (Eoligarry)** on Barra and the car ferry to Eriskay. A few miles to the west of Ludag, at **Pol a' Charra (Pollachar)** is the charming **C** *Polachar Inn*, T700215, F700768, which has great views across the Sound of Barra and its own beach close by. At **Cille Bhríghde (West Kilbride)** nearby is *Hebridean Croft Originals*, which has a wide range of local crafts on show, as well as a photographic display of local history. It's open daily and has a tearoom.

Eirisgeidh (Eriskay)

The tiny island of Eriskay, with a population of less than 200, gives its name to the native breed of pony, said to have been ridden by King Robert the Bruce at the Battle of Bannockburn in 1314. In the late 1970s it nearly became extinct but one surviving stallion saved the breed and numbers are growing. A series of paths take you round the island in about three hours. For more details, see the *Cuairt Eirisgeidh* leaflet published by the Western Isles Tourist Board and available at the Lochboisdale Tourist Information Centre.

Phone code: 01878
Colour map 3,
grid A1

Most people come to Eriskay to pay a visit to **Coilleag a' Phrionnsa (Prince's beach)**, the sandy beach on the west coast. This is where Bonnie Prince Charlie first stepped on to Scottish soil, on July 23, 1745, at the start of the ill-fated Jacobite Rebellion. The rare pink convolvulus which grows there today is said to have been planted by the Prince himself from seeds brought from France. A small memorial cairn situated in the dunes behind the beach was erected by the local school to commemorate the occasion.

As well as the wreck of the *SS Politican* (see box), another sight worth seeing is **St Michael's**, the Roman Catholic church, built in 1903 and funded by the local fishing fleet.

Eriskay is reached by a frequent car ferry from Ludag (Mon-Sat only; for times, T01878-720261), which lands at the ferry jetty at **Haun**. Construction of a new causeway linking Eriskay to South Uist commenced in 2000 and will replace the ferry when it opens in August 2001.

Getting there

There is a B&B on the island (T720232), a self-catering flat (T720274) or you can wild camp though there are few amenities, other than a shop, pub and post office.

Sleeping

Tight little island

Between Eriskay and South Uist is the wreck of the famous SS Politician, the island's other claim to fame. In 1941, the 12,000 ton ship went aground just off the island of Calvey and sank with its cargo, which included 20,000 cases of whisky. This not only provided many islanders with a supply of whisky for many years, but also provided the plot for Compton Mackenzie's book

Whisky Galore!, which was later made into the famous Ealing comedy of the same name (it was called Tight Little Island in the US) and filmed on Barra. Part of the wreck can be seen at low tide and there's more information on the famous incident on display in the appropriately named Am Politician pub (open 1230-1430), in the main settlement of Baile (Balla).

Bharraigh (Barra)

Population: 1,316
Phone code: 01871
Colour map 3, grid A1

It may be tempting to overlook the little island of Barra, only about eight miles long by five miles wide, but this would be a great mistake, as it's one of the most beautiful of all the islands in the Outer Hebrides. Here you'll find the best of the islands in miniature – beaches, machair, peat-covered hills, tiny crofting communities and neolithic remains – and a couple of days spent on Barra gives a real taster of Hebridean life. Gaelic culture is also strong here, but with its Catholic tradition, Barra is a bit more laid-back than many of the other islands in the Outer Hebrides and doesn't follow the others' strict Sabbatrianism.

Ins and outs

Getting there The best way to arrive by **air** at Tràigh Mhòr ('Cockle Strand'), the famous airstrip on the beach at the north end of the island. This is the only airport in the UK where flight schedules are shown as 'subject to tides'. For flight details see page 318. Barra is reached by **car ferry** from Oban and Mallaig on the mainland (for more details, see page 318) and also by car ferry from Lochboisdale on South Uist, and by passenger-only ferry from Ludag on South Uist (see page 319).

Getting around There is a regular bus/postbus service (5-8 times per day Mon-Sat) that runs from Castlebay to the ferry port of Eòlaigearraidh, via the **aiport**. There are also buses (3-4 per day Mon-Sat) from Castlebay to Bhatarsaigh (Vatersay). You can also hire a car or a bicycle to tour the island at your leisure (see below).

Bàgh a' Chaisteil (Castlebay)

Colour map 3, grid A1 The main settlement is Castlebay, on the southern side of the island, situated in a wide sheltered bay and overlooked by **Sheabhal** (383 m), on top of which is a marble statue of the Blessed Virgin and Child. It's a short but steep walk up to the top from the town and the views are well worth it. The once-thriving herring port is also overlooked by the large Roman Catholic church, Our Lady, Star of the Sea.

As the main ferry port, Castlebay provides the full range of services: hotels, B&Bs, shops, a bank (but no ATM) and post office. The **tourist information centre** is on the main street near the ferry terminal. It has information on local walks and will book accommodation. ■ *T810223. Apr to mid-Oct Mon-Sat 0900-1700; also open for the arrival of the evening ferry.*

Castlebay's most notable feature is the impressive 15th-century **Kisimul Castle**, built on an island in the middle of the harbour. This was the ancient home of the Chief of the MacNeils, one of the oldest Scottish clans, who owned the island from 1427 till 1838. It was then sold to the notorious Colonel Gordon of Cluny, along with neighbouring South Uist and Benbecula (see page 346), and the poor people of Barra suffered the same cruel fate, 600 of them being shipped to Canada to starve. One hundred years later the castle and much of the island was bought back for the MacNeils by an American architect, Robert Lister MacNeil, who became the 45th Clan Chief and restored the castle to its present state before his death in 1970. His son, the new Clan Chief, uses it as his residence when visiting, though it is now in the care of Historic Scotland.
■ *The castle can be visited by boat from the pier, weather permitting, Apr-Sep daily 0930-1830; Oct Mon-Wed 0930-1630, Thu 0930-1230, Sat 0930-1630, Sun 1400-1630. Adult £3, concession £2.30, children £1.T810313.*

If you're interested in finding out about the island's history, you should visit the **Barra Heritage Centre**. ■ *Apr-Sep Mon-Fri 1100-1700. Adult £1. T810403.*

It's a good idea to book in advance if arriving on the evening ferry from Oban or Mallaig. The best place to stay is the **D** *Castlebay Hotel*, by the ferry terminal (T810223, F810445). 14 rooms, friendly, good food, good value and a great bar. A few miles west of Castlebay is the modern, purpose-built **B-C** *Isle of Barra Hotel* (T810383, F810385, BarraHotel@aol.com) 30 rooms, open Apr-Oct, overlooking a lovely beach with fantastic sea views. **D** *Craigard Hotel*, T810200, a family-run hotel with hearty home cooking.

There are also several guesthouses and B&Bs in and around Castlebay, including **E** *Grianamul*, T810416, F810319,ronnie.macneil@virgin.net **E** *Ceol Mara*, T810294, and **E** *Terra Nova*, T810458, which is situated a 10 min walk from the ferry in Nask. At the moment there are no independent hostels or a Gatliff Trust Hostel on Barra. Although there are also no official campsites on Barra, there are endless opportunities for **wild camping** across the island with the most popular spots to be found on the machair at Traigh Mhor (north Barra), Borve Point (west Barra), and Ledaig (Castlebay). Generally, no permission is required from the landowner but ensure all waste and litter is removed when you leave the site. For campers, there are 2 or 3 well-stocked mini-supermarkets in Castlebay.

The best food is available at the *Castelbay Hotel* and *Isle of Barra Hotel*, both of which offer excellent local fish and seafood at mid-range prices. For something a lot cheaper, try the *Kismul Galley* on the main street, T810645, which offers all-day breakfasts, snacks and home baking and is open Mon-Sat 0900-2100 and Sun 1000-1800. There's also a tearoom at the airport.

Car hire is available from £20 per day at *Barra Car Hire*, T810243, and *MacMillan Self Drive*, T890366. **Bicycles** can be hired at *Barra Cycle Hire*, T810284. **Taxi services** and **island tours** with *Hatcher's Taxis*, T810486, and *Nellie's Taxi*, T810302.

Around Bharraigh

The A888 makes a circular route of 14 miles around the island, making an ideal day's bike tour from Castlebay. Heading west, it passes the turning for the causeway to **Vatersay** (see below), then runs northwest between two hills (**Sheabhal** to the east and **Beinn Tangabhal** to the west) to the west coast, where you'll find the nicest beaches. One of these is at **Halaman Bay**, near the village of **Tangasdal (Tangasdale)**, overlooked by the *Isle of Barra Hotel* (see above). At the turning for **Borgh (Borve)** there are standing stones. Next is the turning for the small settlement of **Baile Na Creige (Craigston)**, where you'll find the **Thatched Cottage Museum**, an original 'blackhouse' and the chambered burial cairn of **Dun Bharpa**. ■ *Museum open Easter-Oct, Mon-Fri 1100-1700. £1.* From Dun Bharpa there are pleasant walks into the surrounding hills with the summit of **Sheabhal** offering tremendous views from the highest point on the island.

North of the turning, near **Allathsdal (Allasdale)** is another lovely beach, and just beyond are the remains of **Dun Cuier**, an Iron-age fort. Make a short detour atGrean follow the headland to the rugged cliffs at Greian Head.

Tràigh Mhor & The A888 then heads east to **Bagh a Tuath (Northbay)**, where a branch left
Eòlaigearraidh leads to the village of Eòlaigearraidh (Eoligarry), near the northern tip sur-
(Eoligarry) rounded by sandy bays washed by Atlantic rollers. A private passenger ferry leaves from here to Ludag on South Uist.

The road to Eoligarry passes the island's airport at Tràigh Mhòr, the 'cockle strand', which once provided 100 to 200 cartloads of delicious cockles each day. Now, the cockleshells are gathered and used for harling, the roughcast wall covering used on many Scottish houses. By the beach is the house that was once the home of Compton MacKnzie, author of *Whisky Galore!* (see page 347). He lies buried at **Cille Bhara**, to the west of the village of Eòlaigearraidh, along with members of the MacNeil clan. This was one of the most important religious complexes in the Outer Hebrides, built in the 12th century, and consists of a church and two chapels. One of these, St Mary's, has been re-roofed and houses several carved medieval tombstones and a copy of a runic stone. The original is in the Museum of Scotland in Edinburgh.

Bhatarsaigh (Vatersay) and Mingulay

A worthwhile trip from Castlebay is to the island of Vatersay, now linked to Barra by a causeway built in an effort to stabilise the island community (the present population is around 70). The island boasts two lovely shell-sand beaches backed by beautiful machair, only a few hundred yards apart on either side of the narrow isthmus that leads to the main settlement of Vatersay. On the west beach, Bagh Siar, is the **Annie Jane Monument**, which commemorates the terrible tragedy in 1853, when the emigrant ship *Annie Jane* was wrecked off the coast of Vatersay, with the loss of 333 lives, many of them islanders.

On a clear day from Vatersay you can enjoy the view of the smaller islands to the south – Sandray, Pabbay and **Mingulay**. The latter was inhabited until 1912, but can still be visited from Barra. It has recently been acquired by the National Trust for Scotland.

Day trips to Mingulay can be arranged with Mr John Allan MacNeil in Castlebay, T810449, (approximately £15 per person) who sails to the island in settled weather when sufficient people can be found to fill the boat. It is one of the most rewarding excursions in the Outer Hebrides, particularly during the puffin season from June to early August. The trip normally includes a two hour sail from Barra past the neighbouring islands of Sandray and Pabbay, a circumnavigation of Mingulay to view the spectacularly high western sea cliffs and a landing on the east coast for a three- hour exploration of the beautiful beach of Mingulay Bay, the deserted village and surrounding hills and coast. There are also fine views to the lighthouse on Barra Head, the most southerly outpost of the Outer Hebrides island chain. Similar boat trips can also be organised by Mr George McLeod at the Castlebay Hotel, T810223, or ask at the tourist office in Castlebay.

St Kilda

Over 40 miles west of the Outer Hebrides lie the spectacular and isolated islands of St Kilda, Scotland's first UNESCO World Heritage Site. St Kilda captures the imagination of most visitors to the Outer Hebrides whether they actually get there or just dream about romantic voyages to mysterious lands across perilous seas.

The largest of the islands, **Hirta**, was the remotest community in Britain, if not Europe, until 1930, when the remaining 36 Gaelic-speaking inhabitants were evacuated at their own request, in one of the most poignant episodes of Scottish history.

In 1957 the islands become the property of the National Trust for Scotland, who in turn leased them to the Nature Conservancy (the forerunner of Scottish Natural Heritage) as a National Nature Reserve. St Kilda is the most important seabird breeding station in northwest Europe. The islands are home to the largest colony of gannets in the world, the largest colony of fulmars in Britain and the largest colony of puffins. These huge numbers of seabirds were vital to the islanders' survival. Their eggs provided food in the summer and gannets and fulmers were caught each season to be plucked, dried and stored for the winter. Their feathers and oil were kept for export to generate income, whilst their bones were shaped into useful tools and skins into shoes.

Today, Hirta is partly occupied by the army as a radar-tracking station for the rocket range on South Uist and managed by **Scottish Natural Heritage**. For more information, contact Scottish Natural Heritage, 135 Stilligarry, South Uist, HS8 5RS, T01870-620238. For details of tours, ask at one of the main tourist informatiob centres in the Outer Hebrides.

Getting there

The biggest problem apart from accessibility is cost although it is definitely possible if you're prepared to break the bank. *Island Cruising* in Uig, on Lewis (T01851-672381, F672212) arranges boat trips to St Kilda from April to October starting from about £300 (4-day all-inclusive). The tour comprises the journey to and from St Kilda and a landing on Hirta with a visit to the museum, the old village and a wider exploration of the island including a climb up to the highest sea cliffs in the British Isles at Conachair (430 m).

The *National Trust for Scotland* also organises two-week long voluntary Work Parties throughout the summer every year to undertake restoration, maintenance and archaeology projects around the old village on Hirta. The groups are very popular and each volunteer must complete an application form, but apply early. The fortnight costs between £450 and £500 and this covers transport from Oban to St Kilda and all food and lodgings costs while on the island. For details contact National Trust for Scotland in Oban (T01631-570000, F570011, stkilda@nts.org.uk

Outer Hebrides

How St Kilda was killed off

Friday 29th August 1930 was the end of the life of St Kilda as it had been for centuries. For a least 1,000 years, the inhabitants of this remote group of islands had been tenants of the Macleods of Dunvegan on Skye. In earlier days, the trip from Skye, undertaken in longboats, would require 16 hours of rigorous rowing and sailing. Even now, the trip to St Kilda is no easy matter.

St Kilda consists of several islands. Hirta, the main habitable island, is now a permanent home only to the largest colony of fulmars in Britain. Across a narrow channel lies Dun. Nearby Boreray is home to the world's largest colony of gannets. Soay virtually completes the group. There are several dramatic 'stacs' rising sheer from the Atlantic Ocean. At 430 m the sea cliffs at Conachair are the highest in the British Isles.

Until 1930, the islanders had been supported by the mainland by the provision of a nurse and a post office. But the Scottish Office decided that their subsidy of the islands was no longer economic. This meant that life for the residents without those facilities would be untenable. Now owned by the National trust for Scotland, St Kilda is a National Nature reserve. Each year, during the brief summer months when travel to the islands is possible, teams of volunteers work on Hirta, maintaining what remains of the abandoned houses, studying the wildlife and glorying in the peace and isolation of the place.

But in 1930, to the younger of the 36 residents, including a man with nine children, evacuation was an attractive prospect. There would be better schooling for the children, and better health care. Although many had never seen a tree, a new life in forestry appealed. The more elderly residents, most of whom had never left the island and who could not speak

English, must have viewed the drastic change with alarm. But the younger majority view prevailed and evacuation was planned.

There were five hundred Soay sheep to be moved first. Their coats of fine wool were not sheared but plucked by the inhabitants with just the help of a penknife. The resultant locally woven tweed, either shipped ashore or sold to rare visitors, had provided the inhabitants' only contact with actual money. No taxes on income or on anything else were paid. Their internal economy took the form of barter. The plentiful supply of gannets, when dried, provided winter food. No inhabitant had ever fought in any war. Their distance and isolation earned them no consideration by the rest of Scotland.

Despite protestations by The Canine Defence League, all dogs were destroyed. Just two were put down by injections of hydrocyanic acid. The rest, at the islanders' insistence, had stones tied around their necks and were hurled from the jetty. Small boats, holding only a dozen or so sheep, were used to ferry them out to the SS Dunara Castle. Ten cows with four calves were also evacuated. Then HMS Harebell, of the Fishery Protection Service came on the final day to take the islanders to the mainland. The Under Secretary of State for Scotland imposed a ban on photography, thus sparing the people of St Kilda privacy during the evacuation. It was not possible to house all of the inhabitants in Argyll, as had been hoped, so the community was split, their communal lives coming to an end.

The history of the island has been documented in a number of scholarly works, including The Life and Death of St Kilda *by Tom Steel and* Island on the Edge of the World, *by Charles Maclean.*

Orkney and Shetland

9

Orkney and Shetland

To some these two archipelagos will never be anything more than distant and overlooked specks of land peppering the wild north Atlantic, above an already remote north coast of mainland Scotland. It is true – they are remote and they have maintained a social and political, as well as geographical, distance from the rest of Scotland which goes a long way to explaining the relatively few numbers of visitors each year.

Orkney was under Norse rule until the mid-13th century, and Shetland was only 'given' (as part of a princess' dowry) to Scotland in 1469. Somehow, seeing them as a part of Scotland can be very misleading and each must be seen within the context of its own unique cultural background and unusual geography.

It is these two qualities that make the islands worth visiting and the ones that the tourist boards are keen to plug. Both Orkney and Shetland are littered with outstanding archaeological evidence, not just of Norse occupation, such as at **Jarlshof** at the very southern tip of Shetland, but also of life back in 3000 BC at **Skara Brae** and the **Knap of Howar** in the Orkneys. They are also the best places in Britain to see wildlife as yet untamed by the 21st century. Here you can sail alongside porpoises and seals and watch a million migratory seabirds nest and bring up their young during the summer months. And, thanks to fast and frequent transport links, it doesn't take an Arctic expedition to get here.

Orkney

Orkney may only be a short step away from John O' Groats, but to the fiercely independent Orcadians, 'Mainland' means the largest of the Orkney islands and not the Scottish mainland.

*Mainland is the largest of the Orkney islands and site of the two main towns and ferry terminals; the capital Kirkwall and the beautiful, old fishing port of Stromness. Here, you'll also find many of Orkney's most precious archaeological treasures: the **Stones of Stenness**; **Maes Howe**; the **Broch of Gurness**; and the remarkable Neolithic village of **Skara Brae.***

*Aside from Mainland, there are a dozen smaller islands to explore, including **Hoy**, with its wild, spectacular coastal scenery. The even more remote northerly islands offer miles of deserted beaches, and nothing but the calls of myriad birds to shatter the all-pervading peace and quiet.*

Ins and outs

Getting there

Air There are direct flights to **Kirkwall** airport daily except Sun from Aberdeen, Edinburgh, Glasgow, Inverness and Shetland, with connections to London Heathrow, Birmingham, Manchester and Belfast. All these flights are operated by *Loganair/British Regional Airlines* and can be booked through *British Airways*, T0845-7222111.

Boat There are several ferry routes to Orkney from the mainland. *P&O Scottish Ferries*, T01856-850655, sail from **Aberdeen** to **Stromness** (8 hrs) twice weekly (Tue and Sat) in 'standard season' (Jun-Aug) and once a week (Sat) the rest of the year. From Aberdeen a standard season passenger fare costs £43.50 single and a car costs £113. There's a 20% discount on passenger fares, and 50% on vehicle fares, for midweek sailings. Cars should be booked in advance.

P&O also sail from **Scrabster** to **Stromness** (2 hrs) twice a day (Mon-Sat; once on Sun) from Apr-Oct and twice a day (Mon-Fri; once on Sat) from Nov-Mar. A standard season passenger fare costs £16.50 single and a car costs £51. A shuttle bus links Scrabster with the nearby town of Thurso, on the north coast. There are regular bus and train services to Thurso from Inverness (see page 273).

P&O sail from **Lerwick** (Shetland) to **Stromness** (8 hrs) on Fri (all year) and Wed (Jun-Aug), returning on Sun (all year) and Tue (Jun-Aug). A passenger fare costs £40.50 single and a car costs £95. There is a 10% student/senior citizen discount on all *P&O* ferries to Orkney.

John o'Groats Ferries, T01955-611353, www.jogferry.co.uk, operate a passenger-only (and bicycles) ferry service from **John o' Groats** to **Burwick** (2-4 times per day; 45 mins) on South Ronaldsay, from May to Sep. A single fare costs £16 (bicycles an extra £3). An **off-peak return** from John o' Groats to Kirkwall, departing at 1600 or 1800 costs £25. No bookings required. A free bus meets the afternoon train from Thurso at 1430 and connects with the 1600 or 1800 ferry to Orkney. There are bus connections between Burwick and Kirkwall (45 mins) for all ferry sailings. They also operate the **Orkney Bus**, a daily direct bus/ferry/bus service between **Inverness** and Kirkwall, via John o' Groats. It leaves Inverness at 0730 and 1420 from Jun-Sep (at 1420 only in May). It costs £40 return. Journey time 5 hrs. Advance booking is essential.

Things to do on Orkney and Shetland

- Visit the amazing archaeological wonders of **Maes Howe** and **Skara Brae**.
- Explore the winding streets of **Stromness**, one of the most fasinating fishing villages in Scotland.
- Take time to reflect in the incredible little **Italian Chapel**, on the island of Lamb Holm.
- Take the spectacular clifftop walk to meet the **Old Man of Hoy**.

- Fly from Westray to **Papa Westray**, which takes all of two minutes!
- Visit the tiny island of **Mousa** to see the best-preserved broch in Scotland.
- Brave the white-knuckle boat trip to **Fair Isle**, one of the best places on earth for birdwatching.
- Explore the dramatic coastal scenery of **Hermaness National Nature Reserve**, from where you can look out to Muckle Flugga, site of the most northeryl lighthouse in the British Isles.

Getting around

Air There are **inter-island flights** which are operated by *Loganair*, T01856-872494. Eight-seater aircraft fly from Kirkwall daily except Sun to **Stronsay**, **Sanday**, **North Ronaldsay**, **Westray** and **Papa Westray**, and on Wed to **Eday**. To Papa Westray and North Ronaldsay costs only £15 single, and to the other islands listed costs £31 single. Inter-island flights not leaving from Kirkwall cost £14. There are **sightseeing flights** in Jul and Aug which fly over all these islands and cost £30. There's also an *Orkney Adventure ticket* which allows you to fly to 3 islands for £66. Flight schedules are given under each relevant destination in this chapter.

Bus Buses on the Orkney islands are very limited. Apart from the daily service between **Burwick** and **Kirkwall** which connects with the ferry, there are buses from Kirkwall to **Stromness**, **Evie/Tingwall**, **Dounby**, **St Margaret's Hope**, **Deerness** and **East Holm**. There's also a bus to **Houton** (Hoy) which connects with the ferry. Bus details are given under each relevant destination and on page 364.

Boat *Orkney Ferries*, T01856-872044, operates daily car and passenger ferries to **Rousay**, **Egilsay** and **Wyre** from Tingwall; to **Shapinsay**, **Eday**, **Stronsay**, **Sanday**, **Westray** and **Papa Westray** from Kirkwall; to **Graemsay** and **Hoy** from Stromness; and to **Hoy** and **Flotta** from Houton. There's a ferry on Fri to **North Ronaldsay** from Kirkwall.
Fares: to **Rousay**, **Egilsay**, **Wyre**, **Shapinsay**, **Hoy**, **Graemsay** and **Flotta** costs £2.40 per passenger one-way and £7.20 per car. Inter-island fares are £1.20 per passenger. A round-trip costs £4.80. To **Eday**, **Stronsay**, **Sanday**, **Westray**, **Papa Westray** and **North Ronaldsay** costs £4.80 per passenger one-way and £10.80 per car. An inter-island fare is £2.40, and round-trip costs £9.60. There are also additional Sun sailings in summer (May-Sep); contact *Orkney Ferries* or the tourist board for the latest schedules. Those travelling by car should book all ferry journeys in advance. Ferry details are given under the relevant destination.

Car Only the main population centres on Mainland are served by public transport and having a car is essential to visit many of the most interesting sights. Bringing a car to Orkney is expensive, but there are several **car hire** firms on the Mainland and on the other islands. Car hire firms are listed under each particular town.

Bicycle Orkney is relatively flat and most of its roads are quiet which makes it ideal for touring by bike, though the wind can make it difficult if it's blowing in the wrong direction. Bicycles

Orkney & Shetland

Orkney

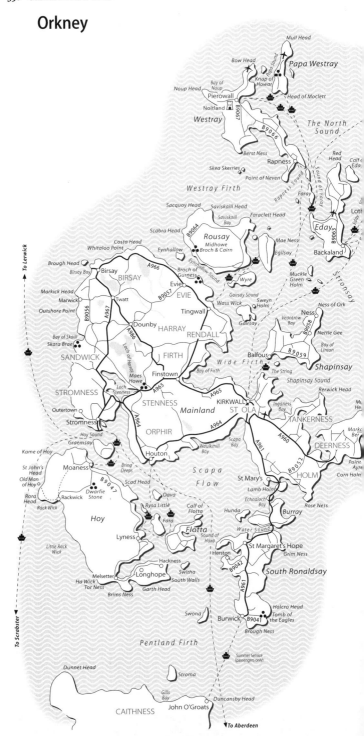

can be hired in Kirkwall, Stromness and on many of the other islands. Details are given in the relevant section.

Organized tours

Those with limited time may prefer to book a tour of the islands. Both general sightseeing tours and special interest tours are available. *Go-Orkney*, South Cannigall, St Ola, T01856-871871, www.orknet.co.uk/orkney-tours, runs a series of tours of Mainland and also to Hoy and Rousay. *Wildabout Orkney*, 5 Clouston corner, Stenness, T01856-851011, www. wildabout.orknet.co.uk, offers highly- rated wildlife, historical, folklore and environmental tours of Mainland for around £16 per person for a full day. *Discover Orkney Tours*, T/F01856-872865, also offer tours of Mainland as well as trips to Westray and Papa Westray.

Tourist information

The **Orkney Tourist Board** (www.visitorkney.com) has tourist offices in Kirkwall and Stromness. They will book accommodation for you, or provide a list of what's available, though many B&Bs are not included in the tourist board scheme. They can also provide information on various sights, walks and the islands' wildlife. Those wishing to leave Mainland and visit the smaller islands should pick up a free copy of the tourist board's excellent information and travel guide, *The Islands of Orkney*. For more background reading, see the *Orkney Guide Book* by Dr C Tait (£14.95).

Many of Orkney's monuments are managed by Historic Scotland. They include Bishop and Earl's Palaces, Broch of Gurness, Maes Howe, Skara Brae and Skaill House, Brough of Birsay and Noltland Castle. You can buy a joint ticket for all these monuments: summer; adult £11, concession £8, children £3.50; winter (Skaill closed) adult £10, concession £7, children £3.

Orkney & Shetland

Viking heritage

The history of Orkney and Shetland is bound up with the history of the Vikings, who first came to the islands in the latter half of the ninth century and stayed for about 650 years. This was part of a great Viking expansion westwards and in less than a century emigrants from Norway and Denmark settled in Orkney, Shetland, Iceland, Greenland, Caithness, the Western Isles, Isle of Man and parts of Ireland and the northern half of England.

In 872, the king of Norway set up a Norse earldom in Orkney, from which the Vikings ruled Orkney, Shetland and the Western Isles and took part in raids around Britain and Europe, creating the popular image of Vikings as aggressive, bloodthirsty invaders. At home, however, they lived a peaceful life, adhering to the laws of their parliament, the ting, and many converted to Christianity.

In the late 14th century, Norway, Denmark and Sweden were united under a Danish king. In 1469, the Royal estates and prerogatives in Orkney and Shetland were pledged to Scotland as part of the marriage dowry of Margaret, daughter of the King of Denmark, on her marriage to Prince James of Scotland, later to become King James III. Orkney and Shetland were to revert to rule by the kings of Norway when the debt was paid, but the pledge was never redeemed and the islands remained under Scottish control.

Soon after assuming control, the Scots began to change the old Norse laws which they had agreed to maintain and Scottish influence grew. In 1564, Mary, Queen of Scots granted the control and revenues from Orkney and Shetland to her half-brother, Robert Stewart. His prime motivation however was to extract as much money as possible through taxes. He was succeeded by his son, the infamous Patrick Stewart, who demanded even more rents, dues and fines. Earl Patrick eventually got his come-uppance when he was executed in Edinburgh for treason, but the changes he had made continued and Scots and English gradually began to usurp Old Norse as the native language of the islands.

Kirkwall

Phone code: 01856
Population: 7,000

Orkney's capital is built around a wide sheltered bay and is the main departure point for ferries to the northern islands. First impressions are a little misleading, as the harbour area has been blighted by modern development. More appealing, however, are the narrow winding streets and lanes of the old town, which has not changed much over the centuries. There are many houses dating from the 16th, 17th and 18th centuries, as well as Kirkwall's greatest attraction, its magnificent **cathedral**, *the finest medieval building in northern Scotland.*

Ins and outs

Getting around
For full details see Transport on page 364

The town is compact and it's easy to get around on foot. The **bus station** is 5 mins walk west of the town centre. The **airport**, T872421, is 3 miles southeast of Kirkwall on the A960. There are no buses to and from town. A taxi will cost around £6.

The **main street** changes its name from Bridge St, to Albert St, to Broad St and Victoria St as it twists its way south from the busy harbour. The cathedral is on Broad St and most of the shops and banks are on Broad St and Albert St.

Tourist Information Centre

On Broad St, near the cathedral, is the very helpful TIC, T872856, info@ otb.ossian.net They will book accommodation and change money and also provide various useful free leaflets including *The Islands of Orkney* and the *Kirkwall Heritage*

Viking place names

Despite the disappearance of the Norse language, many of the Viking place names have survived. Here are some of the most common Old Norse elements which will help explain the meaning of many place names:

a(y)	island	*geo*	creek
a, o	stream	*grind*	gate
aith	isthmus	*ham(n)*	anchorage
ayre	beach	*holm*	small island
bard	headland	*houb*	lagoon
bister	farm	*howe*	mound
brae, brei	broad	*kirk*	church
fell, field	hill	*lax*	salmon
fors	waterfall	*ler*	mud, clay
garth	farm	*lyng*	heather
		minn	mouth
		mool, noup	headland
		setter	farm
		ting	parliament
		toft	house site
		voe	sea inlet
		wick	bay

Guide. They also stock a wide range of guide books and maps and have details of forth-coming events. Another good source is the weekly newspaper *The Orcadian*. Open Apr-Sep daily 0830-2000; Oct- Mar Mon-Sat 0930-1700.

Sights

The town's outstanding sight is the huge and impressive red sandstone St Magnus Cathedral, built by masons who had worked on Durham Cathedral in the north of England. It was founded in 1137 by Rognvald Kolson, Earl of Orkney, in memory of his uncle, Magnus Erlendson, who was slain by his cousin, Haakon Paulson, on Egilsay, in 1115. Magnus was buried at Birsay and it is said that heavenly light was seen over his grave. It soon became a shrine, attracting pilgrims from as far afield as Norway. Magnus was canonized in 1133, and four years later his nephew commissioned construction of the cathedral. The building wasn't completed until the 14th century and major additions were made during the intervening centuries. The most recent addition was a new west window for the nave, in 1987 to celebrate the cathedral's 850th anniversary.

St Magnus Cathedral

The bones of St Magnus now lie in the north choir pillar, while those of St Rognvald lie in the south one. There's also a memorial to John Rae, the 19th-century Arctic explorer, who is buried in the graveyard, as well as a monument to the 833 men of the HMS *Royal Oak* who died when it was torpedoed in Scapa Flow in 1939. ■ *Apr-Sep Mon-Sat 0900-1800, Sun 1400-1800; Oct-Mar Mon-Sat 0900-1300 and 1400-1700, Sun service at 1115.*

Looming impressively nearby are the ruins of the Bishop's Palace, built in the 12th century as the first Kirkwall residence of the Bishop of Orkney. Here King Haakon of Norway died in 1263 after his defeat at the Battle of Largs. The palace was repaired and extended in the mid-16th century by Bishop Reid and most of what you see dates from that period. There's a good view of the town from the top of the '*Moosie Too'r*'.

Bishop's Palace

The adjacent **Earl's Palace** was built around 1600 by the notorious Patrick Stewart, Earl of Orkney using forced labour. Still very much intact, it is one of

Orkney & Shetland

Scotland's most elegant Renaissance buildings and was occupied by the tyrannical Stewart only for a very short time, until he was imprisoned and later executed. Wandering around both these spectacularly impressive, and solid, buildings is a very good way to get a feel for a period of Orkney's history that is very often ignored, with the likes of Skara Brae just up the road.

■ *Apr-Sep daily 0930-1830. Adult £2, concession £1.50, children £0.75. Joint ticket for all Orkney monuments also available. T871918.*

Tankerness House & Gardens Opposite St Magnus Cathedral is Tankerness House and Gardens, a 16th-century former manse which has been restored and now houses the **Orkney Museum**, which features various archaeological artefacts from Neolithic times to the Vikings. If you are spending any time in Kirkwall at the beginning of your stay, then this is an exceedingly worthwhile exhibition. It is a great way to whet your appetite for the archaeological gems that are lying in

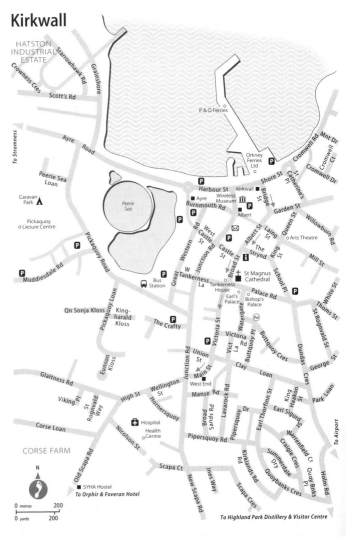

Kirkwall

wait for you all over the islands, and it also puts them all into a useful chronological context. ■ *Oct-Mar Mon-Sat 1030-1230, 1330-1700; Apr-Sep 1030-1700; May-Sep also Sun 1400-1700. Free. T873191.*

Old radio buffs should not miss the Orkney Wireless Museum, at Kiln Corner, at the harbour end of Junction Road, which houses a jumble of domestic and wartime communications equipment from the 1930s onwards. ■ *Apr-Sep Mon-Sat 1000-1630, Sun 1400-1630. Adult £2, children £1.*

Orkney Wireless Museum

A mile south of the town centre on the road to South Ronaldsay is the 200-year-old Highland Park Distillery, the most northerly of Scotland's whisky distilleries. There are guided tours of the distillery, one of the few that still has its own floor maltings, and a wee dram of this particularly fine single malt at the end. ■ *Tours every half hour Apr-Oct Mon-Fri 1000-1700 (last tour at 1600); Jul and Aug also Sat and Sun 1200-1700; Nov, Dec and Mar Mon-Fri at 1400 and 1530 only. Adult £3, concession £2, children £1.50. T874619.*

Highland Park Distillery

Essentials

The top hotel in Kirkwall is the very comfortable **B-C** *Ayre Hotel*, T873001, www.ayrehotel.co.uk, on the harbour front. Another good option is the **B-D** *Albert Hotel*, T876000, enquiries@alberthotel.co.uk, on Mounthoolie Lane in the centre of town. It also has a restaurant and a couple of lively bars (see below).

Sleeping

Two miles from town on the A964 Orphir road at St Ola is the **D** *Foveran Hotel*, T872389, www.foveranhotel.com, overlooking Scapa Flow. It is friendly and comfortable and also offers very good food, including vegetarian. The **D** *West End Hotel*, Main St, T872368, www.orkneyisles.co.uk/westendhotel, is central and serves good bar meals.

There are also plenty of cheap **B&Bs**, though most rooms are small and don't have en suite facilities. **E** *Whiteclett*, St Catherine's Pl, T874193. A 200-year-old listed house near the harbour, and **E-F** *Arundel*, Inganess Rd, T873148. A modern bungalow on a quiet road about a mile from the town centre.

F *SYHA Youth Hostel*, T872243, open Apr-Sep. This large, well-equipped youth hostel is on Old Scapa Rd, about 15 mins walk from the town centre. There's also **camping** at *Pickaquoy Caravan & Camping Site*, T873535. Open May-Sep, on the western outskirts of Kirkwall, off the A965.

Kirkwall is no gastronome's paradise and you'll be hard-pushed to find somewhere decent to eat in town. The best place to eat is probably the *Foveran Hotel* (see above). Otherwise, the *Albert Hotel* (see above) serves bar meals (made with home-grown produce, cheap to mid-range) as does the *West End Hotel*. The islands' only Indian restaurant is the *Mumtaz*, on Bridge St. The best place for a snack is the *St Magnus Café*, opposite the cathedral. This is a true cafeteria-style café, serving substantial soups and rolls in a bustling and very friendly atmosphere.

Eating

The *Bothy Bar* at the *Albert Hotel* is a good place for a drink and sometimes has live folk music. The hotel's *Matchmakers Bar* has a disco at weekends. The *Ayre Hotel* also stages folk music nights. Check details in *The Orcadian*. The town's *New Phoenix* **cinema** is housed in the *Pickaquoy Leisure Centre*, T879900, on Pickaquoy Rd. It also has **sports** and fitness facilities and a café and bar.

Bars & nighlife
Nightlife is Kirkwall revolves around its lively pubs

Orkney & Shetland

Never a dull moment

There are numerous events which take place throughout the year.

Amongst the best-known annual events is **The Ba'** (ball), held on Christmas Day and New Year's Day in Kirkwall. It is a bit like rugby, basketball and a full-scale riot all rolled into one and is contested between two sides – the Uppies and the Doonies – representing different districts of the town. As many as 200 'players' may be involved and a game can last up to seven hours as both sides attempt to jostle the ball along the streets until one reaches their 'goal' to win the prized ba'. One of the most entertaining events on Orkney is the excellent **Orkney Folk Festival,** which takes place at various locations throughout the islands over three days at the end of May.

The most prestigious and popular event is the acclaimed **St Magnus Festival,** held in June in Kirkwall. It consists of six days of music, drama, literature and the visual arts and features many internationally renowned performers.

During July there are several **regattas** held on most of the islands, while August is marked by numerous **agricultural shows**, culminating in the **Festival of the Horse and Boys' Ploughing Match** on South Ronaldsay (see page 373).

The **Orkney Science Festival** is held in the first week in September, T01856-876214. For details of what's going on and when, buy a copy of The Orcadian, which comes out on Thursdays, or pick up a free copy of the Tourist Board's guide.

Transport For details of flights and ferries to Orkney, see page 356. Details of inter-island flights and ferries are given in the relevant island sections.

There's a limited **bus** service around the Mainland. *Peace Coaches*, T872866, runs regular buses Mon-Sat from Kirkwall bus station to **Stromness** 30 mins. They also run 3-5 buses a day, Mon-Sat, to **Houton**, 30 mins, which connect with ferries to Hoy; and a daily bus, Mon-Sat, to **East Holm**, 25 mins, and **Stromness via Dounby**, 55 mins. *Causeway Coaches*, T831444, runs 2-4 buses a day, Mon-Sat, to **St Margaret's Hope**, 30 mins. *Rosie Coaches*, T751227, runs buses to **Tingwall** and **Evie**. The bus service between Kirkwall and **Burwick** is run by *Shalders Coaches*, T850809. Note that there is no Sun bus service on Orkney.

Car hire *Scarth Car Hire*, Great Western Rd, T872125. *WR Tullock*, Castle St, T876262, and Kirkwall airport, T875500. **Cycle hire** *Bobby's Cycle Centre*, Tankerness Lane, T/F875777. Mountain bikes from £8 per day.

Directory **Banks** Branches of the 3 main Scottish banks with cash machines are on Broad St and Albert St. Exchange also at the tourist office. **Communications** Post office: Junction Rd. Open Mon-Fri 0900-1700, Sat 0930-1230. **Laundry** *The Launderama*, Albert St, T872982. Open Mon-Fri 0830-1730, Sat 0900-1700. **Medical facilities** Balfour Hospital, Health Centre and Dental Clinic, New Scapa Rd, T885400.

West Mainland

Phone code: 01856 Everything west of Kirkwall is known as West Mainland, an area of rich farmland, rolling hills and moorland, fringed by spectacular cliffs along the Atlantic coastline and with the greatest concentration of pre-historic monuments in Britain. Here you'll find, amongst many others, the well-preserved Neolithic village of **Skara Brae**, silent monuments to human endeavour in the form of the standing **Stones of Stenness** and the **Ring of Brodgar**, and the chambered tomb of **Maes Howe**, with its many still unresolved mysteries. The sights below are listed in an anti-clockwise direction starting from Kirkwall.

Nine miles northwest of Kirkwall is the tiny village of Evie. A track leads from the village towards the coast, past a sandy beach, to the **Broch of Gurness**. Standing on a lonely, exposed headland on the north coast with warm, gentle views across towards the island of Rousay, this is the best-preserved broch on Orkney, thought to date from around 100 BC. It is surrounded by an Iron Age village whose houses are also remarkably well-preserved, with the original hearths, beds, cupboards and even a toilet still in evidence. The broch and village were occupied by the Picts right up till Viking times, around 900 AD. Many Pictish artefacts have been found on the site and the grave of a ninth-century Norse woman was also discovered. ■ *Apr-Sep daily 0930-1830. Adult £2.80, concession £2, children £1. T751414 (HS).*

Evie & the Broch of Gurness

To the southwest of Evie is the **Birsay Moors RSPB Reserve** and at **Lowrie's Water** on Burgar Hill there's a bird-hide from where you can watch breeding red-throated divers. Also on Burgar Hill you'll see several huge aerogenerators built to take advantage of Orkney's fierce winds.

Sleeping D *Woodwick House*, T751330, a very comfortable country house hotel offering good food and occasional cultural events. Good value. The *Eviedale Centre* beside the junction of the road to Dounby, T751270, open April-October, has a small **bothy** and **campsite**. *The Mistra* is the local village shop, post office and pub.

At the far northwestern corner of the Mainland is the parish of Birsay which was a favourite residence of the Earls of Orkney in Viking times as well as the first seat of the Bishop, before the building of St Magnus Cathedral in Kirkwall. Earl Thorfinn the Mighty lived here (1014-64) and built Orkney's first cathedral, **Christchurch**, for the new Bishop.

Birsay

In the centre of the village are the ruins of the **Earl's Palace**, built by the infamous Earl Robert Stewart in the late 16th century and once described as "a sumptuous and stately dwelling". Not much remains today but enough to give some idea of the sheer scale of the place. ■ *Open at all times. Free. T01856-721205.*

Close by is **St Magnus church**, built in 1760 on the site of an earlier church, which in turn was built on the foundations of what is believed to be the original Christchurch. Also in Birsay, just south of the A966 and A967 junction, is **Barony Mills**, the last working water-powered mill in Orkney. ■ *Apr-Sep daily 1000-1300 and 1400-1700. Adult £1.50.*

Lying half a mile off the coast near the village is the **Brough of Birsay**, a tidal island, jutting out into the north Atlantic and visible from several other points all the way down the west cost of the mainland. It is only accessible for a couple of hours at low tide (times available from Kirkwall and Stromness tourist offices) but, if possible, it is best seen at the end of the day, as the sun sets – and you'll probably have the whole island to yourself. Pick your way over the shell and bladderack-strewn causeway and wander at your leisure (but don't forget the tide!) amongst the remnants of a Pictish, and then Viking, community. The island was an important Pictish settlement from around the sixth century and many artefacts have been found here. Some of these can be seen at the

Orkney & Shetland

Ring of Brodgar

small ticket office at the entrance to the island. The Brough was also the site of an important Viking settlement and there are extensive remains, including the 12th-century **St Peter's church**, where St Magnus was buried after his murder on Egilsay. You can also walk out to the island's **lighthouse** along the top of the cliffs and see puffins (amongst other migrating seabirds) and possibly Minke whales, Pilot whales and Killer whales. ■ *The tidal island is now managed by Historic Scotland. Open (when tides permit) 11 Jun-30 Sep, daily 0930-1830. Adult £1.50, concession £1.10, children £0.50. Phone the Earl's Palace (see above).*

Markwick Head At the southern end of Birsay Bay are the wild and spectacular 300 ft-high cliffs of Marwick Head, topped by the distinctive **Kitchener Memorial**, erected after the First World War to commemorate Lord Kitchener and the crew of the *HMS Hampshire*, which was sunk by a German mine off the coast in 1916 with the loss of all but 12 of her crew. Marwick Head is also an **RSPB Reserve** and during the nesting season in early summer is home to many thousands of guillemots, razorbills, kittiwakes and fulmars, as well as a few puffins.

A mile inland, by the Loch of Isibister, is another RSPB reserve, **The Loons**, an area of marshland where you can see breeding and migrating wildfowl and waders. Further east, between Boarhouse Loch and Hundland Loch, is the **Kirbuster Farm Museum**, the last surviving Orkney 'black-house' which was lived-in till the 1960s and gives an insight into 19th-century rural life on the islands. ■ *Mar-Oct Mon-Sat 1030-1300 and 1400-1700, Sun 1400-1900. Free.*

Sleeping Accommodation is limited to the **D-E** *Barony Hotel*, T721327, baronyhotel@btinternet.com Open May-Sep, on the north shore of Boardhouse Loch. It specializes in fishing holidays and is about the only place to offering **food** in these parts. There's also **E-F** *Primrose Cottage*, T/F721384, i.clouston@talk21.com, a comfortable **B&B** overlooking Marwick Bay.

Transport On Mon there's a **bus** between Kirkwall and Birsay with *Shalder Coaches*, T850809.

Skara Brae and Skaill House

South of Birsay, eight miles north of Stromness, in the magnificent setting of the dazzling white sands of the Bay of Skaill, is Skara Brae, the best preserved Stone Age village in northern Europe. First revealed in 1850 after a violent storm blew away the dunes, the site dates from around 5,000 years ago and was occupied for about 600 years.

The houses contain stone furniture, fireplaces, drains, beds, dressers and even have damp-proof coursing in the foundations. The whole complex presents a unique picture of the lifestyle of its inhabitants and there's also a replica 'house' that you can enter, and wander around in through the gloom, empathizing with that 3000 BC lifestyle.

The swish, modern visitor centre has a useful introductory video and exhibition which is definitely worth seeing before you look round the site (and it's also worth buying their guidebook). After leaving the visitor centre, you walk down a 'path of time', which takes you back through landmark achievements of the last seven millennia, gradually building up the suspense and putting the achievements of Skara Brae in perspective - they may only be rudimentary buildings that once had turf for their rooves, but they were built 2000 years before the pyramids of Egypt, and in one of the world's most northerly outposts.

During the summer, a ticket to Skara Brae includes admission to nearby **Skaill House**, an early 17th-century mansion which contains a few old artefacts, including Captain Cook's dinner service from the *Resolution*, but is a bit of a let-down after what you will have just witnessed, not 300 yards away at Skara Brae.

■ *Skara Brae and Skaill House Apr-Sep daily 0930-1830. Adult £4.50, concession £3.30, children £1.30. Oct-Mar (Skara Brae only) Mon-Sat 0930-1630 and Sun 1400-1630. Adult £3.50, concession £2.60, children £1.20. Joint ticket for all Orkney Historic Scotland monuments also available. T841815.*

There are a few **B&Bs** close to Skara Brae, including **E** *Kierfiold House*, T/F841583, near Loch Harray, and **E-F** *Netherstove*, T/F841625, ann.poke@virgin.net, overlooking the Bay of Skaill. To get to Skara Brae you'll need your own transport, or you can visit as part of a guided tour (see page 357), or walk north along the coast from Stromness, via Yesnaby.

Sleeping

A short distance inland from here, at **Sandwick**, is Orkney's only brewery, housed in the old Quayloo School. It brews the island's *Raven Ale* and various bottled beers, including *Skull-splitter*, named after the Viking Earl, Thorfinn Skull-splitter.

South of the Bay of Skaill is **Yesnaby**, one of the most spectacular places on the islands, where the cliffs have been eroded into a series of stacks and *geos* by the fierce Atlantic seas. An exhilarating, and precarious, half mile walk south from the car park and old Second World War lookout post brings you to **Yesnaby Castle**, a huge sea stack similar to the Old Man of Hoy. It's a dramatic sight, especially in a full force gale.

Northeast of Stromness, on the road to Kirkwall, is the tiny village of **Stenness**, near some of Orkney's most interesting prehistoric sites. The Standing Stones of Stenness comprise the four remaining stones from an original circle of 12 stones, dating from 3000 BC. The largest of the stones stands over 15 ft high. ■ *Free*. A path leads from the stones to the nearby **Barnhouse Settlement**, a recently- excavated Neolithic village.

Standing Stones of Stenness

About a mile northwest of Stenness is another stone circle, the Ring of Brodgar. This is a particularly impressive henge monument. It is over 100yds in diameter and 27 of the original 60 stones are still standing, some of them up to 15 ft high. Given the importance of these sites it is particularly refreshing to realize when you get there that you can walk about amongst the stones in the still calm of a summer evening, with only a few oyster catchers for company, but both do get busy with coach parties during the day. ■ *Free*.

Ring of Brodgar

Orkney & Shetland

Maes Howe

Less than a mile northeast of the Stones of Stenness is Maes Howe, the finest Neolithic burial chamber in Europe. It was built around 2750 BC, making it contemporary with the Standing Stones and Skara Brae, and is amazingly well preserved. A huge mound covers a stone-built entrance passage which leads into a central chamber – over 12 ft square and the same in height – with three smaller cells built into the walls of the tomb. A fascinating feature of the site is that the winter solstice sun sets directly over the Barnhouse Stone, half a mile away, and shines down the entrance passage of Maes Howe and onto the back wall of one of the cells.

Orkney Chair

One of Scotland's most distinctive pieces of furniture is the Orkney chair. Starting as a 'needs must' object, the chairs were originally made of driftwood and backed with oat straw. Their half moon shape ingeniously gave protection from the many draughts in a house. Very often the back was extended upwards into a cowl, so that the chair looked rather like an upended cradle. This gave added protection. It was often been said that what an Orkney man could not make from straw was not worth having. The straw, which came from black oats, was particularly important as trees are not plentiful on Orkney. Even today bringing timber from across the Pentland Firth is an expensive business. Heavy storms still yield windfall wood but not such a variety as in the days of wooden ships which too often perished in these waters.

When it was opened, in 1861, no human remains or artefacts were found, giving no clues as to its usage. However, in the 12th century, Vikings returning from the Crusades broke into the tomb searching for treasure. They found nothing but left behind one of the largest collections of runic graffiti anywhere in the world, as well as carvings of a dragon, serpent and walrus. Many of the inscriptions are pretty basic, along the lines of "Thorfinn wrote these runes" but some are more intriguing, such as "Many a woman has come stooping in here no matter how pompous a person she was".

A guide gives you an excellent overview of the chamber's mysterious architectural attributes, but the fact remains that the history of this extraordinary place is still largely unsolved – something that obviously adds to the site's attraction. Unfortunately, you do not get the chance to spend very much time in the chamber, so you are unlikely to uncover any great secrets.

■ *Tickets to Maes Howe from Tormiston Mill, on the other side of the road, where there's a an exhibition, introductory video and café. Apr-Sep daily 0930-1830; Oct-Mar Mon-Sat 0930-1630 and Sun 1400-1630. Adult £2.80, concession £2, children £1. Joint ticket for all Orkney Historic Scotland monuments also available. T761606.*

Sleeping There are a few places to stay around **Stenness**. On the shores of Loch Harray is the **B** *Merkister Hotel*, T771366, merkisterhotel@ecos.co, which is a favourite with anglers. It has a very good restaurant and a popular bar. On the shores of Loch Stenness is the **D-C** *Standing Stones Hotel*, T850449, standingstones@sol.co.uk There's also the lovely **D-E** *Mill of Eyreland*, T850136, www.orknet.co.uk/mill, a converted mill 3 miles from Stromness.

Orphir

On the southern shores of West Mainland, overlooking Scapa Flow, is the scattered community of Orphir, which has a few sights worth visiting, especially if you're heading across to Hoy from the ferry terminal at **Houton**, a little further west.

Orkneyinga Saga Centre The main point of interest in Orphir is the Orkneyinga Saga Centre, where a small exhibition and video introduces the saga, written circa 1200, possibly by an Icelander, which tells the history of the Viking Earls of Orkney from around 900 AD to 1200 AD, when the islands became a part of Scotland rather than Norway. As you would expect, there's plenty of gore and Machievellian goings-on, including an assassination attempt that went disastrously wrong, when a poinsoned shirt meant for Earl Harold was unwittingly and fatally worn by his brother Paul instead. ■ *All year daily 0900-1700. Free.*

Behind the centre is **The Earl's Bu**, looking out across Orphir Bay south to Cava Island. These are the 12th-century foundations of the home of the Norse Earls of Orkney written about in the saga. Inside the cemetery gates is a section of the circular church built by Haakon and modelled on the rotunda of the Church of the Holy Sepulchre in Jerusalem.

For details of **ferries** to Hoy and Flotta, see page 375. For details of **buses** to Houton, see page 364.   **Transport**

Stromness

Ferries from Scrabster arrive in Stromness and the newcomer is greeted by rows of stone-built houses hugging the shore, each with their own jetty. Stromness is a much more attractive than Kirkwall and its narrow, winding main street, its wynds and closes, its fascinating shops, and its unique atmosphere make it the ideal base for exploring the West Mainland.

Phone code: 01856
Population: 2,500

Ins and outs

For details of **ferries** to Scrabster, Aberdeen and Lerwick, see page 356. For ferries to Hoy, see page 375.   **Getting there**

The TIC is at the new the ferry terminal, T850716. Its exhibition *This Place Called Orkney* is a useful introduction to the islands and its free *Stromness Heritage Guide* takes you round all the buildings of interest in the town. Apr-Oct Mon-Sat 0800-1800, Sun 0900-1600; Nov-Mar Mon-Fri 0900-1700.   **Tourist Information Centre**

History

Though referred to in the Viking Saga as Hamnavoe, the town dates from the 17th century. Its importance as a trading port grew in the 18th century when wars and privateers made the English Channel too dangerous and ships used the northern route across the Atlantic, calling in at Stromness to take on food and water and to hire local men as crew. Until the late 19th-century ships of the Hudson Bay Company made Stromness their main base for supplies and used **Login's Well** as a source of fresh water. Whaling ships bound for Greenland also hired local labour. By the late 19th century the herring boom had reached Stromness and there were 400 boats using its harbour, but within two decades the boom was over due to over-fishing. Today, Stromness remains a fishing port, as well as Orkney's main ferry terminal and the headquarters of the Northern Lighthouse Board.

Sights

Stromness consists largely of one narrow, winding main street, paved with flagstones, which hugs the shoreline. Running off the street are numerous little lanes and alleyways, many with fascinating names such as **Khyber Pass**, and full of interesting buildings which reflect the town's proud maritime heritage. The houses on the seaward side of the street are gable end to the

Stromness is one of the classic Scottish fishing villages and a perfect introduction to Orkney

Orkney & Shetland

waterfront and each has its own jetty. The town is not designed for the motor car, so you'll have to park by the harbour and explore its delights on foot. The main street changes its name from Victoria Street to Graham Place, Dundas Street, Alfred Street and South End as it runs south from the harbour.

The **Stromness Museum**, at 52 Albert Street, has exhibitions on natural and maritime history and contains artefacts from Scapa Flow and the days of the Hudson Bay company. ■ *May-Sep daily 1000-1700; Oct-Apr Mon-Sat 1030-1230 and 1330-1700. Adult £2.50, children £0.50. T850025.* , Opposite the museum is the house where **George Mackay Brown** (1921-96), Orkney's most famous poet and story-writer, spent the last two decades of his life (see also page 372).

On a jetty to the south of the new harbour is the excellent **Pier Arts Centre**, housing a permanent collection of works of the St Ives school, including Barbara Hepworth, Ben Nicholson and Patrick Heron amongst others in a lovely gallery. ■ *Tue-Sat 1030-1230 and 1330-1700; Jul and Aug also Sun 1400-1700. Free.*

Essentials

Sleeping The best hotel in town is the **C-D** *Stromness Hotel*, T850298, www.Stromnesshotel.com, an imposing old building overlooking the harbour, recently refurbished and offering good value meals.

Also near the ferry terminal, on John St, is the **E** *Ferry Inn*, T850280, www.ferryinn.com/ which serves food and has a lively bar. There are several B&B options, including **E-D** *Stenigar*, T850438. Open Apr-Oct, a converted boatyard on Ness Rd, just before the campsite, with views of Hoy, and **E** *Mrs Worthington*, T850215. Open Apr-Oct, a traditional gable-ended house at 2 South End. On Victoria St near the harbour is **E** *Orca Hotel*, T850447, www.theoakleigh.com Also has a bistro (*Bistro 76*) serving good food. A few miles behind Stromness, at Innertown, is **E** *Thira*, T851181. A comfortable, friendly and non-smoking modern bungalow with spectacular views of Hoy. Also serves an excellent cooked breakfast and will provide a fantastic dinner made from the finest local ingredients on request.

F *Brown's Hostel*, 45 Victoria St, T850661. This popular independent hostel has no curfew and is open all year round unlike the **F** *SYHA Hostel*, on Hellihole Rd, a 10-min walk south from the ferry terminal, T850589. Open Mar-Oct. There's a **campsite**, T873535, open May to mid-Sep, at Ness Point, a mile south of the ferry terminal. It's well equipped and has incomparable views but is very exposed.

Eating & The best place to eat is the *Hamnavoe Restaurant*, at 35 Graham Pl, T850606. It spe-
drinking cializes in local seafood but also offers good vegetarian dishes. Mid-range. Open Mar-Oct Tue-Sun from 1900. The *Stromness Hotel* bar serves good, cheap meals. The *Ferry Inn* also serves cheap bar food. The *Orca Hotel* (see above) has a good cellar bistro. Near the ferry terminal on John St, is the popular *Coffee Shop* which serves good, cheap grub. Open Mon-Sat 0900-1830, Sun 0900-1700 (Mon-Sat till 1700 in winter). The best places for a drink are the downstairs bar of the *Stromness Hotel*, the *Ferry Inn* and the bar of the *Royal Hotel*.

Sports **Diving** *The Diving Cellar*, 4 Victoria St, T850055. Offers diving packages, equipment rental and boat charters. Open Mon-Fri 1100-1400 and 1700-1900, Sat 1300-1700. *Scapa Scuba*, 13 Ness Rd, T/F851218. Diving course, guided dives, night dives and boat charters.

The graveyard of Scapa Flow

The huge natural harbour of Scapa Flow has been used since Viking times and in the years leading up to the First World War the Royal Navy held exercises there, sometimes involving up to 100 ships. But Scapa was vulnerable to attack and over the course of the war defences were improved with 21 blockships sunk at the eastern approaches. Scapa Flow continued to be used as the main naval base in the Second World War, but the blockships were not enough to prevent a German U-boat from torpedoing HMS Royal Oak and the huge task of building the Churchill Barriers began (see page 373).

Scapa Flow's most famous incident happened at the end of the First World War, when, under the terms of the Armistice, Germany agreed to surrender most of her navy. Seventy-four German

ships were interred in Scapa Flow, awaiting the final decision, but as the deadline approached the German commander, Admiral Von Reuter gave the order for all the ships to be scuttled and every ship was beached or sank.

The scuttled German fleet, however, proved a hazard for fishing and a massive salvage operation began. Today, seven German ships remain at the bottom of Scapa Flow – three battleships and four light cruisers – along with four destroyers and a U-boat and the Royal Navy battleships HMS Royal Oak and HMS Vanguard, which blew up in 1917. This makes Scapa Flow one of the world's great **scuba diving** sites. Two companies in Stromness (see page 371) offer diving courses for beginners and wreck diving for experienced divers.

There are several **buses** daily (Mon-Sat) between Stromness and **Kirkwall**, 30 mins. **Transport**
There's also a bus from Stromness to **Birsay** on Mon only, with *Shalder Coaches*,
T850809. **Car hire** *Brass's Car Hire*, Blue Star Garage, North End Rd, T850850. **Cycle**
hire *Orkney Cycle Hire*, 54 Dundas St, T850255. £4.50-8.50 per day.

Banks There are branches of *Bank of Scotland* and *Royal Bank of Scotland*, both with **Directory**
cash machines, on Victoria St. **Laundry** Next to the *Coffee Shop*, T850904. Self-service or
service washes.

East Mainland

The East Mainland is mainly agricultural land, and though it contains little of the Phone code: 01856
amazing archaeological wealth of its western counterpart, there are some attrac-
tive fishing villages, fine coastal walks and many poignant reminders of Orkney's
important wartime role.

Deerness

There is not much to see inland on the road running southeast from Kirkwall
past the airport, but head on towards the Deerness Peninsula and you will be
richly rewarded by a truly serene, gentle beauty. There are sandy bays, which
make for very pleasant short walks and picnics (if you can find a sheltered
spot), jutting cliffs and a great variety of birdlife. The peninsula makes the
West Mainland seem like a mad, hectic whirl by comparison and is one of the
best places on the Mainland to 'get away from it all'.

When the weather's good, the view southwest from Sandside Bay to the Isle
of **Copinsay** (an RSPB reserve) is glorious, and, as it emerges slowly and
gracefully from the wild North Sea, is a perfect example of the whale-like

Orkney Writers

For its size, Orkney has produced a disproportionate number of well loved and much read authors.

Born to a farming family in 1887, **Edwin Muir** was the youngest of six children. He spent his first fourteen years on the lovely island of Wyre before the family moved to Glasgow. His father, mother and two brothers died within four years. Muir then resorted to a number of soul destroying clerical jobs in order to keep body and soul together. For consolation, he turned to literature, writing and socialism.

In 1919 he married Willa Anderson who chronicled their life together touchingly in 'The Belonging.' The couple eventually moved to London, where Muir became drama critic of The Scotsman and also assistant to AR Orage, editor of New Age. Life soon led them to Europe, where they spent time in Czechoslovakia, Germany, Italy, France and Austria. After their return to England in 1927, their son Gavin was born. Translations became the couple's forte and they worked on Kafka's 'The Castle'. During the Second World War, Muir worked in Edinburgh for the British Council. In 1949, he was appointed director of the British Institute in Rome. Eventually returning to Scotland in 1950, he was appointed head of Newbattle Abbey College in Dalkeith, having for the previous year held the Professorship of Poetry at Harvard.

Because of his significant contribution to Scottish poetry he received an MBE in 1953. Having by then published seven volumes of verse, he was recognized as one of the most distinguished poets of his century. He died in 1959 whilst living in Cambridgeshire.

George Mackay Brown's works gained even more popularity after the posthumous publication of his autobiography following his death in 1996. Dogged by tuberculosis in his youth he later found inspiration through alcohol. Unlike Edwin Muir, he rarely left his native Orkney. Their paths eventually crossed when Muir invited him to study at Newbattle Abbey. Thanks to this he went on to Edinburgh University to learn more of literature. He also formed a close partnership with Peter Maxwell Davies, who used his words to enhance his musical works.

The son of a master mariner from Dounby on Orkney, but born in Wales himself, **Eric Linklater** eventually settled in the Orkneys. Born in 1899, he was educated at Aberdeen Grammar School and began studying medicine at the university there. In the First World War, he absented himself and, under age, joined the Black Watch. However, after a serious head wound he returned to change subjects and graduate in English literature. Bent on a career in writing, he went to work for The Times of India. After his return, he became an assistant lecturer in English at Aberdeen. Always popular, he was voted rector of Aberdeen University from 1945-48. Many of his copious output of books and poems are on Scottish subjects.

properties that have been attributed to the Orkneys by the islands' most famous poet George Mackay Brown. There is a **footpath** following the coast from Sandside Bay to Mull Head (a Nature Reserve) and round the tip of the peninsula to the Covenanters Memorial (1679), a five mile circular walk.

The Gloup If you continue along the B9050, the road ends at The Gloup car park at Skaill Bay, from where it's a 200 yard-walk to The Gloup, a dramatic collapsed sea cave, separated from the sea by a land bridge about 80 yards wide. The word comes from the Old Norse *'gluppa'* meaning chasm, the local name for a blow-hole. A network of signposted footpaths cover the northeastern part of the peninsula and there are circular walks of between two to five miles which start from The Gloup car park. At the northeastern tip is **Mull Head**, a clifftop nature reserve which is home to guillemots, shags, fulmars, razorbills, terns and skuas.

On the south coast of East Mainland, near the northern end of the Churchill Barriers, is the old fishing village of **St Mary's**, once a busy little place but largely forgotten since the building of the causeways. To the east of the village is the **Norwood Museum**, which features the large and eclectic antique collection of local stonemason Norris Wood. ■ *May-Sep Tue-Thu and Sun 1400-1700 and 1800-2000. Adult £3, children £1. T781217.*

Sleeping and eating The only place to stay or eat around here is the **E** *Commodore Motel*, T781319.

East Mainland is linked to a string of islands to the south by four causeways, known as the Churchill Barriers, built on the orders of Prime Minister Winston Churchill during the Second World War as anti-submarine barriers to protect the British Navy which was based in Scapa Flow at the time. His decision was prompted by the sinking of the battleship *HMS Royal Oak* in October 1939 by a German U-boat which had slipped between the old blockships, deliberately sunk during the First World War to protect Scapa Flow, and the shore. After the war, a road was built on top of the causeways, linking the islands of Lamb Holm, Glimps Holm, Burray and South Ronaldsay to Mainland.

The Churchill Barriers

On the island of Lamb Holm camps were built to accommodate the men working on the construction of the barriers, many of whom were Italian Prisoners of War. The camps have long since gone but the Italians left behind the remarkable **Italian Chapel**, fittingly known as 'The Miracle of Camp 60'. It is difficult to believe that such a beautiful building could have been made using two Nissen huts, concrete and bits of scrap metal and the chapel's enduring popularity with visitors is a tribute to the considerable artistic skill of the men involved. One of them, Domenico Chiochetti, returned in 1960 to restore the interior paintwork. ■ *Open all year during daylight hours. Free.*

On the island of Burray the road passes the **Orkney Fossil and Vintage Centre**, which houses a bizarre collection of old furniture, various relics and 350 million-year-old fish fossils found locally. There's also an archive room where you can browse through old books and photographs, and a coffee shop. Not really something to go out of your way for, but worth a look if its raining. ■ *Apr-Sep daily 1000-1800; Oct Wed-Sun 1030-1800. Adult £2.*

Burray

Sleeping and eating In Burray village, on the south coast of the island, there's **B&B** accommodation at **E** *Vestlaybanks*, T731305, vestlaybanks@btinternet.com, which also provides evening meals. Alternatively, you can eat at the *Sands Motel*, T731298.

South Ronaldsay

South Ronaldsay is the southernmost of the Orkney islands, only six miles from the Scottish mainland, across the stormy Pentland Firth, the most dangerous stretch of water in the British Isles. A small passenger ferry crosses to **Burwick** on the southern tip of the island from John O' Groats (for details see page 356).

Phone code: 01856

St Margaret's Hope The main settlement is the picturesque little village of St Margaret's Hope on the north coast. It is said to be named after Margaret, Maid of Norway, who died near here in 1290 at the age of seven while on her way to marry Prince Edward, later Edward II of England. She had already been proclaimed Queen of Scotland and her premature death was a major factor in the long Wars of Independence with England. The word 'hope' comes from the Old Norse word '*hjop*' meaning bay.

The village smithy has been turned into the **Smiddy Museum**, with lots of old blacksmith's tools to try out. ■ *Open May and Sep daily 1400-1600; Jun-Aug 1200-1600; Oct Sun 1400-1600. Free.* The museum also features a small exhibition on the annual **Boys' Ploughing Match**, a hugely popular event first held in circa 1860. Each year in August, boys from the village (and now girls as well) dress up as horses and parade in the village square (prizes are given for the best costume). Afterwards the boys and their fathers, or grandfathers, head for the **Sand of Wright** a few miles west and have a ploughing match with miniature ploughs, which are usually family heirlooms. The categories are: best ploughed ring, best *feering* or guiding furrow, neatest ends and best kept plough. This sheltered beach is well worth a visit anyway, ploughing or no ploughing. The views stretch in a spectacular 180 degree panorama, south across the Pentland Firth to Caithness on mainland Scotland, west to South Walls and Cantick Head on Hoy and northwest to Flotta and the west Mainland. It is also yet another good place to spot snipe, lapwing, curlew and redshank. Arctic terns also nest nearby and you can spot them diving dramatically as they fish in the bay.

To the north of the beach is the **Howe of Hoxa**, a ruined broch where Earl Thorfinn Skull-Splitter was buried in AD 963, according to the Orkneyinga saga. South Ronaldsay is a good place to buy local arts and crafts and there are several workshops dotted around the island. One of these is the **Hoxa Tapestry Gallery**, three miles west of the village, on the way to Hoxa Head. Local artist Leila Thompson's huge tapestries are well worth a visit, you may not like the style, but you cannot help but marvel at the extraordinary amount of work and dedication involved in their creation; many of them take years to finish. ■ *Apr-Sep Mon-Fri 1000-1730, Sat and Sun 1400-1800. Adult £2, concession £1.50, children under 12free . T/F831395.*

Sleeping and eating There's a good selection of accommodation in St Margaret's Hope. Best of the lot is the award-winning **D** *Creel Restaurant & Rooms*, T831311, www.thecreel.co.uk, on Front Rd. It offers comfortable rooms and superb, though expensive, food using deliciously fresh, locally grown ingredients. Dinner only. For cheaper meals, try the bar of the **E** *Murray Arms Hotel*, T831205, on Back Rd. For a good **B&B** try **E** *Bellevue Guest House*, T831294, or **E** *The Fisher's Gill*, T831711, which also offers seafood dishes. For cheap and basic **hostel** accommodation, head for the *Wheems Bothy*, T831537, open Apr-Oct, which is now an organic farm at Wheems, Eastside, a few miles southeast of St Margaret's Hope.

Transport Details of **buses** between Kirkwall and St Margaret's Hope on page 364.

Tomb of the Eagles At the southeastern corner of South Ronaldsay is the recently-excavated Tomb of the Eagles, one of the most interesting archaeological sights on Orkney. The 5,000-year-old chambered cairn was discovered by local farmer and amateur archaeologist, Ronald Simison, whose family now runs the privately-owned site and museum. The interior contents of the tomb were practically intact and there were up to 340 people buried here, along with carcasses and talons of sea eagles, hence the name. Various objects were also found outside the tomb, including stone tools and polished stone axes.

Before visiting the tomb you can handle the skulls and various other artefacts at the small 'museum' in the family home, which actually means, their front porch! Then you walk for about five to 10 minutes through a field to visit a **burnt mound**, a kind of Bronze Age kitchen, where Ronald Simison will regail you with all manner of fascinating insider information about the excavation process, before walking out along the cliff edge to the spectacularly-sited tomb which you must enter by lying on a trolley and pulling yourself in using an overhead rope. It is particularly eerie being here because there is generally no-one else around, and as you haul yourself into the tomb, with the sound of the North Sea crashing into the cliffs nearby, you wonder to yourself how those buried here met their fate. There is also a lovely, but generally wild and windy, walk back along the cliffs, via a different route back to the car park. ■ *Apr-Oct daily 1000-2000; Nov-Mar 1000-1200. £2.50.*

Hoy

To the southwest of the Mainland is Hoy, the second largest of the Orkney islands. The name is derived from the Norse Ha-ey, meaning High Island, which is appropriate as much of the island is more reminiscent of the Scottish highlands than Orkney, with only the southern end being typically low and fertile.

Phone code: 01856

There are 2 **ferry** services to Hoy, both run by *Orkney Ferries*, T850624. Transport on Hoy limited to a minibus between Moaness Pier and Rackwick. **Car and bike hire** is available from *Halyel Car Hire* in Lyness, T791240.

Ins & outs
See Transport on next page

Orkney's highest point, **Ward Hill** (1,571 ft) is in the north of the island and the north and west coasts are bounded by spectacular cliffs. At **St John's Head** the sheer cliffs rise out of the sea to a height of 1,150 ft, the highest vertical cliffs in Britain. The island is most famous for its **Old Man of Hoy**, a great rock stack rising to 450 ft. This northern part of Hoy forms the **North Hoy RSPB Reserve** which has a variety of habitats ranging from woodland to tundra-like hill-tops and sea cliffs. The reserve is home to a huge variety of birds including great skuas and Arctic skuas, Manx shearwaters and puffins. On the hills there are red grouse, curlews, golden plovers and dunlins, as well as peregrine falcons, merlins, kestrels and even golden eagles. Mountain hares are quite common and if you are very lucky, you can also see otters along the Scapa Flow coastline.

Hoy's great attraction is its many excellent **walking** opportunities. A minibus runs between **Moaness Pier**, where the ferry from Stromness docks (see Transport below) and **Rackwick**, on the opposite side of the island, but it's a lovely two-hour walk by road through beautiful **Rackwick Glen**, once populated by crofters and fishermen, but now quiet and isolated. On the way you'll pass the **Dwarfie Stone**, a huge, lonely block of sandstone which is the only rock-cut tomb in Britain, dating from around 3000 BC. Be careful, though, because according to Sir Walter Scott, this is the residence of the *Trolld*, a dwarf from Norse legend. On your return you can take a different route through a narrow valley between the **Cuilags** (1,421 ft) and **Ward Hill** and **Berriedale Wood**, the most northerly woodland in Britain. The most popular walk on Hoy is the spectacular three-hour hike from Rackwick to the cliffs facing the **Old Man of Hoy**. The path climbs steeply westwards from the old

Walks on Hoy

Orkney & Shetland

crofting township then turns northwards before gradually descending to the cliff edge.

Lyness & South Walls On the southeast coast of the island is Lyness, site of a large naval base during both world wars when the British fleet was based in Scapa Flow. Many of the old dilapidated buildings have gone but the harbour area is still scarred with the scattered remains of concrete structures and there's also the unattractive sight of the huge oil terminal on **Flotta**. Lyness has a large **Naval Cemetery**, last resting place of those who died at Jutland, of Germans killed during the scuttle and of the crew of *HMS Royal Oak*. The old pump house opposite the new ferry terminal is now the **Scapa Flow Visitor Centre**, a fascinating naval museum with old photographs, various wartime artefacts, a section devoted to the scuttling of the German Fleet and an audio-visual feature on the history of Scapa Flow. Well worth a visit. ■ *Mid-May to mid-Sep Mon-Sat 0900-1630, Sun 1030-1545; Jul and Aug Mon-Sat 0900-1630, Sun 0945-1800; mid-Sept to mid-May Mon-Fri 0900-1630. Adult £2. T791300.*

At South Walls overlooking Longhope Bay, is **Hackness Martello Tower and Battery** which, along with another tower on the north side at Crockness, was built in 1815 to protect British ships in Longhope Bay against attack by American and French privateers while they waited for a Royal Navy escort on their journey to Baltic ports. ■ *The tower is open to the public. If locked, a sign on the door will tell you where to get the key from.*

Essentials

Sleeping & eating There's not much accommodation in the north of the island, except for the two SYHA hostels. The larger of the two, **F** *Hoy Youth Hostel* is about a mile from Moaness Pier. It's open from May-Sep. The smaller hostel is **F** *Rackwick Youth Hostel* in Rackwick Glen (open mid-Mar to mid-Sep). To book ahead for both hostels, contact Orkney Council, T873535, ext 2404. Near the pier and post office is the *Hoy Inn*, T791313, a bar and restaurant which serves good seafood (closed Mon). There's also an RSPB information centre here.

There are a few very good **B&Bs** in the south of the island. South of **Lyness** is **E** *Stoneyquoy*, T/F791234, www.visithoy.com The owner Louise Budge also runs guided tours of the island for £40 for up to 4 people, including lunch. On the other side of the bay in Longhope is **E-F** *Burnhouse*, T701263. Also in Longhope is the **E-F** *Old Custom House*, T701358. Near the ferry terminal in Lyness is **E** *The Hoy Hotel*, T791377. Open Apr-Oct, which serves meals. The *Anchor Bar*, T791356, in Lyness serves lunches. There are shops/petrol stations in Lyness and Longhope.

Transport A passenger ferry sails between **Stromness** and Moaness Pier in the north (30 mins) 3 times a day Mon-Fri and twice on Fri evenings, twice daily Sat and Sun. There's a reduced winter service (mid-Sep to mid-May). There's also a car and passenger service between **Houton** and Lyness and Longhope (45 mins) up to 6 times daily (Mon-Sat). There's a limited Sun service from mid-May to mid-Sep.

Transport on Hoy is very limited. *North Hoy Transport*, T791315, runs a **minibus** service between Moaness Pier and Rackwick, which meets the 1000 ferry from Stromness. Call the same number for a taxi around the island.

Rousay, Egilsay and Wyre

These three islands lie a short distance off the northeast coast of Mainland and, together with Shapinsay to the southeast, are the closest of Orkney's North Isles to Kirkwall.

Phone code: 01856

Rousay

Rousay is a hilly island about five miles in diameter and known as the 'Egypt of the North' due to the large number archaeological sites. It also has the important **Trumland RSPB Reserve**, home to merlins, hen harriers, peregrine falcons, short-eared owls and red-throated divers, and its three lochs offer good trout fishing.

Getting around You can take one of the very informative **minibus tours** run by *Rousay Traveller*, T821234. These run from Jun-early Sep, Tue-Fri, meeting the 1040 ferry from Tingwall and lasting 6 hrs. Tours: adult £15, students/OAPs £12, children £6. **Bike hire** is available from *Arts, Crafts & Bike Hire* at the pier, T821398.

Ins & outs

A road runs right around the island, and makes a pleasant 13 mile bike run, but most of the sights are within walking distance of the ferry pier on the southeast side of the island where most of the 200 inhabitants live. A short distance west of the pier by the road is **Tavershoe Tuick**, an unusual two-storey burial cairn, which was discovered in the late 19th century by Mrs Burroughs, wife of General Traill Burroughs who lived at nearby Trumland House. A mile further west, to the north of the road, is **Blackhammer**, a stalled Neolithic burial cairn. Further west, and a steep climb up from the road, is **Knowe of Yarso**, another stalled cairn, which contained the remains of at least 21 people. The tomb dates from around 2900 BC.

Most of the island's archaeological sights are to be found along the **Westness Walk**, a mile-long walk which starts from Westness Farm, about four miles west of the ferry pier, and ends at the remarkable Midhowe Cairn. The walk is described in detail in a leaflet available from the tourist offices on Mainland. **Midhowe Cairn** is the largest and longest thus far excavated on Orkney – over 100 ft long and 40 ft wide – and like the others, dates from around 3000 BC. Housed in a large building to protect it, the 'Great Ship of Death', as it is known, contained the remains of 25 people, in crouched position on or under the eastern shelves of the chamber which is divided into 12 sections. Standing nearby, with fine views across to Eynehallow island, is **Midhowe Broch**, one of the best-preserved brochs on Orkney, occupied from around 200 BC to 200AD. The outer walls are about 60 ft in diameter and up to 14 ft high in places.

Another fine walk on the island is around the **RSPB Reserve**. A footpath leads from beside Trumland House and heads up towards the island's highest point, **Blotchnie Fiold** (821 ft). A leaflet describing the walk is available from the tourist offices on Mainland or the **Trumland Orientation Centre** by the pier.

Orkney & Shetland

Accommodation on Rousay is very limited. Near Knowe of Yarso, about 2 miles west of the pier, is the **E-D** *Taversoe Hotel*, T821325, which offers excellent value meals. The seafood is particularly recommended (closed Mon to non-residents). The only other option is the **F** *Rousay Hostel* at Trumland Organic Farm, T821252, open all year and half a mile from the ferry. It has laundry facilities and you can also camp. The *Pier Restaurant* beside the pier serves food at lunchtime (cheap to mid-range).

Sleeping & eating

Transport A small car **ferry** sails from **Tingwall** (20 mins) to **Rousay** 6 times a day (Mon-Sat; 5 times on Sun). Most of the ferries call in at **Egilsay** and **Wyre** but some are on demand only and should be booked in advance, T751360. A bus connects Tingwall and Kirkwall (see page 364).

Egilsay and Wyre

These two small islands lie to the east of Rousay and have a couple of interesting sights of their own. Egilsay's claim to fame is the murder here of St Magnus, in 1115, and a **cenotaph** marks the spot where he was slain. The island is dominated by the 12th-century **St Magnus church**, built on the site of an earlier church, possibly as a shrine to St Magnus. It is the only surviving example on Orkney of a round-towered Viking church.

Much of Egilsay has been bought by the RSPB as a reserve to preserve the habitat of the very rare **corncrake**, whose distinctive rasping call may be heard.

Tiny Wyre features strongly in the Viking saga as the domain of Kolbein Hruga and the remains of his 12th-century stronghold, **Cubbie Roo's Castle**, and nearby **St Mary's chapel** can be still be seen. Kolbein's home, or *Bu*, was on the site of the nearby **Bu Farm**, where the poet **Edwin Muir** (1887-1959) spent part of his childhood. The far westerly point of the island, known as **the Taing**, is a favourite haunt of seals and a great place to enjoy a summer sunset.

Shapinsay

Phone code: 01856 Less than 30 minutes by ferry from Kirkwall is the fertile, low-lying island of Shapinsay. The main attraction is **Balfour Castle**, an imposing baronial pile which is in fact a Victorian extension to a much older house called 'Cliffdale'. The house, and the rest of the island, was bought by successive generations of the Balfour family who had made their fortune in India. Today, the castle is the home of the Zawadski family and can only be visited as part of an inclusive half-day tour. ■ *Tour leaves from Kirkwall on Wed and Sun May-Sep, on the 1415 ferry. Tours must be arranged in advance at the tourist office in Kirkwall. They cost around £15 per person which includes ferry ticket, guided tour of the castle and gardens (at 1500) and complimentary tea and cakes in the servants' quarters. You can take an earlier ferry if you wish to explore the island. T872856.*

In the village, built by the Balfours to house their estate workers, is the **Shapinsay Heritage Centre**, in the old Smithy. It has displays on the island's history and a tearoom upstairs. ■ *Mon, Tue and Thu-Sat 1200-1630, Wed and Sun till 1730. Free. T711258.*

A mile north of the village is the **Mill Dam RSPB Reserve**, where there's a hide overlooking a loch from which you can see many species of wildfowl and waders. Four miles from the pier, at the far northeast corner of the island, is the well-preserved **Burroughston Broch** with good views of seals sunning themselves on the nearby rocks. West of here, at **Quholme**, is the original birthplace of the father of **Washington Irving**, author of *Rip Van Winkle*.

Essentials

Sleeping & eating You can stay at **C** *Balfour Castle*, T711282, www.balfourcastle.co.uk, and enjoy all that Victorian splendour. The price includes dinner. The castle has a private chapel and a boat is available for bird watching and fishing trips for residents. Alternatively, there's comfortable B&B in the humbler surroundings of **E** *Girnigoe*, T711256, near the northern end of Veantro Bay. It also offers evening meals. There's a pub in the village, in the old gatehouse. Also 2 shops and a post office.

The small car **ferry** makes 6 sailings daily (including Sun in summer) from **Kirkwall** (25 mins).

Transport

Eday

The long, thin and sparsely-populated island of Eday lies at the centre of the North Isles group. It is less fertile than the other islands but its heather-covered hills in the centre have provided peat for the other peatless Orkney islands. Eday's sandstone has also been quarried and was used in the building of St Magnus Cathedral in Kirkwall.

Phone code: 01857

Getting there   There are **flights** from **Kirkwall** to Eday airport (called London Airport) There are also **ferries** from **Kirkwall**. The ferry pier is at Backaland, on the southeast of the island, a long way from the main sights. **Getting around** *Orkney Ferries*, T872044, also run the **Eday Heritage Tour**.

Ins & outs
See Transport on next page

The island has numerous chambered cairns and these, along with the other attractions, are concentrated in the northern part. These are all covered in the signposted five-mile **Eday Heritage Walk** which starts from *Community Enterprises Shop* and leads up to the Cliffs of Red Head at the northern tip. The walk takes about three hours to complete and it's worth picking up the *Eday Heritage Walk* leaflet.

The walk starts at Mill Bay and heads past **Mill Loch** where an RSPB hide allows you to watch rare red-throated divers breeding in spring and summer. Further north is the huge, 15-ft tall **Stone of Setter**, the largest standing stone in Orkney and visible from most of the chambered cairns. Close by are the **Fold of Setter**, a circular enclosure dating back to 2000 BC, and the **Braeside** and **Huntersquoy** chambered cairns. Further north along the path is **Vinquoy Chambered Cairn**, one of the finest in Orkney and similar to the better-known tomb at Maes Howe, dating from around the same time. An acrylic dome provides light to the main chamber, which can be entered by a narrow underground passage.

The path continues to the summit of **Vinquoy Hill**, which commands excellent views of the surrounding islands of Westray and Sanday. From here you can continue north to the spectacular red sandstone cliffs at **Red Head**, home to nesting guillemots, razorbills and puffins in summer, or head southeast along the coast to **Carrick House**. Built for Lord Kinclaven, Earl of Carrick, in 1633, the house is best known for its associations with the pirate, John Gow, whose ship ran aground during a failed attack on the house. He was captured and taken to London for trial and hanged. Sir Walter Scott's novel, *The Pirate*, is based on this story. ■ *Mid-Jun to mid-Sep, guided tour at 1400. £2. T622260.*

Essentials

There's B&B at **E** *Mrs Poppelwell's*, T622248, at Blett, Carrick Bay, opposite the Calf of Eday. She also provides evening meal and packed lunch, and has a self-catering cottage nearby for up to 3. Also **D** *Mrs Cockram*, T622271. Open Jun-Mar, at Skaill Farm, just south of the airport. Price includes dinner. There's a basic *Youth Hostel*, T622206, open Apr-Sep, run by Eday Community Enterprises, just north of the airport.

Sleeping & eating

Orkney & Shetland

Transport There are **flights** from **Kirkwall** to Eday with *Loganair*, T872494, on Wed only. There are **ferries** from **Kirkwall** (1 hr 15 mins to 2 hrs) twice daily via **Sanday** or **Stronsay**.

Orkney Ferries, T872044, also run the **Eday Heritage Tour** every Sun from mid-Jun to mid-Sep. It leaves Kirkwall at 0920 and return at 1955 and costs around £30 per person, which includes ferries, guided walks or minibus tour, entry to Carrick House and lunch. Book with *Orkney Ferries* or at the tourist office in Kirkwall. You can hire a **taxi** from Mr A Stewart by the pier, T622206, or **hire bikes** from Mr Burkett at Hamarr, near the Post Office south of Mill Loch.

Sanday

Phone code: 01857 Sanday is the largest of the North Isles, 12 miles long, and flat as a pancake except for the cliffs at Spurness. It is well-named, as its most notable feature is its sweeping bays of sparkling white sand backed by machair, and turquoise seas.

Ins & outs There are **flights** to Sanday from Kirkwall and also a **ferry** service. The ferry arrives at **Loth**, at the southern tip of the island, and is met by a **minibus** which will take you to most places.

There are numerous burial mounds all over the island, the most impressive being **Quoyness Chambered Cairn**, a 5,000 year-old tomb similar to Maes Howe. The 13 ft-high structure contains a large main chamber with six smaller cells opening through low entrances. Most of the burial tombs remain unexcavated, such as those at **Tofts Ness**, at the far northeastern tip, where there are over 500 cairns, making it potentially one of the most important prehistoric sites in Britain. At **Scar**, in Burness, a spectacular Viking find was made recently, and at **Pool** a major excavation has uncovered the remains of at least 14 Stone-age houses.

Sanday is known for its **knitwear**, though the factory unfortunately closed down recently. You can still visit *Orkney Angora craft shop*, in Upper Breckan, near the northern tip of the island, T600421.

Essentials

Sleeping & eating There are a couple of hotels, the **E** *Belsair Hotel*, T600206, joy:@sanday.quista.net, which serves meals, and the **E** *Kettletoft Hotel*, T/F600217, which also serves meals and has a lively bar. Both are in Kettletoft, where the ferry used to dock. There's also a handful of **B&Bs** including **E-F** *Quivals*, T600467, run by Tina and Bernie Flett. Tina also runs the ferry bus service and Bernie runs a **car and bike hire** service, T600418. Bernie also runs full-day **tours** of the island, on Wed and Fri, from mid-May to early Sep, departing from **Kirkwall** pier at 1010 and returning at 1940 (around £30 per person, minimum of 4 people).

Transport There are *Loganair* **flights** to Sanday from **Kirkwall** twice daily Mon-Fri and once on Sat. There's a **ferry** service twice daily from **Kirkwall** (1 hr 30 mins).

Orkney & Shetland

Stronsay

The peaceful, low-lying island of Stronsay has some fine sandy beaches and cliffs which attract large colonies of grey seals and nesting seabirds. There are few real sights on this largely agricultural island but the coastline has some pleasant walks. One of the best is to the **Vat of Kirbister** in the southeast, a spectacular '*gloup*' or blow-hole spanned by the finest natural arch in Orkney. To the south of here, at **Burgh Head**, you'll find nesting puffins and the remains of a ruined broch, and at the southeastern tip, at **Lamb Head**, is a large colony of grey seals, lots of seabirds and several archaeological sites.

Phone code: 01857

There are **flights** to Stronsay from Kirkwall, as well as a **ferry** service. See also Transport below. **Ins & outs**

The main settlement is the quiet village of **Whitehall**, on the northeast coast where the ferry arrives. It's hard to believe it now but this was one of the largest herring ports in Europe. During the boom years of the early 20th century 300 steam drifters were working out of Whitehall and nearly 4,000 fishing crew and shore workers were employed. In the peak year of 1924 over 12,000 tons of herring were landed here, to be cured (salted) and exported to Russia and Eastern Europe. Whitehall developed considerably and *Stronsay Hotel* was said to have the longest bar in Scotland. On Sundays during July and August there were so many boats tied up that it was possible to walk across them to the little island of **Papa Stronsay**. By the 1930s, however, herring stocks were severely depleted and the industry was in decline. The old **Fish Mart** by the pier houses a **heritage centre** with photos and artefacts from the herring boom days. It also has a café and hostel (see below). Note that at the time of writing it was closed and a new operator was expected to take over in May-June, 2001. ■ *May-Sep 1100-1700. Free. T616360.*

Prior to the herring boom, Stronsay's economic mainstay was the **kelp industry**. By the end of the 18th century 3,000 people were employed in the collection of seaweed and production of kelp for export to be used in making iodine, soap and glass.

Essentials

The **F** *Stronsay Fish Mart Hostel*, T616360. Open all year, is well-equipped and comfortable (see above). The **E** *Stronsay Hotel*, T616213, www.stronsayhotel.com, is being refurbished and offers cheap bar food. There's **B&B** at **F** *Stronsay Bird Reserve*, T616363. On Mill Bay to the south of Whitehall, where you can also **camp** overlooking the wide sandy bay. At the southern end of the island is the very basic and very cheap *Torness Camping Barn*, T616314, on the shore of Holland Bay near Lea-shun Loch. They also organize nature walks to the nearby seal-hide. Phone for pick-up from the ferry. Other eating options are the café at the *Fish Mart*, which does cheap meals, and the *Woodlea Takeaway* along the shore (open Wed 2130-2300, Fri-Sun 1630-1830 and 2100-2300). **Sleeping & eating**

There are *Loganair* **flights** to Stronsay from Kirkwall, twice daily Mon-Fri. A **ferry** service runs from **Kirkwall** (1 hr 30 mins) twice daily Mon-Sat (once on Sun) and once daily Mon-Sat from Eday (35 mins). **Transport**

Car hire and **taxis** are available from *DS Peace*, T616335. Taxis and **island minibus tours** are available from M Williamson, T616255.

Orkney & Shetland

Westray

Westray is the second largest of the North Isles with a varied landscape of farmland, hilly moorland, sandy beaches and dramatic cliffs. It is also the most prosperous of the North Isles, producing beef, fish and seafood and supports a population of 700. The main settlement is **Pierowall**, in the north of the island, but though it has one of the best harbours in Orkney, the main ferry terminal is at **Rapness**, on the south coast.

Ins & outs
Getting there There are **flights** to Westray from Kirkwall. The airport is in the far northeastern corner of the island. There's a **car ferry** service from **Kirkwall** to Rapness, on the south coast of the island.

Getting around There are **guided minibus tours** of Westray which connect with ferry at Rapness. For more information and details of cycle hire and other tours, see next page.

Pierowall
Pierowall is a relatively large village for the North Isles and there are several shops, a post office, a hotel and the **Westray Heritage Centre**, with displays on local and natural history and a tearoom. ■ *Early May to late Sep Tue-Sat 0930-1230 and 1400-1700. £2.* Also in the village is the ruined 17th-century **St Mary's church**. About a mile west of the village is Westray's most notable ruin, the impressive **Notland Castle**, a fine example of a 16th-century fortified Z-plan tower-house. ■ *The castle is managed by Historic Scotland. 11 Jun-30 Sep, daily 0930-1830. Adult £1.50, concession £1.10, children £0.50. Phone Skara Brae T01856-841815.*

Walks on the island
There are some great coastal **walks** on the island, particularly to the spectacular sea cliffs at **Noup Head**, at the far northwestern tip, which are an **RSPB Reserve** and second only to St Kilda in terms of breeding seabirds, with huge colonies of guillemots, razorbills, kittiwakes and fulmars, as well as puffins. The cliffs on the west coast of Westray are five miles long and there's an excellent walk down the coast from Noup Head, past **Gentleman's Cave**, used as a hiding place by four Jacobite lairds in 1746. Near the southern end of the walk is **Fitty Hill** (554 ft), the highest point on the island, which you can climb for great views, and the walk ends at **Inga Ness**, where you can also see puffins. The best place to see puffins is at **Castle o' Burrian**, a sea stack on **Stanger Head**, on the southeastern coast near the Rapness ferry terminal.

Essentials

Sleeping
The best place to stay is **C-D** *Cleaton House Hotel*, T677508, www.orknet.co.uk/cleaton A converted Victorian manse about 2 miles southeast of Pierowall. It serves excellent meals in the restaurant (1900-2100) and in the bar (1200-1400, 1800-2100). In the village is the **E** *Pierowall Hotel*, T677208, www.orknet.co.uk/pierwall, which is less stylish but comfortable and friendly. It also serves good value bar meals. There are also several B&Bs, including **E-F** *Sand o'Gill*, T677374, where you can also camp or hire their self-catering caravan.

Transport
Flights to Westray with *Loganair* depart Kirkwall twice daily Mon-Fri and once on Sat. There's a **car ferry** service from **Kirkwall** to Rapness, on the south coast of the island (1 hr 30 mins). It sails twice daily in summer (mid-May to mid-Sep) and once daily in winter. There's also a **passenger ferry** from Pierowall to **Papa Westray** (see below).

There are **guided minibus tours** of Westray with Alex Costie of *Island Explorer*, T677355, which connect with ferry at Rapness and cost £20 for a full day. *J & M Marcus* at Pierowall also run bus tours and offer **car hire**. For **cycle hire** contact Mrs Groat at *Sand o' Gill* (see above) or Mrs Bain at *Twiness*, T677319. For **boat trips** to Papa Westray contact Tom Rendall, T677216. *Discover Orkney*, T/F01856-872865, run **day tours** on a Sun to Westray from Kirkwall, leaving at 0940 and returning at 2015, and costing around £30 per person including ferry. The also run a day tour on a Mon to Papa Westray.

Papa Westray

Tiny Papa Westray, known locally as 'Papay', can be reached on the world's shortest scheduled flight – all of two minutes – from Westray, but there are other reasons to visit this little island, one of the most remote of the Orkney group.

Phone code: 01857

As well as the above-mentioned 2-minute **flight** from Westray, there is also a direct flight **Kirkwall**. There's a **passenger ferry** from **Pierowall** on Westray and **car ferry** from **Kirkwall**.

Ins & outs
See Transport below

Papay is home to Europe's oldest house, the **Knap of Howar**, which was built around 5,500 years ago and is still standing (they knew how to build 'em in those days). It's on the west coast, just south of the airport. Half a mile north is **St Boniface Kirk**, one of the oldest Christian sites in the north of Scotland, founded in the 8th century, though most of the recently-restored building dates from the 12th century. Inland from the Knap of Howar is **Holland Farm**, former home of the lairds of the island, where you can rummage around the farm buildings and the small **museum**. ■ *Open at all times. Free.*

Papay is famous for its birds and **North Hill**, on the north of the island, is an important **RSPB Reserve**. The cliffs are home to many thousands of breeding seabirds and at Fowl Craig, on the east coast you can see nesting puffins. The interior is home to the largest arctic tern colony in Europe as well as many arctic skuas. If you wish to explore you have to contact the warden at Rose Cottage, T644240, who runs regular guided walks.

It's worth taking a boat trip to the even tinier, deserted **Holm of Papay**, off the east coast. This is the site of several Neolithic burial cairns, including one of the largest **chambered cairns** on Orkney. You enter the tomb down a ladder into the main chamber which is nearly 70 ft long, with a dozen side-cells. ■ *Contact Jim Davidson, T644259, for boat trips between May and Sep.*

Essentials

There are few options for sleeping. One is the **D-E** *Beltane House Guest House*, T644267, a row of converted farm workers' cottages to the east of Holland House. It offers dinner (mid-range). It's run by the island community Co-operative, as is the 16-bed **F** *Papa Westray Hostel*, T644267. Open all year, housed in the same complex at Beltane. The co-operative also runs a shop and restaurant serving lunch and evening meals. They have a **minibus** which takes ferry passengers from the pier to anywhere on the island.

Sleeping & eating

The famous **flight** from Westray leaves twice daily Mon-Sat (£14 one-way). There is also a direct flight to Papay from **Kirkwall** daily Mon-Sat, except Fri (£15 one-way). There's a **passenger ferry** from **Pierowall** on Westray 3-6 times daily (25 mins). The **car ferry** from Kirkwall to Westray continues to Papa Westray on Tue and Fri (2 ¼ hrs).

Transport

Orkney & Shetland

h Ronaldsay

e and storm-battered North Ronaldsay is the most northerly of the
y islands and a place where old Orcadian traditions remain. It seems
kable that anyone should live here at all in these extreme conditions
be North Ron' as it is known locally has been inhabited for many centuries
and continues to be heavily farmed. The island's sheep are a hardy lot and
live exclusively off the seaweed on a narrow strip of beach, outside a 13-mile
stone dyke which surrounds the island. This gives their meat a unique,
'gamey' flavour.

This small, flat island, only three miles long, has few real attractions,
except to keen ornithologists who flock here to catch a glimpse of its rare
migrants. From late March to early June and mid-August to early November there are huge numbers of migratory birds. The **Bird Observatory**, in
the southwest corner of the island by the ferry pier, gives information on
which species have been sighted, as well as providing accommodation.
There are also colonies of grey seals and cormorants at **Seal Skerry**, on the
northeast tip of the island.

Essentials

Sleeping You can stay at the **E** *North Ronaldsay Bird Observatory*, T633200, alison@
& eating nrbo.prestel.co.uk It offers wind and solar-powered full-board accommodation in private rooms or dorms. Full-board accommodation is also available at **D-E** *Garso House*,
T633244, christine.muir@virgin.net, about 3 miles from the ferry pier. They also have a
self-catering cottage (up to 5 people) and can arrange **car hire, taxis** or **minibus
tours**. The *Burrian Inn and Restaurant* is the island's pub and also serves **food**.
Camping is possible on the island, contact, T633222.

Transport There are *Loganair* **flights** from **Kirkwall** twice daily Mon-Sat, T01856-872494. There's
a car and passenger **ferry** which sails from **Kirkwall** (2 hrs 40 mins) once a week (usually Fri) and also on some Sun between May and Sep. Contact *Orkney Ferries* for
details, T01856-872044.

Shetland

*Shetland is so far removed from the rest of Scotland, it can only be shown as an
inset on maps. In fact, it is easier and quicker to get there from Norway than it is
from London. This seems entirely appropriate, for Shetland is historically and
culturally closer to Scandinavia than Britain. Many of its place-names are of
Norse origin and people still celebrate ancient Viking festivals, such as Up
Helly-Aa.*

*Modern day visitors tend to come by plane rather than longboat and usually
bring binoculars, for Shetland is a birdwatchers' paradise. It is home to countless
bird species, many of them seeking refuge from the madding crowds. And let's face
it, there's no better place than here to really get away from it all.*

Island tours

Shetland Wildlife Tours, T01950-422483, www.shetland-wildlife-tours.zetnet.co.uk *Offer a number of guided tours to see the islands' outstandingly rich selection of wildlife; ranging from the excellent value £20 trip around Noss and Bressay, where , if you go at the right time of year, you are almost guaranteed to see seals, porpoises and the astounding gannetry on the spectacular cliffs of Noss' east coast to the more upmarket week-long 'Ultimate Shetland' tour, at around £700.*

There are also Noss & Bressay Wildlife Cruises with **Bressaboats**, *T01595-693434, and* **Shetland Sea Charters** *(same phone number) which costs around £20. Bressaboats and Shetland Wildlife Tours both run a full-day Hermaness and Muckle Flugga Cruise which costs around £70 per person. A variety of* **bus tours** *are available with* **John Leask & Son**, *The Esplanade, Lerwick, T01595-693162. These cost from around £10 up to £20 depending on the destination.*

Ins and outs

Getting there

Shetland has good air connections with the rest of the UK. There are regular flights to **Air** and from several mainland airports which are operated by *British Airways* franchise partners *Loganair* and *British Regional Airlines*, T0845-773 3377. Shetland's main airport is at **Sumburgh**, 25 miles south of Lerwick, T01950-460654.

There are direct daily flights from **Aberdeen** (4 Mon-Fri; 2 on Sat and Sun), which has frequent services to all other major British airports. There are also direct flights from **Glasgow** (daily), **Edinburgh** (daily except Sun), **London Heathrow** (daily), **Inverness** (Mon-Fri), **Orkney** (daily except Sun), **Wick** (Mon-Sat) and **Belfast** (daily except Sat). There are also international flights to and from **Bergen** and **Oslo** (Norway) on Thu and Sun.

Flying to Shetland is expensive. From Aberdeen a special return fare costs £110-180 and a standard one-way ticket is around £125. A special tourist fare of £80-90 return is available between Orkney and Shetland. For details of the excellent value **Highland Rover Pass**, see page 43.

P&O Scottish Ferries, T01224-572615, www.poscottishferries.co.uk, operate car ferries **Boat** to **Lerwick** from **Aberdeen** and **Stromness** (Orkney). There are sailings from Aberdeen once a day Mon-Fri; the journey takes 14 hrs. Passenger fares for a seat with no accommodation cost from £58 one-way (return costs double), depending on the times of year. Cars cost from £179-188 return. For details of ferries from Stromness, see page 356. Children aged 4-14 travel for half price and under 4s go free. There are also ferries from **Norway**, **Iceland** and the **Faroe Isles**, see page 35.

There's a 50% discount on vehicle fares on some midweek sailings

Getting around

There is a regular scheduled inter-island service from **Tingwall Airport** near Lerwick, **Air** with *Loganair*, T01595-840246, to the islands of **Foula** (£42 return), **Fair Isle** (£74 return), **Papa Stour** (£32 return) and **Out Skerries** (£36 return).

Orkney & Shetland

Shetland

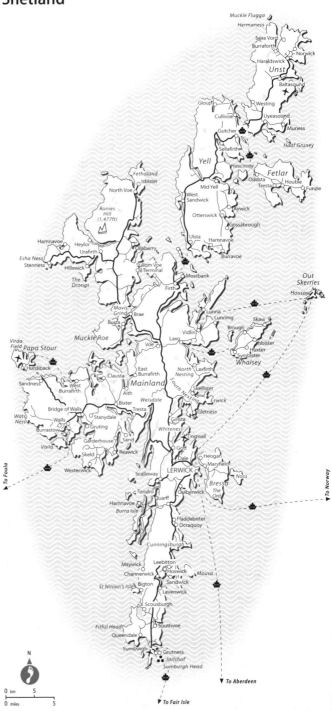

Birds in paradise

Shetland is famous for its birds. As well its huge seabird colonies, the islands attract Arctic species and are an important crossroads for migrating birds. Over 340 species have been recorded on Fair Isle, including rare and exotic birds from Asia and America. Twenty-one out of the 24 seabirds common to Britian breed in Shetland. These can be found around the coastline but the largest colonies are at the **Hermaness** *and* **Noss** *reserves.*

Amongst the many species which can be seen are the puffin. About one fifth of Scotland's puffins breed in Shetland. Its cousins in the auk family, guillemots, and razorbills, are also here in abundance during the summer months, along with kittiwakes, shags and that most common of seabirds, the fulmar. Britain's largest seabird, the gannet, can be seen diving spectacularly for fish at Hermaness, Noss, Fair Isle and Foula, while its smallest seabird, the storm petrel, is best seen around dusk on the tiny island of Mousa.

Summer heralds the return of the Arctic tern which breeds along low coastlines, as do the eider, oystercatcher, ringed plover and black guillemot, or tystie, which stays here all year round. The best place to see waders and shelduck are the nutrient-rich

tidal mudflats at the Pool of Virkie in the South Mainland.

Many birds breed on agricultural land and these include the lapwing, skylark, meadow pipit and wheater. The hills and moorland provide breeding grounds for many summer visitors such as that pirate of the skies, the great skua, or bonxie, and the Arctic skua. Another Arcitc species, the whimbrel, also nests here, mainly in Unst, Yell and Fetlar. Moorland habitats are also favoured by the curlew, golden plover and merlin, Shetland's only bird of prey, while the lochs are home to large numbers of red-throated divers. Fetlar is home to 90% of the population of one of Britain's rarest birds, the red-necked phalarope.

Many of Shetland's bird habitats are protected as **RSPB Reserves** *and* **National Nature Reserves** *and it is an offence to disturb the birds and their young at or near their nests. You also risk being dive-bombed by some of the more aggressively protective species. For a full list of all species recorded on the islands and more practical birdwatching information, be sure to get a copy of the* **Shetland Bird Chart** *, by Joyce Gammack, available from the tourist office in Lerwick.*

Boat

A frequent ferry service links the larger islands with the Shetland Mainland

There are regular daily car ferries between **Lerwick** and **Bressay** (5 mins), **East Mainland** and **Whalsay** (30 mins), **North Mainland** and **Yell** (20 mins), **Yell** and **Unst** (10 mins) and **Yell** and **Fetlar** (25 mins). Fares on all these routes are £1.20 per passenger and £2.90 per car. There's a less frequent car ferry service between **East Mainland** and **Skerries** (Mon, Fri, Sat and Sun; 1 hr 30 mins), and **Lerwick** and **Skerries** (Tue and Thu; 2 hrs 30 mins). Fares on these routes are £2.10 per passenger and £2.90 per car. Bookings are essential. There's also a passenger/cargo ferry service between **West Mainland** and **Papa Stour** (Mon, Wed, Fri, Sat and Sun; 40 mins), **West Mainland** and **Foula** (Tue, Sat and alternate Thu; 2 hrs), **Scalloway** and **Foula** (alternate Thu; 3 hrs), **South Mainland** and **Fair Isle** (Tue, Sat and alternate Thu; 2 hrs 30 mins) and **Lerwick** and **Fair Isle** (alternate Thu; 4 ½ hrs). Fares on these routes are £2.20 for an adult single and bookings are also essential.

Road

Shetland has around 500 miles of good roads and an extensive public **bus service** links Lerwick with all towns, villages and tourist sights. There are several bus operators. For detailed information on all bus services, call 01595-694100 (Mon-Sat 0900-1715). A Shetland Transport Timetable, published by Shetland Islands Council, contains details of all air, sea and bus services throughout the islands. It is available from the tourist office in Lerwick

Orkney & Shetland

The best way to explore the islands is with your own **private car**. It is cheaper to **hire** a car in Lerwick rather than at the airport. For a list of car hire firms see page 391. **Cycling** is a good way to experience the islands, though most places are very exposed and the winds can be strong. **Hitching** is also a feasible way to get around and is relatively safe.

Lerwick

Phone code: 01595
Population: 7,600
Colour map 6, grid B2

Lerwick is the capital and administrative centre of Shetland and the only sizeable town. Though the islands have been inhabited for many centuries, Lerwick only dates from the 17th century, when it began to grow as a trading port for Dutch herring fishermen, thanks to its superb natural sheltered harbour, the Bressay Sound. The town spread along the waterfront, where merchants built their *lodberries*, which were houses and warehouses with their own piers so that they could trade directly with visiting ships. By the late 19th century, Lerwick had become the main herring port in northern Europe.

Ins & outs
Ferries from Aberdeen arrive at the main Holmsgarth terminal, which is about a mile north of the old harbour. There's a regular **bus** service between Lerwick and **Sumburgh airport** (50 mins) run by *John Leask & Son*, T693162. **Taxis** (around £25) and **car hire** are also available. All island bus services start and end at the Viking bus station, which is on Commercial Road, a short distance north of the town centre. The town is small and everything is within easy walking distance.

The main **Tourist Information Centre** is at Market Cross, on Commercial St, T693434, www.shetland-tourism.co.uk As well as booking accommodation, they are an excellent source of information, books, maps and leaflets and will change foreign currency. Open May-Sep Mon-Fri 0800-1800, Sat 0800-1600, Sun 1000-1300; Oct-Apr Mon-Fri 0900-1700.

Lerwick has continued to grow and is now home to a third of Shetland's population. The discovery of **oil** in the North Sea in the early 1970s led to building of the **Sullom Voe Oil Terminal** and the effect on Lerwick has been dramatic. It is now the main transit point to the North Sea oil rigs and there have been major extensions to the harbour area, bringing increased shipping and prosperity to the town.

Sights

The town's heart is the attractive **Commercial Street**, which runs parallel to the Esplanade. At the southern end are many old houses and *lodberries* and you can continue south along the cliffs to the **Knab** or to the lovely **Bain's beach**. *Lerwick Walks* is a leaflet detailing many interesting walks in and around town.

Overlooking the north end of Commercial Street is **Fort Charlotte**, built in 1665 and later rebuilt in 1780 and named after Queen Charlotte, George III's consort. It has since been used as a prison and Royal Naval Reserve base and though there's little to see in the fort there are fine views of the harbour from the battlements. ■ *Jun-Sep daily 0900-2200; Oct-May 0900-1600. Free.* One of Lerwick's most impressive buildings is the Victorian **town hall**, on Hillhead. The stained glass windows of the main hall depict episodes from Shetland's history. ■ *Mon-Fri 1000-1200 and 1400-1530. Free.*

Opposite the town hall, above the library, is the **Shetland Museum**, which gives a useful introduction to the islands' history. Amongst the artefacts on display is a replica of the St Ninian's Isle treasure. ■ *Mon, Wed and Fri 1000-1900; Tue, Thu and Sat till 1700. Free. T695057.*

Also in town is the **Up Helly-Aa Exhibition**, in the Galley Shed off St Sunniva Street. This gives a taste of the famous Viking fire festival held annually in Lerwick on the last Tuesday in January when a torch-lit procession through the town by hundreds of people dressed in Viking costumes (*guizers*) is followed by a replica Viking longship built especially for the event. At the end of the procession the ship is set ablaze when the *guizers* throw their flaming torches onto it. ■ *Mid-May to mid-Sep Tue 1400-1600 and 1700-1900, Fri 1700-1900, Sat 1400-1600. Adult £2.50, concession £1.*

A mile west of town are the substantial remains of **Clickimin Broch**, a fortified site occupied from 700 BC to around the fifth or sixth century AD. A path leads to the site from opposite the *Safeway* supermarket on the A970. ■ *Always open. Free.*

About a mile north of the ferry terminal is the **Böd of Gremista**, a restored 18th-century fishing *böd* (booth) which was the birthplace of Arthur Anderson (1791-1868), co-founder of the Peninsular and Oriental Steam Navigation Company, now *P&O*. One of the rooms features an exhibition on Anderson's life and involvement with *P&O*. ■ *Jun to mid-Sep, Wed and Sun 1000-1300 and 1400-1700. Free..*

Essentials

Sleeping

Shetland's best accommodation is outside Lerwick, whose hotels are mostly geared towards the oil industry. During the peak months of Jul and Aug and the Folk Festival in Apr, it's a good idea to book in advance.

The most luxurious hotel in town is the **B** *Kveldsro House Hotel*, Greenfield Pl, T692195, www.kghotels.co.uk Pronounced 'kel-ro', it overlooks the harbour and has an upmarket (and expensive) restaurant as well as cheaper bar food. Directly opposite the ferry terminal is the modern **B** *Shetland Hotel*, T695515, and 10 mins from the centre is the **B** *Lerwick Hotel*, 15 South Rd, T692166, reception@lerwickhotel.co.uk,

Orkney & Shetland

Lerwick

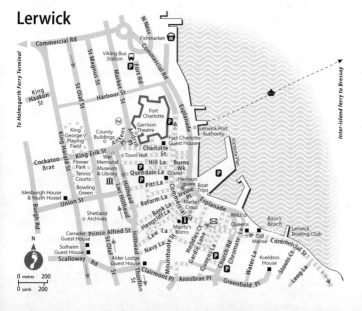

Bedsin Böds

There is only one youth hostel in Shetland, but budget travellers shouldn't panic. The Shetland Camping Böd project has developed a network of camping böds (pronounced 'burd') which provide basic and cheap accommodation throughout the islands.

A Böd was a building used to house fishermen and their gear during the fishing season and the name has been used to describe these types of accommodation which are similar to English 'camping barns'. They are all located in scenically attractive places and

each has its own fascinating history.

They are very basic and the more remote ones have no electricity or lighting. You'll need to bring a stove, cooking and eating utensils, sleeping bag and torch (flashlight). All böds must be booked in advance through the tourist office in Lerwick. They cost £5 per person per night, though they can also be booked for exclusive use by large groups. They are open from the beginning of April till the end of September. There are at present six camping böds on Shetland and these are listed in the relevant places.

which has a reputation for fine cuisine. In the centre is the **B** *Grand Hotel*, Commercial St, T692826, which features Shetland's only nightclub, and by the harbour is the rather faded **B-C** *Queen's Hotel*, Commercial St, T692826.

There are several pleasant guest houses and B&Bs, including **D-E** *Fort Charlotte Guest House*, 1 Charlotte St, T695956, **D** *The Old Manse*, 9 Commercial St, T696301, **D** *Alder Lodge Guest House*, 6 Clairmont Pl, T695705, **D-E** *Carradel Guest House*, 36 King Harald St, T692251, and next door, **D-E** *Solheim Guest House*, T695275. Lerwick's clean, well-run **F** *SYHA hostel* is at Islesburgh House, King Harald St, T692114, open Apr-Sep.

There's **camping** at *Clickimin Caravan & Camp Site*, T741000, near Clickimin Leisure Centre and loch on the western edge of town.

Eating

Despite a ready supply of fresh local produce, Shetland is a gastronomic desert

The best place to eat in Lerwick is *Monty's Bistro & Deli*, 5 Mounthooly St, T696655. It offers good modern Scottish cooking in a cosy, informal setting. Lunch cheap; dinner mid-range. Closed Sun. The next best choice is dinner or bar lunch at the *Kveldsro Hotel* and *Lerwick Hotel* (see above). Best place for a curry is the moderately-priced *Raba* Indian Restaurant, 26 Commercial Rd, T695585. *Osla's Café*, T696005, on Mounthooly St, is a cosy café serving a wide range of coffees, pancakes and other snacks and boasting the islands' only beer garden. Open Mon-Sat till at least 1900, Sun 1200-1600.

Bars & entertainment

The best place for a drink is the upstairs bar in the *Lounge*, on Mounthooly St near the tourist office, where local musicians usually play on Sat lunchtimes and some evenings. The town's only **nightclub** is *Posers*, at the *Grand Hotel*. **Folk music** has a strong following in Shetland and the islands play host to 2 of Scotland's top folk events. In **mid-Apr** the islands are alive with the sound of music as musicians from around the globe come to play at the *Shetland Folk Festival*. Later, in **mid-Oct**, is the *Shetland Accordion and Fiddle Festival*. For details of both events, contact the Folk Festival office, 5 Burns Lane, Lerwick, T694757. To find out what's going on, buy a copy of the *Shetland Times* on Fri, or check out their website, www.shetland-times.co.uk Also check the tourist board's Events phoneline, T694200.

Sport

Clickimin Centre, Lochside, T741000. Sports and fitness centre open daily 0800-2300.

Orkney & Shetland

There are regular daily **buses** (Nos 3 and 4) to and from **Sumburgh airport** which connect with flights. These buses also stop at several main sights, including **Jarlshof**, **Sandwick** (for Mousa Broch) and **St Ninian's Isle**. Bus No 2 runs to **Scalloway** (Mon-Sat). There are also buses (daily except Sun) to **Walls, Sandness, Aith, Skeld, North Roe, Hillswick, Vidlin, Toft** and **Mossbank**. Buses depart from the Viking bus station. Full details are given in the **Shetland Transport Timetable**.

   Car hire *Bolts Car Hire*, Toll clock Shopping Centre, 26 North Rd, T693636. *John Leask & Son*, Esplanade, T693162. *Star Rent-a-Car*, 22 Commercial Rd, T692075. Both also have offices at Sumburgh Airport. **Cycle hire** *Grantfield Garage*, North Rd, T692709, Mon-Sat 0800-1300 and 1400-1700. There are several **taxi** companies in Lerwick: *6050 Cabs*, T696050; *Sheilds Taxis*, T695276; *Abbys Taxis*, T696666.

Banks *Bank of Scotland*, Clydesdale and Royal are on Commercial St. *Lloyds TSB* is on the Esplanade. **Communications Post office** Commercial St (open Mon-Fri 0900-1700, Sat 0900-1200), also in Toll clock Shopping Centre, 26 North Rd. **Embassies and consulates** Denmark, Iceland, Netherlands and Sweden at *Hay & Company*, 66 Commercial Rd, T692533; Finland, France, Germany and Norway at *Shearer Shipping Services*, Garthspool, T692556. **Laundry** *Lerwick Laundry*, 36 Market St, T693043, closed Sun. Service washes only. **Medical facilities** *Gilbert Bain Hospital*, Scalloway Rd, T743000. Opposite is the *Lerwick Health Centre*, T693201. **Travel agents** *John Leask & Son*, Esplanade, T693162.

Transport *See page 385 for details of ferries and flights to and from Lerwick*

Directory

Around Lerwick

Lying to the east of Lerwick across the Bressay Sound is the island of Bressay (pronounced 'bressah'), which creates a sheltered harbour for the capital and led to its establishment as a major trading port. Bressay is only seven miles long by three miles wide and makes an ideal day trip for **cyclists**. Another good way to get around is on foot and there's a fine walk to the top of **Ward Hill** (742 ft), the highest point, from where you get great views of the island and as far afield as Foula and Out Skerries. There are also some good coastal walks, particularly along the cliffs from Noss Sound south to **Bard Head**, **The Ord** and **Bressay Lighthouse**, where you can see large colonies of seabirds.

   Serious birdwatchers should head for **Noss**, a tiny, uninhabited island off the east coast of Bressay which is a **National Nature Reserve** with over 100,000 pairs of breeding seabirds. A walk around the perimeter of the island takes at least three hours but is highly recommended. At the east side is the **Noup of Noss**, where the 600 ft cliffs are packed full of nesting gannets. The reserve is managed by Scottish Natural Heritage who have a small **visitor centre** at Gungstie.

Bressay & Noss *Colour map 6, grid B2/3*

Sleeping **D-E** *Maryfield House Hotel*, T820207, near the ferry terminal.

Transport Noss can only be visited from late May to late Aug daily except Mon and Thu, from 1000-1700. There are regular car **ferries** from the old harbour in Lerwick to Bressay (see page 387). From the 'Wait here' sign overlooking Noss sound on the east side of Bressay an inflatable dinghy shuttles back and forth to Noss during the island's opening hours (see above). The trip costs £3 return. In bad weather, call the tourist office, T693434, to check if it's sailing. A **post car** service runs once a day (except Sunday) from Maryfield ferry terminal to Noss Sound, T820200.

Orkney & Shetland

Central Mainland

Scalloway

Phone code: 01595
Colour map 6, grid B2

The Central Mainland is Shetland's slim waist and only a few miles of land separates the east and west coast. Six miles from Lerwick, on the west coast, is Scalloway, once the capital of Shetland and now a fishing port and fish-processing centre. In 1942, during The Second World War, Scalloway became the headquarters of the **Shetland Bus** operations. This was the name given to the Norwegian fishing boats which sailed to Shetland during the night from German-occupied Norway bringing refugees to safety and returning with ammunition and resistance fighters. An interesting exhibition on the 'Shetland Bus' can be seen at **Scalloway Museum** on Main Street. ■ *May to Sep Tue-Thu 1400-1630, Sat 1000-1230 and 1400-1630. Donation requested.*

The harbour is dominated by the ruins of **Scalloway Castle**, built in 1600 by the notorious Earl Patrick Stewart using local slave labour (see page 360). After his execution the castle fell into disrepair though the four-storey main block and one wing remain. Inside, an interpretative display explains its history. Next to the castle is the **Shetland Woollen Company**, T880243, where you can buy the famous Shetland wool and Fair Isle sweaters.

South of Scalloway lie the islands of **Trondra** and **Burra**, now connected to the Mainland by bridges. At Burland on Trondra is the **Spirit of Shetland**, T880437, where you buy Shetland knitwear, while on West Burra is the attractive little fishing village of **Hamnavoe**.

Sleeping & eating
There are a few places to stay in Scalloway. In the upper part of the village is **E** *Hildasay Guest House*, T880822. The latter had disabled facilities and arranges fishing trips. Eating options are limited to a bar meal at the *Scalloway Hotel* or *Kiln Bar*, or *Da Haaf Restaurant*, T880328, which is a canteen-style restaurant in the North Atlantic Fisheries college and specializes in (yes, you guessed it) seafood. Does a good fish supper, as well as having a more up market menu for the evenings. Open Mon-Fri 0900-2000.

Transport
There are several daily **buses** (except Sun) between Lerwick and Scalloway, operated by *Shalder Coaches*, T880217.

Tingwall

Phone code: 01595
Colour map 6, grid B2

North of Scalloway the B9074 runs through the fertile Tingwall Valley, past a nine-hole **golf course** at Asta, and the **Loch of Tingwall**, which is good for brown trout fishing and also home to swans and otters. At the northern end of the loch is a promontory called **Law Ting Holm**, which was the site of the *Althing*, or parliament, during the period of Norse rule. Overlooking the loch is **Tingwall Kirk**, built in the late 18th century on the site of the earlier church of St Magnus which dated back to the early period of Norse Christianity. In the graveyard is the old burial vault with several interesting old grave slabs. Nearby is **Tingwall Agricultural Museum**, which houses a collection of old crofting implements. ■ *Jun-Aug Mon-Sat 1000-1300 and 1400-1700. Adult £1.50.*

Sleeping
Near the airport, by the crossroads, is the **C** *Herrislea House Hotel*, T840208, www.herrislea-house.shetland.co.uk, which offers good home cooking daily till 2100 and live music in its *Starboard Tack* bar. In nearby Wormadale is the modern **C-D** *Westings Hotel*, T840242, www.westings.shetland.co.uk, which is a good place to stop for lunch.

North of the museum is **Tingwall Airport,** T840246, which has flights to most of the **Transport** smaller islands (see page 385). Getting to and from the airport is straightforward as regular buses between Lerwick and Westside (see below) stop in Tingwall.

Weisdale

The A971 continues northwest towards Weisdale. At the head of **Weisdale** *Phone code: 01595* **Voe** the B9075 branches north to **Weisdale Mill** which now houses the *Colour map 6, grid B2* **Bonhoga Gallery**, a purpose-built art gallery featuring varied exhibitions of local, national and international works. There's also a nice café serving snacks. ■ *Wed-Sat 1030-1630, Sun 1200-1630. T830400.*

Weisdale Mill was part of the Kergord estate, known until 1945 as Fleming-ton, and was built from the stones of evacuated crofthouses. Over 300 crofters were forcibly evicted in the mid-19th century during the 'Clearances' when lairds expanded their more profitable sheep-farming activities. In 1940 the mill was requisitioned as the intelligence and administrative HQ for the 'Shet-land Bus' operations (see Scalloway above). The Kergord estate today is larg-est area of woodland in Shetland and attracts a variety of migratory birds.

On the west shore of Weisdale Voe, south of the mill, are the ruins of the house where **John Clunies Ross** (1786-1854) was born. He settled in the Cocos Islands in the Indian Ocean in 1827 and proclaimed himself 'King'. After his death, the islands were ruled by his offspring until they became Aus-tralian territory, no doubt to the relief of the islanders.

The Westside

The western Mainland of Shetland, stretching west from Weisdale to *OS Landranger* Sandness, is known as The Westside. This part of Shetland is notable for its *maps Nos 3 & 4* varied landscape of spectacular sea cliffs, rolling green hills, bleak moorland, peaty freshwater lochs and numerous long sea lochs, or *voes*. This is excellent **walking** country, with many fine coastal routes, especially around **Culswick** and **Dale of Walls**. It is also great for **birdwatching** and **trout fishing** and there are many opportunities for spotting **whales, dolphins** and **otters**.

There are a few interesting archaeological sites here, too. At **Stanydale**, signposted from the road between the villages of **Bixter** and **Walls**, is the site of a Neolithic settlement with the remains of houses, field boundaries and clearance cairns. Near the **Brig o' Waas**, just north of Walls, is the **Scord of Brouster**, prehistoric farm site which has been excavated.

The pretty little village **Walls** (pronounced 'waas') is set around a sheltered **Walls** natural harbour and is a popular spot with visiting yachts. It also attracts *Phone code: 01595* many visitors during its Agricultural Show in August, the biggest such event *Colour map 6, grid B1* on Shetland.

Sleeping Walls also boasts the best accommodation on the Westside. Two miles southwest of the village is **B** *Burrastow House*, T809307, burr.hs.hotel@zetnet.co.uk, a restored 18th-century house overlooking Vaila Sound. It's full of character and has a reputation for serving superb cuisine (some say the best on the islands, so you'll need to book ahead). There's a **camping böd** in Walls, at *Voe House*, a restored 18th-century house overlooking the village. Open Apr-Sep. Book through Lerwick tourist office. A mile or so north of the village is **E** *Skeoverick*, T803349, a friendly B&B. At Gruting, east of Brig o' Waas is **E-F** *Pomona*, T810438.

Transport There are daily **buses** to Walls from Lerwick, Mon-Sat, with *Shalder Coaches*, T01595-880217. A **minibus** runs to Sandness from Walls once a day (except Sun). Contact Mr P Isbister, T809268.

Sandness   Northwest of Walls, the A971 crosses bleak moorland before descending to the crofting township of Sandness (pronounced 'saa-ness'), surrounded by fertile land and facing little Papa Stour, about a mile offshore. There's a good **beach** here and also a **woollen spinning mill**, where you can watch how they spin the famously fine wool into yarn. ■ *Mon-Fri 0800-1700, free.*

Foula

Walls is the departure point for **ferries** to the remote island of Foula, whose name derives from the Norse *fugl ey*, meaning 'bird island'. Lying 15 miles west of the Shetland Mainland, tiny Foula is the second most remote inhabited island after Fair Isle. It supports a population of around 40 people, who are greatly out numbered by many thousands of seabirds, including a small colony of gannets and the rare Leach's petrel. There are also about 2,500 pairs of great skuas, the largest colony in the UK.

The island is dominated by its sheer cliffs which reach their most awe-inspiring peak at **The Kame** (1,220 ft), the second highest sea cliffs in Britain after St Kilda.

An interesting feature of the island's people is that they still observe the old **Julian calendar**, replaced in 1752 in Britain by the present Gregorian system which deleted 11 days from the year. Remote areas of the country kept to the old calendar, adding an extra day in 1800, which was a leap year, and some parts of Shetland continued to observe festivals 12 days after the dates in the new calendar. The most remote areas kept to the old calendar longest, and the people of Foula still celebrate Christmas on 6 January and New Year's Day on 13 January.

Sleeping   Those wishing to celebrate 2 Christmases or New Year's Days, or to stay and admire the bird life, can stay on the island at **E** *Leraback*, T753226, which includes dinner in the price. There is also self catering accommodation available on the island £90-150 per week for a cottage sleeping 4-6 people. Contact Mr R Holbourn, T753232.

Transport   For details of **ferries** and **flights** to Foula, see page 385.

Papa Stour

Colour map 6, grid B1   A ferry sails from **West Burrafirth** on the Westside, near Sandness, to the little island of Papa Stour, only a mile offshore. The island, which has a population of around 30, is mostly made up of volcanic rock which has been eroded to form an amazing coastline of stacks, arches and caves, most spectacular of which is **Kirstan's Hole**. The island is home large colonies of auks, terns and skuas and also has a fascinating history of its own. Pick up the island trails leaflet from the tourist office in Lerwick.

Essentials   You can stay on the island at **D** *North House*, T873238, which offers full board. There's no shop on the island. For details of **ferries** and **flights** to Papa Stour, see page 385. Ferries should be booked with *W Clark*, T810460.

South Mainland

From Lerwick a long, narrow finger of land points south. The main road runs down the east coast for 25 miles till it ends at **Sumburgh Head**, near Shetland's main airport. This southern part of the Shetland Mainland holds the islands' two most important archaeological sights and main tourist attractions.

Phone code: 01950

About 10 miles south of Lerwick, just to the south of **Cunningsburgh**, is the **Catpund Quarries**, where soft soapstone was quarried from Neolithic to medieval times and made into a variety of stone implements and utensils.

Mousa

Fifteen miles south of Lerwick, the scattered crofting communities of **Sandwick** look across to the **Isle of Mousa**, site of the best-preserved broch in Scotland. This fortified tower was built around 2,000 years ago and still stands close to its original height of 45 ft. It's a very impressive structure when you see it from the inside and has chambers, galleries, an internal staircase and a parapet. The broch features in a Viking saga of the 12th century when the mother of Harald, Earl of Orkney, took refuge there with her lover. The Earl, who did not approve of the liaison, laid siege to the broch but it proved impregnable and he gave up.

Colour map 6, grid C2
Entry to the broch is free

Mousa island is also home to many seabirds and waders, most notably the Storm Petrel, which is best seen at dusk as they return to their nests amongst the beach rocks. You can also see seals on the white-sand beach at West Voe. If you have time, it's a good idea to walk right around the coast, starting from the landing stage at West Ham and first heading south to the broch. A **passenger ferry** sails to the island from **Leebitton harbour** in Sandwick daily from mid-April to mid-September, weather permitting, at 0930, 1230 and 1400, allowing visitors 2½ hours to see the island. The trip takes 15 minutes and costs £6.50 per adult. For bookings, call Tom Jamieson.

Allow about two hours and watch out for dive-bombing terns

There's accommodation in Sandwick at the **E** *Barclay Arms Hotel*, T431226, which offers evening meals, and **F-E** *Solbrekke*, T431410.

Sleeping

There are several daily **buses** (Mon-Sat; 2-3 on Sun) between Lerwick, Sandwick and Sumburgh Airport.

Transport

At Hoswick, between Sandwick and Levenwick, is **Da Warp and Weft Visitor Centre**, which houses an exhibition on weaving, crofting, fishing and island life. ■ *May-Sep Mon-Sat 1000-1700, Sun 1200-1700. Free.* Next door is the **Shetland Woollen Company**, where you can buy knitwear.

South of Sandwick

Further south on the east coast, at Boddam, is the **Shetland Crofthouse Museum**, a restored thatched crofthouse with 19th-century furniture and utensils. ■ *May-Sep daily 1000-1300 and 1400-1700. Adult £2.*

St Ninian's Isle to Quendale

On the west coast, near Bigton village, a signposted track leads to the spectacular sandy causeway (known as a tombolo) which leads to St Ninian's Isle. The tombolo is the best example of its kind in Britain and you can walk across

Colour map 6, grid C2

Orkney & Shetland

Battling Betty

Betty Mouat was quite a woman. In 1886, at the age of 60, she was on a boat heading for Lerwick when the captain was swept overboard and the two crewmen went to rescue him, leaving Betty alone. They were unable to get back to the boat which drifted for nine days before ending up in Norway. Betty survived the ordeal.

to the island which is best known for the hoard of Pictish treasure which was discovered in 1958 in the ruins of the 12th-century church. The 28 silver objects included bowls, a spoon and brooches, probably dating from around 800 AD and are now on display in the Royal Scottish Museum in Edinburgh, though you can see replicas in the Shetland Museum in Lerwick. Two daily **buses** (not Sunday) run to Bigton from Lerwick, though you have to change at Channerwick junction.

The west coast south of Bigton is beautiful with long, sandy beaches interspersed with dramatic cliff scenery. On the other side of the road from the long, sheltered beach at **Scousburgh Sands** is the **Loch of Spiggie RSPB Reserve**. The loch is an important winter wildfowl refuge, particularly for Whooper Swans and during the summer you can see various ducks, waders, gulls, terns and skuas. There's a hide on the northern shore with an information board. Nearby is the *Spiggie Hotel*, T01950-460409, which offers bar meals, afternoon tea or dinner.

A few miles south of the loch is the village of **Quendale** overlooking a wide, sandy bay. Here you'll find the beautifully-restored and fully working 19th-century **Quendale Mill**, the last of Shetland's watermills. ■ *May-Sep daily 1000-1700. Adult £1.50.*

Not far from here, between Garth's Ness and Fitful Head, lies the wreck of the *Braer* oil tanker which ran onto the rocks in 1993. A disaster of epic proportions was averted by the hurricane-force gales which dispersed the huge oil spillage.

Transport Two **buses** daily (Mon-Sat) run to Quendale from Lerwick, with a change at Channerwick junction.

Sumburgh and Jarlshof

Colour map 6, grid C2 At the southern tip of Mainland is the village of Sumburgh, site of Shetland's main **airport** for external passenger flights and for helicopters and planes servicing the North Sea oil industry. South of the airport is Shetland's prime archaeological site, Jarlshof, a hugely impressive place which spans 4,000 years of occupation, from Neolithic times through Norse settlement to the 16th century. The original Stone Age dwellings are topped by a medieval broch, Pictish wheelhouses, Viking longhouses and, towering over the whole complex, the ruins of a 16th-century mansion. This remarkable site was only discovered at the end of the 19th century when a violent storm ripped off the top layer of turf. Jarlshof is, in fact, not a genuine name, but the exotic invention of Sir Walter Scott in his novel *The Pirate*. A helpful guidebook available from the visitor centre helps to bring the place to life. ■ *Apr-Sep daily 0930-1830. Adult £2.80, concession £2, children £1. T460112 (HS).*

South of Jarlshof is the Mainland ends abruptly at **Sumburgh Head**, an RSPB Reserve. The **lighthouse** on top of the cliff was built by Robert Stevenson in 1821 and the keepers' cottages are now rented out as

Orkney & Shetland

self-catering accommodation. The lighthouse isn't open to the public but from its grounds you can see many nesting seabirds such as puffins, kittiwakes, fulmars, guillemots and razorbills. Just to the east of the airport is **Pool of Virkie**, another good birdwatching area.

Accommodation is limited. There's the **C** *Sumburgh Hotel*, T460201, next to Jarlshof in a converted laird's house. It has a bar and restaurant. There's also a **camping böd** in *Betty Mouat's Cottage*, next to a recently-excavated site at Scatness next to the airport. It sleeps up to 8 and is open Apr-Sep. Book through Lerwick tourist office. **Sleeping**

There are regular daily **buses** from Lerwick, which stop at the hotel, Scatness and Grutness Pier (for Fair Isle) en route to the airport. **Transport**

Fair Isle

Fair Isle is the most isolated of Britain's inhabited islands. Only three miles long by 1½ miles wide, the island has a population of around 70 and is best known for its intricately-patterned knitwear, which is still produced by a co-operative, Fair Isle Crafts. Co-operative could be said to sum up the friendly islanders, whose lifestyle is based on mutual help and community effort.

*Phone code: 01595
24 miles SW of
Sumburgh & 27 miles
NE of North Ronaldsay
in Orkney*

Getting to Fair Isle requires patience, persistence and a strong stomach to survive the white-knuckle 4 ½-hr **ferry** sailing. There are also **flights** from Tingwall Airport. See Transport below. **Ins & outs**

For more information on Fair Isle visit www.fairisle.org.uk or call the National Trust for Scotland (T0141-616 2266, www.thenationaltrustforscotland.org.uk)

Fair Isle is a paradise for **birdwatchers** and keen ornithologists form the majority of the island's visitors. Celebrity birdwatcher and former Goodie, Bill Oddie, has dubbed it the "the Hilton of the bird world". It stands in the flight path of many thousands of migrating birds and over 340 species have been recorded here at the **Fair Isle Bird Observatory** which also offers accommodation and where visitors are welcome to take part. As well as the almost obscenely rich birdlife there are around 240 species of flowering plants, making the island an especially beautiful haven for naturalists. Fair Isle's coastline, especially in the north and west, also boasts some outstanding cliff scenery.

The bird observatory was the brainchild of George Waterston, an ornithologist who first visited in 1935 and then bought the island in 1948 to begin his task of building the observatory. The island was given to the National Trust for Scotland in 1954 and declared a National Scenic Area. It was recently designated a place of outstanding natural beauty and cultural heritage by the Council of Europe. The **George Waterston Memorial Centre** has exhibits and photographs detailing the island's natural history as well as the history of crofting, fishing, archaeology and knitwear. ■ *May to mid-Sep Mon and Fri 1400-1600, Wed 1030-1200. Donations welcome.*

Orkney & Shetland

There are a few places to stay on the island, but accommodation must be booked in advance and includes meals. The **C** *Fair Isle Lodge and Bird Observatory*, T760258, www.fairislebirdobs.co.uk, offers full board accommodation in private rooms or in a dormitory (**E**). Alternatively, there's full board at **D** *Schoolton*, T760250, and **D** *Upper Leogh*, T760248, kathleen.coull@lineone.net There's also a self-catering cottage for 4 from £210 weekly (T760248). There are no hotels, pubs or restaurants. **Sleeping**

Transport For details of **ferries** to Fair Isle from **Grutness** (near Sumburgh) or Lerwick, and **flights** from **Tingwall Airport**, see page 387. A day return flight allows about 6 hrs on the island. You can also fly from **Kirkwall** on Orkney, which allows 2 ½ hrs on the island, T01856-872420. Ferries should be booked with *J W Stout*, T760222.

North Mainland

Voe
Phone code: 01806
Colour map 6, grid B2

The main road north from Lerwick branches at **Voe**, a peaceful and colourful little village nestling in a bay at the head of the Olna Firth. One branch leads to the Yell car and passenger ferry terminal at **Toft**, past the turn-off to the massive **Sullom Voe Oil Terminal**, the largest oil and liquefied gas terminal in Europe. The other road heads northwest to Brae (see below).

Sleeping and eating You can stay in Voe at the *Sail Loft* by the pier. This former fishing store is now Shetland's largest **camping böd**, open Apr-Sep. Food is available at the *Pierhead Restaurant and Bar*, T588332.

Transport Regular **buses** from **Lerwick** to Brae and Hillswick to the northwest, and Toft and Mossbank to the north, pass through Voe daily except Sun.

Brae
Colour map 6, grid B2

Brae is not a very pretty place and was built to accommodate workers at the nearby Sullom Voe oil terminal. It does boast a good selection of accommodation and decent facilities, though, and makes a good base from which to explore the wild and wonderful coastal scenery around the Northmavine peninsula to the north. There's also good walking and spectacularly good westerly views around the island of **Muckle Roe** to the southwest and up the island's small hill, South Ward (554 ft). But be careful of the overly protective bonxies, or great skuas, which will attack if you get too close. The island is attached to the mainland by a bridge.

Sleeping The best place to stay around Brae, or anywhere else on Shetland, is the **B** *Busta House Hotel*, T522506, www.mes.co.uk/busta A luxurious and wonderfully-atmospheric 16th-century country house overlooking Busta Voe about 1½ miles from Brae village. The superb restaurant (mid-range to expensive) is the finest on Shetland with a selection of malts to match, and there are also meals in the bar. There are also several B&Bs to choose from, including **D** *Valleyfield Guest House*, T522563, and **E** *Drumquin Guest House*, T522621, both with dinner available. On Muckle Roe is **E** *Westayre*, T522368, which is a working croft. A good place to **eat**, other than *Busta House* is the *Mid Brae Inn* which serves great food daily till 2100.

Transport **Buses** from **Lerwick** to Hillswick (see below) and to **Toft/Mossbank** (see under Yell below) stop in Brae.

Northmavine

This is one of Shetland's most dramatic and beautiful areas, with rugged scenery, spectacular coastline and wide empty spaces

Mavis Grind, the narrow isthmus where it's claimed you can throw a stone from the Atlantic to the North Sea, leads into Northmavine, the northwest peninsula of North Mainland. This is excellent **walking** country and it's a good idea to abandon the car and explore it on foot. **Hillswick Ness**, to the south of **Hillswick** village, is a nice walk but further west, around the coastline of **Eshaness**, is the most spectacular cliff scenery and amazing natural features, all with unusual and evocative names.

North of the lighthouse are the **Holes of Scraada**, **Grind o' da Navir** and the **Villians of Hamnavoe**, which are not the local gangs but eroded lava cliffs with blowholes, arches and caves. East of Eshaness are the **Heads of Grocken** and **The Drongs**, a series of exposed sea stacks, which offer superb diving. Further north, overlooking the deep sea inlet of **Ronies Voe**, is the dramatic red granite bulk of **Ronies Hill** (1,477 ft), with a well-preserved burial cairn at the summit. The coastal scenery to the north and west of here is even more breathtaking but very remote and exposed. You should be well equipped before setting out. A useful guide is *Walking the Coastline of Northmavine* by Peter Guy.

Between Eshaness and Hillswick, a side road leads south to the **Tangwick Haa Museum**, which features displays and photographs on the history of fishing and whaling and the hardships of life in these parts. ■ *May-Sep Mon-Fri 1300-1700, Sat and Sun 1100-1900. Free.*

Accommodation is available at **E** *Almara*, T503261, at Upper Urafirth. In Hillswick is *The Booth*, Shetland's oldest pub, which serves food daily in summer.

In **Hamnavoe**, reached by a side road which branches north from the road between Hillswick and Eshaness, you can stay at *Johnny Notion's Camping Böd*, birthplace of John Williamson, known as 'Johnny Notions', an 18th-century craftsman who developed an effective innoculation against smallpox. It's open Apr-Sep and has no electricity. Book through Lerwick tourist office.

Sleeping & eating

There is a daily **bus** service from **Lerwick** to Hillswick (Mon-Sat; £1.90), departing at 1710 and arriving at 1825. From there, a feeder service continues to **Eshaness** (20 minutes). Contact *Whites Coaches*, T809443.

Transport

Whalsay and Out Skerries

South of Voe, the B9071 branches east to **Laxo**, the ferry terminal for the island of **Whalsay**, one of Shetland's most prosperous small islands owing to its thriving fishing industry which helps support a population of around 1,000. The fleet is based at **Symbister**, the island's main settlement. Beside the harbour at Symbister is the **Pier House**, a restored böd which was used by the Hanseatic League, a commercial association of German merchants who traded in Shetland from the Middle Ages to the early 18th century. Inside is an exhibition explaining the history of the Hanseatic trade and general information on the island. ■ *Mon-Sat 0900-1300 and 1400-1700, Sun 1400-1700. 50p.*

Phone code: 01806
Colour map 6, grid B3

In the seas around Whalsay you can see porpoises, dolphins, minke whales and orcas, hence its Viking name which means 'island of whales'

One of Scotland's great poets **Hugh McDiarmid** (Christopher Grieve) spent most of the 1930s in Whalsay, where he wrote much of his finest poetry, until he was called for war work in 1942, never to return. His former home, at Sodom, near Symbister, is now a **camping böd**. It's open April-September and has no electricity.

There are regular daily car and passenger **ferries** between **Laxo** and **Symbister** (see page 387). To book, call T566259. There are daily **buses** to Laxo and and **Vidlin** (see below) from Lerwick, run by *Whites Coaches*, T01595-809443.

Transport

Out Skerries

The Out Skerries are a small group of rocky islands about five miles from Whalsay and 10 miles east of Shetland Mainland. It's made up of three main islands: the larger islands of **Housay** and **Bruray**, which are connected by a road bridge; and the uninhabited island of **Grunay**. The Skerries boast some spectacular and rugged sea cliffs which are home to many rare migrant sea-birds in spring and autumn.

Transport There are **ferries** to the Skerries from **Lerwick** and also from **Vidlin**, about 3 miles northeast of Laxo (see page 387). For bookings, call *G W Henderson*, T515226. There are also **flights** from Tingwall Airport (see page 385).

Yell

Phone code: 01957
Colour map 6,
grid A/B 2

Yell, the second largest of the Shetland islands, was described rather damningly by Shetland-born writer Eric Linklater as 'dull and dark'. And it's true that the interior is consistently desolate peat moorland. But the coastline is greener and more pleasant and provides an ideal habitat for the island's large **otter** population. Yell is also home a rich variety of birds and offers some good coastal and hill walks, especially around the rugged coastline of **The Herra**, a peninsula about half way up the west coast.

At **Burravoe**, about five miles east of the ferry terminal at **Ulsta**, is the **Old Haa Museum**, housed in Yell's oldest building which dates from 1672. It contains an interesting display on local flora and fauna and history. ■ *Late Apr-Sep Tue-Thu and Sat 1000-1600, Sun 1400-1700. Free. T722339*

The island's largest village, **Mid Yell**, has a couple of shops, a pub and a leisure centre with a good swimming pool. About a mile northwest, on the hillside above the main road, are the reputedly haunted ruins of **Windhouse**, dating from 1707. To the north is the **RSPB Lumbister Reserve**, where red-throated divers, merlins, great and Arctic skuas and many other bird species come to breed. The reserve is also home to a large number of otters. A pleasant walk leads along the nearby steep and narrow gorge, known as the **Daal of Lumbister**, filled with many colourful flowers. The area to the north of the reserve provides good walking over remote moorland and coastline.

The road continues north past the reserve and around **Basta Voe** where you can see otters. North of **Gutcher**, the ferry port for Unst, is the village of **Cullivoe**, with some good walks along the attractive coastline.

Sleeping
& eating

There's accommodation on Yell at **E** *Hillhead*, T722274, in Burravoe; at **E** *Pinewood Guest House*, T702427, in South Aywick, between Burravoe and Mid Yell; and at the friendly **E-F** *Post Office*, T744201, in Gutcher. You can also stay at *Windhouse Lodge*, which is a **camping böd** below the ruins of haunted Windhouse. It's well-equipped and open Apr-Sep. Eating options are limited to the café in the *Old Haa Museum*, the *Seaview Café* in Gutcher, or the *Hilltop Restaurant and Bar* in Mid Yell.

Transport

There are frequent car and passenger **ferries** from **Toft** on North Mainland to **Ulsta** on the south coast of Yell (see page 387). It's not essential, but a good idea to book in advance, T722259. Three **buses** daily (Mon-Fri; 2 on Sat, 1 on Sun) run between Lerwick and Toft (1 hr; £1.90). There's a bus service on Yell which runs between Ulsta and Cullivoe and stops at villages in between, T744214.

Fetlar

Phone code: 01957
Colour map 6, grid A3

Fetlar is the smallest of the North Isles but the most fertile, and known as 'the garden of Shetland'. Indeed, the name derives from Norse meaning 'fat land' as there is good grazing and croftland and a rich variety of plant and bird life. The whole island is good for birdwatching but the prime place is the 1,700 acres of **North Fetlar RSPB Reserve** around Vord Hill (522 ft) in the north of the island. This area has restricted access during the summer months and visitors should contact the warden at Bealance, T733246. The warden will also let you know if and when you can see the one or two female Snowy Owls which sometimes visit.

The north cliffs of the reserve are home to large colonies of breeding seabirds, including auks, gulls and shags, and you can also see common and grey seals on the beaches in late autumn. Fetlar is home to one of Britain's rarest birds, the **red-necked phalarope**, which breeds in the loch near **Funzie** (pronounced 'finnie') in the east of the island. You can watch them from the RSPB hide in the nearby marshes. Red-throated divers and whimbrel also breed here. The island is also good for **walking** and a leaflet describing some of the walks is available from the tourist office in Lerwick.

The main settlement on the island is **Houbie**, on the south coast. Here you'll see a house called Leagarth, which was built by the island's most famous son, Sir William Watson Cheyne, who with Lord Lister pioneered antiseptic surgery. Nearby is the excellent **Fetlar Interpretive Centre** which presents the island's history and gives information on its bounteous birdlife. ■ *May-Sep Tue-Sun 1200-1700. Free.*

There's **B&B** at **E** *The Gord*, T733227, in Houbie, and at **E** *The Glebe*, T733242, a lovely   **Sleeping** old house overlooking Papil Water. You can also **camp** at *Gerth's Campsite*, T733227,   **& eating** which overlooks the beach at Tresta and has good facilities.

There are regular car and passenger **ferries** between **Oddsta** in the northwest of the island   **Transport** and **Gutcher** on Yell and **Belmont** on Unst (see page 387). There's a **post car** service which runs around the island from the ferry once a day on Mon, Wed and Fri, T733227.

Unst

Unst is the most northerly inhabited island in Britain but there is more to the   *Phone code: 01957* island than its many 'most northerly' attractions. It is scenically one of the   *Colour map 6,* most varied of the Shetland islands with spectacular cliffs, sea stacks, sheltered   *grid A3* inlets, sandy beaches, heather-clad hills, fertile farmland, freshwater lochs and even a sub-arctic desert. Such a variety of habitats supports over 400 plant species and a rich variety of wildlife. Unst is a major breeding site for gannets, puffins, guillemots, razorbills, kittiwakes, shags, Arctic and great skuas and whimbrels amongst others and in the surrounding waters you can see seals, porpoises, otters and even killer whales.

In the east of the island, north of **Baltasound**, is the Keen of Hamar National   **Keen of Hamar** Nature Reserve, 74 acres of serpentine rock which breaks into tiny fragments   **National** known as 'debris', giving the landscape a strange, lunar-like appearance. This   **Nature Reserve** bleak 'desert' is actually home to some of the rarest plants in Britain. Baltasound is the island's main settlement, with an airport, hotel, pub, post office, leisure centre with pool and Britain's most northerly brewery, the **Valhalla Brewery** which can be visited by appointment, T711348.

To the north of here is the village of Haroldswick, home of Britain's most   **Haroldswick** northerly post office, where your postcards are sent with a special stamp to inform everyone of this fact. Here also is **Unst Boat Haven**, where you can see a beautifully-presented collection of traditional boats and fishing artefacts. ■ *May-Sep daily 1400-1700. Free.* A little way further north is the **Unst Heritage Centre**, which has a museum of local history and island life. ■ *Same opening hours as Boat Haven and also free.* Nearby is an RAF radar tracking station at Saxa Vord. The road ends at Skaw, where there's a lovely beach and Britain's most northerly house. The road northwest from Haroldswick leads to the head of **Burra Firth**, a sea inlet flanked by high cliffs and site of Britain's most northerly golf course.

Hermaness National Nature Reserve
To the west of Burra Firth is the remote Hermaness National Nature Reserve, 2,422 acres of dramatic coastal scenery and wild moorland which is home to over 100,000 nesting seabirds including gannets, and the largest number of puffins and great skuas (or 'bonxies') in Shetland. There's an excellent **visitor centre** in the former lighthouse keeper's shore station where you can pick up a leaflet which shows the marked route into the reserve, and see the local artistic efforts of many of Unst's children. Whilst in the reserve, make sure you keep to the marked paths to avoid being attacked by bonxies, they are highly protective and rest assured that they will attack if they think that their territory is being threatened. ■ *Daily late Apr to mid-Sep 0830-1800. T711278.*

The views from Hermaness are wonderful, out to the offshore stacks and skerries including **Muckle Flugga**, and then to the wide open north Atlantic ocean. Muckle Flugga is the site of the most northerly lighthouse in Britain, built in 1857-58 by Thomas Stevenson, father of Robert Louis Stevenson. The writer visited the island in 1869 and the illustrated map in his novel *Treasure Island* bears a striking similarity to the outline of Unst. Beyond the lighthouse is **Out Stack**, which marks the most northerly point on the British Isles. With nothing between you and the North Pole but water, this is the place to sit and contemplate what it feels like to be at the end of the world.

Essentials

Sleeping & eating
There's a decent selection of accommodation on Unst. Top choice has to be **D** *Buness House*, T711315, buness@zetnet.co.uk, a lovely old 17th-century Haa in Baltasound. Staying here is a bizarre and rather surreal experience, given that you are on the most northerly island in Britain. The house is crammed full of Indian Raj relics, and the stuffed eagle, tiger and leopard skins hanging in the hallway is a wildlife close-up almost as impressive, though considerably more unsettling and un-'PC', as the Hermaness Nature Reserve in the north of the island that the family own. The food is excellent and the accommodation comfortable. Another good place is **E** *Prestegaard*, T755234, a Victorian house at Uyeasound on the south coast near the ferry. Also in Baltasound is the **E** *Cligera Guest House*, T711579, and the independent *Gardiesfauld Hostel*, T755259; open Apr-Sep, which also **hires bikes**.

There's also **B&B** in Haroldswick at **E** *Gerratoun*, T711323. Eating options are limited, though all the B&Bs serve evening meals on request. The **D** *Baltasound Hotel*, T711334, serves meals and drinks to non-residents.

Transport
There are regular car and passenger **ferries** to Belmont from **Gutcher** on Yell. Booking is advised, T722259. There's an island **bus** service which runs a few times daily (except Sun) between **Baltasound**, **Belmont** and **Haroldswick**, T711666.

Background

10

Background

History

Prehistoric times

The rubbish dumps of shellfish-eating cave dwellers on the islands of Oronsay and Kerrera in the Outer Hebrides have provided rich pickings for archaeologists who conclude that these hunter-gatherers of around 6000-5000 BC are Scotland's earliest known inhabitants. By 2000-1500 BC these Mesolithic people had been joined by **Beaker folk**, so named from their distinctive pottery, and grain cultivating Megalithic people, arriving by sea via Spain and Portugal, who were tempted to settle by a then prevailing near-Mediterranean climate. Several climate changes for the worse, triggered much population movement and also, along with extensive deforestation, caused the formation of peaty soil, now characteristic of much of Scotland, by around 1000 BC.

The pottery and other artefacts of the Beaker people have been found in burial mounds or cairns, such as **Maeshowe** on Orkney Mainland (see page 367) from around this time and suggest a complex social structure and perhaps, more importantly, a belief in the afterlife, as do the prehistoric settlements and monuments in Caithness, Orkney, Shetland and the Outer Hebrides, notably at **Skara Brae** (page 366), **Stenness**, and the **Ring of Brodgar** on Orkney Mainland and **Callanish** on Lewis (see page 329). But throughout Scotland there are hundreds of standing stones and circles, a legacy of the megalithic peoples. In Aberdeenshire surveys reveal precise orientations indicating their use as observatories charting lunar cycles and eclipses. The layout of **Clava Cairns**, near Inverness (see page 93), bears similarities to the great temple at Newgrange in Ireland. And at **Kilmartin**, in Argyll (see page 206), cup and ring marks, stone alignments and burial cairns, formed in a complete 'landscape temple', suggest a geomantic sophistication that has now been forgotten.

At the beginning of the first millenium BC, **Bronze Age** traders from far afield were busy along the coasts. Celts arrived from Germany, bringing with them new agricultural technology and weaponry, such as swords and shields, which in turn necessitated impressive earthwork defences in the form of hillforts and crannogs (see page 418) as competition for land increased. In about 200-100 BC more Celts arrived with superior iron working skills and consequently, more fortifications were also built. The **brochs**, or towers, the remains of many of which can still be seen dotted along the west coast and in the islands, date from this time (see also page 418).

The Picts and the Romans

Indigenous iron age tribes, or as myth relates, Scythians who arrived via Ireland, inhabited most of the country and were identified by the Romans as 'Picts' – possibly meaning 'painted, or tattooed, people'. They thwarted Roman imperial ambition in Alba, the land north of the Forth and Clyde, in around 80 AD and a string of Roman military outposts along the highland line remain from this abandoned campaign.

At **Fortingall**, near Aberfeldy, the ancient yew tree is said to mark the birthplace of Pontius Pilate, possibly the son of a Roman soldier, and cousin of King Caractacus, who later found preferment in Rome. To add credence to this theory, a gravestone marked 'PP' was found.

Defensive **walls** built by Emperors **Hadrian** (built circa 123 AD from the Solway Firth to the Tyne) and **Antoninus** (from the Clyde to the Forth circa 143 AD) against the Picts inadvertently set a precedent for the eventual polarization of Scotland and England, beginning around the ninth century, out of the mass of tribal kingdoms. An endlessly disputed border led to centuries of retaliatory raids and devastation on either side.

Picts south of the Antonine wall became semi-Romanized and were known as **Britons**, kin to the Welsh. Their kingdom of Strathclyde, with a stronghold on **Dumbarton Rock**, near Glasgow, once extended into Lancashire and retained a separate identity into the 11th century. The Lothians, territory of the British Gododdin, was overrun by Anglians from Northumbria. In the seventh century the Anglians challenged the Picts in Alba and were finally defeated at Dunnichen.

Meanwhile an Irish tribe, **the Scots**, who claimed descent from an Egyptian Pharaoh's daughter, had been settling in Pictish territory in Argyll from around the fourth century. Once in Argyll, the sons of the Scots' leader, Erc, established a kingdom called **Dalriada**, sharing it between themselves under a high king at **Dunadd** (see page 94). When their fellow countryman, **Columba**, arrived in the sixth century on **Iona**, they were aided in their cause by his diplomatic skills at the hostile Pictish court of King Brude, in Inverness. In the ninth century, the Scots under **Kenneth MacAlpin** took over the Picts. Although their written records were destroyed, or falsified by the conquering Scots, they left a rich legacy of unique sculptured stones denoting a civilized and artistic culture. When Kenneth set up at **Scone**, and Alba became Scotland, the seven kingdoms of Pictland in the north and east survived as great earldoms.

The early Church

Some claim Joseph of Arimathea brought Christianity to **Whithorn** in Galloway which had been a religious centre since the first century. Around 397 AD **Ninian** founded a Christian Mission in Whithorn, along eastern Mediterranean monastic lines vastly different from the Roman model. From here he and countless missionaries such as Kentigern, Moluag and Comgan went north to convert the Picts, as far as St Ninian's Isle in Shetland. Their communities, oak churches and cells are remembered in innumerable place names, wells and simple cross-marked stones, often established on pre-Christian sacred sites.

In 563 AD Columba arrived on **Iona** (see page 127), where he went on to found the Celtic Church, or the Church of the Culdees, with centres throughout Scotland, which differed in many ways from the Church of Rome. Iona became known as 'Cradle of Christianity in Scotland', but the arrival of the Vikings inhibited sea travel and the monks were driven from Iona. About this time, the Scots took over the Pictish nation and the Columban church moved to **Dunkeld**, with Columba's relics transported in the *breacbannoch*, or Monymusk reliquary. This was carried at Bannockburn and is now in the Museum of Scotland in Edinburgh.

St Andrews later became the principal seat of the church, although Iona retained special status. Communities of Culdees (one of which was at St Andrews) survived into the 13th century, outwith the Columban and later Roman church. These were thought to be adherents of Ninian's church, preserving elements of pre-Christian druid religion.

A common origin for the cross symbol found on both the **Pictish cross slabs** and the free standing crosses of **Iona and Islay** is the chi-ro, or wheeled cross, as found at Whithorn. However the enigmatic symbols, vivid hunting scenes and mythical beasts of the Pictish stones found throughout Pictland are unique, and their function remains a mystery.

Another mystery is the brief flourishing in the early 13th century of an accomplished school of sculptors around Loch Awe, in Argyll. In ancient burial grounds throughout **Knapdale** are found grave slabs depicting swords, warriors, and foreign ships thought to mark the graves of the **Knights Templar** who fled here from France.

The Vikings

Pagan Norsemen in dragonships are first heard of in Argyll in 795 AD, the first of many such coastal raids of unimaginable savagery, which included ritual killings. Colonies of monks were not spared; 68 suffered the 'red martyrdom' on Iona in 807, and its library, 'a shop window crammed with the loot of centuries' was a magnet for raiders.

By the late ninth century, Norsemen had colonized **Orkney** (see page 360), and from Birsay Palace Earl Sigurd wielded power as far south as Moray. A renegade bunch of mixed Norse and Gaelic ancestry, the **Gall-Gaels**, appeared in the Hebrides and Galloway. Some of these, like chieftain Ketil Flatnose's family, became early settlers of Iceland.

Once surrounded by aggressive Norse colonies, now also in Dublin and York, the newly formed 'Scotland' survived through a combination of fighting spirit and a network of shifting alliances with the various Norse powers. Some of these alliances were enduring. In the ninth century 'Torf' Einar, credited with introducing peat cutting, founded a dynasty from which sprang the Earls of Angus.

After the Dublin colony collapsed in 1014, a Viking kingdom of 'Man and the Sudreys' (Hebrides) filled the vacuum, and the isles continued to be ravaged by warring Norsemen. By around 1100 Norwegian king Magnus Barelegs' empire included the entire northern and western seaboard. Against this backdrop, pursuing his own interests, appears **Somerled**, Hebridean hero of Norse-Gaelic blood, progenitor of Clan Donald and the powerful Lordship of the Isles. In 1153, he supported a rebellion against the Scottish crown. Later, in the early 13th century he built a series of castles around the coast, such as Sween, Tioram, Mingary and Dunstaffnage, which foiled the intermittent attempts made by the Scottish crown to assert control.

The last of the great Norse kings, Hakon, was defeated by the Scots in 1263 at Largs, with the aid of bad winter weather. Orkney and Shetland were only returned to Scotland in the 15th century. A Norse dialect was spoken there into the 18th century and vestiges of Norwegian law still survive, as does the Viking St Magnus Cathedral, in Kirkwall.

Macbeth and the battle for kingship

Macbeth, the earl-king of the vast land of Moray, rose to high kingship with popular support, reigning for a relatively long (1040-57) and peaceful time with his queen Gruoch, grand-daughter of Kenneth III of Scots. The popular image of Macbeth as portrayed by Shakespeare is, in fact, a false one. The great bard vilified Macbeth in order to please his James VI, who claimed descent from Duncan, Macbeth's rival. But it was Duncan who was the nasty piece of work, and he was slain not at Glamis, as in the famous play, but on the battlefield, while invading Macbeth's territory. Indeed Duncan is remembered in the *Orkneyinga saga*, the 'bible' of Viking history, as Karl Hundason, 'low-born son of the hound'.

Competition for the throne was a part of Pictish custom. A suitable 'tanist' or candidate was elected from anyone whose great-grandfather had been king and the candidates would then fight it out: in practice survival of the fittest. This competition for the right to be king was complicated by the ancient dynastic rivalry among the Dalriadic Scots and perpetuated when they merged with the Picts under Kenneth MacAlpin. This later precipitated the Wars of Independence.

One part of Shakespeare's Macbeth which is historical fact is the Birnam Wood incident, when Malcolm, Duncan's son, and his Northumbrian allies used tree branches as camouflage to advance on Macbeth in his Dunsinnan stronghold near Perth. He was later hunted down and slain at Lumphanan by Malcolm's ally, MacDuff, Earl of Fife, and is buried on Iona.

Background

Macbeth, the last truly Celtic king, was also one of the most able early kings. He was the first to establish and implement a fair legal system and a firm supporter of the Celtic church, he went on pilgrimage to Rome where an Irish monk observed him liberally scattering money to the poor. Further evidence of the great disservice done to his memory by Shakespeare.

The Canmores and the Norman conquest

Macbeth's usurper, the uncouth **Malcolm III**, Canmore (meaning 'big head'), was an illegitimate son of Duncan and a miller's daughter. In 1067 Malcolm married Margaret, a Saxon princess born in Hungary and sister of Edgar Atheling, the English heir to the throne, who had fled north with his family to escape William the Conqueror and the Norman conquest. Margaret was a devout Catholic and was largely responsible for introducing the religious ideas of the Roman Catholic Church into Scotland, for which she was canonized in 1251. In 1072 she founded **Dunfermline Abbey** and introduced southern manners to the Scottish court. Her private chapel survives in Edinburgh castle and is one of the oldest surviving buildings in Scotland.

Malcolm's belligerent instincts were not curbed by the influence of the saintly Margaret, however, and one of his many raids into Northumberland provoked a visit from William the Conqueror. The result was that Malcolm was forced to swear allegiance to William, an oath he didn't take too seriously, as he continued to raid England at whim, but one which would lead to a greater degree of southern interference in Scottish constitutional matters.

The Normans began to exert their influence over Scotland in many other ways. They were granted land as far as the Highland fringes, establishing a feudal system based on loyalty to the crown. The traditional patriarchal tribal culture was eroded, causing constant rebellions in the North and Galloway. The Norman successor to the Scottish throne, **David I**, like many of his Norman friends, had English estates, acquired through his wife. This wealth built the great Border abbeys and established the Roman church more fully. New parishes and dioceses revolutionized administration, and burghs were founded to develop international trade, attracting **Flemish** settlers. Society in Medieval Scotland became more typically European than England or even France.

One of the depressingly familiar themes running through Scottish history has been the unwillingness of the Scots nobility to resist English ambitions towards Scotland. This has always been their Achilles heel and, in 1290, it provoked a crisis of succession, when the new child queen, Margaret, Maid of Norway, died en route from Norway. Margaret had been recognised as heiress of Scotland, the Hebrides and the Isle of Man, but was taken ill on her way to England and a child marriage to the prince who would become Edward II, son of Edward I. Following her death, no fewer than 13 rival contestants materialized. Two main factions emerged: the Balliols and Comyns against the Bruces. But instead of reverting to the traditional method of tanistry, or 'natural selection', the pusillanimous Scots nobles appealed to Edward I of England to adjudicate.

Wallace and Bruce: the Wars of Succession

Edward eventually chose John Balliol, and he was crowned king at Scone in June 1292. Balliol was anxious to prove to his fellow Scots that he was not as weak as they claimed him to be. He negotiated a defensive agreement with the French, the beginning of the Auld Alliance. He then invaded Cumberland in 1296, but in retaliation, Edward attacked Berwick and slaughtered its inhabitants. The Scottish army was then defeated at Dunbar, and thereafter the castles of Edinburgh, Roxburgh Perth and Stirling were captured.

In the same year, Balliol abdicated at Stracathro and went into exile. Edward then destroyed the great Seal of Scotland and, worse still, moved the Stone of Destiny, the traditional crowning throne for all Scottish kings, to Westminster Abbey, where it lay under the Coronation Chair for 700 years. Scotland, as a result, was left in disarray.

However, resistance found a leader in **William Wallace**, son of a Renfrew laird. He began a revolt against the English in 1297 and built up a substantial army. By September of that year he he had secured a small but strategic victory against English forces at **Stirling Bridge**. This galvanized support and he was quickly declared 'Guardian of the Realm'. Following his defeat at Falkirk he was betrayed to Edward by one of the Scots noblemen, captured and taken south to be executed (disembowelled, then hung, drawn and quartered) in Smithfield, London, in 1305.

This stirred **Robert Bruce** to take up the cause of independence. Encountering his treacherous rival, 'Red' Comyn, in a Dumfries church, he seized the initiative, stabbing him at the altar. With Comyn dead, and the support of patriotic church leaders, as well as Sir James, 'The Black Douglas', Bruce was able to consolidate his gains, and he was crowned king with full ceremony at Scone before the inevitable blow of Papal excommunication fell. But not only did Rome refuse to recongize Bruce as king. Edward I, the self-proclaimed 'Hammer of the Scots', was not best pleased and for the next seven years Bruce was a virtual outlaw fighting a guerrilla campaign against Edward from hiding in the west.

During this time the indomitable Edward died, and Bruce felt bold and confident enough to raid the northern counties of England as far south as Appleby and Richmond. Of his castles captured by the English, only Stirling remained to be wrested from Edward's successor, Edward II. So the scene was set for the most significant battle in Scottish history, at **Bannockburn**, near Stirling, in 1314, where Bruce confronted Edward II's vastly superior army. His incredible victory, aided by Angus Og of the Isles, and a number of Knights Templar recently arrived seeking sanctuary from persecution in France, has ensured him a place in the heart of every patriotic Scot.

Bannockburn brought the Scots a rare victory over their southern enemy, and led to the signing of the **Declaration of Arbroath**, manifesto of Scotland's independence, in 1320. There followed a temporary peace with England, and Bruce was finally recognized as king by the Pope, before he died in 1329. His friend Douglas, as requested, took Bruce's heart on pilgrimage to the Holy Land but when Douglas died en route it was returned to **Melrose Abbey**.

The Stewart Dynasty

From Robert Bruce's title of 'High Steward' sprang the dynasty of Stewart kings. The early Jameses (of whom there were seven in all) all followed a tragic pattern: succeeding as infant kings, imprisoned throughout childhood, and suffering untimely deaths. James I and III were both murdered, and James II blew himself up accidentally with a cannon. Unscrupulous regents frequently took charge and hugely powerful nobles like the house of Douglas competed both amongst themselves and against the king. James II hot-bloodedly murdered the earl of Douglas over dinner at Stirling Castle by throwing him out the window. The Lords of the Isles were put down by the Earl of Mar and his followers in one of the bloodiest battles of all, 'Red Harlaw' near Inverurie. Like the Douglases, they, too, were finally forfeited, in 1543.

However, the early Stewarts made progress towards rescuing the country from anarchy, by laying the foundations for a modern state through a series of constitutional reforms. They embodied the democratic 'Kings of Scots', answerable first to the common people. Mostly cultured and progressive, they found time to write poetry (James I wrote the *King's Quair*), to build Renaissance palaces, and to father sufficient illegitimate 'James Stewarts' to fill numerous ecclesiastical sinecures

Background

(James IV and V). James IV was a true Renaissance prince with a glittering court, but a self-destructive streak led to his early death along with most of the nobility at Flodden, in 1513, sacrificed for the long-standing 'Auld Alliance' with France.

Mary, Queen of Scots

There is no more tragic and romantic figure in Scottish history than Mary, Queen of Scots. Raised in France for safekeeping as a Catholic, her brief reign was dogged by bad luck, bad judgement and bad timing. She arrived back in Scotland in 1561, a young widow, at the height of Reformation turmoil in which both France and Catholicism were inimical. Something of a loose cannon, she was embroiled in a power struggle not helped by her disastrous choice of husbands. Implicated in the celebrated murder of the first one, her cousin, Henry Lord Darnley, she then swiftly married one of the chief suspects, the Earl of Bothwell, incurring the fury of everyone else. Imprisoned after the Battle of Carberry on the island fortress of Loch Leven, she escaped only to throw herself on the mercy of her cousin Queen Elizabeth I, who, mindful that in Catholic eyes Mary had the better claim to the English throne, locked her up at Fotheringhay for 19 years before deciding to do away with her altogether.

Reformation and the roots of Scottish education

The Reformation, converting the Catholic church to Protestant, came relatively late to Scotland and the motives were as much political as religious, though, of course, in 16th-century terms the two were inextricably linked. A pro-English Protestant faction had grown over decades, opposing the French Catholic Regent, Mary of Guise, and a rebel parliament in 1560 banned Catholic Mass. Thus shattering for good the Auld Alliance with France, first formalized in 1295.

The casualties of the Reformation were countless and included religious buildings, works of art and even whole libraries. It amounted to a complete obliteration of the past over which even today amnesia prevails, though unlike England, there were very few martyrs. So began 100 years of bitter struggle to establish the reformed church. Cue the Protestant exile, **John Knox**, a Calvinist rabble-rouser of dubious character and little diplomacy who was prone to blasting his trumpet off against the 'monstrous regiment of women,' namely Mary, Queen of Scots. Knox's skills as a colourful orator, and his self-appointed role as official historian of the Reformation have allowed him to eclipse the real hero, **Andrew Melville**, who sacrificed his career of reforming university education, to devote himself to the nuts and bolts of church reform.

Schooling for all as a passport to intellectual freedom and moral probity was a dream of the reformers. While grammar and song schools already existed, by the end of the 17th century most parishes had schools using the bible as textbook. The 'Dominie' (schoolmaster) was until recently a hugely influential community figure. Prior to the Reformation the **Universities** of St Andrews (1412), Glasgow (1451) and Aberdeen (1495) had been established and Edinburgh University was added to the list in the 1580's.

James VI and the Union of Crowns

After Elizabeth's death, Mary's son became James VI of Scotland. **Jacobean Scotland** was vibrant and vigorously European. Religious extremists were checked by James VI, the 'Wisest fool in Christendom,' and unprecedented peace allowed Renaissance culture to blossom. but trouble was brewing. In 1603 James VI ascended to the English throne as James I, with the Union of Crowns. At this time, the

Scottish Parliament had so little power that James VI/I was able to write from his palace in London: "Here I sit and govern Scotland with my pen. I write and it is done." In contrast, the English parliament had begun to assume some genuine power.

Charles I and the Covenanters

James believed in the Divine Right of kings – the God given right of monarchs to rule their subjects. It was a belief that he passed on to his son Charles I, who succeeded in 1625 and quickly proved that he had little desire to consult parliament in either Scotland or England. Although he was born in Dunfermline, he showed little interest in Scotland and was essentially an absentee monarch. He did not even bother to come to Scotland to be crowned until 1633, calling a parliament at the same time – and then overseeing proceedings, making sure that the voting went his way.

Charles also showed little tact and diplomacy in matters ecclesiastical and by reasserting the powers of the bishops he rode roughshod over the authority of the General Assembly of the Church of Scotland. Not surprisingly, the rumblings of revolution could soon be heard.

The struggle of the kirk (church) against the king erupted into full scale civil war, with hostility towards bishops the recurrent theme. A riot in St Giles in Edinburgh expressed public feeling and resulted in **The National Covenant**, signed in Edinburgh in 1638, pledging faith to 'the true religion' and affirming the authority of the powerful General Assembly of the Church of Scotland in all matters spiritual. Covenanters and king came to blows, followed by an extremist group of Presbyterians allying with the English parliament against the king, in the **Solemn League and Covenant**. Battle-hardened Scots flooded back from European campaigns to take up arms.

A supporter of the original Covenant, **Montrose**, led a spirited but doomed campaign for the king against the extremists. At Ardvreck, in Assynt, he was betrayed to his arch-enemy 'King Campbell', Duke of Argyll, who gave him a traitor's death in Edinburgh. After the Restoration Argyll found himself on the wrong side and met the same end on the same spot.

Civil War

Throughout the 17th century the dark side of religious idealism – fanaticism and paranoia – were epitomized by the 'kirk sessions' courts in which the church conducted an orgy of scapegoating and witch-hunts. Fundamental differences of ideology, constitution and culture between two countries only recently 'twinned', opened cracks in the alliance with the Parliamentarians. The following year, Civil War broke out in England, with parliamentarians led by **Oliver Cromwell** fighting to wrest power from the king. In 1649 Charles was executed and England became a republic. The Scots, however, wanted to keep the monarchy and proclaimed his son, Charles II as their king, despite falling under Cromwell's military 'Protectorate'. Cromwell acted swiftly to bring the country under his control. In 1651 he forbade the Scots from holding their own parliament – forcing them to send representatives to Westminster instead.

Charles II and Restoration

The Commonwealth under Cromwell lasted until 1660, when Charles II was restored to the English throne. The Scottish Parliament was revived and met again in 1661. This time the Presbyterian Covenanters, who had gained such control of Parliament prior to the Commonwealth, were tamed. The Scottish Parliament was again largely run by nobles loyal to the king.

Background

Although Charles II's was greeted with wild rejoicing, the reinstatement of the bishops once again proved problematic. Some unconsenting ministers of the church were outlawed and finding a loyal following, especially in the southwest, they held illegal services, 'Conventicles', in the open air. Crippling fines and brutal persecution from officers of the crown, including Graham of Claverhouse merely increased their resistance, and many died in the 'Killing Times' as martyrs to high principle.

Religion and the Monarchy

Scotland and England continued to disagree, both about the succession and about religion. Charles II's brother and successor, James VII/II, was a Roman Catholic and in 1687 he tried to introduce more tolerant policies towards Catholics. His actions were seen as a threat to the privileged position held by the Church of England, which since the time of Henry VIII had been the official church in England, and also displeased Presbyterians in Scotland. At first, the feeling was that this state of affairs wouldn't last: James was ageing, and as both his daughters were Protestants, the Protestant succession seemed safe. However, when his heir James Francis Edward was born and brought up as a Catholic, a crisis was precipitated and James was ousted from the throne, fled ignominiously in 1689. His Protestant daughter Mary and her husband William of Orange, were invited to take the throne of England, and were later reluctantly accepted by the Scots under the terms of the **Revolution Settlement**.

The Darién Scheme

Although both countries shared a monarch, England was growing significantly wealthier than Scotland. Like other European countries, it was thriving economically through trade generated by its colonies. Scotland, however, had no colonies of its own. To remedy this, a monopoly company was founded with the approval of the King, modelled on the English East India Company. Wealthy Scots helped to fund it, but much of the capital was raised in England. However, the English East India Company, exercised its considerable power to protect its monopoly. Strings were pulled and the House of Commons soon threatened to prosecute the Scottish company's English directors. The King, who had agreed to its establishment, now came under pressure to oppose it. Not surprisingly, most of the English backers withdrew and Scotland saw it as a matter of national pride to raise the starting capital itself – a sum of £400,000, roughly half the nation's capital.

The intention of the scheme was to establish a permanent colony at Darién, on the Panama Isthmus in Central America. Darien was a strategically important site and the plan was that goods sent to and from Europe would sail to Panama, be carried overland across the isthmus, then reshipped – the new Scottish company carrying out this lucrative work.

However, the project had not been thoroughly researched. For one thing, the land was owned by Spain, a major world power who King William could not afford to offend. Consequently, he ordered English colonists in the area not to help the Scottish settlers defend their new home against the Spanish. In addition the terrain was hostile (which was why the Spanish had not set up a similar scheme already) and diseases like malaria and yellow fever were rife. Within months large numbers of colonists had died. Another attempt was made and was also unsuccessful, and by 1700 the colony had been abandoned.

The consequences were far reaching. Scotland lost a vast proportion of her wealth; national pride and confidence were dented, and the country lost faith in the dual monarchy. The King had sided with his wealthiest subjects – and Scotland felt betrayed.

Press gangs

This enforced form of recruitment was widely suffered around the coasts of Scotland, dating from the time of the Napoleonic wars. Gangs of 'heavies' from anchored ships would go ashore and grab any able bodied young men for forcible service in the navy. Easiest targets were found in the public houses! Whenever Britian went to war, there came a new calling for men. During the Seven Year War (1756-1815) recruitment was regularised to the extent that the government demanded that every fifth man in any town or village was to serve in the Navy. The Napoleonic Wars (1799-1815) also required huge numbers of sailors. Men sailed out to sea at dawn and by noon found themselves ganged by His Majesty's ship-of-war. They would probably not see their families again for several years. Their 'disappearance' resulted in a serious depletion in the number of fishermen and consequently great misery and increased poverty for the communities affected.

Often, if rumours reached a village that the gangs were coming along the shore by foot, the women would lie in wait and stone the gangs, thus giving the men time to hide. A number of young fishermen went off to the collieries of Fife and other places in order to escape this inhumane practice.

In 1801, recognising the depletion in numbers of fishermen, Parliament passed an act making it illegal to press gang any person engaged in taking, curing or selling fish. Pressing did continue as a means of recruitment until the end of the war with France in 1815 when it was not used so often. A few years later it was abolished.

Union of Parliaments

While Darién produced much anti-English feeling, a number of Scots began to feel that greater co-operation with England could be economically advantageous. At around the same time a further constitutional crisis was brewing. William of Orange had no children and was to be succeeded by James VII/II's daughter Anne who was Protestant. However, Anne had no surviving children and English politicians began to search for an heir – who had to be both Protestant and have Stuart blood. They decided on the Hanoverians, who were descended from the daughter of James VI/I. In 1701 the English parliament passed the **Act of Settlement**, ruling that on Anne's death the throne should pass to the House of Hanover. In 1702 William died and the throne passed to Anne.

The assumption was that the Scots would follow England's lead and accept the Hanoverian succession. But the nation was still smarting over Darién, and as Anne turned out to have little interest in Scotland, relations were strained. The difficulties over having two separate governments under one monarch would not go away. In 1703 the Scottish parliament passed the **Act of Security** which declared that on Anne's death, Scotland would take a different successor to England unless some settlement could be agreed upon that restored 'the honour and sovereignty of this Crown and Kingdom'. They wanted to guarantee the power of the Scottish parliament; the freedom of Scottish religion, and freedom of trade. In addition Parliament ordered people to arm themselves and prepare to fight. It was sabre rattling that the English could hardly ignore.

Although Anne signed the Act of Security, Scotland's triumph was shortlived. England passed the **Alien Act**, which declared that all Scots except those resident in England should be treated as aliens, and Scottish trade with England was to be blocked. The Act was to remain in force until Scotland agreed to make moves towards parliamentary union, or accepted Hanoverian succession.

There were obvious economic advantages to closer ties with England, and Scotland was in a weakened position. Not only had the Darién venture weakened the economy, the country was also suffering from several years of harvest failure which had led to famine. Although public opinion was against union with England that counted for little. It certainly appealed to many in parliament. Financial inducements were offered – and accepted, causing Robert Burns to comment later that Scotland had been "bought and sold for English gold". The Church of Scotland, initially suspicious of Union, withdrew its objections when it was assured that Presbyterianism would be safeguarded. A propaganda campaign was carried out on both sides of the border, many of the pamphlets being written by the author Daniel Defoe. The English were assured that union would end the threat of invasion from Scotland; the Scots assured of great economic benefits.

The people were not swayed. There were violent demonstrations in the streets, and riots in Glasgow, Dumfries and Edinburgh. Opponents even went as far as claiming that union would be sinful. The riots in Edinburgh were particularly violent causing Defoe, who was acting as a spy for the English government, to say: "A Scots rabble is the worst of its kind.'The Scots', he said, 'were a hardened and terrible people'. Pro union MPs were attacked and plans were made in Lanarkshire to raise an army to march on Edinburgh. But public opinion was not of consequence. The Duke of Argyll, for instance, made paper kites out of anti-union petitions and flew them around Parliament. Although some members , notably Andrew Fletcher of Saltoun, were opposed to union, the treaty was comfortably passed by the Scottish Parliament on 16th January 1707. It had to be signed in secret in Edinburgh to protect politicians from the mob.

In April, the act was passed in the English Parliament and on 1st May 1707 the Union came into effect. The Kingdoms of Scotland and England were united into Great Britain, though Scotland preserved its separate legal system, educational system and church. Despite the vigorous opposition, threats and bribery assured that a bankrupt and exhausted Scotland was, in popular mythology, sold to England for £398,085 – part compensation for Darien, part wages for the Commissioners who closed the deal.

Jacobite rebellion and the Clearances

Rebellion against the imposition of William of Orange began in 1689, when William's government redcoats clashed with supporters of James II (the Jacobites) at **Killiecrankie** (see page160). They were led by Graham of Claverhouse, 'Bonnie Dundee', who was killed in the battle. In 1692, an expedition to weed out the Jacobites in the Highlands resulted in the **Glencoe massacre**, which provoked unprecedented public outcry (see page 233).

The Act of Settlement was not forgotten and dwindling trade and increased taxation fuelled dissatisfaction with the Union. A lively underground resistance, aided by long-standing French connections, revolved around the Jacobite court in exile at St Germain. Sympathy also came from English quarters.

Four attempts ensued to reinstate a Stewart monarchy, supported erratically by France, and culminating at **Culloden**, in 1746 (see page 205). Much support came from north of the Tay, which was Catholic and Episcopalian country. The term 'Jacobite' popularly denoted anti-establishment and Episcopalian. Also, pejoratively, Highlander, and was evocative of a linguistic, social and cultural divide between Lowlander and Highlander whihch had grown since the 15th century.

Highland culture and independence was not diminished after the demise of the Lords of the Isles, hence the rise of the Campbells to enormous power as government agents, dealing for instance with the troublesome MacGregors. Claiming descent from

General Wade's Bridges

Most major roads in Scotland were planned in 1724 by George Wade. He was appointed Commander of His Majesty's forces in Scotland because of his far seeing plans for moving troops . The network began with 250 miles of roads in the Highlands, the first engineered since Roman days. Eventually Wade's roads covered over 1,000. Every summer, he deployed five hundred men to the task.

But he is best remembered for his substantial bridges, still sturdy and much used. The often painted bridge at Braemar is perhaps the best known. But his bridge at Aberfeldy spanning the Tay, Scotland's longest river, was his first. Designed by William Adam and built of local stone, it is nearly 400-miles long, with five arches. By present day prices it cost around £1 million, which is good value over 250 years!

Kenneth MacAlpin, the MacGregors were almost annihilated in 1603, and outlawed until 1774. They played a significant part in the Jacobite rebellions (see also page 156).

Although traditionally indifferent to the monarchy, many clans came out in support for the Prince Charles (of 'Bonnie Prince Charlie' fame) in 1745. After defeat at Culloden, savage reprisals were led by the 'Butcher' Cumberland. Rebels were beheaded or hanged, estates confiscated and the pipes and Highland dress proscribed until 1782. Clansmen were enlisted into Highland regiments and 1,150 were exiled, swelling the ranks of emigrants to the colonies. Gaelic culture was effectively expunged and Scotland as a whole suffered disgrace.

Rise and fall of Bonnie Prince Charlie

Charles Edward Stuart, the 'Young Pretender', grandson of James II was born in Italy. First setting foot on Scottish soil, aged 23, with seven companions (the Seven Men of Moidart), his forceful personality persuaded reluctant clan chiefs to join him in raising the Standard at Glenfinnan for his father in 1745. Inadequately prepared government troops under 'Johnny Cope' (of ballad fame) enabled his swift progress to Edinburgh, where he held court at Holyrood, dazzling the populace with a grand ball. Edinburgh was charmed but embarrassed.

With sights set on the English throne, he reached Derby. Encouraging reports about panic in London were offset by news of advancing government troops which prompted retreat. The pursuing redcoats were outwitted as far as Inverness, and the ensuing bloodbath at **Culloden**, though Charles' only defeat, was decisive. Fleeing to the Hebrides, he was given shelter by **Flora MacDonald** (see page 299) and then spent a summer as a lone fugitive. Despite a £30,000 reward for his capture, he managed to escape on a French frigate in 1746. Too late by a fortnight, 40,000 louis d'ors then arrived from France, enough to revive the whole campaign.

This failure has been ascribed to a fatal weakness of character and a collapse of resolve at Derby. He ended his days a degenerate and broken man, ensuring the complete collapse of the Jacobite cause. But Bonnie Prince Charlie is remembered in numerous nostalgic songs, a toast to 'the King over the Water' and a host of memorabilia.

The Enlightenment

Intellectual life flourished in late 18th century Scotland. Embracing all the arts, its roots lay in the philosophical nature, shaped by European thought, underlying Scots law, education and the church. The sceptic **David Hume** (1711-76) was the foremost of a school of philosophers, best known for his *Treatise on Human Nature* and *Essays, Moral*

Background

Great Scots

For such a small country, Scotland has produced a remarkable number of intellectual geniuses who have been peculiarly influential. Many of them were great scientists, like **James Clerk Maxwell**, *described by Einstein as the most important physicist after Newton, who by paving the way for Einstein's theory of relativity, practically invented the modern world. There was also* **John Napier**, *the inventor of logarithms,* **Lord Kelvin**, *who devised the second law of thermodynamics, and* **James Hutton**, **Roderick Murchison** *and* **Charles Lyell**, *who together created modern geology.*

In medicine, Scotland led the world. **Robert Liston** *and* **James Young Simpson** *discovered the benefits of chloroform and* **Alexander Fleming** *discovered penicillin, the most effective antibiotic ever devised. The number of technologists is incredible and includes* **James Watt**, *who developed the steam engine,* **R W Thomson** *who invented the fountain pen and pneumatic tyre,* **John Macadam**, *who gave the world the metalled road,* **Charles Mackintosh** *who invented waterproof fabric,* **Alexander Graham Bell** *who invented the telephone and not forgetting* **John Logie Baird**, *the father of television.*

Scotland has also given the world the Bank of England, the decimal point, colour photographs, the fax machine, the photocopier, the bicycle, the bus, the thermos flask, the thermometer, the gas mask, the gravitating compass, interferon and insulin.

and Political. Kirkcaldy born **Adam Smith** pioneered political economy in his *Wealth of Nations* (1776), a powerful impetus to later political reform.

An emphasis on research and practicality in the sciences fostered inventiveness in applied science, contributing much to industry and agriculture. **James Watt** (1736-1819) developed the steam engine which powered the machinery of the Industrial Revolution, medicine flourished at Edinburgh university, and further generations spawned engineers and inventors like **Alexander Graham Bell** and **John Logie Baird**, inventors of the telephone and television respectively.

Classicism was espoused in architecture and by painters like **Allan Ramsay, Raeburn** and **Nasymth**, and gave way in literature to the Romanticism of **Robert Burns** whose work profoundly influenced popular culture and notions of democracy.

Sir Walter Scott's best selling historical novels worked miracles for Scotland's public image. It was he who stage-managed the visit of George IV, who sportingly donned a kilt and, for modesty's sake, pink tights for the occasion. Later on, Queen Victoria was inspired to adopt a Highland home, and with the craze for 'Balmorality', the Highlands assumed a romantic glamour, becoming a fashionable resort for southern sportsmen.

Industrial revolution

Until around 1750, half of Scotland's population lived north of the Clyde and Tay. **Emigration** to the lowlands or North America was already a problem as a money economy threatened traditional ways of life. The decision of landlords to resettle their tenants on the coasts, replacing black cattle with sheep, was a disastrous economic and social experiment, with brutal evictions in some areas – although popular myth forgets that famine, disease and overpopulation were rife and many went willingly. Eventually, in 1886, crofters' rights were to some extent recognized (see also page 308).

The gap between Highland and Lowland life continued to widen as overgrazing, deforestation for industry, and deer 'forests', led to desolation in the Highlands, while improvements and drainage transformed lowland agriculture.

At the same time **industrialization** was soon to bring a massive population shift. Wool cloth and linen, long established as cottage industries, were undergoing mechanization. By 1820 mills were established in the coalfields of Lanark, Renfrew, and Ayr. Linen declined in favour of cotton spun and woven in Paisley and New Lanark, while tweed was first woven in Galashiels, in 1830. Dundee substituted jute for linen and Kirkcaldy developed linoleum. Thriving on trade with America, Glasgow's population mushroomed, absorbing many from the Highlands, also thousands of Irish refugees from the potato famine of the 1840's. Poor housing, overcrowding and disease became chronic.

20th-century Scotland

By 1900 iron and later steel, mainly in the west, had become manufacturing mainstays, serviced by new canals, railways and roads. As well as emigrants, Scotland supplied goods to North America: locomotives, girders, bridges, textile machinery and tools.

Shipyards flourished on the **Clyde**. The first iron steam ships were launched around 1800, although fast wooden clippers like the Cutty Sark were still competitive in the mid-19th century, when major shipping companies such as Cunard came to the fore. From 1880, skilled labour built steel ships for world markets as well as for the Royal Navy. Business boomed during the First World War, when political activity among skilled workers inspired by the Bolshevik revolution, led by Marxist and Scottish Nationalist **John Maclean**, gave rise to the myth of 'Red Clydeside'.

Post-war slump hit all industries in the 1920's from which they never really recovered. A dangerous dependency on mining, metalworking and heavy engineering was a crucial factor in industrial decline and the innovative spirit of the 19th century is only now re-emerging among pioneering computer software development companies in the central belt.

The rise of nationalism and the new Parliament

In a long Liberal tradition dedicated to political reform, the issue of Home Rule reared its head repeatedly after the 1880's. The first stirrings of nationalism were heard after the First World War and voiced by writers in the 1920's, such as Lewis Spence, Hugh MacDiarmid, Grassic Gibbon and Neil Gunn. These sentiments took political shape as the **Scottish National Party** (SNP)in 1934. Support grew through the 1950s and 1960s, and in 1967 the SNP was revealed as a potent political force when Winifred Ewing won the Hamilton by-election.

Nationalist fervour reached its height in the 1970s, roused by expectations that revenue from the **oil and gas** recently discovered in the North Sea would reverse economic decline. These hopes were dashed by oil revenues disappearing into the British Treasury at Westminster. In 1974, 11 SNP MPs were elected to Westminster – and although many felt that this was a protest vote, Labour felt concerned. In 1979 it held a referendum on the establishment of a Scottish Assembly. Turnout was low and support was lukewarm, so no assembly was established.

Labour were soon ousted from office and the Thatcher government swept to power in 1979, bringing with them a disdain for Scotland that was to have far reaching consequences. The new Conservative government also introduced policies that did not sit easily with most Scots. When the unpopular Poll Tax, which notoriously taxed 'dukes the same as dustmen' was introduced in Scotland a year earlier than in the rest of Britain, the country felt that it was increasingly being governed by politicians who cared little for its people. Years of Tory rule served only to widen the gap between Scotland and Westminster, and it was almost inevitable that some form of devolution would follow.

Background

Twenty years on, the Scots voted emphatically in favour of devolution and the **Scottish Parliament** reconvened after 292 years on 12 May, 1999. The new Parliament has 129 MSPs (Members of the Scottish Parliament) who were elected by proportional representation. It has the power to pass legislation and to alter the rate of taxation. However defence and foreign affairs are still handled by Westminster. The early years of the Parliament have not been without controversy and its relationship with Westminster has at times proved frosty. The most pressing issue is the so called 'West Lothian Question', the anomaly that allows Scottish MPs at Westminster to vote on issues solely affecting England, while English MPs cannot vote on solely Scottish issues. MSPs, for example, recently voted to fund all care for all elderly people in Scotland. Yet this went against the policy of the Labour government, leading to the possible scenario of Scottish Labour MPs at Westminster voting *against* such funding for the elderly in England. As one commentator said: "The English have been the silent and uninvited guests at the devolutionary feast". In addition, Scotland still benefits from higher spending per head than any other part of Britain – a situation which is almost certain to change.

The new parliamentary building has also attracted controversy as its estimated £50 million construction costs have spiralled to around £300 million. And although it was due to be completed in summer 2001, it is now unlikely to be finished until December 2003.

However, despite these inevitable teething troubles, Scotland's Parliament is finding its feet – and there's no chance that an arrogant monarch (or arrogant Prime Minister) will succeed in controlling it again. Whether devolution is a step on the road to full independence remains to be seen.

Culture

Architecture

Background

Early structures: from brochs to towers A thousand years before Stonehenge, a Neolithic architect was supervising the construction of **Maes Howe** (see page 367) in Orkney. Dramatically accompanied by two stone circles, its massive precision-cut stonework houses a tomb. Religious architecture evolved into the Bronze Age and over 22 centuries of chambered tombs survive, notably at **Camster** and **Kilmartin**. Henges and stone circles, as at Cairnpapple, also abound. At **Skara Brae** (see page 366) is a 5,000 year-old village, a Neolithic Pompeii where stone furniture and utensils survive in rooms straight out of the 'Flintstones'.

Brochs, fortresses not dissimilar to diminutive industrial cooling towers such as at **Mousa** on Shetland (see page 396), appeared around 75 BC. A staircase ascended within double walls and a well often provided water for the besieged within. On duns and hilltops, timber laced forts, built from 700 BC into the Middle Ages, are sometimes found to have been fired to such an extent that stonework fused solid or vitrified. Whether this was intentional, or the result of attack, remains a mystery.

Ninth-century wheelhouses, with stone piers radiating from a central hearth, are visible at **Jarlshof** on Shetland, and appeared later in the Hebrides. Timber began to be used for Pictish hall houses, **crannogs** – lake dwellings on wooden rafts – and early churches (such as at Whithorn).

In the 11th century, **round towers**, such as those at Brechin and Abernethy, were used for defence and as belfries by Culdee communities. Around this time the first cathedrals were built. The one at Birsay on Orkney, founded in 1050 by Earl Thorfinn, was soon replaced by another in Kirkwall commemorating the Norse **St Magnus** (see page 361). This was built by masons from Durham Cathedral after working at Dunfermline Abbey, also Romanesque, built for St Margaret. She also commissioned St Rule's in St Andrews, whose tall square tower suggests Northumbrian influence, echoed in those at Muthill, Dunning (in Strathearn) and Dunblane.

David I (1124-53) granted land to Roman monastic orders and two centuries of abbey and cathedral building ensued, though mostly in the lowlands. Years of neglect and depredations by English troops and iconoclastic reformers leave many as picturesque ruins, stripped of magnificent wood and stone carving, stained glass and wallpainting. The wallpaintings at Fowlis Easter, 15th-century collegiate churches, is a rare survivor. The ruins of Oronsay Priory and the Valerian clad cloisters of **Iona's** nunnery (see page 129) are legacy of the Augustinians.

Abbeys & cathedrals

Symbols of feudalism built by Norman settlers appear in the form of timber motte and bailey fortresses – timber towers with defensive earthworks, though they are found mostly south of the Forth and Clyde.

Medieval castles

Square or oblong tower houses, with a defensive entry at first floor level, barrel vaulting and great hall were to be an enduring form of dwelling, evolving from the 14th century into the 17th. More elaborate are L-plan and Z-plan versions, with one or two towers added at corners to defend the entry.

While ordinary folk lived in thatched turf and stone hovels (some into the 20th century), the cosmopolitan and cultured Stewart kings set about building new palaces and improving existing residences.

Renaissance palaces

The old castle at **Linlithgow** had emerged by 1540, a wholly residential Renaissance palace ranged around a quadrangle, which even impressed the French Mary of Guise. While the Great Hall at **Stirling** is a triumph of late Gothic, the later Palace block (1540-42) reveals many Renaissance features, such as the recessed bays along the exterior with sculpted figures, and the famous carved wooden ceiling medallions, the 'Stirling Heads'.

A minor building boom in the late 16th century was a result of church land being transferred over a long period into private hands. The old tower house formula found favour, preferred over earlier royal examples of Renaissance innovation. Everyone from nobility to minor gentry was afforded both defence against troublesome neighbours as well as gracious living. **Claypotts** in Dundee is a good example of 'the castle with a country house built on top', while at **Craigievar** (see page 178), finished as late as 1626, idiosyncratic inventiveness reaches its apogée where the roofline explodes in a flurry of fairytale turrets. Families of masons developed individual styles detectable in Aberdeenshire where many tower houses, great and small, are still inhabited or have been recently revived. Defensive features like gun loops (apertures for guns) survived less out of necessity than as status symbols, and interiors, especially timber ceilings, were vividly painted, with exuberant imagery, as at **Crathes** (see page 171).

The Tower house

Background

'New towns' to promote trade were established by David I and settled with English and Flemish merchants, with a strict hierarchy of trading rights and privileges. Stone houses first replaced wood in the east coast burghs in the 16th century, setting a precedent for future urban design. Every burgh had its symbols of commerce and government at its centre: the Mercat (market) cross and the Tolbooth (town hall).

16th-century townhouses

Two centuries later, the spirit of vernacular architecture had not changed dramatically. Nor had urban layout, many houses still being built gable end on to the street. The multi-storey tenement became a distinctive feature of urban living, pioneered in Edinburgh's Canongate, where buildings such as Gladstone's Land are still intact.

William Bruce & the 17th-century mansion

Less defensive and more comfortable was the country mansion, a concept pioneered by Alexander Seton, paragon of a new kind of architectural patron, at **Pinkie House** in Musselburgh, a daring essay in elegance and erudition. In an urban setting, **Culross Palace** and **Argyll's Ludgings** in Stirling, are outstanding examples of grand town houses.

Post Restoration, William Bruce exemplifies a new concept: the architect. Introducing classical symmetry to existing buildings such as Holyrood and Thirlestane, he also designed **Hopetoun** in 1699-1703. The innovative oblong shape and hipped roof of Kinross are characteristic of his many other country house designs with their Anglo-Dutch interiors and plasterwork. He also revolutionized garden and landscape design.

Bruce's protege, James Smith, was a pioneer of British Palladianism. Rising from master mason to King's Master of Works and private architect, his own house, Newhailes (c1690), was the inspiration for countless lairds' houses, both grand and humble, built throughout Scotland in the 18th century.

Victorian Baronial

Not content with Classicism, architects raided the Gothic, Tudor, Jacobean and Scottish past, even Asia and Europe, for ideas. Late 18th-century country houses by Gillespie Graham were assymetrial and castellated. Inspired by the picturesque movement, they are the harbingers of the High Victorian revival of Scottish baronial which reached its peak in the 1860's. New and unprecedented wealth found industrial tycoons and landowners beating a path to the doors of fashionable architects like Burn and Bryce, to build colossal and fantastic country seats with room for entertaining on a huge scale and the latest in comforts, like plumbing. Some followed Queen Victoria's example at Balmoral, building extravagant Highland shooting lodges. Most eclectic of all is **Mount Stuart** on Bute (1870's) a neo-Gothic/Renaissance palace whose sumptuous interior even includes details from Charlemagne's tomb (see page 74).

Flamboyant design extended to monumental industrial buildings like textile mills and foundries, also railway stations, viaducts and bridges.

Glasgow's heyday: Thomson & Mackintosh

Glasgow grew phenomenally through the 19th century to become the 'Second City of the Empire'. While acres of tenements housed artisans and middle class families, earlier Georgian suburbs were abandoned for commodious villas for the prosperous, designed by leading architects in areas like Kelvingrove. Many, especially on the south side, were designed by Alexander 'Greek' Thomson using Classical Greece and Egypt as inspiration. The best known of his public works is the Greek Revival church in St Vincent St (1858). The originality of his work is itself currently enjoying an long-overdue revival.

While **Glasgow University** (1870) by Gilbert Scott was inspired by medieval Flemish cloth halls, banks were modelled on Renaissance palazzos. Thomson designed Egyptian-style warehouses, and Burnet in the 1890's returned from New York to design tall, narrow-fronted buildings with steel frames. By 1896 and Charles Rennie Mackintosh's debut, Glasgow had the most exciting architecture in Europe.

20th century: Traditionalism & modernism

The forward-looking Beaux-Arts rationalism of Burnet and company was challenged by Traditionalists reacting against aggressive modernity and advocating traditional building materials and craftsmanship, and referring back to 16th- and 17th-century vernacular architecture. **Rennie Mackintosh** was a leading, if independent exponent, as exemplified at **Hill House** in Helensburgh (see page 68) while a more mainstream Arts and Crafts aesthetic was adopted by **Robert Lorimer** who 'restored' many early houses, as well as designing anew.

In contrast, Art Déco was favoured by architects such as Glasgow's **Jack Coia**, and by the mid-century, **Basil Spence** was a champion of Modernism. Traditionalism versus Modernism was to become an enduring theme.

Economic depression and dramatic social change brought an urgent need for solutions to both rural depopulation, and urban overpopulation and decay. Already by the 1930's two contrasting visions of social progress were being proposed: restoration of organic unity, versus modernist utopia.

A desperate need for housing resulted in massive building projects into the 1970's transforming cities. Many historic buildings were demolished and city centres gutted in an effort to remedy post-war dereliction. Edinburgh had the worst slums in Europe where overpopulated tenements were literally collapsing. The first residential tower-blocks, the epitome of the Modern Functionalist brave new world, appeared, most notoriously in Glasgow's Gorbals. Urban over-spill was re-housed in New Towns such as Cumbernauld, which although internationally acclaimed in the 1960's, was unpopular with its inhabitants.

Post-war to present day

Traditionalists meanwhile continued to advocate experiments in vernacular style and a move was made to protect historic buildings.

Most prominent of recent public buildings is the new wing of the **Museum of Scotland in Edinburgh**. Completed at a time of renewed national confidence and cultural awareness, historical references are foremost. The sandstone-clad exterior is reminiscent of a medieval fortress, and from within the view over the adjacent Greyfriar's church, scene of the signing of the National Covenant in 1638, has been emphasized.

With the building of the **Scottish Parliament** at Holyrood by Eric Miralles still under way, it is not inappropriate that its temporary home is in the Assembly Rooms of the Church of Scotland, that most democratic of institutions.

Literature

Robert Burns

Any overview, no matter how brief, of Scotland's literary tradition must begin with a poet who has become inextricably linked with the image of Scotland and all things Scottish across the globe. Robert Burns was born on 25 January 1759, in a small cottage in Alloway, Ayrshire, where he lived until the age of eight. His father was a market gardener and Burns later referred to himself as 'a very poor man's son'. During this time, he and his brother were placed under the instruction of a village tutor but, following the family's move to a farm a few miles away, Robert's attendance at school was interrupted by the need to work the farm. But his father was keen that his son's education continue, be it from a brief spell with a tutor or under his own instruction.

Another move and a few weeks at school in Kirkoswald followed, while Robert continued to labour for his father, although in this time he had shown signs of his talent in a succession of love poems and poems based on day-to-day incidents of his life.

Following the death of their father in 1784, Robert and Gilbert rented another farm but luck wasn't on their side, as they fought against failing crops and an increasing struggle to provide for the family. To combat the anxiety of this situation, Burns found a refuge in his writing. Within the next two years, he had composed poetry which encompassed many subjects but mainly concerned itself with life as he was living it. He was also keen to point out what he saw as a kinship between all living things, such as in his famous 'To A Mouse', which was written, 'On turning her up in her nest with the plough, November, 1785'. The most frequently quoted lines of this poem; 'The best laid schemes o' mice an' men – Gang aft a-gley,' has entered the language, as have many sayings originated by Burns, and perfectly sum up his point.

Burns wrote in the dialect of plain country people and about the lives they led, but the emotions he described were so genuine that they appealed to all classes. The first three shilling volume of his poetry was released in July, 1786, by a publisher in Kilmarnock and his wife, Jean Armour, but only got as far as Greenock. However, by this time he had made a reputation for himself in Edinburgh and changed course for the capital to seek his fortune.

The 'ploughman-poet' was fêted by the cultured Edinburgh society. But, despite these attentions and his growing popularity, he remained a son of the soil at heart, unimpressed by the fuss his presence caused. In a letter of March, 1787, he wrote, "Scottish themes and Scottish story are the themes I could wish to sing," and while expressing a desire "to make leisurely pilgrimages through Caledonia," he preferred "to return to my old acquaintance the plough; and, if I can meet with a lease by which I can live, to commence a farmer".

In 1788 Burns and his wife set up a home at Ellisland, but given his previous lack of success as a farmer, he accepted a job as an Exciseman in Dumfriesshire, seizing contraband and checking on licences for the sale of alcohol. It was during this period, possibly inspired by coming into contact with so many people through his job, that he wrote of the joys of human companionship in what is perhaps his most celebrated work, *Auld Lang Syne*. Sung or spoken, this poem stands to this day as a symbol of friendship and is practically an anthem when friends gather to celebrate New Year around the world. His love of the companionship of friends is also a focus of *Tam O'Shanter*, which also serves as a cautionary warning against overindulgence and is a ghost story in the tradition of the mythic, while his irritation against the assumed superiority of some was put into words in *A Man's A Man For A' That*, which also returns to his theme of kinship:

> *"It's coming yet, for a' that,*
> *That man to man, the world o'er.*
> *Shall brothers be for a' that".*

In 1791, Burns quit farming and moved to Dumfries. His poems of this period were a return to the form of traditional ballads, such as *Bannockburn* (often mistakenly referred to as *Scots, Wha Hae*) which celebrates the resolute spirit of his ancestors during the battle.

After a period of ill health, Burns died on 21 July 1796, and was buried in St Michael's Churchyard, Dumfries. A statue was erected in his honour by the citizens of Dumfries in 1822 and, to this day, visitors may still be shown around Burns' Cottage in Alloway and view the poet's birthplace, while his memory is celebrated every year on 25 January, his date of birth, now referred to as Burns Night.

Sir Walter Scott

Burns was famously described as having eyes which "were large and glowed... when he spoke with such feeling and interest. I have never seen such eyes in a human head," by another man regarded as one of the nation's greatest literary figures, Sir Walter Scott. The two men had met while Scott was still in his teens and it was to have a profound effect on him which lasted throughout his life.

Scott was the son of a wealthy Edinburgh lawyer and was born there in 1771, the sixth surviving child of 12. He contracted polio as a child, leaving him lame in the right leg, the Old Town at the time being disease-ridden. His parents then moved to the New Town, while young Scott was sent to his uncle's farm at Sandyknowe in the Borders for a period of recuperation. This period was to last five years, during which time he immersed himself in tales and ballads of Jacobites and Border heroes, giving him a passion for history which would infuse his later work.

Following spells at Edinburgh High School and University, Scott became a solicitor in his father's firm before becoming an advocate in 1792, while devoting his spare time to the love of poetry and literature which had seen him writing verse at the age of 11 and translating poems from their original German.

In 1797, he married Charlotte Carpenter and the marriage was to last for the rest of her life. At the time, he had been collecting local material which would eventually become poems in his three volumes of *Minstrelsy Of The Scottish Border'* which established his name as a literary figure. Other romantic poetic works followed, such as *The Lady Of The Lake*, as with Burns, employing the Scottish dialect.

Apart from these works, he also acted as editor on others' works, wrote contemporary history, biographies and collected historical documents. He was appointed Clerk to the Court of Session in 1806.

In 1811, Scott purchased Abbotsford, a farmhouse near Melrose, and his alterations and rebuilding were to drain his finances over the next 14 years. It was during this period that he would find the style which would remain his best remembered contribution to literature, the historical novel. Collectively known as the *Waverley* novels, these included *Old Mortality*, *Rob Roy* and *The Heart Of Midlothian*.

The original *Waverley* was a romantic tale of the Jacobite Rebellion of 1745 and the Highland society of the time. By 1819, Scott had moved beyond purely Scottish history and wrote *Ivanhoe*, set in 12th-century England. It remains his most enduring work and he followed it with *Kenilworth*, *Redgauntlet* and *The Talisman*.

Scott's fascination with history went beyond his fictional work and, in 1817, he and some friends discovered the ancient Honours of Scotland, the royal sword, crown and sceptre, which had remained hidden behind a sealed door at Edinburgh Castle since the days of Charles II.

In 1825, Scott was the victim of multiple tragedies. His publishers and a printing company, in which he was a partner, collapsed with disastrous financial consequences. Added to that, his beloved Charlotte died and he threw himself into his work so ferociously that he suffered four strokes.

Trips to Malta and Italy didn't succeed in improving his health and he died at Abbotsford on 21 September 1832. His huge popularity was believed to have kept the spirit of Scotland alive and he is commemorated by the Scott Monument in Princes Street, Edinburgh. This is an impressive architectural achievement and, if you have the stamina, affords a breathtaking view of Scott's native city.

Robert Louis Stevenson

Scott is best remembered for his romantic historical adventures. This tradition was to continue in the work of another of the nation's most famous authors. Robert Louis Stevenson was born at 8 Howard Place, Edinburgh, on November 13th, 1850. Like Scott, he was trained in law. He was also fond of travel.

It was these travels which led to his employment as a writer of travel articles and essays. However, while staying in Braemar in 1881, his young stepson, Lloyd Osbourne, asked him "to try to write something interesting instead". The rented house had a playroom, where Stevenson drew pirate maps of an island. These became the basis of his tale, which had the working title of *The Sea Cook*. When he offered it to *Young Folks* magazine, the editor suggested a new title and so, in the autumn of 1881, *Treasure Island* appeared in serial form, written by one 'Captain George North', a suitably seafaring pseudonym for Stevenson.

Two years after the serial appeared, it was released as a novel, under Stevenson's own name this time, and sold out almost immediately. For Stevenson, it was just the first of the many adventure tales, including *Kidnapped*, its sequel, *Catriona* and *The Master of Ballantrae*, he wrote before his death in Samoa on 3 December 1894.

Apart from adventure stories, he was also fond of the macabre, as shown in stories like *The Bottle Imp* and *The Bodysnatcher*, and he was responsible for one of the classics of horror literature, *The Strange Case of Doctor Jeckyll and Mister Hyde*, at once an update of the werewolf myth of man-turning-beast as well as exploration of the dual nature of man. The tale was inspired by Edinburgh's notorious Deacon Brodie, a respectable pillar of the community by day and a robber and highway man by night. Stevenson wrote the first draft in a few days but it shocked his wife to such an extent that he burned it and rewrote it, injecting some moral points to appease his spouse.

Arthur Conan Doyle

Sherlock Holmes is regarded by many as the quintessential English detective, even though his creator, Sir Arthur Conan Doyle, was very much a Scot. Born at Picardy Place, Edinburgh, on 22 May 1859, Conan Doyle was schooled in Lancashire before returning to study medicine at Edinburgh University in 1876. It was while serving as an out-patient clerk at Edinburgh Royal Infirmary that Doyle met the man who was to influence most the creation of his famous character, Doctor Joseph Bell. "His strong point", Doyle later noted, "was diagnosis, not only of disease, but of occupation and character".

Doyle was living in London and had published several short stories and essays when memories of his former mentor, combined with a love of the detective fiction of Edgar Allan Poe, inspired him to write *A Study In Scarlet*, which first appeared in the 1887 edition of *Beeton's Christmas Annual*. Doctor Watson recounted Sherlock Holmes' unique detective skills in this, followed by a further three novels and 56 short stories, with all but *The Sign Of Four* making their initial appearance in *The Strand Magazine*.

Holmes became a phenomenon that not even Doyle could control. In fact, by 1893 he was so annoyed that his more serious literary endeavours were being neglected that he achieved what many criminals had failed to do. He killed Holmes.

Following publication of *The Final Problem*, in which Holmes and his mortal foe, Professor Moriarty plunged over the Reichenbach Falls, there were public displays of grief and mourning. It was clear that the public were not going to let Holmes rest in peace and eventually Doyle was forced to find an ingenious way of reviving the character. He penned his last Holmes story in 1927, a mere three years before his own death. In memory of a much loved son and his famous creation, a statue of Holmes was recently erected in Edinburgh.

Despite Doyle's reluctance to continue with the character, Holmes has taken on a life of his own. Of all fictional characters, he has been the subject of most films. He has also been played on stage, radio, television, in musicals and has been the subject, or victim, of countless parodies or pastiches by numerous authors, from Agatha Christie to Stephen King.

Other Scottish writers

Doyle's personal favourites of these parodies were written by his 'older literary friend', **JM Barrie**. Born in Kirriemuir in 1860, James Matthew Barrie was the son of a weaver. Educated at Glasgow Academy and Edinburgh University, Barrie spent some years in Nottingham as a journalist before returning to Kirriemuir to write. He moved to London in 1885, and it was there that he wrote his first novel, *Better Dead*. More novels and plays followed, best known of which is *Peter Pan, or The Boy Who*

Wouldn't Grow Old. First published in 1904, it was written for the children of a friend, Llewlyn Davis. Barrie returned to Kirriemuir. Before his death in 1937, he bequeathed the copyright for *Peter Pan* to Great Ormond Street Hospital in London.

The tradition of the adventure story has continued throughout the 20th century, in the works of Perth-born **John Buchan,** author of *The Thirty-Nine Steps*. It was also the major theme in Glasgow-born **Alistair MacLean's** many novels, of which the most famous are *The Guns of Navarone*, *Ice Station Zebra* and *Where Eagles Dare*.

Other important Scottish books include: *The House with the Green Shutters*, by **George Douglas Brown**, *Sunset Song* by **Lewis Grassic Gibbon**, *The Silver Darlings* by **Neil Gunn**, *The Prime of Miss Jean Brodie* by **Muriel Spark** and **James Hogg's** *Confessions of a Justified Sinner*. Aside from Robert Burns, there are many fine **poets**, and the Selected Poems of **Norman McCaig**, **Hugh McDiarmid** and **George Mackay Brown** are all recommended.

Many of the writers living and working in Scotland today use their environment for inspiration. **Iain Banks**, author of *The Wasp Factory*, *The Crow Road* and many others (as well as science fiction novels written under the name Iain M Banks) based his fantasy, *The Bridge*, on the structure of the Forth Railway Bridge. **Irvine Welsh** has explored the capital's drug culture in the likes of *Trainspotting*, while **Ian Rankin's** crime novels take place in the real streets and bars of Edinburgh. Other notable contemporary works of fiction include *Lanark*, by **Alisdair Gray**, **William MacIlvanney's** *Docherty*, **James Kelman's** Booker prize-winning *How Late It Was, How Late*, **Janice Galloway's** *The Trick is to Keep Breathing*, **A L Kennedy's** *Night Geometry and the Garscadden Trains*, and **Alan Warner's** *Morvern Caller*.

Music

It could easily be argued that, in its music, Scotland produces the finest and clearest expression of its culture. All tastes are currently catered for within its music scene, reflecting the cosmopolitan nature of a country standing at the threshold of a new era with its own parliament and a deep sense of love of its history and traditions, while keeping a weather eye on the future. Although the words 'Scottish music' often conjure up images of a tartan-clad piper on a mist-covered moor, that same piper is just as likely to be found supplying stirring melodies to the decidedly nineties edge of 'drums and bass' styles heard in clubs around the country. And that's not all – the sheer number of options available to those seeking any style of music, ranging from folk to funk, from 'Tattoo' to 'T In The Park', is truly remarkable.

Yet, despite the fact a new millennium has come and gone, bringing with it so many changes in music and technology, Scotland as a nation still responds, virtually as one, to the skirl of a full set of highland **bagpipes**. Little wonder the pipes have been a dominant instrument for centuries, in celebration, in battle, in mourning, and are never far from the traveller's notion of all things Scottish. Indeed, in practically all the major cities and towns 364 days a year, a piper can be found busking on the main thoroughfares, come rain or shine.

The pipes' unique sound is enjoyed the world over, not just in Scotland – witness the large numbers of pipe bands in the USA, Canada, across Europe, Australia and New Zealand. However, perhaps the best way to enjoy the pipes is to visit the country in summer when, accompanied by a full complement of drummers, many pipe bands can be seen taking part in competitions or playing at Highland Games in the open air – a real treat for the traveller from near or far.

Indoors, unfortunately, acoustic bagpipes are a little too loud for the average music fan, and another instrument comes to the fore – the violin, or 'fiddle'. Whichever way one hears it, solo or accompanied by guitar, accordion, voice or best of all more violins – fewer sweeter sounds can be heard than a well-played fiddle. Traditional Scottish music can be passionate or jocular, mournful or joyous. In the hands of a good player, few instruments compare to the fiddle's wealth of expression. For confirmation, simply seek out the work of **Ally Bain**. With **The Boys Of The Lough**, **Phil Cunningham** or solo, his handling of all traditional Scottish styles is superb. Your Discman will never be the same again!

Delving a little deeper into Scotland's music, one may come across **Strathspey and Reel societies**. These are groups of fiddlers, large or small, which are well attended across the length and breadth of Scotland, regardless of the size of town. Most welcome visitors to their meetings to enjoy the music and, as most of these take place in pubs, and hotels, to enjoy the local brew, too! If this turns out to be impractical, a night spent at a ceilidh can be even more entertaining.

A **ceilidh** (pronounced '*kay*-lee') is an evening of Scottish music and dancing, the music provided by a ceilidh band, which normally consists of a fiddler, an accordionist, a drummer and a singer. One can then spend the evening sampling the delights of Gay Gordons or Dashing White Sergeants. In case you're wondering, these aren't people who frequent these events – they are actually Scottish country dances which, along with eightsome reels, figure prominently in the ceilidh dance-band repertoire. Beware the well-meaning local lad or lassie bearing gifts of whisky, however – an excellent evening enjoying the music can often lead to a spectacular hangover the following morning!

In a similar vein (though with a slightly less frenetic style), folk music clubs still thrive in Scotland although, sadly, seem to be restricted to an 'early-in-the-week' slot of a Monday or Tuesday evening in bars around Scotland as landlords attempt to bring in customers on what are generally quieter nights for business. Even the Scots, with their fearsome (and well earned) reputation for partying, can't do it *every* night of the week! Thankfully, this does not take away from the enthusiasm shown by the participants as fiddles, whistles, guitars, mandolins and bhodrans are produced and traditional songs and tunes are belted out by lusty voices and nimble fingers.

Folk festivals

Thankfully, folk music is not just confined to pubs on Monday evenings in Scotland. Folk festivals take place all over the country, from Arran to Shetland, and are great fun. Musicians from all over the country gather to play the tunes, sing the songs and maybe, just maybe, drink the odd beer or two. Amongst the best of the folk festivals is the **Shetland Folk Festival** held over a long weekend in mid-April. Also recommended are those held in **Inverness** in July and August, **Killin** at the end of June, **Islay** during the last two weeks in May, **Arran** in early June, **Skye** at the end of July and **Kirriemuir** on the first weekend in September. Details of these festivals, and many others, are available from the Scottish Area Tourist Boards (see page 21).

Art and crafts

Many of the handicrafts you'll see during your visit to the highlands and Islands, such as pottery and jewellery, though undeniably beautiful, are produced by non-indigenous residents. Two traditional craft skills which have survived are weaving and knitting. Two areas where these skills reach their apotheosis are Harris and Orkney and Shetland and Fair Isle.

Clans and tartans

Before Culloden and the Clearances, Highland tradition decreed that a person's loyalty lay first and foremost with their own particular clan, or family group. There were two classes of clan: clansmen of the clan who were related by blood and shared the same family name, and individuals and groups who sought and obtained the protection of the clan. This resulted in a clan having septs, or sub-groups, of different surnames. Most Scottish surnames can be traced to a clan name, each with their own particular tartan.

Clan tartans are patterns for general use by clanspeople, but there are also variations of clan tartans which are used for specific purposes. Dress tartans were originally worn by the women of the clan who preferred light-coloured patterns, and were woven on a white background.

Hunting tartans are worn for sport and outdoor activities, with brown or some other dark hue as the predominant colour, in order to give some form of camouflage. Rather confusingly, ancient clan tartan does not signify an older pattern, but is merely a term used to describe a tartan woven in lighter-coloured shades.

For a comprehensive history of Scottish clans and families, see Scottish Family History, by Margaret Stuart and James Balfour Paul (Edinburgh, 1930), or The Surnames of Scotland: their origin, meaning and history by George Black (New York, 1940). These books are available in most public libraries. Those wishing to trace their Scottish ancestry should start at the Scots Ancestry Research Society, 20 York Place, Edinburgh.

Knitting

Scottish sheep, particularly Orkney and Shetland, are characterized by their fine wool. The sheep of the original breed of Orkney and Shetlands, small bodied with low carcass weights, were probably a cross with Scandinavian animals. These Moorit sheep still thrive on North Ronaldsay, protected by the Rare Breeds Survival Trust. For most of the year they feed on seaweed but are moved on to grass in the lambing season. All the males and 20% of the females are horned.

Gossamer fine shawls made from Shetland wool are soft but hardwearing. Shetland wool is very loosely spun, which adds to the lightness of the finished garment. Knitted on fine needles the famed characteristic of the shawls is that they can be pulled effortlessly through a wedding ring.

Intricate patterns in bright colours characterise Fairisle knitting. When not being worked into the design, the wool in the spare colour is taken across the back of the work, caught at regular intervals in the stitches so that there are no long loops. It is important for the tension to be correct as too tight carrying of the spare wool would distort the finished garment. This double use of wool also means that Fairisle garments as well as being extremely colourful, are very warm, consisting as they do of two or more layers of wool.

Before the advent of mass produced fleece clothing and other warm store bought wear, a Scottish fisherman wore a sea jersey, sometimes known as a Guernsey or a Gansey. Tradition says that each village had its own peculiar design. Thus, if a man were lost at sea, his jersey pattern might the only means of identification if he were not found very quickly. But in reality, every family and knitter in that family would have their own pattern. Cable stitch represented rope, hearts, anchors and waves could also be part of a design. The jerseys were made from five ply Yorkshire 'wheeling', still available from Richard Poppleton of Wakefield, Yorkshire. This is a pure wool worsted yarn, tightly spun which makes it warm and hardwearing. When unwashed, the wool would contain lanoline, the natural oil, which would make garments practically water proof too. Wool with the natural oils would be widely used for the knitting of seaboot stockings.

The jerseys are knitted in the round on four or five needles. There is no sewing together of the garment, all is done by knitting. Some jerseys have three little pearl buttons to close the neck. The sleeves are knitted from the armholes downwards and are never too long as they get wet as the seamen work with the nets. Also, when the wrist edges eventually become frayed, the knitter unravels the cuff and knits it up afresh.

The needles are long as more than 500 stitches are cast on. In order to make the work easier to handle, the right hand needle would be anchored at the waist by a 'shield', a pouch of straw or a bunch of feathers. Quite an intricate design might be woven into the shields and they fetch a good price in auctions today. Alternatively, a knitting stick or knitting goose would anchor a needle under the right arm.

It is said that Kaffe Fasset, now one the world's leading knitwear designers, began his career thanks to Scottish wools. He was in the north and saw for sale wools of every delicious colour. Knowing little about knitting at that point, he nevertheless bought wool of every shade and also two needles. Boarding the train from Inverness back to London, he was in a carriage with several women. Soon after they began the journey he said 'I'm sure that some of you ladies can knit?' Indeed they could. By the time that they reached London, they had shown Kaffe Fasset how to cast on and off and how to increase and decrease. This was all that was needed to start his amazingly successful career. To this day, his designs use no complicated stitches, their unique beauty derived from inspired use of vibrant or subtle colours.

Religion

The Highlands and Islands of Scotland are largely Protestant and religion, as in the rest of the country, plays a relatively small part in the lives of most people. This does not apply, however, in the Outer Hebrides, where religion plays a vitally important role in the islanders' lives, and priests and ministers still wield considerable power in the community, particularly in the Calvinist Protestant islands of North Uist, Harris and Lewis, which still strictly adhere to the creed of Sabbatariansim.

Here, Sunday is the Lord's Day and the whole community stops work. But despite the fact that the Outer Hebrides are sharply divided between the Protestant northern islands and the Roman Catholic southern islands of Benbecula, Barra and South Uist, there has been little confrontation.

The only conflict has arisen within the Presbyterian Church of Scotland (or Kirk) itself, which has split into various factions over the years. The main split had its roots in the 1712 Patronage act, which allowed a landlord the right to choose the parish minister, thus breaking the fundamental rule of the church ministers and elders. In 1843, in protest at the state's refusal to change the Patronage act, a third of Scottish ministers walked out of the established Church of Scotland to form the Free Church of Scotland – the so-called 1843 Disruption. In 1893 a second disruption occurred, this time within the Free Church of Scotland itself when a minority seceded and formed the Free Presbyterian Church. Now it becomes really confusing. In 1900 most congregations in the Free Church of Scotland and the United Presbyterian Church joined together to form the United Free Church of Scotland. However, a large proportion of people in Lewis were opposed to this union and the largest congregations decided to continue as the Free Church of Scotland, or 'Wee Frees' as they are popularly known. Later, in 1929, the United Free Church joined with the Established Church of Scotland. And it doesn't end there. As recently as 1988, the Wee Frees split over the threatened expulsion of a minister who attended a requiem mass during the Catholic funeral of a friend. He and his supporters have since formed the breakaway Associated Presbyterian Churches.

Now all this may seem pedantic in the extreme to many outsiders, but to the people of Lewis, Harris and North Uist (and also much of Skye and Raasay), the Free Church is of enormous social and cultural, as well as spiritual, importance. Not only did it organize resistance to the infamous Highland Clearances but it has also done the most to preserve the Gaelic language.

Language

Though the vast majority of Scots speak English, one ancient Scottish language which survives is **Scottish Gaelic** (*Gaidhlig,* pronounced 'Gallic'). Preceded by the speech of the Celts, it is now Scotland's oldest surviving language. Often referred to as the national language, it has been spoken the longest. Introduced to the country by Irish immigrants in the third and fourth centuries, its use soon spread and became well established. The language is spoken by about 85,000 people in Scotland (about 2% of the population). This is in the *Gaidhealtachd,* the Gaelic-speaking areas of the Outer Hebrides, parts of Skye and a few of the smaller Hebridean islands. Gaelic is one of the Celtic languages, which has included Irish Gaelic, Manx, Welsh, Cornish and Breton. Today, only Scottish and Irish Gaelic, Welsh and Breton survive.

Argyll takes its name from the Irish, Dal Rioda, and was the prime Gaelic speaking area from the time Columba landed there in 563. Scottish Gaelic expanded greatly from the fifth century to around the 12th century and became the national language, spoken throughout most of the country with the exception of the Norse-speaking Orkney and Shetland isles. Galloway had a Gaelic community which was separated from the Highlands but the language died out there about 17th century.

From that point, Gaelic began a steady decline over the following centuries and even before Union with England was being usurped by English as more and more wealth and power passed into non-Gaelic hands. This transfer of power was given a major boost by the Reformation in the mid-16th century as strong anti-Gaelic feeling was a to the fore in of the Church of Scotland.

Gaelic culture still flourished in the Highlands but the failure of two successive Jacobite rebellions in the 18th century helped to seal its fate. In the wake of Culloden, all features of traditional Gaelic culture were proscribed and the clean sweep by government and landlords culminated in the Highland Clearances of the 19th century. The final nail in the coffin came in 1872 with the Education Act that gave no official recognition to Gaelic.

After two centuries of decline, Gaelic is now staging a comeback, thanks to financial help from government agencies and the EU which has enabled the introduction of bilingual primary and nursery schools and a massive increase in broadcasting time given to Gaelic language programmes. An increased interest in the 1960's and 1970's led to new organisations being set up in 1980's. Comann an Luchdionnsaghaidh in particular provided provision for learning the language by adults. This Renaissance can also be seen, and heard, in the fields of music and literature, and the recent return of the Scottish Parliament can surely only help to strengthen the position of Gaelic in Scottish society. Gaelic psalm singing survives from post reformation times. The tune is 'lined out' by a precentor, the tempo is slow. Psalms are sung in unison (or octaves) with local, ancient variants known as 'free heverophony', their nearest parallels being Copts in the Middle East.

The largest concentration of Gaelic culture, language and identity is in Na h-Eileanan an Iar (the Western Isles or Outer Hebrides), Highland and the former Strathclyde region. The rest of Gaelic speakers are scattered around the country, mainly in Edinburgh. In 1997,Comunn na Gaidhlig suggested to the Scottish Office ways to ensure Gaelic's continuance. No national minority languages have 'state' or 'official' status in Scotland but the government is strongly committed to the support of Gaelic.

The census of 1981 dealt with statistics but the questions themselves may have led to some inaccurate information. But it did confirm, not surprisingly, that the Western Isles are the stronghold, with 80% being native speakers, the percentage of those who also can read and write Gaelic is roughly 42%. By 1991, the census found the number of those over three years old that could speak, read or write the language to be 69,510.

Those who are interested in the language are soon inspired to learn it for themselves as it nearly always suffers in translation. Sabhal Mor Ostaig, Skye's Gaelic College has been such a success that a branch has been opened on Islay. Part of the Highlands and Islands University, it offers correspondence courses, a summer school and soon there may be scholarships for young pupils. The first CD Rom for Gaelic speakers has been launched. It will be distributed free to every secondary school in Scotland and is on sale through Canan Ltd., which is based at Sabhal Mor Ostaig.

It is said that most present day Scots would have had a parent or grandparent who was a Gaelic speaker. Even today, few will not have come into contact or worked with a Gaelic speaker.

Land and environment

Geographically, Scotland can be divided into three areas: Southern Uplands, Central Lowlands and Highlands. The **Southern Uplands** is the area south from Edinburgh and Glasgow to the English border, and consists of a series of hill ranges sandwiched between fertile coastal plains. The **Central Lowlands**, the triangle formed by Edinburgh, Glasgow and Dundee to the north, contains most of the population and is the country's industrial heartland. The Highland Boundary Fault is the geographical division running northeast from Helensburgh (west of Glasgow) to Stonehaven (south of Aberdeen). To the north of this line lie the **Highlands and Islands**, which comprise roughly two-thirds of the country. This is an area of high mountain ranges punctuated by steep-sided valleys, or glens, and deep lochs. The northwest coastline is indented by numerous steep, fjord-like sea lochs and offshore are some 790 islands, 130 of which are inhabited. These are grouped into the Outer Hebrides, or Western Isles, the Inner Hebrides, and, to the north, the Orkney and Shetland Islands.

Vegetation

Much of Scotland was long ago covered by the **Caledonian forest**, which consisted mainly of the **Scots pine**, along with **oak**, **birch** and other hardwoods. Over the centuries, the trees were felled for timber and to accommodate livestock and now only around 1% of this ancient forest still remains. Small pockets of native Scots pine can be found scattered around the Highlands, at Rothiemurchus, near Aviemore, at Glen Tanar, near Ballater in Deeside, around Braemar, at Strathtyre near Callander and Achray Forest near Aberfoyle, at Rowardennan on Loch Lomond, in Glen Affric and on the shores of Loch Maree.

Several decades ago, the **Forestry Commission**, a government body, set about fencing off large areas of moorland for reforestation. Now much of the landscape is dominated by regimented rows of fast-growing sitka spruce, which are not particularly attractive. There are also serious concerns over the damage coniferization causes to the unique habitats in many areas, in particular to large areas of bogland in the "Flow Country" of Caithness and Sutherland, a unique natural environment as precious as any tropical rainforest. This and other endangered habitats are registered as an SSSI – a site of Special Scientific Interest – but this has proved less than adequate. The only real guarantee of protection is for such areas to be owned or managed by environmental organizations such as *Scottish Natural Heritage*, the *Scottish Wildlife Trust*, the *Royal Society for the Protection of Birds*, the *Woodland Trust* and *John Muir Trust* (see page 57).

Tourism can also have a damaging effect on the fragile ecology of the Highlands. The unique alpine flora of the Cairngorms is threatened by the hordes of summer visitors using the ski lifts, and controversy rages over proposals to replace the Cairngorm ski lift with a funicular railway.

Wildlife

The Highlands and Islands of Scotland contain many of Britain's remotest areas and wildest scenery. As a result it is also home to many of the country's rarest animals and its most exotic wildlife. For example, **pine martens**, golden and sea **eagles**, **ospreys**, **killer whales** or **orcas**, **red deer** and **red squirrels**, amongst others, are all best seen in the Scottish Highlands and Islands.

As for the **wildcat**, it is debatable whether or not such a thing really exists now because of interbreeding with feral domestic cats. The **water-vole** (best known as "Ratty" in The Wind in the Willows) is now a threatened species throughout Britain but has its last strongholds in the northwest of Scotland in areas not yet colonised by the invading American mink. Both the harbour or **common seal** and the larger **grey seal** can be found living and breeding in Scottish waters. The latter is especially friendly and curious so will often be seen following small boats.

Red deer occur in large numbers throughout Scotland and are of great importance to the local economies of many parts of the Highlands where stalking estates cover much of the land. Males (stags) are larger than the females (hinds) and are characterized by impressive antlers, which are used in the autumn rut to compete for mates. Each year in late winter the antlers are cast and stags must grow a new pair during the summer. Whilst growing, the antlers appear soft and velvety. During the rut, the glens resound with the sound of roaring stags, their antlers clashing, each trying to out-do his neighbouring rival. Red deer are most easily seen in winter, when they are forced down off the mountains in search of food. Large numbers can be seen on Rannoch Moor and between Blair Atholl and Drumochter Pass from the A9 Perth-Inverness road.

Sika deer which are slightly smaller than red deer and spotted in summer can now also been seen in some places, having escaped from deer parks. They have even been known to hybridize with red deer. **Roe deer**, meanwhile, are widespread.

Golden eagles can be seen throughout the Highlands and Islands, especially on Skye, Mull, the Outer Hebrides, around Aviemore and Deeside and in the northwest. Far less prevalent is the **sea eagle**, recently re-introduced after having been extinct for much of this century. Much larger even the golden eagle, the sea eagle eats fish, but also takes large mammals including domestic livestock, which ultimately led to its persecution. Sea eagles can be seen on the Hebridean islands of Rùm and Canna, as well as parts of the west coast, around Argyll and Loch Maree.

The **osprey**, known in North America as the 'fish hawk' and also a member of the eagle family, has a famous nesting site at the RSPB reserve at **Loch Garten**, near Aviemore in Strathspey (see page 189). Also in the reserve, which is a lovely example of Caledonian pine forest, can be found other Scottish specialities such as **crossbills**, so called because of the shape of their beaks, designed for extracting seeds from pine cones. **Capercaillie**, the largest member of the grouse family and the size of a large turkey, is now very rare and runs the risk of extinction largely due to loss of habitat. Male capercaillies display at "leks", where groups of courting males fan their tails and try to attract females.

The Caledonian forest is also home to pine-martens and red squirrels. The **pine-marten** is a giant tree weasel, about the size of a cat, and reddish in colour with a white throat. It now has a very limited distribution, being most abundant in **Beinn Eighe Nature Reserve** in Wester Ross (see page 252). **Red squirrels** are much more widespread and common throughout natural and plantation coniferous forests in Scotland, especially on Speyside and Deeside. They are smaller than the invading north American grey squirrel, and have tufts on their ears, and sometimes whitish tails.

Like red deer, **grouse** are very important to the local economy, and so responsible for the land management of much of southern, central and northeastern Scotland. Grouse moors can be recognized from a distance by the mosaic of burnt, young and mature heather patches providing an environment to maximize the number of breeding territories.

Grouse moors are also home to other species, the most notable of which are perhaps the **ptarmigan** and **mountain hare**, both of which turn white in winter. The ptarmigan is another species of grouse which tends to live at a higher altitude, in snowy areas. However, it may often be seen looking very out of place when the snow has melted. Mountain hares, with shorter ears than brown hares and without black on the tail, will always run uphill when disturbed. Both ptarmigan and mountain hares are abundant in the **Cairngorms** and can be seen easily from **Glen Shee**.

Otters, live both on rivers and along the coast and are most easily seen on the islands and the west coast. The best place to see them is **Skye**, especially at the Otter Haven at **Kylerhea**. Otters eat fish and other marine life, and can be seen swimming or scampering along the shore. Their droppings which are usually found on prominent places along the shore, have a very characteristic smell.

Many species such as foxes and badgers, common in England, can be found throughout Scotland as well, although they haven't reached some of the islands. However, in some cases animals have been introduced to the islands to the detriment of the local wildlife. For example, the hedgehog is regarded by some as a pest in the Outer Hebrides where it eats the eggs of many ground-nesting birds, especially waders, which have evolved in the absence of such predators. And one mammal which is soon to be re-introduced to the Highlands of Scotland is the European **beaver**.

The seas around the north of Scotland are some of the best places in Europe to see **whales, dolphins** and **porpoises**. The best area is the **Moray** and **Cromarty Firths**, near Inverness, which are home to Europe's largest population of **bottlenose dolphins**. Dolphins can be seen all year round, but the best months are between May and September. Other good places for sighting dolphins, porpoises and whales is the coast around **Gairloch**, in Wester Ross, where you may see **minke whales**, and if you're lucky, **killer whales**, and around **Bressay, Noss** and **Mousa** on **Shetland**. For details of where to see birds , see page 57.

Footnotes

11

Footnotes

Index

Shorts

Map index

Will you help us?

We try as hard as we can to make each Footprint Handbook as
up-to-date and accurate as possible but, of course, things always
change. Many people email or write to us – with corrections, new
information, or simply comments. If you want to let us know about
your experiences and adventures – be they good, bad or ugly –
then don't delay; we're dying to hear from you. And please try to
include all the relevant details and juicy bits. Your help will be
greatly appreciated, especially by other travellers. In return we will
send you details about our special guidebook offer.

email Footprint at:
schi1_online@footprintbooks.com

or write to:

Elizabeth Taylor
Footprint Handbooks
6 Riverside Court
Lower Bristol Road
Bath
BA2 3DZ
UK

Sales & distribution

Footprint Handbooks
6 Riverside Court
Lower Bristol Road
Bath BA2 3DZ England
T 01225 469141
F 01225 469461
discover
@footprintbooks.com

Australia
Peribo Pty
58 Beaumont Road
Mt Kuring-Gai
NSW 2080
T 02 9457 0011
F 02 9457 0022

Austria
Freytag-Berndt Artaria
Kohlmarkt 9
A-1010 Wien
T 01533 2094
F 01533 8685

Freytag-Berndt
Sporgasse 29
A-8010 Graz
T 0316 818230
F 3016 818230-30

Belgium
Craenen BVBA
Mechelsesteenweg 633
B-3020 Herent
T 016 23 90 90
F 016 23 97 11

Waterstones
The English Bookshop
Blvd Adolphe Max 71-75
B-1000 Brussels
T 02 219 5034

Canada
Ulysses Travel Publications
4176 rue Saint-Denis
Montréal
Québec H2W 2M5
T 514 843 9882
F 514 843 9448

Europe
Bill Bailey
16 Devon Square
Newton Abbot
Devon TQ12 2HR. UK
T 01626 331079
F 01626 331080

Denmark
Nordisk Korthandel
Studiestraede 26-30 B
DK-1455 Copenhagen K
T 3338 2638
F 3338 2648

Scanvik Books
Esplanaden 8B
DK-1263 Copenhagen K
T 3312 7766
F 3391 2882

Finland
Akateeminen Kirjakauppa
Keskuskatu 1
FIN-00100 Helsinki
T 09 121 4151
F 09 121 4441

Suomalainen Kirjakauppa
Koivuvaarankuja 2
01640 Vantaa 64
F 09 852751

France
FNAC – major branches

L'Astrolabe
46 rue de Provence
F-75009 Paris 9e
T 01 42 85 42 95
F 01 45 75 92 51

VILO Diffusion
25 rue Ginoux
F-75015 Paris
T 01 45 77 08 05
F 01 45 79 97 15

Germany
GeoCenter ILH
Schockenriedstrasse 44
D-70565 Stuttgart
T 0711 781 94610
F 0711 781 94654

Brettschneider
Feldkirchnerstrasse 2
D-85551 Heimstetten
T 089 990 20330
F 089 990 20331

Geobuch
Rosental 6
D-80331 München
T 089 265030
F 089 263713

Gleumes
Hohenstaufenring 47-51
D-50674 Köln
T 0221 215650

Globetrotter Ausrustungen
Wiesendamm 1
D-22305 Hamburg
T040 679 66190
F 040 679 66183

Dr Götze
Bleichenbrücke 9
D-2000 Hamburg 1
T 040 3031 1009-0

Hugendubel Buchhandlung
Nymphenburgerstrasse 25
D-80335 München
T 089 238 9412
F 089 550 1853

Kiepert Buchhandlung
Hardenbergstrasse 4-5
D-10623 Berlin 12
T 030 311 880
F 030 311 88120

Greece
GC Eleftheroudakis
17 Panepistemiou
Athens 105 64
T 01 331 4180-83
F 01 323 9821

India
India Book Distributors
1007/1008 Arcadia
195 Nariman Point
Mumbai 400 021
T 91 22 282 5220
F 91 22 287 2531

Israel
Eco Trips
8 Tverya Street
Tel Aviv 63144
T 03 528 4113
F 03 528 8269

For a fuller list, see www.footprintbooks.com

Italy
Librimport
Via Biondelli 9
I-20141 Milano
T 02 8950 1422
F 02 8950 2811

Libreria del Viaggiatore
Via dell Pelegrino 78
I-00186 Roma
T/F 06 688 01048

Netherlands
Nilsson & Lamm bv
Postbus 195
Pampuslaan 212
N-1380 AD Weesp
T 0294 494949
F 0294 494455

Waterstones
Kalverstraat 152
1012 XE Amsterdam
T 020 638 3821

New Zealand
Auckland Map Centre
Dymocks

Norway
Schibsteds Forlag A/S
Akersgata 32 - 5th Floor
Postboks 1178 Sentrum
N-0107 Oslo
T 22 86 30 00
F 22 42 54 92

Tanum
Karl Johansgate 37-41
PO Box 1177 Sentrum
N-0107 Oslo 1
T 22 41 11 00
F 22 33 32 75

Olaf Norlis
Universitetsgt 24
N-1062 Oslo
T 22 00 43 00

Pakistan
Pak-American Commercial
Hamid Chambers
Zaib-un Nisa Street
Saddar, PO Box 7359
Karachi
T 21 566 0418
F 21 568 3611

South Africa
Faradawn CC
PO Box 1903
Saxonwold 2132
T 011 885 1787
F 011 885 1829

South America
Humphrys Roberts
Associates
Caixa Postal 801-0
Ag. Jardim da Gloria
06700-970 Cotia SP
Brazil
T 011 492 4496
F 011 492 6896

Southeast Asia
APA Publications
38 Joo Koon Road
Singapore 628990
T 865 1600
F 861 6438

In Hong Kong, Malaysia,
Singapore and Thailand:
MPH, Kinokuniya, Times

Spain
Altaïr
C/Balmes 69
08007 Barcelona
T 933 233062
F 934 512559

Altaïr
Gaztambide 31
28015 Madrid
T 0915 435300
F 0915 443498

Libros de Viaje
C/Serrano no 41
28001 Madrid
T 01 91 577 9899
F 01 91 577 5756

Il Corte Inglés – major
branches

Sweden
Hedengrens Bokhandel
PO Box 5509
S-11485 Stockholm
T 08 611 5132

Kart Centrum
Vasagatan 16
S-11120 Stockholm
T 08 411 1697

Kartforlaget
Skolgangen 10
S-80183 Gavle
T 026 633000
F 026 124204

Lantmateriet Kartbutiken
Kungsgatan 74
S-11122 Stockholm
T 08 202 303
F 08 202 711

Switzerland
Office du Livre OLF
ZI3, Corminboeuf
CH-1701 Fribourg
T 026 467 5111
F 026 467 5666

Schweizer Buchzentrum
Postfach
CH-4601 Olten
T 062 209 2525
F 062 209 2627

Travel Bookshop
Rindermarkt 20
Postfach 216
CH-8001 Zürich
T 01 252 3883
F 01 252 3832

Tanzania
A Novel Idea
The Slipway
PO Box 76513
Dar es Salaam
T/F 051 601088

USA
Publishers Group West
1700 Fourth Street
Berkeley
CA 94710
T 510 528 1444
F 510 528 9555

Barnes & Noble, Borders,
specialist travel bookstores

Footprint travel list

Footprint publish travel guides to over 120 countries worldwide. Each guide is packed with practical, concise and colourful information for everybody from first-time travellers to travel aficionados . The list is growing fast and current titles are noted below. For further information check out the website **www.footprintbooks.com**

Andalucía Handbook	Rajasthan Handbook
Argentina Handbook	Rio de Janeiro Handbook
Bali & the Eastern Isles Hbk	Scotland Handbook
Bangkok & the Beaches Hbk	Scotland Highlands & Islands Hbk
Bolivia Handbook	Singapore Handbook
Brazil Handbook	South Africa Handbook
Cambodia Handbook	South American Handbook
Caribbean Islands Handbook	South India Handbook
Chile Handbook	Sri Lanka Handbook
Colombia Handbook	Sumatra Handbook
Cuba Handbook	Syria & Lebanon Handbook
Dominican Republic Handbook	Thailand Handbook
East Africa Handbook	Tibet Handbook
Ecuador & Galápagos Handbook	Tunisia Handbook
Edinburgh Handbook	Turkey Handbook
Egypt Handbook	Venezuela Handbook
Goa Handbook	Vietnam Handbook
India Handbook	
Indian Himalaya Handbook	
Indonesia Handbook	**In the pipeline** – Costa Rica,
Ireland Handbook	Guatemala, Nicaragua, Barcelona
Israel Handbook	& New Zealand
Jordan Handbook	
Jordan, Syria & Lebanon Hbk	**Also available from Footprint**
Laos Handbook	Traveller's Handbook
Libya Handbook	Traveller's Healthbook
London Handbook	
Malaysia Handbook	
Myanmar Handbook	
Mexico Handbook	
Mexico & Central America Hbk	
Morocco Handbook	
Namibia Handbook	
Nepal Handbook	
Pakistan Handbook	
Peru Handbook	

Available at all good bookshops

Caledonian MacBrayne
Hebridean and Clyde Ferries

Scottish

Island

Discover

a different kind of world
with Caledonian MacBrayne

SCOTLAND

1851-2001

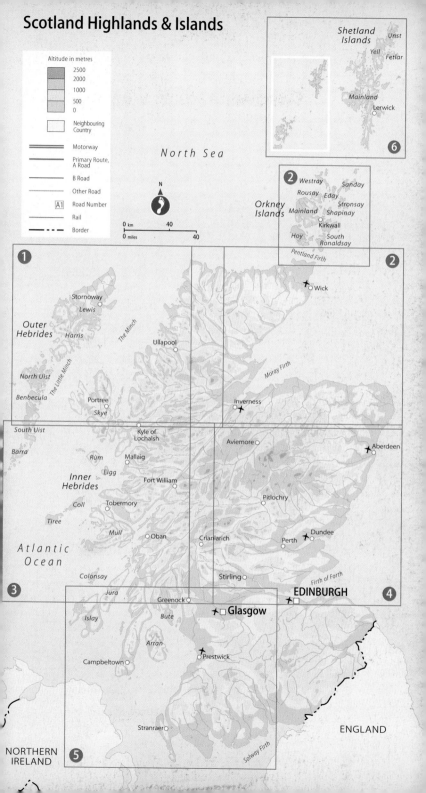

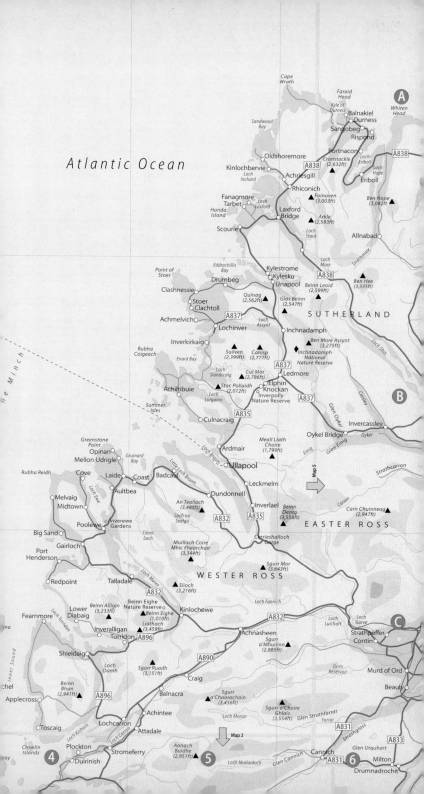

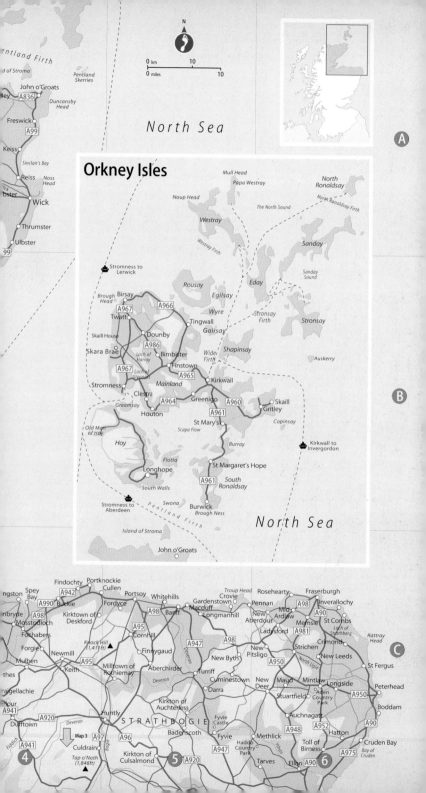

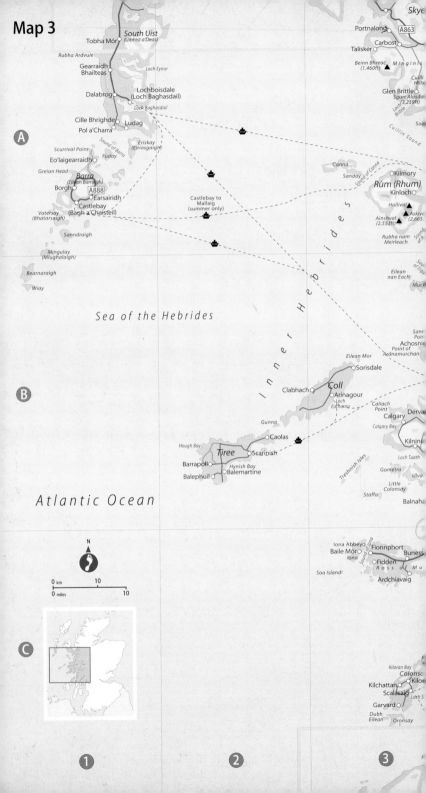

Map 3

Skye

Portnalong
Carbost
A863
Talisker

Beinn Bhreac *Minginis*
(1,460ft)
Cuilli
Hills
Glen Brittle
Sgurr Alasdair
(3,259ft)
Loch
Brittle
Cuillin Sound
Soo

South Uist
(Uibhist a'Deas)
Tobha Mór

Rubha Ardvule

Gearraidh
Bhailteas
Loch Eynor

Dalabrog
Lochboisdale
(Loch Baghasdail)

Cille Bhrighde
Loch Baghasdail

A

Pol a'Charra
Ludag

Canna
Sound of Canna
Kilmory
Sanday
Rùm (Rhum)
Kinloch

Scurrival Point
Eriskay
(Eiriosgaigh)
Eo'laigearraidh
Fuday

Greian Head
Barra
(Eilean Barraigh)
Borgh
A888
Earsairidh
Castlebay
(Bagh a'Chaisteil)

*Castlebay to
Mallaig
(summer only)*

Hallival
Askiva
(2,553ft)
Ainshval
(2,665

*Vatersay
(Bhatarsaigh)*

Sanndraigh

*Rubha nam
Meirleach*

*Mingulay
(Mughalaigh)*

Bearnaraigh

Eilean
nan Each
Muc

Wiay

Sea of the Hebrides

Inner Hebrides

Sanr
Poir
Achosni
Point of
Ardnamurchan

Eilean Mor
Sorisdale

Clabhach
Coll
Arinagour
Loch
Eathaina

Caliach
Point
Calgary
Derva

Calgary Bay

B

Gunna
Caolas
Kilnini

Hough Bay
Tiree
Scarinish
Loch Tuath

Barrapoll
Hynish Bay
Balemartine
Balephuil

Gometra
Ulva

Treshnish Isles

Little
Colonsay

Staffa
Balnaha

Atlantic Ocean

Iona Abbey
Fionnphort
Baile Mór
Buness
Iona
Fidden
Ross
Mu
Ardchiavaig

Soa Island

N

0 km   10
0 miles   10

C

Kiloran Bay
Colonse
Kilchattan
Kilo
Scalasaig
Loch S
Garvard
Dubh
Eilean
Oronsay

1   **2**   **3**

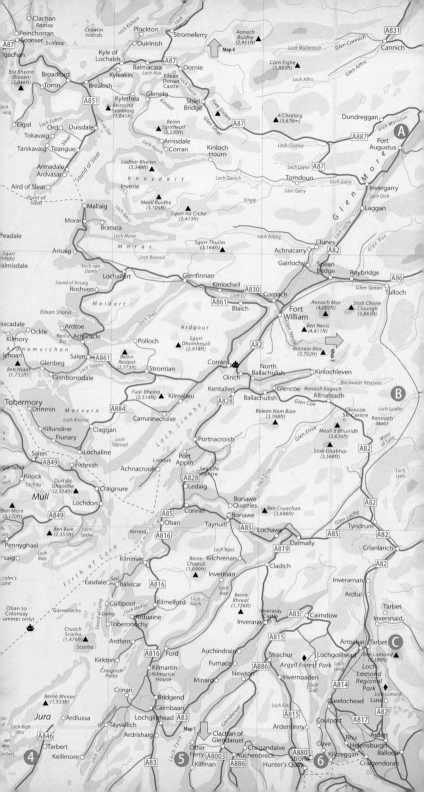

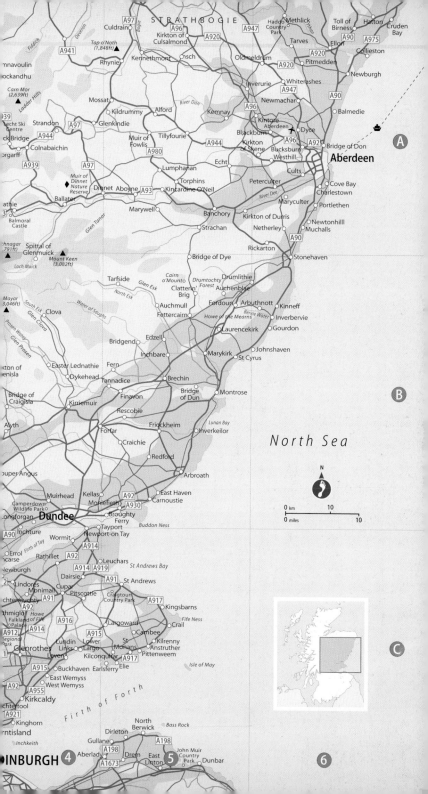

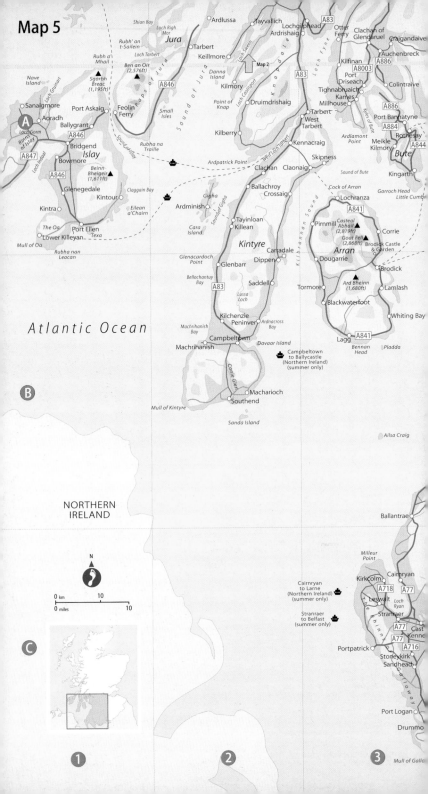

Map 5

Atlantic Ocean

NORTHERN IRELAND

N

0 km   10
0 miles   10

Islay

Nave Island
Loch Gruinart
Sanaigmore
Aoradh
Ballygrant
Port Askaig
Feolin Ferry
A846
A847
Bridgend
Bowmore
Loch Gorm
Rinns of Islay
A846
Glenegedale
Kintour
Kintra
A846
Port Ellen
The Oa
Lower Killeyan
Mull of Oa
Rubha nan Leacan
Beinn Bheigeir (1,611ft)
Claggain Bay
Eilean a'Chairn
Texa

Jura

Shian Bay
Loch Righ Mor
Rubh' an t-Sailein
Rubh a' Mhàil
Ardlussa
Tarbert
Keillmore
Ben an Oir (2,576ft)
Sgarbh Breac (1,195ft)
A846
Danna Island
Kilmory
Point of Knap
Small Isles
Sound of Jura
Sound of Islay
Rubha na Traille
Ardpatrick Point
Paps of Jura

Knapdale

Tayvallich
Lochgilphead
Ardrishaig
A83
Loch Sween
Loch Caolisport
Druimdrishaig
Kilberry
West Tarbert
Tarbert
Kennacraig
Clachan
Claonaig
Skipness
Ballachroy
Crossaig
A83
Map 2

Kintyre

Gigha
Ardminish
Cara Island
Sound of Gigha
Tayinloan
Killean
Carradale
Dippen
Glenbarr
Saddell
Glenacardoch Point
Bellochantuy Bay
Lussa Loch
Kilchenzie
Peninver
Ardnacross Bay
Machrihanish Bay
Campbeltown
Machrihanish
Conie Glen
Macharioch
Southend
Mull of Kintyre
Davaar Island
Sanda Island
Campbeltown to Ballycastle (Northern Ireland) (summer only)

Arran

Lochranza
A841
Pirnmill
Casteal Abhail (2,819ft)
Goat Fell (2,868ft)
Corrie
Brodick Castle & Garden
Dougarrie
Brodick
Tormore
Ard Bheinn (1,680ft)
Lamlash
Blackwaterfoot
Whiting Bay
Lagg
A841
Bennan Head
Pladda
Cock of Arran
Sound of Bute
Kilbrannan Sound

Loch Fyne

Otter Ferry
Clachan of Glendaruel
Craigandaive
Auchenbreck
Kilfinan
A8003
Port Driseach
Tighnabruaich
Kames
Millhouse
Ardlamont Point

Bute

Port Bannatyne
A886
A884
Meikle Kilmory
Rothesay
A844
Kingarth
Garroch Head
Little Cumb...
Kyles of Bute

Ballantrae
Milleur Point
Cairnryan
Kirkcolm
A718
A77
Leswalt
Loch Ryan
Stranraer
A77
Cast...
Kenne...
A716
Portpatrick
Stoneykirk
Sandhead
Rhinns of Galloway
Port Logan
Drummo...
Mull of Gallo...
Ailsa Craig

Cairnryan to Larne (Northern Ireland) (summer only)

Stranraer to Belfast (summer only)

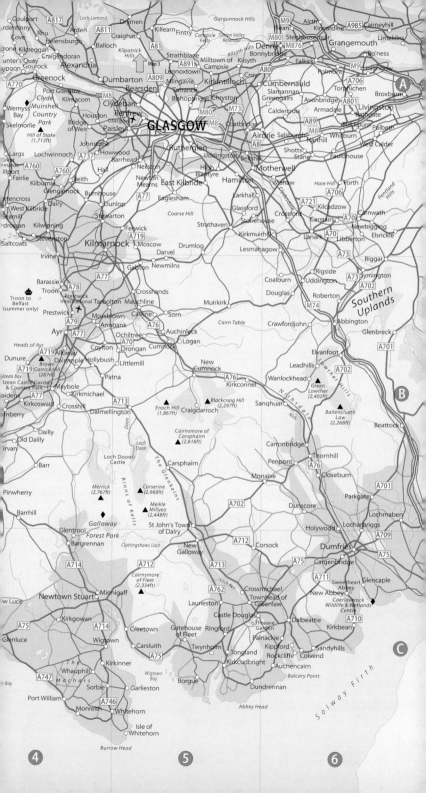

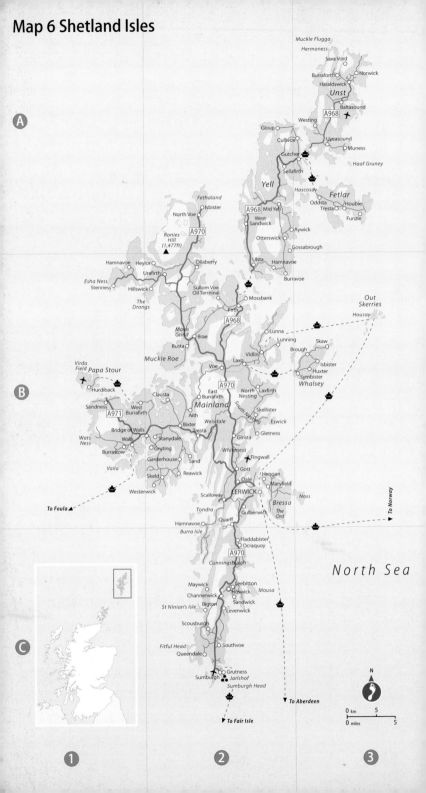

Map 6 Shetland Isles

Muckle Flugga
Hermaness
Saxa Vord
Burraforth
Haraldswick
Norwick
Unst
A968
Baltasound
Westing
Uyeasound
Gloup
Cullivoe
Muness
Gutcher
Sellafirth
Haaf Gruney

Yell
Hascosay
Fetlar
Oddsta
Tresta
Houbie
A968
Mid Yell
West
Sandwick
Aywick
Funzie
Otterswick
Gossabrough
Fethaland
Isbister
North Voe
Ulsta
Hamnavoe
A970
Ronies Hill
(1,477ft)
Burravoe

Hamnavoe
Heylor
Ollaberry
Urafirth
Esha Ness
Stenness
Hillswick
Sullom Voe
Oil Terminal
Mossbank
The Drongs
Firth
Out Skerries
Housay
Mavis Grind
Brae
A968
Lunna
Lunning
Skaw
Busta
Voe
Vidlin
Brough
Muckle Roe
Laxo
Isbister
Huxter
Virda Field
Papa Stour
East
Burrafirth
North Nesting
Laxfirth
Symbister
Whalsey
Hurdiback
Clausta
Aith
Mainland
Skellister
Weisdale
Bixter
Tresta
Eswick
Sandness
South Nesting
West
Burrafirth
A971
Girlsta
Gletness
Wats Ness
Bridge of Walls
Stanydale
Whiteness
Walls
Gruting
Tingwall
Vaila
Burrastow
Garderhouse
Sand
Gott
Heogan
Skeld
Reawick
Dale
Maryfield
Westerwick
To Foula
Scalloway
LERWICK
Noss
Tondra
Bressa
The Ord
Quarff
Gulberwick
To Norway
Hamnavoe
Burra Isle
Fladdabister
Ocraquoy
A970
North Sea
Cunningsburgh
Maywick
Leebitton
Channerwick
Hoswick
Mousa
Bigton
Sandwick
St Ninian's Isle
Levenwick
Scousburgh
Fitful Head
Southvoe
Queendale
Grutness
Sumburgh
Jarlshof
Sumburgh Head
To Aberdeen
To Fair Isle

N

0 km   5
0 miles   5

A   B   C

1   2   3

www.footprintbooks.com
A new place to visit

"*As valuable to Scots wanting to explore their own country as to tourists discovering it for the first time.*"
Highlands News Group

"*Footprint can be depended on for accurate travel information and for imparting a deep sense of respect for the lands and people they cover.*"
World News

"*Footprint Handbooks, the best of the best.*"
Le Monde, Paris

"*Well worth the wait. Triumphs over the competition.*"
The Sunday Telegraph

Mail order
Available worldwide in bookshops and on-line. Footprint travel guides can also be ordered directly from us in Bath, via our website **www.footprintbooks.com** or from the address on the imprint page of this book.

Acknowledgements

Alan would like to thank all those helped in the research, writing and preparation of this guidebook. Norma Rowlerson, Suzy Kennard and Rebecca Ford for their contributions to the History section. Norma also researched and wrote many of the new walks as well as several of the Shorts. Thanks Susie Kennard for the Architecture section, Duncan Lindsay for the Music section, Jos Milner for the Wildlife section and Frank Nicholas for the Literature section. Nigel Easton for updating the Outer Hebrides chapter and providing new information on environmental issues. Sid Kimbrough for his sterling work updating all the Sleeping and Transport sections. Thanks also to all the staff at the various tourist information centres who were so willing and helpful, the staff at Caledonia MacBrayne, the National Trust for Scotland and Historic Scotland. Finally, a big shout to all at Footprint, especially Lambchop for not wanting the moon on a stick.

About the author

When **Alan Murphy** upped sticks and left the fleshpots of Dundee to start his own seaweed collecting business on a remote island croft, many saw it as a cry for kelp. But Alan not only survived several bleak Hebridean winters, he went on to found a sanctuary for wayward seal pups and devoted the next ten years to working with young delinquent marine mammals. Later, Alan turned his hand to travel writing and now spends his summers researching and writing Footprint Handbooks to Scotland, Edinburgh and Scotland Highlands & Islands, and winters travelling around South America to research Footprint guides to Bolivia, Peru and Venezuela. He currently lives in Bath with his Burmese cats, Geoffrey and Brian.